CCH Preparing FRS 102 Company Accounts

CCH Preparing FRS 102
Company Accounts

James Lole FCA

© 2016 Wolters Kluwer (UK) Ltd
Wolters Kluwer (UK) Limited
145 London Road
Kingston upon Thames KT2 6SR
Tel: 0844 561 8166
Fax: 0208 547 2638
E-mail: cch@wolterskluwer.co.uk
www.cch.co.uk

© Financial Reporting Council (FRC). Financial Reporting Council material is adapted and reproduced with the kind permission of the Financial Reporting Council. All rights reserved. For further information, please visit www.frc.org.uk or call +44 (0)20 7492 2300.

ISBN 978-1-78540-258-6

British Library Cataloguing-in-Publication Data

A catalogue record for this book is available from the British Library.

Typeset by Innodata Inc., India.

Printed by Gutenberg Press Ltd, Malta.

Preface

This is the third edition of *Preparing FRS 102 Company Accounts*. It focuses on the UK financial reporting standard FRS 102 *The Financial Reporting Standard applicable in the UK and Republic of Ireland* within the UK financial reporting framework contained in FRS 100 *Application of Financial Reporting Requirements* which is mandatory for accounting periods commencing on or after 1 January 2015.

Since the publication of the first edition, the FRC has gone ahead with its reforms to the accounting requirements for small entities. This was driven partly by the UK Government implementing EU accounting directives for small entities. As a result, *The Financial Reporting Standard for Smaller Entities* (FRSSE) has been withdrawn for accounting periods commencing on or after 1 January 2016 to be replaced with the accounting principles of FRS 102 but with the option of some disclosure relaxations. At the same time, the FRC has introduced a simpler reporting regime for the smallest entities in the form of FRS 105 *The Financial Reporting Standard for Micro Entities*.

FRS 102 therefore applies to those entities which either are not required (or do not choose) to apply EU-adopted International Financial Reporting Standards (IFRS) or are not eligible (or do not choose) to apply FRS 105. It replaces what has come to be known as 'UK GAAP' and will, in time, become known as UK GAAP in its own right. Financial reporting in the UK continues to be underpinned by the statutory accounting framework of the *Companies Act* 2006.

The main objective of this book is to be a companion rather than a comprehensive technical commentary in its own right – a quick and, we hope, relatively straightforward guide concentrating on the presentation and disclosure requirements of FRS 102 together with the statutory disclosures of the *Companies Act* 2006 and other Regulations. The book will highlight those disclosures which are not mandatory for small entities.

FRS 102 implements the principles of IFRS into UK GAAP for the first time. The standard is based on the *IFRS for SMEs* which was published by the IASB in July 2009 and is intended to be a self-contained standard designed to meet the needs and capabilities of private or non-publicly accountable small and medium-sized entities (SMEs). It is, to a certain extent, a simplification of the principles of IFRS for recognising and measuring assets, liabilities, income and expenses and in most situations uses the simpler accounting treatment where IFRS permits options, contains fewer disclosures and is drafted more succinctly. In adapting the IFRS for SMEs standard for the UK, the FRC made amendments to ensure consistency with companies' legislation, and took into consideration the comments from respondents during the exposure draft stage.

The FRC has announced that the first triennial review of FRS 102 will take place in 2017–18 to provide a three-year stable platform for small entities applying FRS 102 for the first time from 1 January 2016. Any changes to FRS 102 arising from the triennial review are not expected to take effect before 1 January 2019.

Comments on any aspect of FRS 102 and its implementation, or any other UK and Ireland accounting standard can be sent to ukfrsreview@frc.org.uk. This might include views on the benefits of the new standards, as well as suggestions for improvements or areas where implementation was challenging.

The comments received will be used to inform the development of proposals for changes to accounting standards, which will be subject to formal consultation at a later date, expected to be during 2017. Comments may be provided at any time during the triennial review process. Those received by 31 October 2016 will be taken into account in developing formal proposals for changes; comments received after this date will be taken into account in the later stages of the review.

About the authors

James Lole FCA is a freelance technical consultant and trainer on financial reporting, auditing and ethical matters. His previous experience as National Technical Director at a top ten firm provided him with an ideal background to join Wolters Kluwer's expanding team of technical writers.

SWAT UK, who provided the model accounts and disclosure checklist for this book, are the largest independent provider of accountancy training and compliance reviews in the UK. As well as client-facing work, they write and update a number of technical accountancy publications, including the *CCH Interactive Company Accounts Disclosure Checklist* and *Model Accounts* products.

Note on scope of book

CCH Preparing FRS 102 Company Accounts 2016–17 is concerned with the accounts of large, medium-sized and small companies (that is companies not defined as 'micro companies' by CA 2006 and companies not choosing to prepare financial statements under IFRS) for financial years beginning on or after 1 January 2016.

Statutory references are to CA 2006 itself (as amended from time to time) or to Regulations made under the Act, unless otherwise indicated.

Changes to legislation and to accounting standards issued up to 31 May 2016 have been considered in the writing of *Preparing FRS 102 Company Accounts 2016–17.* As a result, the book considers the impact of FRS 100 *Application of Financial Reporting Requirements,* FRS 101 *Reduced Disclosure Framework* and, in more detail, the requirements of FRS 102 *The Financial Reporting Standard applicable in the UK and Republic of Ireland.*

The following topics are considered peripheral to this main objective and are not therefore covered in detail:

International financial reporting standards and FRS 101: Although the new UK GAAP contained in FRS 102 is based on the principles of measurement and recognition contained in IFRS, it is not fully aligned. Companies of any size have the option, within Company Law to prepare 'IAS Accounts' and would therefore fall within the scope of the full suite of IFRS.

The CCH publication *Preparing IFRS Accounts* is available from www.cch.co.uk/books.

Chapter 5 contains an overview of FRS 101 and the disclosure exemptions from EU-adopted IFRS for qualifying entities. Further detail and guidance is available in the CCH publication *Preparing FRS 101 Accounts.*

Small companies: Whilst this book does refer to the application of FRS 102 to the accounts of small companies, it is mainly concerned with large and medium-sized companies. More detail including example accounts and disclosures can be found in the companion publication *CCH Preparing Company Accounts – Small and Micros* available from www.cch.co.uk/books.

Micro-entities: In November 2013, the Government introduced regulations allowing the smallest companies to take certain exemptions relating to the preparation of their financial statements for periods ending on or after 30 September 2013. The regulations are contained in the *Small Companies (Micro-Entities' Accounts) Regulations* 2013 (SI 2013/3008) available on CCH Online. The FRC has also issued FRS 105 *The Financial Reporting Standard applicable to the Micro-entities Regime* which contains the accounting and reporting framework for micro-entities.

The companion publication *CCH Preparing Company Accounts – Small and Micros* also covers the accounting and reporting provisions of the 'micro entities' regime and FRS 105.

Audit and assurance: Preparing FRS 102 Company Accounts 2016–17 does not purport to provide professional guidance on auditing or the provision of assurance services by auditors. Many subsidiary companies and small companies are now able to take advantage of audit exemption regardless of the financial reporting framework they choose to adopt, however most medium-sized and large companies continue to require audit. Consequently, the book does not comment in detail on audit exemption, audit reports and on the reporting requirements of auditors in circumstances where an audit is required. **Chapter 14** provides information on the content and examples of auditors reports on company accounts. The latest 2016 auditing, ethical and quality control standards are available on CCH Online and in *Auditing and Reporting 2016–17*, with detailed guidance in *Implementing GAAS 2016–17* published by Wolters Kluwer.

Charities: *Preparing FRS 102 Company Accounts 2016–17* does not cover the requirements of incorporated charities. Accounting for charities (incorporated or otherwise) has generally been brought under one roof by the introduction of the *Charities Act* 2011, which supersedes the *Charities Act* 1993 and the *Charities Act* 2006, and, to which reference should be made where appropriate. The requirements for Charities are set out in the CCH publication *CCH Preparing Charity Accounts 2016–17* available from www.cch.co.uk/books.

Further information on charity accounts including audit work programmes, example accounts and relevant legislation is available on CCH Online.

Limited Liability Partnerships (LLPs): *Preparing FRS 102 Company Accounts 2016–17* does not cover all the requirements for LLPs. The CA 2006 is applicable to LLPs for accounting periods starting on or after 1 October 2008. The key regulations which set out how the CA 2006 applies to LLPs are *The Limited Liability Partnerships (Accounts and Audit) (Application of Companies Act 2006) Regulations* 2008 (SI 2008/1911), available on CCH Online. In May 2016, FRS 105 was amended to bring LLPs and qualifying partnerships within the scope of the micro-entities regime.

The requirements for LLPs are set out in the CCH publication *Preparing Accounts for LLPs, Third Edition* available from www.cch.co.uk/books.

Abbreviations

AAC	Audit and Assurance Council (part of the FRC)
APB	Auditing Practices Board (disbanded in July 2012, replaced by the FRC's Audit and Assurance Council)
ASB	Accounting Standards Board (disbanded in July 2012, replaced by the FRC's Accounting Council)
BIS	Department for Business, Innovation and Skills
C(AICE) 2004	*Companies (Audit, Investigations and Community Enterprise) Act* 2004
CA 2006	*Companies Act* 2006
CCAB	Consultative Committee of Accountancy Bodies
EC	European Commission
EEA	European Economic Area
ESOP	Employee share ownership plan
EU	European Union
EU Regulation	Regulation (EC) No. 1606/2002 of the European Parliament (dated 19 July 2002) on the application of international accounting standards
FA	Finance Act
FASB	US Financial Accounting Standards Board
FRC	Financial Reporting Council
FRED	Financial Reporting Exposure Draft
FRRP	Financial Reporting Review Panel (disbanded in July 2012, replaced by the FRC Monitoring Committee)
FRS	Financial Reporting Standard
FRSSE	Financial Reporting Standard for Smaller Entities (being the 'FRSSE (effective April 2008)' or 'FRSSE (effective January 2015)' as indicated or as the circumstances dictate)
FSMA	*Financial Services and Markets Act 2000*
GAAP	Generally accepted accounting practice (or principles) (see also 'UK GAAP')
HMRC	Her Majesty's Revenue and Customs
IAASB	International Auditing and Assurance Standards Board
IAS	International Accounting Standards issued or adopted by IASB
IAS Regulation	Regulation (EC) No. 1606/2002 of the European Parliament (dated 19 July 2002) on the application of international accounting standards
IASB	International Accounting Standards Board
ICTA	*Income and Corporation Taxes Act 1988*
IFRIC	International Financial Reporting Interpretations Committee (an IASB committee)
IFRS	International Financial Reporting Standards (including IAS and interpretations adopted by IASB)
IFRS for SMEs	International Financial Reporting Standard for Small and Medium-sized Entities

ISA	International Standard on Auditing ('ISA (UK and Ireland)': an ISA applicable within the UK and Ireland). For the purpose of this book, these are the ISAs applicable in the UK and Ireland for financial periods starting before 17 June 2016.
NIC	National Insurance Contribution
MiFID	MiFID investment firm – an investment firm within the meaning of Directive 2004/39/EC, art. 4.1.1 of the European Parliament and of the Council of 21 April 2004 on markets in financial instruments (but see CA 2006, s. 474)
OCI	Other comprehensive income
OFR	Operating and Financial Review
OPSI	Office of Public Sector Information
P & L account	Profit and loss account
PAYE	Pay as you earn
PN	APB Practice Note
POB	Professional Oversight Board (part of the FRC) (disbanded in July 2012, replaced by the FRC Conduct Committee)
Reg.	Regulation (for example, SI 2008/409 reg. 4(2) means regulation 4(2) of SI 2008/409)
s.	section (unless otherwise stated, section references refer to CA 2006, as amended or inserted from time to time)
Sch.	Schedule (for example: 'CA 2006, Sch. 7.7(2)' means Companies Act 2006, Schedule 7, paragraph 7(2); or for SI 2008/409, 'SI 2008/409, Sch. 4.5(2)' or simply 'Sch. 4.5(2)' means Schedule 4, paragraph 5(2))
SI	Statutory instrument
SIC	Standing Interpretation Committee of IASB (or an interpretation of SIC e.g. 'SIC-1')
SME	Small or medium-sized entity (or enterprise)
SORP	Statement of Recommended Practice
SSAP	Statement of Standard Accounting Practice
SSRA	Statement of Standards for Reporting Accountants
STRGL	Statement of total recognised gains and losses
UCITS	Undertaking for Collective Investment in Transferable Securities (see CA 2006, s. 471(1))
UITF	Urgent Issues Task Force (part of FRC since July 2012, previously part of the ASB)
UK GAAP	Financial reporting requirements (as specified by the FRC) in the United Kingdom and the Republic of Ireland (see 'GAAP')
VAT	Value added tax

Statutory instruments

SI 2015/1672	*Companies, Partnerships and Groups (Accounts and Reports) (No. 2) Regulations* 2015
SI 2015/980	*Companies, Partnerships and Groups (Accounts and Reports) Regulations* 2015
SI 2013/3008	*Small Companies (Micro-Entities' Accounts) Regulations* 2013
SI 2013/1970	*Companies Act 2006 (Strategic Report and Directors' Report) Regulations* 2013

SI 2012/2301	*Companies and Limited Liability Partnerships (Accounts and Audit Exemptions and Change of Accounting Framework) Regulations 2012*
SI 2012/952	*Companies Act 2006 (Amendment of Part 23) (Investment Companies) Regulations 2012*
SI 2011/2198	*Companies (Disclosure of Auditor Remuneration and Liability Limitation Agreements) (Amendment) Regulations 2011*
SI 2009/1802	*Companies Act 2006 (Part 35) (Consequential Amendments, Transitional Provisions and Savings) Order 2009*
SI 2009/1581	*Companies Act 2006 (Accounts, Reports and Audit) Regulations 2009*
SI 2008/2860	*Companies Act 2006 (Commencement No. 8, Transitional Provisions and Savings) Order 2008*
SI 2008/489	*Companies (Disclosure of Auditor Remuneration and Liability Limitation Agreements) Regulations 2008*
SI 2008/410	*Large and Medium-sized Companies and Groups (Accounts and Reports) Regulations 2008*
SI 2008/409	*Small Companies and Groups (Accounts and Directors' Report) Regulations 2008*
SI 2008/393	*Companies Act 2006 (Amendment) (Accounts and Reports) Regulations 2008*
SI 2008/374	*Companies (Summary Financial Statement) Regulations 2008*
SI 2007/3495	*Companies Act 2006 (Commencement No. 5, Transitional Provisions and Savings) Order 2007*

EC Regulations and Directives

EC 1004/2008	Adoption of certain IASs in accordance with regulation EC 1606/2002 (amending regulation EC 1725/2003) (15 October 2008)
EC 707/2004	Adoption of certain IASs in accordance with regulation EC 1606/2002 (amending regulation EC 1725/2003) (6 April 2004)
EC 1606/2002	Requirement for use of IASs by listed companies (by 2005) (19 September 2002)
2003/51/EC	The 'Modernisation Directive' amending earlier Directives on annual and consolidated accounts (18 June 2003)
2001/65/EC	The 'Fair Value Directive' on valuation rules for annual and consolidated accounts of certain companies (21 September 2001)

Summary of implementation dates

Company Law

The *Companies Act* 2006 received Royal Assent on 8 November 2006. Provisions under the Act were introduced by commencement orders and regulations. All parts of the Act were brought into force by 1 October 2009.

Accounts and reports – generally, the requirements on the form and content of accounts and reports in CA 2006, Pt. 15 (Accounts and reports) and new regulations made under it (including, for example, SI 2008/410 for large and medium-sized companies) were effective for accounts and reports for **financial periods beginning on or after 6 April 2008**.

In March 2015, SI 2015/980 was issued implementing obligations in Directive 2013/34/EU ('the Directive') of the European Parliament and of the Council of 26 June 2013 on the annual financial statements, consolidated financial statements and related reports of certain types of undertakings, coming into force on 6 April 2015. These regulations make certain changes to the form and content of accounts and redefine the criteria for companies qualifying as medium-sized, small and micro which will apply for **financial periods beginning on or after 1 January 2016**.

Audit – the provisions of CA 2006, Pt. 16 (Audit) were effective on 6 April 2008, and, following the approach in Pt. 15 (Accounts and reports) above, most of the provisions became applicable to the audits of accounts for **financial periods beginning on or after 6 April 2008**.

The Companies Act 2006 and the ***Regulations*** are available on CCH Online in Companies Legislation.

Financial Reporting Standards

The following Financial Reporting Standards (and subsequent amendments) are mandatory for **financial periods commencing on or after 1 January 2015**:

FRS 100 *Application of Financial Reporting Requirements*

FRS 101 *Reduced Disclosure Framework*

FRS 102 *The Financial Reporting Standard applicable in the UK and Republic of Ireland*

FRS 103 *Insurance Contracts*

FRS 104 *Interim Financial Reporting*

In 2015, in conjunction with the changes to the Companies Act in respect of small and micro entities, the FRC issued a new section 1A to FRS 102 to implement the standard with reduced mandatory disclosures for small entities. At the same time, it also issued a new standard applicable to micro-entities:

FRS 105 *The Financial Reporting Standard applicable to the Micro-entities Regime*

Both FRS 105 and section 1A to FRS 102 are mandatory for **financial periods beginning on or after 1 January 2016** (although they may be earlier adopted for financial periods beginning on or after 1 January 2015).

FRS 105 was amended in May 2016 to bring limited liability partnerships and qualifying partnerships within the scope of the micro-entities regime. These amendments are applicable for accounting periods beginning on or after 1 January 2016, with early application permitted from 1 January 2015 if the new legislation the *Limited Liability Partnerships, Partnerships and Groups (Accounts and Audit) Regulations* 2016 are also applied from that date.

The full text of the standards and amendments are available on CCH Online in Accounting Standards.

International Accounting Standards and IFRS for SMEs

In accordance with SI 2004/2947, *Companies Act 1985 (International Accounting Standards and Other Accounting Amendments) Regulations* 2004, from 1 January 2005 all UK companies (other than charities and those automatically covered by the EU IAS Regulation) were permitted (but not required) to use international accounting standards (forming 'IAS accounts') as an alternative to the UK domestic reporting accounting framework ('Companies Act accounts').

In July 2009, the IASB issued the *IFRS for SMEs – International Financial Reporting Standard for Small and Medium-sized Entities*. The *IFRS for SMEs* has not been adopted for use in the EU and therefore cannot be applied in the UK, however much of FRS 102 was originally based on this standard.

Contents

		Page
Preface		*v*
About the authors		*vi*
Note on scope of book		*vii*
Abbreviations		*ix*
Summary of implementation dates		*xiii*

PART I GENERAL		**1**
1	**Introduction and purpose of this book**	**3**
2	**Companies Act 2006**	**5**
	2.1 Annual accounts under Companies Act 2006	5
	2.2 Companies Act accounts	6
	2.3 Contents of annual accounts and reports	9
	2.4 Auditing and audit reports	9
3	**General accounting provisions**	**11**
	3.1 Introduction	11
	3.2 Annual accounts	11
	3.3 'True and fair' view	12
	3.4 Format of accounts	13
	3.5 Accounting principles	14
	3.6 Notes to accounts – disclosures	15
	3.7 Strategic report and directors' report – contents and requirements	16
	3.8 Group accounts	16
	3.9 Audit requirements	17
	3.10 Adequate accounting records	18
	3.11 Approval and signature of accounts	19
	3.12 Publication of statutory and non-statutory accounts	19
4	**Financial Reporting Framework in UK and Republic of Ireland**	**21**
	4.1 The new financial reporting standards	21
	4.2 Application of financial reporting requirements (FRS 100)	21
	4.3 Summary of financial reporting framework	21
	4.4 Statement of compliance	22
	4.5 Consistency with company law	22
	4.6 Effective date and transitional arrangements	22
5	**Reduced disclosure framework**	**25**
	5.1 Qualifying entities	25
	5.2 Criteria	25
	5.3 Financial institutions	25
	5.4 Consolidated accounts	26
	5.5 Equivalent disclosures	26
	5.6 Specific disclosure exemptions	27

PART II FRS 102 – THE FINANCIAL REPORTING STANDARD APPLICABLE IN THE UK AND REPUBLIC OF IRELAND		**29**
6	**Introduction**	**31**
	6.1 Scope of the standard	31
	6.2 Basis of preparation of accounts	31
	6.3 Reduced disclosures for subsidiaries and ultimate parents	32

Contents

7   Concepts and pervasive principles   35
   7.1   Objective of accounts   35
   7.2   Qualitative characteristics of accounts information   35
   7.3   Financial position   36
   7.4   Performance   36
   7.5   Recognition of assets, liabilities, income and expenses   36
   7.6   Measurement of assets, liabilities, income and expenses   37
   7.7   Offsetting   37

8   Accounts presentation   39
   8.1   Fair presentation ('true and fair view')   39
   8.2   Composition of a set of accounts   39
   8.3   Compliance with the FRS   40
   8.4   Going concern   41
   8.5   Frequency of reporting and comparative information   41
   8.6   Consistency of presentation   41
   8.7   Materiality and aggregation   42

9   Format of accounts   43
   9.1   Statement of Financial Position   43
   9.2   Statement of Comprehensive Income   47
   9.3   Statement of Changes in Equity and Statement of Income and Retained Earnings   50
   9.4   Statement of Cash Flows   52
   9.5   Notes to the accounts   57
   9.6   Example accounts   58
   9.7   Small companies: abridged accounts   58

10 Consolidated and separate accounts (FRS 102 section 9)   59
   10.1   Definition of parent and subsidiary   59
   10.2   Requirement to present consolidated accounts   59
   10.3   Specific disclosures in consolidated accounts   62
   10.4   Individual and separate accounts   62
   10.5   Intermediate payment arrangements   63

11 Disclosure requirements of FRS 102   65
   11.1   Accounting policies, estimates and errors (FRS 102 section 10)   65
   11.2   Financial instruments (FRS 102 sections 11, 12 and 22)   66
   11.3   Inventories (FRS 102 section 13)   72
   11.4   Investments in associates (FRS 102 section 14)   73
   11.5   Investments in joint ventures (FRS 102 section 15)   74
   11.6   Investment property (FRS 102 section 16)   75
   11.7   Property, plant and equipment (FRS 102 section 17)   77
   11.8   Intangible assets other than goodwill (FRS 102 section 18) 79
   11.9   Business combinations and goodwill (FRS 102 section 19)   81
   11.10 Leases (FRS 102 section 20)   83
   11.11 Provisions and contingencies (FRS 102 section 21)   85
   11.12 Revenue (FRS 102 section 23)   87
   11.13 Government grants (FRS 102 section 24)   89
   11.14 Share-based payment (FRS 102 section 26)   89
   11.15 Impairment of assets (FRS 102 section 27)   91
   11.16 Employee benefits (FRS 102 section 28)   92
   11.17 Income tax (FRS 102 section 29)   95
   11.18 Foreign currency translation (FRS 102 section 30)   96
   11.19 Hyperinflation (FRS 102 section 31)   97
   11.20 Events after the end of the reporting period (FRS 102 sections 32)   97
   11.21 Related party disclosures (FRS 102 section 33)   98

| | 11.22 | Specialised activities (FRS 102 section 34) | 101 |
| | 11.23 | Transition to FRS 102 (FRS 102 section 35) | 102 |

PART III DIRECTOR AND AUDITOR REPORTS | | | 103

12 Strategic Report and Directors' Report | | | 105
| | 12.1 | Strategic Report | 105 |
| | 12.2 | Directors' Report | 106 |

13 Auditor's Report | | | 109
	13.1	Auditor's reports now and in the future	109
	13.2	ISA (UK and Ireland) 700 The Independent Auditor's Report on Financial Statements	111
	13.3	Example Auditor's Report of a medium-sized (or large) company	112
	13.4	Example Auditor's Report of a small company	114

PART IV FILING OF ACCOUNTS | | | 117

14 Filing exemptions for small and medium-sized companies | | | 119
| | 14.1 | Abbreviated accounts | 119 |
| | 14.2 | Filing exemptions for small companies only | 119 |

15 Filing of accounts | | | 121
	15.1	Introduction and electronic filing	121
	15.2	Filing deadlines	121
	15.3	Registrar of Companies	122
	15.4	Filing accounts in paper form	123
	15.5	Common reasons for accounts rejections at Companies House	123
	15.6	Filing accounts in electronic form	124
	15.7	Amended accounts	124
	15.8	HMRC	125
	15.9	Electronic tagging of accounts (iXBRL)	125

APPENDICES | | 127

Appendix A	Example accounts	129
Appendix B	FRS 102 Disclosure checklist	159
Appendix C	Large and Medium-sized Companies and Groups (Accounts and Reports) Regulations 2008 (SI 2008/410)	239
Appendix D	Glossary of terms used in FRS 102	413
Appendix E	Selected reading and reference material	433

INDEX | | 435

Part I   General

Chapter 1   Introduction and purpose of this book

This book is concerned with the accounts of companies preparing accounts under 'new' UK GAAP (i.e. FRS 102 *The Financial Reporting Standard applicable in the UK and Ireland*).

All UK companies are eligible to prepare their individual accounts in accordance with this Financial Reporting Standard. However, there are other options available:

- any company may elect to prepare 'IAS Accounts', i.e. in accordance with International Accounting Standards;

- 'small companies' may elect to prepare accounts with less detailed information, i.e. in accordance with the 'small companies' regime' and section 1A of FRS 102;

- 'micro-entities' may elect to prepare simple accounts with minimal information, i.e. in accordance with the 'micro-entities regime' and FRS 105.

A company is treated as micro or small (or medium-sized) if it does not exceed more than one of the following criteria in its first accounting period or in two successive periods:

	Micro	Small	Medium-sized
Turnover	£632,000	£10.2m	£36m
Balance sheet total	£316,000	£5.1m	£18m
Average number of employees (on a monthly basis)	10	50	250

Certain categories of company, regardless of size, are not entitled to any exemptions. These are:

- public companies;

- members of 'ineligible' (basically, public or regulated) groups;

- companies carrying on an insurance market activity; and

- companies that are authorised insurance companies, banking companies, e-money issuers, MiFID investment firms or UCITS management companies.

More detailed information concerning the qualification as micro or small is available in the companion publication *CCH Preparing Company Accounts 2016–17 – Small and Micros* available from www.cch.co.uk/books.

See **Chapter 2** for an explanation of the framework for preparing accounts and the options available.

This book aims to provide an explanation of the requirements for company accounts prepared in accordance with FRS 102 within the statutory provisions of the Companies Act. While not purporting to give a comprehensive explanation of all accounting provisions contained in the standard the objective is to explain many of the accounting requirements that apply to most companies and matters of practical relevance.

It is intended as a stand-alone guide to the disclosure requirements of the new standard and not a detailed comparison of the changes from the suite of SSAPs and FRSs which remain extant for accounting periods which commenced before 1 January 2015. Similarly, it does not include a comparison of the changes from the FRSSE which can still be used for accounting periods which commenced before 1 January 2016. The book will, however, explain differences from 'old' UK GAAP where this detail is considered necessary. A useful overview comparison between the accounting standards is available in *CCH New UK GAAP: An at a glance comparison between new and old UK GAAP and IFRS*.

The book is written from the perspective of a UK company whose equity or debt is not listed on any recognised stock exchange or equivalent market. It provides the following:

- a summary of the statutory company accounts provisions in general;

- an explanation of the framework for the preparation of accounts in the UK and Republic of Ireland (FRS 100);

- guidelines and definitions – for accounting presentation, disclosure and terminology;

- illustrative examples including example full statutory company accounts; and

- a disclosure checklist for an individual company preparing accounts in accordance with FRS 102.

This book refers briefly to the disclosure requirements for small companies preparing accounts in accordance with section 1A of FRS 102; more detailed information is available in the companion publication *CCH Preparing Company Accounts 2016–17 – Small and Micros.*

Chapter 2   Companies Act 2006

2.1   Annual accounts under Companies Act 2006

2.1.1   Basic approach

The *Companies Act* 2006 received Royal Assent on 8 November 2006. Running to 701 pages of primary legislation together with 59 pages of index and comprising 47 Parts, 1,300 sections and 16 Schedules, it was the longest Act ever. It consolidated virtually all existing companies legislation, introduced many reforms and company law was re-written and re-presented to make it easier to understand and more flexible – especially for smaller companies.

Working on the 'think small first' approach, company law is presented on a basis that clearly recognises each of the following categories of company or group (CA 2006, s. 380):

- micro entities (a subset of small companies);
- small companies;
- larger private companies;
- public companies (other than quoted companies);
- quoted public companies;
- all companies.

Different provisions apply to different kinds of company; the main distinctions are between:

- companies subject to the 'micro entities regime' (CA 2006, s. 384A) or 'small companies' regime' (CA 2006, s. 381) and companies that are not subject to either regime; and
- quoted companies (CA 2006, s. 385) and companies that are not quoted.

Provisions applying to companies subject to the small companies' regime appear in the legislation before the provisions applying to other companies (CA 2006, s. 380(4)).

The law, both within the Act itself and in supporting legislation issued in regulations under it, is clearly presented in its application. There are separate comprehensive codes of accounting and reporting requirements for small and larger companies, defining the generally accepted accounting practice relevant to them.

2.1.2   Implementation

Provisions of CA 2006 were introduced by statutory instrument by means of 'commencement orders' and other supporting regulations in the months leading up to October 2009, the date by which all parts of the Act came into force.

The accounts and report provisions of the Act relate to financial years *commencing on or after 6 April 2008*.

2.1.3   Accounts and audit

The Act covers accounts and audit within:

- Part 15 (s. 380–474) – 'Accounts and reports'; and
- Part 16 (s. 475–539) – 'Audit' (where relevant, subject to audit exemption rules).

2.1.4 Applicable accounting framework

CA 2006, s. 395 specifies that all companies prepare accounts that are either in accordance with:

- CA 2006, s. 396 ('Companies Act accounts'); or

- International accounting standards ('IAS accounts').

Charitable companies may only prepare Companies Act accounts.

If a company has prepared IAS accounts then it must continue to do so and may only revert to Companies Act accounts if there has been a relevant change of circumstances (CA 2006, s. 395(3)). A relevant change of circumstances occurs when a company becomes a subsidiary of another that does not prepare IAS accounts, a company ceases to be a subsidiary undertaking or a company (or its parent) ceases to have its shares traded on a regulated market.

Any company may revert from IAS Accounts to Companies Act accounts without a relevant change of circumstances provided that they have not done so in the previous five years.

2.2 Companies Act accounts

This book is concerned with the preparation of Companies Act accounts and not IAS accounts.

The preparation of accounts is governed by:

- CA 2006, Pt. 15 (relevant sections) (the 'primary legislation'); and

- Regulations made under statutory instruments ('secondary legislation') covering the form and content of accounts and directors' report. In particular for large and medium-sized companies – the *Large and Medium-sized Companies and Groups (Accounts and Reports) Regulations* 2008 (SI 2008/410) and for small companies – the *Small Companies and Groups (Accounts and Directors' Report) Regulations* 2008 (SI 2008/409).

The regulations were amended in 2015 by the *Companies, Partnerships and Groups (Accounts and Reports) Regulations* 2015 (SI 2015/980). All references hereinafter are made to the regulations as amended.

2.2.1 Structure of SI 2008/410

The *Large and Medium-sized Companies and Groups (Accounts and Reports) Regulations* 2008 (SI 2008/410) specify the form and content of the accounts and directors' report of companies not subject to the small companies regime under of the CA 2006, Pt. 15. The contents and structure of SI 2008/410 the regulations are as follows:

Table 2.1 Large and Medium-sized Companies and Groups (Accounts and Reports) Regulations 2008 (SI 2008/410)

Part 1 – Introduction

Part 2 – Form and content of accounts

Part 3 – Directors' report

Part 4 – Directors' remuneration report

Part 5 – Interpretation

Schedules:

Schedule 1 – *Companies Act individual accounts: companies which are not banking or insurance companies*

- general rules and formats
- accounting principles and rules
- notes to the accounts
- special provision where company is a parent or subsidiary undertaking
- special provisions where company is an investment company

Schedule 2 – *Banking companies: Companies Act individual accounts*

- general rules and formats
- accounting principles and rules
- notes to the accounts
- interpretation of this schedule

Schedule 3 – *Insurance companies: Companies Act individual accounts*

- general rules and formats
- accounting principles and rules
- notes to the accounts
- interpretation of this schedule

Schedule 4 – *Information on related undertakings required whether preparing Companies Act or IAS accounts*

- provisions applying to all companies
- companies not required to prepare group accounts
- companies required to prepare group accounts
- additional disclosures for banking companies and groups
- interpretation of references to 'beneficial interest'

Schedule 5 – *Information about benefits of directors*

- provisions applying to quoted and unquoted companies
- provisions applying only to unquoted companies
- supplementary provisions

Schedule 6 – *Companies Act group accounts*

- general rules
- modifications for banking groups
- modifications for insurance groups

Schedule 7 – *Matters to be dealt with in Directors' Report*

- matters of a general nature
- disclosure required by company acquiring its own shares, etc.
- disclosure concerning employment, etc. of disabled persons
- employee involvement
- policy and practice on payment of creditors
- disclosure required by certain publicly traded companies

Schedule 8 – *Quoted companies: Directors' remuneration report*

- introductory
- information not subject to audit
- information subject to audit
- interpretation and supplementary

Schedule 9 – *Interpretation of term 'provisions'*

- part 1 meaning for purposes of these regulations
- part 2 meaning for purposes of parts 18 and 23 of the 2006 Act

Schedule 10 – *General information*

The *Large and Medium-sized Companies and Groups (Accounts and Reports) Regulations* 2008 (SI 2008/410) are reproduced in full in **Appendix C**.

2.2.2   Structure of SI 2008/409

The *Small Companies and Groups (Accounts and Directors' Report) Regulations* 2008 (SI 2008/409) specify the form and content of the accounts and directors' report of companies subject to the small companies regime under of the CA 2006, Pt. 15. The contents and structure of the regulations are as follows.

Table 2.2 The Small Companies and Groups (Accounts and Directors' Report) Regulations 2008 (SI 2008/409)

Part 1 – Introduction

Part 2 – Form and content of accounts

Part 3 – Directors' report

Part 4 – Directors' remuneration report

Part 5 – Interpretation

Schedules:

Schedule 1 – *Companies Act individual accounts*

- general rules and formats
- accounting principles and rules
- notes to the accounts

Schedule 2 [*omitted*]

Schedule 3 [*omitted*]

Schedule 4 [*omitted*]

Schedule 5 – *Matters to be dealt with in Directors' Report*

Schedule 6 – *Group accounts*

- form and content of companies act group accounts
- information about related undertakings where company preparing group accounts (companies act or IAS accounts)

Schedule 7 – *Interpretation of term 'provisions'*

- part 1 meaning for purposes of these regulations
- part 2 meaning for purposes of parts 18 and 23 of the 2006 Act

Schedule 8 – *General interpretation*

The *Small Companies and Groups (Accounts and Directors' Report) Regulations* 2008 (SI 2008/409) are available on CCH Online and in the book *CCH Preparing Company Accounts: Small and micros.*

2.3   Contents of annual accounts and reports

The content and structure of annual accounts and reports is governed not only by the requirements of the Companies Act and secondary legislation but also by applicable accounting standards.

See **Chapter 4** for a detailed explanation of the options available to companies on the accounting standards applicable to Companies Act accounts.

2.4   Auditing and audit reports

Audit is covered in CA 2006, Pt. 16, which contains provisions concerning, for example, the requirement for audited accounts, the appointment of auditors, the auditor's report, the duties and rights of auditors, and removal, resignation, etc.

The audit report must include an introduction identifying the annual accounts and the financial reporting framework under which they are prepared, together with a description of the scope of the audit identifying the auditing standards adopted.

In essence, under CA 2006, s. 495, the auditor is required to report his opinion on four elements.

- *True and fair view* – whether the annual accounts show a 'true and fair view' (having regard to the directors' statutory duty under CA 2006, s. 393(1)).

- *Relevant reporting framework* – whether the accounts have been prepared in accordance with the relevant financial reporting framework.

- *Appropriate legislation* – whether the accounts have been prepared in accordance with CA 2006 (Pt. 15) or IAS (IAS Regulation, art. 4), if applicable.

- *Form of report or emphasis* – whether the report is 'unqualified or qualified' or contains reference to any emphasis of any matters without qualifying the report.

The auditor's report must state the name of the auditor and be signed and dated. Where the auditor is a firm, the report must be signed by the 'senior statutory auditor' in his own name, for and on behalf of the auditor (CA 2006, s. 504). This only applies to the set of the accounts provided to the members of the company. A signature is not required on the set of accounts delivered to Companies House. However, if the auditor wishes to physically sign the accounts for Companies House, they can be signed in the name of the firm rather than the individual.

The form of report by auditors to be adopted with respect to Companies Act accounts is determined by CA 2006 and also by international auditing standards applicable within the UK. Following the adoption of International Standards on Auditing (ISAs), auditors' reports on accounts are required to follow, inter alia, ISA (UK and Ireland) 700 (Revised) *The Auditor's Report on Financial Statements*, as commented on within **Chapter 13**.

Chapter 3   General accounting provisions

3.1   Introduction

This chapter summarises the accounting provisions of CA 2006 which relate to the prescriptive formats of accounts, the content of accounts and the principles and rules for determining amounts included in the accounts.

Annual accounts may be prepared:

- as 'Companies Act individual accounts' (CA 2006, s. 396) or 'Companies Act group accounts' (CA 2006, s. 404); or

- in accordance with international accounting standards ('IAS individual accounts' or 'IAS group accounts') (CA 2006, s. 395(1)).

The chapter summarises accounts provisions of CA 2006, insofar as they relate to accounts ('individual accounts') which the directors of the company have a duty to prepare in accordance with CA 2006, s. 394.

'Abridged accounts' (available to small companies only) are considered separately in **Chapter 14**.

Consolidated accounts prepared by groups are covered in **Chapter 10**.

3.2   Annual accounts

Accounts must be prepared for members for all companies, irrespective of size (except dormant subsidiary companies, subject to certain criteria – see CA 2006, s. 394A).

A company qualifying as 'small' may, in addition, present a reduced form of accounts for filing with the Registrar of Companies (see **Chapter 14**).

Depending on certain size criteria, small companies may be exempt from the requirement for audit. Certain subsidiaries and dormant companies may also take advantage of audit exemption (see **Chapter 13**).

Company accounts are produced from the company's underlying financial records ('adequate accounting records') as explained at 3.10 (CA 2006, s. 386–389 'Accounting Records').

Table 3.1 summarises the requirements which directors must follow in respect of a company's 'individual accounts' which are set out in CA 2006, s. 396.

Table 3.1 Individual accounts (CA 2006, s. 396)

For each financial year, the directors must prepare individual accounts comprising:

- a balance sheet; and

- a profit and loss account;

showing a true and fair view of:

- the state of affairs at the year end; and

- the profit or loss for the financial year;

complying with:

> - the provisions of the *Large and Medium-sized Companies and Groups (Accounts and Reports) Regulations* 2008 (SI 2008/410) or the *Small Companies and Groups (Accounts and Directors' Report) Regulations* 2008 (SI 2008/409) as to form, content and notes;
>
> containing:
>
> - any additional information (or departure from requirement) necessary to show a true and fair view.

3.3   'True and fair' view

As shown in **Table 3.1**, there is a fundamental requirement for full accounts (individual accounts or group accounts) to show a 'true and fair' view, a term that has never been defined in statute or case law (but see **8.1**).

The directors of a company must not approve accounts unless they are satisfied that they give a true and fair view of the company's assets, liabilities, financial position and profit or loss.

The requirement for full accounts to show a 'true and fair' view applies irrespective of whether or not the accounts are subject to audit. Any decision concerning the method of accounting or means of disclosing information must take this fundamental requirement into account.

In essence, accounts may be considered to present a 'true and fair view' if they:

- comply with any relevant legislation or regulatory requirement;
- comply with accounting standards and generally accepted accounting practice;
- provide an unbiased (fair and reasonable) presentation;
- are compiled with sufficient accuracy within the bounds of materiality; and
- faithfully represent the underlying commercial activity (the concept of 'substance over legal form').

However, please refer to **8.1** to see how this applies to small companies preparing accounts in accordance with FRS 102 section 1A.

The requirement for accounts to give a 'true and fair view' is also embodied within European Accounting Directives. In the case of IAS accounts, there is a requirement under international accounting standards that such accounts must achieve a 'fair presentation' which in all practical aspects is the same as true and fair.

A 'true and fair view' is required to be given of the state of affairs of the company (and/or consolidated undertakings) as at the end of the financial year and of the profit or loss of the company (and/or consolidated undertakings so far as concerns members of the parent company) for the financial year.

Where compliance with the provisions of CA 2006 as to the matters to be included in 'annual accounts' ('individual accounts' or 'group accounts') or the notes would not be sufficient to give a true and fair view, the necessary additional information must be given in the accounts or in a note to them.

If in special circumstances such compliance is inconsistent with the requirement to show a 'true and fair view', the directors must depart from the relevant provision of CA 2006 to the extent necessary to show a 'true and fair view' and must explain such departure in a note to the accounts (the true and fair 'override' principle). One common example of this circumstance which arose in old UK GAAP concerned the non-depreciation of fixed asset investment properties in accordance with SSAP 19.

The 'true and fair view' has the ultimate legal override; a company may override accounting standards only to give a 'true and fair view' and this would be only in exceptional circumstances. A departure from an accounting standard must be justified and explained.

3.4   Format of accounts

The form and content of accounts is governed by regulations made under CA 2006.

The form and content of Companies Act accounts for companies that do not qualify for, or choose not to apply the small companies' regime is determined in accordance with the *Large and Medium-sized Companies and Groups (Accounts and Reports) Regulations* 2008 (SI 2008/410).

Schedules within SI 2008/410 prescribe the required formats from which companies may choose for Companies Act individual accounts (Sch. 1) and group accounts (Sch. 6).

The full text of SI 2008/410 is reprinted in **Appendix C**.

The form and content of Companies Act accounts for small companies is determined in accordance with the *Small Companies and Groups (Accounts and Directors' Report) Regulations* 2008 (SI 2008/409).

Schedules within SI 2008/409 prescribe the required formats from which companies may choose for Companies Act individual accounts (Sch. 1) and group accounts (Sch. 6).

Once a format has been adopted, the company must use the same format for subsequent years unless, in the directors' opinion, there are special reasons for changing; these must be disclosed in the year of change.

The accounts must show the items listed in the adopted format if they apply either in the financial year or the preceding year.

Adopting a particular format is not as restricting as it may seem, as there are a variety of options, for example:

- departure from the format is allowed if it is made to ensure a true and fair view (see above);
- certain headings (which the Schedules identify by the use of Arabic numbers) may be combined (provided combination is disclosed);
- immaterial items may be disregarded;
- information can be given in greater detail than prescribed and items not listed in a format may be included, if directors so wish; and
- certain information may be given in notes instead of on the face of the accounts.

The balance sheet format may be adapted to distinguish between current and non-current items in a different way and the profit and loss account format may be adapted, provided that:

(a) the information given is at least equivalent to that which would have been required by the use of such format had it not been thus adapted; and

(b) the presentation of those items is in accordance with generally accepted accounting principles or practice.

Where there is no amount to be shown for a format item for the financial year, a heading or sub-heading corresponding to the item must not be included, unless an amount can be shown for the item in question for the immediately preceding financial year under the relevant format heading or sub-heading.

For every item shown in the current period, the corresponding amount for the immediately preceding financial year must also be shown. Where that corresponding preceding year amount is not comparable, the prior year amount may be adjusted, but particulars of the non-comparability and of any adjustment must be disclosed in a note to the accounts.

Every profit and loss account must show the amount of a company's profit or loss before taxation (see **Chapter 9** at **9.2**).

3.5   Accounting principles

Company accounts are required to be prepared in accordance with the principles set out in:

- SI 2008/410, Sch. 1 – for medium-sized and large companies; and
- SI 2008/410, Sch. 6 – for medium-sized and large groups;

or:

- SI 2008/409, Sch. 1 – for small companies;
- SI 2008/409, Sch. 6 – for small groups.

These principles are the fundamental accounting concepts that underlie accounts and are also incorporated within accounting standards generally.

The basic statutory accounting principles to SI 2008/410, Sch. 1 and SI 2008/409, Sch. 1 (together 'the Regulations') are as follows:

(1)   Going concern – the company is presumed to be carrying on business as a going concern.

(2)   Consistency – accounting policies must be applied consistently within the same accounts and from one financial year to the next.

(3)   Prudence – the amount of any item must be determined on a prudent basis and in particular:

    (a)   only profits realised at the balance sheet date must be included in the profit and loss account; and

    (b)   all liabilities having arisen in respect of the financial year (or preceding financial years) must be taken into account (including those liabilities becoming apparent up to the date of approval of the accounts (in accordance with CA 2006, s. 414)).

(4)   Accruals – all income and charges relating to the financial year to which the accounts relate must be taken into account, without regard to the date of receipt or payment.

(5)   Individual determination – in determining the aggregate amount of any item, the amount of each individual asset or liability that is taken into account must be determined separately.

(6)   Netting – amounts in respect of items representing assets or income must not be set off against amounts in respect of items representing liabilities or expenditure (as the case may be), or vice versa.

(7)   Substance of transactions – in determining how amounts are presented within the accounts, regard should be had to the substance of the reported transaction or arrangement in accordance with GAAP.

If it appears to the company's directors that there are special reasons for departing from any of the accounting principles in preparing the company's accounts in respect of any financial year, they may do so. Particulars of the departure, the reasons for it and its effect must be given in a note to the accounts.

Accounting standards enhance the above principles by determining that accounting policies adopted should be relevant, reliable, comparable and understandable.

For fixed assets, stocks, investments and goodwill, rules regarding valuation, accounting and disclosure are laid down in the Regulations (supplemented where relevant by accounting standards).

Historical cost principles are stated as the normal method of accounting but alternative bases (e.g. revaluation and current cost) are allowed provided that details and related historical cost figures are disclosed. The 'alternative accounting rules' and 'fair value accounting' rules are set out in the Regulations.

Only 'realised' profits can be included in the profit and loss account subject to the fair value accounting rules which permit certain fair value gains and losses to be shown in the profit and loss account where the required by accounting standards. This is particularly pertinent as FRS 102 requires or permits more assets and liabilities to be measured at fair value with gains or losses being taken through profit and loss.

In determining for accounting purposes 'realised profits' (and 'realised losses'), such profits or losses mean profits or losses of the company that fall to be treated as realised in accordance with principles generally accepted at the time when the accounts are prepared, unless the CA 2006 specifies some other treatment.

3.6　Notes to accounts – disclosures

The Regulations also set out information required to be disclosed in the notes to company's accounts, covering the following heads (only items marked with an asterisk (*) are required for small companies):

- reserves and dividends;
- disclosure of accounting policies;
- share capital and debentures;
- fixed assets*;
- investments;
- assets and liabilities valued at fair value*;
- investment property and living animals and plants at fair value;
- reserves and provisions;
- provision for taxation;
- details of indebtedness (including payments by instalments and nature of security)*;
- guarantees and other financial commitments*;
- separate statement and analysis of interest and similar charges;
- particulars (analysis) of tax;
- particulars (analysis) of turnover;
- prior period adjustments included in profit and loss account – effect of inclusion*;
- exceptional items*;
- sums denominated in foreign currencies – basis of translation into sterling;
- dormant companies acting as agent;
- related party transactions* (see below);
- post balance sheet events*; and
- particulars of proposed appropriations of profit or treatment of loss.

Note that some disclosures not necessarily required by the Regulations for small companies are still required by FRS 102 (e.g. related party transactions).

In the case of related party transactions, small companies need only disclose those that are material and not conducted under normal market conditions.

3.7 Strategic report and directors' report – contents and requirements

In addition to the accounts, the directors of a company must prepare a strategic report and directors' report for each financial year of the company.

Where the company is a parent company, and the directors of the company prepare group accounts, the reports must be consolidated reports (e.g. 'group strategic report') covering all the undertakings included in the consolidation. A group report may, where appropriate, give greater emphasis to matters that are significant to the undertakings included in the consolidation, taken as a whole.

Small companies or those companies which would otherwise qualify as small but for being members of an ineligible group are exempt from the requirement to prepare a strategic report.

For accounting periods ending on or after 30 September 2013, the strategic report is required as a separate report under CA 2006, s. 414A. For earlier accounting periods, the information required to be included in a strategic report is contained in the 'business review' section of the directors' report.

Quoted companies are also required to prepare a directors' remuneration report (s. 421), covering aspects of directors' remuneration such as remuneration details, company policy, service contracts, share options and pension disclosures. Those requirements are outside the scope of this book.

In accordance with s. 385, a 'quoted company' means a company whose equity share capital has been included in the official list in accordance with the provisions of the *Financial Services and Markets Act* 2000 (c. 8), Pt. 6, or is officially listed in an EEA state, or is admitted to dealing on either the New York Stock Exchange or the NASDAQ.

Details of required components of the strategic report and directors' report are given in **Chapter 12**.

3.8 Group accounts

A parent company (other than a small parent company) which has 'subsidiary undertakings' is required (subject to some exceptions) to prepare group accounts in the form of consolidated accounts of the company and its subsidiary undertakings. Consolidation is not restricted to subsidiaries which are companies.

Group accounts (when prepared) are required to comply with the provisions of CA 2006 as to the form and content of consolidated accounts and additional information to be given. Regulations under CA 2006 provided by SI 2008/410, Sch. 4 and 6 require the following accounting for consolidations:

- elimination of group transactions;
- provisions for acquisition and merger accounting;
- treatment and disclosure of 'minority interests';
- non-consolidated subsidiary undertakings;
- joint ventures and associated undertakings; and
- preparation 'as if' he group were a single company.

A subsidiary may be excluded from consolidation on the grounds of immateriality and must be excluded in the following circumstances:

- severe long-term restrictions; or

- temporary control – holding with a view to subsequent resale.

Exemptions from the requirement to prepare consolidated accounts otherwise available for groups generally are under:

- s. 400 (company included in EEA accounts of larger group);

- s. 401 (company included in non-EEA accounts of larger group); and

- s. 402 (company none of whose subsidiary undertakings need be included in the consolidation).

A parent of a small group may voluntarily prepare group accounts. Regulations are provided in SI 2008/409 which are equivalent to those noted above.

Further details about group accounts are given in **Chapter 10**.

3.9   Audit requirements

Full statutory accounts (together with an audit report, if appropriate) are required for members for all companies.

A company's accounts for a financial period must be audited unless the company may claim exemption under:

- s. 477 (small companies);

- s. 479A (certain subsidiary companies subject to certain qualifying conditions); or

- s. 480 (dormant companies).

Audit exemption limits have increased in line with the limits set out in **Chapter 1** for accounting purposes with effect for periods beginning on or after 1 January 2016. Note that although the new limits can be applied for accounting purposes voluntarily from 1 January 2015, this option is not available for audit purposes.

In addition certain non-profit-making companies subject to public sector audit may also be exempt.

A company is not entitled to any such exemption unless its balance sheet contains a statement by the directors immediately above the signature confirming it is exempt and that:

- the members have not required the company to obtain an audit of its accounts for the year in question in accordance with s. 476; and

- the directors acknowledge their responsibilities for complying with the requirements of the Companies Act with respect to accounting records and the preparation of accounts.

The auditor must state clearly whether, in the auditor's opinion, the annual accounts:

- give a true and fair view:

  - in the case of an individual balance sheet, of the state of affairs of the company as at the end of the financial year;

  - in the case of an individual profit and loss account, of the profit or loss of the company for the financial year;

  – in the case of group accounts, of the state of affairs as at the end of the financial year and of the profit or loss for the financial year of the undertakings included in the consolidation as a whole, so far as concerns members of the company;

- have been properly prepared in accordance with the relevant financial reporting framework; and

- have been prepared in accordance with the requirements of the Companies Act.

The auditor must also consider whether the information given in the strategic report (if applicable) and directors' report is consistent with the accounts or contains any apparent misstatements and must state that fact in their report. There is no requirement to state in what respect it is inconsistent however an indication of apparent misstatements must be given.

In the case of a quoted company the auditor must report to the company's members on the auditable part of the directors' remuneration report and state whether in the auditor's opinion that part of the directors' remuneration report has been properly prepared in accordance with the Companies Act. The 'auditable part' of a directors' remuneration report is the part identified as such by regulations under CA 2006, s. 421.

Where a company subject to audit takes advantage of the filing exemptions available to small companies (see **Chapter 14**), and does not deliver to the registrar a copy of the company's profit and loss accounts (and consequently also not file the auditor's report), the copy of the balance sheet delivered to the registrar must disclose that fact, and:

- state whether the auditor's report was qualified or unqualified;

- where that report was qualified, disclose the basis of the qualification; and

- state the name of the auditor and (where the auditor is a firm) the name of the person who signed the auditor's report as senior statutory auditor.

Please note that the option to prepare and file abbreviated accounts is withdrawn for periods commencing on or after 1 January 2016.

3.10 Adequate accounting records

Companies are required to keep 'adequate accounting records' in accordance with CA 2006, s. 386. Company accounts are produced from these underlying financial records.

CA 2006, s. 386 is summarised in **Table 3.2**.

Table 3.2 Adequate accounting records

A company is required to keep accounting records ('adequate accounting records') which are sufficient to show and explain the company's transactions. The accounting records must:

- disclose with reasonable accuracy, at any time, the financial position of the company at that time;

- enable the directors to ensure that any accounts required to be prepared comply with the requirements of CA 2006;

- contain entries from day to day of all receipts and expenditure (with sufficient identifying detail); and

- contain a record of company assets and liabilities.

If the company deals in goods, the accounting records must also contain statements of:

- stock held at the year end;

- stocktaking (records and procedures) underlying the year end stock; and

- all goods sold and purchased (except for retail sales), in sufficient detail to identify the goods and the buyers and sellers.

A parent company must ensure that any subsidiary undertaking keeps such accounting records as ensure compliance with CA 2006.

(Directors should be constantly aware of the company's financial position and progress. The exact nature and extent of the accounting systems and management information needed to exercise adequate control will depend on the nature, complexity and extent of the company's business.)

Adequate control over records and transactions involves monitoring:

- cash;
- debtors and creditors;
- stock and work in progress;
- capital expenditure;
- contractual arrangements; and
- plans and budgets.

Accounting records are required by CA 2006, s. 388(4) to be preserved for:

- three years (private company); or
- six years (public company).

From the date on which they are made; although, having regard to other legislation, it is generally considered that documents should be kept for at least six years (and 12 years in the event of contracts under seal).

3.11   Approval and signature of accounts

The strategic report (if applicable), directors' report, statutory accounts and the auditor's report all require appropriate approval and signature.

A company's annual accounts must be approved by the board of directors and signed on behalf of the board by a director of the company. The signature must be on the company's individual balance sheet and the name of the signatory must be stated.

The strategic report (if applicable) and directors' report must also be approved by the board of directors and signed on their behalf by a director or the secretary of the company; the name of the signatory must be similarly stated. On occasions when the secretary signs the directors' report this is generally 'by order of the board'.

The above requirements also apply to the approval and directors' signature of abbreviated accounts.

The auditor's report must state the name of the auditor and be signed and dated. Where the auditor is an individual, the report must be signed by him. Where the auditor is a firm, the report delivered to the members must be signed by the senior statutory auditor in his own name, for and on behalf of the firm of auditors.

3.12   Publication of statutory and non-statutory accounts

If a company publishes any of its statutory accounts (other than a summary financial statement under s. 426), they must be accompanied by the auditor's report on those accounts (unless the company is exempt from audit and the directors have taken advantage of that exemption).

A company that prepares statutory group accounts for a financial year must not publish its statutory individual accounts for that year without also publishing with them its statutory group accounts.

If a company publishes non-statutory accounts, it must publish with them a statement indicating:

- that they are not the company's statutory accounts;
- whether statutory accounts dealing with any financial year with which the non-statutory accounts purport to deal have been delivered to the Registrar of Companies; and
- whether an auditor's report has been made on the company's statutory accounts for any such financial year, and if so whether the report:
  - was qualified or unqualified, or included a reference to any matters to which the auditor drew attention by way of emphasis without qualifying the report; or
  - contained a statement under CA 2006, s. 498(2) (accounting records or returns inadequate or accounts or directors' remuneration report (where applicable) not agreeing with records and returns), or CA 2006, s. 498(3) (failure to obtain necessary information and explanations).

A company must not publish with any non-statutory accounts the auditor's report (i.e. the full audit report) on the company's statutory accounts.

'Non-statutory accounts' are accounts or other published financial information that are not the company's statutory accounts (e.g. simplified accounting information such as an account in any form purporting to be a balance sheet or profit and loss account relating to the financial year of a company or group).

Chapter 4   Financial Reporting Framework
        in UK and Republic of Ireland

4.1   The new financial reporting standards

As set out in the Summary of implementation dates, the relevant suite of financial reporting standards in the UK now consists of:

- FRS 100 – *Application of financial reporting requirements*;

- FRS 101 – *Reduced disclosure framework*;

- FRS 102 – *The financial reporting standard applicable in the UK and Republic of Ireland*;

- FRS 103 – *Insurance contracts*;

- FRS 104 – *Interim financial statements*; and

- FRS 105 – *The financial reporting standard applicable to the micro-entities regime*.

These standards replaced all extant Statements of Standard Accounting Practice (SSAPs), Financial Reporting Standards (FRSs) and Urgent Issues Task Force Abstracts (UITFs) with effect from accounting periods commencing 1 January 2015.

The Financial Reporting Standard for Smaller Entities (FRSSE 2015) was withdrawn for periods commencing on or after 1 January 2016 and was replaced by FRS 102 section 1A (for small companies) and FRS 105 (for micro-entities).

4.2   Application of financial reporting requirements (FRS 100)

FRS 100 sets out the financial reporting requirements for UK and Republic of Ireland entities preparing accounts that are intended to give a true and fair view of the assets, liabilities, financial position and profit or loss for a period.

The standard requires entities prepare their accounts, depending on eligibility, in accordance with either EU-adopted IFRS, FRS 101, 102 or 105.

- EU-adopted IFRS is applied when required by law or regulation e.g. in consolidated accounts of fully listed or AIM companies. It is optional for other entities.

- FRS 101 sets out a reduced disclosure framework for individual accounts of qualifying entities that apply EU-adopted IFRS for recognition and measurement.

- FRS 102 replaces the current suite of standards which comprise UK GAAP. It includes a reduced disclosure requirements for small companies and other disclosure exemptions for qualifying group entities.

- FRS 105 may be applied by eligible micro entities.

4.3   Summary of financial reporting framework

The following table summarises the options available to entities.

Table 4.1 Summary of financial reporting framework options

Accounting regime	Applicable to	Expected users
EU-adopted IFRS	• Those required by law or regulation • Optional for others other than charities	• Group accounts of fully listed or AIM companies
FRS 101 (EU-adopted IFRS with reduced disclosures)	• Individual financial statements of qualifying group companies	• Parent company and subsidiaries of fully listed or AIM groups
FRS 102	• Group and individual accounts of companies not required by law or regulation to apply EU-adopted IFRS	• Large and medium-sized companies and groups
FRS 102 with reduced disclosures	• Individual financial statements of qualifying group companies	• Parent and subsidiaries of private groups
FRS 102 with disclosures set out in section 1A	• Group and individual accounts of small companies	• Small private companies
FRS 105	• Eligible micro companies	• Micro private companies

Section 1A of FRS 102 is applicable to companies which are eligible for the small companies' regime under CA 2006. It sets out the disclosure requirements of FRS 102 which are mandated for small companies. All the accounting requirements of FRS 102 are, therefore, applicable to small companies with no relaxations. See **Chapter 11** for a description of the disclosure requirements of FRS 102 noting which are mandatory for small companies applying section 1A.

See **Chapter 5** for the definition of a qualifying company for the reduced disclosure framework of FRS 101 or 102.

4.4   Statement of compliance

Companies are required to include a statement of compliance in the notes to the accounts specifying whether they are applying FRS 101, FRS 102, FRS 102 with reduced disclosures, FRS 102 section 1A or FRS 105. Note that small companies applying FRS 102 section 1A are only encouraged to make this statement but are not mandatorily required to.

Companies applying EU-adopted IFRS are required by IAS 1 to make an equivalent statement of compliance.

4.5   Consistency with company law

CA 2006, s. 395 requires that companies prepare either 'Companies Act accounts' or 'IAS accounts'. Accounts prepared in accordance with FRS 101, FRS 102, FRS 102 with reduced disclosures, FRS 102 section 1A or the FRS 105 are 'Companies Act accounts'. Only those accounts prepared under EU-adopted IFRS (with full disclosures) are 'IAS accounts'. Charitable companies are prohibited by company law from applying EU-adopted IFRS and must prepare 'Companies Act accounts'.

4.6   Effective date and transitional arrangements

FRS 100 is applicable to accounting periods commencing on or after 1 January 2015. Early adoption is available subject to provisions set out in FRS 101, 102 and 105. A company applying the standard early is required to state that fact.

On first application of FRS 100, a company shall apply the following transitional arrangements if transitioning to:

- EU-adopted IFRS – the requirements of IFRS 1;

- FRS 101 unless the company previously applied EU-adopted IFRS – IFRS 1 para. 6–33;

- FRS 101 where the company previously applied EU-adopted IFRS – the company does not re-apply IFRS 1 but considers whether adjustments are necessary to comply with FRS 101.5(b);

- FRS 102 – the transitional arrangements set out in FRS 102 section 35;

- FRS 105 – the transitional arrangements set out in FRS 105 section 28.

Companies eligible to apply FRS 101 are likely to apply that standard early, particularly if they currently already prepare their accounts under EU-adopted IFRS and would benefit from the exemption from certain disclosures.

FRS 102 is only likely to be early adopted by recently incorporated companies about to prepare accounts for their first period to avoid the needless conversion from 'old' UK GAAP to 'new' UK GAAP after one or two accounting periods.

Chapter 5 Reduced disclosure framework

FRS 100 permits a reduced disclosure framework in the individual accounts of qualifying entities provided certain criteria are met.

Qualifying entities will either apply FRS 101 (if preparing accounts under the recognition and measurement principles of EU-adopted IFRS) or the relevant disclosure exemptions available in FRS 102 if preparing accounts under that standard.

The specific disclosure exemptions available in FRS 102 are discussed in **Chapter 6** at **6.3**.

5.1 Qualifying entities

A qualifying entity is defined as a member of a group where the parent of that group prepares publicly available consolidated accounts that are intended to give a true and fair view (of the assets, liabilities, financial position and profit or loss) and that member is included in the consolidation.

A charity may be a qualifying entity for the purposes of the disclosure exemptions in FRS 102, however, a charity may not be a qualifying entity under FRS 101.

Qualifying entities will therefore be subsidiaries or the parent as the term 'included in the consolidation' means that the company is included on a full consolidation basis and not proportional.

5.2 Criteria

A qualifying company may apply the reduced disclosure framework of FRS 101 or 102 if the following conditions are met:

- shareholders have been notified in writing about, and do not object to, the disclosure exemptions; and

- the accounts summarise in narrative form the exemptions applied and clearly identify the consolidated financial statements in which the company is consolidated.

Holders of 5% or more of the allotted share capital or holders of more than half of the allotted share capital not owned by the immediate parent may raise an objection and the company must specify a reasonable time-frame in which an objection can be raised.

5.3 Financial institutions

A qualifying company which is a financial institution may not apply the disclosure exemptions in respect of financial assets or financial liabilities (see **Table 5.1** or **Table 6.1**).

A financial institution is defined as any of the following:

- a bank which is:
  - a firm with a Part IV permission (FSMA 2000, s. 40) which includes accepting deposits and:
    - which is a credit institution; or
    - whose Part IV permission includes a requirement that it complies with the rules in the General Prudential sourcebook and the Prudential sourcebook for Banks, Building Societies and Investment Firms relating to banks, but which is not a building society, a friendly society or a credit union;
  - an EEA bank which is a full credit institution;

- a building society which is defined in the *Building Societies Act* 1986, s. 119(1) as a building society incorporated (or deemed to be incorporated) under that Act;

- a credit union, being a body corporate registered under the *Industrial and Provident Societies Act* 1965 as a credit union in accordance with the *Credit Unions Act* 1979, which is an authorised person;

- a custodian bank, broker-dealer or stockbroker;

- a company that undertakes the business of effecting or carrying out insurance contracts, including general and life assurance entities;

- an incorporated friendly society incorporated under the *Friendly Societies Act* 1992 or a registered friendly society registered under the *Friendly Societies Act* 1974, s. 7(1)(a) or any enactment which it replaced, including any registered branches;

- an investment trust, Irish Investment Company, venture capital trust, mutual fund, exchange traded fund, unit trust, open-ended investment company (OEIC);

- a retirement benefit plan; or

- any other company whose principal activity is to generate wealth or manage risk through financial instruments. This is intended to cover entities that have business activities similar to those listed above but are not specifically included in the list above.

A parent company whose sole activity is to hold investments in other group entities is not a financial institution.

5.4 Consolidated accounts

A qualifying company which is required to prepare consolidated accounts (e.g. an intermediate holding company which is not eligible to the exemptions in CA 2006, s. 400–402) or which voluntarily chooses to do so, may not take advantage of the reduced disclosure exemptions.

5.5 Equivalent disclosures

Certain of the disclosure exemptions require that equivalent disclosures are provided in the consolidated accounts of the group in which the company is consolidated.

In deciding whether the consolidated accounts of the parent provide equivalent disclosures, it is necessary to consider whether the consolidated accounts meet the basic disclosure requirements. It is not necessary to ensure each and every disclosure requirement is covered in detail. This is particularly relevant if the consolidated accounts are prepared under a different country's GAAP.

Disclosure exemptions are permitted where the relevant consolidated disclosures are made in aggregate or in an abbreviated form. If, however, no disclosure is made in the consolidated accounts on the grounds of immateriality, the relevant disclosures should be made in the qualifying entity's accounts if material to those accounts.

5.6   Specific disclosure exemptions

A qualifying company may take advantage of the following disclosure exemptions.

Table 5.1 FRS 101 Disclosure exemptions from EU-adopted IFRS for qualifying entities		
Area	**Exemption**	**Notes**
Share-based payment	The analysis of number and weighted average exercise price analysis and narrative information concerning share-based payment arrangements.	Provided that for a qualifying company that is: (i) a subsidiary, the share-based payment arrangement concerns equity instruments of another group company; (ii) an ultimate parent, the share-based payment arrangement concerns its own equity instruments and its separate financial statements are presented alongside the consolidated financial statements of the group;and, in both cases, provided that equivalent disclosures are included in the consolidated financial statements of the group in which the company is consolidated.
Business combinations	Detailed information about the nature and financial effect of business combinations that occur either during or after the financial period or where adjustments are made for business combinations in previous periods.	Provided that equivalent disclosures are included in the consolidated financial statements of the group in which the company is consolidated.
Non-current assets Held for Sale and Discontinued Operations	The net cash flows attributable to the activities of discontinued operations.	Provided that equivalent disclosures are included in the consolidated financial statements of the group in which the company is consolidated.
Financial instruments	All requirements of IFRS 7 *Financial Instruments: Disclosures*.	Provided that equivalent disclosures are included in the consolidated financial statements of the group in which the company is consolidated.
Fair value measurements	All disclosure requirements of IFRS 13 *Fair Value Measurements*.	Provided that equivalent disclosures are included in the consolidated financial statements of the group in which the company is consolidated.
Presentation of financial statements	Comparative information in respect of: – for share capital the number of shares outstanding at the beginning and end of the period; – for non-current assets the reconciliations of the carrying amounts at the beginning and end of the period.	
Statement of cash flows	All requirements of IAS 7 *Statement of Cash Flows*.	

Area	Exemption	Notes
Accounting policies	Information relating to standards not applied which have been issued but are not yet effective	
Key management personnel	Details of key management personnel compensation.	Covered by CA 2006 Directors' remuneration disclosures.
Related party transactions	Transactions entered into between two or more members of a group provided any subsidiary is wholly owned.	
Impairment of assets	Detailed information about key assumptions and calculations used in measuring recoverable amounts of cash generating units containing goodwill or intangible assets with indefinite useful lives.	Provided that equivalent disclosures are included in the consolidated financial statements of the group in which the company is consolidated.

The specific disclosure exemptions available in FRS 102 are discussed in **Chapter 6** at **6.3**.

Part II   FRS 102 – The Financial Reporting Standard Applicable in The UK and Republic of Ireland

Chapter 6   Introduction

The chapters in this part do not set out to provide an in-depth commentary on the recognition and measurement requirements of FRS 102 but rather to provide the essential elements of presentation and disclosure making cross references to the Standard where necessary. Reference will also be made to the requirements of CA 2006 and the Regulations (SI 2008/410 or SI 2008/409 as applicable) where this is considered necessary to understand the interaction of the underlying company legislation.

For more detailed guidance on the differences between FRS 102, current UK GAAP and IFRS, please see the Deloitte UK GAAP series of books available from www.cch.co.uk/books.

The full text of the latest Standard is included in the CCH publication *Accounting Standards* and in the online *Accounting Standards* service.

FRS 102 is a single financial reporting standard, organised by topic in separate sections, and applies to the accounts of entities not applying EU-adopted IFRS, FRS 101 or FRS 105. It aims to provide succinct financial reporting requirements which are consistent with international accounting standards.

6.1   Scope of the standard

FRS 102 was issued by the FRC to replace all extant standards in the UK and Republic of Ireland following a sustained and detailed period of consultation. Evidence from consultation supported a move towards a framework based on international standards but one that was more proportionate to the needs of preparers and users.

The FRS applies to accounts that are intended to give a true and fair view of the company's financial position and profit or loss for the reporting period.

Reduced disclosures are available to qualifying entities under certain criteria. These are explained in section **6.3** below.

The standard is mandatory for reporting periods commencing on or after 1 January 2015 for large and medium-sized companies and for periods commencing on or after 1 January 2016 for small companies including micro-entities not adopting FRS 105. Early adoption is permitted by large and medium-sized companies for periods ending on or after 31 December 2012. If the standard is early adopted, that fact must be stated in the accounts.

6.2   Basis of preparation of accounts

As noted in **Chapter 4**, all UK and Irish companies are within the scope of FRS 100 which provides the following instruction on the accounting framework options available to companies.

A company that is required by EU Regulation or other legislation or regulation (e.g. AIM rules) to prepare consolidated financial statements in accordance with EU-adopted IFRS must do so. The individual financial statements of such companies and the individual or consolidated accounts of any other company within the scope of FRS 100 must be prepared in accordance with the following requirements:

- micro companies that are eligible to apply the FRS 105, may prepare the accounts in accordance with that standard;

- all other companies (including those that are eligible but choose not to apply the FRS 105) must prepare accounts in accordance with:

- FRS 102 (see **Chapters 7–11**);

- EU-adopted IFRS (not in the scope of this book); or

- FRS 101 (see **Chapter 5**).

As some aspects of EU-adopted IFRS are not covered in FRS 102, companies are required to apply the following specific IFRS standards, if applicable.

- IAS 33 Earnings per share – a company whose ordinary shares or potential ordinary shares are publicly traded, or that files, or is in the process of filing its accounts with a securities commission or other regulatory organisation for the purpose of issuing ordinary shares in a public market, or a company that chooses to disclose earnings per share.

- IFRS 8 Operating segments – a company whose debt or equity instruments are publicly traded, or that files, or is in the process of filing its accounts with a securities commission or other regulatory organisation for the purpose of issuing any class of instruments in a public market, or a company that chooses to provide information described as segment information. If a company discloses disaggregated information, but the information does not comply with the requirements of IFRS 8 then it shall not describe the information as segment information.

- IFRS 6 Exploration for and evaluation of mineral resources – a company engaged in extractive activities.

Note: When applying IAS 33, IFRS 8 or IFRS 6, references to other IFRSs within those standards shall be taken as references to the relevant sections of FRS 102.

6.3   Reduced disclosures for subsidiaries and ultimate parents

FRS 102 contains similar provisions to FRS 101 to allow qualifying subsidiaries (and the individual accounts of parents preparing consolidated accounts) to reduced disclosure in certain areas.

See **Chapter 5** for the definitions and criteria to be satisfied.

6.3.1   Specific disclosure exemptions

A qualifying company may take advantage of the following disclosure exemptions.

Table 6.1 Disclosure exemptions from FRS 102 for qualifying entities		
Area	**Exemption**	**Notes**
Presentation of financial statements (see **9.1.4**)	A reconciliation of the number of shares outstanding at the beginning and end of the period.	
Statement of cash flows (see **9.4**)	All requirements of *Statement of Cash Flow,* section 7.	
Financial instruments (no financial instruments held at fair value) (see **11.2**)	All disclosure requirements of *Basic financial instruments,* section 11 and *Other financial instruments,* section 12.	Provided that equivalent disclosures are included in the consolidated financial statements of the group in which the company is consolidated.

Area	Exemption	Notes
Financial instruments (with financial instruments held at fair value)	Exemption as above applies to: • financial assets required to be held at fair value, such as held for trading assets and derivatives; • financial liabilities held as part of a trading portfolio; and • financial liabilities that are derivatives. However, for financial instruments held at fair value under SI 2008/410, Sch. 1, para. 36(4) the exemption is restricted – disclosure requirements of section 11 must be applied to those financial instruments held at fair value.	Restricted exemption applies to financial instruments such as: • financial liabilities not held as part of a trading portfolio or derivatives; • financial assets that would not normally be carried at fair value but which are permitted to be if certain criteria are met under IAS 39.
Share-based payment (see **11.14**)	The analysis of number and weighted average exercise price analysis and narrative information concerning share-based payment arrangements. Information on the fair value measurement method and reasons in respect of equity settled share-based payments. Information on the liability measurement in respect of cash settled share-based payments. Information on modifications to share-based payment arrangements. The total expense recognised in profit or loss and the total carrying amount at the end of the period for liabilities arising.	Provided that for a qualifying company that is: (i) a subsidiary, the share-based payment arrangement concerns equity instruments of another group company; (ii) an ultimate parent, the share-based payment arrangement concerns its own equity instruments and its separate financial statements are presented alongside the consolidated financial statements of the group; and, in both cases, provided that equivalent disclosures are included in the consolidated financial statements of the group in which the company is consolidated.
Related party transactions (see **11.20.2**)	Disclosure of key management personnel compensation in total. Transactions and balances between two or more members of a group.	Disclosures required by CA 2006 and SI 2008/410 are not exempted and therefore still apply. Any subsidiary which is a party to the transaction is a wholly owned subsidiary.

A qualifying company which is a financial institution may not apply the disclosure exemptions in respect of financial instruments (see **Table 6.1**). Discussion of how a financial institution is defined is included in **Chapter 5** (see **5.3**).

Chapter 7   Concepts and pervasive principles

This section summarises the objectives, concepts and basic principles of accounts set out in section 2 of FRS 102. These apply equally to entities applying FRS 102 and those eligible small companies applying FRS 102 section 1A.

7.1   Objective of accounts

The objective of accounts is to provide information about the financial position, performance and cash flows of a company that is useful for economic decision making by a broad range of users and stakeholders who are not in a position to be able to obtain reports specific to their needs, such as management.

Accounts also reflect the stewardship by management, i.e. their accountability of the management of resources entrusted to them.

7.2   Qualitative characteristics of accounts information

The standard provides ten fundamental qualitative characteristics of information in accounts.

- **Understandability** – information should be presented in a way that is comprehensible by reasonably knowledgeable users. The need for understandability does not, however, allow information to be omitted on the grounds it may be too difficult for users to understand.

- **Relevance** – information must be relevant to the decision making needs of users by helping them evaluate past, present or future events or by confirming or correcting their past evaluations.

- **Materiality** – information is material, and is therefore relevant, if its omission or misstatement could influence the decisions of users based on that information. Materiality depends on either the size or nature of the item or a combination of the two. It is, however, inappropriate to make or leave uncorrected immaterial departures from the FRS to achieve a particular presentation of the company's position, performance or cash flows.

- **Reliability** – information must be free from material error and bias and represents faithfully that which it purports to represent or could reasonably be expected to represent.

- **Substance over form** – to enhance reliability, transactions, events and conditions should be accounted for and presented in accordance with their substance, not merely the legal form.

- **Prudence** – the inclusion of a certain degree of caution in the exercise of judgments needed in making estimates when circumstances are uncertain. Prudence does not permit bias by the deliberate understatement of assets or income or the deliberate overstatement of liabilities or expenses.

- **Completeness** – information must be complete within the bounds of materiality and cost in order to be reliable.

- **Comparability** – accounts should be capable of being compared from period to period in order for users to identify trends. Similarly accounts of different entities should be capable of being compared in order for users to evaluate their relative position, performance and cash flows.

- **Timeliness** – to be relevant financial information must be provided to enable users to make economic decisions within the decision time-frame. Management must balance the need to provide timely information with the need to provide reliable information.

- **Balance between benefit and cost** – the benefits derived from information should outweigh the costs of providing it. This is a judgmental process bearing in mind the costs will not necessarily be borne by those enjoying the benefits.

7.3 Financial position

The relationship of the assets, liabilities and equity at a specific point in time.

- **Asset** – a resource controlled by the company as a result of past events and from which future economic benefits are expected to flow to the company.

  Future economic benefit is the potential to contribute, directly or indirectly, to future cash flows either from use of the asset (e.g. raw material inventories, property, plant and equipment) or from the disposing of it (e.g. finished goods, trade receivables).

  The right of ownership of an asset is not essential to the existence of it, e.g. a lease is an asset if the company controls the benefits that are expected to derive from its use.

- **Liability** – a present obligation arising from past events, the settlement of which is expected to result in an outflow of resources.

  An essential characteristic is that the company has a present obligation to perform or act in a particular way. The obligation may be legal or constructive. Legal in that it is legally enforceable as a consequence of a binding contract or statutory requirement. Constructive when it is derived from an established practice, published policy or current statement that indicates to other parties the company will accept certain responsibilities and has created a valid expectation to those other parties that it will discharge the responsibilities.

- **Equity** – the residual interest in the company's assets after deducting its liabilities.

  Equity may be sub-divided in a company's statement of financial position into funds contributed by shareholders, retained earnings and accumulated gains or losses recognised in other comprehensive income.

7.4 Performance

The relationship of income and expenses of the company during the reporting period. FRS 102 permits performance to be presented either as a single statement of comprehensive income or as two separate statements: an income statement (or profit and loss account) and a statement of comprehensive income.

- **Income** – increases in economic benefits in the form of inflows or enhancements of assets or decreases in liabilities that result in the increase in equity (other than that derived from contributions from investors).

  Income is made up of two parts: revenue and gains. Revenue is income derived from the course of normal activities typically referred to as sales, fees, interest, dividends, royalties and rent. Gains are other items of income that are not revenue, e.g. enhancements in the value of assets or decreases in the value of liabilities.

- **Expenses** – decreases in economic benefits in the form of outflows, depletions of assets or incurrences of liabilities that result in a decrease of equity (other than that occurring from distribution to investors).

  Expenses comprise losses as well as expenses incurred in the course of normal activities, e.g. cost of sales, wages, overhead costs and depreciation.

7.5 Recognition of assets, liabilities, income and expenses

There are two criteria for the recognition of assets, liabilities, income or expenses: probability and reliability.

It must be probable that future economic benefit associated with the item will flow to or from the company. Probability takes into account the degree of uncertainty that economic benefits may flow to or from the company. Judgments exercised will take into account the evidence available when the accounts are prepared that relate to conditions that existed at the end of the reporting period. If it is not probable that economic benefit will flow then the item is not recognised.

The second criterion is cost or value can be measured reliably. In many cases, the cost or value will be known; however, in some cases, it will be necessary to make a reasonable estimate. When a reasonable estimate cannot be made the item is not recognised.

If an item is not recognised because it fails either of the criteria it may qualify for recognition at a later date and may nonetheless warrant disclosure in the notes to the accounts for the current period. This is appropriate if knowledge of the item is relevant to the users of the accounts.

7.6   Measurement of assets, liabilities, income and expenses

Measurement is the process of determining the monetary amounts at which a company records assets, liabilities, income and expenses and the FRS specifies the measurement basis for many types of these items.

The two common measurement principles are historical cost and fair value.

- **Historical cost** is the amount of cash or cash equivalents paid or received or the fair value of non-cash consideration given or received at the time either an asset is received or an obligation incurred. For certain liabilities (e.g. corporation tax), it is the amounts of cash or cash equivalents expected to be paid to settle the obligation in the normal course of business.

- **Fair value** is the amount for which an asset could be exchanged, a liability settled or an equity instrument granted could be exchanged between knowledgeable, willing parties in an arm's length transaction.

7.7   Offsetting

The general principle is that assets and liabilities, or income and expenses shall not be offset, unless specifically required or permitted in the standard.

Offsetting does not include the measurement of assets net of provisions for diminution in value (e.g. allowances for inventory obsolescence or allowances for irrecoverable debts).

Similarly, where the company's operating activities do not include the buying and selling of property plant and equipment or investments then gains or losses are reported at the net amount of proceeds of disposal less the carrying amount and related selling costs.

Chapter 8   Accounts presentation

The following principles apply to the presentation of accounts prepared in accordance with FRS 102. There are some differences for small companies preparing accounts in accordance with section 1A of FRS 102 which are noted below where relevant.

8.1   Fair presentation ('true and fair view')

The financial position, performance and cash flows of a company shall be presented fairly. This requires the faithful representation of the effects of transactions, other events and conditions in accordance with the concepts and pervasive principles noted in section 2 of the standard.

It is presumed that the application of FRS 102 with additional disclosure where required achieves a fair presentation of financial position, performance and cash flows.

8.1.1   FRS 102.1A Small Companies

The financial statements of a small company preparing accounts in accordance with section 1A of FRS 102 shall give a true and fair view. Although this requirement is worded differently, in practical terms the terms 'true and fair view' and 'fair presentation' are equivalent.

The significant difference however lies in the fact that the mandatory requirements of section 1A of FRS 102 in terms of the disclosures required in the primary statements and notes to the accounts are not 'deemed' or 'presumed' to show a true and fair view and therefore directors of small companies must consider whether the additional disclosures required for larger companies might be necessary.

8.2   Composition of a set of accounts

8.2.1   FRS 102

A complete set of accounts for large and medium-sized companies for the reporting period shall comprise:

- a statement of financial position at the reporting date;
- either:
  - a single statement of comprehensive income showing a subtotal of items recognised in determining profit or loss followed by other items of comprehensive income; or
  - a separate income statement and statement of comprehensive income (which begins with profit or loss for the period followed by other items of comprehensive income);
- a statement of changes in equity;
- a statement of cash flows; and
- notes to the accounts including a summary of the significant accounting policies.

If the only changes in equity for the periods presented in the accounts (current and preceding) are the profit or loss for the period, the payment of dividends, and prior period adjustment for correction of and/or changes in accounting policies then the company may present a single 'statement of income and retained earnings' in place of the statement of comprehensive income and statement of changes in equity.

If there are no items of other comprehensive income then the separate statement of comprehensive income may be excluded. In such situations the total profit for the year would be described as 'Profit and total comprehensive income for the financial period'.

Each statement shall have equal prominence and shall be clearly identified.

The titles of the primary statements used in FRS 102 follow the conventions used in IFRS however they are not mandatory. Other titles may be used so long as their meaning is not misleading. This addresses the apparent discrepancy with the titles of the formats suggested by CA 2006 and the Regulations and allows companies to continue to use statement titles such as 'Balance Sheet' and 'Profit and Loss Account' if they wish. For the purpose of this book, the titles in FRS 102 will be used.

The following information is also necessary (repeated on each page as necessary):

- name of the company and any change since the last reporting period;

- whether the accounts cover the company only or a group of companies;

- the date of the end of the period and the length of the period covered; and

- the presentational currency and the level of rounding used.

The notes to the accounts must also disclose the legal form of the company, its country of incorporation, registered office and principal place of business if different from the registered office.

A description of the nature of the company's operations and principal activities must also be provided if not provided in the business review.

8.2.2   FRS 102.1A Small Companies

A complete set of accounts for small companies for the reporting period shall comprise:

- a statement of financial position at the reporting date;

- an income statement for the reporting period; and

- notes to the accounts including a summary of the significant accounting policies.

Small companies are exempt from the requirement to present the other information shown in **8.2.1** above however there are certain situations where they are encouraged to make additional disclosures. These are discussed in **Chapter 9** below.

8.3   Compliance with the FRS

The company must make an explicit and unreserved statement in the notes to the accounts of compliance with FRS 102 (small companies are encouraged to make an equivalent statement with regard to FRS 102 section 1A) and this statement cannot be made unless the accounts comply with all requirements of the FRS.

In rare circumstances where management concludes that compliance with a particular requirement the FRS would be misleading and conflict with the objective of accounts and pervasive principles then management may depart from that requirement and made the following disclosures:

- that it has concluded the accounts present fairly the financial position, performance and cash flows;

- that it has complied with the FRS or applicable legislation except it has departed from a particular requirement to achieve a fair presentation; and

- a description of the departure, including the treatment the FRS or legislation would require, the reason why this would be misleading and the treatment adopted.

This is similar to the necessary disclosures required by the 'true and fair' override provisions of CA 2006 (s. 396(5) and 404(5)) if in special circumstances the requirements of the Act or regulations is inconsistent with the obligation to present a true and fair view.

8.4   Going concern

When preparing accounts, management must make an assessment of the company's ability to continue as a going concern. A company is a going concern unless management either intends to liquidate the company or cease trading or has no realistic alternative but to do so.

In making that assessment, management must take into account all available information about the future which is at least (but not limited to) 12 months from the date of approval of the accounts.

No explicit disclosure is required that the company is a going concern unless management is aware of material uncertainties which may cast significant doubt on the company's ability to continue as a going concern. In such cases, disclosure of those uncertainties is required (and is encouraged for small companies applying FRS 102 section 1A).

If the company is not a going concern and the accounts are prepared accordingly, management must disclose the fact, the reasons why and the basis on which the accounts are prepared.

8.5   Frequency of reporting and comparative information

Accounts must be prepared at least annually including comparative information for the preceding period for all items presented in the current period. Comparative information should also be provided for narrative information where this is considered relevant to an understanding of the current period's accounts.

Where the reporting period is not one year, management must disclose the fact, the reason for this and the fact that the comparative period is not entirely comparable.

8.6   Consistency of presentation

The presentation and classification of items in the accounts shall remain consistent from one period to the next.

Exceptions to this principle may be applied in two situations:

- when there has been a significant change in the nature of the company's operations or following a review of the accounts it is clear that another presentation or classification is more appropriate; or

- when FRS 102 (or another applicable FRS or FRC abstract) requires a change in presentation. This typically will occur when the FRS is amended or an abstract is issued.

In such situations, the comparative information shall also be changed (unless impracticable) and disclosures included in the accounts detailing the nature of the change, the amounts reclassified and the reasons given. If the reclassification of comparatives is impracticable the reasons why shall be stated.

8.7 Materiality and aggregation

Items of similar nature or function are aggregated and each material class of similar items shall be presented separately.

If a line item in the accounts is immaterial it need not be presented but is aggregated with other items; however, separate presentation may be necessary in the notes to the accounts.

If a specific disclosure is required by FRS 102 it need not be given if the information is not material.

Chapter 9   Format of accounts

Sections 4–8 of FRS 102 set out the information to be presented in the accounts. These sections specify the basic information to be presented which is drawn from the underlying legislative requirements where appropriate. The content and disclosure requirements are then augmented by the later sections of the standard for specific areas.

As stated in **Chapter 3**, the format of the Statement of Financial Position (Balance Sheet) and that part of the Statement of Comprehensive Income which relates to the profit or loss (Profit and Loss Account) and certain note disclosures are specifically set out in schedules to the Regulations.

The other primary statements (Statement of Other Comprehensive Income, Statement of Cash Flows, and Statement of Changes in Equity) are all specifically required by FRS 102 and are not referred to by company legislation.

It has already been noted in **Chapter 8** that FRS 102 uses titles which are common to international standards (such as 'statement of financial position') which differ from those used in the underlying company legislation. This extends to the description component areas of financial statements e.g. 'Property, Plant and Equipment' for 'Tangible Fixed Assets', 'Inventories' for 'Stock'. FRS 102 does not prescribe the names to be used for the principal line items in the primary statement therefore for the purposes of this chapter we will continue to use the terms used in CA 2006 and the Regulations in example disclosures.

As already discussed, small companies are allowed certain exemptions in the presentation of the primary statements and notes to the accounts and where relevant these are discussed below.

9.1   Statement of Financial Position

9.1.1   Information to be presented

The Regulations allow two alternative formats. Both are shown below in **Table 9.1** for comparison.

Table 9.1 Statement of Financial Position formats prescribed by SI 2008/410, Sch. 1

The items shown in bold in Format 1 need not be disclosed in Format 2. For illustrative purposes, the Arabic number sub-headings (which are common to both formats) are not reproduced in this table but are shown in **Table 9.2**.

Format 1		Format 2	
		ASSETS	
A	Called up share capital not paid	A	Called up share capital not paid
B	Fixed assets	B	Fixed assets
	I Intangible assets		I Intangible assets
	II Tangible assets		II Tangible assets
	III Investments		III Investments
C	Current assets	C	Current assets
	I Stocks		I Stocks
	II Debtors		II Debtors
	III Investments		III Investments
	IV Cash at bank and in hand		IV Cash at bank and in hand
D	Prepayments and accrued income	D	Prepayments and accrued income

---

Format 1		Format 2	
E	Creditors: amounts falling due within one year		

F	**Net current assets (liabilities)**		
G	**Total assets less current liabilities**		
			CAPITAL, RESERVES AND LIABILITIES
H	Creditors: amounts falling due after more than one year	A	Capital and reserves
			I Called up share capital
			II Share premium account
			III Revaluation reserve
			IV Other reserves, including the fair value reserve
			V Profit and loss account
			Minority interests
I	Provisions for liabilities	B	Provisions for liabilities
J	Accruals and deferred income		
[ ]	Minority interests [*Alternative* (1)]		

K	Capital and reserves	C	Creditors
	I Called up share capital		[*Amounts falling due within one year and after one year must be shown separately for each of the items in creditors and in aggregate unless the aggregate amounts within one year and after one year are disclosed in the notes.*]
	II Share premium account		
	III Revaluation reserve		
	IV Other reserves, including the fair value reserve		
	V Profit and loss account		
[ ]	Minority interests [*Alternative* (2)]	D	Accruals and deferred income

The dotted line above in Format 1 illustrates the usual 'break-point' in the balance sheet, although in practice the balance sheet total could be 'struck' after item G. Format 2 requires balance sheet totals of ASSETS and LIABILITIES to be given.

Table 9.2 Balance sheet – Arabic number sub-headings

The sub-headings may be presented either on the face of the balance sheet or in the notes to the accounts.

B I INTANGIBLE ASSETS

    1   Development costs

    2   Concessions, patents, licences, trademarks and similar rights and assets

    3   Goodwill

    4   Payments on account

B II TANGIBLE ASSETS

    1   Land and buildings

    2   Plant and machinery

    3   Fixtures, fittings, tools and equipment

    Payments on account and assets in the course of construction

B III INVESTMENTS

    1   Shares in group undertakings

    2   Loans to group undertakings

    3   Participating interests *

    4   Loans to undertakings in which the company has a participating interest

    5   Other investments other than loans

    6   Other loans

    7   Own shares

C I STOCKS

    1   Raw materials and consumables

    2   Work in progress

    3   Finished goods and goods for resale

    4   Payments on account

C II DEBTORS

    1   Trade debtors

    2   Amounts owed by group undertakings

    3   Amounts owed by undertakings in which the company has a participating interest

    4   Other debtors

    5   Called up share capital not paid

    6   Prepayments and accrued income

C III INVESTMENTS

    1   Shares in group undertakings

    2   Own shares

    3   Other investments

E AND H CREDITORS: AMOUNTS FALLING DUE WITHIN AND AFTER MORE THAN ONE YEAR

    1   Debenture loans

    2   Bank loans and overdrafts

    3   Payments received on account

    4   Trade creditors

    5   Bills of exchange payable

    6   Amounts owed to group undertakings

    7   Amounts owed to undertakings in which the company has a participating interest

    8   Other creditors including taxation and social security

    9   Accruals and deferred income

* *In group accounts, in a consolidated Statement of Financial Position this item is replaced by two items: 'Interests in associated undertakings' and 'other participating interests'.*

9.1.2   Debtors due after more than one year

Where the amount of debtors due after more than one year is so material in the context of total net assets, that amount may be separately disclosed on the face of the Statement of Financial Position. In most cases, it should be sufficient to disclose the amount within the notes to the accounts.

9.1.3   Creditors: amounts falling due within one year

Creditors shall be classified as falling due within one year when the company does not have an unconditional right, at the end of the reporting period, to defer settlement of the creditor for at least 12 months after the reporting date.

9.1.4   Share capital and reserves

If the company has share capital or reserves the following must be disclosed, either in the Statement of Financial Position or in the notes.

(a)   For each class of share capital:

    (i)   the number of shares issued and fully paid, and issued and not fully paid;

    (ii)   par or nominal value per share (or that the shares have no par value);

    (iii)   a reconciliation of the number of shares outstanding at the beginning and end of the period. Prior year amounts do not need to be stated;

    (iv)   the rights, preferences and restrictions attaching to that class including restrictions on the distribution of dividends and the repayment of capital;

    (v)   shares in the company held by itself or by its subsidiaries, associates or joint ventures;

    (vi)   shares reserved for issue under options and contracts for the sale of shares including the terms and amounts.

(b)   A description of each reserve within equity.

9.1.5   Major disposal of assets or a disposal group

Where the company, at the reporting date, has a binding sale agreement for a major disposal of assets or a disposal group, the following shall be presented in the notes:

(a)   a description of the asset(s) or disposal group;

(b)   a description of the facts and circumstances of the sale; and

(c)   the carrying amount of the assets or, for the disposal group, the carrying amount of the underlying assets and liabilities.

9.1.6   Small companies

As stated in **Chapter 3**, the format of the Statement of Financial Position (Balance Sheet) and certain note disclosures are specifically set out in schedules to the *Small Companies and Groups (Accounts and Directors' Report) Regulations* 2008 (SI 2008/409).

These Regulations similarly allow two alternative formats which are the same as those shown in **Table 9.1** above. The Arabic number sub-headings are, however, reduced and are shown below in **Table 9.3** below.

Table 9.3 Balance sheet – Arabic number sub-headings for small companies

The sub-headings may be presented either on the face of the balance sheet or in the notes to the accounts.

B I   INTANGIBLE ASSETS

  1   Goodwill

  2   Other intangible assets

B II   TANGIBLE ASSETS

  1   Land and buildings

  2   Plant and machinery, etc.

B III   INVESTMENTS

  1   Shares in group undertakings and participating interests

  2   Loans to group undertakings and undertakings in which the company has a participating interest

  3   Other investments other than loans

  4   Other investments

C I   STOCKS

  1   Stocks

  2   Payments on account

C II   DEBTORS

  1   Trade debtors

  2   Amounts owed by group undertakings and undertakings in which the company has a participating interest

  3   Other debtors

C III   INVESTMENTS

  1   Shares in group undertakings

  2   Other investments

E AND H CREDITORS: AMOUNTS FALLING DUE WITHIN AND AFTER MORE THAN ONE YEAR

  1   Bank loans and overdrafts

  2   Trade creditors

  3   Amounts owed to group undertakings and undertakings in which the company has a participating interest

  4   Other creditors

9.2   Statement of Comprehensive Income

9.2.1   *Information to be presented*

A company shall present its total comprehensive income for the period either:

(a)   in a single Statement of Comprehensive Income which presents all items of income and expense; or

(b)   in two statements – an Income Statement (which is referred to as a Profit and Loss Account in the Act and Regulations) and a Statement of Comprehensive Income.

Small companies are only required to present an income statement for the period however when (only as permitted by FRS 102) a small company recognises gains or losses in other comprehensive income it is encouraged to present a statement of total comprehensive income as if it were not a small company.

The Regulations for small companies (SI 2008/409) and large and medium-sized companies (SI 2008/410) are similar and allow two alternative formats for that part of the Statement of Comprehensive Income that relates to the profit or loss for the period (single statement approach) or the Income Statement (two statement approach).

Format 1 categorises expenses by function as part of cost of sales, distribution costs or administrative expenses. Formats 2 categorises by nature (e.g. depreciation, raw materials and consumables and staff costs). The standard requires that a company presents the analysis of expenses, i.e. the format of the Income Statement, based on either their function or nature, whichever provides information that is reliable and more relevant.

The layout of the formats are shown in **Table 9.4** below.

Table 9.4 Income Statement Formats 1 and 2 prescribed by SI 2008/410, Sch. 1

Items shown in bold below show the differences in disclosure required by the formats. Notes are shown in *italics*.

Format 1	Format 2
1. Turnover	1. Turnover
2. Cost of sales	**2. Change in stocks of finished goods and in work in progress**
3. Gross profit or loss	**3. Own work capitalised**
4. Distribution costs	
5. Administrative expenses	
6. Other operating income	4. Other operating income
	5. (a) Raw materials and consumables
	(b) Other external charges
In Format 1 staff costs must be allocated over items 2, 4 and 5	**6. Staff costs**
	(a) wages and salaries
	(b) social security costs
	(c) other pension costs
In Format 1 depreciation must be allocated over items 2, 4 and 5	7. (a) Depreciation and other amounts written off tangible and intangible fixed assets
	(b) Exceptional amounts written off current assets
	8. Other operating charges
7. Income from shares in group undertakings	9. Income from shares in group undertakings
8. Income from participating interests	10. Income from participating interests
9. Income from other fixed asset investments	11. Income from other fixed asset investments (15)
10. Other interest receivable and similar income	12. Other interest receivable and similar income (15)
11. Amounts written off investments	13. Amounts written off investments
12. Interest payable and similar expenses	14. Interest payable and similar expenses (16)
12A. Profit or loss before taxation	**14A. Profit or loss before taxation**
13. Tax on profit or loss	15. Tax on profit or loss

<table>
<tr><td>Format 1</td><td>Format 2</td></tr>
<tr><td>14. Profit or loss after taxation</td><td>16. Profit or loss after taxation</td></tr>
<tr><td>19. Other taxes not shown under the above items</td><td>21. Other taxes not shown under the above items</td></tr>
<tr><td>20. Profit or loss for the financial year</td><td>22. Profit or loss for the financial year</td></tr>
</table>

Profit or loss on ordinary activities before taxation must also be disclosed.

Items 15–18 (Format 1) and 17–20 (Format 2) relating to extraordinary items were removed by SI 2015/980 with effect from 1 January 2016.

In addition the company shall include in the statement of comprehensive income, either below the line 'Profit or loss for the financial year' (single statement approach) or as a separate Statement of Comprehensive Income (two statement approach), line items that present the following amounts for the period.

- Classified by nature (excluding amounts in (b)), the components of other comprehensive income recognised as part of total comprehensive income outside profit or loss as permitted or required by the FRS. A company may present the components of other comprehensive income either:

  - net of related tax effects; or

  - before the related tax effects with one amount shown for the aggregate amount of income tax relating to those components.

- Its share of the other comprehensive income of associates and jointly controlled entities accounted for by the equity method.

- Total comprehensive income.

The company shall present the following items as allocations of profit or loss and other comprehensive income in the Statement of Comprehensive Income for the period.

- Profit or loss for the period attributable to:

  - non-controlling interest; and

  - owners of the parent.

- Total comprehensive income for the period attributable to:

  - non-controlling interest; and

  - owners of the parent.

Where the company takes the two statement approach. The Statement of Comprehensive Income shall begin with the profit and loss for the financial period as its first line.

9.2.2 Discontinued operations

A company must disclose on the face of the Income Statement an amount comprising the total of post-tax profit or loss of discontinued operations and the post-tax gain or loss attributable to the impairment or on the disposal of the assets or disposal groups constituting discontinued operations.

In addition, a line by line analysis shall be presented in a column identified as relating to discontinued operations separately from continuing operations together with a total column.

The amounts for prior periods relating to operations discontinued by the end of the reporting period shall be re-presented for disclosure in the comparative information.

9.2.3   Prior period adjustments

Material errors and effects of changes in accounting policy shall be presented as adjustments to prior periods rather than as part of the profit or loss for the current period.

9.2.4   Exceptional items

The term 'exceptional items' is not included or defined in the standard. However, the standard provides the following allowances for a proper understanding of the company's performance.

- Additional line items headings and subtotals may be included in the Statement of Comprehensive Income (or Income Statement if presented) where presentation is relevant to an understanding of the company's performance.

- When items included in Total Comprehensive Income are material a company shall disclose their nature and amount separately in the Statement of Comprehensive Income (or Income Statement if presented) or in the notes.

Small companies that prepare accounts in accordance with FRS 102 section 1A are similarly required to state the amount and nature of individual items of income or expense of exceptional size or incidence.

9.2.5   Operating profit

There is no requirement to present a sub-total for 'Operating profit' (which is typically struck below item 6 in Format 1 and item 8 in Format 2). If it is presented the company must ensure that the amount disclosed is representative of the activities which would normally be regarded as 'operating'. It would therefore be inappropriate to exclude from operating profit items such as inventory write downs, restructuring costs, relocation expenses, etc. because they occur infrequently or are unusual in amount. Similarly it would not be appropriate to exclude items such as depreciation and amortisation on the grounds that they do not involve cash flows.

9.3   Statement of Changes in Equity and Statement of Income and Retained Earnings

The statement of changes in equity presents a company's profit or loss for a reporting period, other comprehensive income for the period, the effects of changes in accounting policies and corrections of material errors recognised in the period, and the amounts of investments by, and dividends and other distributions to, equity investors during the period.

Small companies that prepare accounts in accordance with FRS 102 section 1A are exempt from the requirements of section 6, however FRS 102 para. 1A.9(b) states that when a small company has transactions with equity holders it is encouraged to present a statement of changes in equity, or a statement of income and retained earnings in accordance with section 6.

9.3.1   Statement of Changes in Equity – information to be presented

- total comprehensive income for the period, showing separately the total amounts attributable to owners of the parent and to non-controlling interests;

- for each component of equity, the effects of retrospective application or retrospective restatement recognised arising from changes in accounting policies or material errors; and

- for each component of equity, a reconciliation between the carrying amount at the beginning and the end of the period, separately disclosing changes resulting from:

– profit or loss;

– other comprehensive income (with sub-analysis by item for each component of equity either on the face of the statement or in the notes); and

– the amounts of investments by, and dividends and other distributions to, owners, showing separately issues of shares, purchase of own share transactions, dividends and other distributions to owners, and changes in ownership interests in subsidiaries that do not result in a loss of control.

Table 9.5 Example Statement of Changes in Equity

	Notes	Share capital £'000	Share premium £'000	Other reserves £'000	Retained earnings £'000	Total £'000
At 1 January 2015		875	70	—	124	1,069
Profit for the year and total comprehensive income		—	—	—	417	417
At 1 January 2016		875	70	—	541	1,486
Profit for the year		—	—	—	541	541
Capital contribution arising on loan from parent	X	—	—	—	89	89
Gain on revaluation of land & buildings	X	—	—	144	—	144
Deferred tax arising from revaluation of land & buildings	X	—	—	(25)	—	(25)
Other comprehensive income for the year		—	—	119	89	208
Total comprehensive income for the year		—	—	119	630	749
New shares issued in the year	X	35	17	—	—	52
At 31 December 2016		910	87	119	1,171	2,287

9.3.2 Statement of income and retained earnings – information to be presented

If the only changes in equity in the periods presented arise from:

- profit or loss;

- payment of dividends;

- corrections of prior period material errors; or

- changes in accounting policy

then the company may present a Statement of Income and Retained Earnings in place of the Statement of Comprehensive Income and Statement of Changes in Equity.

As shown in **Table 9.6**, the Statement of Income and Retained Earnings should include:

- the information required to be presented in the Statement of Comprehensive Income or Income Statement – see **9.2** above;

- retained earnings at the beginning of the reporting period;

- dividends declared and paid or payable during the period;

- restatements of retained earnings for corrections of prior period material errors;

- restatements of retained earnings for changes in accounting policy; and

- retained earnings at the end of the reporting period.

	Notes	2016 £'000	2015 £'000
Table 9.6 Example Statement of Income and Retained Earnings for the year ended 31 December 2016			
Turnover	X	11,087	7,579
Cost of sales		(5,995)	(3,533)
Gross profit		5,092	4,046
Administrative expenses		(4,327)	(3,449)
Other operating income	X	46	29
Operating profit		811	626
Interest payable and similar expenses	X	(74)	(39)
Profit on before tax		737	587
Taxation	X	(196)	(170)
Profit after taxation and total comprehensive income for the financial year		541	417
Retained earnings brought forward		2,754	2,457
Dividends paid	X	(140)	(120)
Retained earnings carried forward		3,115	2,754

9.4   Statement of Cash Flows

The Statement of Cash Flows provides information about the changes in cash and cash equivalents showing separately the changes arising from operating, investing and financing activities.

The format of the Statement of Cash Flows differs substantially from the Cash Flow Statement previously required by FRS 1 (see **Table 9.7**) as there are now only three categories of cash flow, not nine and the statement reconciles the movement in 'cash and cash equivalents'.

Cash flow statements are an area of particular focus of regulators as errors are often noted in classification and calculation therefore it is important that sufficient attention is given to the preparation of this statement.

Small companies that prepare accounts in accordance with FRS 102 section 1A are exempt from the requirement to prepare a statement of cash flows. If the directors of a small company voluntarily prepare a statement of cash flows, then the requirements of section 7 should be adopted.

9.4.1   Cash equivalents

Cash equivalents are short-term highly liquid investments that are readily convertible to known amounts of cash and that are subject to an insignificant risk of changes in value. An investment normally qualifies as a cash equivalent only if it has a relatively short maturity (typically less than three months) from the date of acquisition.

Bank overdrafts are normally classified as financing activities similar to borrowings. However, if they are repayable on demand and form an integral part of the company's cash management, bank overdrafts are a component of cash and cash equivalents.

9.4.2   Information to be presented

The Statement of Cash Flows shall present cash flows for a company classified into three categories: operating activities, investing activities and financing activities.

9.4.2.1   Operating activities

Operating activities are the principal revenue producing activities of the company and therefore generally, but not exclusively, result from the transactions and other events relating to the profit or loss for the period. Some transactions such as the sale of an item of plant and machinery may give rise to a gain or loss that is included in profit and loss however these cash flows are from investing activities. Examples of operating activity cash flows are:

- cash receipts from the sale of goods or rendering of services;

- cash receipts from royalties, fees, commissions and other revenue;

- cash payments to suppliers of goods and services;

- cash payments to and on behalf of employees;

- cash payments or refunds of income tax (e.g. UK Corporation Tax) unless specifically identified as investing or financing activities;

- cash receipts and payments from investments, loans and other contracts held for dealing or trading purposes; and

- cash advances and loans made to other parties by financial institutions.

Some transactions such as the sale of an item of plant and machinery may give rise to a gain or loss which is included in profit and loss. These cash flows are from investing activities.

9.4.2.2   Investing activities

Investing activities are the acquisition and disposal of long-term assets and other investments which are not included as cash equivalents. Examples include:

- cash payments to acquire property, plant and equipment (including self-constructed property, plant and equipment and capitalised development costs), intangible assets and other long-term assets;

- cash receipts from sales of property, plant and equipment, intangibles and other long-term assets;

- cash payments to acquire equity or debt instruments of other entities and interests in joint ventures (other than payments for those instruments classified as cash equivalents or held for dealing or trading);

- cash receipts from sales of equity or debt instruments of other entities and interests in joint ventures (other than receipts for those instruments classified as cash equivalents or held for dealing or trading);

- cash advances and loans made to other parties (except those made by financial institutions – see paragraph **9.4.2.1**);

- cash receipts from the repayment of advances and loans made to other parties;

- cash payments for futures contracts, forward contracts, option contracts and swap contracts, except when the contracts are held for dealing or trading, or the payments are classified as financing activities; and

- cash receipts from futures contracts, forward contracts, option contracts and swap contracts, except when the contracts are held for dealing or trading, or the receipts are classified as financing activities.

When a contract is accounted for as a hedge, the cash flows of the contract are accounted for in the same category as the hedged item.

9.4.2.3   Financing activities

Financing activities result in changes in the size and composition of the contributed equity and borrowings of the company. Examples include:

- cash proceeds from issuing shares or other equity instruments;

- cash payments to owners to acquire or redeem the company's shares;

- cash proceeds from issuing debentures, loans, notes, bonds, mortgages and other short-term or long-term borrowings;

- cash repayments of amounts borrowed; and

- cash payments by a lessee for the reduction of the outstanding liability relating to a finance lease.

9.4.3   Operating activities: Direct vs Indirect

Cash flows from operating activities may be presented using either the indirect method or direct method.

The indirect method adjusts the profit and loss for the effects of changes in:

- inventories and operating receivables and payables;

- other non-cash items such as depreciation, provisions, deferred tax, accrued income or expenses not yet paid or received in cash, unrealised foreign currency gains and losses, undistributed profits of associates and non-controlling interests; and

- items where the cash effects are investing or financing activities.

The direct method discloses the major classes of gross cash receipts and gross cash payments obtained from the accounting records if these are maintained on a cash basis or by adjusting sales, cost of sales and other items in the Statement of Comprehensive income for changes in inventories, operating receivables and payables, other non-cash items and items where the cash effects are investing or financing activities.

In the UK, most companies and other entities traditionally use the indirect method to disclose operating activity cash flows by providing a reconciliation of the profit or loss for the year to cash flow from operating activity.

9.4.4   Reporting cash flows from investing and financing activities

The major classes of gross cash receipts and gross cash payments shall be presented separately.

Aggregate cash flows from acquisitions and disposals of subsidiaries and other business units shall be presented separately, classified as investing activities.

9.4.5   Reporting cash flows on a net basis

Cash flows arising from certain operating, investing or financing activities may be reported on a net basis.

- Cash receipts and payments on behalf of customers when the cash flows reflect the activities of the customer rather than those of the company.

  For example, the acceptance and repayment of demand deposits of a bank; funds held for customers by an investment company; and rents collected on behalf of, and paid over to, the owners of properties.

- Cash receipts and payments for items in which the turnover is quick, the amounts are large, and the maturities are short.

  For example, principal amounts relating to credit card customers; the purchase and sale of investments; and other short-term borrowings, for example, those which have a maturity period of three months or less.

9.4.6   Foreign currency cash flows

Cash flows arising from foreign currency transactions or the cash flows of a foreign subsidiary shall be translated into the company's functional currency at the exchange rate at the date of the cash flow or at an exchange rate which approximates the actual rate (e.g. a weighted average rate for the period).

Unrealised gains or losses arising from changes in foreign currency rates are not cash flows. However, to reconcile the opening and closing cash and cash equivalent balances remeasured at the relevant period end rates the unrealised gain or loss shall be presented separately from operating, investing and financing cash flows.

9.4.7   Interest and dividends

The cash flows from interest and dividends paid and received shall be presented separately within the relevant classification.

Interest and dividends received and interest paid may be classified as operating cash flows as they are included in profit or loss and similarly dividends paid as they are paid out of operating cash flows.

Alternatively, interest and dividends paid may be considered financing cash flows because they are a cost of obtaining financial resources and interest and dividends received may be considered investing cash flows because they are returns on investment.

However, the company chooses to classify these cash flows, it should present them consistently as such year on year.

9.4.8   Income tax

Cash flows from income taxes shall also be presented separately and within operating cash flows unless they can be specifically identified with financing or investing activities. When allocated over more than one classification, the total amount of taxes paid shall be disclosed.

9.4.9   Non-cash transactions

Investing and financing activities that do not require the use of cash and cash equivalents shall be excluded from the Statement of Cash Flows however they shall be disclosed in the accounts in a way that provides all relevant information about those activities.

Some companies investing or financing activities may have a major impact on the capital or assets structure however their exclusion is wholly in accordance with the objective of the Statement of Cash Flows. Examples include:

- acquisition of assets by assuming directly related liabilities or by means of a finance lease;

- acquisition of an entity by means of an equity issue; and

- conversion of debt to equity.

9.4.10   Components of cash and cash equivalents

Disclosure is required of the components of cash and cash equivalents and a reconciliation of the amounts presented in the Statement of Cash Flows to the amounts presented in the Statement of Financial Position (e.g. cash and cash equivalents includes bank overdrafts included in Creditors).

This reconciliation is not required if the amount is identical to the amount similarly described in the Statement of Financial Position.

9.4.11   Other disclosures

Other disclosures and appropriate commentary by management are required for the amount of significant cash and cash equivalents held but not available for use by the company. This may be the case for example where foreign exchange controls exist or other legal restrictions are in place.

Table 9.7 Example Statement of Cash Flows for the year ended 31 December 2016

	Notes	2016 £'000	2015 £'000
Cash flows from operating activities			
Operating profit		811	737
Adjustments for:			
Provisions		120	—
Depreciation and amortisation		191	150
Profit on disposal of property, plant and equipment		(26)	(17)
		1,276	759
Movements in working capital			
(Increase)/decrease in inventories		(225)	25
Increase in trade and other receivables		(288)	(218)
Decrease in trade and other payables		(255)	(429)
Cash generated from operations		508	137
Interest paid		(34)	(65)
Income taxes paid		(177)	(124)
Net cash generated by/(used in) operating activities		297	(52)
Cash flows from investing activities			
Proceeds from sale of property, plant and equipment		67	29
Payments for property, plant and equipment		(387)	(186)
Payments for other intangible assets		(50)	—
Net cash used in investing activities		(370)	(157)

	Notes	2016 £'000	2015 £'000
Cash flows from financing activities			
Proceeds from issue of new share capital		52	—
Repayments of bank borrowings		(114)	(31)
Proceeds from bank borrowings		664	—
Net cash generated by/(used in) financing activities		602	(31)
Net increase/(decrease) in cash and cash equivalents		529	(240)
Cash and cash equivalents at the beginning of the year		(106)	134
Cash and cash equivalents at the end of the year		**423**	**(106)**
Cash and bank balances		502	4
Bank overdrafts	**19**	(79)	(110)
Net cash used in financing activities		**423**	**(106)**

9.5   Notes to the accounts

Section 8 of FRS 102 sets out the principles underlying the information to be presented in the notes to the financial statements which provide additional information, narrative descriptions or a disaggregation of items presented in the primary financial statements. The notes will also present information about items that do not qualify for recognition in those statements.

Small companies preparing their accounts in accordance with FRS 102 section 1A are exempt from the requirements of section 8 however FRS 102 para. 1AC.3 does require that a small company must state the accounting policies adopted. The disclosure requirements of section 8 are similar and should therefore be followed as best practice.

9.5.1   Structure

The notes shall:

- present information about the basis of preparation of the accounts and the specific accounting policies used;

- disclose the information required by FRS 102 that is not otherwise presented in the accounts; and

- provide information that is not presented in the elsewhere in the accounts but is relevant to an understanding of any item.

The notes shall, as far as possible, be presented in a systematic manner and the items in the primary financial statements shall be cross referenced to related information elsewhere in the notes.

Notes are normally presented in the following order:

- a statement that the accounts have been prepared in accordance with FRS 102;

- a summary of the significant accounting policies, judgments and key sources of estimation uncertainty applied;

- supporting information for items presented in the accounts in the sequence in which each statement and line item is presented; and

- any other disclosures.

9.5.2   Accounting policies

Accounting policies shall disclose:

- the measurement basis or bases used in preparing the accounts;

- other accounting policies that are relevant to an understanding of the accounts;

- judgments (except those in respect of estimation uncertainty) that management has made in the process of applying the accounting policies that have the most significant effect on the amounts recognised in the accounts.

9.5.3   Key sources of estimation uncertainty

Disclosure is required in the notes of information about key assumptions concerning the future or other key sources of estimation uncertainty that have a significant risk of causing material adjustment to the assets or liabilities in the next financial year.

In respect of those assets and liabilities, the notes shall include details of their nature and the carrying amount as at the end of the reporting period.

9.6   Example accounts

See **Appendix A** for an example set of typical company financial statements showing the appropriate layout of the primary statements included in this chapter.

The model accounts do not include all of the elements illustrated in some of the examples shown in the tables above, for example the Statement of Income and Retained Earnings.

9.7   Small companies: abridged accounts

Small companies preparing accounts in accordance with the small companies' regime have the option, when appropriate to the circumstances of the company, to prepare for members an abridged statement of financial position, an abridged income statement or both. This option is only available for individual accounts and not group accounts.

The decision to prepare abridged accounts (either all or in part) must be agreed by all members and the agreement must be obtained each year.

The abridged statement of financial position need only include those items designated with letters or Roman numerals (see **Table 9.1** above) but not the details designated by Arabic numbers (see **Table 9.3** above).

The abridged income statement will combine certain line items under one heading 'Gross profit or loss' depending on which format is used. Companies using Format 1 will combine turnover, cost of sales and other operating income. Companies using Format 2 will combine turnover, changes in stocks of finished goods and in work in progress, own work capitalised, other operating income, raw materials and consumables, and other external charges (see **Table 9.4**).

It should be noted that companies choosing to prepare abridged accounts must still comply with the requirement for accounts to show a true and fair view. There is no guidance available, however, the appendices to FRS 102 section 1A note that in order to meet the requirement, abridged accounts should provide additional information in the notes, for example, in relation to disaggregating the information in the statement of financial position, disaggregating the income statement, and disclosing turnover.

Chapter 10 Consolidated and separate accounts (FRS 102 section 9)

Section 9 of FRS 102 sets out the requirements for the preparation of consolidated accounts by parent companies intended to give a true and fair view of the financial position and profit or loss of the group.

As noted below, a parent of a small group may be exempt from the requirement to prepare group accounts and therefore the requirements of section 9 do not apply to such companies.

Where a small company voluntarily prepares group accounts it must apply the consolidation procedures set out in section 9 and is encouraged to provide the necessary disclosures.

10.1 Definition of parent and subsidiary

FRS 102 defines a parent as a company that has one or more subsidiaries. A subsidiary is a company (including an unincorporated entity) that is controlled by another entity.

Control of an entity is defined in FRS 102 as the power to govern the financial and operating policies of an entity so as to obtain benefits from its activities.

Control is presumed to exist when the parent owns, directly or indirectly through subsidiaries, more than half of the voting power of an entity. That presumption may be overcome in exceptional circumstances if it can be clearly demonstrated that such ownership does not constitute control. Control also exists when the parent owns half or less of the voting power of an entity but it has:

- power over more than half of the voting rights by virtue of an agreement with other investors;

- power to govern the financial and operating policies of the entity under a statute or an agreement;

- power to appoint or remove the majority of the members of the board of directors or equivalent governing body and control of the entity is by that board or body; or

- power to cast the majority of votes at meetings of the board of directors or equivalent governing body and control of the entity is by that board or body.

Control can also be achieved by having options or convertible instruments that are currently exercisable or by having an agent with the ability to direct the activities for the benefit of the controlling entity.

Control can also exist when the parent has the power to exercise, or actually exercises, dominant influence or control over the undertaking or it and the undertaking are managed on a unified basis.

10.2 Requirement to present consolidated accounts

A parent company shall present consolidated accounts in which it consolidates all its investments in subsidiaries. A parent company need only prepare consolidated accounts under the Act if it is a parent at the period end.

However, a parent is exempt from the requirement to prepare consolidated accounts on any one of the following grounds:

- the parent is itself a subsidiary and certain conditions are met;

- the parent and the group headed by it qualifies as small within the meaning of the Act;

- all of the parent's subsidiaries are required to be excluded from consolidation; or

- for parents not reporting under the Act, if its statutory framework does not require the preparation of consolidated accounts.

The first three of these exemptions are explained below.

10.2.1   Intermediate parent entities

Under s. 400 and 401 of the Act, a company is exempt from the requirement to prepare consolidated accounts if it is itself a subsidiary undertaking and its immediate parent undertaking is established under the law of an EEA state (s. 400) or not in an EEA state (s. 401), in the following cases:

- where the company is a wholly-owned subsidiary of that parent undertaking;

- where that parent undertaking holds 90% or more of the allotted shares and the remaining shareholders have approved the exemption;

- where that parent undertaking holds more than 50% (but less than 90%) of the allotted shares and notice requesting the preparation of group accounts has not been served on the company by shareholders holding in aggregate at least 5% of the allotted shares.

Exemption is conditional upon compliance with all of the following conditions:

- the company must be included in consolidated accounts for a larger group drawn up to the same date, or to an earlier date in the same financial year, by a parent undertaking established under the law of an EEA state;

- those accounts must be drawn up and audited, and that parent undertaking's annual report must be drawn up, according to that law:

  - in accordance with the provisions of the Seventh Directive (83/349/EEC) (as modified, where relevant, by the provisions of the Bank Accounts Directive (86/635/EEC) or the Insurance Accounts Directive (91/674/EEC)); or

  - in accordance with international accounting standards;

- the company must disclose in its individual accounts that it is exempt from the obligation to prepare and deliver group accounts;

- the company must state in its individual accounts the name of the parent undertaking that draws up the group accounts referred to above and:

  - if it is incorporated outside the United Kingdom, the country in which it is incorporated; or

  - if it is unincorporated, the address of its principal place of business;

- the company must deliver to the registrar, within the period for filing its accounts and reports for the financial year in question, copies of:

  - those group accounts; and

  - the parent undertaking's annual report, together with the auditor's report on them;

  any requirement of Pt. 35 of the Act as to the delivery to the registrar of a certified translation into English must be met in relation to any of these documents.

The exemption does not apply to a company any of whose securities are admitted to trading on a regulated market in an EEA state.

10.2.2   Small groups

CA 2006, s. 383 and 384 set out the conditions to be met by a group for the parent company to qualify as 'small'.

A parent company qualifies as a small company in relation to a financial year only if the group headed by it qualifies as a small group. A group must also be eligible to be small. A group is ineligible if any of its members is:

- a public company (but see below);

- a body corporate (other than a company) whose shares are admitted to trading on a regulated market in an EEA state;

- a person (other than a small company) who has permission under the *Financial Services and Markets Act* 2000, Pt. 4 to carry on a regulated activity;

- a small company that is an authorised insurance company, a banking company, an e-money issuer, a MiFID investment firm or a UCITS management company; or

- a person who carries on insurance market activity.

A parent company of a small group that is a public company may still be exempt from preparing group accounts if it would be subject to the small companies' regime but for being a public company and it is not a traded company, i.e. one whose transferrable securities are traded on a regulated market.

The size classification of a parent company is determined with regard to the aggregate qualifying criteria of the group taken as a whole (parent company and subsidiary undertakings), irrespective of the actual size qualification of the parent company itself.

A group qualifies as small in relation to the parent company's first financial year if the qualifying conditions are met in that year. In subsequent years, a group qualifies as small if the qualifying conditions:

- are met in that year and the preceding financial year;

- are met in that year and the group qualified as small in relation to the preceding financial year; or

- were met in the preceding financial year and the group qualified as small in relation to that year s. 383(2)–(3).

A group meets the qualifying conditions (and is, therefore, exempt from producing group (consolidated) accounts as a small group) if it does not exceed more than one of the following criteria on one or other of the following two bases:

Criteria	**(The bases may be mixed)**	
	Net basis	*Gross basis*
Turnover	£10.2m	£12.2m
Balance sheet total	£5.1m	£6.1m
Average monthly number of employees	50	50

These criteria apply for accounting periods beginning on or after 1 January 2016.

The alternative bases for turnover and balance sheet totals (as qualifying conditions for exemption) are:

- 'net' basis – aggregate figures for turnover and balance sheet totals after any set-offs and consolidation adjustments made for the elimination of group transactions in accordance with CA 2006, s. 404 and the regulations thereunder (Companies Act group accounts) or international accounting standards (IAS group accounts); and

- 'gross' basis – aggregate figures for turnover and balance sheet totals without such set-offs and consolidation adjustments.

CA 2006 under SI 2008/410, Sch. 6 consolidation adjustments include:

- elimination of intra-group transactions and assets and liabilities;

- elimination of intra-group unrealised profits or losses; and

- adjustments to effect uniform accounting policies within the group.

It is important to note that the 'net' and 'gross' bases may be mixed in determining whether the criteria have been met. For example, if a group has a turnover of £8m (gross) and £6m (net), a balance sheet total of £3.8m (gross) and £3.5m (net) and 60 employees, on the size criteria the group would qualify as a small group. Although it exceeds the employee number threshold, it does not exceed the net turnover threshold or gross balance sheet threshold.

The aggregate figures are ascertained by aggregating the relevant figures from individual statutory accounts (determined in accordance with CA 2006, s. 382) for each member of the group.

10.2.3   Subsidiaries excluded from consolidation

A subsidiary shall only be excluded from consolidation where:

- severe long-term restrictions substantially hinder the exercise of the rights of the parent over the assets or management of the subsidiary; or

- the interest in the subsidiary is held exclusively with a view to subsequent resale; and the subsidiary has not previously been consolidated in the consolidated accounts.

A subsidiary is not excluded from consolidation because its business activities are dissimilar to those of the other entities within the consolidation. Relevant information is provided by consolidating such subsidiaries and disclosing additional information in the consolidated accounts about the different business activities of subsidiaries.

A subsidiary is not excluded from consolidation because the information necessary for the preparation of consolidated accounts cannot be obtained without disproportionate expense or undue delay, unless its inclusion is not material (individually or collectively for more than one subsidiary) for the purposes of giving a true and fair view in the context of the group.

10.3   Specific disclosures in consolidated accounts

The following disclosures are required in consolidated accounts:

- the fact that the statements are consolidated accounts;

- the basis for concluding that control exists when the parent does not own, directly or indirectly through subsidiaries, more than half of the voting power;

- any difference in the reporting date of the accounts of the parent and its subsidiaries used in the preparation of the consolidated accounts;

- the nature and extent of any significant restrictions (e.g. resulting from borrowing arrangements or regulatory requirements) on the ability of subsidiaries to transfer funds to the parent in the form of cash dividends or to repay loans; and

- the name of any subsidiary excluded from consolidation and the reason for exclusion.

10.4   Individual and separate accounts

There is a subtle difference between separate accounts and individual accounts when prepared by a parent.

Individual accounts are those that are required to be prepared by a company in accordance with CA 2006, s. 394.

Separate accounts (which are a sub-group within 'individual accounts') are 'those prepared by a parent in which the investments in subsidiaries, associates and joint ventures are accounted for either at cost or fair value rather than on the basis of the reported results and net assets of the investees'.

In the UK, when a parent files consolidated accounts at Companies House, it is required to include its individual accounts too. These would be classified as separate accounts.

Equally, when a parent is exempt from preparing consolidated accounts, the 'company only' accounts are treated as separate.

Conversely, where a company has no subsidiaries (even if it has associates or joint ventures) then it does not prepare consolidated accounts and its company only accounts are not separate accounts as the company is not a parent.

The above considerations are relevant to the necessary disclosure requirements for separate accounts. It is necessary to:

- disclose the fact that they are separate accounts;

- provide a description of the methods used to account for the investments in subsidiaries, jointly controlled entities and associates;

- if exemption from consolidation is claimed, it must disclose the grounds on which it is exempt; and

- if the policy choice is adopted to measure investments in subsidiaries, associates or jointly controlled entities at fair value through profit or loss, the disclosure requirements of FRS 102, section 11 apply to those investments (see **11.2** below).

10.5   Intermediate payment arrangements

Intermediate payment arrangements do not feature in the *IFRS for SMEs*, but were inserted by the FRC in recognition of the fact that these are a relatively common type of arrangement in the UK.

The most common example of an intermediate payment arrangement is a trust set up by a company to make payments to employees, although section 9 does allow for the possibility of other types of structure and other types of beneficiary. The main principle of the requirements is that, in general, a payment that a company makes into this type of arrangement will not usually give rise to an expense for the company until the time when payments are made to the beneficiaries.

This presumed treatment can only be rebutted if the company can demonstrate that either it will not at any point obtain future economic benefits from the amounts transferred or that it does not control the right or access to benefits it expects to receive.

The resulting accounting treatment is to effectively treat the assets and liabilities of the intermediary as those of the sponsoring company and any shares of the sponsoring company held by the intermediary are deducted from equity (equivalent to treasury shares).

Where a company is the sponsor of an intermediate payment arrangement, the following disclosures are required:

- a description of the main features of the intermediary including the arrangements for making payments and for distributing equity instruments;

- any restrictions relating to the assets and liabilities of the intermediary;

- the amount and nature of the assets and liabilities held by the intermediary, which have not yet vested unconditionally with the beneficiaries of the arrangement;

- the amount that has been deducted from equity and the number of equity instruments held by the intermediary, which have not yet vested unconditionally with the beneficiaries of the arrangement;

- for companies that have their equity instruments listed or publicly traded on a stock exchange or market, the market value of the equity instruments held by the intermediary which have not yet vested unconditionally with employees;

- the extent to which the equity instruments are under option to employees, or have been conditionally gifted to them; and

- the amount that has been deducted from the aggregate dividends paid by the sponsoring company.

Chapter 11   Disclosure requirements of FRS 102

As explained earlier in this book, the recognition and measurement requirements of FRS 102 apply to all companies other than those preparing their accounts in accordance with IFRS, FRS 101 or 105.

This chapter sets out the disclosure requirements of FRS 102 sections 10–35 which are applicable to all companies preparing accounts in accordance with the standard except those that are eligible for the small companies' regime and choose to present their accounts in accordance with FRS 102 section 1A.

Appendix C to section 1A of FRS 102 sets out minimum the disclosure requirements for small companies based on the requirements of company law. Directors of small companies are, however, encouraged to make other disclosures in order that the accounts show a true and fair view. Therefore, they will need to consider whether any non-mandatory disclosures of FRS 102 would be necessary in the accounts.

Throughout this chapter, we will indicate those disclosures that are mandatory for small companies and those which are not mandatory but encouraged.

11.1   Accounting policies, estimates and errors (FRS 102 section 10)

11.1.1   Accounting policies

Accounting policies are the specific principles, bases, conventions, rules and practices applied by a company in preparing and presenting financial statements.

A company shall disclose as its accounting policies:

- the measurement basis or bases used in preparing the accounts; and

- other accounting policies that are relevant to an understanding of the accounts.

Changes in accounting policy arise when either:

- it is required by a FRS or FRC Abstract; or

- the directors consider it results in the accounts providing reliable and more relevant information about the effects of transactions, other events or conditions on the company's financial position, financial performance or cash flows.

The disclosures required following a change in accounting policy for the reasons above differ slightly. When an amendment to an FRS or FRC Abstract has an effect on the current period or any prior period, or might have an effect on future periods, a company shall disclose the following:

- the nature of the change in accounting policy;

- or the current period and each prior period presented, to the extent practicable, the amount of the adjustment for each financial statement line item affected;

- the amount of the adjustment relating to periods before those presented, to the extent practicable; and

- an explanation if it is impracticable to determine the above amounts to be disclosed.

When a voluntary change in accounting policy has an effect on the current period or any prior period, a company shall disclose the following:

- the nature of the change in accounting policy;

- the reasons why applying the new accounting policy provides reliable and more relevant information;

- to the extent practicable, the amount of the adjustment for each financial statement line item affected, shown separately:

  - for the current period;

  - for each prior period presented;

  - in the aggregate for periods before those presented; and

- an explanation if it is impracticable to determine the above amounts to be disclosed.

In both cases, accounts of subsequent periods need not repeat these disclosures.

11.1.2   Changes in accounting estimates

A company shall disclose the nature of a change in an accounting estimate and the effects of the change on assets, liabilities, income and expenses for the current period. If practicable for the company to estimate the effects of the change on one or more future periods, the company shall disclose those estimates.

11.1.3   Corrections of prior period errors

The following disclosure is required of material prior period errors:

- the nature of the prior period error;

- to the extent practicable, for each prior period presented the amount of the correction for each line in the accounts affected;

- to the extent practicable, the amount of the correction at the beginning of the earliest period presented; and

- if not practicable, an explanation to determine the amounts to be disclosed above.

Accounts of subsequent periods need not repeat these disclosures.

11.1.4   Small companies

> **Small companies**
>
> Small companies are exempt from the presentation and disclosure requirements of section 10, however the specific requirements for small companies contained in FRS 102 paragraphs 1AC.3–1AC.10 are equivalent to the disclosures noted above.

11.2   Financial instruments (FRS 102 sections 11, 12 and 22)

Financial instruments is a potentially complex area of accounting in FRS 102 as it brings into UK GAAP the principles of IFRS accounting for such instruments for the first time for many companies. Sections 11 and 12 deal with 'basic' and 'other' (i.e. non-basic) financial instruments respectively. Section 22 covers the classification of liabilities and equity.

11.2.1   Definitions and scope

Whilst a detailed commentary of the recognition and measurement of financial instruments is outside the scope of this book, in broad terms instruments are categorised according to their nature and measured at either amortised cost, cost less impairment or at fair value through profit and loss. We therefore set out a brief analysis of the key definitions.

A financial instrument is a contract that gives rise to a financial asset of one company and a financial liability or equity instrument of another.

A financial asset is any asset that is:

- cash;

- an equity instrument of another entity;

- a contractual right:

  - to receive cash or another financial asset from another entity; or

  - to exchange financial assets or financial liabilities with another entity under conditions that are potentially favourable to the entity; or

- a contract that will or may be settled in the entity's own equity instruments and:

  - under which the entity is or may be obliged to receive a variable number of the entity's own equity instruments; or

  - that will or may be settled other than by the exchange of a fixed amount of cash or another financial asset for a fixed number of the entity's own equity instruments.

For this purpose, the entity's own equity instruments do not include instruments that are themselves contracts for the future receipt or delivery of the entity's own equity instruments.

A financial liability is any liability that is:

- a contractual obligation:

  - to deliver cash or another financial asset to another entity; or

  - to exchange financial assets or financial liabilities with another entity under conditions that are potentially unfavourable to the entity; or

- a contract that will or may be settled in the entity's own equity instruments and:

  - under which the entity is or may be obliged to deliver a variable number of the entity's own equity instruments; or

  - will or may be settled other than by the exchange of a fixed amount of cash or another financial asset for a fixed number of the entity's own equity instruments. For this purpose the entity's own equity instruments do not include instruments that are themselves contracts for the future receipt or delivery of the entity's own equity instruments.

Equity is the residual interest in the assets of the entity after deducting all its liabilities.

Typical examples of financial assets and liabilities in a relatively uncomplicated set of accounts might include:

- cash;

- trade debtors (receivables);

- trade creditors (payables);

- bank loans payable;

- investments in shares or debt of other companies;

- forward currency contracts; and

- interest rate swaps.

The definitions are very broad and therefore relevant to almost all preparers of accounts, not just those with complex financial arrangements.

The recognition and measurement principles of financial instruments vary depending on whether they are categorised as 'basic' or 'other'. Specific rules on the categorisation are given in FRS 102 section 11.

There are however certain categories of financial instruments which are scoped out of sections 11 and 12 as they are covered in greater detail elsewhere in the standard:

- investments in subsidiaries, associates and joint ventures (sections 9, 14 and 15);

- instruments meeting the definition of own equity (sections 22 and 26);

- leases (section 20) – although there are some aspects of lease contracts that may still give rise to an asset or liability in the scope of section 11 or 12;

- rights and obligations under employee benefit plans (section 28);

- share based payment arrangements (section 26) except those explicitly scoped into section 12;

- contracts for contingent consideration in a business combination (the exemption is for the acquirer, not the vendor);

- any forward contract between an acquirer and a selling shareholder to buy or sell an acquiree that will result in a business combination at a future acquisition date; and

- most rights under insurance contracts are scoped out of section 12, but obligations under them are included.

Contracts to buy and sell non-financial items are generally outside the scope however section 12 does cover 'contracts to buy or sell non-financial items if the contract can be settled net in cash or another financial instrument, or by exchanging financial instruments as if the contracts were financial instruments'. In other words, if a company speculates on commodity prices by contracting to buy at a fixed price but has an agreement that it is not obliged to take delivery of the commodity but may settle the contract by paying or receiving the difference with spot price at completion, then the derivative instrument is scoped into section 12.

However, this would not be the case for contracts entered into and which continue to be held for the purpose of the receipt or delivery of the non-financial item in accordance with the company's expected purchase, sale or usage requirements. Therefore, a company which uses, for example, rubber as a raw material and enters into a forward contract to meet its expected purchase needs but there is a net settlement in cash provision as a safety measure, would not account for the contract under section 12 but rather as a normal purchase transaction.

11.2.2   Disclosure requirements

The disclosure requirements of the sections of the standard are quite extensive owing to the large number of possible types of instruments and accounting choices. The requirements have therefore been broken down into areas.

These disclosure requirements do not apply to investments in subsidiaries which are accounted for at cost less impairment or at fair value with changes recognised in OCI (see **10.4** above). Investments in subsidiaries which are accounted for at fair value with changes recognised in profit or loss shall follow the disclosure requirements shown below.

Accounting policies

A company shall disclose, in the summary of significant accounting policies, the measurement basis (or bases) used for financial instruments and the other accounting policies used for financial instruments that are relevant to an understanding of the accounts.

Statement of financial position

The total carrying amounts of each of the following categories of financial instrument at the reporting date must be disclosed either on the face of the statement or in the notes:

- financial assets measured at fair value through profit or loss;

- financial assets that are debt instruments measured at amortised cost;

- financial assets that are equity instruments measured at cost less impairment;

- financial liabilities measured at fair value through profit or loss. Financial liabilities that are not held as part of a trading portfolio and are not derivatives shall be shown separately;

- financial liabilities measured at amortised cost; and

- loan commitments measured at cost less impairment.

A company shall disclose information that enables users of the accounts to evaluate the significance of financial instruments for its financial position and performance. For example, for long-term debt such information would normally include the terms and conditions of the debt instrument (such as interest rate, maturity, repayment schedule, and restrictions that the debt instrument imposes on the entity).

Note that the above requirement uses an example, designed to encourage judgment on which matters require disclosure.

For all financial assets and financial liabilities measured at fair value, the company shall disclose the basis for determining the fair value (e.g. quoted market price in an active market or a valuation technique). When a valuation technique is used, the company shall disclose the assumptions applied in determining fair value for each class of financial assets or financial liabilities. For example, if applicable, a company discloses information about the assumptions relating to prepayment rates, rates of estimated credit losses, and interest rates or discount rates.

If a reliable measure of fair value is no longer available for ordinary or preference shares measured at fair value through profit or loss, the company shall disclose that fact.

Derecognition

If a company has transferred financial assets to another party in a transaction that does not qualify for derecognition (e.g. debt factoring with full recourse), the company shall disclose the following for each class of such financial assets:

- the nature of the assets;

- the nature of the risks and rewards of ownership to which the company remains exposed; and

- the carrying amounts of the assets and of any associated liabilities that the company continues to recognise.

Collateral

When a company has pledged financial assets as collateral for liabilities or contingent liabilities, it shall disclose the following:

- the carrying amount of the financial assets pledged as collateral; and

- the terms and conditions relating to its pledge.

For loans payable recognised at the reporting date for which there is a breach of terms or default of principal, interest, sinking fund, or redemption terms that has not been remedied by the reporting date, disclosure is required of the following:

- details of that breach or default;

- the carrying amount of the related loans payable at the reporting date; and

- whether the breach or default was remedied, or the terms of the loans payable were renegotiated, before the financial statements were authorised for issue.

Items of income, expense, gains or losses

A company shall disclose the following items of income, expense, gains or losses:

- income, expense, net gains or net losses, including changes in fair value, recognised on:

  - financial assets measured at fair value through profit or loss;

  - financial liabilities measured at fair value through profit or loss (with separate disclosure of movements on those which are not held as part of a trading portfolio and are not derivatives);

  - financial assets measured at amortised cost; and

  - financial liabilities measured at amortised cost;

- total interest income and total interest expense (calculated using the effective interest method) for financial assets or financial liabilities that are not measured at fair value through profit or loss; and

- the amount of any impairment loss for each class of financial asset. A class of financial asset is a grouping that is appropriate to the nature of the information disclosed and that takes into account the characteristics of the financial assets.

Financial instruments at fair value through profit or loss (FRS 102 11.48A)

The following disclosures are required only for financial instruments measured at fair value through profit or loss in accordance with paragraph 36(4) of Schedule 1 to the Regulations. This does not include financial liabilities held as part of a trading portfolio nor derivatives.

- The amount of change, during the period and cumulatively, in the fair value of the financial instrument that is attributable to changes in the credit risk of that instrument, determined either:

  - as the amount of change in its fair value that is not attributable to changes in market conditions that give rise to market risk; or

  - using an alternative method the company believes more faithfully represents the amount of change in its fair value that is attributable to changes in the credit risk of the instrument.

- The method used to establish the amount of change attributable to changes in own credit risk, or, if the change cannot be measured reliably or is not material, that fact.

- For a financial liability, the difference between the financial liability's carrying amount and the amount the company would be contractually required to pay at maturity to the holder of the obligation.

- If an instrument contains both a liability and an equity feature, and the instrument has multiple features that substantially modify the cash flows and the values of those features are interdependent (such as a callable convertible debt instrument), the existence of those features.

- If there is a difference between the fair value of a financial instrument at initial recognition and the amount determined at that date using a valuation technique, the aggregate difference yet to be recognised in profit or loss at the beginning and end of the period and a reconciliation of the changes in the balance of this difference.

- Information that enables users of the company's financial statements to evaluate the nature and extent of relevant risks arising from financial instruments to which the company is exposed at the end of the reporting period. These risks typically include, but are not limited to, credit risk, liquidity risk and market risk. The disclosure should include both the company's exposure to each type of risk and how it manages those risks.

This requirement was inserted specifically to ensure compliance with EU/UK law, and will be of only limited relevance to most UK preparers. In general, for a financial asset or liability to qualify to be held at FVTPL, it will either be a derivative or will be part of portfolio, meaning 11.48A will not apply: the disclosures are only relevant where an item has been designated at FVTPL based on 11.48(b)(i), i.e. because it eliminates or significantly reduces an accounting mismatch.

Hedge accounting

If a company uses hedge accounting (covered in s. 12) then the following disclosures apply.

A company shall disclose the following separately for hedging relationship described in FRS 102, para. 12.19:

- a description of the hedge;
- a description of the financial instruments designated as hedging instruments and their fair values at the reporting date; and
- the nature of the risks being hedged, including a description of the hedged item.

If a company uses hedge accounting for a fair value hedge it shall disclose the following:

- the amount of the change in fair value of the hedging instrument recognised in profit or loss for the period; and
- the amount of the change in fair value of the hedged item recognised in profit or loss for the period.

If a company uses hedge accounting for a cash flow hedge it shall disclose the following:

- the periods when the cash flows are expected to occur and when they are expected to affect profit or loss;
- a description of any forecast transaction for which hedge accounting had previously been used, but which is no longer expected to occur;
- the amount of the change in fair value of the hedging instrument that was recognised in other comprehensive income during the period;
- the amount that was reclassified from other comprehensive income to profit or loss for the period; and
- the amount of any excess of the fair value of the hedging instrument over the change in the fair value of the expected cash flows that was recognised in profit or loss for the period.

If an entity uses hedge accounting for a net investment in a foreign operation it shall disclose separately the amounts recognised in other comprehensive income in accordance with FRS 102 para. 12.24(a) and the amounts recognised in profit or loss in accordance with FRS 102 para. 12.24(b).

The conditional situations in which the above hedge accounting disclosures apply are not explained here as it is felt they are of limited relevance to the users of this book.

11.2.3   Small companies

Small companies

Small companies are exempt from the presentation and disclosure requirements of sections 11, 12 and 22.

The disclosure requirements for financial instruments of small companies relate to those measured at fair value and are contained in FRS 102 para. 1AC.22–1AC.26. These requirements are summarised below.

Where financial instruments or other assets have been measured at fair value through profit or loss there must be stated:

- the significant assumptions underlying the valuation models and techniques used to determine the fair values;

- for each category of financial instrument or other asset, the fair value of the assets in that category and the change in value:

  – included directly in the income statement; or

  – credited to or (as the case may be) debited from the fair value reserve, in respect of those assets.

This does not apply where financial instruments or other assets are measured at fair value only on initial recognition.

This applies where financial instruments are subsequently measured at fair value through profit or loss.

Where financial instruments or other assets have been measured at fair value through profit or loss there must be stated for each class of derivatives, the extent and nature of the instruments, including significant terms and conditions that may affect the amount, timing and certainty of future cash flows.

Where any amount is transferred to or from the fair value reserve during the reporting period, there must be stated in tabular form:

- the amount of the reserve as at the beginning of the reporting period and as at the reporting date respectively; and

- the amount transferred to or from the reserve during that year.

The treatment for taxation purposes of amounts credited or debited to the fair value reserve must be disclosed in a note to the financial statements.

Financial instruments which under international accounting standards may be included in accounts at fair value, may be so included, provided that the disclosures required by such accounting standards are made. This only applies in certain circumstances; for example, it does not apply to derivatives. It applies where investments in subsidiaries, associates and joint ventures are measured at fair value through profit or loss. When it applies, the disclosures required by FRS 102 section 11 that relate to financial assets and financial liabilities measured at fair value, including para. 11.48A, shall be given.

Directors of a small company should consider whether any of the other disclosures of section 11, 12 or 22 noted above are necessary in order for the accounts to show a true and fair view.

11.3   Inventories (FRS 102 section 13)

The following disclosures are required:

- the accounting policies adopted in measuring inventories, including the cost formula used. The cost formula will typically be:

  – first in, first out (FIFO);

  – weighted average cost; or

  – specific identification of cost of inventories not ordinarily interchangeable and goods or services produced and segregated for specific projects;

- total carrying amount of inventories and the carrying amount in classifications appropriate to the company;

- the amount of inventories recognised as an expense during the period;

- impairment losses recognised or reversed during the period;

- total carrying amount pledged as security for liabilities.

Small companies

Small companies are exempt from the presentation and disclosure requirements of section 13.

Small companies are only required to state the accounting policy adopted in measuring inventories, however the directors of a small company should consider whether the other disclosures noted above are necessary in order that the accounts show a true and fair view.

11.4 Investments in associates (FRS 102 section 14)

An associate is an entity over which an investor has significant influence and that is neither a subsidiary nor an interest in a joint venture.

A parent company shall, in its consolidated accounts, account for all investments in associates using the equity method, i.e. to reflect the investor's share of the profit and loss, other comprehensive income and equity of the associate. Except in cases where the investment is held as part of an investment portfolio in which case they are accounted for at fair value through profit and loss.

A company that is not a parent has the choice whether to account for its investments in associates at cost or at fair value.

The accounts shall disclose:

- the accounting policy for investments in associates;

- the carrying amount of investments in associates; and

- the fair value of investments in associates accounted for using the equity method for which there are published price quotations.

Where the cost model is used, disclosure of the amount of dividends and other distributions recognised in income. Where the equity method is used, disclosure of the investor's share of the profit or loss of such associates and its share of any discontinued operations.

Where the fair value model is used, the relevant financial instruments disclosures must be included.

Finally, the individual accounts statements of an investor that is not a parent must provide summarised financial information about the investments in the associates, along with the effect of including those investments as if they had been accounted for using the equity method. Investing entities that are exempt from preparing consolidated financial statements, or would be exempt if they had subsidiaries, are exempt from this requirement. In other words, typically a medium-sized or large company that is not itself a subsidiary would need to provide summarised financial information.

Small companies

Small companies are exempt from the presentation and disclosure requirements of section 14 and 15 (below).

The specific disclosure requirements are contained in FRS 102 para. 1AC.12–1AC.13 and relate to the aggregate amount of fixed asset investment in subsidiaries, associates and joint ventures.

- the effect on any amount shown in the statement of financial position in respect of that item of:

  - any revision of the amount in respect of any assets included under that item made during the reporting period as a result of revaluation;

  - acquisitions during the reporting period of any assets;

  - disposals during the reporting period of any assets; and

  - any transfers of assets of the small entity to and from that item during the reporting period.

There must also be stated:

  - the cumulative amount of provisions for depreciation and impairment of assets included under that item as at the date of the beginning of the reporting period and as at the reporting date respectively;

  - the amount of any such provisions made in respect of the reporting period;

  - the amount of any adjustments made in respect of any such provisions during the reporting period in consequence of the disposal of any assets; and

  - the amount of any other adjustments made in respect of any such provisions during the reporting period.

The directors of a small company should consider whether the other disclosures noted above are necessary in order that the accounts show a true and fair view.

11.5   Investments in joint ventures (FRS 102 section 15)

A joint venture is a contractual arrangement whereby two or more parties undertake an economic activity that is subject to joint control. Joint ventures can take the form of jointly controlled operations, jointly controlled assets, or jointly controlled entities.

Joint control is the contractually agreed sharing of control over an economic activity, and exists only when the strategic financial and operating decisions relating to the activity require the unanimous consent of the parties sharing control (the venturers).

The three sub-categories of joint venture may be summarised as follows:

Jointly controlled operations involve the use of the assets and other resources of the venturers rather than the establishment of a corporation, partnership or other entity, or a financial structure that is separate from the venturers themselves. The key feature is the lack of a distinct legal or financial structure, so although there is a definable business, it is not ring fenced or self-contained.

Jointly controlled assets are jointly controlled, and often also jointly owned, by the investors, and is dedicated to the purposes of the joint venture.

Jointly controlled operations and assets are accounted for by the investor by recognising its share of the relevant assets, liabilities, income and expenses classified according to their nature. There are no specific disclosure requirements.

Jointly controlled entities are any joint ventures where the operations are run through a distinct corporation, partnership or other entity in which each venturer has an interest.

A venture that is a parent company shall, in its consolidated accounts, account for all investments in associates using the equity method in the same way as for investments in associates. A similar exemption exists where the investments are held as part of an investment portfolio in which case they shall be accounted for at fair value though profit and loss.

A venturer that is not a parent has the choice whether to account for its investments in associates at cost or at fair value.

The accounts shall disclose:

- the accounting policy for investments in jointly controlled entities;

- the carrying amount of investments in jointly controlled entities;

- the fair value of investments in associates accounted for using the equity method for which there are published price quotations; and

- the aggregate amount of its commitments relating to joint ventures, including its share on the capital commitments that have been incurred jointly with other venturers, as well at its share of the capital commitments of the joint ventures themselves.

Where the equity method is used, disclosure of the investor's share of the profit or loss of such associates and its share of any discontinued operations of jointly controlled entities.

Where the fair value model is used, the relevant financial instruments disclosures must be included.

Finally, the individual accounts statements of an investor that is not a parent must provide summarised financial information about the investments in the associates, along with the effect of including those investments as if they had been accounted for using the equity method. Investing entities that are exempt from preparing consolidated financial statements, or would be exempt if they had subsidiaries, are exempt from this requirement.

Small companies

Please see the small companies note in **11.4 Investments in associates (FRS 102 section 14)** above.

11.6   Investment property (FRS 102 section 16)

Investment property is property held by its owner or a lessee under a finance lease to earn rentals or for capital appreciation or both, rather than for use in the production or supply of the goods or services, for administrative purposes or for sale in the ordinary course of business.

Investment property shall be accounted for at fair value through profit and loss. Exemptions from this model are available where the fair value cannot be obtained without undue cost or effort or where the property is held primarily for the provision of social benefit, e.g. social housing held by a public benefit entity. If the fair value model is not used the property is accounted for under a cost model in accordance with FRS 102 section 17 'Property, plant and equipment' (see **11.7**) and the relevant disclosures of that section apply.

The following disclosures apply for investment property accounted for at fair value through profit and loss:

- the methods and significant assumptions applied in determining the fair value of investment property;

- the extent to which the fair value of investment property (as measured or disclosed in the accounts) is based on a valuation by an independent valuer who holds a recognised and relevant professional qualification and has recent experience in the location and class of the investment property being valued. If there has been no such valuation, that fact shall be disclosed;

- the existence and amounts of restrictions on the realisability of investment property or the remittance of income and proceeds of disposal;

- contractual obligations to purchase, construct or develop investment property or for repairs, maintenance or enhancements; and

- a reconciliation between the carrying amounts of investment property at the beginning and end of the period, showing separately:

  - additions, disclosing separately those additions resulting from acquisitions through business combinations;

  - net gains or losses from fair value adjustments;

  - transfers to property, plant and equipment when a reliable measure of fair value is no longer available without undue cost or effort;

  - transfers to and from inventories and owner-occupied property; and

  - other changes.

This reconciliation need only be presented for the current period, i.e. it is not required for prior periods.

A company shall also give all relevant disclosures about leases it has entered into as required by FRS 102 section 20 both as a lessor and lessee.

True and fair override

Paragraph 39(2) of Schedule 1 to the Regulations allows investment properties to be measured at fair value under UK GAAP with movements in fair value recognised in the profit and loss account. There is no requirement to provide depreciation. This treatment is consistent with FRS 102. As a result, there is now no need for a true and fair override to be given in UK GAAP accounts prepared under FRS 102 because of the non-provision of depreciation.

Previously the treatment required by SSAP 19 was consistent with paragraph 32(2) of Schedule 1 to the Regulations which allows tangible fixed assets to be measured under the alternative accounting rules at 'a market value determined as at the date of their last valuation or at their current cost'. All gains and losses resulting from movements in an asset's value (other than those relating to permanent diminutions in value) were recognised in the revaluation reserve. However, paragraph 33 still required the depreciation rules to be applied in such circumstances – hence the need, under SSAP 19, for a true and fair override to be given because of the non-provision of depreciation.

Small companies

Small companies are exempt from the presentation and disclosure requirements of section 16.

The specific disclosure requirements for small companies are covered in FRS 102 paragraphs 1AC.12–1AC.13 however the disclosures are similar to those noted above.

11.7 Property, plant and equipment (FRS 102 section 17)

Property, plant and equipment are tangible assets:

- held for use in the production or supply of goods or services, for rental to others or for administrative purposes; and

- expected to be used during more than one period.

This section also applies to investment property whose fair value cannot be measured reliably without undue cost of effort (see **11.6**).

None of the following are within the scope of FRS 102, section 17 but are all within the scope of section 34, Specialised Activities:

- biological assets related to agricultural activity;

- heritage assets; and

- mineral rights and mineral reserves, such as oil, natural gas and similar non-regenerative resources.

Property , plant and equipment may be measured under a cost model or a revaluation model using fair value less accumulated depreciation and accumulated impairment losses. Under a revaluation model, gains are recognised in other comprehensive income and accumulated in equity. Losses are recognised in profit and loss to the extent they exceed any previously accumulated revaluation gains.

A company must present its property, plant and equipment in accordance with the Regulations. This requires 'Tangible assets' to be presented on the face of the statement of financial position with the notes giving an analysis of the following categories:

- land and buildings;

- plant and machinery;

- fixtures, fittings, tools and equipment; and

- payments on account and assets in course of construction.

Several disclosures are required for each class of property, plant and equipment:

- the measurement bases used for determining the gross carrying amount;

- the depreciation methods used;

- the useful lives or the depreciation rates used;

- the gross carrying amount and the accumulated depreciation (aggregated with accumulated impairment losses) at the beginning and end of the reporting period;

- a reconciliation of the carrying amount at the beginning and end of the reporting period showing separately:

  - additions;

  - disposals;

  - acquisitions through business combinations;

  - revaluations;

  - transfers to or from investment property if a reliable measure of fair value becomes available or unavailable;

- impairment losses recognised or reversed in profit or loss in accordance with FRS 102 section 27 Impairment of Assets;

- depreciation; and

- other changes.

This reconciliation need not be presented for prior periods.

In addition, the company shall also disclose the following:

- the existence and carrying amounts of property, plant and equipment to which the company has restricted title or that is pledged as security for liabilities; and

- the amount of contractual commitments for the acquisition of property, plant and equipment.

For items of property, plant and equipment stated at revalued amounts, the following shall be disclosed:

- the effective date of the revaluation (see also SI 2008/410, Sch. 1, para. 53(a) which requires disclosure of the years (so far as they are known to the directors) in which the assets were severally valued and those several values);

- whether an independent valuer was involved;

- the methods and significant assumptions applied in estimating the items' fair values; and

- for each revalued class of property, plant and equipment, the carrying amount that would have been recognised had the assets been carried under the cost model.

In addition, in the case of assets that have been valued during the financial year, SI 2008/410 Sch. 1, para. 53(b) requires disclosure of the names of the persons who valued them or particulars of their qualifications for doing so and (whichever is stated) the bases of valuation used by them.

There are also some additional disclosures required by the Companies Act which are not referred to in FRS 102. These are:

- Paragraph 2(1) of Schedule 7 to SI 2008/410 which requires disclosure in the Directors' Report of any substantial differences between the market value of properties and their carrying value, if the directors think the difference is of such significance that members should be made aware of it. This could arise where, for instance, land and buildings are held at historical cost and market values have significantly increased or decreased since the date of acquisition or last valuation or there is a more valuable alternative use to an item of owner-occupied property; and

- SI 2008/410, Sch. 1, para. 53 which requires disclosures in respect of land and buildings to include an analysis of freehold, long leasehold (i.e. those leases with 50 years or more to run at the end of the reporting year) and short leasehold property.

Small companies

Small companies are exempt from the presentation and disclosure requirements of section 17.

The specific disclosure requirements for small companies are covered in FRS 102 paragraphs 1AC.12–1AC.19, however, the disclosures are similar to those noted above except that there is no need to separate the classes of tangible assets and no requirement to disclose in the Directors' Report any substantial difference between the market value of properties and their carrying value

The directors of a small company should consider whether the other disclosures noted above are necessary in order that the accounts show a true and fair view.

11.8   Intangible assets other than goodwill (FRS 102 section 18)

An intangible asset is an identifiable non-monetary asset without physical substance. Such an asset is identifiable when:

- it is separable, i.e. capable of being separated or divided from the company and sold, transferred, licensed, rented or exchanged, either individually or together with a related contract, asset or liability; or

- it arises from contractual or other legal rights, regardless of whether those rights are transferable or separable from the company or from other rights and obligations.

None of the following are within the scope of FRS 102 section 18:

- financial assets (sections 11 and 12);

- heritage assets (section 34);

- mineral rights and mineral reserves, such as oil, natural gas and similar non-regenerative resources (section 34);

- goodwill (which is an intangible asset but is dealt with in section 19); and

- intangible assets held by a company for sale in the ordinary course of business are accounted for and disclosed as Inventories (section 13).

Intangible assets other than goodwill may be measured under a cost model or a revaluation model using fair value less accumulated depreciation and accumulated impairment losses. A revaluation model is only possible where the fair value can be determined by reference to an active market. Under a revaluation model, gains are recognised in other comprehensive income and accumulated in equity. Losses are recognised in profit and loss to the extent they exceed any previously accumulated revaluation gains.

The disclosure requirements for intangible assets are largely similar to those for property, plant and equipment (see **11.7**). Much of the disclosure is governed by the Regulations. This requires 'Intangible assets' to be presented on the face of the statement of financial position with the notes giving an analysis of the following sub-headings:

- Concessions, patents, licences, trademarks, and similar rights and assets;

- Development costs;

- Goodwill;

- Payments on account.

The requirements in FRS 102 refer to disclosures for each 'class' of intangible assets. A class is a grouping of assets of a similar nature and use in a company's operations, for example:

- brand names;

- mastheads and publishing titles;

- computer software;

- licences and franchises;

- copyrights, patents and other industrial property rights, services and operating rights;

- recipes, formulas, models, designs and prototypes; and

- intangible assets under development.

The disclosures required for each class are as follows:

- the useful lives or the amortisation rates used and the reasons for choosing those periods;

- the amortisation methods used;

- the gross carrying amount and any accumulated amortisation (aggregated with accumulated impairment losses) at the beginning and end of the reporting period;

- the line item(s) in the statement of comprehensive income (or in the income statement, if presented) in which any amortisation of intangible assets is included; and

- a reconciliation of the carrying amount at the beginning and end of the reporting period showing separately:

  - additions, indicating separately those from internal development and those acquired separately;

  - disposals;

  - acquisitions through business combinations;

  - amortisation (see also SI 2008/410, Sch. 1, para. 51(2) and 51(3));

  - revaluations (see also SI 2008/410, Sch. 1, para. 51(1)(b)(i));

  - impairment losses recognised or reversed in profit or loss in accordance with section 27; and

  - other changes.

  This reconciliation does not need to be presented for prior periods.

The following disclosures are also required:

- a description, the carrying amount and remaining amortisation period of any individual intangible asset that is material to the company's financial statements;

- for intangible assets acquired by way of a grant and initially recognised at fair value;

  - the fair value initially recognised for these assets; and

  - their carrying amounts;

- the existence and carrying amounts of intangible assets to which the company has restricted title or that are pledged as security for liabilities; and

- the amount of contractual commitments for the acquisition of intangible assets.

A company shall disclose the aggregate amount of research and development expenditure recognised as an expense during the period (i.e. the amount of expenditure incurred internally on research and development that has not been capitalised as an intangible asset or as part of the cost of another asset that meets the recognition criteria in the standard).

Finally, the FRC added para. 18.29A to match with the new permission to revalue an intangible asset. For any intangible assets accounted for at a revalued amount, a company shall disclose the items below:

- the effective date of the revaluation (see also SI 2008/410, Sch. 1, para. 52(a) which requires disclosure of the years (so far as they are known to the directors) in which the assets were severally valued and those several values);

- whether an independent valuer was involved;

- the methods and significant assumptions applied in estimating the assets' fair values; and

- for each revalued class of intangible assets, the carrying amount that would have been recognised had the assets been carried under the cost model.

In addition to the above requirements from section 18, in the case of assets that have been valued during the financial year, SI 2008/410, Sch. 1, para. 53(b) requires disclosure of the names of the persons who valued them or particulars of their qualifications for doing so and (whichever is stated) the bases of valuation used by them.

Small companies

Small companies are exempt from the presentation and disclosure requirements of section 18.

The specific disclosure requirements for small companies are covered in FRS 102 paragraphs 1AC.12–1AC.19, however, the disclosures are similar to those noted above except that there is no need to separate the classes of intangible assets and no requirement to specify the amount of research and development expenditure recognised as an expense during the period.

In addition, if a small company capitalises development costs in its statement of financial position, it shall state the period over which the costs are being written off and the reasons for capitalising the costs in question.

The directors of a small company should consider whether the other disclosures noted above are necessary in order that the accounts show a true and fair view.

11.9   Business combinations and goodwill (FRS 102 section 19)

A business combination is defined as 'the bringing together of separate entities or businesses into one reporting company'. This covers a range of situations, including the acquisition of shares, purchase of net assets, assumption of liabilities, or purchase of a group of assets constituting a business. The term 'business combination' and the relevant disclosures apply equally to consolidated accounts (in the case of the acquisition of a subsidiary) and to individual accounts in the case of the acquisition of a business.

All business combinations shall be accounted for using the purchase method except for group reconstructions which may be accounted for using the merger accounting method.

Under the purchase method, the acquirer shall allocate the cost of a business combination by recognising the acquiree's identifiable assets (including intangible assets), liabilities and contingent liabilities in accordance with the recognition criteria specified in FRS 102 which in most cases refer to fair value. Under the merger accounting method the carrying values of the assets and liabilities of the parties to the combination are not required to be adjusted to fair value (although adjustments may be required to achieve uniform accounting policies).

Goodwill is the amount of goodwill acquired plus any excess of the cost of acquisition over the acquirer's interest in the net amount of identifiable assets, liabilities and contingent liabilities and is carried at its cost less accumulated amortisation and cumulated impairment losses.

Negative goodwill can arise if the interest in the net amount of identifiable assets, liabilities and contingent liabilities exceeds the cost of the business combination. The credit balance is released to profit or loss as follows: amounts up to the fair value of the non-monetary assets (for instance property, plant and equipment, which are likely to give rise to most significant fair value adjustments) are released over the periods in which the assets' fair values are recovered; and any excess over those amounts is released in the periods expected to be benefited. The carrying value is disclosed separately on the face of the Statement of Financial Position immediately after amounts of positive goodwill.

The disclosure requirements in the Regulations notes for intangible assets are equally applicable to goodwill. FRS 102 also requires a reconciliation of the opening and closing carrying amounts of positive goodwill, showing separately:

- changes arising from new business combinations;
- amortisation;
- impairment losses;
- disposals of previously acquired businesses; and
- other changes.

In the case of negative goodwill, a reconciliation of the opening and closing carrying amounts of positive goodwill, showing separately:

- changes arising from new business combinations;
- amounts recognised in profit or loss in accordance with FRS 102, para. 19.24(c);
- disposals of previously acquired businesses; and
- other changes.

These reconciliations need not be presented for prior periods.

Detailed disclosures are required for business combinations (excluding group reconstructions) effected during the reporting period as follows:

- the names and descriptions of the combining entities or businesses;
- the acquisition date;
- the percentage of voting equity instruments acquired;
- the cost of the combination and a description of the components of that cost (such as cash, equity instruments and debt instruments);
- the amounts recognised at the acquisition date for each class of the acquiree's assets, liabilities and contingent liabilities, including goodwill;
- the useful life of goodwill, and if this cannot be reliably estimated, supporting reasons for the period chosen; and
- the periods in which the excess recognised in accordance with paragraph 19.24 will be recognised in profit or loss.

Then, for each material business combination in the period, disclosure of the revenue and profit or loss of the acquiree since the acquisition date included in the consolidated statement of comprehensive income for the period.

For group reconstructions (that do not qualify as business combinations):

- the names of the combining entities (other than the reporting company);
- whether the combination has been accounted for as an acquisition or a merger; and
- the date of the combination.

Small companies

Small companies are exempt from the presentation and disclosure requirements of section 19.

The specific disclosure requirements for small companies are covered in FRS 102 paragraphs 1AC.12–1AC.13 and relate to the disclosures required by the Regulations.

- a reconciliation of the opening and closing carrying amounts of positive goodwill, showing separately:

    - changes arising from new business combinations;

    - amortisation;

    - impairment losses;

    - disposals of previously acquired businesses; and

    - other changes;

- in the case of negative goodwill, a reconciliation of the opening and closing carrying amounts of positive goodwill, showing separately:

    - changes arising from new business combinations;

    - amounts recognised in profit or loss in accordance with FRS 102, para. 19.24(c);

    - disposals of previously acquired businesses; and

    - other changes.

These reconciliations need not be presented for prior periods.

The directors of a small company should consider whether the other disclosures noted above are necessary in order that the accounts show a true and fair view.

11.10   Leases (FRS 102 section 20)

A lease is an agreement whereby the lessor conveys to the lessee, in return for a payment or series of payments, the right to use an asset for an agreed period of time.

Leases are classified as operating leases or finance leases.

Different disclosures are required for lessees and lessors.

11.10.1   Lessees

A lessee shall make the following disclosures for finance leases:

- for each class of asset, the net carrying amount at the end of the reporting period;

- the total of future minimum lease payments at the end of the reporting period, for each of the following periods:

    - not later than one year;

    - later than one year and not later than five years; and

    - later than five years; and

- a general description of the lessee's significant leasing arrangements including, for example, information about contingent rent, renewal or purchase options and escalation clauses, subleases, and restrictions imposed by lease arrangements.

A lessee shall make the following disclosures for operating leases:

- the total of future minimum lease payments under non-cancellable operating leases for each of the following periods:

    - not later than one year;

    - later than one year and not later than five years; and

    - later than five years; and

- lease payments recognised as an expense.

11.10.2 Lessors

A lessor shall make the following disclosures for finance leases:

- a reconciliation between the gross investment in the lease at the end of the reporting period, and the present value of minimum lease payments receivable at the end of the reporting period. In addition, a lessor shall disclose the gross investment in the lease and the present value of minimum lease payments receivable at the end of the reporting period, for each of the following periods:

  - not later than one year;

  - later than one year and not later than five years; and

  - later than five years;

- unearned finance income (i.e. the gross investment in the lease less the net investment in the lease);

- the unguaranteed residual values accruing to the benefit of the lessor;

- the accumulated allowance for uncollectible minimum lease payments receivable;

- contingent rents recognised as income in the period; and

- a general description of the lessor's significant leasing arrangements, including, for example, information about contingent rent, renewal or purchase options and escalation clauses, subleases, and restrictions imposed by lease arrangements.

A lessor shall disclose the following for operating leases:

- the future minimum lease payments under non-cancellable operating leases for each of the following periods:

  - not later than one year;

  - later than one year and not later than five years; and

  - later than five years;

- total contingent rents recognised as income; and

- a general description of the lessor's significant leasing arrangements, including for example, information about contingent rent, renewal or purchase options and escalation clauses, and restrictions imposed by lease arrangements.

11.10.3 Small companies

Small companies

Small companies are exempt from the presentation and disclosure requirements of section 20. The disclosure of commitments and contingencies is however required by the requirements of paragraph 1AC.29 which is discussed in section **11.11.6** below

The directors of a small company should consider whether any of the other disclosure requirements noted above are necessary in order that the accounts show a true and fair view.

11.11 Provisions and contingencies (FRS 102 section 21)

A provision is a liability of uncertain timing or amount. A contingency is a possible asset or liability that arises from past events whose existence will be confirmed only by the occurrence or non-occurrence of one or more uncertain future events not wholly within the control of the company. A contingent liability also arises from a present obligation that arises from past events but cannot be recognised because it is not probable that economic outflow will be required to settle the obligation or the amount cannot be reliably estimated.

11.11.1 Provisions

For each class of provision, the following must be disclosed (comparative information is not required):

- a reconciliation showing:

    - the carrying amount at the beginning and end of the period;

    - additions during the period, including adjustments that result from changes in measuring the discounted amount;

    - amounts charged against the provision during the period;

    - unused amounts reversed during the period;

- a brief description of the nature of the obligation and the expected amount and timing of any resulting economic outflows;

- an indication of the uncertainties about the amount or timing of those outflows; and

- the amount of any expected reimbursement, stating the amount of any asset that has been recognised for that expected reimbursement.

Note that para. 8.6 and 8.7 of the standard require disclosure of judgments made by management and the key assumptions concerning the future and other key sources of estimation uncertainty (see **9.5.3**). This is usually included in the accounting policies section of the notes to the financial statements, with the other disclosures above usually given in a provisions note.

11.11.2 Contingent liabilities

For each class of contingent liability, unless the possibility of an outflow of economic benefits is remote, the following must be disclosed:

- a brief description of the nature of the contingent liability;

- an estimate of its financial effect, measured in accordance with the guidance for measuring provisions;

- an indication of the uncertainties about the amount or timing of the outflows; and

- the possibility of any reimbursement. (Note that this only requires a statement of the possibility of a reimbursement, rather than the amount as required for disclosures about provisions.)

If it is impracticable to make any of the disclosures other than the nature of the contingent liability then this fact must be stated. 'Impracticable' is defined in the glossary to FRS 102 as being unable to comply with a requirement 'after making every reasonable effort to do so'. The IFRS Foundation notes that 'impracticable is a high hurdle'.

The *Companies Act* 2006 also requires disclosure of the details of any valuable security provided by the company in connection with a contingent liability.

11.11.3   Contingent assets

For contingent assets the following must be disclosed:

- a description of the nature of the contingent assets; and

- an estimate of their financial effect measured in accordance with the guidance for measuring provisions.

If it is impracticable to make the financial disclosure then this fact must be stated.

11.11.4   Prejudicial disclosures

The standard recognises that disclosing some or all of the information required by the standard could prejudice seriously the position of an company in a dispute with other parties on the matter which has given rise to the provision, contingent liability or contingent asset, although the standard advises that such a situation will be 'extremely rare'.

In such circumstances the company need not disclose all of the particulars required above insofar as it relates to the dispute, but instead must disclose at least the following:

- In relation to provisions, the following information shall be given:

  - a table showing the reconciliation required by FRS 102 para. 21.14(a) in aggregate, including the source and application of any amounts transferred to or from provisions during the reporting period;

  - particulars of each provision in any case where the amount of the provision is material; and

  - the fact that, and reason why, the information required by FRS 102 para. 21.14 has not been disclosed.

- In relation to contingent liabilities, the following information shall be given:

  - particulars and the total amount of any contingent liabilities (excluding those which arise out of insurance contracts) that are not included in the statement of financial position;

  - the total amount of contingent liabilities which are undertaken on behalf of or for the benefit of:

    (a) any parent or fellow subsidiary of the entity;

    (b) any subsidiary of the entity; or

    (c) any entity in which the reporting entity has a participating interest, shall each be stated separately; and

  - the fact that, and reason why, the information required by paragraph 21.15 has not been disclosed.

- In relation to contingent assets, the entity shall disclose the general nature of the dispute, together with the fact that, and reason why, the information required by paragraph 21.16 has not been disclosed.

11.11.5   Commitments

The *Companies Act* 2006 requires disclosure of the aggregate amount or estimated amount of contracts for capital expenditure not provided for, certain details in respect of pension commitments not provided for, and also the particulars of any other financial commitments that are not provided for and are relevant to assessing the state of the company's affairs.

11.11.6   Small companies

Small companies: Indebtedness, guarantees and financial commitments

The disclosure requirements for small companies are taken from the requirements of SI 2008/409 and are reproduced in FRS 102 at paragraphs 1AC.27–1AC.31 and are summarised below.

For the aggregate of all items shown under 'creditors' in the statement of financial position there must be stated the aggregate of the following amounts:

- the amount of any debts included under 'creditors' which are payable or repayable otherwise than by instalments and fall due for payment or repayment after the end of the period of five years beginning with the day next following the reporting date; and

- in the case of any debts so included which are payable or repayable by instalments, the amount of any instalments which fall due for payment after the end of that period.

In respect of each item shown under 'creditors' in the statement of financial position there must be stated the aggregate amount of any debts included under that item in respect of which any security has been given by the small entity with an indication of the nature and form of any such security.

The total amount of any financial commitments, guarantees and contingencies that are not included in the statement of financial position must be stated.

The total amount of any commitments concerning pensions must be separately disclosed.

The total amount of any commitments which are undertaken on behalf of or for the benefit of:

- any parent, fellow subsidiary or any subsidiary of the company; or

- any undertaking in which the company has a participating interest,

must each be separately stated.

Such commitments can arise in a variety of situations, including in relation to group entities, investments, property, plant and equipment, leases and pension obligations.

An indication of the nature and form of any valuable security given by the company entity in respect of commitments, guarantees and contingencies noted above must be given.

If in any reporting period a small entity is or has been party to arrangements that are not reflected in its statement of financial position and at the reporting date the risks or benefits arising from those arrangements are material the nature and business purpose of the arrangements must be given in the notes to the financial statements to the extent necessary for enabling the financial position of the small entity to be assessed.

Examples of off-balance sheet arrangements include risk and benefit-sharing arrangements or obligations arising from a contract such as debt factoring, combined sale and repurchase arrangements, consignment stock arrangements, take or pay arrangements, securitisation arranged through separate entities, pledged assets, operating lease arrangements, outsourcing and the like. In many cases the disclosures about financial commitments and contingencies required above will also address such arrangements.

11.12   Revenue (FRS 102 section 23)

Revenue is the gross inflow of economic benefits during the period arising in the course of the ordinary activities of a company when those inflows result in increases in equity, other than increases relating to contributions from equity participants.

Section 23 deals with the accounting for revenue from the sale of goods, rendering of services, construction contracts (where the company is the contractor) and returns from the use of the company's assets by others yielding interest, royalties and dividends.

Other sections of FRS 102 deal with the accounting for other revenue or income:

- lease agreements (section 20);

- income from equity accounted investments (section 14);

- changes in the fair value of financial assets or liabilities (sections 11 and 12);

- changes in the fair value of investment property (section 16);

- initial recognition and subsequent changes in fair value of biological assets (section 34);

- initial recognition of agricultural produce (section 34); and

- insurance contracts (FRS 103).

Disclosure is required of the following:

- the accounting policies adopted for the recognition of revenue, including the methods adopted to determine the stage of completion of transactions involving the rendering of services; and

- the amount of each category of revenue recognised during the period, showing separately, at a minimum, revenue arising from:

  - the sale of goods;

  - the rendering of services;

  - interest;

  - royalties;

  - dividends;

  - commissions;

  - grants; and

  - any other significant types of revenue.

Further disclosures are required for construction contracts as follows:

- the amount of contract revenue recognised as revenue in the period;

- the methods used to determine the contract revenue recognised in the period; and

- the methods used to determine the stage of completion of contracts in progress, and separate presentation of:

- the gross amount due from customers for contract work, as an asset; and

- the gross amount due to customers for contract work, as a liability.

11.12.1 Particulars of turnover

Companies' legislation requires an analysis of particulars of turnover (SI 2008/410, Sch. 1, para. 68) as follows.

- If in the course of the financial year the company has carried on business of two or more classes that, in the opinion of the directors, differ substantially from each other, the amount of the turnover attributable to each class must be stated and the class described.

- If in the course of the financial year the company has supplied geographical markets that, in the opinion of the directors, differ substantially from each other, the amount of the turnover attributable to each such market must also be stated.

In making this analysis the source (in terms of class of business or in terms of market) of turnover, the directors of the company must have regard to the manner in which the company's activities are organised.

Classes of business which, in the opinion of the directors, do not differ substantially from each other must be treated as one class. Similarly geographical markets which, in the opinion of the directors, do not differ substantially from each other must be treated as one market.

There is an exemption available where, in the opinion of the directors, the disclosure of any of this information would be seriously prejudicial to the interests of the company. In such cases the information need not be disclosed, but the fact that any such information has not been disclosed must be stated.

Small companies

Small companies are exempt from the presentation and disclosure requirements of section 23, however the directors of a small company should consider whether the disclosures noted above are necessary in order that the accounts show a true and fair view.

11.13   Government grants (FRS 102 section 24)

Government grants are assistance by government in the form of transfers of resources to a company in return for past or future compliance with specified conditions relating to the operating activities of the company. Government refers to government, government agencies and similar bodies whether local, national or international.

There are two aspects of the definition. The first is it applies to grants from governmental bodies. The second is that it only applies to grants related to a company's operating activities. Operating activities are defined as 'the principal revenue-producing activities of the company and other activities that are not investing or financing activities'.

The following shall be disclosed:

- the accounting policy adopted for grants;

- the nature and amounts of grants recognised in the financial statements;

- unfulfilled conditions and other contingencies attaching to grants that have been recognised in income; and

- an indication of other forms of government assistance from which the company has directly benefited.

Small companies

Small companies are exempt from the presentation and disclosure requirements of section 24, however the directors of a small company should consider whether the disclosures noted above are necessary in order that the accounts show a true and fair view.

11.14   Share-based payment (FRS 102 section 26)

A share-based payment is a transaction in which the company:

- receives goods or services (including employee services) as consideration for its own equity instruments (including shares or share options); or

- receives goods or services but has no obligation to settle the transaction with supplier; or

- acquires goods or services by incurring liabilities to the supplier of those goods or services for amounts that are based on the price (or value) of the company's shares or other equity instruments of the company or another group company.

FRS 102 requires a charge where a company provides some form of benefit under a share-based payment transaction. This applies whether the benefits provided are in the form of equity, or in cash at an amount that is based upon equity.

Disclosures required in respect of share-based payments are as follows:

In all cases, a company must disclose the following in respect of all arrangements that were in place during the period:

- a description of each type of arrangement that was in place during the period, including the general terms and conditions of each arrangement, such as vesting requirements, the maximum term of options granted, and the method of settlement (e.g. whether cash or equity). This information may be aggregated where an company has a number of such arrangements;

- the number and weighted average exercise prices of share options for each of the following groups of options:
    - outstanding at the beginning of the period;
    - granted during the period;
    - forfeited during the period;
    - exercised during the period;
    - expired during the period;
    - outstanding at the end of the period; and
    - exercisable at the end of the period;

- the total expense that has been recognised in profit or loss for the period in respect of share-based payment transactions; and

- the total carrying amount at the end of the period for liabilities arising from share-based payment transactions.

Where a company has modified any of its share-based payment arrangements during the period it has to provide an explanation of the modification.

Where a company has equity-settled share-based payment arrangements it must disclose information about how it measured the fair value of the goods or services received or the value of the equity instruments which were granted, as appropriate. Where valuation methodology has been used the company shall disclose the method and the reasons why that methodology was adopted.

Where a company has cash-settled share-based payment arrangements it needs to provide information about how the liability has been measured.

Where the company is a member of a group share-based payment plan, and has taken advantage of the option to measure its share-based payment expense of the basis of a reasonable allocation of the group expense than that fact needs to be disclosed together with the basis on which the expense has been allocated.

Small companies

Small companies are exempt from the presentation and disclosure requirements of section 26, however the directors of a small company should consider whether the disclosures noted above are necessary in order that the accounts show a true and fair view.

11.15   Impairment of assets (FRS 102 section 27)

An impairment loss occurs when the carrying amount of an asset exceeds its recoverable amount.

Section 27 is applied typically to assets such as inventories, property, plant and equipment, intangible assets and investments in subsidiaries, joint ventures and associates.

Section 27 does not apply to the following assets where impairment requirements are contained in other sections:

- assets arising from construction contracts (section 23);

- deferred tax assets (section 29);

- assets arising from employee benefits (section 28);

- financial assets within the scope of section 11 Basic Financial Instruments or section 12 Other Financial Instruments Issues;

- investment property measured at fair value (section 16); and

- biological assets related to agricultural activity measured at fair value less estimated costs to sell (section 24).

For each of the following classes of assets indicated below, disclosure is required of both the amount of impairment losses and the reversals of those impairment losses that are recognised in profit or loss during the period as well as the line item(s) in the statement of comprehensive income (or in the income statement, if presented) in which those impairment losses are included or reversed:

- inventories;

- property, plant and equipment (including investment property accounted for by the cost method);

- goodwill;

- intangible assets other than goodwill;

- investments in associates; and

- investments in joint ventures.

A company shall also disclose a description of the events and circumstances that led to the recognition or reversal of the impairment loss.

There are no specific references to disclosures for investments in subsidiaries as these are covered in section 9 of the standard.

There are further disclosure requirements contained in the Regulations. Provisions for diminution in value are made in respect of any fixed asset that has diminished in value if the reduction in its value is expected to be permanent. Where such provisions are not shown explicitly in the profit and loss account, SI 2008/410, Sch. 1, para. 19 and 20 require that they are disclosed (either separately or in aggregate) in a note to the accounts. Specific disclosure requirements are also given in SI 2008/410, Sch. 1, para. 51(53). These disclosures are:

- the cumulative amount of provisions for depreciation or diminution in value of assets included under that item at the beginning of the financial year and at the balance sheet date;

- the amount of any such provisions made in respect of the financial year;

- the amount of any adjustments made in respect of any such provisions during that year in consequence of the disposal of any assets; and

- the amount of any other adjustments made in respect of any such provisions during that year.

Small companies

Small companies are required to disclose:

- provisions for impairment of fixed assets (including fixed asset investments) separately in a note to the accounts if not shown separately in the income statement; and

- any provisions for impairment of fixed assets that are reversed because the reasons for which they were made have ceased to apply (either separately or in aggregate) in a note to the accounts if not shown separately in the income statement.

Small companies are exempt from the presentation and disclosure requirements of section 27, however the directors of a small company should consider whether the other disclosures noted above are necessary in order that the accounts show a true and fair view.

11.16   Employee benefits (FRS 102 section 28)

Employee benefits are all forms of consideration given by a company in exchange for service rendered by employees, including directors and management.

Although this definition would include amounts payable to directors and other management, disclosure of these items is dealt with in section 33 related party transactions.

Section 28 applies to all employee benefits other than those that arise as a result of share-based payment transactions, which are dealt with separately in section 26.

All other employee benefits are divided into four categories:

- short-term employee benefits – those benefits (other than termination benefits) which are expected to be settled wholly within twelve months of the end of the reporting period in which the services have been provided by the employees;

- post-employment benefits – those benefits (other than termination and short-term benefits) which are payable after the completion of employment. This will primarily relate to pensions, but may cover other benefits such as post-retirement healthcare;

- other long-term employee benefits – all benefits other than short-term, post-employment or termination. This would include longer term incentive schemes; and

- termination benefits – those benefits provided in exchange for the termination of an employee's employment, whether this arises from a decision to terminate an employee's employment before the normal retirement date or an employee's decision to accept voluntary redundancy in exchange for those benefits.

11.16.1   *Short-term employee benefits*

There are no disclosure requirements in FRS 102 relating to short-term employee benefits, however, companies must follow the requirements of company law. The statutory disclosures in this area are a requirement to analyse the staff costs between wages and salaries, social security costs and other pension costs, and to provide details of staff numbers analysed by category.

There are additional disclosures in respect of the remuneration of directors, and connected matters, which are contained in Sch. 5 to SI 2008/410 (see **Appendix C**).

11.16.2   Post-employment benefits

Post-employment benefits disclosures vary depending on whether the company has a defined contribution scheme (or 'money purchase' scheme) or a defined benefits scheme.

For a defined contribution scheme the only disclosure is the requirement to show the amount recognised in profit or loss as an expense in respect of the scheme.

If a company is party to a defined benefit multi-employer scheme but treats it as though it were a defined contribution scheme on the basis that it has insufficient information to enable it to apply defined benefit accounting, the company must also disclose:

- the fact that it is a defined benefit scheme;

- the reason why the scheme has been accounted for as defined contribution scheme;

- any available information about the surplus or deficit in the scheme as a whole and the implications, if any, that this has for the company;

- a description of the extent to which the company can be liable to the scheme for other entities' obligations under the terms and conditions of the scheme; and

- how any liability recognised in respect of a funding arrangement to deal with a deficit has been determined.

For a defined benefit scheme, other than a multi-employer scheme treated as though it is a defined contribution scheme, there are far more disclosures necessary. If there is more than one scheme disclosure may be in aggregate, separate or by groupings where these are considered most useful.

The disclosures required are:

- a general description of the type of scheme, including the funding policy;

- the date of the most recent comprehensive actuarial valuation;

- if the most recent comprehensive actuarial valuation was not undertaken as at the reporting date then a description of the adjustments that have been made to measure the defined benefit obligation at the current reporting date;

- a reconciliation of the opening closing balances for each of the following;

  - the defined benefit obligation;

  - the fair value of scheme assets; and

  - any reimbursement right which has been recognised as an asset;

- in each of the relevant reconciliations as set out above:

  - the change in the defined benefit liability that arises from employee service rendered during the period and that has been recorded in profit or loss;

  - interest income or expense;

  - re-measurement of the defined benefit liability, showing separately the actuarial gains and losses and the return on scheme assets less amounts included within interest income or expense;

  - scheme introductions, changes, curtailments or settlements;

- the total cost of defined benefit schemes in the period, split between:
  - the amounts recognised in profit or loss as an expense; and
  - the amounts that have been included in the cost of an asset;
- for each major class of scheme assets the percentage or amount that each major class constitutes of the fair value of the total scheme assets at the reporting date. This analysis must include, but is not limited to, an analysis between equity instruments, debt instruments, property and all other assets;
- the amounts, if any, that have been included in the fair value of scheme assets for:
  - each class of the company's own financial instruments; and
  - any property occupied by, or other assets used by, the company;
- the return on scheme assets;
- the principal actuarial assumptions used, including where appropriate:
  - the discount rates applied;
  - the expected rates of salary increases;
  - medical cost trends rates; and
  - any other material actuarial assumptions which have been used.

Comparatives are not required for the reconciliations.

Where a company participates in a defined benefit scheme that shares risk between entities under common control it has to disclose the following:

- the contractual agreement or details of the stated policy for charging the cost of a defined benefit scheme, or a statement that there is no such agreement or policy;
- the policy for determining the contribution that has to be paid by the company;
- if the company accounts for an allocation of the net defined benefit cost then the information that would normally be required for any other type of defined benefit scheme; and
- if the company accounts for the contributions payable for the period then the following information about the scheme as a whole:
  - a general description of the type of scheme, including the funding policy;
  - the date of the most recent comprehensive actuarial valuation;
  - if the most recent comprehensive actuarial valuation was not undertaken as at the reporting date then a description of the adjustments that have been made to measure the defined benefit obligation at the current reporting date;
  - for each major class of scheme assets the percentage or amount that each major class constitutes of the fair value of the total scheme assets at the reporting date. This analysis must include, but is not limited to, an analysis between equity instruments, debt instruments, property and all other assets; and
  - the amounts, if any, that have been included in the fair value of scheme assets for:
    - each class of the company's own financial instruments; and
    - any property occupied by, or other assets used by, the company.

This information does not always have to be provided in the financial statements of the individual company. It can be included by cross-reference to disclosures that are provided in the financial statements of another group company if:

- that group company's financial statements separately identify and disclose the information required about the scheme; and

- that group company's financial statements are available to users of financial statements and the same as those for the company and at the same time or earlier.

11.16.3 Other long-term benefits

Where a company has provided any other long-term benefits to its employees it must disclose:

- the nature of the benefits;

- the amount of its obligation; and

- the extent of funding at the reporting date.

11.16.4 Termination benefits

Where a company has provided termination benefits to its employees it must disclose:

- the nature of the benefits;

- the accounting policy that has been applied;

- the amount of its obligation at the reporting date; and

- the extent of funding at the reporting date.

Where there is an uncertainty about the number of employees who might accept an offer of termination benefits then the liability is a contingent liability. All of the disclosures which are normally required in relation to a contingent liability must also be provided (see **11.11**).

11.16.5 Small companies

> **Small companies**
>
> Small companies are required to disclose the average number of persons employed by the company in the reporting period.
>
> Small companies are exempt from the presentation and disclosure requirements of section 29, however the directors of a small company should consider whether the other disclosures noted above are necessary in order that the accounts show a true and fair view.

11.17 Income tax (FRS 102 section 29)

For the purpose of the standard, income tax is all domestic and foreign taxes that are based on taxable profit. In the UK, this would typically relate to corporation tax. It also includes such withholding taxes payable by subsidiaries, associates and joint ventures on distributions to the reporting company.

A company is required to recognise the current and future tax consequences of transactions and other events that have been recognised in the accounts, i.e. current tax and deferred tax. Deferred tax is also required to be recognised in respect of assets (excluding goodwill) and liabilities recognised as a result of business combinations.

The major components of tax expense or income must be disclosed, which may include:

- current tax expense or income;

- adjustments recognised in the period for current tax of prior periods;

- the amount of deferred tax expense or income relating to the origination and reversal of timing differences;

- the amount of deferred tax expense or income relating to changes in tax rates or the imposition of new taxes;

- adjustments to deferred tax expense arising from a change in the tax status of an company or its shareholders; and

- the amount of tax expense relating to changes in accounting policies or errors.

This list is not exhaustive. Judgment is needed on whether another component is major, qualitatively or quantitatively.

A number of specific details are also required, if they are material:

- the aggregate current and deferred tax relating to items that are included in other comprehensive income;

- a reconciliation between the total expense or income reported in profit and the product of profits and the applicable tax rate;

- the quantum of net reversals of deferred tax balances expected in the following year;

- an explanation of changes in the applicable tax rates from the previous period;

- the amount of deferred tax liabilities and deferred tax assets at the end of the reporting period for each type of timing difference and each type of unused tax losses and tax credits;

- the expiry date, if any, of timing differences, unused tax losses and unused tax credits; and

- an explanation of the potential income tax consequences that would result from the payment of dividends to shareholders.

The final point only becomes relevant in situations where the payment out of dividends to shareholders triggers the application of a different tax rate from the retention of profits in the company, which is not relevant under current UK tax legislation.

> **Small companies**
>
> Small companies are exempt from the presentation and disclosure requirements of section 29, however the directors of a small company should consider whether the disclosures noted above are necessary in order that the accounts show a true and fair view.

11.18   Foreign currency translation (FRS 102 section 30)

There are three situations where foreign currency issues are relevant to a company's accounts: it may have transactions in foreign currencies; it may have foreign operations; or it may present its accounts in a presentational foreign currency which is different from its functional currency.

A company must disclose:

- The amount of exchange differences recognised in profit or loss during the period, except for those arising on financial instruments measured at fair value through profit or loss in accordance with sections 11 and 12.

- The amount of exchange differences arising during the period and classified in equity at the end of the period.

The currency in which the financial statements are presented must be disclosed, as must the functional currency if it is different, with an explanation for the difference.

If the functional currency changes, the fact of the change and the reasons for it must be disclosed.

Small companies

Small companies are exempt from the presentation and disclosure requirements of section 30, however the directors of a small company should consider whether the disclosures noted above are necessary in order that the accounts show a true and fair view.

11.19 Hyperinflation (FRS 102 section 31)

Section 31 deals with the accounting requirements of a company whose functional currency is in a hyperinflationary economy and requires the accounts to be adjusted for the effects of hyperinflation. This is considered to be of limited relevancy to preparers of UK accounts and not covered here.

11.20 Events after the end of the reporting period (FRS 102 sections 32)

Events after the end of the reporting period and before the accounts are authorised for issue fall into two categories:

- those that provide evidence of conditions existing at the reporting date (adjusting events); and

- those that are indicative of conditions that arose after the end of the reporting period (non-adjusting events).

The date when the accounts were authorised for issue shall be disclosed, this is usually done as part of the approval statement and signature on the statement of financial position.

There are no specific disclosure requirements for adjusting events as the relevant line items in the primary statements and note disclosures will include the effects of such events.

Disclosure is required of each category of non-adjusting event stating the nature of the event and an estimate of the financial effect (or a statement that such an estimate cannot be made).

The following examples are given in the standard of non-adjusting events. Disclosures will reflect the information that becomes known after the end of the reporting period:

- a major business combination or disposal of a major subsidiary;

- announcement of a plan to discontinue an operation;

- major purchases of assets, disposals or plans to dispose of assets, or expropriation of major assets by government;

- the destruction of a major production plant by a fire;

- announcement, or commencement of the implementation, of a major restructuring;

- issues or repurchases of an company's debt or equity instruments;

- abnormally large changes in asset prices or foreign exchange rates;

- changes in tax rates or tax laws enacted or announced that have a significant effect on current and deferred tax assets and liabilities;

- entering into significant commitments or contingent liabilities, for example, by issuing significant guarantees; and

- commencement of major litigation arising solely out of events that occurred after the end of the reporting period.

Small companies

Small companies are exempt from the presentation and disclosure requirements of section 32, the directors of a small company should consider whether the disclosures noted above are necessary in order that the accounts show a true and fair view.

11.21   Related party disclosures (FRS 102 section 33)

Disclosures are required concerning related parties of the company and the transactions and outstanding balances with those parties to draw attention to the possibility that the company's financial position and results have been affected.

Certain disclosures required by the standard are similar to and may be satisfied by Company Law disclosures. There are also some additional disclosures required by CA 2006 or the Regulations.

Disclosures required by the standard need not be given for two or more members of a group provided that any subsidiary which is party to the transaction is a wholly owned subsidiary.

11.21.1   Parent-subsidiary relationships

Section 33 requires the disclosure of the name of the parent company and, if different, of the ultimate controlling party. If neither of these higher companies produces publicly available accounts, then the name of the highest company in the chain that does produce them must be disclosed. This does not seem to be affected by whether or not the relevant parent company prepares consolidated accounts.

However, SI 2008/410, Sch. 4, para. 8 and 9 are more prescriptive and are required in addition to the above.

Where the company is a subsidiary undertaking, the following information must be given with respect to the parent undertaking of the largest group of undertakings for which group accounts are drawn up and of which the company is a member, and the smallest such group of undertakings.

- The name of the parent undertaking must be stated.
- There must also be stated:
  - if the undertaking is incorporated outside the United Kingdom, the country in which it is incorporated;
  - if it is unincorporated, the address of its principal place of business.
- If copies of the group accounts referred to above are available to the public, there must also be stated the addresses from which copies of the accounts can be obtained.

Where the company is a subsidiary undertaking, the following information must be given with respect to the company (if any) regarded by the directors as being the company's ultimate parent company.

- The name of that company must be stated.
- If that company is incorporated outside the United Kingdom, the country in which it is incorporated must be stated (if known to the directors).
- In this paragraph 'company' includes any body corporate.

Section 33 would appear to only require disclosure of the ultimate controlling party where this is different to the parent of a subsidiary company and would suggest therefore that disclosure is not required of a controlling party (if any) in the accounts of a stand-alone company or the ultimate parent of a group.

11.21.2   Disclosure of key management personnel compensation

The standard requires just one line of information being the total of key management personnel compensation. At first sight, it would appear that this would be covered by the requirements in the Regulation relating to remuneration of directors (see **11.16**); however, the definitions of key management personnel and compensation may be wider than just the directors and their remuneration as required by company law.

Key management personnel is defined as 'those persons having authority and responsibility for planning, directing and controlling the activities of the company, directly or indirectly, including any director (whether executive or otherwise) of that company'. Companies would need to decide whether any other senior management would be defined as such.

The standard also explains that compensation includes all employee benefits (as defined in FRS 102 section 28) including share based payments which is excluded from the legal definition of directors remuneration.

In practical terms the company law disclosures may be augmented with the additional requirements of FRS 102 with clear explanation to ensure both requirements are satisfied.

11.21.3   Related party transactions

A related party transaction is defined as 'a transfer of resources, services or obligations between a reporting company and a related party, regardless of whether a price is charged'. This includes, but is not limited to, normal sales and purchases, transfers of fixed assets, payments for services, lease arrangements and the resulting transactions, financing transactions such as the issue of loans, payment of dividends, and the taking on of commitments such as guarantees.

The minimum information to be disclosed about related party transactions is:

- the amount of the transactions;
- the amount of outstanding balances and:
  - their terms and conditions, including whether they are secured, and the nature of the consideration to be provided in settlement; and
  - details of any guarantees given or received;
- provisions for uncollectible receivables related to the amount of outstanding balances;
- the expense recognised during the period in respect of bad or doubtful debts due from related parties.

There is no specific requirement to name the related parties involved, instead the standard requires that the disclosures are provided separately for the following categories of related party:

- investors in the company (those which have control, joint control or significant influence);
- investees of the company (subsidiaries, joint ventures or associates);
- key management personnel (see **11.21.2** above); and
- entities which provide key management personnel services to the company; and
- other related parties (this would include, among others, fellow subsidiaries in a group, close family of key management personnel, and pension schemes).

A company may also aggregate items of a similar nature within these groupings, however separate disclosure is required where this is necessary for a full understanding of the effects of related party transactions on the accounts. For example, a company that guarantees the debts both of one of its fellow subsidiaries and a close family member of one of the directors would, in theory, be able to aggregate the disclosures of these items in the category 'other related parties'. This aggregation, though, would obscure the uncommon nature of the guarantee for the family member and therefore one would expect separate presentation.

Depending on the volume and diversity of a company's related parties and its transactions with them, the most efficient and readable way of providing the required disclosures will vary. For entities with a small number of simple arrangements, a few lines of narrative with figures may be sufficient; if the situation is more complex, though, a matrix presentation is easier to read at a glance, and can be augmented if necessary with additional narrative.

Companies should be careful not to state that related party transactions are made on terms equivalent to an arm's length basis as the standard only allows such statements if those terms can be substantiated.

11.21.4   Information about directors' benefits: advances, credit and guarantees

CA 2006, s. 413 also requires disclosures relating to advances and credits granted by the company (or its subsidiaries) to its directors and guarantees of any kind entered into by the company (or its subsidiaries) on behalf of its directors.

The details required of an advance or credit are:

- its amount (and total);

- an indication of the interest rate;

- its main conditions; and

- any amounts (and total) repaid.

The details required of a guarantee are:

- its main terms;

- the amount of the maximum liability (and total maximum liability) that may be incurred by the company (or its subsidiary); and

- any amount (and total amount) paid and any liabilities incurred by the company (or its subsidiary) for the purpose of fulfilling the guarantee (including any loss incurred by reason of enforcement of the guarantee).

These disclosures are required for any person who was a director at any time in the financial year to which the accounts relate.

The disclosures also relate to every advance, credit or guarantee subsisting at any time in the financial year to which the accounts relate: whenever it was entered into, whether or not the person concerned was a director of the company in question at the time it was entered into, and in the case of an advance, credit or guarantee involving a subsidiary undertaking of that company, whether or not that undertaking was such a subsidiary undertaking at the time it was entered into.

These requirements are not covered by the FRS 102 principle of materiality as they arise from CA 2006 and the wording of the legislation would suggest disclosure of every single advance and repayment thereof. In larger organisations this may be possible as advances to directors are not common place. However in smaller, owner managed companies there may be a significant number of advances and repayments between a company and a director and therefore general consensus is that the disclosure requirements are satisfied on an aggregated basis which might also coincide with the FRS 102 section 33 disclosure requirements. For example:

'During the year, the company made total advances to Mr X of £5,600 of which £2,600 has been repaid. At the end of the reporting period the company was owed £3,000.'

11.21.5   Small companies

Small companies

Small companies are exempt from the presentation and disclosure requirements of section 33 but detailed requirements are given in FRS 102 paragraphs 1AC.34–1AC.36. Those requirements are not summarised here as they are similar to those summarised above and any small company following the requirements of section 33 would be compliant.

One important difference is that the related party transactions disclosures (see **11.21.3** above) need only be disclosed where those transactions have not been concluded under normal market conditions.

11.22   Specialised activities (FRS 102 section 34)

Section 34 provides the accounting requirements and specific disclosures for the following types of specialised activities:

- Agriculture;
- Extractive Activities;
- Service Concession Arrangements;
- Financial Institutions;
- Retirement Benefit Plans: Financial Statements;
- Heritage Assets;
- Funding Commitments;
- Incoming Resources from Non-Exchange Transactions;
- Public Benefit Entity Combinations;
- Public Benefit Entity Concessionary Loans.

These activities are considered to be less relevant to the preparation of general company accounts and are therefore not summarised in this book. Please see the full text of FRS 102 at:

www.frc.org.uk/Our-Work/Publications/Accounting-and-Reporting-Policy/FRS-102-The-Financial-Reporting-Standard-applicab.pdf.

Small companies

Small companies are exempt from the presentation and disclosure requirements of section 34. The directors of any small company engaged in any of the specialised activities noted above should refer to the relevant disclosures and consider whether they are necessary in order that the accounts show a true and fair view.

11.23   Transition to FRS 102 (FRS 102 section 35)

On first adoption of FRS 102, the accounts must include an explanation of how the transition from the old to the new financial reporting framework has affected the company's financial position, financial performance and cash flows.

The explanation in the first financial statements under the standard shall include:

- a description of the nature of each change in accounting policy;

- reconciliations of the company's equity determined in accordance with its previous financial reporting framework to its equity determined in accordance with this FRS for both of the following dates:

    - the date of transition to this FRS; and

    - the end of the latest period presented in the company's most recent annual financial statements determined in accordance with its previous financial reporting framework;

- a reconciliation of the profit or loss determined in accordance with its previous financial reporting framework for the latest period in the company's most recent annual financial statements to its profit or loss determined in accordance with this FRS for the same period.

In the reconciliations, the effect of changing accounting policies on adoption of FRS 102 should, where practicable, be distinguished from any restatements of errors picked up as part of the transition process.

Depending on the size and complexity of the company and the level of adjustments required, the disclosures may be presented by a simple reconciliation of retained earnings for the prior period and the opening (transition date) and closing equity for the prior period so long as the explanations clearly show how the primary statements would be affected.

Alternatively, it may be more appropriate to present the full prior period statement of comprehensive income and the transition date and prior period statements of financial position with a columnar presentation of the adjustments (plus narrative explanation of the adjustments).

Small companies

Small companies are exempt from the presentation and disclosure requirements of section 35, however FRS 102 paragraph 1AD.1 encourages small companies to present an explanation of how the transition to FRS 102 has affected its financial position and financial performance as set out above.

Part III   Director and Auditor Reports

Chapter 12 Strategic Report and Directors' Report

The requirement to prepare a Strategic Report and Directors' Report is contained in CA 2006, s. 414–419A.

The requirement for a separate Strategic Report was introduced for accounting periods ending before 30 September 2013, however, the information to be presented in this report was previously required within the Directors' Report (CA 2006, s. 417).

12.1 Strategic Report

The directors of a company must prepare a Strategic Report for each financial year of the company.

Companies entitled to the small companies' exemption are exempt from the requirement to prepare a Strategic Report. A company is entitled to small companies' exemption if:

- it is entitled to prepare accounts for the year in accordance with the small companies regime; or

- it would be so entitled but for being or having been a member of an ineligible group.

A company which is a parent company and the directors of the company prepare group accounts, must prepare a consolidated Strategic Report relating to all the undertakings included in the consolidation and may, where appropriate, give greater emphasis to the matters that are significant to the undertakings included in the consolidation, taken as a whole.

The purpose of the strategic report is to inform members of the company and help them assess how the directors have performed their duty under s. 172 (duty to promote the success of the company).

12.1.1 Content of the Strategic Report

The strategic report must contain a fair review of the company's business and a description of the principal risks and uncertainties facing the company.

The review required is a balanced and comprehensive analysis, consistent with the size and complexity of the business, of the development and performance of the company's business during the financial year and the position of the company's business at the end of that year.

The review must, to the extent necessary for an understanding of the development, performance or position of the company's business, include analysis using financial key performance indicators and, where appropriate, analysis using other key performance indicators, including information relating to environmental matters and employee matters.

'Key performance indicators' means factors by reference to which the development, performance or position of the company's business can be measured effectively.

Where a company qualifies as medium-sized in relation to a financial year, the review for the year need not provide the analysis using non-financial key performance indicators.

There are additional disclosure requirements for quoted companies.

The report must, where appropriate, include references to, and additional explanations of, amounts included in the company's annual accounts, e.g. turnover and profit measures.

12.2   Directors' Report

The directors of a company must prepare a Directors' Report for each financial year of the company.

As a result of the removal of the strategic and business review from the Directors' Report to the Strategic Report for periods ending on or after 30 September 2013 the Directors' Report now contains primarily factual and statutory information about the company.

Companies entitled to the small companies' exemption are exempt from disclosing most of the information otherwise required for large and medium-sized companies. A company is entitled to small companies' exemption if:

- it is entitled to prepare accounts for the year in accordance with the small companies regime; or

- it would be so entitled but for being or having been a member of an ineligible group.

If a small company is taking advantage of the small companies' exemption, the directors' report must contain a statement to that effect in a prominent position above the signature.

12.2.1   Content of the Directors' Report

The Directors' Report must always contain:

- the names of the persons who, at any time during the financial year, were directors of the company;

- the amount (if any) that the directors recommend should be paid by way of dividend (not required for companies entitled to the small companies exemption – see **9.6.1**);

- where the weekly average number of UK-based employees exceeds 250, a statement describing the company's policy on the hiring, continuing employment and training, career development and promotion of disabled persons.

In addition SI 2008/410, Sch. 7 also requires large and medium-sized companies to provide the following information:

- details of political donations or expenditure where the aggregate exceeds £2,000;

- with regard to the use of financial instruments, an indication of:

  - the financial risk management objectives and policies of the company, including the policy for hedging each major type of forecasted transaction for which hedge accounting is used; and

  - the exposure of the company to price risk, credit risk, liquidity risk and cash flow risk, unless such information is not material for the assessment of the assets, liabilities, financial position and profit or loss of the company;

- particulars of any important events affecting the company which have occurred since the end of the financial year;

- an indication of likely future developments in the business of the company;

- an indication of the activities (if any) of the company in the field of research and development; and

- an indication of the existence of branches (as defined in s. 1046(3) of the 2006 Act) of the company outside the United Kingdom;

- where the weekly average number of UK based employees exceeds 250, for employees working wholly or mainly in the UK, a description of the action that has been taken during the financial year to introduce, maintain or develop arrangements aimed at:

- providing employees systematically with information on matters of concern to them as employees;

- consulting employees or their representatives on a regular basis so that the views of employees can be taken into account in making decisions which are likely to affect their interests;

- encouraging the involvement of employees in the company's performance through an employees' share scheme or by some other means;

- achieving a common awareness on the part of all employees of the financial and economic factors affecting the performance of the company.

Any of the information required by SI 2008/410, Sch. 7 may be presented in the Strategic Report if the directors consider it to be of strategic importance to the company. If so, the directors shall state in the Directors' Report that they have done so and in respect of which information they have done so.

12.2.2   Statement of disclosure of information to auditors

For audited companies, the directors' report must contain a statement that so far as each of the directors, at the time the report is approved, is aware:

- there is no relevant audit information of which the company's auditor is unaware; and

- the directors have taken all steps that they each ought to have taken to make themselves aware of any relevant audit information and to establish that the company's auditor is aware of that information.

12.2.3   Statement of Directors' responsibilities

Where a company is subject to audit, it is necessary (in order to accord with International Standards on Auditing (UK and Ireland)) to prepare a detailed statement appearing, generally, within the directors' report. Alternatively, the statement may be presented as a separate page.

ISA (UK and Ireland) 700, *The auditor's report on financial statements*, requires the auditor's report to include a statement that those charged with governance are responsible for the preparation of the financial statements and a statement that the responsibility of the auditor is to audit and express an opinion on the financial statements in accordance with applicable legal requirements and International Standards on Auditing (UK and Ireland).

APB Bulletin 2010/2, *Compendium of illustrative auditor's reports on United Kingdom private sector financial statements for periods ended on or after 15 December 2010 (revised)* envisages a 'Directors' Responsibilities Statement' within the financial statements or accompanying information (for example, in the directors' report) to include an adequate statement of directors' responsibilities. Specific reference is made to this statement in the auditor's report.

Example 12.1 provides an example directors' responsibilities statement based on APB Bulletin 2010/2 (Revised) (APB Bulletin Appendix 17 Example 47).

Example 12.1 Example Directors' Responsibilities Statement

The directors are responsible for preparing the Directors' Report and the financial statements in accordance with applicable law and regulations.

Company law requires the directors to prepare financial statements for each financial year. Under that law the directors have elected to prepare the financial statements in accordance with United Kingdom Generally Accepted Accounting Practice (United Kingdom Accounting Standards and applicable law). Under company law the directors must not approve the financial statements unless they are satisfied that

---

they give a true and fair view of the state of affairs of the company and of the profit or loss of the company for that period.

In preparing these financial statements, the directors are required to:

- select suitable accounting policies and then apply them consistently;

- make judgments and estimates that are reasonable and prudent;

- state whether applicable UK Accounting Standards have been followed, subject to any material departures disclosed and explained in the financial statements *[not applicable for companies subject to the small companies regime and medium sized companies]*; and

- prepare the financial statements on the going concern basis unless it is inappropriate to presume that the company will continue in business *[included where no separate statement on going concern is made by the directors]*.

The directors are responsible for keeping adequate accounting records that are sufficient to show and explain the company's transactions and disclose with reasonable accuracy at any time the financial position of the company and enable them to ensure that the financial statements comply with the *Companies Act* 2006. They are also responsible for safeguarding the assets of the company and hence for taking reasonable steps for the prevention and detection of fraud and other irregularities.

[Where the financial statements are published on the internet] [The directors are responsible for the maintenance and integrity of the corporate and financial information included on the company's website. Legislation in the United Kingdom governing the preparation and dissemination of financial statements may differ from legislation in other jurisdictions.]

[Author's note – this paragraph is not illustrated in APB Bulletin 2010/2].

Chapter 13   Auditor's Report

13.1   Auditor's reports now and in the future

This chapter comments on, and provides examples of audit reports of unlisted small, medium-sized and large companies. Audit reports must be prepared having regard to International Standards on Auditing (UK and Ireland) (ISAs) which are published by the FRC.

Where an audit report is included, the directors are required to make a detailed statement of directors' responsibilities by the ISAs and this should appear either as a separate statement or as part of the directors' report (see **12.2.3**).

This chapter is only a summary of the key aspects; for more detailed guidance, please see the publication *CCH Audit Reports Handbook 2015* available from www.cch.co.uk/books.

In June 2016, the FRC finalised a number of revised Auditing Standards to reflect the introduction of the statutory instrument bringing into force the new EU Audit Directive & Regulation in the UK. Included were revisions to ISA 700 and its accompanying standards (ISAs 701–720) which will alter the layout and format of auditor's reports. The revised standards are applicable for audits of financial statements for periods commencing on or after 17 June 2016.

The new final ISAs are applicable in the UK only as the Irish regulator, IAASA, has been appointed as the Competent Authority for Audit in Ireland, and will be responsible for issuing standards for use in Ireland.

At the time, the FRC updated 23 of the existing 35 ISAs, with only 12 remaining unchanged. The standards have been revised to simplify the language and the application material has been expanded to clarify the inter-relationship between the ISA requirements and the requirements of the directive.

The example reports illustrated below and in the model financial statements in **Appendix A** do not reflect these forthcoming changes which will be included in the next edition of this book.

For more detailed guidance on the new standards and reports, please see the publications *Implementing GAAS 2016–17* and *Preparing Audit Reports 2016–17* also available from www.cch. co.uk/books.

13.1.1   Audit – CA 2006, Pt. 16

Audit is covered in CA 2006, Pt. 16, which contains provisions (s. 475–539) concerning the requirement for audited accounts and the auditor's report.

13.1.2   Elements of an auditor's report

An auditor's report must include an introduction identifying the annual accounts and the financial reporting framework under which they are prepared, together with a description of the scope of the audit identifying the auditing standards adopted.

In essence, under CA 2006, s. 495, the auditor is required to report his opinion on these elements.

(1) *True and fair view* – whether the annual accounts show a 'true and fair view' (having regard to the directors' statutory duty under CA 2006, s. 393(1)).

(2) *Relevant reporting framework* – whether the accounts have been prepared in accordance with the relevant financial reporting framework.

(3) *Appropriate legislation* – whether the accounts have been prepared in accordance with CA 2006 (Pt. 15) and if applicable IFRS as adopted in the EU.

The auditor's report must be either 'unqualified' or 'qualified' and may contain reference to any emphasis of matters which the auditor may wish to include without qualifying the report.

In addition, the auditor must report on the strategic report (if applicable) and the directors' report. Whilst it is not a requirement for the strategic report and directors' report to be audited, the auditor must consider, in the light of the work undertaken in the course of the audit of the accounts and his knowledge of the company, whether the reports are consistent with the accounts, are prepared in accordance with legal requirements and whether they contain any material misstatements.

13.1.3 Auditor's report – CA 2006, s. 495 and 496

The form of report to be adopted with respect to Companies Act accounts is determined by CA 2006 and by the International Standards on Auditing as applicable within the UK. Following the adoption of International Standards on Auditing (ISAs), an auditor's report on accounts is required to follow ISA (UK and Ireland) 700, *The Auditor's Report on Financial Statements*. Example reports are issued by the Auditing Practices Board (APB) – see **Example 13.1**.

CA 2006, s. 495 (Auditor's report on company's annual accounts) and 496 (Auditor's report on strategic report and directors' report) are reproduced in full in **Table 13.1**.

Table 13.1 Auditor's report on annual accounts CA 2006, s. 495

495 Auditor's report on company's annual accounts

(1) A company's auditor must make a report to the company's members on all annual accounts of the company of which copies are, during his tenure of office–

 (a) in the case of a private company, to be sent out to members under section 423;

 (b) in the case of a public company, to be laid before the company in general meeting under section 437.

(2) The auditor's report must include–

 (a) an introduction identifying the annual accounts that are the subject of the audit and the financial reporting framework that has been applied in their preparation, and

 (b) a description of the scope of the audit identifying the auditing standards in accordance with which the audit was conducted.

(3) The report must state clearly whether, in the auditor's opinion, the annual accounts–

 (a) give a true and fair view–

  (i) in the case of an individual balance sheet, of the state of affairs of the company as at the end of the financial year;

  (ii) in the case of an individual profit and loss account, of the profit or loss of the company for the financial year;

  (iii) in the case of group accounts, of the state of affairs as at the end of the financial year and of the profit or loss for the financial year of the undertakings included in the consolidation as a whole, so far as concerns members of the company;

 (b) have been properly prepared in accordance with the relevant financial reporting framework; and

 (c) have been prepared in accordance with the requirements of this Act (and, where applicable, Article 4 of the IAS Regulation).

Expressions used in this subsection that are defined for the purposes of Part 15 (see section 474) have the same meaning as in that Part.

(4)   The auditor's report–

    (a)   must be either unqualified or qualified; and

    (b)   must include a reference to any matters to which the auditor wishes to draw attention by way of emphasis without qualifying the report.

496 Auditor's report on strategic report and directors' report

In his report on the company's annual accounts, the auditor must–

(a)   state whether, in his opinion, based on the work undertaken in the course of the audit–

    (i)   the information given in the strategic report (if any) and the directors' report for the financial year for which the accounts are prepared is consistent with those accounts, and

    (ii)   such strategic report and the directors' report have been prepared in accordance with applicable legal requirements,

(b)   state whether, in the light of the knowledge and understanding of the company and its environment obtained in the course of the audit, he has identified material misstatements in the strategic report (if any) and the directors' report, and

(c)   if applicable, give an indication of the nature of each of the misstatements referred to in paragraph (b).

13.1.4   Identifying the annual accounts subject to audit

The auditor's report should refer to the names of the primary statements and related notes. Where the audited entity does not publish accounts on a website or if it does so in a 'PDF' format then the auditor may refer to the page numbers where the primary statements and related notes may be found.

13.1.5   Signature of auditor's report

The auditor's report must state the name of the auditor and be signed and dated. However, where the auditor is a firm, the report delivered to the members must be signed by the 'senior statutory auditor' in his own name, for and on behalf of the auditor. (CA 2006, s. 504).

Although the set of the financial statements filed with the Registrar of Companies must contain the original signatures of the directors who have signed the financial statements on behalf of the board of directors (where the paper accounts are being filed), a physical signature is not required on the auditor's report. In practice many auditors still prefer that the set submitted to the Registrar of Companies contains a signature. Where the auditor is a firm, the set filed with the Registrar of Companies can be signed in the name of the firm rather that in the name of the senior statutory auditor, although the name of the senior statutory auditor should be included.

The Registrar of Companies has requested that all signatures with the report and accounts should be in black ink.

13.2   ISA (UK and Ireland) 700 The Independent Auditor's Report on Financial Statements

13.2.1   ISAs (UK and Ireland) and the auditor's report

The report of an auditor is required to follow ISA (UK and Ireland) 700, *The Independent Auditor's Report on Financial Statements*.

ISA (UK and Ireland) 700, although generally prescriptive as to the form and content of the auditor's report, does not preclude some flexibility when using the format and wording of the example reports prescribed by the Statement. The use of the term 'accounts', for example, in preference to 'financial statements' accords with the CA 2006 and is essentially a question of personal choice, permissible provided the term is adequately defined.

The APB* issued from time to time a Bulletin providing illustrative examples of auditor's reports. The APB Bulletin 2010/02 (Revised), *Compendium of Illustrative Auditor's Reports on United Kingdom Private Sector Financial Statements for periods ended on or after 15 December 2010 (Revised)* is the most recent bulletin and was issued in March 2012 and is applicable for periods ended on or after 23 March 2011.

ISA (UK and Ireland) 700, *The Independent Auditor's Report on Financial Statements*, facilitates, but does not mandate, a more concise auditor's report. This may be achieved by permitting the description of the scope of an audit and the auditor's reporting responsibilities to be made either within the body of the auditor's report (as was previously the norm) or by cross-reference to the FRC website (where a relevant statement of scope is maintained) or by cross-reference to a 'Statement of the Scope of an Audit' that is included elsewhere within the Annual Report.

13.3   Example Auditor's Report of a medium-sized (or large) company

Example 13.1 is based on APB Bulletin 2010/2 Revised (March 2012) (at Appendix 1, Example 2) as modified by the FRC Bulletin 4. It illustrates an 'unqualified' report with no 'emphasis of matter' paragraph of a non-publicly traded company where the audit is performed in accordance with International Standards on Auditing (UK and Ireland) issued by the FRC. The example assumes:

- the company is not a quoted company;

- the company either does not qualify as a small company or qualifies as a small company but chooses not to prepare its financial statements in accordance with the small companies regime;

- the company does not prepare group financial statements;

- the company prepares a strategic report and directors' report but no other 'surround information' (for example chairman's report, corporate governance statement or other financial commentary);

- the company adopts UK GAAP (and not IAS).

Amendments in the example made (by the author), for completeness and illustrative purposes, are presented in **[bold text]**.

Example 13.1

INDEPENDENT AUDITOR'S REPORT TO THE MEMBERS OF [MEDIUM COMPANY LIMITED]

We have audited the financial statements of **[Medium Company Limited]** for the year ended **[31 December 2016]** which comprise **[the Statement of Total Comprehensive Income, the Statement of Financial Position, the Statement of Changes in Equity, the Statement of Cash Flows]** and the related notes. The financial reporting framework that has been applied in their preparation is applicable law and United Kingdom Accounting Standards (United Kingdom Generally Accepted Accounting Practice).

This report is made solely to the company's members, as a body, in accordance the *Companies Act* **2006, Ch. 3, Pt. 16. Our audit work has been undertaken so that we might state to the company's members those matters that we are required to state to them in an auditor's report and for no other purpose. To the fullest extent permitted by law, we do not accept or assume responsibility to anyone other than the company and the company's members as a body, for our audit work, for this report, or for the opinions we have formed.**

[Author's note (1)]

---

* Note that the APB was disbanded in July 2012. The function of the APB is now performed by the FRC's Audit and Assurance Council.

Respective responsibilities of directors and auditor

As explained more fully in the Directors' Responsibilities Statement **[set out on page xx]**, the directors are responsible for the preparation of the financial statements and for being satisfied that they give a true and fair view. Our responsibility is to audit and express an opinion on the financial statements in accordance with applicable law and International Standards on Auditing (UK and Ireland). Those standards require us to comply with the Financial Reporting Council's [(FRCS's)] Ethical Standards for Auditors.

Scope of the audit of the financial statements

Either:

A description of the scope of an audit of financial statements is [provided on the FRC's website at www. frc.org.uk/apb/scope/private.cfm]/[set out **[on page x]** of the Annual Report].

Or:

An audit involves obtaining evidence about the amounts and disclosures in the financial statements sufficient to give reasonable assurance that the financial statements are free from material misstatement, whether caused by fraud or error. This includes an assessment of: whether the accounting policies are appropriate to the **[company's]** circumstances and have been consistently applied and adequately disclosed; the reasonableness of significant accounting estimates made by **[the directors]**; and the overall presentation of the financial statements. In addition, we read all the financial and non-financial information in the **[Strategic Report and Directors' Report]** to identify material inconsistencies with the audited financial statements and to identify any information that is apparently materially incorrect based on, or materially inconsistent with, the knowledge acquired by us in the course of performing the audit. If we become aware of any apparent material misstatements or inconsistencies we consider the implications for our report.

[Author's note (2)]

Opinion on financial statements

In our opinion the financial statements:

- give a true and fair view of the state of the company's affairs as at **[31 December 2016]** and of its profit [loss] for the year then ended;

- have been properly prepared in accordance with United Kingdom Generally Accepted Accounting Practice; and

- have been prepared in accordance with the requirements of the *Companies Act* 2006.

Opinion on other matter prescribed by the Companies Act 2006

In our opinion, based on the work undertaken in the course of the audit, the information given in the Strategic Report and , the information given in the Strategic Report and Directors' Report for the financial year for which the financial statements are prepared:

- is consistent with the financial statements;

- have been prepared in accordance with applicable legal requirements; and

- in the light of knowledge and understanding of the company and its environment obtained during the course of the audit, we have not identified any material misstatements in the Strategic Report and Directors' Report.

Matters on which we are required to report by exception

We have nothing to report in respect of the following matters where the Companies Act 2006 requires us to report to you if, in our opinion:

- adequate accounting records have not been kept, or returns adequate for our audit have not been received from branches not visited by us; or

- the financial statements are not in agreement with the accounting records and returns; or

- certain disclosures of directors' remuneration specified by law are not made; or

- we have not received all the information and explanations we require for our audit.

Lucy Caldwell   *[Author's note (3)]*

....

Lucy Caldwell (Senior Statutory Auditor)

for and on behalf of TRUE & FAIRVIEW LLP

Statutory Auditor

17 Queens Place,

LONDON EC4P 3BC   23 April 2017

Author's notes and commentary to **Example 13.1**.

*(1) **Duty of care to third parties** – the ICAEW recommends that auditors include additional wording in audit reports in order to clarify auditors' responsibilities to third parties – that is, other than to the members (or the directors, as the case may be) as a body. (Audit 1/03 – The Audit Report and The Auditors' Duty of Care to Third Parties.) (January 2003, most recent update January 2010.)*

*(2) **Description of the scope of an audit of financial statements** – ISA (UK and Ireland) 700 requires that an auditor's report should either: cross refer to a Statement of the scope of an audit maintained on the APB's (now FRC's) website; or cross refer to such a scope statement that is included elsewhere within the Annual Report; or include a prescribed description of the scope of an audit.*

*The prescribed description of the scope of an audit (as illustrated in **Example 13.1**) is set out in ISA (UK and Ireland) 700.*

*(3) **Signature and dating of auditor's report** – CA 2006, s. 503 and ISA (UK and Ireland) 700, para. 23–26.*

13.4   Example Auditor's Report of a small company

Example 13.1 is based on APB Bulletin 2010/2 Revised (March 2012) (at Appendix 1, Example 1) as modified by FRC Bulletin 4. It illustrates an 'unqualified' report with no 'emphasis of matter' paragraph of a non-publicly traded small company where the audit is performed in accordance with International Standards on Auditing (UK and Ireland) issued by the FRC. The example assumes:

- the company is not a quoted company;

- the company qualifies as a small company and chooses to prepare its financial statements in accordance with the small companies regime;

- the company does not prepare group financial statements;

- the company prepares a directors' report but no other 'surround information'; and

- the company adopts UK GAAP (and not IAS).

Amendments in the example made (by the author), for completeness and illustrative purposes, are presented in **[bold text]**.

Example 13.1

INDEPENDENT AUDITOR'S REPORT TO THE MEMBERS OF [SMALL COMPANY LIMITED]

We have audited the financial statements of **[Small Company Limited]** for the year ended **[31 December 2016]** which comprise **[the Income Statement, the Statement of Financial Position,]** and the related notes. The financial reporting framework that has been applied in their preparation is applicable law and United Kingdom Accounting Standards (United Kingdom Generally Accepted Accounting Practice).

> This report is made solely to the company's members, as a body, in accordance the Companies Act 2006, Ch. 3, Pt. 16. Our audit work has been undertaken so that we might state to the company's members those matters that we are required to state to them in an auditor's report and for no other purpose. To the fullest extent permitted by law, we do not accept or assume responsibility to anyone other than the company and the company's members as a body, for our audit work, for this report, or for the opinions we have formed. *[Author's note (1)]*

Respective responsibilities of directors and auditor

Explained more fully in the Directors' Responsibilities Statement **[set out on page xx]**, the directors are responsible for the preparation of the financial statements and for being satisfied that they give a true and fair view. Our responsibility is to audit and express an opinion on the financial statements in accordance with applicable law and International Standards on Auditing (UK and Ireland). Those standards require us to comply with the Financial Reporting Council's [(FRCS's)] Ethical Standards for Auditors.

Scope of the audit of the financial statements

Either:

> A description of the scope of an audit of financial statements is [provided on the FRC's website at www.frc.org.uk/apb/scope/private.cfm]/ [set out **[on page x]** of the Annual Report].

Or:

> An audit involves obtaining evidence about the amounts and disclosures in the financial statements sufficient to give reasonable assurance that the financial statements are free from material misstatement, whether caused by fraud or error. This includes an assessment of: whether the accounting policies are appropriate to the [company's] circumstances and have been consistently applied and adequately disclosed; the reasonableness of significant accounting estimates made by [the directors]; and the overall presentation of the financial statements. In addition, we read all the financial and non-financial information in the [Strategic Report and Directors' Report] to identify material inconsistencies with the audited financial statements and to identify any information that is apparently materially incorrect based on, or materially inconsistent with, the knowledge acquired by us in the course of performing the audit. If we become aware of any apparent material misstatements or inconsistencies we consider the implications for our report.

[Author's note (2)]

Opinion on financial statements

In our opinion the financial statements:

- give a true and fair view of the state of the company's affairs as at **[31 December 2016]** and of its profit [loss] for the year then ended;

- have been properly prepared in accordance with United Kingdom Generally Accepted Accounting Practice; and

- have been prepared in accordance with the requirements of the *Companies Act* 2006.

Opinion on other matter prescribed by the Companies Act 2006

In our opinion, based on the work undertaken in the course of the audit, the information given in the Directors' Report for the financial year for which the financial statements are prepared:

- is consistent with the financial statements;

- have been prepared in accordance with applicable legal requirements; and

- in the light of knowledge and understanding of the company and its environment obtained during the course of the audit, we have not identified and material misstatements in the Directors' Report.

[Author's note (3)]

Matters on which we are required to report by exception

We have nothing to report in respect of the following matters where the *Companies Act* 2006 requires us to report to you if, in our opinion:

- adequate accounting records have not been kept, or returns adequate for our audit have not been received from branches not visited by us; or

- the financial statements are not in agreement with the accounting records and returns; or

- certain disclosures of directors' remuneration specified by law are not made; or

- we have not received all the information and explanations we require for our audit;

- the directors were not entitled to [prepare the financial statements in accordance with the small companies regime] [and] [take advantage of the small companies' exemption in preparing the directors' report] [and] [take advantage of the small companies exemption from the requirement to prepare a strategic report.

Lucy Caldwell   *[Author's note (4)]*

....

Lucy Caldwell (Senior Statutory Auditor)

for and on behalf of TRUE & FAIRVIEW LLP

Statutory Auditor

17 Queens Place,

LONDON EC4P 3BC   23 April 2017

Author's notes and commentary to **Example 13.1**.

*(1) **Duty of care to third parties** – the ICAEW recommends that auditors include additional wording in audit reports in order to clarify auditors' responsibilities to third parties – that is, other than to the members (or the directors, as the case may be) as a body. (Audit 1/03 – The Audit Report and The Auditors' Duty of Care to Third Parties.) (January 2003, most recent update January 2010.)*

*(2) **Description of the scope of an audit of financial statements** – ISA (UK and Ireland) 700 requires that an auditor's report should either: cross refer to a Statement of the scope of an audit maintained on the APB's (now FRC's) website; or cross refer to such a scope statement that is included elsewhere within the Annual Report; or include a prescribed description of the scope of an audit.*

*The prescribed description of the scope of an audit (as illustrated in **Example 13.1**) is set out in ISA (UK and Ireland) 700.*

*(3) **Signature and dating of auditor's report** – CA 2006, s. 503 and ISA (UK and Ireland) 700, para. 23–26.*

Part IV   Filing of Accounts

Chapter 14 Filing exemptions for small and medium-sized companies

14.1 Abbreviated accounts

For periods commencing on or after 1 January 2016, a company classified as small or medium-sized is no longer permitted to deliver 'abbreviated accounts' in place of full statutory accounts ('individual accounts') to the Registrar of Companies.

Under the new regulations, companies must deliver a copy of the accounts which were prepared for the members however small companies are still able to take advantage of certain filing exemptions. There are no filing exemptions available to medium-sized companies.

14.2 Filing exemptions for small companies only

As this book is concerned mainly with the requirements of large and medium-sized companies, the following is a brief summary of the exemptions available to small companies. More detail can be found in the book *CCH Preparing Company Accounts – Small and Micros*.

14.2.1 Abridged accounts

As explained in **Chapter 9**, a small company has the option to prepare for its members abridged accounts consisting of an abridged statement of financial position and/or abridged income statement. If a company chooses to do this and does not take advantage of any further filing exemptions (explained below), the directors must also deliver to the Registrar of Companies a statement by the company that all of the members have consented to the abridgement. No guidance is yet available where this statement should be positioned or whether it should be a separate statement.

14.2.2 Directors' report and income statement

Irrespective of whether the company prepares full or abridged accounts for its members, a small company also has the option (under CA 2006, s. 444) not to file with the Registrar of Companies a copy of the directors' report and/or the income statement.

If the company does not file a copy of the income statement, there should be disclosure of that fact on statement of financial position that is filed.

14.2.3 Audit report

A small company need only file with the Registrar of Companies a copy of the audit report (when applicable) if it chooses to file a copy of the income statement.

If the company has taken advantage of the exemption explained in **14.2.2** above and chooses not to file a copy of the income statement and therefore does not file the audit report, the statement of financial position which it files must disclose the following:

- whether the auditor's report was qualified or unqualified;

- if qualified, the basis of the qualification;

- if unqualified, whether a reference was made to any matters to which the auditor drew attention my way of emphasis; and

- the name of the auditor and the name of the person who signed the auditor's report as senior statutory auditor.

Chapter 15   Filing of accounts

15.1   Introduction and electronic filing

This book does not aim to cover the finer details of the filing requirements for the accounts of companies but this chapter gives guidance on filing with both the Registrar of Companies and HMRC and explains some of the current filing methods as these organisations continue to work together to provide a joint filing facility. Further details can be found on CCH Online in the *Company Secretary's Factbook*.

In general, company accounts need to be filed:

- with the Registrar of Companies within the filing deadline (see below); and

- with HMRC with the company's tax return (if the company is required to file a tax return) not more than 12 months following the end of the year to which they relate.

For a number of years now, the Registrar of Companies has accepted electronic filing of some types of accounts. Paper filing can still be used optionally in all cases and in some cases it is the only way that certain sets of accounts can currently be filed, though Companies House is working in a staged approach towards a fully electronic filing service. A significant proportion (almost 85% during 2015) of the accounts submitted are now being filed electronically.

From a practical point of view, there are many advantages in filing electronically, including the certainty that accounts have been accepted quickly, the inbuilt checks to prevent errors and the avoidance of delays or loss in the post. Companies House report that there are fewer rejections of accounts when filed electronically (2.1% in 2015) compared to paper (12.8% in 2015) as the software checks a number of the elements prior to filing. This also results in fewer late filing penalties, as rejected accounts often cause deadlines to be missed. In addition, credit reference agencies use Companies House data and where it is available electronically the agencies can upload such information in their systems the day after it goes live on Companies House, allowing much more accurate and relevant data to be quickly available.

It can only be anticipated that electronic filing will increase 'voluntarily' and will, indeed, become a requirement over the coming years. In the meantime, Companies House will be adding facilities for charities, LLPs and new UK GAAP accounts, including abridged accounts to be filed electronically.

15.2   Filing deadlines

15.2.1   Private companies

In general, private companies are required to file accounts with the Registrar of Companies within nine months from the end of the accounting period (accounting reference date or ARD).

When filing the company's first accounts, the deadline for delivery is nine months after the anniversary of incorporation (i.e. 21 months). The deadline remains the same even if this company extends its first accounting period to the maximum of 18 months. It is calculated to the exact corresponding date in the 21st month following the incorporation. For example, a company incorporated on 29 January 2013 has until midnight on 29 October 2014 to submit its first accounts.

When the accounting period is extended, other than for the first accounts, the filing deadline remains as nine months after the end of the period. However, when a private company shortens the accounting period, the filing deadline for that period is the longer of the following:

- nine months after the new ARD; or

- three months after the date of the notice of the ARD change being delivered to the Registrar.

Companies submitting their accounts after the filing deadline has passed will incur a late filing penalty of at least £150. The penalty increases in line with the period of late submission. The maximum penalty for a private company which submits accounts six months after the normal filing deadline is £1,500. However, if the company files its accounts late two years in a row, the penalty in the second year is doubled. Further information is available on the Companies House website www.gov.uk/government/organisations/companies-house.

15.2.2   Public companies

The regulations in respect of public companies are the broadly the same as above with the following exceptions:

- the period allowed for filing is six months (not nine); and

- the late filing penalties are greater, starting at £750 up to a maximum of £7,500.

15.3   Registrar of Companies

The Registrar of Companies is given authority under CA 2006 to make rules governing the filing of documents at Companies House. These 'Registrar's Rules' are secondary legislation, made under s. 1117 of the Act, and include the form, delivery and method of authentication for documents (including accounts) to be delivered to the Registrar.

The rules specify differing filing requirements for hard copy and electronic filings. For example, although the Companies Act requirement for an original signature to be included on the accounts that are filed was repealed as from 1 October 2009, signatures are still required by the Registrar's Rules to be included on balance sheets filed in paper form.

Furthermore, Companies House has recently reviewed its policy on filing documents with original signatures and has concluded that the Registrar of Companies will not reject documents 'simply because the signature does not appear to be original'.

A detailed list of the Registrar's Rules, including when amendments came into force, is available at www.gov.uk/government/publications/company-registrars-rules-and-powers.

The current version of these rules is GP 6 September 2014 which itself was updated in December 2014. The registrar encourages entities to use either software filing or WebFiling services. Software filing means using an external provider's software, such as CCH's Accounts Production, to create iXBRL versions of accounts for filing. WebFiling is Companies House's own service, designed for use by the smallest and simplest of entities who might not be expected to have access to specialist software.

Table 15.1 The Registrar's Rules

The Registrar's Rules consist of the following five volumes www.gov.uk/guidance/registrars-rules:

Registrar's (Electronic Form) Rules 2012 Volume 1 – Documents delivered in electronic form;

Registrar's Rules 2009 Volume 2 – Documents delivered in paper form;

Registrar's Rules 2009 Volume 3 – Documents (or parts thereof) delivered on a CD-ROM or DVD-ROM;

Registrar's Rules 2009 Volume 4 – Informal correction of a document delivered to the registrar;

Registrar's Rules 2009 Volume 5 – Authentication of a certificate sent by the Registrar by electronic means.

The website above also lists a table of changes to the filing requirements.

15.4   Filing accounts in paper form

Of particular relevance to the filing of accounts on paper at Companies House are the following rules relating to registered number, signatures and the form and content of documents.

Table 15.2 Filing accounts at Companies House

The Registrar's (requirements for paper documents) Rules 2009

Registered number

Paragraph 22(3) of Volume 2 of the amended Registrar's Rules 2009 lists the documents (delivered on paper) which must contain the name and registered number of the company to which the document relates (but only one of the documents filed must show this information).

Only one of the following documents filed must contain the name and registered number of the company:

- copy of balance sheet or abbreviated accounts;
- (where applicable): copy of profit and loss account; copy of directors' report; or directors' remuneration report;
- copy of auditor's report.

The company name or registered number required as above must be in black typescript or handwritten in black ink in a 'prominent position' in the document filed; this does **not**, however, include, for example, the cover of an annual accounts package.

Signature – the following documents (filed in paper form) must be signed by a director:

- copy of balance sheet;
- abbreviated accounts; or
- annual accounts.

The signature must be applied to the document in a prominent position, **at the end of the balance sheet**.

Form and content of documents:

Generally, paper documents sent to Companies House must state in a prominent position the registered name and number of the company. Paper documents must be:

- on A4 size, plain white paper with a matt finish (note – Companies House does usually accept accounts on US letter sized paper and off-white paper as long as the document can be scanned legibly to A4);
- **black**, clear and legible text, of uniform density; and
- clear and legible bold letters and numbers.

Documents should not be poor lettering or photocopies, carbon copies, or produced from a dot matrix printer (note – as this may cause problems scanning the documents).

15.5   Common reasons for accounts rejections at Companies House

Companies House regularly report, in webinars via the ICAEW for example, details of rejection reasons for accounts. The following are the main reasons in 2015 why paper accounts had been rejected:

- Made Up to Date is the same date as the last set of accounts;
- balance sheet signature is not present or as required;
- the Accounting Reference Date or Made Up to Date are incorrect or absent;
- the company number is invalid;
- not all relevant documents are filed.

For electronic accounts, only a very small percent (2.1% in 2015) are rejected and this is primarily due to the following reasons:

- Made Up to Date is a duplicate;

- the Accounting Reference Date or Made Up to Date are incorrect or absent;

- abbreviated or micro accounts submitted for a plc.

If such accounts are submitted close to the filing deadline and the corrected accounts cannot be returned before the filing deadline expires, an automatic late filing penalty will be issued.

15.6   Filing accounts in electronic form

At present, the filing of accounts in electronic format at Companies House is only available to dormant company accounts or audit exempt small or micro-entity accounts and is therefore not covered in this book. Details are available in the publication *CCH Preparing Company Accounts – Small and Micros*.

15.7   Amended accounts

If it is found that a set of accounts submitted to Companies House is defective (i.e. containing errors or not compliant with a requirement of the Companies Act), then the directors may submit amending financial statements to the Registrar of Companies. This may be because the company has realised that the accounts are defective or because the Registrar has written to the directors to request that they either give a satisfactory explanation for the accounts or prepare revised accounts.

The rules relating to revised accounts are set out in CA 2006 (s. 454–459) and the *Companies (Revision of Defective Accounts and Reports) Regulations* 2008 (SI 2008/373).

Revised accounts sent to Companies House must be marked as 'amending'. It is recommended that the 'amending' is very clearly marked (to prevent rejection by Companies House for being made up to the same date as a set of accounts that has previously been filed). The highlighting should not obscure any part of the accounts, however, as they could then be rejected if they do not scan legibly.

The amending accounts must contain the following statements (in a prominent position):

- the revised accounts replace the original accounts for the financial year (specifying it);

- the revised accounts are now the statutory accounts for that year; and

- the revised accounts have been prepared as at the date of the original accounts, and not as at the date of the revision and accordingly do not deal with events between those dates.

The accounts must also contain details (in a prominent position) of:

- the way in which the original accounts did not comply with the requirements of CA 2006; and

- any significant amendments made as a result of correcting the defects (SI 2008/373, Pt. 2, reg. 4).

If the original accounts were audited, the amending accounts must contain an audit report on the revised accounts. This report differs from the original report and includes statements of whether:

- in the auditor's opinion, the revised accounts have been properly prepared in accordance with CA 2006;

- the revised accounts give a true and fair view to the individual balance sheet and profit and loss (consolidated in the case of group accounts), seen as at the date the original accounts were approved; and

- the original accounts failed to comply with the requirements of the CA 2006 in the respects identified by the directors. SI 2008/373, Pt. 2, reg. 5.

Where a revised directors' report is prepared, the report must also state whether, in the auditor's opinion, the information given in that revised report is consistent with the accounts for the financial year.

If the previous set of accounts was not audited, but the revised set is found not to be exempt from audit, the company must also deliver an auditor's report to Companies House within 28 days after the date of revision of the accounts.

The original (defective) accounts will remain on the public record. Removing incorrect documents from the public record requires a court order (unless Companies House, in error, accepted an item which should have been rejected).

Companies House provides further guidance at http://resources.companieshouse.gov.uk/infoAndGuide/faq/amendingAccounts.shtml (Archived content).

15.8   HMRC

A UK Corporation Tax Return for a limited company (preparing Companies Act or IAS individual accounts) includes form CT600, the accounts and the tax computation together with any accompanying information as required. This must be submitted to HMRC electronically. The accounts forming part of the return must be in iXBRL format.

iXBRL tagging of UK statutory financial statements has been required for tax purposes since 2011.

A dormant company will not have to deliver a return unless it is sent a statutory notice to do so. In most cases, if HMRC has been notified that a company is dormant, no notice to deliver a return will be issued.

Overseas companies resident in the UK must deliver the accounts required by a notice to deliver a return in iXBRL. Also a company not resident in the UK, but carrying on a trade in the UK through a permanent establishment, branch or agency in the UK, must deliver any trading and profit and loss account and any balance sheet of the UK establishment, branch or agency required as part of its return in iXBRL format.

Further guidance on HMRC requirements is available in *Tax Reporter*, CCH Online's direct tax commentary service.

15.9   Electronic tagging of accounts (iXBRL)

Inline Extensible Business Reporting Language (iXBRL) is an electronic format for embedding XBRL 'tags' into financial statements. XBRL itself is an open and global standard for exchanging business information.

The accounts tagged under iXBRL are still in a format which can be read 'manually' (as opposed to by a computer only): this is what the 'inline' refers to – the tags applied are hidden behind the scenes, in line with the normal text.

Embedding tags into an annual report and accounts document can by performed in a variety of ways:

- using an accounts preparation package which has the tagging facility built in;

- using tagging software to apply the tags to accounts created in a word-processed document; or

- engaging a third party tagging firm or accountant to create the iXBRL file from the word processed document file ('managed tagging').

HMRC maintain a list of approved providers of software and managed tagging providers at www. gov.uk/government/publications/corporation-tax-commercial-software-suppliers.

Taxonomies have been created for UK GAAP (both old and new) and IFRS which set out the available tags to be used in a set of financial statements. The FRC has taken over the function of dealing with UK GAAP taxonomies whilst the IASB look after the IFRS ones (which are available on CCH Online – *International Accounting Standards*). Up until now charity accounts haven't had suitable 'tagging' terms within these taxonomies, but the FRC has recently issued a charities taxonomy and so Companies House expect soon to be able to offer an electronic filing option for charity accounts under new UK GAAP.

The FRC has issued a guide to taxonomies which can be found here www.frc.org.uk/Our-Work/ Publications/Accounting-and-Reporting-Policy/FRC-Taxonomies-Tagging-Guide.pdf as well as the taxonomies themselves. However, the latter are mostly only required for the software companies writing iXBRL compatible accounts production programmes.

Appendices

Appendix A   Example accounts

The following example accounts prepared in accordance with FRS 102 are for a medium-sized manufacturing company which is not a parent company. They are intended to illustrate some of the more unusual situations which might apply to companies. However, they are not intended to be comprehensive. The accounts are regularly updated on CCH Online in the *Model Accounts* product authored by SWAT UK, which also contains guidance notes and accounts under FRS 101, FRS 102 section 1A and FRS 105.

The accounts relate to the year ended 31 December 2015 and is the first year of adoption of FRS 102.

The company has adopted the single Statement of Comprehensive Income layout showing other comprehensive income after the profit for the financial year.

Directors' report

The directors present their annual report and the audited financial statements for the year ended 31 December 2015.

Principal place of business

Manufacturing Company Limited is a company incorporated and domiciled in England and has its registered office and principal place of business at Sound House, Sea View, Plymouth, PL1 2CD.

Results and appropriations

The results and the state of affairs of the company for the year are set out in the financial statements on pages 5 to 28. The directors do not recommend the payment of a dividend. The profit for the financial year of £542,000 will therefore be taken to reserves.

Directors

The directors of the company throughout the year were:

Mr Raymond Chard

Ms Adeline Long

Mr Anthony Hope

In accordance with Article 84(a) of the Company's Articles of Association, all directors shall retire and, being eligible, offer themselves for re-election.

Statement of directors' responsibilities

The directors are responsible for preparing the Directors' Report, the Strategic Report and the financial statements in accordance with applicable law and regulations and in accordance with United Kingdom Generally Accepted Accounting Practice.

Company law requires the directors to prepare financial statements for each financial year. Under that law the directors have elected to prepare the financial statements in accordance with United Kingdom Generally Accepted Accounting Practice (Financial Reporting Standard 102). Under company law the directors must not approve the financial statements unless they are satisfied that they give a true and fair view of the state of affairs of the company and the profit or loss of the company for that period.

In preparing these financial statements, the directors are required to:

- select suitable accounting policies and then apply them consistently;

- make judgments and accounting estimates that are reasonable and prudent; and

- prepare the financial statements on the going concern basis unless it is inappropriate to presume that the company will continue in business.

The directors are responsible for keeping adequate accounting records that are sufficient to show and explain the company's transactions and disclose with reasonable accuracy at any time the financial position of the company and enable them to ensure that the financial statements comply with the *Companies Act* 2006. They are also responsible for safeguarding the assets of the company and hence for taking reasonable steps for the prevention and detection of fraud and other irregularities.

The directors are responsible for the maintenance and integrity of the corporate and financial information included on the company's website. Legislation in the United Kingdom, governing the preparation and dissemination of financial statements, may differ from legislation in other jurisdictions.

Post balance sheet events

There are no matters to report as post balance sheet events.

Strategic Report

The company has chosen in accordance with *Companies Act* 2006, s. 414C(11) to set out in the company's strategic report information required by the *Large and Medium-sized Companies and Groups (Accounts and Reports) Regulations* 2008, Sch. 7 to be contained in the directors' report. It has done so in respect of future developments, research & development and financial instruments.

Statement of disclosure of information to auditors

Each of the persons who is a director at the date of approval of this report confirms that:

- so far as the director is aware, there is no relevant audit information of which the company's auditors are unaware; and

- the director has taken all the steps that they ought to have taken as a director in order to make themselves aware of any relevant audit information and to establish that the company's auditors are aware of that information.

Auditors

Nickleby & Chuzzlewitt will be deemed to continue in office under the *Companies Act* 2006, s. 487(2).

On behalf of the Board

R.Chard

Director

25 April 2016

Strategic report

Business Review

The company has four product divisions and the directors consider that the key financial performance indicators are those that monitor the performance in respect of each of these divisions. The turnover of the company from the sale of products analysed by division is as follows:

	2015	2014 (as restated)
	£'000	£'000
Sound & graphics	5,488	3,198
Network	2,395	2,217
WiFi and Bluetooth	1,327	153
USB Memory Sticks	1,877	2,011
	11,087	7,579

The Sound & graphics divisions and the network divisions have shown growth of 72% and 8% respectively which were in line with the directors' expectations. The directors are pleased to see the growth of products for the WiFi and Bluetooth market which was a new market in 2014. All product lines are sold in a competitive market and the directors believe that it is in the best interests of the company for it to operate predominately in the UK.

Due to a sustained downward turn in sales, the Board of Directors sold the Memory Sticks division in December 2015. The results of this division are shown separately in the accounts as discontinued activities. The loss on disposal of discontinued activities represents the loss on the sale of goodwill and plant in that division.

The operating profit of the company has increased from £618,000 to £812,000, with those excluding the Memory Sticks division showing an increase from £741,000 to £1,288,000. The profit after taxation showed an increase from £417,000 to £542,000.

The company faces a number of risks and uncertainties and the directors believe that the key business risks are in respect of competition from both UK and international businesses and in ensuring product development and availability. In view of these risks and uncertainties, the directors are aware that the development of the company may be affected by factors outside their control.

Principal risks and uncertainties

The company faces a number of business risks and uncertainties due to worsening trading conditions and new competition. In view of this, the directors are looking carefully at both existing and potential new markets.

Future developments

The directors anticipate the business environment will remain competitive. They believe that the company is in a good financial position and they remain confident that the company will continue to grow, although not necessarily at the rate achieved in the current year.

Financial instruments

The company has a normal level of exposure to price, credit, liquidity and cash flow risks arising from trading activities which are only conducted in sterling. The company does not enter into any hedging transactions.

Research and development

The company is currently undertaking research and development to improve the performance of its network cards, Bluetooth dongles and WiFi extenders.

On behalf of the Board

R. Chard

Director

25 April 2016

Independent auditor's report

Independent auditor's report to the members of Manufacturing Company Limited

We have audited the financial statements of Manufacturing Company Limited for the year ended 31 December 2015 set out on pages 5 to 27. The financial reporting framework that has been applied in their preparation is applicable law and United Kingdom Accounting Standards (United Kingdom Generally Accepted Accounting Practice), including FRS 102 'The Financial Reporting Standard applicable in the UK and Republic of Ireland'.

This report is made solely to the company's members, as a body, in accordance with the *Companies Act* 2006, Pt. 16, Ch. 3. Our audit work has been undertaken so that we might state to the company's members those matters we are required to state to them in an auditor's report and for no other purpose. To the fullest extent permitted by law, we do not accept or assume responsibility to anyone other than the company and the company's members as a body, for our audit work , for this report, or for the opinions we have formed.

Respective responsibilities of directors and auditors

As explained more fully in the Directors' Responsibilities Statement, set out on pages from one to three, the directors are responsible for the preparation of the financial statements and for being satisfied that they give a true and fair view. Our responsibility is to audit and express an opinion on the financial statements in accordance with applicable law and International Standards on Auditing (UK and Ireland). Those standards require us to comply with the Financial Reporting Council's Ethical Standards for Auditors.

Scope of the audit of the financial statements

A description of the scope of an audit of financial statements is provided on the Financial Reporting Council's website at www.frc.org.uk/auditscopeukprivate.

Opinion on the financial statements

In our opinion the financial statements:

- give a true and fair view of the state of the company's affairs as at 31 December 2015 and of its profit for the year then ended;
- have been properly prepared in accordance with United Kingdom Generally Accepted Accounting Practice; and
- have been prepared in accordance with the requirements of the *Companies Act* 2006.

Opinion on other matter prescribed by the Companies Act 2006

In our opinion, the information given in the Directors' Report and the Strategic Report for the financial year for which the financial statements are prepared is consistent with the financial statements.

Matters on which we are required to report by exception

We have nothing to report in respect of the following matters where the *Companies Act* 2006 requires us to report to you if, in our opinion:

- adequate accounting records have not been kept, or returns adequate for our audit have not been received from branches not visited by us; or
- the financial statements are not in agreement with the accounting records and returns; or

- certain disclosures of directors remuneration specified by law are not made; or
- we have not received all the information and explanations we require for our audit.

R Lee

Robert Lee

Senior Statutory Auditor

for and on behalf of Nickleby & Chuzzlewitt

Chartered Accountants and Statutory Auditors

Plymouth

25 April 2016

Statement of Comprehensive Income

Statement of comprehensive income for the year ended 31 December 2015

| | | 2015 | | | 2014 (as restated) | | |
| | | Continuing operations | Discontinued operations | Total | Continuing operations | Discontinued operations | Total |
Continuing operations	Notes	£'000	£'000	£'000	£'000	£'000	£'000
Turnover	3	9,210	1,877	11,087	5,568	2,011	7,579
Cost of sales		(4,076)	(1,919)	(5,995)	(1,728)	(1,805)	(3,533)
Gross profit		5,134	(42)	5,092	3,840	206	4,046
Distribution costs and selling expenses		(778)	(138)	(916)	(708)	(130)	(838)
Administrative expenses		(3,115)	(116)	(3,231)	(2,412)	(199)	(2,611)
Other operating income	4	46	–	46	29	–	29
Loss on disposal of operation	8	–	(180)	(180)	–	–	–
Operating profit		1,287	(476)	811	749	(123)	626
Interest payable and similar charges	5	(74)	–	(74)	(39)	–	(39)
Profit on ordinary activities before tax		1,213	(476)	737	710	(123)	587
Taxation	6	(196)	–	(196)	(170)	–	(170)
Profit on ordinary activities after taxation and profit for the financial year	9	1,017	(476)	541	540	(123)	417
Other comprehensive income							
Gain on revaluation of land and buildings				144			–
Deferred taxation arising from revaluation of land and buildings				(25)			–
Total comprehensive income for the year				660			417

136

Statement of Financial Position

Statement of financial position at 31 December 2015

	Notes	2015 £'000	2014 (as restated) £'000
Fixed assets			
Intangible assets	**12**	102	102
Tangible assets	**13**	1,374	1,105
		1,476	1,207
Current assets			
Stocks	**14**	1,080	855
Debtors	**15**	1,499	1,211
Cash at bank and in hand		502	4
Total current assets		3,081	2,070
Creditors: amount falling due within one year	**17**	(1,314)	(1,533)
Net current assets		1,767	537
Total assets less current liabilities		3,243	1,744
Creditors: amount falling due more than one year	**18**	(770)	(209)
Provision for liabilities			
Deferred taxation	**7**	(66)	(49)
Other provisions	**21**	(120)	–
		(186)	(49)
TOTAL ASSETS		**2,287**	**1,486**
Capital and reserves			
Called up share capital	**22**	910	875
Share premium account	**22**	87	70
Other reserves	**23**	119	–
Profit and loss account	**23**	1,171	541
TOTAL EQUITY		**2,287**	**1,486**

The financial statements were approved by the board of directors on 25 April 2016 and signed on its behalf by:

R. Chard

Director

Company number 7654321

Statement of Changes in Equity

Statement of changes in equity for the year ended 31 December 2015

	Notes	Share capital	Share premium	Other reserves	Retained earnings	Total
		£'000	£'000	£'000	£'000	£'000
At 1 January 2014		875	70	–	124	1,069
Profit for the year and total comprehensive income		–	–	–	417	417
At 1 January 2015		875	70	–	541	1,486
Profit for the year		–	–	–	541	541
Gain on revaluation of land & buildings	12	–	–	144	–	144
Deferred tax arising from revaluation of land & buildings	7	–	–	(25)	–	(25)
Other comprehensive income for the year		–	–	119	89	208
Total comprehensive income for the year		–	–	119	541	660
New shares issued in the year	21	35	17	–	–	52
Capital contribution arising on loan from parent	23	–	–	–	89	89
At 31 December 2015		910	87	119	1,171	2,287

Statement of Cash Flows

Statement of cash flows for the year ended 31 December 2015

		Notes	2015	2014 (as restated)
			£'000	£'000
Cash flows from operating activities				
Operating profit	from continuing operations		1,287	749
	from discontinued operations		(476)	(12)
Adjustments for:				
Provisions			120	–
Depreciation and amortisation			191	129
Impairment loss on goodwill			–	21
Loss on disposal of discontinued operation			180	–
Profit on disposal of property, plant and equipment			(26)	(17)
			1,276	759
Movements in working capital				
(Increase)/decrease in inventories			(225)	25
Increase in trade and other receivables			(288)	(218)
Decrease in trade and other payables			(255)	(429)
Cash generated from operations			508	137
Interest paid			(34)	(65)
Income taxes paid			(177)	(124)
Net cash generated by/ (used in) operating activities			297	(52)
Cash flows from investing activities				
Proceeds from sale of discontinued operations		8	35	–
Proceeds from sale of property, plant and equipment			32	29
Payments for property, plant and equipment			(387)	(186)
Payments for other intangible assets			(50)	–
Net cash used in investing activities			(370)	(157)
Cash flows from financing activities				
Proceeds from issue of new share capital			52	–
Repayments of bank borrowings			(73)	(10)
Proceeds from bank borrowings			664	–
Repayments of obligations under finance leases			(41)	(21)
Net cash generated by/(used in) financing activities			602	(31)
Net increase/(decrease) in cash and cash equivalents			529	(240)
Cash and cash equivalents at the beginning of the year			(106)	134
Cash and cash equivalents at the end of the year			**423**	**(106)**
Cash and bank balances			502	4
Bank overdrafts		19	(79)	(110)
Net cash used in financing activities			**423**	**(106)**

Notes to the financial statements

1. Significant accounting policies

(a) Basis of accounting

The financial statements have been prepared under the historical cost convention as modified by the revaluation of land and buildings and certain financial instruments measured at fair value in accordance with the accounting policies set out below.

These financial statements have been prepared in compliance with FRS 102 – The Financial Reporting Standard applicable in the UK and Republic of Ireland and the *Companies Act* 2006.

This is the first year in which the financial statements have been prepared under FRS 102. Details of the transition to FRS 102 are disclosed in note 28.

(b) Revenue recognition

Revenue is measured at the fair value of the consideration received or receivable. Revenue is reduced for estimated customer returns, rebates and other similar allowances.

Revenue from the sale of computer components as specified in the strategic report is recognised when all the following conditions are satisfied:

- the Company has transferred to the buyer the significant risks and rewards of ownership of the goods;

- the Company retains neither continuing managerial involvement to the degree usually associated with ownership nor effective control over the goods sold;

- the amount of revenue can be measured reliably;

- it is probable that the economic benefits associated with the transaction will flow to the Company; and

- the costs incurred or to be incurred in respect of the transaction can be measured reliably.

Specifically, revenue from the sale of goods is recognised when goods are delivered and legal title is passed.

(c) Borrowing costs

Borrowing costs directly attributable to the acquisition, construction or production of qualifying assets, which are assets that necessarily take a substantial period of time to get ready for their intended use or sale, are added to the cost of those assets, until such time as the assets are substantially ready for their intended use or sale.

Investment income earned on the temporary investment of specific borrowings pending their expenditure on qualifying assets is deducted from the borrowing costs eligible for capitalisation. All other borrowing costs are recognised in profit or loss in the period in which they are incurred.

(d) Taxation

Income tax expense represents the sum of the tax currently payable and deferred tax.

The tax currently payable is based on taxable profit for the year. Taxable profit differs from profit as reported in the statement of comprehensive income because of items of income or expense that are taxable or deductible in other years and items that are never taxable or deductible. The Company's liability for current tax is calculated using tax rates that have been enacted or substantively enacted by the end of the reporting period.

Deferred tax is recognised on timing differences between the carrying amounts of assets and liabilities in the financial statements and the corresponding tax bases used in the computation of taxable profit. Deferred tax liabilities are generally recognised for all taxable temporary differences. Deferred tax assets are generally recognised for all deductible timing differences to the extent that it is probable that taxable profits will be available against which those deductible temporary differences can be utilised. The carrying amount of deferred tax assets is reviewed at the end of each reporting period and reduced to the extent that it is no longer probable that sufficient taxable profits will be available to allow all or part of the asset to be recovered.

Deferred tax assets and liabilities are measured at the tax rates that are expected to apply in the period in which the liability is settled or the asset realised, based on tax rates (and tax laws) that have been enacted or substantively enacted by the end of the reporting period. The measurement of deferred tax liabilities and assets reflects the tax consequences that would follow from the manner in which the Company expects, at the end of the reporting period, to recover or settle the carrying amount of its assets and liabilities.

Current or deferred tax for the year is recognised in profit or loss, except when they relate to items that are recognised in other comprehensive income or directly in equity, in which case, the current and deferred tax is also recognised in other comprehensive income or directly in equity respectively.

(e) Intangible assets

Development expenditure

Development of products is capitalised where there is expected to be a benefit to future periods and the following conditions are met:

(i)   It is technically feasible to complete the research or development so that the product will be available for use or sale.

(ii) It is intended to use or sell the product being developed.

(iii) The Company is able to use or sell the product.

(iv) It can be demonstrated that the product will generate probable future economic benefits.

(v)   Adequate technical, financial and other resources exist so that product development can be completed and subsequently used or sold.

(vi) Expenditure attributable to the research and development work can be reliably measured.

Capitalised development expenditure is stated at cost less accumulated amortisation and impairment losses and amortised over its useful economic life. Assessments of useful economic life range from 5 to 15 years.

All other research and development expenditure is recognised as an expense in the period in which it is incurred.

Goodwill

Goodwill arising on an acquisition of a business is carried at cost less accumulated amortisation and impairment losses, if any. Amortisation is calculated on a straight-line basis over the useful economic life of 10 years.

For the purposes of impairment testing, goodwill is allocated to each of the Company's cash-generating units (or groups of cash-generating units) that is expected to benefit from the synergies of the combination.

(f) Tangible assets

Land and buildings held and used in the Company's own activities for production and supply of goods or for administrative purposes are stated in the statement of financial position at their revalued amounts. The revalued amounts equate to the fair value at the date of revaluation, less any depreciation or impairment losses subsequently accumulated. Revaluations are carried out regularly so that the carrying amounts do not materially differ from using the fair value at the date of the statement of financial position.

Any revaluation increase or decrease on land and buildings is credited to the property revaluation reserve in 'other reserves'.

Depreciation on revalued buildings is charged to profit or loss so as to write off their value, less residual value, over their estimated useful life of 50 years, using the straight-line method.

Once a revalued property is sold or retired any attributable revaluation surplus that is remaining in the property revaluation reserve is transferred to retained earnings. No transfer is made from the revaluation reserve to retained earnings unless an asset is derecognised.

Plant and equipment are stated at cost less accumulated depreciation and accumulated impairment losses.

Depreciation on plant and equipment is charged to profit or loss so as to write off their value, over their estimated useful lives of between 5 and 20 years using the straight-line method.

Assets held under finance leases are depreciated in the same manner as owned assets.

At each balance sheet date, the Company reviews the carrying amounts of its property, plant and equipment to determine whether there is any indication that any items of property, plant and equipment have suffered an impairment loss. If any such indication exists, the recoverable amount of an asset is estimated in order to determine the extent of the impairment loss, if any. Where it is not possible to estimate the recoverable amount of the asset, the Company estimates the recoverable amount of the cash-generating unit to which the asset belongs.

If the recoverable amount of an asset is estimated to be less than its carrying amount, the carrying amount of the asset is reduced to its recoverable amount. Impairment loss is recognised as an expense immediately.

Where an impairment loss subsequently reverses, the carrying amount of the asset is increased to the revised estimate of its recoverable amount, to the extent that the increased carrying amount does not exceed the carrying amount that would have been determined (net of depreciation) had no impairment loss been recognised for the asset in prior years. A reversal of an impairment loss is recognised as income immediately.

(g) Stocks

Stocks are stated at the lower of cost and estimated selling price less costs to complete and sell. Costs, which comprise direct production costs, are based on the method most appropriate to the type of inventory class, but usually on a first-in-first-out basis. Overheads are charged to profit or loss as incurred. Net realisable value is based on the estimated selling price less any estimated completion or selling costs.

When stocks are sold, the carrying amount of those stocks is recognised as an expense in the period in which the related revenue is recognised. The amount of any write-down of stocks to net realisable value and all losses of stocks are recognised as an expense in the period in which the write-down or loss occurs. The amount of any reversal of any write-down of stocks is recognised as a reduction in the amount of inventories recognised as an expense in the period in which the reversal occurs.

(h) Trade and other debtors

Trade and other debtors are initially recognised at the transaction price and thereafter stated at amortised cost using the effective interest method, less impairment losses for bad and doubtful debts except where the effect of discounting would be immaterial. In such cases, the debtors are stated at cost less impairment losses for bad and doubtful debts.

(i) Cash and cash equivalents

Cash and cash equivalents comprise cash at bank and on hand, demand deposits with banks and other short-term highly liquid investments with original maturities of three months or less and bank overdrafts. In the statement of financial position, bank overdrafts are shown within borrowings or current liabilities.

(j) Impairment of financial assets

Financial assets, are assessed for indicators of impairment at the end of each reporting period. Financial assets are considered to be impaired when there is objective evidence that, as a result of one or more events that occurred after the initial recognition of the financial asset, the estimated future cash flows of the investment have been affected.

For all other financial assets, objective evidence of impairment could include:

- significant financial difficulty of the issuer or counterparty; or

- breach of contract, such as a default or delinquency in interest or principal payments; or

- it becoming probable that the borrower will enter bankruptcy or financial re-organisation; or

- the disappearance of an active market for that financial asset because of financial difficulties.

For certain categories of financial asset, such as trade receivables, assets that are assessed not to be impaired individually are, in addition, assessed for impairment on a collective basis. Objective evidence of impairment for a portfolio of receivables could include the Company's past experience of collecting payments, an increase in the number of delayed payments in the portfolio past the average credit period of 50 days, as well as observable changes in national or local economic conditions that correlate with default on receivables.

For financial assets carried at amortised cost, the amount of the impairment loss recognised is the difference between the asset's carrying amount and the present value of estimated future cash flows, discounted at the financial asset's original effective interest rate. The impairment loss is recognised in profit or loss.

For financial assets carried at cost, the amount of the impairment loss is measured as the difference between the asset's carrying amount and the present value of the estimated future cash flows discounted at the current market rate of return for a similar financial asset. Such impairment loss will not be reversed in subsequent periods.

The carrying amount of the financial asset is reduced by the impairment loss directly for all financial assets with the exception of trade receivables, where the carrying amount is reduced through the use of an allowance account. When a trade receivable is considered uncollectible, it is written off against the allowance account. Subsequent recoveries of amounts previously written off are credited against the allowance account. Changes in the carrying amount of the allowance account are recognised in profit or loss.

For financial assets measured at amortised cost, if, in a subsequent period, the amount of the impairment loss decreases and the decrease can be related objectively to an event occurring after the impairment was recognised, the previously recognised impairment loss is reversed through profit or loss to the extent that the carrying amount of the investment at the date the impairment is

143

reversed does not exceed what the amortised cost would have been had the impairment not been recognised.

(k) Trade and other creditors

Trade and other creditors are initially recognised at fair value and thereafter stated at amortised cost using the effective interest method unless the effect of discounting would be immaterial, in which case they are stated at cost.

(l) Interest bearing borrowings

Interest-bearing borrowings are recognised initially at fair value less attributable transaction costs. Subsequent to initial recognition, interest-bearing borrowings are stated at amortised cost with any difference between the amount initially recognised and redemption value being recognised in the statement of comprehensive income over the period of the borrowings, together with any interest and fees payable, using the effective interest method.

(m) Derivative financial instruments

The company uses forward foreign currency contracts to reduce exposure to foreign exchange rates.

Derivatives are initially recognised at fair value on the date a derivative contract is entered into and are subsequently re-measured at their fair value. Changes in the fair value of derivatives are recognised in profit and loss in finance costs or income as appropriate.

The company does not currently apply hedge accounting for foreign exchange derivatives.

(n) Related parties

For the purposes of these financial statements, a party is considered to be related to the Company if:

(i)   the party has the ability, directly or indirectly, through one or more intermediaries, to control the Company or exercise significant influence over the company in making financial and operating policy decisions, or has joint control over the Company;

(ii)   the Company and the party are subject to common control;

(iii) the party is an associate of the Company or a joint venture in which the Company is a venturer;

(iv)   the party is a member of key management personnel of the Company or the Company's parent, or a close family member of such an individual, or is an entity under the control, joint control or significant influence of such individuals;

(v)   the party is a close family member of a party referred to in (i) or is an entity under the control, joint control or significant influence of such individuals;

(vi)   the party is a post-employment benefit plan which is for the benefit of employees of the Company or of any entity that is a related party of the Company; or

(vii) the party, or any member of a group of which it is part, provides key management personnel services to the company or its parent.

Close family members of an individual are those family members who may be expected to influence, or be influenced by, that individual in their dealings with the entity.

(o) Leased assets

Assets that are held by Company under leases which transfer to the Company substantially all the risks and rewards of ownership are classified as being held under finance leases. Leases which do not transfer substantially all the risks and rewards of ownership to the Company are classified as operating leases.

Assets held under finance leases are initially recognised as assets of the Company at their fair value at the inception of the lease or, if lower, at the present value of the minimum lease payments. The corresponding liability to the lessor is included in the statement of financial position as a finance lease obligation. Lease payments are apportioned between finance expenses and reduction of the lease obligation so as to achieve a constant rate of interest on the remaining balance of the liability. Finance expenses are recognised immediately in profit or loss, unless they are directly attributable to qualifying assets, in which case they are capitalised in accordance with the Company's policy on borrowing costs (see the accounting policy above). Contingent rentals are recognised as expenses in the periods in which they are incurred.

Operating lease payments are recognised as an expense on a straight-line basis over the lease term, except where another systematic basis is more representative of the time pattern in which economic benefits from the leased asset are consumed. Contingent rentals arising under operating leases are recognised as an expense in the period in which they are incurred.

In the event that lease incentives are received to enter into operating leases, such incentives are recognised as a liability. The aggregate benefit of incentives is recognised as a reduction of rental expense on a straight-line basis, except where another systematic basis is more representative of the time pattern in which economic benefits from the leased asset are consumed.

(p) Foreign currencies

The financial statements are presented in Sterling, which is also the functional currency of the Company. Transactions in currencies, other than the functional currency of the Company, are recorded at the rate of exchange on the date the transaction occurred. Monetary items denominated in other currencies are translated at the rate prevailing at the end of the reporting period. All differences are taken to the statement of comprehensive income. Non-monetary items that are measured at historic cost in a foreign currency are not retranslated.

(q) Employee benefits

Short-term employee benefits are recognised as an expense in the period in which they are incurred.

The obligations for contributions to defined contribution scheme are recognised as an expense in the period they are incurred. The assets of the scheme are held separately from those of the Company in an independent administered fund.

(r) Discontinued operation

A discontinued operation is a component of the Company's business, the operations and cash flows of which can be clearly distinguished from the rest of the Company and which represents a separate major line of business or geographical area of operations, or is part of a single coordinated disposal of a separate major line of business or geographical area of operations, or is a subsidiary acquired exclusively with a review to resale.

(s) Provisions

Provisions are recognised when the Company has a present legal or constructive obligation arising as a result of a past event, it is probable that an outflow of economic benefits will be required to settle the obligation and a reliable estimate can be made. Provisions are measured at the present value of the expenditures expected to be required to settle the obligation using a pre-tax rate that reflects current market assessments of the time value of money and the risks specific to the obligation. The increase in the provision due to passage of time is recognised as interest expense.

2. Critical accounting judgements and key sources of estimation uncertainty

In the application of the Company's accounting policies, which are described in note 1, management is required to make judgements, estimates and assumptions about the carrying values of assets and liabilities that are not readily apparent from other sources. The estimates and underlying assumptions are based on historical experience and other factors that are considered to be relevant. Actual results may differ from these estimates.

The estimates and underlying assumptions are reviewed on an ongoing basis. Revisions to accounting estimates are recognised in the period in which the estimate is revised if the revision affects only that period, or in the period of the revision and future periods if the revision affects both current and future periods.

The key sources of estimation uncertainty that have a significant effect on the amounts recognised in the financial statements are described below.

Valuation of land and buildings

As described in note 12 to the financial statements, land and buildings are stated at fair value based on the valuation performed by an independent professional valuer Turner & Co, Chartered Surveyors with recent experience in the location and category of property valued. The valuer used observable market prices adjusted as necessary for any difference in the future, location or condition of the specific asset.

3. Turnover

	2015	2014 (as restated)
Turnover	£'000	£'000
Continuing operations		
Revenue from the sale of goods	9,210	5,568
Discontinued operations		
Revenue from the sale of goods (note 8)	1,877	2,011
	11,087	7,579

4. Other gains and losses

	2015	2014 (as restated)
	£'000	£'000
Gain on disposal of property, plant and equipment	26	17
Foreign exchange gains	20	12
	46	29

5. Finance costs

	2015	2014 (as restated)
Continuing operations:	£'000	£'000
Interest on bank overdrafts and loans:		
Wholly repayable within five years	28	17
Not wholly repayable within five years	11	6

	2015	2014 (as restated)
Interest on obligations under finance leases:		
Wholly repayable within five years	13	8
Losses on derivative financial instruments	22	8
	74	39

6. Taxation

	2015	2014 (as restated)
(a) Analysis of charge in period:	**£'000**	**£'000**
Current tax		
UK corporation tax on profits of the period	197	170
Under-provision in respect of prior year	7	–
Total current tax	204	170
Deferred tax	(8)	–
Total income tax recognised in profit or loss	196	170

(b) Factors affecting tax charge for the period

The tax assessed for the period is higher than the standard rate of corporation tax in the UK.

The differences are explained below.

	2015	2014 (as restated)
	£'000	**£'000**
Profit on ordinary activities before tax	738	587
Profit on ordinary activities multiplied by the standard rate of UK corporation tax 20.25% (2014 – 21.5%)	149	126
Effects of:		
Expenses not deductible for tax purposes	41	51
Marginal tax rates	(1)	(7)
Adjustments to charge in respect of previous periods	7	–
Current tax charge for the period	196	170

(c) Factors that may affect future tax charges

Based on current capital investment plans the company expects to be able to continue to claim capital allowances in excess of depreciation in future years at a slightly lower level than in the current year. The company has used all brought forward tax losses which had reduced tax payments in recent years.

7. Deferred taxation

	Derivative financial instruments £'000	Property revaluation £'000	Accelerated capital allowances £'000	Total £'000
At 1 January 2015	4	–	45	49
Credited to the profit and loss account	–	–	(8)	(8)
Charged to other comprehensive income	–	25	–	25
At 31 December 2015	4	25	37	66

Deferred tax of £29,000 is expected to reverse in the next year.

8. Discontinued operations

Due to a sustained downward turn in sales, the Board of Directors sold the Memory Sticks division in December 2015. The disposal was completed on 31 December 2015 at which date control of the division passed to the acquirer. The results of the discontinued operations are analysed below. The comparative figures have been re-presented to show separately the results of the discontinued operation as included in that period.

	2015 £'000	2014 (as restated) £'000
Loss for the year from discontinued operations		
Revenue	1,877	2,010
Expenses	(2,173)	(2,133)
Loss before tax	(296)	(123)
Loss on disposal of operation	(180)	–
Loss for the year from discontinued operations	(476)	(123)

	2015 £'000	2014 (as restated) £'000
Cash flows from discontinued operations		
Net cash flows from operating activities	(313)	(148)
Net cash flows from financing activities	(8)	(5)
	(321)	(153)

	£'000
Sale of discontinued operations	
Goodwill	35
Property, plant and equipment	180
Net assets disposed of	215
Loss on sale of discontinued operations	(180)
Cash consideration received	35

9. Profit for the year from continuing operations

Profit for the year from continuing operations has been arrived at after charging:

		2015	2014 (as restated)
		£'000	£'000
Auditors' remuneration	Audit services	40	39
	Other services	7	6
Depreciation of property, plant and equipment			
– owned assets		151	88
– assets held under finance lease		24	10
Amortisation of intangible assets		15	30
Impairment loss on goodwill		–	21
Operating lease charges			
– property		240	220
– plant and equipment		165	174
Staff costs including directors' remuneration			
– salaries		1,950	1,495
– defined contribution plans		300	78

10. Staff Costs

The average number of persons employed by the company (including directors) during the year was:

	2015	2014 (as restated)
	No.	No.
Production	29	16
Selling and distribution	6	5
Administration	26	25
	61	46

Their remuneration was:	2015	2014 (as restated)
	£'000	£'000
Wages and salaries	1,779	1,364
Social security costs	170	130
Pension costs	300	75
	2,249	1,569

11. Directors' remuneration

	2015	2014 (as restated)
	£'000	£'000
Aggregate emoluments (including benefits in kind)	225	210
Aggregate of company contributions to defined contribution pension schemes	214	11

	2015	2014 (as restated)
	£'000	£'000
Highest paid director emoluments	80	75
money purchase pension contribution	74	5
Number of directors to whom retirement benefits are accruing:		
Defined contribution schemes	3	3

12. Intangible assets

	Goodwill	Research and development	Total
	£'000	£'000	£'000
Cost			
At 1 January 2015	140	194	334
Additions-Internal development	–	50	50
Disposal of business	(140)	–	(140)
At 31 December 2015	–	244	244
Amortisation and impairment			
At 1 January 2015	105	127	232
Amortisation expense	–	15	15
Disposal of business	(105)	–	(105)
At 31 December 2015	–	142	142
Carrying amount			
At 31 December 2015	–	102	102
At 31 December 2014	35	67	102

The goodwill related to the purchase of the Memory Sticks division which was acquired to expand sales in the Memory Sticks division. The goodwill was sold along with the rest of the division in December 2015.

Research and development expenditure is amortised on a straight-line basis over a period of 12 years and represents the cost of designing products currently being sold by the Company.

Amortisation expense for the year and last year are included in administrative expenses.

13. Tangible assets (property, plant and equipment)

	Freehold land and buildings	Plant and equipment	Finance lease equipment	Total
	£'000	£'000	£'000	£'000
Cost or valuation				
At 1 January 2015	720	516	96	1,332
Additions	–	387	100	487
Disposal of business	–	(295)	–	(295)
Other disposals	–	(64)	–	(64)
Revaluation	127	–	–	127
At 31 December 2015	847	544	196	1,587

	Freehold land and buildings £'000	Plant and equipment £'000	Finance lease equipment £'000	Total £'000
Accumulated depreciation				
At 1 January 2015	17	197	13	227
Charge	17	135	24	176
Disposal of business	–	(115)	–	(115)
Other disposals	–	(58)	–	(58)
Revaluation	(17)	–	–	(17)
At 31 December 2015	17	159	37	213
Carrying amount				
At 31 December 2015	830	385	159	1,374
At 31 December 2014	703	319	83	1,105

The analysis of the cost or valuation at 31 December 2015 and 2014 of the above assets is as follows:

	Land and buildings £'000	Plant and equipment £'000	Finance lease equipment £'000	Total £'000
At 31 December 2015				
At cost	–	544	196	740
At valuation	847	–	–	847
	847	544	196	1,587
At 31 December 2014				
At cost	–	516	96	612
At valuation	720	–	–	720
	720	516	96	1,332

Freehold property was revalued as at 1 December 2015 to £848,000 by Turner & Co, Chartered Surveyors who are independent of the Company and have experience of valuing similar properties. The property has been valued on an open market existing use basis. If freehold property were included in the balance sheet on an historical cost basis, then the carrying amount would be £690,000 (2014 – £704,000).

14. Stocks

	2015 £'000	2014 (as restated) £'000
Raw materials	337	378
Work in progress	158	165
Finished goods	585	312
	1,080	855

The amount of stock recognised as an expense in cost of sales during the year is as follows:

Continuing operations	2015 £'000	2014 (as restated) £'000
Carrying amounts of stock sold	2,852	1,524

Discontinued operations	2015 £'000	2014 (as restated) £'000
Carrying amounts of stocks sold	1,603	1,130

There are no write-downs or reversals of write-downs of inventories in 2015 or 2014.

15. Debtors

	2015 £'000	2014 (as restated) £'000
Trade debtors	1,442	1,081
Allowance for doubtful debts	(54)	(60)
	1,388	1,021
Amount due from a director (note 16)	13	6
Other debtors	3	15
Prepayments	95	169
	1,499	1,211

Included above are amounts due from a related party of £26,587 (2014: nil) (see note 26).

16. Amount due from a director

Director	Term of loan	Balance at 31.12.15 £'000	Balance at 31.12.14 £'000	Maximum amount outstanding during the year £'000
Raymond Chard	Unsecured, no repayment terms and interest free	13	6	13

17. Creditors: amounts falling due within one year

	2015 £'000	2014 (as restated) £'000
Bank loans and overdrafts (Note 19)	87	118
Trade creditors	803	963
Taxation and social security	266	231
Obligations under finance leases (Note 20)	47	31
Derivative financial instruments (Note 23)	7	8
Accruals	104	182
	1,314	1,533

18. Creditors: amounts falling due after more than one year

	2015 £'000	2014 (as restated) £'000
Bank loans (Note 19)	259	168
Amounts owed to group undertakings	427	–
Obligations under finance leases (Note 20)	84	41
	770	209

19. Borrowings

	2015 £'000	2014 (as restated) £'000
Current		
Bank loans – secured	8	8
Bank overdrafts, repayable on demand – unsecured	79	110
	87	118
Non-current		
Bank loans – secured	259	168
	346	286
Carrying amount repayable		
Wholly within five years	87	177
Not wholly repayable within five years	259	109
	346	286

	Carrying amount repayable	
Wholly within five years	87	177
Not wholly repayable within five years	259	109
	346	286

Bank loans comprise:	Maturity date	Effective interest rate	Carrying amount 2015 £'000	2014 (as restated) £'000
Floating rate bank loan	2019	4.8%	95	111
Floating rate bank loan	2017	4.0%	–	57
Floating rate bank loan	2024	4.8%	164	–
Total bank loans			259	168

The bank loans are secured by the Company's land and buildings which have a carrying value of £830,200 (2014: £703,500). Bank loans include a new loan drawn down in March 2015 of £164,000, however capital repayments will not commence until March 2018. The loan bears interest at the prime rate less 0.2% and is repayable over 15 years. The directors consider that the carrying amounts of the bank loans and overdraft approximate to their fair value.

20. Obligations under finance leases

Finance leases relate to manufacturing and warehousing equipment as well as motor vehicles. The Company has options to purchase the equipment for a nominal amount at the conclusion of the lease agreements. Interest rates underlying all obligations under finance leases are fixed at respective contract rates ranging from 8.9% to 12.9% (2014: 9.9% to 12.9%).

	Minimum lease payments		Present value of minimum lease payments	
	2015	2014 (as restated)	2015	2014 (as restated)
	£'000	£'000	£'000	£'000
Within one year	58	38	47	31
Between one and five years	95	45	84	41
	153	83	131	72
Less: future finance charges	(22)	(11)	–	–
Present value of lease obligations	131	72	131	72
Included in the financial statements as:				
Current obligations under finance leases			47	31
Non-current obligations under finance leases			84	41
			131	72

The finance leases are secured by the lessors' title to the leased assets which have a carrying value of £159,500 (2012: £82,600).

The directors consider that the carrying amount of the obligations under finance leases approximate to their fair value.

21. Other provisions

	2015	2014 (as restated)
	£'000	£'000
Provision for faulty Ethernet cards		
Balance at 1 January	–	–
Provision made during the year	120	–
Balance at 31 December	120	–

The provision for faulty Ethernet cards represents the directors' best estimate of the present value of the cost to the Company due to the recall and replacement of faulty Ethernet cards.

The expected time period of each claim is up to 2 years. At the lapse of the time period, the provision will be adjusted to Profit & loss account.

22. Called up share capital

	No. of shares	Called up share capital £'000	Share premium £'000
Issued and fully paid:			
Ordinary shares of par value of £1 each			
At 1 January 2014, 31 December 2014 and 1 January 2015	875,000	875	70
Shares issued in year	35,000	35	17
At 31 December 2015	910,000	910	87

During the year, 35,000 ordinary shares of £1.00 each were issued fully paid for cash at £1.50.

The holders of ordinary shares are entitled to receive dividends as declared from time to time and are entitled to one vote per share at meetings of the Company. All ordinary shares rank equally with regard to the Company's residual assets.

Called-up share capital represents the nominal value of shares that have been issued.

The share premium reserve contains the premium arising on issue of equity shares, net of issue expenses.

23. Reserves

	Capital contribution £'000	Property revaluation reserve £'000	Profit & loss account £'000	Total £'000
At 1 January 2014	–	–	124	124
Profit for the year	–	–	417	417
At 31 December 2014 and 1 January 2015	–	–	541	541
Loan from parent	89	–	–	89
Gain on revaluation of land and buildings	–	145	–	145
Deferred taxation	–	(25)	–	(25)
Profit for the year	–	–	542	542
At 31 December 2015	89	120	1,083	1,292

The profit and loss reserve includes all current and prior retained period profits and losses.

24. Financial instruments

	2015 £'000	2014 (as restated) £'000
Financial instruments that are debt instruments measured at amortised cost:		
Trade debtors	1,388	1,021
Other debtors	3	15
Cash at bank and in hand	502	4

	2015	2014 (as restated)
Financial liabilities measured at fair value through profit and loss:		
Forward foreign currency contracts	8	8
Financial liabilities measured at amortised cost:		
Bank overdraft	87	110
Bank loans	267	176
Finance leases and hire purchase contracts	131	72
Trade creditors	803	963

Derivative financial instruments – forward contracts

The company enters into foreign currency contracts to mitigate the exchange rate risk for certain foreign currency debtors. At 31 December 2015, the outstanding contract matures within 3 months (2014: 3 months) of the year end. The company is committed to sell €200,000 and received a fixed sterling amount (2014: €175,000).

The forward currency contracts are measured at fair value using quoted forward exchange rates.

25. Operating leases

The total future minimum lease payments under non-cancellable operating leases are payable as follows:

	2015 £'000	2014 (as restated) £'000
Within one year	405	394
After one year but within five years	777	1,019
	1,182	1,413

26. Parent undertaking and related parties

The immediate and ultimate parent undertaking is Manufacturing Company Parent Limited, which prepares group financial statements. Copies can be obtained from 20 The Strand, London EC14 2HA.

Amounts owed by a director are disclosed in note 16.

During the year the Company made sales of £115,100 on agreed terms to a subsidiary of a company that is owned by the wife of Mr Raymond Chard. The amount due from that company at 31 December 2013 is shown in note 15. The company was not a related party in 2014.

Key management personnel compensation

The remuneration of directors and other members of key management during the year was as follows:

	2015 £'000	2014 (as restated) £'000
Short-term benefits	295	270
Post employment benefits	254	46
	549	316

27. Employer Pension Scheme

The company is operating a defined contribution scheme. During the year the company contributed £300K (2014: £75K).

28. Transition to FRS 102

This is the first year that the company has presented its results under FRS 102. The last financial statements under previous UK GAAP were for the year ended 31 December 2014 and the date of transition to FRS 102 was 1 January 2014. Set out below are the changes in accounting policies which reconcile profit for the financial year ended 31 December 2014 and the total equity as at 1 January 2014 and 31 December 2014 between UK GAAP as previously reported and under FRS 102 in these financial statements.

Reconciliation of equity

	31 December 2014	1 January 2014
	£'000	£'000
Under UK GAAP – as previously reported	1,508	1,093
Derivative financial instruments	(8)	(13)
Holiday pay accrual	(10)	(7)
Deferred tax impact of adjustments		
Derivative financial instruments	(2)	(3)
Holiday pay accrual	(2)	(1)
Under FRS 102	1,486	1,069

Reconciliation of profit and loss for the year ended 31 December 2014

	31 December 2014
	£'000
Under UK GAAP – as previously reported	415
Derivative financial instruments	5
Holiday pay accrual	(3)
Deferred tax impact of adjustments	
Derivative financial instruments	1
Holiday pay accrual	(1)
Under FRS 102	417

Derivative financial instruments

The company's derivative financial instruments comprise forward foreign currency contracts. FRS 102 requires derivative financial instruments to be recognised at fair value. Previously under UK GAAP the company did not recognise these instruments in the financial statements. Accordingly at transition a liability of £12,820 was recognised and a gain of £4,898 was recognised in the profit and loss account for the year ended 31 December 2014. A liability of £7,922 was recognised at that date.

Holiday pay accrual

Prior to applying FRS 102, the company did not make provision for holiday pay which comprises holiday earned but not taken prior to the year-end. FRS 102 requires short term employee benefits to be charged to the profit and loss account as the employee service is received. This has resulted in the company recognising a liability for holiday pay of £7,310 on transition to FRS 102.

The provision at 31 December 2014 increased to £10,350 so the effect on profit for the year ended 31 December 2014 is an additional expense of £3,040.

Deferred tax

The company has accounted for deferred taxation on transition as follows:

(a) Derivative financial instruments – Deferred tax of £2,564 has been recognised at 20% on the liability recognised on transition at 1 January 2014. In the year ended 31 December 2014 the company has recognised a credit of £980 in the profit and loss account in respect of the reduction in the value of the derivative liability recognised in the profit and loss account.

(b) Holiday pay accrual – Deferred tax of £1,462 has been recognised at 20% on the liability recognised on transition at 1 January 2014. In the year ended 31 December 2014 the company has recognised a charge of £608 in the profit and loss account in respect of the increase in the holiday pay accrual.

29. General information

Manufacturing Company Limited is a limited company incorporated in England and has its registered office and principal place of business at Sound House, Sea View, Plymouth, PL1 2CD.

The principal activity of the Company is the manufacture and supply of computer components. The manufacture of Memory Sticks drives was discontinued in the current year.

Appendix B   FRS 102 Disclosure checklist

FRS 102 ACCOUNTS

This checklist is for a company or LLP preparing accounts in accordance with the full disclosure requirements of FRS 102, not taking account of the lesser disclosure available in company law for small companies. Exemptions available to eligible companies or LLPs applying the reduced disclsoure framework are marked with an 'R'. They are also listed in Appendix 10.

This checklist includes disclosures that apply to companies and LLPs. Those disclosures that only apply to companies are marked with a 'C' and those that only apply to LLPs with a 'L'.

Disclosures shown by this checklist should be marked with a 'Y' to indicate Yes correct disclosure, a 'N' for No incorrect disclosure and 'NA' for Not Applicable.

The references to legislation and financial reporting standards shown in this checklist are as follows:

s = Companies Act 2006 section number.

R-C = Accounts Regulations for Companies in SI 2008/410 The Large and Medium-sized Companies and Groups (Accounts and Reports) Regulations 2008 as amended by SI 2015/980 The Companies, Partnerships and Groups (Accounts and Reports) Regulations 2015.

R-L = Accounts Regulations for LLPs in SI 2008/1913 The Large and Medium-sized Limited Liability Partnerships (Accounts) Regulations 2008 as amended by SI 2016/575 The Limited Liability Partnerships, Partnerships and Groups (Accounts and Audit) Regulations 2016.

FRS 102 = FRS 102 The Financial Reporting Standard applicable in the UK and the Republic of Ireland.

SORP = Statement of Recommended Practice – Accounting by Limited Liability Partnerships (2014).

This checklist consists of a main checklist and 11 appendices. The main checklist should be completed on all companies and LLPs. Each appendix should only be completed if applicable. The appendices are as follows:

1. A parent not preparing group accounts.

2. A parent preparing group accounts.

3. Statement of cash flows.

4. Share based payment.

5. Defined benefit plans.

6. Agriculture.

7. Financial institution.

8. Funding commitments.

9. Transition to FRS 102.

10. Reduced disclosure framework.

11. Strategic report with supplementary material.

COMPLETION

I have completed the checklist in accordance with our procedures.

I am satisfied that the answers given to the questions in this checklist are correct and that all significant matters have been adequately documented through comments and supporting working papers.

I confirm that this checklist (and supporting working papers, if any) contains sufficient documentation for review and evidence purposes.

Name: _____

Date: _____

Signature: _____

Client:		Year-end:

Main checklist

			Reference	Y, N, N/A	C L	R

1 **DIRECTORS' REPORT/STRATEGIC REPORT/MEMBERS' REPORT**

Directors' report requirements

1.01 The directors' report for a financial year must state:

    (a) the names of the persons who, at any time during the financial year, were directors of the company; and   s416(1)a   ☐ C

    (b) the amount (if any) that the directors recommend should be paid by way of dividend.   s416(3)   ☐ C

1.02 Where the company is a parent company and prepares consolidated accounts:

    (a) the directors' report must be a consolidated report (a 'group directors' report') relating to the company and its subsidiary undertakings included in the consolidation;   s415(2)   ☐ C

    (b) a group directors' report may, where appropriate, give greater emphasis to the matters that are significant to the company and its subsidiary undertakings included in the consolidation, taken as a whole; and   s415(3)   ☐ C

    (c) In relation to a group directors' report, (a) and (b) should be completed with references to the company being treated as references to the group.   s417(9)   ☐ C

1.03 Disclose particulars of any important post-balance sheet events affecting the company (and subsidiary undertakings).   R-C Sch 7.7(1)a   ☐ C

1.04 Give an indication of the likely future developments in the business of the company (and subsidiary undertakings).   R-C Sch 7.7(1)b   ☐ C

1.05 Give an indication of any research and development activities of the company (and subsidiary undertakings).   R-C Sch 7.7(1)c   ☐ C

1.06 Unless the company is an unlimited company, give an indication of the existence of branches of the company outside the UK.   R-C Sch 7.7(1)d   ☐ C

1.07 If the company employs more than an average monthly number of 250 UK employees, give a statement describing:

    (a) the policy during the year in respect of disabled persons regarding consideration to applications for employment, continuing their employment and their training, career development and promotion; and   R-C Sch 7.10(3)   ☐ C

    (b) the action taken during the year to introduce, maintain or develop arrangements in connection with employees, in respect of the provision of information, consultation, involvement in performance and awareness of factors affecting the company.   R-C Sch 7.11(3)   ☐ C

Political donations

1.08 Where the company is not itself the wholly owned subsidiary of a UK incorporated company and has made any donation to any EU political party, other EU political organisation or independent election candidate, or incurred any political expenditure, and it does not have subsidiaries which have made such contributions, and the amount of the donation or expenditure, or the aggregate amount of all such donations, exceeds £2,000 disclose: R-C Sch 7.3(2)

		Reference	Y, N, N/A	C L	C	R

(a) the name of each EU political party, other EU political organisation or independent election candidate to whom any such donation has been made; — C

(b) the total amount given to that party, organisation or candidate by way of such donations in the financial year; and — C

(c) the total amount of political expenditure incurred within the financial year. — C

1.09 Where the company is not itself the wholly owned subsidiary of a UK incorporated company and any of the company's subsidiaries have made any donation to any EU political party, other EU political organisation or independent election candidate, or incurred any political expenditure, and the total amount of any such donations or expenditure (or both) made or incurred in that year by the company and the subsidiaries between them exceeds £2,000, the company must disclose in respect of it and its subsidiaries: — R-C Sch 7.3(3)

(a) the name of each EU political party, other EU political organisation or independent election candidate to whom any such donation has been made; — C

(b) the total amount given to that party, organisation or candidate by way of such donations in the financial year; and — C

(c) the total amount of political expenditure incurred within the financial year. — C

1.10 Where the company is not itself the wholly owned subsidiary of a UK incorporated company and the company has made any contribution to a non-EU political party, and it does not have any subsidiaries which have made such contributions, disclose: — R-C Sch 7.4(1)

(a) a statement of the amount of the contribution; or — C

(b) where the company has made two or more such contributions in the year, a statement of the total amount of the contributions. — C

[Guidance]
Contribution, in relation to an organisation, means:
(a) any gift of money to the organisation (whether made directly or indirectly);
(b) any subscription or other fee paid for affiliation to, or membership of, the organisation; or
(c) any money spent (otherwise than by the organisation or a person acting on its behalf) in paying any expenses incurred directly or indirectly by the organisation.
Non-EU political party means any political party which carries on, or proposes to carry on, its activities wholly outside the EU member states.
(SI 2008/410-L Sch 7.4(3)&(4))

1.11 Where any of the company's subsidiaries have made any contribution to a non-EU political party, disclose the total amount of the contributions made in the year by the company and the subsidiaries between them. — R-C Sch 7.4(2) — C

		Reference	Y, N, N/A	C L	R

Other areas of the Directors' report

1.12 In relation to the use of financial instruments by a company and by its subsidiary undertakings, the directors' report must contain an indication of: R-C Sch 7.6

   (a) the financial risk management objectives and policies of the company and its subsidiary undertakings included in the consolidation, including the policy for hedging each major type of forecasted transaction for which hedge accounting is used; and   ☐ C

   (b) the exposure of the company and its subsidiary undertakings included in the consolidation to price risk, credit risk, liquidity risk and cash flow risk.   ☐ C

This is unless such information is not material for the assessment of the assets, liabilities, financial position and profit or loss of the company and its subsidiary undertakings included in the consolidation.   ☐ C

1.13 Where a company has chosen to set out in the strategic report information required to be stated in the directors' report: R-C Sch 7.1A

   (a) state in the directors' report that it has done so; and   ☐ C

   (b) specify the information concerned.   ☐ C

1.14 Include a statement of directors' responsibilities either as part of the directors' report or as a separate statement. This statement should include the following points: Bulletin-2010/2

   (a) that the directors are responsible for preparing the Directors' Report and the financial statements in accordance with applicable law and regulations and in accordance with United Kingdom Generally Accepted Accounting Practice;   ☐ C

   (b) that company law requires the directors must not approve the financial statements unless they are satisfied that they give a true and fair view of the state of affairs of the company and of the profit or loss of the company for that period;   ☐ C

   (c) that in preparing the financial statements the directors are required to:

      (i) select suitable accounting policies and then apply them consistently;   ☐ C

      (ii) make judgements and accounting estimates that are reasonable and prudent;   ☐ C

      (iii) state whether applicable accounting standards have been followed, subject to any material departures disclosed and explained in the financial statements; and   ☐ C

   NB. Does not apply to small and medium-sized companies.

      (iv) prepare the financial statements on the going concern basis unless it is inappropriate to presume that the company will continue in business.   ☐ C

   (d) that the directors are responsible for keeping adequate accounting records that are sufficient to show and explain the company's transactions and disclose with reasonable accuracy at any time the financial position of the company and that enable them to ensure that the financial statements comply with the Companies Act;   ☐ C

   (e) that the directors are responsible for safeguarding the assets of the company and hence for taking reasonable steps for the prevention and detection of fraud and other irregularities; and   ☐ C

	Reference	*Y, N, N/A*	*C L*	*R*

(f)   that, where appropriate, the directors are responsible for the maintenance and integrity of the corporate and financial information included on the company's website. It is important to bear in mind that legislation in the United Kingdom governing the preparation and dissemination of financial statements may differ from legislation in other jurisdictions. | | □ | C

[Guidance]
The requirements of FRC Bulletin 2010/2 (Revised March 2012) are persuasive rather than prescriptive; however they do represent best practice, hence they are included in this checklist.

1.15   The directors' report must contain a statement to the effect that, in the case of each of the persons who are directors at the time when the report is approved, the following applies: s418(2)

(a)   so far as each director is aware, there is no relevant audit information (information needed by the company's auditors in connection with preparing their report) of which the company's auditors are unaware; and   □ C

(b)   each director has taken all the steps that he ought to have taken as a director in order to make himself aware of any relevant audit information and to establish that the company's auditors are aware of that information.   □ C

1.16   A statement must be made where a qualifying third party indemnity provision is, at the time the report is approved, or was, at any time during the financial year, in force for the benefit of one or more directors of the company or of an associated company.   s236(1)   □ C

1.17   The name of the director or secretary who has signed the directors' report on behalf of the board of directors to indicate their approval of the report.   s419(1)   □ C

[Guidance]
If a copy of the directors' report is sent to Companies House this copy does not have to be signed by that director or secretary.

Strategic report requirements

1.18   The strategic report for a financial year must contain:

(a)   a fair review of the company's business;   s414C(2)a   □ C

(b)   a description of the principal risks and uncertainties facing the company;   s414C(2)b   □ C

(c)   the review required is a balanced and comprehensive analysis, consistent with the size and complexity of the business, of:

    (i)   the development and performance of the business of the company during the financial year; and   s414C(3)a   □ C

    (ii)   the position of the company's business at the end of that year;   s414C(3)b   □ C

(d)   the review must, to the extent necessary for an understanding of the development, performance or position of the company's business, include:

    (i)   analysis using financial key performance indicators; and   s414C(4)a   □ C

    (ii)   where appropriate, analysis using other key performance indicators, including information relating to environmental matters and employee matters;   s414C(4)b   □ C

			Reference	Y, N, N/A	C L	R

[Guidance]
Key performance indicators means factors by reference to which the development, performance or position of the business of the company can be measured effectively.

NB. Medium-sized companies need not comply in so far as they relate to non-financial information. (CA 06 Co. s.414C(6))

(e)	the report may also contain such of the matters otherwise required to be disclosed in the directors' report as the directors consider are of strategic importance to the company;	s414C(11)	☐	C
(f)	the report must, where appropriate, include references to, and additional explanations of, amounts included in the company's annual accounts;	s414C(12)	☐	C
(g)	in relation to a group strategic report, references to the company should be treated as references to the undertakings included in the consolidation;	s414C(13)	☐	C
(h)	nothing in this section requires the disclosure of information about impending developments or matters in the course of negotiation if the disclosure would, in the opinion of the directors, be seriously prejudicial to the interests of the company.	s414C(14)	☐	C
1.19	The name of the director or secretary who has signed the strategic report on behalf of the board of directors to indicate their approval of the report.	s414D	☐	C

LLP Members' report

1.20	The LLP should disclose the following information:			
(a)	the principal activities of the LLP and its subsidiary undertakings;	SORP-30	☐	L
(b)	any significant changes during the year;	SORP-30	☐	L
(c)	the existence of any branches outside the UK;	SORP-30	☐	L
(d)	the identity of anyone who was a designated member during the year;	SORP-30	☐	L
(e)	the overall policy of the LLP regarding members' drawings; and	SORP-30, 69	☐	L
(f)	the policy of the LLP regarding subscription and repayment of members' capital.	SORP-30, 69	☐	L

[Guidance]
The disclosures required by LLP SORP (2014), paragraphs 30 and 69, may now be disclosed anywhere in the annual report. Although not a statutory requirement, a separate Members' Report offers one possible vehicle for such communication. (LLP SORP (2014)-31)

1.21	The statement of members' responsibilities, when stating that the financial statements comply with the Companies Act 2006, should add 'as applied to limited liability partnerships by the Limited Liability Partnerships (Accounts and Audit) (Application of Companies Act 2006) Regulations 2008'.	SI 2008/1911-3(2)b	☐	L

2   AUDITOR'S REPORTS

2.01	An ISA style report in accordance with FRC Bulletin 2010/2 (Revised March 2012).	Bulletin-2010/2	☐

[Guidance]
The requirements of FRC Bulletin 2010/2 (Revised March 2012) are persuasive rather than prescriptive; however they do represent best practice, hence they are included in this checklist.

2.02	The term 'Independent Auditor' should be used in the title of the auditors' report.	Bulletin-2010/2	☐

			Reference	Y, N, N/A	C L	R
2.03		The auditor's report should include an explanation of the respective responsibilities of directors and auditor.	ISA 700-15, Bulletin-2010/2	☐		
2.04		The auditor's report shall either:	s495(2)b, ISA 700-16, Bulletin-2010/2			
	(a)	Cross refer to a 'Statement of the Scope of an Audit' that is maintained on the FRC's website; or		☐		
	(b)	Cross refer to a 'Statement of the Scope of an Audit' that is included elsewhere within the Annual Report; or		☐		
	(c)	Include the description of the scope of an audit included in Bulletin 2010/2 (Revised March 2012), as amended by FRC Bulletin 4 (April 2014).		☐		
2.05		The auditor's report must:				
	(a)	have an appropriate title;	ISA 700-12	☐		
	(b)	be appropriately addressed;	ISA 700-13	☐		
	(c)	identify the financial statements of the entity that have been audited, including the date of, and period covered by, the financial statements and include an introduction identifying the financial reporting framework that has been applied in their preparation;	s495(2)a, ISA 700-14	☐		
	(d)	include a statement that those charged with governance are responsible for the preparation of the financial statements and a statement that the responsibility of the auditor is to audit and express an opinion on the financial statements in accordance with applicable legal requirements and International Standards on Auditing (UK and Ireland);	ISA 700-15	☐		
	(e)	state that those Standards on Auditing require the auditor to comply with the APB's Ethical Standards for Auditors;	ISA 700-15	☐		
	(f)	state clearly whether in the auditor's opinion the annual accounts have been properly prepared in accordance with the requirements of this Act;	s495(3)c, ISA 700-17	☐		
	(g)	state in particular whether the annual accounts give a true and fair view, in accordance with the relevant financial reporting framework:	ISA 700-18			
		(i) in the case of an individual balance sheet, of the state of affairs of the company as at the end of the financial year;	s495(3)a(i)	☐		
		(ii) in the case of an individual profit and loss account, of the profit or loss of the company for the financial year;	s495(3)a(ii)	☐		
		(iii) in the case of group accounts, of the state of affairs as at the end of the financial year and of the profit or loss for the financial year, of the undertakings included in the consolidation as a whole, so far as concerns members of the company;	s495(3)a(iii)	☐		
		(iv) have been properly prepared in accordance with the relevant financial reporting framework;	s495(3)b	☐		
	(h)	state whether, in his opinion, based on the work undertaken in the course of the audit:				
		(i) the information given in the strategic report (if any) and the directors' report is consistent with the financial statements; and	s496(a)(i)	☐	C	
		(ii) any such strategic report and the directors' report have been prepared in accordance with applicable legal requirements;	s496(a)(ii)	☐	C	
	(i)	state whether, in the light of the knowledge and understanding of the company and its environment obtained in the course of the audit, he has identified material misstatements in the strategic report (if any) and the directors' report;	s496(b)	☐	C	
	(j)	if applicable, give an indication of the nature of each of the misstatements referred to in (i) above.	s496(c)	☐	C	

		Reference	Y, N, N/A	C L	R
(k)	be either unqualified or qualified;	s495(4)a	☐		
(l)	include a reference to any matters to which the auditor wishes to draw attention by way of emphasis without qualifying the report;	s495(4)b	☐		
(m)	when an auditor is engaged to issue an opinion on the compliance of the financial statements with an additional financial reporting framework the second opinion shall be clearly separated from the first opinion on the financial statements, by use of an appropriate heading;	ISA 700-19	☐		
(n)	when the auditor addresses other reporting responsibilities within the auditor's report on the financial statements, the opinion arising from such other responsibilities shall be set out in a separate section of the auditor's report following the opinion[s] on the financial statements;	ISA 700-21	☐		
(o)	if the auditor is required to report on certain matters by exception the auditor shall describe its responsibilities under the heading 'Matters on which we are required to report by exception' and incorporate a suitable conclusion in respect of such matters;	ISA 700-22	☐		
(p)	the date of an auditor's report on a reporting entity's financial statements shall be the date on which the auditor signed the report expressing an opinion on those financial statements;	ISA 700-23	☐		
(q)	the auditor shall not sign, and hence date, the report earlier than the date on which all other information contained in a report of which the audited financial statements form a part have been approved by those charged with governance and the auditor has considered all necessary available evidence;	ISA 700-24	☐		
(r)	the report shall name the location of the office where the auditor is based; and	ISA 700-25			
(s)	the auditor's report shall state the name of the auditor and be signed and dated.	ISA 700-26	☐		
2.06	The auditor must state in his report if in his opinion:		☐		
(a)	adequate accounting records have not been kept by the company;	s498(2)a	☐		
(b)	proper returns adequate for their audit have not been received from branches not visited by him;	s498(2)a	☐		
(c)	the company's accounts are not in agreement with the accounting records and returns; and	s498(2)b	☐		
(d)	all the information and explanations necessary for the purposes of his audit have not been obtained.	s498(3)	☐		
2.07	If the disclosure requirements concerning directors' emoluments are not complied with in the annual accounts, the auditor must give the required particulars in his report, so far as he is reasonably able to do so.	s498(4)	☐	C	
2.08	If the audit report is qualified and the company proposes to make a distribution, the auditor must state whether, in his opinion, the matter in respect of which his report is qualified is material for determining whether the distribution would contravene the Companies Act provisions. This may form part of the normal audit report, or be submitted subsequently in writing.	s837(4)a	☐	C	
2.09	Include the Bannerman wording as recommended by ICAEW Technical Release Audit 1/03.		☐		
2.10	For the name of auditor, state:				
(a)	where the auditor is not an individual, the name of the senior statutory auditor;	s503(3), s505(1)a	☐		
(b)	where the auditor is not an individual, the name of the audit firm; and	s505(1)a	☐		
(c)	that the firm are Statutory Auditors.	s505	☐		

	Reference	*Y, N,*	*C*	*R*
		N/A	*L*	

[Guidance]
The signed copy of the report issued to the client must be signed personally by the senior statutory auditor in their own name for and on behalf of the firm.

[Guidance]
The copy of the report delivered to Companies House need not be signed (by the senior statutory auditor or the audit firm). Signed copies of the report for other purposes may be signed in the name of the firm by any RI.

2.11   When the prior year's financial statements are not audited, the incoming auditor should state in the auditor's report that the corresponding figures are unaudited.   ISA 700-19   ☐

LLP auditor's report

2.12   The auditor's report, when referring to either Chapter 3 of Part 16 of the Companies Act 2006 or that the financial statements have been prepared in accordance with the requirements of the Companies Act 2006, should add "as applied to limited liability partnerships by the Limited Liability Partnerships (Accounts and Audit) (Application of Companies Act 2006) Regulations 2008".   Bulletin-2010/2   ☐ L

3   FINANCIAL STATEMENTS PRESENTATION

Compliance with FRS 102

3.01   The accounts must disclose any additional information that is necessary to show a true and fair view.   s396(4), FRS 102-3.2   ☐

3.02   An entity whose financial statements comply with FRS 102 shall make an explicit and unreserved statement of such compliance in the notes.   R-C Sch 1.45, R-L Sch 1.45, FRS 102-3.8   ☐

3.03   When an entity departs from a requirement of FRS 102 in accordance with paragraph 3.4, or from a requirement of applicable legislation, it shall disclose the following: s396(5), R-C Sch 1.45, R-L Sch 1.45, FRS 102-3.5

(a)   that management has concluded that the financial statements give a true and fair view of the entity's financial position, financial performance and when required to be presented, cash flows;   ☐

(b)   that it has complied with FRS 102 or applicable legislation, except that it has departed from a particular requirement of this FRS or applicable legislation to the extent necessary to give a true and fair view;   ☐

(c)   the nature and effect of the departure;   ☐

(d)   the treatment that FRS 102 or applicable legislation would require;   ☐

(e)   the reason why that treatment would be so misleading in the circumstances that it would conflict with the objective of financial statements set out in Section 2 of FRS 102; and   ☐

(f)   the treatment adopted.   ☐

3.04   When an entity has departed from a requirement of FRS 102 or applicable legislation in a prior period, and that departure affects the amounts recognised in the financial statements for the current period, it shall disclose: FRS 102-3.6

(a)   the nature of the departure;   ☐

(b)   the treatment that FRS 102 or applicable legislation would require;   ☐

		Reference	Y, N, N/A	C L	R

(c) the reason why that treatment would be so misleading in the circumstances that it would conflict with the objective of financial statements set out in Section 2 of FRS 102; and

(d) the treatment adopted.

Compliance with LLP SORP (2014)

3.05 A note to the financial statements which deals with accounting policies should state that: — SORP-132

(a) the LLP's accounts have been prepared in compliance with the LLP SORP (2014); or — L

(b) detail the areas of non compliance and any reasons therefore. — L

Going concern

3.06 Disclose any material uncertainties related to events or conditions that cast significant doubt upon the entity's ability to continue as a going concern. — FRS 102-3.9

3.07 Where an entity does not prepare financial statements on a going concern basis, it shall disclose: — FRS 102-3.9

(a) that fact;

(b) the basis on which it prepared the financial statements; and

(c) the reason why the entity is not regarded as a going concern.

Frequency of reporting

3.08 When the end of the reporting period changes and the annual financial statements are presented for a period longer or shorter than one year, disclose the following: — FRS 102-3.10

(a) that fact;

(b) the reason for using a longer or shorter period; and

(c) the fact that comparative amounts presented in the financial statements (including the related notes) are not entirely comparable.

Consistency of presentation

3.09 When comparative amounts are reclassified, disclose the following: — R-C Sch 1.7(2), R-L Sch 1.7(2), FRS 102-3.12

(a) the nature of the reclassification;

(b) the amount of each item or class of items that is reclassified; and

(c) the reason for the reclassification.

3.10 If it is impracticable to reclassify comparative amounts, disclose why reclassification was not practicable. — FRS 102-3.13

Comparative information

3.11 Present comparative information in respect of the preceding period: — R-C Sch 1.7(1), R-L Sch 1.7(1), FRS 102-3.14

(a) for all amounts presented in the current period's financial statements; and

(b) for narrative and descriptive information when it is relevant to an understanding of the current period's financial statements.

| | | *Reference* | *Y, N,* | *C* | *R* |
| | | | *N/A* | *L* | |

Materiality and aggregation

3.12   In respect of any individual item of income or expenditure which is of exceptional size or incidence, state:

Reference: R-C Sch 1.69(2), R-L 1.67(2), FRS 102-3.15

    (a)   the amount; ☐

    (b)   the nature; and ☐

    (c)   the effect. ☐

Identification of the financial statements

3.13   Display the following information prominently, and repeat it when necessary for an understanding of the information presented: FRS 102-3.23

    (a)   the name of the reporting entity; ☐

    (b)   any change in its name since the end of the preceding reporting period; ☐

    (c)   whether the financial statements cover the individual entity or a group of entities; ☐

    (d)   the date of the end of the reporting period and the period covered by the financial statements; ☐

    (e)   the presentation currency, as defined in Section 30 of FRS 102; and ☐

    (f)   the level of rounding, if any, used in presenting amounts in the financial statements. ☐

3.14   Disclose the following in the notes:

    (a)   the legal form of the entity, e.g. whether the company is a public or private company and whether it is limited by shares or by guarantee;   FRS 102-3.24, s396(A1) ☐

    (b)   its country of incorporation and, if the UK, the part of the UK in which the company is registered;   FRS 102-3.24, s396(A1) ☐

    (c)   the entity's registered number;   s396(A1) ☐

    (d)   the address of its registered office (or principal place of business, if different from the registered office);   FRS 102-3.24, s396(A1) ☐

    (e)   a description of the nature of the entity's operations, unless this is disclosed in the business review (or similar statement) accompanying the financial statements; and   FRS 102-3.24 ☐

    (f)   a description of the nature of the entity's principal activities, unless this is disclosed in the business review (or similar statement) accompanying the financial statements.   FRS 102-3.24 ☐

    (g)   where appropriate, the fact that the entity is being wound up.   s396(A1) ☐

3.15   The registered number of the entity must be shown in a prominent position on the balance sheet or one of the other documents required to be filed under the Companies Act.   s1068(3)c ☐

Formats

3.16   Disclose in the notes to the accounts the directors' reasons for any change from one format to another.   R-C Sch 1.2(2), R-L Sch 1.2(2) ☐

		Reference	Y, N, N/A	C L	R

LLP Annual report

3.17   The annual report should comprise: SORP-25

(a)   the financial statements;   ☐ L

(b)   a statement of members' responsibilities in relation to the production of financial statements; and   ☐ L

(c)   a report on the financial statements by a registered auditor.   ☐ L

3.18   The financial statements will normally comprise: SORP-26

(a)   either:

     (i)   a single statement of comprehensive income displaying all items of income and expense recognised during the period including those items recognised in determining profit or loss and items of other comprehensive income; or   ☐ L

     (ii)   a separate income statement and a separate statement of comprehensive income;   ☐ L

(b)   a statement of changes in equity;   ☐ L

[Guidance]
In certain circumstances, paragraph 3.18 of FRS 102 allows entities to present a single statement of income and retained earnings in place of the statement of comprehensive income and statement of changes in equity. However, the SORP does not recommend this approach for LLPs as it will be of little benefit to users of LLP financial statements in most cases. (LLP SORP (2015)-26A)

(c)   a statement of cash flows;   ☐ L

(d)   a statement of financial position; and   ☐ L

(e)   notes, comprising a summary of significant accounting policies and other explanatory information.   ☐ L

4   STATEMENT OF FINANCIAL POSITION

Balance sheet formats

4.01   The balance sheet must include the following items, unless there is no amount for that heading in the current and preceding year: R-C Sch 1(Part 1) Section B, R-L Sch 1(Part1) Section B

(a)   Called up share capital not paid.   ☐ C

(b)   Fixed assets.   ☐

(c)   Current assets.   ☐

(d)   Prepayments and accrued income.   ☐

(e)   Creditors: amounts falling due within one year.   ☐

(f)   Creditors: amounts falling due after more than one year.   ☐

(g)   Provisions for liabilities.   ☐

(h)   Accruals and deferred income.   ☐

(i)   Capital and reserves.   ☐

(j)   Minority interests.   ☐

		Reference	Y, N, N/A	C L	R

LLP Members' Interests

4.02   The following should be disclosed separately on the face of the balance sheet:

(a)	loans and other debts due to members (which includes 'loans and other debts due to members' and 'members' capital' in so far as it is classified as a liability);	R-L Sch 1(Part1) Section B, SORP-55	☐	L
(b)	members' other interests, including the following where classified as equity:	R-L Sch 1(Part1) Section B, SORP-55	☐	L
	(i) members' capital;	SORP-55	☐	L
	(ii) revaluation reserve; and	SORP-55	☐	L
	(iii) other reserves.	SORP-55	☐	L

4.03   The following should also be disclosed separately on the face of the balance sheet:

(a)	the net assets of the LLP attributable to members (by including a sub-total of balance sheet items A to I); and	SORP-58	☐	L
(b)	total members' interests' (being the total of items J and K less any amounts due from members in debtors) should be disclosed as a memorandum item.	SORP-58	☐	L

4.04   The following amounts must be shown separately under 'Loans and other debts due to members':

(a)	the aggregate amount of money advanced to the LLP by the members by way of loan;	SORP-66	☐	L
(b)	the aggregate amount of money owed to members by the LLP in respect of profits;	SORP-66	☐	L
(c)	any other amounts;	SORP-66	☐	L
(d)	the aggregate amount of loans and other debts due to members that fall due after one year.	R-L Sch 1.47(f), SORP-65	☐	L

4.05   The amount of debts owing to the LLP by members should be disclosed.   SORP-67   ☐ L

Share Capital

4.06   An entity with share capital shall disclose the following, either in the statement of financial position or in the notes: R-C Sch 1 Section B(12), 1.47(1)(a), FRS 102-4.12

(a)	For each class of share capital:		
	(i) the number of shares allotted/issued and fully paid;	☐	C
	(ii) the number of shares allotted/issued but not fully paid;	☐	C
	(iii) where shares are not fully paid: any amount that has not been called;	☐	C
	(iv) par value per share, or that the shares have no par value;	☐	C
	(v) a reconciliation of the number of shares outstanding at the beginning and at the end of the period;	☐	C
	[Guidance] *This reconciliation need not be presented for prior periods.*		
	(vi) the rights, preferences and restrictions attaching to that class including restrictions on the distribution of dividends and the repayment of capital;	☐	C

		Reference	Y, N, N/A	C L	R

	(vii)	shares in the entity held by the entity or by its subsidiaries, associates, or joint ventures; and		☐	C
	(viii)	shares reserved for issue under options and contracts for the sale of shares, including the terms and amounts;		☐	C
(b)		A description of each reserve within equity.		☐	C
4.07		If the company has allotted any shares during the year, state the classes of shares allotted and, for each class, the number allotted, their aggregate nominal value and the consideration received.	R-C Sch 1.48	☐	C
4.08		Where redeemable shares are in issue, show the earliest and latest dates of redemption, whether redemption is mandatory, or at the company's or shareholders' option, and the amount, and any premium payable.	R-C Sch 1.47(2)	☐	C
4.09		For options on unallotted shares, show the number, amount and description of shares under option, the price and the period during which the option is exercisable.	R-C Sch 1.49	☐	C

Entity without share capital

| 4.10 | An entity without share capital, such as a partnership or trust, shall disclose information equivalent to that required by paragraph 4.12(a) of FRS 102, showing changes during the period in each category of equity, and the rights, preferences and restrictions attaching to each category of equity. | FRS 102-4.13 | ☐ | | |

Purchase of and interest in own shares

4.11		Where a company purchases any of its own shares during the year, disclose in the directors' report:	R-C Sch 7.9		
	(a)	the number and nominal value of the shares purchased;		☐	C
	(b)	the aggregate amount of the consideration paid;		☐	C
	(c)	the reasons for the purchase; and		☐	C
	(d)	the percentage of the called up share capital which the shares represent.		☐	C
4.12		Where a company acquires (other than purchases) its shares through a nominee, or provides financial assistance to purchase its shares, such that it obtains a beneficial interest, or a lien or charge over its shares, state in the directors' report:	R-C Sch 7.9		
	(a)	the number and nominal value of the shares acquired or charged during the year;		☐	C
	(b)	the maximum number and nominal value of the shares held by or on behalf of the company or charged at any time of the year; and		☐	C
	(c)	the percentage of the called up share capital which the shares represent.		☐	C
4.13		Where shares are disposed of or cancelled, having been acquired by the company, or having been acquired by another person such that the company obtains a beneficial interest, or having been charged, disclose in the directors' report:	R-C Sch 7.9		
	(a)	the number and nominal value of the shares disposed of or cancelled; and		☐	C
	(b)	the amount or value of the consideration in each case.		☐	C
4.14		Where any of the shares have been charged, state in the directors' report the amount of the charge in each case.	R-C Sch 7.9	☐	C

		Reference	Y, N, N/A	C L	R

General

4.15 If, at the reporting date, an entity has a binding sale agreement for a major disposal of assets, or a disposal group, disclose the following information: — FRS 102-4.14

   (a)   a description of the asset(s) or the disposal group; — ☐

   (b)   a description of the facts and circumstances of the sale; and — ☐

   (c)   the carrying amount of the assets or, for a disposal group, the carrying amounts of the underlying assets and liabilities. — ☐

4.16 Give particulars where the original purchase price or production cost of an asset is unknown, and the earliest known cost is used in its place. — R-C Sch 1.64(1), R-L Sch 1.61 — ☐

[Guidance]
All fixed assets should be included at purchase price or production cost (SI 2008/1913 L Sch 1.17(1); SI 2008/410 L Sch 1.17(1)), unless revalued.

4.17 Disclose details where a distribution by an investment company reduces its net assets to below the amount of its called-up share capital and undistributable reserves. — s833, R-C Sch 1.75 — ☐ C

4.18 If a material illegal dividend was paid during the year or is proposed, disclose the fact that it is illegal, and the consequences (i.e. that it may be repayable by the shareholders). — ☐ C

[Guidance]
This disclosure is not required by legislation but it does need to be considered in order to ensure that the accounts give a true and fair view.

5 STATEMENT OF COMPREHENSIVE INCOME AND INCOME STATEMENT

Single-statement approach

5.01 Include, in the statement of comprehensive income, line items that present the following amounts for the period: — FRS 102-5.5A

   (a)   an entity should present the components of other comprehensive income recognised as part total comprehensive income outside profit or loss as permitted or required by FRS 102, either:

      (i)   net of related tax effects; or — ☐

      (ii)   before the related tax effects with one amount shown for the aggregate amount of income tax relating to those components. — ☐

   (b)   its share of the other comprehensive income of associates and jointly controlled entities accounted for by the equity method; and — ☐

   (c)   total comprehensive income. — ☐

5.02 Present the following items as allocations of profit or loss and other comprehensive income in the statement of comprehensive income for the period: — FRS 102-5.6

   (a)   profit or loss for the period attributable to:

      (i)   non-controlling interest; and — ☐

      (ii)   owners of the parent. — ☐

   (b)   total comprehensive income for the period attributable to:

      (i)   non-controlling interest; and — ☐

      (ii)   owners of the parent. — ☐

		Reference	Y, N, N/A	C L	R

Two-statement approach

5.03   If an entity presents profit or loss in an income statement, it shall present the profit or loss for the period attributable to: FRS 102-5.7A

(a)   non-controlling interest; and

(b)   owners of the parent.

Requirements applicable to both approaches

5.04   Every profit and loss account must show:

(a)   the amount of a company's/LLPs profit or loss before taxation; and   R-C Sch 1.6, R-L Sch 1.6

(b)   the amount of profit or loss attributable to non-controlling interests.   R-C Sch 6.17(3)   C

5.05   Disclose on the face of the income statement (or statement of comprehensive income if presented) an amount comprising the total of: FRS 102-5.7D

(a)   the post-tax profit or loss of discontinued operations; and

(b)   the post-tax gain or loss attributable to the impairment or on the disposal of the assets or disposal group(s) constituting discontinued operations.

5.06   A line-by-line analysis shall be presented in the income statement (or statement of comprehensive income if presented), in a columnar format with columns for each of continuing, discontinued and total.   FRS 102-5.7D

5.07   An entity shall re-present the disclosures by paragraph 5.7D of FRS 102 for prior periods presented in the financial statements so that the disclosures relate to all operations that have been discontinued by the end of the reporting period for the latest period presented.   FRS 102-5.7E

5.08   In the rare circumstances where extraordinary items exist, state the amount and description of each item.   FRS 102-5.9A, 5.10A, 5.10B

LLP Members' Remuneration

5.09   The following should be disclosed on the face of the profit and loss account (or statement of comprehensive income):

(a)   profit or loss for the financial year before members' remuneration and profit shares;   R-L Sch 1, Part 1, Section B SORP-51   L

(b)   members' remuneration charged as an expense; and   SORP-51   L

(c)   profit or loss for the financial year available for discretionary division among members.   SORP-51   L

6   STATEMENT OF CHANGES IN EQUITY AND STATEMENT OF INCOME AND RETAINED EARNINGS

Information to be presented in the statement of changes in equity

6.01   Present a statement of changes in equity showing in the statement: FRS 102-6.3

(a)   total comprehensive income for the period, showing separately:

(i)   the total amounts attributable to owners of the parent; and

(ii)   the total amounts attributable to non-controlling interests;

				Reference	*Y, N, N/A*	*C L*	*R*

(b) for each component of equity, the effects of retrospective application or retrospective restatement recognised in accordance with Section 10 of FRS 102 Accounting Policies, Estimates and Errors; and

☐

(c) for each component of equity, a reconciliation between the carrying amount at the beginning and the end of the period, separately disclosing changes resulting from:

   (i) profit or loss;

☐

   (ii) other comprehensive income;

☐

   (iii) the amounts of investments by owners, showing separately:

     – issues of shares

☐

     – purchase of own share transactions

☐

     – changes in ownership interests in subsidiaries that do not result in a loss of control; and

☐

   (iv) the amounts of dividends and other distributions to owners.

☐

Information to be presented in the statement of income and retained earnings

6.02 Present, in the statement of income and retained earnings, the following items in addition to the information required by Section 5 of FRS 102 Statement of Comprehensive Income and Income Statement: FRS 102-6.5

(a) retained earnings at the beginning of the reporting period;   R-C Sch 1.59(2), R-L Sch 1.57(2) ☐

(b) dividends declared and paid or payable during the period;   R-C Sch 1.43, R-L Sch 1.43 ☐

(c) restatements of retained earnings for corrections of prior period material errors; ☐

(d) restatements of retained earnings for changes in accounting policy; and ☐

(e) retained earnings at the end of the reporting period.   R-C Sch 1.59(2), R-L Sch 1.57(2) ☐

LLP Members' Other interests

6.03 A statement of changes in equity should be presented as a primary statement (paragraph 6.3 of FRS 102) detailing the movements in 'Members' other interests' (balance sheet item K).   SORP-59 ☐ L

6.04 Regarding the reconciliation of members' interests, for each of the items the notes should disclose: SORP-60, 60A

(a) the amount brought forward from the previous year; ☐ L

(b) the change in the year arising from the profit or loss for the financial year available for division among members; ☐ L

(c) any amounts contributed by members during the financial year; ☐ L

(d) any amounts allocated to members during the year; ☐ L

(e) any amounts withdrawn by members or applied on behalf of members during the year; ☐ L

(f) the balance carried forward at the end of the year. ☐ L

		Reference	Y, N, N/A	C L	R

(g) The above reconciliation of members' interests may be presented as a primary statement instead of a statement of changes in equity. Where this option is taken, comparative amounts should be presented by way of the full table relating to the prior period. — □ L

6.05 Additional categories of members' interests or types of movements to those set out above should be disclosed, where this aids clarity or circumstances require it. — SORP-60 — □ L

6.06 Any unallocated profits should appear under 'Other reserves' in 'Members' other interests'. — SORP-61 — □ L

6.07 Where the LLP makes a loss for the financial year that is not allocated to the members, the amount should be deducted from 'Other reserves'. — SORP-61 — □ L

7 STATEMENT OF CASH FLOWS

If the entity prepares a statement of cash flows, complete Appendix 3. — □

8 NOTES TO THE FINANCIAL STATEMENTS

Disclosure of accounting policies

8.01 Disclose the following in the summary of significant accounting policies: — R-C Sch 1.44, R-L Sch 1.44, FRS 102-8.5

(a) the measurement basis (or bases) used in preparing the financial statements; and — □

(b) the other accounting policies used that are relevant to an understanding of the financial statements. — □

[Guidance]
Changes in accounting policy are dealt with in section 10, 'Accounting policies, estimates and errors'.

Information about judgements

8.02 Disclose, in the summary of significant accounting policies or other notes, the judgements, apart from those involving estimations, that management has made in the process of applying the entity's accounting policies and that have the most significant effect on the amounts recognised in the financial statements. — FRS 102-8.6 — □

Information about key sources of estimation uncertainty

8.03 Disclose in the notes information about the key assumptions concerning the future, and other key sources of estimation uncertainty at the reporting date, that have a significant risk of causing a material adjustment to the carrying amounts of assets and liabilities within the next financial year. — FRS 102-8.7 — □

8.04 In respect of those assets and liabilities, the notes shall include details of: — FRS 102-8.7

(a) their nature; and — □

(b) their carrying amount as at the end of the reporting period. — □

			Reference	Y, N, N/A	C L	R

Auditors remuneration

8.05   Small and medium-sized companies/LLPs should disclose the following in respect of auditors' remuneration: SI 2008/489-4(1), (2),(3), SI 2008/1911-38

    (a)   the amount of any remuneration receivable by the company's auditor for the auditing of the accounts;

    (b)   the nature of any benefits in kind;

    (c)   the estimated monetary value of any benefits in kind; and

    (d)   where more than one person has been appointed as a company's auditor during the period: separate disclosure in respect of the remuneration for each such person.

8.06   A medium-sized company/LLP should provide an analysis of total remuneration receivable by the auditor under the following headings: SI 2008/489-4(4), SI 2008/1911-38

    (a)   The auditing of the accounts in question;

    (b)   Assurance services other than auditing of the company's accounts;

    (c)   Tax advisory services; and

    (d)   Other services.

[Guidance]
The statutory instrument does not actually require the disclosure of (b), (c) and (d) in the accounts, but gives the Secretary of State the power to call for this information if it is not disclosed in the accounts, such disclosure being optional.

8.07   A company/LLP that is not small or medium-sized should disclose the following in respect of auditors remuneration: SI 2011/2198-5, SI 2008/1911-38

    (a)   any remuneration receivable by the company's auditor, or an associate of the company's auditor, for the auditing of the accounts;

    (b)   any remuneration receivable for the supply of other services to the company or its associates by:

       (i)   the company's auditor; or

       (ii)   any person who was, at any time during the period to which the accounts relate, an associate of the company's auditor;

    (c)   the nature of any benefits in kind included above; and

    (d)   the estimated monetary value of any such benefits in kind.

8.08   A company/LLP that is not small or medium-sized should give an analysis of the total remuneration under the categories specified below: SI 2011/2198-5, SI 2008/1911-38

    (a)   the auditing of the accounts in question;

    (b)   the auditing of accounts of any associate of the company;

    (c)   audit-related assurance services;

    (d)   taxation compliance services;

    (e)   all taxation advisory services not falling within (d);

		Reference	Y, N, N/A	C L	R
(f)	internal audit services;		☐		
(g)	all assurance services not falling within (b) to (f);		☐		
(h)	All services relating to corporate finance transactions entered into, or proposed to be entered into, by or on behalf of the company or any of its associates not falling within (b) to (g); and		☐		
(i)	All non-audit services not falling within (c) to (h).		☐		

[Guidance]
Where a service could fall within more than one category, it shall be treated as falling within the first mentioned.

8.09	Disclose separately services supplied to:	SI 2008/489-5(4), SI 2008/1911-38	
	(a) the company and its subsidiaries; and		☐
	(b) associated pension schemes.		☐
8.10	Where more than one person has been appointed as a company's auditor during the period to which the accounts relate, separate disclosure is required in respect of the remuneration of each such person and his associates.	SI 2008/489-5(5), SI 2008/1911-38	☐
8.11	Where a company does not disclose information concerning auditor's remuneration because that information is required to be disclosed in the group accounts on a consolidated basis: give a statement to that effect.	SI 2008/489-6(3), SI 2008/1911-38	☐
8.12	A group that is not medium-sized should disclose the above information required by SI 2008 /489.5(1),(2) in respect of auditor's remuneration as if the undertakings included in the consolidation were a single company.	SI 2008/489-6(1), SI 2008/1911-38	☐
8.13	A company, which has entered into a liability limitation agreement with its auditor, must disclose:	SI 2008/489-8	
	(a) its principal terms;		☐ C
	(b) the date of the resolution approving the agreement; and		☐ C
	(c) in the case of a private company, the date of the resolution waiving the need for such approval.		☐ C

[Guidance]
The accounts in which disclosure is required are those for the financial year to which the agreement relates unless the agreement was entered into too late for it to be reasonably practical for the disclosure to be made, in which case disclosure should be made in the company's next following annual accounts.

Other notes

8.14	State the total charge for depreciation or provision in respect of diminution in value and, if appropriate, the amount of any provision for diminution written back.	R-C Sch 1.17, 19 R-L Sch 1.17, 19	☐
8.15	If the company is or has been party to arrangements that are not reflected in its balance sheet, and at the balance sheet date the risks or benefits arising from those arrangements are material, disclosure should be given of:	s410A(2)	
	(a) the nature and business purpose of the arrangements; and		☐
	(b) the financial impact of the arrangements on the company.		☐

[Guidance]
If the company prepares group accounts then the above applies in relation to the group accounts as if the undertakings included in the consolidation were a single company.

		Reference	*Y, N,*	*C*	*R*
			N/A	*L*	

8.16   If the company is a subsidiary undertaking at the year end, disclose:

(a)   the name of the ultimate parent company or body corporate, and (if known to the directors) the country of incorporation (if non-GB); and   R-C Sch 4.9, R-L Sch 2.7

(b)   for the parent undertaking of both the largest and the smallest group for which group accounts are drawn up and of which the company is a member: R-C Sch 4.8, R-L Sch 2.6

     (i)   the name of the parent undertaking;

     (ii)   the name of the country of incorporation (if non-GB), or the principal place of business (if unincorporated); and

     (iii)   the address from which copies of the accounts can be obtained (if available to the public).

8.17   If not shown in the Statement of Changes in Equity, disclose for each class of reserves: R-C Sch 1.43,59(2), R-L Sch 1.43,57(2)

(a)   the amount transferred to or from the reserve during the year;

(b)   the source and application of any such movement;

(c)   the aggregate amount of dividends that the company is liable to pay at the balance sheet date; and

(d)   the aggregate amount of dividends that are proposed before the date of approval of the accounts, and not otherwise disclosed.

9A   CONSOLIDATED FINANCIAL STATEMENTS

A parent preparing group accounts should complete Part 1 of Appendix 2.

9B   INDIVIDUAL FINANCIAL STATEMENTS OF PARENT

A parent not preparing group accounts should complete Appendix 1.

10   ACCOUNTING POLICIES, ESTIMATES AND ERRORS

Disclosure of a change in accounting policy

10.01   When an amendment to an FRS or FRC Abstract has an effect on the current period or any prior period, or might have an effect on future periods, disclose the following: FRS 102-10.13

(a)   the nature of the change in accounting policy;

(b)   for the current period and each prior period presented, to the extent practicable, the amount of the adjustment for each financial statement line item affected;

(c)   the amount of the adjustment relating to periods before those presented, to the extent practicable; and

(d)   an explanation if it is impracticable to determine the amounts to be disclosed in (b) or (c) above.

[Guidance]
Financial statements of subsequent periods need not repeat these disclosures.

		Reference	Y, N, N/A	C L	R

10.02   When a voluntary change in accounting policy has an effect on the current period or any prior period, disclose the following: FRS 102-10.14

(a)   the nature of the change in accounting policy;

(b)   the reasons why applying the new accounting policy provides reliable and more relevant information;

(c)   to the extent practicable, the amount of the adjustment for each financial statement line item affected, shown separately:

     (i)   for the current period;

     (ii)   for each prior period presented;

     (iii)   in the aggregate for periods before those presented; and

(d)   an explanation if it is impracticable to determine the amounts to be disclosed in (c) above.

[Guidance]
Financial statements of subsequent periods need not repeat these disclosures.

Disclosure of a change in estimate

10.03   Disclose the nature of any change in an accounting estimate and the effect of the change on assets, liabilities, income and expense for the current period.   FRS 102-10.18

10.04   If it is practicable to estimate the effect of the change in one or more future periods, then disclose those estimates.   FRS 102-10.18

Disclosure of prior period errors

10.05   Disclose the following about material prior period errors: R-C Sch 1.7(2), R-L Sch 1.7(2), FRS 102-10.23

(a)   the nature of the prior period error;   R-C Sch 1.69(1), R-L Sch 1.67(1)

(b)   for each prior period presented, to the extent practicable, the amount of the correction for each financial statement line item affected;

(c)   to the extent practicable, the amount of the correction at the beginning of the earliest prior period presented; and

(d)   an explanation if it is not practicable to determine the amounts to be disclosed in (b) or (c) above.

[Guidance]
Financial statements of subsequent periods need not repeat these disclosures.

LLP accounting policies   L

10.06   The disclosures should include:

(a)   an indication of the policy applicable where the cash requirements of the business compete with the need to allow cash drawings by members;   SORP-69   L

(b)   any transfers of members' interests from equity to debt (and vice versa) during the period and up to the date the accounts are approved;   SORP-69   L

(c)   the policy under which members contribute or subscribe amounts to the LLP by way of equity or debt;   SORP-69   L

(d)   the policy under which their contributions and subscriptions are repayable by the LLP; and   SORP-69   L

(e)   the policy in respect of post-retirement payments to members.   SORP-92   L

	Reference	Y, N, N/A	C L	R

11   BASIC FINANCIAL INSTRUMENTS

Disclosure of accounting policies for financial instruments

11.01   Disclose, in the summary of significant accounting policies, the measurement basis (or bases) used for financial instruments and the other accounting policies used for financial instruments that are relevant to an understanding of the financial statements.

Reference: R-C Sch 1.44 & 1.56, R-L Sch 1.44 & 1.54, FRS 102-11.40 — R

Statement of financial position – categories of financial assets and financial liabilities

11.02   Disclose the carrying amounts of each of the following categories of financial assets and financial liabilities at the reporting date, in total, either in the statement of financial position or in the notes:

Reference: FRS 102-11.41

(a)   financial assets measured at fair value through profit or loss;   R

(b)   financial assets that are debt instruments measured at amortised cost;   R

(c)   financial assets that are equity instruments measured at cost less impairment;   R

(d)   financial liabilities measured at fair value through profit or loss;   R

(e)   financial liabilities that are not held as part of a trading portfolio and are not derivatives shall be shown separately;   R

(f)   financial liabilities measured at amortised cost; and   R

(g)   loan commitments measured at cost less impairment.   R

11.03   For each class of fixed asset investment disclose the aggregate of:

Reference: R-C Sch 1.51, R-L Sch 1.49

(a)   cost or valuation at the beginning and end of the year;

(b)   additions during the year;

(c)   disposals during the year;

(d)   transfers during the year;

(e)   revaluations during the year;

(f)   accumulated provision for diminution in value at the beginning and end of the year; and

(g)   provision for diminution in value, the amount released on disposals and other adjustments to provision for diminution in value during the year.

[Guidance]
Comparative figures are not required.

11.04   Disclose information that enables users of its financial statements to evaluate the significance of financial instruments for its financial position and performance.

Reference: FRS 102-11.42 — R

11.05   For all financial assets and financial liabilities measured at fair value, disclose the basis for determining fair value, e.g. quoted market price in an active market or a valuation technique.

Reference: FRS 102-11.43 — R

		Reference	Y, N, N/A	C L	R
11.06	When a valuation technique is used, disclose the assumptions applied in determining fair value for each class of financial assets or financial liabilities.	R-C Sch 1.55 (2)(a), R-L Sch 1.53 (2)(a), FRS 102-11.43	☐		
11.07	Where fixed asset investments are included at a valuation which is not market value (e.g. Directors' valuation), state the method used and the reason for adopting it.	R-C Sch 1.32(3), R-L Sch 1.32(3)	☐		
11.08	If a reliable measure of fair value is no longer available for ordinary or preference shares measured at fair value through profit or loss, disclose that fact.	FRS 102-11.44	☐		R

Derecognition ☐

11.09	If an entity has transferred financial assets to another party in a transaction that does not qualify for derecognition, disclose the following for each class of such financial assets:	FRS 102-11.45			
	(a) the nature of the assets;		☐		R
	(b) the nature of the risks and rewards of ownership to which the entity remains exposed; and		☐		R
	(c) the carrying amounts of the assets and of any associated liabilities that the entity continues to recognise.		☐		R

Collateral

11.10	When an entity has pledged financial assets as collateral for liabilities or contingent liabilities, disclose the following:	FRS 102-11.46			
	(a) the carrying amount of the financial assets pledged as collateral; and		☐		R
	(b) the terms and conditions relating to its pledge.		☐		R

Defaults and breaches on loans payable

11.11	For loans payable recognised at the reporting date for which there is a breach of terms or default of principal, interest, sinking fund, or redemption terms that has not been remedied by the reporting date, disclose the following:	FRS 102-11.47			
	(a) details of that breach or default;		☐		R
	(b) the carrying amount of the related loans payable at the reporting date; and		☐		R
	(c) whether the breach or default was remedied, or the terms of the loans payable were renegotiated, before the financial statements were authorised for issue.		☐		R

Items of income, expense, gains or losses

11.12	Disclose the following items of income, expense, gains or losses:	FRS 102-11.48			
	(a) income, expense, net gains or net losses, including changes in fair value, recognised on:				
	(i) financial assets measured at fair value through profit or loss;		☐		R
	(ii) financial liabilities measured at fair value through profit or loss (with separate disclosure of movements on those which are not held as part of a trading portfolio and are not derivatives);		☐		R
	(iii) financial assets measured at amortised cost; and		☐		R
	(iv) financial liabilities measured at amortised cost;		☐		R

			Reference	Y, N, N/A	C L	R

(b) total interest income and total interest expense (calculated using the effective interest method) for financial assets or financial liabilities that are not measured at fair value through profit or loss; and — — R

(c) the amount of any impairment loss for each class of financial asset. A class of financial asset is a grouping that is appropriate to the nature of the information disclosed and that takes into account the characteristics of the financial assets. — — R

Financial instruments at amortised cost

11.13 For any fall in value of a fixed asset investment where a provision has been made, disclose those provisions not shown in the profit and loss account in a note to the accounts, either separately or in aggregate. — R-C Sch 1.19(3), R-L Sch 1.19(3)

11.14 Where a provision in in respect of a fall in value of a fixed asset investment has been written back as it is no longer necessary, disclose those provisions not shown in the profit and loss account in a note to the accounts either separately or in aggregate. — R-C Sch 1.20, R-L Sch 1.20

11.15 For listed current asset investments disclose: — R-C Sch 1.54, R-L Sch 1.52

(a) the aggregate amount;

(b) the aggregate market value if different; and

(c) for each individual investment where the market value in the accounts exceeds the Stock Exchange value, disclose both values.

Debtors and other current assets

11.16 Disclose for each category of debtor any amounts falling due after one year. — R-C Sch 1.9(5), R-L Sch 1.9(3)

11.17 Disclose separately, for each type of assistance, the aggregate amount of any outstanding loans made by the company to provide financial assistance for the purchase of its own shares. — R-C Sch 1.64(2) — C

11.18 Where the amount repayable on any debt owed by the company exceeds the value of the consideration originally received, and the surplus is treated as an asset, it should be subject to annual amortisation, and fully written off before repayment of the debt. If the current amount is not shown separately in the balance sheet, disclose the assets in a note. — R-C Sch 1.25, R-L Sch 1.25

Creditors

11.19 For each item included under 'creditors' in the balance sheet, show: — R-C Sch 1.61(1), R-L Sch 1.59(1)

(a) the total amount falling due after five years and not repayable by instalments; and

(b) for any amounts payable by instalments, the amount of those instalments which are payable after five years.

(c) For each item included in (a) and (b) above state the terms of repayment, and the rate of interest (unless the directors consider that such a note would be of excessive length, when a general indication of repayment terms and interest rates is sufficient). — R-C Sch 1.61(2) (3), R-L Sch 1.59(2) (3)

		Reference	Y, N, N/A	C L	R

11.20 In respect of each item under 'creditors' in the balance sheet: — R-C Sch 1.61(4), R-L Sch 1.59(4)

   (a)   state the total amount secured; and ☐

   (b)   give an indication of the security given. ☐

11.21 Where debentures have been issued during the year, state the class of debentures issued, and for each class, the amount issued and the consideration received. — R-C Sch 1.50(1), R-L Sch 1.48(1) ☐

11.22 Where any debentures are held by a nominee of or trustee for the company, state the nominal and book value of the holdings. — R-C Sch 1.50(2), R-L Sch 1.48(2) ☐

11.23 The amount of any convertible debts, including debenture loans, must be shown separately from other debts or debentures. — R-C Sch 1.9(7), R-L Sch 1.9(5) ☐

11.24 For arrears of fixed cumulative dividends, show the amount and period of arrears for each class of share. — R-C Sch 1.62 ☐ C

Financial instruments at fair value through profit or loss

11.25 For listed fixed asset investments, disclose: — R-C Sch 1.54, R-L Sch 1.52

   (a)   the aggregate amount; ☐

   (b)   the aggregate market value if different; and ☐

   (c)   for each individual investment where the market value in the accounts exceeds the Stock Exchange value, disclose both values. ☐

11.26 An entity, including an entity that is not a company, shall provide the following disclosures only for financial instruments measured at fair value through profit or loss in accordance with paragraph 36(4) of Schedule 1 to the Regulations. This does not include financial instruments held as part of a trading portfolio nor derivatives. The required disclosures are: — FRS 102-11.48A

   (a)   The amount of change, during the period and cumulatively, in the fair value of the financial instrument that is attributable to changes in the credit risk of that instrument, determined either:

      (i)   as the amount of change in its fair value that is not attributable to changes in market conditions that give rise to market risk; or ☐ R

      (ii)   using an alternative method the entity believes more faithfully represents the amount of change in its fair value that is attributable to changes in the credit risk of the instrument; ☐ R

   (b)   The method used to establish the amount of change attributable to changes in own credit risk, or, if the change cannot be measured reliably or is not material, that fact; ☐ R

   (c)   For a financial liability, the difference between the financial liability's carrying amount and the amount the entity would be contractually required to pay at maturity to the holder of the obligation; ☐ R

   (d)   If an instrument contains both a liability and an equity feature, and the instrument has multiple features that substantially modify the cash flows and the values of those features are interdependent (such as a callable convertible debt instrument), the existence of those features; ☐ R

   (e)   If there is a difference between the fair value of a financial instrument at initial recognition and the amount determined at that date using a valuation technique, the aggregate difference yet to be recognised in profit or loss at the beginning and end of the period and a reconciliation of the changes in the balance of this difference; and ☐ R

		Reference	Y, N, N/A	C L	R

(f) Information that enables users of the entity's financial statements to evaluate the nature and extent of relevant risks arising from financial instruments to which the entity is exposed at the end of the reporting period including:

    (i)   the exposures to risk and how they arise;   ☐ R

    (ii) its objectives, policies and processes for managing the risk and the methods used to measure the risk; and   ☐ R

    (iii) any changes in (i) or (ii) from the previous period.   ☐ R

11.27 For each category of financial instrument or other asset measured at fair value, the fair value of the assets in that category and the changes in value: R-C Sch 1.55(2)(b), R-L Sch 1.53(2)(b)

    (i)   included directly in the profit and loss account; or   ☐

    (ii) credited to or (as the case may be) debited from the fair value reserve.   ☐

11.28 For each class of derivatives, disclose the extent and nature of the instruments, including significant terms and conditions that may affect the amount, timing and certainty of future cash flows.   ☐

11.29 Where any amount is transferred to or from the fair value reserve during the financial year, there must be stated in tabular form: R-C Sch 1.55(3), R-L Sch 1.53(3)

    (a) the amount of the reserve as at the date of the beginning of the financial year and as at the balance sheet date respectively;   ☐

    (b) the amount transferred to or from the reserve during that year; and   ☐

    (c) the source and application respectively of the amounts so transferred.   ☐

11.30 Disclose the treatment for taxation purposes of amounts credited or debited to the fair value reserve.   R-C Sch 1.41(2), R-L Sch 1.41(2)   ☐

Interests in unlimited companies and partnerships

11.31 For all qualifying undertakings at the year end, state: R-C Sch 4.7(2)

    (a) the name and legal form of the undertaking; and   ☐ C

    (b) the address, whether GB or non-GB, of the undertaking's registered office or head office (if no registered office).   ☐ C

[Guidance]
This information need not be given if it is not material. (SI 2008/410-L Sch 4.7(4))

11.32 For a qualifying partnership, state either:

    (a) that a copy of the latest accounts has been, or is to be, appended to a copy of the company's accounts filed with the registrar; or   R-C Sch 4.7(3)a   ☐ C

    (b) the name of at least one body corporate where the accounts of the undertaking have been, or are to be, consolidated; unless   R-C Sch 4.7(3)b   ☐ C

    (c) If a qualifying partnership is being dealt with in the group accounts prepared by a member of the partnership established under the law of an EC member state, or parent undertaking of such a member, the disclosures required by (b) above do not need to be given. The company's accounts must instead disclose that advantage has been taken of the exemption under Regulation 7 of the Partnerships and Unlimited Companies (Accounts) Regulations 1993.   R-C Sch 4.7(5)   ☐ C

		Reference	Y, N, N/A	C L	R

[Guidance]

A qualifying undertaking is either a qualifying company or partnership where:

(a) *a qualifying company is an unlimited company incorporated in Great Britain where each of its members is:*

    (i) *a limited company; or*

    (ii) *another unlimited company, or a Scottish firm, each of whose members is a limited company;*

(b) *a qualifying partnership is one where each of its members is:*

    (i) *a limited company; or*

    (ii) *an unlimited company, or a Scottish firm, each of whose members is a limited company.*

LLP members' interests

		Reference		C/L	
11.33	The notes to the accounts should explain where amounts in 'Loans and other debts due to members' (other than members' capital classified as debt) would rank in relation to other creditors who are unsecured in the event of a winding-up.	SORP-63	☐	L	
11.34	Details of any protection afforded to creditors (other than members) in the event of a winding-up, which is legally enforceable and cannot be revoked solely by a decision of the members.	SORP-63	☐	L	
11.35	Disclose what restrictions or limitations exist on the ability of the members to reduce the amount of 'Members' other interests', or state that there are no such restrictions.	SORP-63	☐	L	

12   OTHER FINANCIAL INSTRUMENTS ISSUES

		Reference			R
12.01	Disclose the following separately for each type of hedging relationship described in paragraph 12.19 of FRS 102:	FRS 102-12.27			
	(a) a description of the hedge;		☐		R
	(b) a description of the financial instruments designated as hedging instruments and their fair values at the reporting date; and		☐		R
	(c) the nature of the risks being hedged, including a description of the hedged item.		☐		R

[Guidance]

FRS 102 paragraph 12.19

There are three types of hedging relationships:

(a) *fair value hedge: a hedge of the exposure to changes in fair value of a recognised asset or liability or an unrecognised firm commitment, or a component of any such item, that are attributable to a particular risk and could affect profit or loss;*

(b) *cash flow hedge: a hedge of the exposure to variability in cash flows that is attributable to a particular risk associated with all, or a component of, a recognised asset or liability (such as all or some future interest payments on variable rate debt) or a highly probable forecast transaction, and could affect profit or loss; and*

(c) *hedge of a net investment in a foreign operation.*

		Reference			R
12.02	If an entity uses hedge accounting for a fair value hedge it shall disclose the following:	FRS 102-12.28			
	(a) the amount of the change in fair value of the hedging instrument recognised in profit or loss for the period; and		☐		R
	(b) the amount of the change in fair value of the hedged item recognised in profit or loss for the period.		☐		R

			Reference	Y, N, N/A	C L	R

12.03   If an entity uses hedge accounting for a cash flow hedge it shall disclose the following: FRS 102-12.29

    (a)   the periods when the cash flows are expected to occur and when they are expected to affect profit or loss;   `[    ]`   R

    (b)   a description of any forecast transaction for which hedge accounting had previously been used, but which is no longer expected to occur;   `[    ]`   R

    (c)   the amount of the change in fair value of the hedging instrument that was recognised in other comprehensive income during the period;   `[    ]`   R

    (d)   the amount, if any, that was reclassified from equity to profit or loss for the period; and   `[    ]`   R

    (e)   the amount, if any, of any excess of the fair value of the hedging instrument over the change in the fair value of the expected cash flows that was recognised in profit or loss for the period.   `[    ]`   R

12.04   If an entity uses hedge accounting for a net investment in a foreign operation it shall disclose separately: FRS 102-12.29A

    (a)   the amounts recognised in other comprehensive income in accordance with paragraph 12.24(a), being the portion of the gain or loss on the hedging instrument that is determined to be an effective hedge; and   `[    ]`   R

    (b)   the amounts recognised in profit or loss in accordance with paragraph 12.24(b), being the ineffective portion.   `[    ]`   R

13   INVENTORIES

13.01   Disclose the following: FRS 102-13.22

    (a)   the accounting policies adopted in measuring inventories, including the cost formula used;   R-C Sch 1.44, R-L Sch 1.44   `[    ]`

    (b)   the total carrying amount of inventories;   `[    ]`

    (c)   the carrying amount in classifications appropriate to the entity;   `[    ]`

    (d)   the amount of inventories recognised as an expense during the period;   `[    ]`

    (e)   impairment losses recognised or reversed in profit or loss; and   `[    ]`

    (f)   the total carrying amount of inventories pledged as security for liabilities.   `[    ]`

13.02   Where the stated value of inventory is materially different from the replacement cost, disclose the amount of the difference.   R-C Sch 1.28(3), R-L Sch 1.28(3)   `[    ]`

14   INVESTMENTS IN ASSOCIATES

A parent with associates preparing group accounts, and an investor with associates that is not a parent, should complete Part 2 in Appendix 2.   `[    ]`

15   INVESTMENTS IN JOINT VENTURES

A parent with joint ventures preparing group accounts, and a venturer that is not a parent, should complete Part 3 in Appendix 2.   `[    ]`

		Reference	Y, N, N/A	C L	R

16   INVESTMENT PROPERTY

16.01   Disclose the methods and significant assumptions applied in determining the fair value of investment property.

R-C Sch 1.44, R-L Sch 1.44, FRS 102-16.10(a)

16.02   Disclose the extent to which the fair value of investment property (as measured or disclosed in the financial statements) is based on a valuation by an independent valuer who holds a recognised and relevant professional qualification and has recent experience in the location and class of the investment property being valued.

FRS 102-16.10(b)

16.03   If the fair value is not based on a valuation by an independent valuer, disclose that fact.

FRS 102-16.10(b)

16.04   Disclose the existence and amounts of restrictions on the realisability of investment property or the remittance of income and proceeds of disposal.

FRS 102-16.10(c)

16.05   Disclose contractual obligations to purchase, construct or develop investment property or for repairs, maintenance or enhancements.

FRS 102-16.10(d)

16.06   Give a reconciliation between the carrying amounts of investment property at the beginning and end of the period, showing separately:

R-C Sch 1.51, R-L Sch 1.49, FRS 102-16.10(e)

(a)   additions, disclosing separately those additions resulting from acquisitions through business combinations;

(b)   net gains or losses from fair value adjustments;

(c)   transfers to property, plant and equipment when a reliable measure of fair value is no longer available without undue cost or effort;

(d)   transfers to and from inventories and owner-occupied property; and

(e)   other changes.

[Guidance]
This reconciliation need not be presented for prior periods.

	Reference	*Y, N,* *N/A*	*C* *L*	*R*

17   PROPERTY, PLANT AND EQUIPMENT

17.01   Disclose the following for each class of property, plant and equipment:

(a)   the measurement bases used for determining the gross carrying amount;   R-C Sch 1.44, R-L Sch 1.44, FRS 102-17.31   ☐

(b)   the depreciation methods used;   R-C Sch 1.44, R-L Sch 1.44,   ☐

(c)   the useful lives or the depreciation rates used;   FRS 102-17.31   ☐

(d)   a reconciliation of the gross carrying amount and the accumulated depreciation (aggregated with accumulated impairment losses) showing separately: R-C Sch 1.51, R-L Sch 1.49, FRS 102-17.31

(i)   the beginning of the reporting period;   ☐

(ii)   additions;   ☐

(iii)   disposals;   ☐

(iv)   acquisitions through business combinations;   ☐

(v)   revaluations;   ☐

(vi)   transfers to or from investment property if a reliable measure of fair value becomes available or unavailable;   ☐

(vii)   impairment losses recognised or reversed in profit or loss;   ☐

(viii)   depreciation;   ☐

(ix)   other changes; and   ☐

(x)   the end of the reporting period.   ☐

[Guidance]
This reconciliation need not be presented for prior periods.

17.02   Disclose the following: FRS 102-17.32

(a)   the existence and carrying amounts of property, plant and equipment to which the entity has restricted title or that is pledged as security for liabilities; and   ☐

(b)   the amount of contractual commitments for the acquisition of property, plant and equipment.   ☐

17.03   If items of property, plant and equipment are stated at revalued amounts:

(a)   state which items;   R-C Sch 1.34, R-L Sch 1.34   ☐

(b)   disclose the effective date of the revaluation;   R-C Sch 1.52, R-L Sch 1.50, FRS 102-17.32A   ☐

(c)   show the amount of each valuation;   R-C Sch 1.52, R-L Sch 1.50   ☐

(d)   disclose whether an independent valuer was involved;   FRS 102-17.32A   ☐

			Reference	Y, N, N/A	C L	R

(e) disclose the methods and significant assumptions applied in estimating the items' fair values;
    R-C Sch 1.34, R-L Sch 1.34, FRS 102-17.32A

(f) if valued during the year, show the names or qualifications of the valuers and the basis of the valuation; and
    R-C Sch 1.52, R-L Sch 1.50

(g) disclose for each revalued class of property, plant and equipment, the carrying amount that would have been recognised had the assets been carried under the cost model.
    R-C Sch 1.34, R-L Sch 1.34, FRS 102-17.32A

17.04 For land and buildings, disclose the separate amounts for freehold, long leasehold (over 50 years unexpired at the balance sheet date) and short leasehold.
    R-C Sch 1.53, R-L Sch 1.51

18 INTANGIBLE ASSETS OTHER THAN GOODWILL

18.01 Disclose the following for each class of intangible assets:

(a) the useful lives or the amortisation rates used and the reasons for choosing those periods;
    R-C Sch 1.44, R-L Sch 1.44, FRS 102-18.27(a)

(b) the amortisation methods used;
    R-C Sch 1.44, R-L Sch 1.44, FRS 102-18.27(b)

(c) the line item(s) in the statement of comprehensive income (or in the income statement, if presented) in which any amortisation of intangible assets is included; and
    R-C Sch 1.51, R-L Sch 1.49, FRS 102-18.27(d)

(d) a reconciliation of the gross carrying amount and accumulated amortisation (aggregated with accumulated impairment losses) showing separately:
    R-C Sch 1.51, R-L Sch 1.49, FRS 102-18.27

    (i) the beginning of the reporting period;

    (ii) additions, indicating separately those from internal development and those acquired separately;

    (iii) disposals;

    (iv) acquisitions through business combinations;

    (v) revaluations;

    (vi) amortisation;

    (vii) impairment losses;

    (viii) other changes; and

    (ix) the end of the reporting period.

[Guidance]
This reconciliation need not be presented for prior periods.

		Reference	Y, N, N/A	C L	R

18.02   In respect of any individual intangible asset that is material to the entity's financial statements give:

     FRS 102-18.28(a)

     (a)   a description of the asset; ☐

     (b)   the carrying amount; and ☐

     (c)   the remaining amortisation period. ☐

18.03   For intangible assets acquired by way of a grant and initially recognised at fair value: FRS 102-18.28(b)

     (a)   the fair value initially recognised for these assets; and ☐

     (b)   their carrying amounts. ☐

18.04   Disclose the existence and carrying amounts of any intangible assets to which the entity has restricted title or that are pledged as security for liabilities.   FRS 102-18.28(c) ☐

18.05   Where the useful economic life of an intangible asset cannot be reliably estimated and it is being written off over a period not exceeding ten years, disclose: R-C Sch 1.22(4), R-L Sch 1.22(4)

     (a)   the period chosen; and ☐

     (b)   the reason for choosing that period. ☐

18.06   Disclose the amount of any contractual commitments for the acquisition of intangible assets.   FRS 102-18.28(d) ☐

18.07   Disclose the aggregate amount of research and development expenditure recognised as an expense during the period.   FRS 102-18.29 ☐

18.08   If intangible assets are accounted for at revalued amounts, disclose the following:

     (a)   the effective date of the revaluation;   R-C Sch 1.52, R-L Sch 1.50, FRS 102-18.29A(a) ☐

     (b)   whether an independent valuer was involved;   FRS 102-18.29A(b) ☐

     (c)   the amount of each valuation;   R-C Sch 1.52, R-L Sch 1.50 ☐

     (d)   the methods and significant assumptions applied in estimating the assets' fair values;   FRS 102-18.29A(c) ☐

     (e)   if valued during the year, the names or qualifications of the valuers and the basis of the valuation; and   R-C Sch 1.52, R-L Sch 1.50 ☐

     (f)   for each revalued class of intangible assets, the carrying amount that would have been recognised had the assets been carried under the cost model.   FRS 102-18.29A(d) ☐

18.09   For development costs include in the note on accounting policies:

     (a)   the period of write off; and   R-C Sch 1.21(2)(a), R-L Sch 1.21(2)(a) ☐

     (b)   the reason for capitalising.   R-C Sch 1.21(2)(b), R-L Sch 1.21(2)(b) ☐

			Reference	Y, N, N/A	C L	R

18.10   If special circumstances exist to justify why capitalised development costs are not to be treated as a realised loss when determining distributable reserves, state this fact and disclose the special circumstances.   s844(3)

19   BUSINESS COMBINATIONS AND GOODWILL

A parent preparing group accounts containing any business combinations should complete Part 4 in Appendix 2.

20A   LESSEES

Finance leases

20A.01   A lessee shall make the following disclosures for finance leases: FRS 102-20.13

     (a)   for each class of asset, the net carrying amount at the end of the reporting period;

     (b)   the total of future minimum lease payments at the end of the reporting period, for each of the following periods:

         (i)   not later than one year;

         (ii)   later than one year and not later than five years;

         (iii)   later than five years; and

     (c)   a general description of the lessee's significant finance leasing arrangements.

20A.02   Disclose the finance charges on finance leases and hire-purchase agreements.   R-C Sch 1.66(1), R-L Sch 1.63(1)

Operating leases

20A.03   A lessee shall make the following disclosures for operating leases: FRS 102-20.16

     (a)   the total of future minimum lease payments under non-cancellable operating leases for each of the following periods:

         (i)   not later than one year;

         (ii)   later than one year and not later than five years;

         (iii)   later than five years; and

     (b)   lease payments recognised as an expense.

All leases

20A.04   The required description of significant finance and operating leasing arrangements should include a description of unique or unusual provisions of the agreement or terms of the sale and leaseback transactions.   FRS 102-20.35

20B   LESSORS

Finance leases

20B.01   A lessor shall make the following disclosures for finance leases: FRS 102-20.23

     (a)   a reconciliation between the gross investment in the lease at the end of the reporting period, and the present value of minimum lease payments receivable at the end of the reporting period;

	Reference	Y, N, N/A	C L	R

(b) in addition, a lessor shall disclose the gross investment in the lease and the present value of minimum lease payments receivable at the end of the reporting period, for each of the following periods:

    (i) not later than one year; □

    (ii) later than one year and not later than five years; and □

    (iii) later than five years; □

(c) unearned finance income; □

(d) the unguaranteed residual values accruing to the benefit of the lessor; □

(e) the accumulated allowance for uncollectible minimum lease payments receivable; □

(f) contingent rents recognised as income in the period; and □

(g) a general description of the lessor's significant finance leasing arrangements. □

Operating leases

20B.02 A lessor shall disclose the following for operating leases: FRS 102-20.30

(a) the future minimum lease payments under non-cancellable operating leases for each of the following periods:

    (i) not later than one year; □

    (ii) later than one year and not later than five years; and □

    (iii) later than five years; □

(b) total contingent rents recognised as income; and □

(c) a general description of the lessor's significant operating leasing arrangements. □

All leases

20B.03 The required description of significant finance and operating leasing arrangements should include a description of unique or unusual provisions of the agreement or terms of the sale and leaseback transactions.   FRS 102-20.35 □

21   PROVISIONS AND CONTINGENCIES

Provisions

21.01 For each class of provision, a company/LLP shall disclose the following: R-C Sch 1.59(2), R-L Sch 1.57(2), FRS 102-21.14

(a) a reconciliation showing:

    (i) the carrying amount at the beginning and end of the period; □

    (ii) additions during the period, including adjustments that result from changes in measuring the discounted amount; □

    (iii) amounts charged against the provision during the period; and □

    (iv) unused amounts reversed during the period; □

	Reference	Y, N, N/A	C L	R

(b)   a brief description of the nature of the obligation;

(c)   the expected amount of any resulting payments;

(d)   the expected timing of any resulting payments;

(e)   an indication of the uncertainties about the amount or timing of those outflows; and

(f)   the amount of any expected reimbursement, stating the amount of any asset that has been recognised for that expected reimbursement.

[Guidance]
Comparative information for prior periods is not required.

Contingent liabilities

21.02   Disclose, for each class of contingent liability at the reporting date: FRS 102-21.15

(a)   a brief description of the nature of the contingent liability:

(b)   and, when practicable:

    (i)   an estimate of its financial effect;

    (ii)   an indication of the uncertainties relating to the amount or timing of any outflow; and

    (iii)   the possibility of any reimbursement.

(c)   whether any valuable security has been given for the liability; and

(d)   if so, details of the security.

21.03   If it is impracticable to make one or more of these disclosures, that fact shall be stated.   FRS 102-21.15

Contingent assets

21.04   If an inflow of economic benefits is probable (more likely than not) but not virtually certain, an entity shall disclose: FRS 102-21.16

(a)   a description of the nature of the contingent assets at the end of the reporting period; and

(b)   when practicable, an estimate of their financial effect.

21.05   If it is impracticable to make this disclosure, that fact shall be stated.   FRS 102-21.16

Prejudicial disclosures

21.06   In extremely rare cases, disclosure of some or all of the information required can be expected to prejudice seriously the position of the entity in a dispute with other parties on the subject matter of the provision, contingent liability or contingent asset. In such cases, an entity need not disclose all of the information required by these paragraphs insofar as it relates to the dispute,, but shall disclose at least the following.   FRS 102-21.17

(a)   In relation to provisions, give the following information:

    (i)   a table showing the reconciliation required by paragraph 21.14(a) in aggregate, including the source and application of any amounts transferred to or from provisions during the reporting period;

    (ii)   particulars of each provision in any case where the amount of the provision is material; and

    (iii)   the fact that, and reason why, the information required by paragraph 21.14 has not been disclosed.

		Reference	*Y, N, N/A*	*C L*	*R*

(b) In relation to contingent liabilities, give the following information:

    (i) particulars and the total amount of any contingent liabilities (excluding those which arise out of insurance contracts) that are not included in the statement of financial position;

    (ii) state separately for each the total amount of contingent liabilities which are undertaken on behalf of or for the benefit of:

        – any parent or fellow subsidiary of the entity;

        – any subsidiary of the entity; or

        – any entity in which the reporting entity has a participating interest;

    (iii) the fact that, and reason why, the information required by paragraph 21.15 has not been disclosed.   C

(c) In relation to contingent assets, disclose the general nature of the dispute, together with the fact that, and reason why, the information required by paragraph 21.16 has not been disclosed.   C

Guarantees and other financial commitments

21.07 In respect of any charge on the assets of the company/LLP to secure the liabilities of any other person, disclose: R-C Sch 1.63(1), R-L Sch 1.60(1)

    (a) particulars; and

    (b) the amount secured.

21.08 In respect of any of the following not included in the balance sheet: R-C Sch 1.63(2), R-L Sch 1.60(2)

    (a) Financial commitments, disclose:

        (i) particulars; and

        (ii) the total amount.

    (b) Guarantees, disclose:

        (i) particulars including the nature and business purpose; and   FRS 102-21.17A

        (ii) the total amount.

    (c) Contingencies, disclose:

        (i) particulars; and

        (ii) the total amount.

21.09 Give an indication of the nature and form of any variable security given by the company/LLP for each class of: R-C Sch 1.63(3), R-L Sch 1.60(3)

    (a) financial commitments;

    (b) guarantees;

    (c) contingencies.

21.10 Disclose the total amount of any commitments included in financial commitments, guarantees or contingencies concerning pensions.   R-C Sch 1.63(4), R-L Sch 1.60(4)

21.11 Give particulars of pension commitments included in the balance sheet.   R-C Sch 1.63(5), R-L Sch 1.60(5)

21.12 Give separate disclosure of particulars of any commitments relating wholly or partly to pensions payable to past directors/members of the company/LLP.   R-C Sch 1.63(6), R-L Sch 1.60(6)

			Reference	Y, N, N/A	C L	R

21.13   Disclose separately the total amount of any commitments, guarantees and contingencies which are undertaken on behalf of or for the benefit of: R-C Sch 1.63(7), R-L Sch 1.60(7)

    (a)   any parent or fellow subsidiary of the company/LLP;   ☐

    (b)   any subsidiary of the company/LLP; or   ☐

    (c)   any undertaking in which the company/LLP has a participating interest.   ☐

LLP Guarantees

21.14   If the LLP has entered into any guarantee or indemnity with respect to the borrowings of a member or members personally, the existence of such a guarantee or indemnity where material should either: SORP-124

    (a)   be disclosed as a note to the accounts (where it is unlikely that the guarantee or indemnity would be called); or   ☐ L

    (b)   provided for in the primary statements where there is an actual or constructive liability as defined under section 21 of FRS 102 and it is probable that the guarantee or indemnity will be called.   ☐ L

22   LIABILITIES AND EQUITY

Distributions to owners

22.01   An entity shall disclose the fair value of any non-cash assets that have been distributed to its owners during the reporting period, except when the non-cash assets are ultimately controlled by the same parties both before and after the distribution.   FRS 102-22.18   ☐

23   REVENUE

23.01   Disclose: FRS 102-23.30

    (a)   the accounting policies adopted for the recognition of revenue;   R-C Sch 1.44, R-L Sch 1.44   ☐

    (b)   the methods adopted to determine the stage of completion of transactions involving the rendering of services;   R-C Sch 1.44, R-L Sch 1.44   ☐

    (c)   the amount of each category of revenue recognised during the period, showing separately, as a minimum, revenue arising from:

        (i)   the sale of goods;   ☐

        (ii)   the rendering of services;   ☐

        (iii)   interest;   ☐

        (iv)   royalties;   ☐

        (v)   dividends;   ☐

        (vi)   commissions;   ☐

        (vii)   grants; and   ☐

        (viii)   any other significant types of revenue.   ☐

23.02   Where, in the opinion of the directors, the company:

    (a)   has substantially different classes of business, disclose the turnover for each class; and   R-C Sch 1.68(1), R-L Sch 1.65(1)   ☐

		Reference	Y, N, N/A	C L	R

(b) supplies substantially different markets, disclose a geographical analysis of turnover for each market; or — R-C Sch 1.68(2), R-L Sch 1.65(2) — ☐

(c) if, in the directors' opinion, such disclosure would be seriously prejudicial to the company's interest, then disclose this fact and do not disclose the details in (a) and (b) above. — R-C Sch 1.68(5), R-L Sch 1.65(5) — ☐

23.03 Disclose that turnover is the amount derived from the provision of goods/services, and stated after trade discounts, other sales taxes and net of VAT. — s474(1) — ☐

Construction contracts — ☐

23.04 Disclose the following: — FRS 102-23.31

(a) the amount of contract revenue recognised as revenue in the period; — ☐

(b) the methods used to determine the contract revenue recognised in the period; and — ☐

(c) the methods used to determine the stage of completion of contracts in progress. — ☐

23.05 Present: — FRS 102-23.32

(a) the gross amount due from customers for contract work, as an asset; and — ☐

(b) the gross amount due to customers for contract work, as a liability. — ☐

24   GRANTS

24.01 Disclose the accounting policy adopted for grants either based on the performance model or the accrual model. — R-C Sch 1.44, R-L Sch 1.44, FRS 102-24.6(a) — ☐

24.02 Disclose the nature and amounts of grants recognised in the financial statements. — FRS 102-24.6(b) — ☐

24.03 Disclose unfulfilled conditions and other contingencies attaching to grants that have been recognised in income. — FRS 102-24.6(c) — ☐

24.04 Give an indication of other forms of government assistance from which the entity has directly benefited. — FRS 102-24.6(d) — ☐

25   BORROWING COSTS

25.01 Where a policy of capitalisation is adopted, disclose: — FRS 102-25.3A

(a) the amount of borrowing costs capitalised in the period; and — ☐

(b) the capitalisation rate used. — ☐

[Guidance]
No disclosures are required by this section when borrowing costs are not capitalised, but see paragraph 48(b) of section 11 which requires disclosure of total interest expense. — ☐

25.02 Disclose the interest payable and similar charges on:

(a) loans from group undertakings; — R-C Sch 1.9(16), R-L Sch 1.9(14) — ☐

(b) bank loans and overdrafts; and — R-C Sch 1.66(1), R-L Sch 1.63(1) — ☐

(c) other loans. — R-C Sch 1.66(1), R-L Sch 1.63(1) — ☐

		Reference	Y, N, N/A	C L	R

[Guidance]
Interest and other amounts payable should be recognised at an amount
that includes any withholding taxes but excludes any other taxes, such as
attributable tax credits, not payable wholly on behalf of the recipient (29.18 of
FRS 102).

25.03   Disclose the amount of any interest capitalised and included in the production cost of any asset.

Reference: R-C Sch 1.27(3) b, R-L Sch 1.27(3)b   ☐

26   SHARE BASED PAYMENT

If there are any share based payments, complete Appendix 4.   ☐

27   IMPAIRMENT OF ASSETS

27.01   Disclose the following for each class of assets: FRS 102-27.32

    (a)   the amount of impairment losses recognised in profit or loss during the period in which those impairment losses are included;   ☐

    (b)   the line item(s) in the statement of comprehensive income (or in the income statement, if presented) in which those impairment losses are included;   ☐

    (c)   the amount of reversals of impairment losses recognised in profit or loss during the period; and   ☐

    (d)   the line item(s) in the statement of comprehensive income (or in the income statement, if presented) in which those impairment losses are reversed.   ☐

27.02   Disclose the information required by the paragraph above for each of the following classes of asset: FRS 102-27.33

    (a)   inventories;   ☐

    (b)   property, plant and equipment (including investment property accounted for by the cost method);   ☐

    (c)   goodwill;   ☐

    (d)   intangible assets other than goodwill;   ☐

    (e)   investments in associates; and   ☐

    (f)   investments in joint ventures.   ☐

27.03   Disclose a description of the events and circumstances that led to the recognition or reversal of the impairment loss.   FRS 102-27.33A   ☐

28A   DIRECTORS'/MEMBERS' REMUNERATION & EMPLOYEE BENEFITS (EXCLUDING DEFINED BENEFIT PENSION PLANS)

Directors' emoluments

28A.01   Disclose for directors' qualifying services (being services as a director of the company and services while director of the company as director of any of its subsidiary undertakings or otherwise in connection with the management of the affairs of the company or any of its subsidiary undertakings):

	Reference	Y, N, N/A	C L	R

(a) the aggregate amount of emoluments paid to or receivable by directors (including 'golden hellos', taxable expense allowances, monetary value of benefits and amounts paid to connected parties for directors' services); — R-C Sch 5.1(1)a — [ ] C

(b) the aggregate amount of money and the net value of other assets received and receivable by directors (other than share options) under long-term incentive schemes; and — R-C Sch 5.1(1)c — [ ] C

(c) the aggregate value of any company contributions paid, or treated as paid, to a money purchase pension scheme. — R-C Sch 5.1(1)d — [ ] C

28A.02 Disclose the number of directors to whom retirement benefits are accruing : — R-C Sch 5.1(2)

(a) under money purchase schemes; and — [ ] C

(b) under defined benefit schemes. — [ ] C

28A.03 Unlisted companies must disclose the number of directors: — R-C Sch 5.1(3)b

(a) who exercised share options; and — [ ] C

(b) in respect of whose qualifying services shares were received or receivable under long term incentive schemes. — [ ] C

28A.04 Where aggregates under Sch 5.1(1)(a) and (c) but excluding Sch 5.1(1)(d) total £200,000 or more, disclose: — R-C Sch 5.2(1)

(a) the amount of that total attributable to the highest-paid director; and — [ ] C

(b) the amount of any money purchase pension contributions paid or payable in respect of the highest-paid director. — [ ] C

28A.05 Where the £200,000 limit is exceeded, and the highest-paid director has performed qualifying services during the year by reference to which the rate or amount of any defined benefits will be calculated, show: — R-C Sch 5.2(2)

(a) the amount at the end of the year of his accrued pension; and — [ ] C

(b) where applicable the amount at the end of the year of his accrued lump sum. — [ ] C

28A.06 Where the £200,000 limit is exceeded, unlisted companies must state whether: — R-C Sch 5.2(3)

(a) the highest paid director exercised any share options; and — [ ] C

(b) any shares were received or receivable by the highest-paid director in respect of qualifying services under a long term incentive scheme. — [ ] C

[Guidance]
A nil statement is not required if the director is not involved in any such transactions. (SI 2008/410 L Sch 5.2(4))

28A.07 Disclose the aggregate amount of any retirement benefits in excess of those to which the directors were entitled on the date the benefits first became available paid to or receivable by:

(a) directors; — R-C Sch 5.3(1) — [ ] C

(b) past directors; — R-C Sch 5.3(1) — [ ] C

(c) disclose the nature of any non-cash benefits. — R-C Sch 5.3(4) — [ ] C

[Guidance]
Any excess paid or payable without recourse to additional contributions, or paid or payable to all pensionable members of the scheme need not be disclosed. (SI 2008/410-L Sch 5.3(2))

				Reference	Y, N, N/A	C L	R

28A.08 Disclose the aggregate amount of any compensation for loss of office. — R-C Sch 5.4(1) — [ ] C

Include any non-cash benefits and disclose the nature of any non-cash compensation. — R-C Sch 5.4(4) — [ ] C

[Guidance]
Include amounts paid or payable in consideration of or in connection with a director's retirement from office, and in the case of breach of contract, any award or settlement. (SI 2008/410-L Sch 5.4(3))

28A.09 Disclose the amount of any sums paid/payable to unconnected third parties for directors' services (including amounts received from the company, subsidiary undertakings and others). — R-C Sch 5.5(1)&(2) — [ ] C

28A.10 Disclose the nature of non-cash benefits included in the sums paid/payable. — R-C Sch 5.5(1)&(2) — [ ] C

LLP Members' remuneration

28A.11 The basis on which each element of remuneration (as defined) has been treated in the accounts should be disclosed and explained by note. — SORP-52 — [ ] L

28A.12 Where it is considered that it will assist in an understanding of the financial performance of the LLP, members' remuneration charged as an expense should be further analysed within the notes to the financial statements. — SORP-54 — [ ] L

28A.13 The average number of members of the LLP during the financial year must be stated. — R-L Sch 1.66(1) — [ ] L

28A.14 Where the amount of profit for the year before members' remuneration and profit shares exceeds £200,000:

(a) the amount of profit (including remuneration) that is attributable to the member with the largest entitlement to profit (including remuneration) should be disclosed. The identity of this member need not be disclosed; and — R-L Sch 1.66(3), SORP-71, — [ ] L

(b) when determining the disclosable amount, the LLP should take account of all the relevant factors and disclose the policy by which the amount was arrived at. — SORP-72 — [ ] L

28A.15 Post-employment benefits awarded to members that are based on the member's salary under an employment contract should be accounted for as required by FRS 102, section 28 Employee Benefits. — SORP-75 — [ ] L

[Guidance]
Where members are not employees, section 28 of FRS 102 does not apply (LLP SORP (2015)-75)

28A.16 Where an LLP has an obligation to provide retirement benefits to members that is unfunded then disclose the following:

(a) Amounts recognised in respect of current members should be charged to the profit and loss account (or statement of comprehensive income) within 'Members remuneration charged as an expense'; — SORP-88 — [ ] L

(b) The recognition of and changes in the liability for post-retirement payments to or in respect of current members and to or in respect of former members should be shown separately; — SORP-88 — [ ] L

(c) The change in the liability in respect of former members should be expensed in the relevant expense item (that is, not in members' remuneration) in the profit and loss account (or statement of comprehensive income); — SORP-88 — [ ] L

			Reference	Y, N, N/A	C L	R

(d) The change in the liability in respect of current members should be charged to the profit and loss account (or statement of comprehensive income) within 'Members' remuneration charged as an expense'; — SORP-88 — ☐ L

(e) The liability for post-retirement payments to or in respect of current members and to or in respect of former members should be shown separately; — SORP-89 — ☐ L

(f) The liability in respect of former members should be shown in the balance sheet under 'Provisions for liabilities' or 'Creditors', as appropriate, as 'Post-retirement payments to former members'; — SORP-89 — ☐ L

(g) The liability in respect of current members should be shown separately, if material, as a component of 'Loans and other debts due to members'; — SORP-89 — ☐ L

(h) In the year in which a member retires, a transfer should be made between the balance in respect of current members and the balance in respect of former members; — SORP-89 — ☐ L

(i) Where the liability has been discounted (as required by FRS 102, section 21 where the effect is material), the unwinding of the discount should be presented as follows: — SORP-90

   (i) where it relates to former members: next to the interest cost line in the profit and loss account (or statement of comprehensive income); — ☐ L

   (ii) where it relates to current members it should be included in 'Members' remuneration charged as an expense'; — ☐ L

(j) Additional annuities granted after the date of a member's retirement should be recognised in full in the profit and loss account (or statement of comprehensive income) within operating profit as soon as the award is granted to the former member. — SORP-91 — ☐ L

28A.17 Where tax (whether current or deferred) to be paid on members' remuneration is a personal liability of the members, it falls within 'Members' interests' on the balance sheet. It should not appear in the profit and loss account (or statement of comprehensive income). — SORP-95 — ☐ L

Employees

28A.18 State the total average monthly number of employees, analysed by categories. — s411(1)(1A) — ☐

28A.19 Disclose separately the aggregate amounts for the year of wages and salaries, social security costs and other pension costs. — s411(5) — ☐

28A.20 Give particulars of any pension commitments: — R-C Sch 1.63(4), R-L Sch 1.60(4)

(a) provided for in the accounts; — ☐

(b) not provided for in the accounts; and — ☐

(c) included in (a) and (b) above which relate to pensions payable to past directors. — ☐

Defined contribution plans

28A.21 Disclose the amount recognised in profit or loss as an expense for defined contribution plans. — FRS 102-28.40 — ☐

		Reference	Y, N, N/A	C L	R

28A.22 If an entity treats a defined benefit multi-employer plan as a defined contribution plan because sufficient information is not available to use defined benefit accounting, it shall: FRS 102-28.40A

  (a) disclose the fact that it is a defined benefit plan: ☐

  (b) disclose the reason why it is being accounted for as a defined contribution plan, along with any available information about the plan's surplus or deficit and the implications, if any, for the entity; ☐

  (c) include a description of the extent to which the entity can be liable to the plan for other entities' obligations under the terms and conditions of the multi-employer plan; and ☐

  (d) disclose how any liability recognised in accordance with paragraph 28.11A of FRS 102 has been determined. ☐

Other long-term benefits

28A.23 For each category of other long-term benefits provided to employees, disclose: FRS 102-28.42

  (a) the nature of the benefit; ☐

  (b) the amount of the obligation; and ☐

  (c) the extent of funding at the reporting date. ☐

Termination benefits

28A.24 For each category of termination benefits provided to employees, disclose: FRS 102-28.43

  (a) the nature of the benefit; ☐

  (b) the accounting policy; ☐

  (c) the amount of the obligation; and ☐

  (d) the extent of funding at the reporting date. ☐

28B **EMPLOYEE BENEFITS (DEFINED BENEFIT PLANS)**

If there are defined benefit plans, complete Appendix 5. ☐

29 **INCOME TAX**

29.01 Disclose information that enables users of the financial statements to evaluate the nature and financial effect of the current and deferred tax consequences of recognised transactions and other events.   FRS 102-29.25 ☐

29.02 Disclose separately the major components of tax expense (income). Such components of tax expense (income) may include: FRS 102-29.26

  (a) current tax expense (income);   R-C Sch 1.67(2)(a), R-L Sch 1.64(2)(a) ☐

  (b) any relief for overseas taxation;   R-C Sch 1.67(2)(b), R-L Sch 1.64(2)(b) ☐

  (c) any adjustments recognised in the period for current tax of prior periods; ☐

  (d) the amount of deferred tax expense (income) relating to the origination and reversal of timing differences; ☐

		Reference	Y, N, N/A	C L	R

(e) the amount of deferred tax expense (income) relating to changes in tax rates or the imposition of new taxes;

(f) adjustments to deferred tax expense (income) arising from a change in the tax status of the entity or its shareholders; and

(g) the amount of tax expense (income) relating to changes in accounting policies and material errors.

29.03 Disclose the following separately: — FRS 102-29.27

(a) the aggregate current and deferred tax relating to items that are recognised as items of other comprehensive income or equity;

(b) a reconciliation between:

(i) the tax expense (income) included in profit or loss; and

(ii) the profit or loss before tax multiplied by the applicable tax rate;

(c) the amount of the net reversal of deferred tax liabilities expected to occur during the year beginning after the reporting period together with a brief explanation for the expected reversal;

(d) the amount of the net reversal of deferred tax assets expected to occur during the year beginning after the reporting period together with a brief explanation for the expected reversal;

(e) an explanation of changes in the applicable tax rate(s) compared with the previous reporting period;

(f) the amount of deferred tax liabilities at the end of the reporting period for each type of timing difference;

(g) the amount of deferred tax assets at the end of the reporting period for each type of timing difference;

(h) the amount of unused tax losses and tax credits;

(i) the expiry date, if any, of timing differences, unused tax losses and unused tax credits; and

(j) in the circumstances described in paragraph 29.14 (different tax rates apply where a profits are distributed) of FRS 102, an explanation of the nature of the potential income tax consequences that would result from the payment of dividends to its shareholders.

29.04 State the amount of UK income tax (as opposed to corporation tax). — R-C Sch 1.67(2)(c), R-L Sch 1.64(2)(c)

29.05 Disclose for overseas taxation the charge in respect of profits, income and (so far as charged to revenue) capital gains. — R-C Sch 1.67(2)(d), R-L Sch 1.64(2)(d)

29.06 Disclose any special circumstances that affected the tax charge or credit for the current period, and quantify the effects. — R-C Sch 1.67(1), R-L Sch 1.64(1)

29.07 Disclose any special circumstances that may affect future periods, and quantify the effects. — R-C Sch 1.67(1), R-L Sch 1.64(1)

29.08 State the tax treatment of any amounts transferred to or from the revaluation reserve. — R-C Sch 1.35(6), R-L Sch 1.35(3)

29.09 Disclose the amount of any provision for deferred taxation separately from the amount of any provision for other taxation. — R-C Sch 1.60, R-L Sch 1.58

	Reference	*Y, N,* *N/A*	*C* *L*	*R*

30   **FOREIGN CURRENCY TRANSLATION**

30.01   Disclose the following: FRS 102-30.25

     (a)   the amount of exchange differences recognised in profit or loss during the period, except for those arising on financial instruments measured at fair value through profit or loss; and

     (b)   the amount of exchange differences arising during the period and classified in equity at the end of the period.

30.02   Disclose the currency in which the financial statements are presented.   FRS 102-30.26

30.03   When the presentation currency is different from the functional currency: FRS 102-30.26

     (a)   state that fact;

     (b)   disclose the functional currency; and

     (c)   disclose the reason for using a different presentation currency.

[Guidance]
In the case of a group, functional currency refers to that of the parent.

30.04   When there is a change in the functional currency of either the reporting entity or a significant foreign operation: FRS 102-30.27

     (a)   disclose that fact; and

     (b)   disclose the reason for the change in functional currency.

31   **HYPERINFLATION**

31.01   Disclose the fact that financial statements and other prior period data have been restated for changes in the general purchasing power of the functional currency.   FRS 102-31.15(a)

31.02   Disclose the identity and level of the price index at the reporting date and changes during the current reporting period and the previous reporting period.   FRS 102-31.15(b)

31.03   Disclose the amount of gain or loss on monetary items.   FRS 102-31.15(c)

32   **EVENTS AFTER THE END OF THE REPORTING PERIOD**

32.01   Give particulars of the proposed appropriation of profit, including dividend declared where relevant, or, where applicable, particulars of the actual appropriation of the profits or treatment of the losses.   R-C Sch 1.72B, R-L Sch 1.70B, FRS 102-32.8

32.02   An entity shall disclose on the balance sheet: s414(1&2), FRS 102-32.9

     (a)   the date when the financial statements were approved by the board of directors/all the members;

     (b)   the name of the director/designated member who signed on behalf of the board/members; and

     (c)   if a copy of the accounts is sent to Companies House, that copy must include the signature of that director/designated member.

32.03   If the entity's owners or others have the power to amend the financial statements after issue, disclose that fact.   FRS 102-32.9

		Reference	Y, N, N/A	C L	R

Non-adjusting events after the end of the reporting period

32.04 Disclose the following for each material non-adjusting event after the end of the reporting period:

R-C Sch 1.72A, R-L Sch 1.70A, FRS 102-32.10

    (a)   the nature of the event; and ☐

    (b)   an estimate of its financial effect or a statement that such an estimate cannot be made. ☐

33 RELATED PARTY DISCLOSURES

Controlling entity disclosures

33.01 Where the reporting entity is controlled by another party (including individuals), disclose:

R-C Sch 4.8&9, R-L Sch 2.6&7, FRS 102-33.5, SORP-131

    (a)   the relationship; ☐

    (b)   the name of that party; ☐

    (c)   if different, the name of the ultimate controlling party; ☐

    (d)   if the name of (b) or (c) is not known, disclose that fact. ☐

33.02 If neither the parent nor the ultimate controlling party produces financial statements available for public use, disclose the name of the next most senior parent that does so (if any).

FRS 102-33.5 ☐

Disclosure of key management personnel compensation

33.03 Disclose key management personnel compensation in total.

FRS 102-33.7, SORP-130A ☐

[Guidance]
Key management personnel will often be more than just the directors or trustees. (See FRS 102 glossary for definition.)

For LLPs, total compensation paid to key management personnel may comprise elements of employee remuneration and profit attributable to members.

Disclosure of related party transactions

33.04 If there are related party transactions, disclose:

FRS 102-33.9

    (a)   the nature of the related party relationship; ☐

    (b)   the amount of the transactions; ☐

    (c)   the amount of outstanding balances; ☐

    (d)   the terms and conditions; ☐

    (e)   whether they are secured; ☐

    (f)   the nature of the consideration to be provided in settlement; ☐

    (g)   details of any guarantees given or received; ☐

    (h)   provisions for uncollectible receivables related to the amount of outstanding balances; and ☐

    (i)   the expense recognised during the period in respect of bad or doubtful debts due from related parties. ☐

		Reference	Y, N, N/A	C L	R

[Guidance]
Note 1. The disclosures need not be given of transactions entered into between two or more members of a group, provided that any subsidiary which is a party to the transaction is wholly owned by such a member.

Note 2. An entity may disclose items of a similar nature in the aggregate except when separate disclosure is necessary for an understanding of the effects of related party transactions on the financial statements of the entity.

33.05   Make the disclosures required by paragraph 33.9 of FRS 102 separately for each of the following categories: FRS 102-33.10

(a)   entities with control, joint control or significant influence over the entity;

(b)   entities over which the entity has control, joint control or significant influence;

(c)   key management personnel of the entity or its parent (in the aggregate);

(d)   entities that provide key management personnel services to the entity; and

(e)   other related parties.

Information about directors' benefits: advances, credit and guarantees

33.06   For a company to its own directors, and in addition, in the case of a parent company preparing group accounts, to the parent's directors by its subsidiaries, disclose details of: s413(1&2)

(a)   for each advance or credit granted by the company to a director disclose: s413(1)(a)&(3)

(i)   its amount;   C

(ii)   an indication of the interest rate;   C

(iii)   its main conditions; and   C

(iv)   any amounts repaid.   C

(b)   also disclose in the notes: s413(5)

(i)   the total of amounts stated in (a)(i);   C

(ii)   the total of the amounts stated in (a)(iv).   C

(c)   guarantees of any kind entered into by the company on behalf of its directors, must be shown in the notes to its individual accounts. For each guarantee disclose: s413(1)(b)&(4)

(i)   its main terms;   C

(ii)   the amount of the maximum liability that may be incurred by the company (or its subsidiary); and   C

(iii)   any amount paid and any liability incurred by the company (or its subsidiary) for the purpose of fulfilling the guarantee (including any loss incurred by reason of enforcement of the guarantee).   C

(d)   also disclose in the notes: s413(5)

(i)   the total of amounts stated in (c)(ii);   C

(ii)   the total of amounts stated in (c)(iii).   C

	Reference	Y, N, N/A	C L	R

[Guidance]

Note 1. The disclosure required re (a) and (c) is in respect of each advance or credit granted or guarantee. There is limited guidance where there are numerous transactions with a director during the year in the form of a director's current account. Where disclosure of such information is given in an aggregated or summarised form, this fact will need to be disclosed.

Note 2. s413 does not require disclosure of the name of the director to whom an advance is made or credit granted. If the advance or credit is material then FRS 102 will require the nature of the relationship to be disclosed as part of the related party transaction disclosure.

34.1 **SPECIALISED ACTIVITIES – AGRICULTURE**

If the entity is engaged in agricultural activity, complete checklist 6.

34.2 **SPECIALISED ACTIVITIES – FINANCIAL INSTITUTIONS: DISCLOSURES**

A financial institution should complete Appendix 7.

34.3 **SPECIALISED ACTIVITIES – FUNDING COMMITMENTS**

If the entity has funding commitments, complete Appendix 8.

35 **TRANSITION TO FRS 102**

If the entity is applying FRS 102 for the first time, complete Appendix 9.

36 **REDUCED DISCLOSURE FRAMEWORK**

An entity that qualifies for and uses the Reduced Disclosure Framework should complete Appendix 10.

37 **STRATEGIC REPORT WITH SUPPLEMENTARY MATERIAL**

A company preparing a strategic report with supplementary material should complete Appendix 11.

Appendix 1

Individual financial statements of parent

		Reference	Y, N, N/A	C L	R

A1.01   When a parent prepares separate financial statements, those separate financial statements shall disclose: FRS 102-9.27

     (a)   that the statements are separate financial statements; and

     (b)   a description of the methods used to account for the investments in subsidiaries, jointly controlled entities and associates.

Intermediate payment arrangements

A1.02   When a sponsoring entity recognises the assets and liabilities held by an intermediary, it should disclose sufficient information in the notes to its financial statements to enable users to understand the significance of the intermediary and the arrangement in the context of the sponsoring entity's financial statements.   FRS 102-9.38

A1.03   This should include: FRS 102-9.38

     (a)   a description of the main features of the intermediary including the arrangements for making payments and for distributing equity instruments;

     (b)   any restrictions relating to the assets and liabilities of the intermediary;

     (c)   in respect of the assets and liabilities held by the intermediary, which have not yet vested unconditionally with the beneficiaries of the arrangement, disclose:

         (i)   the amount; and

         (ii)   their nature.

     (d)   the amount that has been deducted from equity which has not yet vested unconditionally with the beneficiaries of the arrangement;

     (e)   the number of equity instruments held by the intermediary which have not yet vested unconditionally with the beneficiaries of the arrangement;

     (f)   for entities that have their equity instruments listed or publicly traded on a stock exchange or market, the market value of the equity instruments held by the intermediary which have not yet vested unconditionally with employees;

     (g)   the extent to which the equity instruments are under option to employees, or have been conditionally gifted to them; and

     (h)   the amount that has been deducted from the aggregate dividends paid by the sponsoring entity.

Basis of exemption from presenting consolidated financial statements

A1.04   A parent that uses one of the exemptions from presenting consolidated financial statements permitted by FRS 102 shall disclose the grounds on which the parent is exempt.   R-C Sch 4.10(1), R-L Sch 2.8(1), FRS 102-9.27A

		Reference	*Y, N, N/A*	*C L*	*R*

A1.05   If the reason why group accounts are not required is that all subsidiaries fall within the exclusions below, state for each subsidiary undertaking which exclusion applies: R-C Sch 4.10(2), R-L Sch 2.8(2)

     (a)   immaterial (individually and collectively);   ☐

     (b)   severe long-term restrictions; and   ☐

     (c)   held exclusively with a view to resale.   ☐

[Guidance]
The Act also provides for exclusion on the grounds that information cannot be obtained without disproportionate expense or undue delay. However, FRS 102 states that this is not a justifiable reason for not consolidating a subsidiary undertaking unless its inclusion is not material (FRS 102 paragraph 9.8A).

A1.06   Where the company is exempt from the requirement to prepare group accounts because it is itself a subsidiary undertaking, the company must: s400(1&2), s401(1&2)

     (a)   disclose in the notes to its individual accounts that it is exempt from the obligation to prepare and deliver group accounts; and   ☐

     (b)   state in its individual accounts:

         (i)   the name of the parent undertaking which draws up group accounts; and   ☐

         (ii)   the address of the undertaking's registered office (whether in or outside the United Kingdom), or if it is unincorporated , the address of its principal place of business.   ☐

[Guidance]
This exemption is only available if:
(a)   the company is included in consolidated accounts for a larger group which are drawn up in accordance with the requirements of s401(2)(b);
(b)   the consolidated accounts are audited; and
(c)   a copy of the consolidated accounts and audit report are filed at Companies House with a certified translation if not in English.

A1.07   Where advantage is taken of the exemption to restrict information relating to certain foreign undertakings (with the agreement of the Secretary of State), state that fact in a note to the accounts.   s409(5)   ☐

Details of subsidiary undertakings

A1.08   For each subsidiary undertaking, state: R-C Sch 4.1(2)(3), R-L Sch 2.1(2)(3)

     (a)   the name; and   ☐

     (b)   the address of its registered office (whether in or outside the UK) and, if unincorporated, the address of its principal place of business.   ☐

		Reference	Y, N, N/A	C L	R

A1.09 Show separately for each class of shares in each subsidiary undertaking: R-C Sch 4.11, R-L Sch 2.9

    (a)   the identity of the class;

    (b)   the proportion of the nominal value held; and

    (c)   identify separately shares held by the company, and those attributed to the company which are held by subsidiary undertakings.

[Guidance]
Comparative figures are not required.

A1.10 For each subsidiary undertaking, disclose: R-C Sch 4.2(1), R-L Sch 2.2(1)

    (a)   the aggregate amount of its capital and reserves as at the end of its relevant financial year;

[Guidance]
'Relevant financial year' means the year coinciding with or ending last before that of the company's financial year. (R-C Sch 4.2(6), R-L Sch 2.2(6))

    (b)   its profit or loss for that year; and

    (c)   the date on which the last financial year ended (last before the company's financial year) where the financial year does not end with that of the company. R-C Sch 4.12, R-L Sch 2.10

[Guidance]
This disclosure is not required if:
(a)   the company is exempt because it is itself a subsidiary undertaking and included in the accounts of a larger group; or
(b)   the company's investment in the subsidiary undertaking is included in the company's accounts using the equity method of valuation; or
(c)   the company's holding is less than 50% of the nominal value of the shares in the subsidiary undertaking, and the subsidiary undertaking does not publish its balance sheet; or
(d)   it is not material.
(R-C Sch 4.2(2)-(5), R-L Sch 2.2(2)-(5))

A1.11 State the number, description and amount of any shares in the company which are held by subsidiary undertakings, with the exception of certain trustee holdings (see the Act for details). R-C Sch 4.3(1)   C

Appendix 2
Consolidated financial statements

		Reference	*Y, N,* *N/A*	*C* *L*	*R*

Part 1

A2.01 The following disclosures shall be made in consolidated financial statements: — FRS 102-9.23

   (a) the fact that the statements are consolidated financial statements; — ☐

   (b) the basis for concluding that control exists when the parent does not own, directly or indirectly through subsidiaries, more than half of the voting power; — R-C Sch 4.16(3), R-L Sch 2.14(3) — ☐

   (c) any difference in the reporting date of the financial statements of the parent and its subsidiaries used in the preparation of the consolidated financial statements; and — R-C Sch 6.2(2), R-L Sch 3.2(2) — ☐

   (d) the nature and extent of any significant restrictions (e.g. resulting from borrowing arrangements or regulatory requirements) on the ability of subsidiaries to transfer funds to the parent in the form of cash dividends or to repay loans. — ☐

[Guidance]
The disclosure in (a) to (d) above is encouraged but not required for a small group (FRS 102.1A22(c).

A2.02 If the company has subsidiary undertakings and is required to prepare group accounts, these must be in the form of consolidated accounts, and must: — s404(3), R-C Sch 6.1(1), R-L Sch 3.1(1)

   (a) comply as far as practicable with the provisions of the Companies Act as if it were a single company; — ☐

   (b) disclose the auditors' remuneration for the group, including expenses and non-cash benefits; and — ☐

   (c) state the nature of any non-cash benefits provided to the auditors. — ☐

A2.03 The consolidated accounts must show a true and fair view – disclose any additional information necessary to achieve this. — s404(2)(4) — ☐

A2.04 If, in special circumstances, compliance with any provision of the Act is inconsistent with the requirement to give a true and fair view, then depart from that provision to the extent necessary, but disclose in a note to the group accounts: — s404(5)

   (a) the nature of the departure; — ☐

   (b) the reasons for the departure; — ☐

   (c) the effect of the departure. — ☐

A2.05 Where in special circumstances uniform accounting policies have not been adopted on consolidation: — R-C Sch 6.3(2), R-L Sch 3.3(2)

   (a) state the different accounting policies used; — ☐

   (b) give the reasons for the different treatment; and — ☐

   (c) state the effect. — ☐

		Reference	Y, N, N/A	C L	R

| A2.06 | State the method used in translating accounts of foreign enterprises. | R-C Sch 1.70, R-L Sch 1.68 | ☐ | | |

| A2.07 | Disclose: | R-C Sch 6.4, R-L Sch 3.4 | | | |

    (a) any differences in the accounting rules between a parent company's individual accounts and its group accounts; and ☐

    (b) the reasons for the differences. ☐

| A2.08 | Where advantage is taken of the exemption to restrict information relating to certain foreign undertakings (with the agreement of the Secretary of State), state that fact in a note to the accounts. | s409(5) | ☐ | | |

| A2.09 | If a subsidiary company or LLP is exempt from the requirements of Companies Act relating to the audit of its accounts for an accounting period ending on or after 1 October 2012 by virtue of s479A Companies Act 2006, disclose in the notes to the consolidated accounts this fact and the name of the subsidiary company or LLP. | s479A(2)d | ☐ | | |

Details of subsidiary undertakings

| A2.10 | For each subsidiary undertaking, state: | R-C Sch 4.1(2)(3), 4.16(2), R-L Sch 2.1(2)(3), 2.14(2) | | | |

    (a) the name; ☐

    (b) the address of its registered office (whether in or outside the UK) and, if unincorporated, the address of its principal place of business; and ☐

    (c) whether the subsidiary undertaking is included in the consolidated accounts, and if not, state the reason for exclusion. ☐

| A2.11 | For each class of share in a subsidiary undertaking, disclose separately (if different) for shares held by the parent company and those held by the group: | R-C Sch 4.17(2), R-L Sch 2.15(2) | | | |

    (a) the identity of the class of shares held; and ☐

    (b) the proportion of the nominal value and voting rights of that class represented by those shares. ☐

[Guidance]
Comparative figures are not required.

Subsidiary undertakings excluded from consolidation

| A2.12 | For each subsidiary undertaking excluded from the consolidated accounts, other than exclusions (see guidance), disclose: | R-C Sch 4.2(1), R-L Sch 2.2(1) | ☐ | | |

    (a) its name; FRS 102-9.23 ☐

[Guidance]
This disclosure is encouraged but not required for a small group (FRS 102.1A22(c). ☐

    (b) the reason for exclusion; FRS 102-9.23 ☐

	Reference	Y, N, N/A	C L	R

[Guidance]
This disclosure is encouraged but not required for a small group (FRS 102.1A22(c).

(c)   the aggregate amount of its capital and reserves as at the end of its relevant financial year; and

[Guidance]
'Relevant financial year' means the year coinciding with or ending last before that of the company's financial year. (R-C Sch 4.2(6), R-L Sch 2.2(6))

(d) its profit or loss for that year.

[Guidance]
Exclusions from disclosure
The disclosures are not required if:
a)   the subsidiary undertaking is included in the group accounts by way of the equity method of valuation; or
b)   the company's holding is less than 50% of the nominal value of the shares in the subsidiary, and the subsidiary is not required to publish its balance sheet.
(R-C Sch 4.2(4)(5), R-L Sch 2.2(4)(5))

Company's profit and loss

A2.13   Where the company is required to prepare group accounts, and does so, and omits its individual profit and loss account, disclose:

(a)   the company's profit or loss for the year in a note to its individual balance sheet; and — s408(1)b

(b)   in the company's accounts that the exemption conferred by s408 Companies Act 2006 is being relied on. — s408(4)

[Guidance]
Although a company which prepares group accounts may omit its individual profit and loss account from the annual audited accounts laid before the members, it must still prepare one, and it must be approved by the board. (CA 06 – s408(3))

Part 2

Investments in associates

Disclosures in individual and consolidated financial statements

A2.14   The financial statements shall disclose:

(a)   the accounting policy for investments in associates; — R-C Sch 1.44, R-L Sch 1.44, FRS 102-14.12

(b)   the carrying amount of investments in associates; — FRS 102-14.12

(c)   the fair value of investments in associates accounted for using the equity method for which there are published price quotations; — FRS 102-14.12

(d)   the name of the undertaking; and — R-C Sch 4.19(2), R-L Sch 2.17(2)

(e)   the address of its registered office (whether in or outside the UK) and, if incorporated outside the UK, the country in which it is incorporated. — R-C Sch 4.19(3), R-L Sch 2.17(3)

		Reference	Y, N, N/A	C L	R

A2.15 For investments in associates accounted for in accordance with the cost model, disclose: — FRS 102-14.13

   (a) the amount of dividends recognised as income; and — ☐

   (b) the amount of other distributions recognised as income. — ☐

A2.16 For investments in associates accounted for in accordance with the equity method, disclose separately: — R-C Sch 6.21, R-L Sch 3.21, FRS 102-14.14

   (a) the share of the profit or loss of such associates; and — ☐

   (b) the share of any discontinued operations of such associates. — ☐

A2.17 For investments in associates accounted for in accordance with the fair value model, make the following disclosures: — FRS 102-14.15

   (a) the basis for determining fair value, e.g. quoted market price in an active market or a valuation technique; — ☐

   (b) the assumptions applied in determining fair value; and — ☐

   (c) If a reliable measure of fair value is no longer available for ordinary or preference shares measured at fair value through profit or loss, disclose that fact. — ☐

A2.18 The individual financial statements of an investor that is not a parent shall disclose: — FRS 102-14.15A

   (a) summarised financial information about the investments in the associates; and — ☐

   (b) the effect of including those investments as if they had been accounted for using the equity method. — ☐

[Guidance]
Investing entities that are exempt from preparing consolidated financial statements, or would be exempt if they had subsidiaries, are exempt from this requirement.

A2.19 In respect of shares in associates, disclose separately in the financial statements for the investing group: — R-C Sch 4.19(4)(5), R-L Sch 2.17(4)(5)

   (a) the identity of each class of shares held; — ☐

   (b) the proportion of the nominal value of that class held: — ☐

   (c) any special rights or constraints attaching to them; and — ☐

   (d) the accounting period or date of the financial statements used if they differ from those of the investing group. — ☐

Significant holdings other than associated undertakings

A2.20 For all significant holdings, disclose: — R-C Sch 4.5(1)(2), R-L Sch 2.4(1)(2)

   (a) the name of the undertaking; and — ☐

   (b) the address of its registered office (whether in or outside the UK) and, if unincorporated, the address of its principal place of business. — ☐

	Reference	Y, N, N/A	C L	R

[Guidance]
A holding by a parent company or group is significant if it amounts to 20 per cent or more of the nominal value of any class of shares in the undertaking, or the amount of the holding (as stated in the investing company's accounts) exceeds one- fifth of the company's assets.
(SI 2008/410-L Sch 4.4(2), SI 2008/1913-L Sch 2.3(2))

A2.21   For all significant holdings, disclose separately in respect of shares held by the parent undertaking and those held by the group: R-C Sch 4.5(3), R-L Sch 2.4(3)

(a)   the identity of each class of shares held; and

(b)   the proportion of the nominal value of that class held.

[Guidance]
Comparative figures are not required.

A2.22   If the information is material, disclose for all significant holdings the aggregate capital and reserves at the end of its relevant financial year, and the profit or loss for that year.   R-C Sch 4.6(1)(3), R-L Sch 2.5(1)(3)

[Guidance]
'Relevant financial year' means the year coinciding with or ending last before that of the company's financial year. (SI 2008/410-L Sch 4.6(4), SI 2008/1913-L Sch 2.5(4))

This information is not required if the holding is less than 50% and the undertaking is not required to deliver and does not publish its balance sheet.   R-C Sch 4.6(2), R-L Sch 2.5(2)

Part 3

Investments in joint ventures

Disclosures in individual and consolidated financial statements

A2.23   Disclose the following: FRS 102-15.19

(a)   the accounting policy for recognising investments in jointly controlled entities;   R-C Sch 1.44, R-L Sch 1.44

(b)   the carrying amount of investments in jointly controlled entities;

(c)   the fair value of investments in jointly controlled entities accounted for using the equity method for which there are published price quotations;

(d)   the aggregate amount of commitments relating to joint ventures;

(e)   the share in the capital commitments that have been incurred jointly with other venturers; and

(f)   the share of the capital commitments of the joint ventures themselves.

A2.24   For jointly controlled entities accounted for in accordance with the equity method, disclose separately .   FRS 102-15.20

(a)   the share of the profit or loss of such investments; and

(b)   the share of any discontinued operations of such jointly controlled entities.

			Reference	Y, N, N/A	C L	R
A2.25		For jointly controlled entities accounted for in accordance with the fair value model, disclose:	FRS 102-15.21			
	(a)	the basis for determining fair value, e.g. quoted market price in an active market or a valuation technique;	FRS 102-11.43	☐		
	(b)	the assumptions applied in determining fair value; and	FRS 102-11.43	☐		
	(c)	if a reliable measure of fair value is no longer available, disclose that fact.	FRS 102-11.44	☐		
A2.26		The individual financial statements of a venturer that is not a parent shall disclose:	FRS 102-15.21A			
	(a)	summarised financial information about the investments in the jointly controlled entities; and		☐		
	(b)	the effect of including those investments as if they had been accounted for using the equity method.		☐		

[Guidance]
Investing entities that are exempt from preparing consolidated financial statements, or would be exempt if they had subsidiaries, are exempt from this requirement.

Part 4

Business combinations and goodwill

Business combinations effected during the reporting period

			Reference	Y, N, N/A	C L	R
A2.27		For each business combination, excluding any group reconstructions, that was effected during the period, disclose the following:	FRS 102-19.25			
	(a)	the names of the combining entities or businesses;	R-C Sch 6.13(2), R-L Sch 3.13(2), SORP-118	☐		
	(b)	the descriptions of the combining entities or businesses;		☐		
	(c)	the acquisition date;	R-C Sch 6.13(2), R-L Sch 3.13(2), SORP-118	☐		
	(d)	the percentage of voting equity instruments acquired;		☐		
	(e)	the cost of the combination;		☐		
	(f)	a description of the components of that cost (such as cash, equity instruments and debt instruments);	R-C Sch 6.13(3), R-L Sch 3.13(3), SORP-118	☐		
	(g)	the amounts recognised at the acquisition date for each class of the acquiree's assets, liabilities and contingent liabilities, including goodwill;		☐		
	(h)	the periods in which any negative goodwill will be recognised in profit or loss;		☐		
	(i)	the useful life of goodwill; and	R-L Sch 1.22(4)(a)	☐	L	
	(j)	the supporting reasons for the useful economic life chosen.	R-L Sch 1.22(4)(b)	☐	L	

	Reference	Y, N, N/A	C L	R

A2.28   Disclose, separately for each material business combination that occurred during the reporting period, the following in respect of the acquiree since the acquisition date included in the consolidated statement of comprehensive income for the reporting period: FRS 102-19.25A

  (a)   the revenue; and

  (b)   the profit or loss.

[Guidance]
The disclosure may be provided in aggregate for business combinations that occurred during the reporting period which, individually, are not material.

A2.29   For each material acquisition, and in aggregate for other acquisitions where these are material in total, give a table showing: R-C Sch 6.13(4), R-L Sch 3.13(4), SORP-118

  (a)   the book values for each class of asset and liabilities of the acquired entity, immediately prior to acquisition;

  (b)   the fair value adjustments to the above values analysed between revaluations, adjustments to bring accounting policies into line, and any other significant adjustments, giving the reasons for the adjustments;

  (c)   the fair values of each class of assets and liabilities at the date of acquisition;

  (d)   the amount of purchased goodwill or negative consolidation difference arising;

  (e)   provisions for reorganisation and restructuring costs included in the acquired entity's accounts and related asset write-downs made within 12 months of the date of acquisition;

  (f)   details of movements on provisions related to acquisitions, analysed between amounts used and amounts released unused (give sufficient details to show the extent to which the provisions have proved unnecessary);

  (g)   the fact and the reasons, where the fair value of the assets and liabilities, or the consideration, can only be determined on a provisional basis; and

  (h)   any subsequent material adjustments to such provisional fair values, with corresponding adjustments to goodwill, together with an explanation of them.

[Guidance]
Comparative figures are not required.

For all business combinations

A2.30   Disclose a reconciliation of the carrying amount of goodwill at the beginning and end of the reporting period, showing separately: R-C Sch 1.51, R-L Sch 1.49, FRS 102-19.26

  (a)   cost or valuation at the beginning and end of the year;

  (b)   changes arising from new business combinations;

  (c)   disposals of previously acquired businesses;

  (d)   transfers during the year;

  (e)   revaluations during the year;

  (f)   accumulated amortisation at the beginning and end of the year;

		Reference	Y, N, N/A	C L	R

(g)   charge for amortisation, the amount released on disposals and other adjustments to amortisation during the year;   ☐

(h)   impairment losses; and   ☐

(i)   other changes.   ☐

[Guidance]
This reconciliation need not be presented for prior periods.

A2.31   Disclose a reconciliation of the carrying amount of negative goodwill at the beginning and end of the reporting period, showing separately: FRS 102-19.26A

  (a)   changes arising from new business combinations;   ☐

  (b)   amounts recognised in profit or loss;   ☐

  (c)   disposals of previously acquired businesses; and   ☐

  (d)   other changes.

[Guidance]
This reconciliation need not be presented for prior periods.

A2.32   State the cumulative amount of goodwill arising from acquisitions (but net of amounts relating to any disposals) which has been written off otherwise than in the consolidated profit or loss account for current or any earlier financial year.   R-C Sch 6.14, R-L Sch 3.14, SORP-118   ☐

Group reconstructions

A2.33   For each group reconstruction that was effected during the period, the combined entity shall disclose the following: FRS 102-19.33

  (a)   the names of the combining entities (other than the reporting entity);   ☐

  (b)   whether the combination has been accounted for as an acquisition or a merger; and   ☐

  (c)   the date of the combination.   ☐

LLP Business combinations

A2.34   Single-entity LLPs that are formed by the transfer or incorporation of existing undertakings, including partnerships, should disclose:

  (a)   corresponding pro forma amounts in the financial statements of the first period after incorporation. Where such comparative amounts are disclosed, they should be stated on the basis of the accounting policies adopted by the LLP; and   SORP-115   ☐   L

  (b)   a pro forma profit and loss account (or statement of comprehensive income), including corresponding amounts, for the whole of the original entity's accounting period spanning the transfer.   SORP-116   ☐   L

[Guidance]
Where there is a transfer of an existing undertaking to an LLP, it should be accounted for using the merger accounting method provided that the transfer meets the definition of a group reconstruction and the conditions of paragraph 19.27 of FRS 102. (SORP (2015)-114)

Disposals

35   Where a disposal significantly affects the group accounts, disclose:

R-C Sch 6.15,
R-L Sch 3.15,
SORP-118

(a)   the name of the undertaking disposed of, or where a group has been disposed of, the name of the parent undertaking of that group;

(b)   the contribution to the group's profit or loss; and

(c)   the amount of any ownership interest retained.

Appendix 3

Statement of cash flows

		Reference	Y, N, N/A	C L	R
	Statement of cash flows				R
A3.01	An entity shall present a statement of cash flows that presents cash flows for a reporting period classified by operating activities, investing activities and financing activities.	FRS 102-7.3	☐		
A3.02	An entity shall present separately cash flows from interest and dividends received and paid.	FRS 102-7.14	☐		
A3.03	The entity shall classify these cash flows consistently from period to period as operating, investing or financing activities.	FRS 102-7.14	☐		
A3.04	An entity shall present separately cash flows arising from income tax and shall classify them as cash flows from operating activities unless they can be specifically identified with financing and investing activities.	FRS 102-7.17	☐		
A3.05	When tax cash flows are allocated over more than one class of activity, the entity shall disclose the total amount of taxes paid.	FRS 102-7.17	☐		
A3.06	An entity shall exclude from the statement of cash flows investing and financing transactions that do not require the use of cash or cash equivalents and shall disclose such transactions elsewhere in the financial statements in a way that provides all the relevant information about those investing and financing activities.	FRS 102-7.18	☐		
A3.07	An entity shall present the components of cash and cash equivalents and shall present a reconciliation of the amounts presented in the statement of cash flows to the equivalent items presented in the statement of financial position.	FRS 102-7.20	☐		
A3.08	An entity shall disclose, together with a commentary by management, the amount of significant cash and cash equivalent balances held by the entity that are not available for use by the entity.	FRS 102-7.21	☐		
	LLP Statement of cash flows				
A3.09	For an LLP, the following classification of transactions with members (and former members) will generally be shown separately:	SORP-74A			
	(a) Remuneration that is paid under an employment contract – operating cash flow;		☐	L	
	(b) Other remuneration (discretionary or non-discretionary) for services provided - operating cash flow;		☐	L	
	(c) Post-retirement payments to former members - operating cash flow;		☐	L	
	(d) Capital introduced by members (classified as equity or liability) – Financing cash flow;		☐	L	
	(e) Repayment of capital or debt to members – Financing cash flow; and		☐	L	
	(f) Payments to members that represent a return on amounts subscribed or otherwise contributed – Financing cash flow.		☐	L	
A3.10	The LLP should disclose transactions with members (and former members) separately from transactions with non-members.	SORP-74B	☐	L	

		Reference	Y, N, N/A	C L	R

Examples from FRS 102

A3.11 FRS 102 includes examples of cash flows from operating activities; these are included in this checklist for guidance: FRS 102-7.4

(a) cash receipts from the sale of goods and the rendering of services;

(b) cash receipts from royalties, fees, commissions and other revenue;

(c) cash payments to suppliers for goods and services;

(d) cash payments to and on behalf of employees;

(e) cash payments or refunds of income tax, unless they can be specifically identified with financing and investing activities;

(f) cash receipts and payments from investments, loans and other contracts held for dealing or trading purposes, which are similar to inventory acquired specifically for resale; and

(g) cash advances and loans made to other parties by financial institutions.

A3.12 FRS 102 includes examples of cash flows from investing activities; these are included in this checklist for guidance: FRS 102-7.5

(a) cash payments to acquire property, plant and equipment (including self-constructed property, plant and equipment), intangible assets and other long-term assets;

(b) cash receipts from sales of property, plant and equipment, intangibles and other long-term assets;

(c) cash payments to acquire equity or debt instruments of other entities and interests in joint ventures (other than payments for those instruments classified as cash equivalents or held for dealing or trading);

(d) cash receipts from sales of equity or debt instruments of other entities and interests in joint ventures (other than receipts for those instruments classified as cash equivalents or held for dealing or trading);

(e) cash advances and loans made to other parties (except those made by financial institutions);

(f) cash receipts from the repayment of advances and loans made to other parties;

(g) cash payments for futures contracts, forward contracts, option contracts and swap contracts, except when the contracts are held for dealing or trading, or the payments are classified as financing activities; and

(h) cash receipts from futures contracts, forward contracts, option contracts and swap contracts, except when the contracts are held for dealing or trading, or the receipts are classified as financing activities.

A3.13 FRS 102 includes examples of cash flows from financing activities; these are included in this checklist for guidance: FRS 102-7.6

(a) cash proceeds from issuing shares or other equity instruments;

(b) cash payments to owners to acquire or redeem the entity's shares;

(c) cash proceeds from issuing debentures, loans, notes, bonds, mortgages and other short-term or long-term borrowings;

(d) cash repayments of amounts borrowed; and

(e) cash payments by a lessee for the reduction of the outstanding liability relating to a finance lease.

Appendix 4

Share based payment

			Reference	Y, N, N/A	C L	R
A4.01		Disclose the following information about the nature and extent of share-based payment arrangements that existed during the period:	FRS 102-26.18		C	
	(a)	A description of each type of share-based payment arrangement that existed at any time during the period;		☐	C	
	(b)	the general terms and conditions of each arrangement, such as vesting requirements, the maximum term of options granted, and the method of settlement (e.g. whether in cash or equity); and		☐	C	
		[Guidance] *An entity with substantially similar types of share-based payment arrangements may aggregate the information.*				
	(c)	The number and weighted average exercise prices of share options for each of the following groups of options:				
		(i) outstanding at the beginning of the period;		☐	C	R
		(ii) granted during the period;		☐	C	R
		(iii) forfeited during the period;		☐	C	R
		(iv) exercised during the period;		☐	C	R
		(v) expired during the period;		☐	C	R
		(vi) outstanding at the end of the period; and		☐	C	R
		(vii) exercisable at the end of the period.		☐	C	R
A4.02		For equity-settled share-based payment arrangements, disclose information about how it measured the fair value of goods or services received or the value of the equity instruments granted.	FRS 102-26.19	☐	C	R
A4.03		If a valuation methodology was used, disclose:	FRS 102-26.19			
	(a)	the method; and		☐	C	R
	(b)	the reason for choosing it.		☐	C	R
A4.04		For cash-settled share-based payment arrangements, disclose information about how the liability was measured.	FRS 102-26.20	☐	C	R
A4.05		For share-based payment arrangements that were modified during the period, disclose an explanation of those modifications.	FRS 102-26.21	☐	C	R
A4.06		If the entity is part of a group share-based payment plan, and it recognises and measures its share-based payment expense on the basis of a reasonable allocation of the expense recognised for the group, it shall disclose:	FRS 102-26.22			
	(a)	that fact; and		☐	C	
	(b)	the basis for the allocation.		☐	C	

		Reference	*Y, N, N/A*	*C* *L*	*R*
A4.07	Disclose the following information about the effect of share-based payment transactions on the entity's profit or loss for the period and on its financial position:	FRS 102-26.23			
	(a) the total expense recognised in profit or loss for the period; and		☐	C	R
	(b) the total carrying amount at the end of the period for liabilities arising from share-based payment transactions.		☐	C	R

Appendix 5

Employee benefits (Defined benefit plans)

		Reference	*Y, N, N/A*	*C L*	*R*

A5.01 Disclose the following information about defined benefit plans (except for any multi-employer defined benefit plans that are accounted for as a defined contribution plan): — FRS 102-28.41

    (a) A general description of the type of plan, including funding policy;

        (aa) This includes the amount and timing of the future payments to be made by the entity under any agreement with the defined benefit plan to fund a deficit (such as a schedule of contributions);

    (b) The date of the most recent comprehensive actuarial valuation;

    (c) If the date was not as of the reporting date, a description of the adjustments that were made to measure the defined benefit obligation at the reporting date;

    (d) A reconciliation of opening and closing balances for each of the following:
(*Note: this reconciliation need not be presented for prior periods.*)

        (i) the defined benefit obligation;

        (ii) the fair value of plan assets; and

        (iii) any reimbursement right recognised as an asset;

    (e) Each of the reconciliations in the paragraph above shall show each of the following, if applicable:
(*Note: this reconciliation need not be presented for prior period.*)

        (i) the change in the defined benefit liability arising from employee service rendered during the reporting period in profit or loss;

        (ii) interest income or expense;

        (iii) re-measurement of the defined benefit liability, showing separately:

            (1) actuarial gains and losses;

            (2) the return on plan assets less amounts included in (ii) above; and

        (iv) plan introductions, changes, curtailments and settlements;

    (f) The total cost relating to defined benefit plans for the period, disclosing separately the amounts:

        (i) recognised in profit or loss as an expense; and

        (ii) included in the cost of an asset;

    (g) For each major class of plan assets, which shall include, but is not limited to, equity instruments, debt instruments, property, and all other assets, the percentage or amount that each major class constitutes of the fair value of the total plan assets at the reporting date;

			Reference	Y, N, N/A	C L	R

(h)   The amounts included in the fair value of plan assets for:

     (i)   each class of the entity's own financial instruments; and   ☐

     (ii)   any property occupied by, or other assets used by, the entity;   ☐

(i)   The return on plan assets; and

(j)   The principal actuarial assumptions used, including, when applicable:

     (i)   the discount rates;   ☐

     (ii)   the expected rates of salary increases;   ☐

     (iii)   medical cost trend rates; and   ☐

     (iv)   any other material actuarial assumptions used.   ☐

[Guidance]
If an entity has more than one defined benefit plan, these disclosures may be made in aggregate, separately for each plan, or in such groupings as are considered to be the most useful.

A5.02   If an entity participates in a defined benefit plan that shares risks between entities under common control: FRS 102-28.41A

EITHER: it shall disclose the following information in its own financial statements: ☐

OR: it shall disclose the following information by cross reference to disclosures in another group entity's financial statements, if that group entity's financial statements separately identify and disclose the information required about the plan and are available on the same terms and at the same time: ☐

(a)   The contractual agreement or stated policy for charging the cost of a defined benefit plan or the fact that there is no policy;   ☐

(b)   The policy for determining the contribution to be paid by the entity;   ☐

(c)   If the entity accounts for an allocation of the net defined benefit cost, all the information required in paragraph 28.41 of FRS 102; and   ☐

(d)   If the entity accounts for the contributions payable for the period, the information about the plan as a whole required by paragraph 28.41(a), (d), (h) and (i) of FRS 102.   ☐

Appendix 6

Specialised activities – Agriculture

	Reference	*Y, N, N/A*	*C L*	*R*

An entity using FRS 102 that is engaged in agricultural activity shall determine an accounting policy for each class of biological asset and its related agricultural produce.

Disclosures – fair value model

A6.01   Disclose the following for each class of biological asset measured using the fair value model: FRS 102-34.7

    (a)   a description of each class of biological asset; ☐

    (b)   the methods applied in determining the fair value of each class of biological asset; ☐

    (c)   the significant assumptions applied in determining the fair value of each class of biological asset; ☐

    (d)   a reconciliation of changes in the carrying amount of each class of biological asset between the beginning and the end of the current period; and ☐
       (Note: This reconciliation need not be presented for prior periods.)

    (e)   the reconciliation shall include: ☐

       (i)   the gain or loss arising from changes in fair value less costs to sell; ☐

       (ii)   increases resulting from purchases; ☐

       (iii)   decreases attributable to sales; ☐

       (iv)   decreases resulting from harvest; ☐

       (v)   increases resulting from business combinations; and ☐

       (vi)   other changes. ☐

A6.02   If any individual biological assets are measured at cost, explain why fair value cannot be reliably measured.   FRS 102-34.7A ☐

A6.03   If the fair value of such a biological asset becomes reliably measurable during the current period, explain: FRS 102-34.7A

    (a)   why fair value has become reliably measurable; and ☐

    (b)   the effect of the change. ☐

A6.04   Disclose the methods and significant assumptions applied in determining the fair value at the point of harvest of each class of agricultural produce.   FRS 102-34.7B ☐

Disclosures – cost model

A6.05   Disclose the following for each class of biological asset measured using the cost model: FRS 102-34.10

    (a)   a description of each class of biological asset; ☐

    (b)   the depreciation method used; ☐

    (c)   the useful lives or the depreciation rates used; ☐

		Reference	Y, N, N/A	C L	R

(d)   a reconciliation of changes in the carrying amount of each class of biological asset between the beginning and the end of the current period; and

(Note: This reconciliation need not be presented for prior periods.)

(e)   the reconciliation shall include:

    (i)   increases resulting from purchases;

    (ii)   decreases attributable to sales;

    (iii)   decreases resulting from harvest;

    (iv)   increases resulting from business combinations;

    (v)   impairment losses recognised or reversed in profit or loss; and

    (vi)   other changes.

A6.06   Disclose, for any agricultural produce measured at fair value less costs to sell, the following in determining the fair value at the point of harvest of each class of agricultural produce: FRS 102-34.10A

(a)   the methods applied; and

(b)   significant assumptions applied.

Appendix 7

Specialised activities – Financial institutions: Disclosures

		Reference	Y, N, N/A	C L	R
	Significance of financial instruments for financial position and performance				
A7.01	Disclose information that enables users of the financial statements to evaluate the significance of financial instruments for the financial position and performance.	FRS 102-34.19	☐		
A7.02	Disclose a disaggregation of the statement of financial position line item by class of financial instrument.	FRS 102-34.20	☐		
	Impairment				
A7.03	Where a financial institution uses a separate allowance account to record impairments, disclose a reconciliation of changes in that account during the period for each class of financial asset.	FRS 102-34.21	☐		
	Fair value				
A7.04	For financial instruments held at fair value in the statement of financial position, disclose for each class of financial instrument, an analysis of the level in the fair value hierarchy into which the fair value measurements are categorised.	FRS 102-34.22	☐		
	Nature and extent of risks arising from financial instruments				
A7.05	Disclose information that enables users of the financial statements to evaluate the following risks arising from financial instruments to which the financial institution is exposed at the end of the reporting period:	FRS 102-34.23			
	(a) nature of credit risk;		☐		
	(b) extent of credit risk;		☐		
	(c) liquidity risk; and		☐		
	(d) market risk.		☐		
A7.06	For each type of risk arising from financial instruments, disclose:	FRS 102-34.24			
	(a) the exposures to risk and how they arise;		☐		
	(b) its objectives, policies and processes for managing the risk and the methods used to measure the risk; and		☐		
	(c) any changes in (a) or (b) from the previous period.		☐		
	Credit risk				
A7.07	Disclose by class of financial instrument:	FRS 102-34.25			
	(a) The amount that best represents its maximum exposure to credit risk at the end of the reporting period;		☐		
	(b) A description of collateral held as security;		☐		
	(c) A description of other credit enhancements;		☐		
	(d) A description of the extent to which the collateral and other credit enhancements mitigate credit risk;		☐		

		Reference	Y, N, N/A	C L	R

(e)   The amount by which any related credit derivatives or similar instruments mitigate that maximum exposure to credit risk; and

(f)   Information about the credit quality of financial assets that are neither past due nor impaired.

[Guidance]
This disclosure is not required for financial instruments whose carrying amount best represents the maximum exposure to credit risk.

A7.08   Provide, by class of financial asset, an analysis of: FRS 102-34.26

(a)   the age of financial assets that are past due as at the end of the reporting period but not impaired;

(b)   the financial assets that are individually determined to be impaired as at the end of the reporting period; and

(c)   the factors the financial institution considered in determining that they are impaired.

A7.09   When a financial institution obtains financial or non-financial assets during the period by taking possession of collateral it holds as security or calling on other credit enhancements (e.g. guarantees), and such assets meet the recognition criteria in other sections, disclose: FRS 102-34.27

(a)   the nature of the assets obtained;

(b)   the carrying amount of the assets obtained; and

(c)   when the assets are not readily convertible into cash, its policies for disposing of such assets or for using them in its operations.

Liquidity risk

A7.10   Provide a maturity analysis for financial liabilities that shows the remaining contractual maturities at undiscounted amounts separated between: FRS 102-34.28

(a)   derivative; and

(b)   non-derivative financial liabilities.

Market risk

A7.11   Provide a sensitivity analysis for each type of market risk (e.g. interest rate risk, currency risk, other price risk) it is exposed to, showing the impact on profit or loss and equity.   FRS 102-34.29

A7.12   Provide details of the methods and assumptions used in preparing the sensitivity analysis.   FRS 102-34.29

[Guidance]
If a financial institution prepares a sensitivity analysis, such as value-at-risk, that reflects interdependencies between risk variables (e.g. interest rates and exchange rates) and uses it to manage financial risks, it may use that sensitivity analysis instead. (FRS 102-34.30)

Capital

A7.13   Disclose information that enables users of the financial statements to evaluate the entity's objectives, policies and processes for managing capital.   FRS 102-34.31

		Reference	Y, N, N/A	C L	R

A7.14   A financial institution shall disclose the following: FRS 102-34.31

- (a) qualitative information about its objectives, policies and processes for managing capital, including:

  - (i) its objectives for managing capital;

  - (ii) its policies for managing capital;

  - (iii) its processes for managing capital;

  - (iv) a description of what it manages as capital;

  - (v) when an entity is subject to externally imposed capital requirements, the nature of those requirements and how those requirements are incorporated into the management of capital; and

  - (vi) how it is meeting its objectives for managing capital;

- (b) summary quantitative data about what it manages as capital;

- (c) any changes in (a) and (b) from the previous period;

- (d) whether during the period it complied with any externally imposed capital requirements to which it is subject; and

- (e) when the entity has not complied with such externally imposed capital requirements, the consequences of such non-compliance.

Appendix 8

Specialised activities – Funding commitments

		Reference	*Y, N, N/A*	*C*	*R*
				L	

A8.01   An entity that has made a commitment shall disclose the following: FRS 102-34.62

     (a)   the commitment made;   ☐

     (b)   the time-frame of that commitment;   ☐

     (c)   any performance-related conditions attached to that commitment; and   ☐

     (d)   details of how that commitment will be funded.   ☐

[Guidance]
The disclosures may be made in aggregate, providing that such aggregation does not obscure significant information.

A8.02   Give separate disclosure for recognised and unrecognised commitments.   FRS 102-34.63   ☐

[Guidance]
The disclosures may be made in aggregate, providing that such aggregation does not obscure significant information.

Appendix 9

Transition to FRS 102

		Reference	Y, N, N/A	C L	R

Transitional arrangements

A9.01   If an entity applies FRS 102 before 1 January 2015 it shall disclose that fact.   FRS 102-1.14   ▭

Explanation of transition to this FRS

A9.02   An entity shall explain how the transition from its previous financial reporting framework to FRS 102 affected its reported financial position and financial performance.   FRS 102-35.12   ▭

A9.03   An entity's first financial statements prepared using FRS 102 shall include: FRS 102-35.13

   (a)   A description of the nature of each change in accounting policy.   ▭

   (b)   Reconciliations of its equity determined in accordance with its previous financial reporting framework to its equity determined in accordance with FRS 102 for both of the following dates:

     (i)   the date of transition to FRS 102; and   ▭

     (ii)   the end of the latest period presented in the entity's most recent annual financial statements determined in accordance with its previous financial reporting framework.   ▭

   (c)   A reconciliation of the profit or loss determined in accordance with its previous financial reporting framework for the latest period in the entity's most recent annual financial statements to its profit or loss determined in accordance with FRS 102 for the same period.   ▭

A9.04   Where an entity becomes aware of errors made under its previous financial reporting framework, the reconciliations required by FRS 102.35.13 must distinguish the correction of errors from changes in accounting policies.   FRS 102-35.14   ▭

A9.05   If an entity did not present financial statements for previous periods, it shall disclose that fact in its first financial statements that conform to FRS 102.   FRS 102-35.15   ▭

Appendix 10

Reduced disclosure framework

		Reference	*Y, N, N/A*	Checklist 4 reference

Reduced disclosures for subsidiaries and a parent's own accounts

A10.01 A qualifying entity may take advantage of the disclosure exemptions set out in this checklist, provided that it discloses in the notes to its financial statements: — FRS 102-1.11

(a) a brief narrative summary of the disclosure exemptions adopted; ☐

(b) the name of the parent of the group in whose consolidated financial statements its financial statements are consolidated; and ☐

(c) from where the parent's consolidated financial statements may be obtained. ☐

A10.02 The following exemptions from disclosure are available:

(a) a reconciliation of the number of shares outstanding at the beginning and at the end of the period; — FRS 102-1.12(a) — ☐ — 4.06(a)(v)

[Guidance]
Disclosure required by FRS 102 Section 4.12(a)(iv) is exempt

(b) a statement of cash flows; and — FRS 102-1.12(b) — ☐ — A3

[Guidance]
Disclosure required by FRS 102 Section 7.4 to 7.6 is exempt

(c) the disclosure required of key management personnel compensation. — FRS 102-1.12(e) — ☐ — 33.03

[Guidance]
Disclosure required by FRS 102 Section 33.7 is exempt

A10.03 The following disclosures required by Section 11: Basic financial instruments and Section 12: Other financial instruments are exempt from disclosure, providing the equivalent disclosures are included in the consolidated financial statements of the group in which the entity is consolidated: — FRS 102-1.12(c)

(a) in the summary of significant accounting policies, the measurement basis (or bases) used for financial instruments that are relevant to an understanding of the financial statements; — ☐ — 11.01

[Guidance]
Disclosure required by FRS 102 Section 11.40 is exempt

(b) in the summary of significant accounting policies, the other accounting policies used for financial instruments that are relevant to an understanding of the financial statements; — ☐ — 11.01

[Guidance]
Disclosure required by FRS 102 Section 11.40 is exempt

(c) the carrying amounts of each of the categories of financial assets set out in 11.41 of FRS 102 at the reporting date; — ☐ — 11.02

	Reference	Y, N, N/A	Checklist 4 reference

[Guidance]
Disclosure required by FRS 102 Section 11.41 is exempt

(d) the carrying amounts of each of the categories of financial liabilities set out in 11.41 of FRS 102 at the reporting date;   ☐ 11.02

[Guidance]
Disclosure required by FRS 102 Section 11.41 is exempt

(e) information that enables users of its financial statements to evaluate the significance of financial instruments for its financial position and performance;   ☐ 11.04

[Guidance]
Disclosure required by FRS 102 Section 11.42 is exempt

(f) the basis for determining fair value of all financial assets and financial liabilities measured at fair value;   ☐ 11.05

[Guidance]
Disclosure required by FRS 102 Section 11.43 is exempt

(g) if applicable, the fact that a reliable measure of fair value is no longer available for ordinary or preference shares measured at fair value;   ☐ 11.08

[Guidance]
Disclosure required by FRS 102 Section 11.44 is exempt

(h) the disclosures required for each class of financial asset, if an entity has transferred financial assets to another party in a transaction that does not qualify for derecognition;   ☐ 11.09

[Guidance]
Disclosure required by FRS 102 Section 11.45 is exempt

(i) the disclosures required when an entity has pledged financial assets as collateral for liabilities or contingent liabilities;   ☐ 11.10

[Guidance]
Disclosure required by FRS 102 Section 11.46 is exempt

(j) the disclosures required for loans payable recognised at the reporting date for which there is a breach of terms or default of principal, interest, sinking fund, or redemption terms that has not been remedied by the reporting date;   ☐ 11.11

[Guidance]
Disclosure required by FRS 102 Section 11.47 is exempt

(k) the disclosures required in respect of basic financial instruments of income, expense, gains or losses;   ☐ 11.12

[Guidance]
Disclosure required by FRS 102 Section 11.48 is exempt

(l) the disclosures that are only required for financial instruments at fair value through profit or loss that are not held as part of a trading portfolio and are not derivatives;   ☐ 11.28

[Guidance]
Disclosure required by FRS 102 Section 11.48A is exempt

(m) the disclosures required for hedges of each of the four types of risks; and   ☐ 12.01

[Guidance]
Disclosure required by FRS 102 Section 12.27 is exempt

	Reference	Y, N, N/A	Checklist 4 reference

(n) the disclosures required if an entity uses hedge accounting. | | ☐ | 12.02 03,04

[Guidance]
Disclosure required by FRS 102 Section 12.28 to 12.29 is exempt

A10.04 For an ultimate parent, the following disclosures required by Section 26: Share-based payment provided that the share-based payment arrangement concerns its own equity instruments and its separate financial statements are presented alongside the consolidated financial statements of the group, and provided that the equivalent disclosures are included in the consolidated financial statements of the group in which the entity is consolidated: | FRS 102-1.12(d) | |

(a) the number and weighted average exercise prices of share options; | | ☐ | A4. 01(c)

[Guidance]
Disclosure required by FRS 102 Section 26.18(b) is exempt

(b) the disclosures required for equity-settled share-based payment arrangements; | | ☐ | A4. 02,03

[Guidance]
Disclosure required by FRS 102 Section 26.19 is exempt

(c) information about how the liability was measured for cash-settled share-based payment arrangements; | | ☐ | A4. 04

[Guidance]
Disclosure required by FRS 102 Section 26.20 is exempt

(d) an explanation of modifications to share-based payment arrangements; and | | ☐ | A4. 05

[Guidance]
Disclosure required by FRS 102 Section 26.21 is exempt

(e) information about the effect of share-based payment transactions on the entity's profit or loss for the period and on its financial position. | | ☐ | A4. 07

[Guidance]
Disclosure required by FRS 102 Section 26.23 is exempt

A10.05 For a subsidiary, the following disclosures required by Section 26: Share-based payment provided that the share-based payment arrangement concerns equity instruments of another group entity, and provided that the equivalent disclosures are included in the consolidated financial statements of the group in which the entity is consolidated: | FRS 102-1.12(d) | |

(a) the number and weighted average exercise prices of share options; | | ☐ | A4. 01(c)

[Guidance]
Disclosure required by FRS 102 Section 26.18(b) is exempt

(b) the disclosures required for equity-settled share-based payment arrangements; | | ☐ | A4. 02,03

[Guidance]
Disclosure required by FRS 102 Section 26.19 is exempt

(c) information about how the liability was measured for cash-settled share-based payment arrangements; | | ☐ | A4. 04

	Reference	Y, N, N/A	Checklist 4 reference

[Guidance]
Disclosure required by FRS 102 Section 26.20 is exempt

(d) an explanation of modifications to share-based payment arrangements; and

A4. 05

[Guidance]
Disclosure required by FRS 102 Section 26.21 is exempt

(e) information about the effect of share-based payment transactions on the entity's profit or loss for the period and on its financial position.

A4. 07

[Guidance]
Disclosure required by FRS 102 Section 26.23 is exempt

Appendix 11

Strategic report with supplementary material

		Reference	*Y, N, N/A*	*C L*	*R*
A11.01	State that the strategic report is only part of the company's annual accounts and reports.	s426A(2)a	☐	C	
A11.02	State how a person entitled to them can obtain a full copy of the company's annual accounts and reports.	s426A(2)b	☐	C	
A11.03	State whether the auditor's report on the annual accounts:	s426A(2)c			
	(a) was unqualified or qualified; and		☐	C	
	(b) if it was qualified, set out the report in full, together with any further material needed to understand the qualification.		☐	C	
A11.04	State whether, in that report, the auditor's statement under section 496 (whether strategic report and directors' report consistent with the accounts):	s426A(2)d			
	(a) was unqualified or qualified; and		☐	C	
	(b) if it was qualified, set out the qualified statement in full, together with any further material needed to understand the qualification.		☐	C	

Appendix C SI 2008/410 – Large and Medium-sized Companies and Groups (Accounts and Reports) Regulations 2008

SI 2008/410 as amended by SI 2015/980, SI 2015/1672 and SI 2016/575

Made on 19 February 2008 by the Secretary of State, in exercise of the powers conferred by s. 396(3), 404(3), 409(1) to (3), 412(1) to (3), 416(4), 421(1) and (2), 445(3)(a) and (b), 677(3)(a), 712(2)(b)(i), 831(3)(a), 832(4)(a), 836(1)(b)(i) and 1292(1)(a) and (c) of the Companies Act 2006. In accordance with s. 473(3) and 1290 of the Companies Act 2006 a draft of this instrument was laid before Parliament and approved by a resolution of each House of Parliament. Operative from 6 April 2008.

PART 1 – INTRODUCTION
CITATION AND INTERPRETATION

1(1) These Regulations may be cited as the Large and Medium-sized Companies and Groups (Accounts and Reports) Regulations 2008.

1(2) In these Regulations **'the 2006 Act'** means the Companies Act 2006.

COMMENCEMENT AND APPLICATION

2(1) These Regulations come into force on 6th April 2008.

2(2) Subject to paragraph (3), they apply in relation to financial years beginning on or after 6th April 2008.

2(3) The requirement for disclosure in paragraph 4 of Schedule 8 to these Regulations (directors' remuneration report: disclosure relating to consideration of conditions in company and group) applies in relation to financial years beginning on or after 6th April 2009.

2(4) These Regulations apply to companies other than those which are subject to the small companies regime under Part 15 of the 2006 Act.

PART 2 – FORM AND CONTENT OF ACCOUNTS
COMPANIES ACT INDIVIDUAL ACCOUNTS (COMPANIES OTHER THAN BANKING AND INSURANCE COMPANIES)

3(1) Subject to regulation 4, the directors of a company–

(a) for which they are preparing Companies Act individual accounts under section 396 of the 2006 Act (Companies Act: individual accounts), and

(b) which is not a banking company or an insurance company,

must comply with the provisions of Schedule 1 to these Regulations as to the form and content of the balance sheet and profit and loss account, and additional information to be provided by way of notes to the accounts.

3(2) The profit and loss account of a company that falls within section 408 of the 2006 Act (individual profit and loss account where group accounts prepared) need not contain the information specified in paragraphs 65 to 69 of Schedule 1 to these Regulations (information supplementing the profit and loss account).

MEDIUM-SIZED COMPANIES: EXEMPTIONS FOR COMPANIES ACT INDIVIDUAL ACCOUNTS

4(1) This regulation applies to a company–

(a) which qualifies as medium-sized in relation to a financial year under section 465 of the 2006 Act, and

(b) the directors of which are preparing Companies Act individual accounts under section 396 of that Act for that year.

4(2A) The individual accounts for the year need not comply with paragraph 45 (disclosure with respect to compliance with accounting standards) of Schedule 1 to these Regulations.

4(2B) Paragraph 72 (related party transactions) applies with the modification that only particulars of transactions which have not been concluded under normal market conditions with the following must be disclosed–

(a) owners holding a participating interest in the company;

(b) companies in which the company itself has a participating interest; and

(c) the company's directors.

4(3) [Omitted by SI 2015/980, reg. 26(3).]

History – Reg. 4(2A) and (2B) substituted for reg. 4(2) by SI 2015/980, reg. 26(2), with effect in relation to–
(a) financial years beginning on or after 1 January 2016, and
(b) a financial year of a company beginning on or after 1 January 2015, but before 1 January 2016, if the directors of the company so decide.

Reg. 4(3) omitted by SI 2015/980, reg. 26(3), with effect in relation to–
(a) financial years beginning on or after 1 January 2016, and
(b) a financial year of a company beginning on or after 1 January 2015, but before 1 January 2016, if the directors of the company so decide.

Former reg. 4(3) read as follows:

"**4(3)** The directors of the company may deliver to the registrar of companies a copy of the accounts for the year–
(a) which includes a profit and loss account in which the following items listed in the profit and loss account formats set out in Schedule 1 are combined as one item – items 2, 3 and 6 in format 1; items 2 to 5 in format 2; items A.1 and B.2 in format 3; items A.1, A.2 and B.2 to B.4 in format 4;
(b) which does not contain the information required by paragraph 68 of Schedule 1 (particulars of turnover)."

COMPANIES ACT INDIVIDUAL ACCOUNTS: BANKING COMPANIES

5(1) The directors of a company–

(a) for which they are preparing Companies Act individual accounts under section 396 of the 2006 Act, and

(b) which is a banking company,

must comply with the provisions of Schedule 2 to these Regulations as to the form and content of the balance sheet and profit and loss account, and additional information to be provided by way of notes to the accounts.

5(2) The profit and loss account of a banking company that falls within section 408 of the 2006 Act (individual profit and loss account where group accounts prepared) need not contain the information specified in paragraphs 85 to 91 of Schedule 2 to these Regulations (information supplementing the profit and loss account).

5(3) Accounts prepared in accordance with this regulation must contain a statement that they are prepared in accordance with the provisions of these Regulations relating to banking companies.

COMPANIES ACT INDIVIDUAL ACCOUNTS: INSURANCE COMPANIES

6(1) The directors of a company–

(a) for which they are preparing Companies Act individual accounts under section 396 of the 2006 Act, and

(b) which is an insurance company,

must comply with the provisions of Schedule 3 to these Regulations as to the form and content of the balance sheet and profit and loss account, and additional information to be provided by way of notes to the accounts.

6(2) The profit and loss account of a company that falls within section 408 of the 2006 Act (individual profit and loss account where group accounts prepared)(a) need not contain the information specified in paragraphs 83 to 89 of Schedule 3 to these Regulations (information supplementing the profit and loss account).

6(3) Accounts prepared in accordance with this regulation must contain a statement that they are prepared in accordance with the provisions of these Regulations relating to insurance companies.

INFORMATION ABOUT RELATED UNDERTAKINGS (COMPANIES ACT OR IAS INDIVIDUAL OR GROUP ACCOUNTS)

7(1) Companies Act or IAS individual or group accounts must comply with the provisions of Schedule 4 to these Regulations as to information about related undertakings to be given in notes to the company's accounts.

7(2) In Schedule 4–

Part 1 contains provisions applying to all companies

Part 2 contains provisions applying only to companies not required to prepare group accounts

Part 3 contains provisions applying only to companies required to prepare group accounts

Part 4 contains additional disclosures for banking companies and groups

Part 5 contains interpretative provisions.

7(3) Information otherwise required to be given by Schedule 4 need not be disclosed with respect to an undertaking that–

(a) is established under the law of a country outside the United Kingdom, or

(b) carries on business outside the United Kingdom,

if the conditions specified in section 409(4) of the 2006 Act are met (see section 409(5) of the 2006 Act for disclosure required where advantage taken of this exemption).

This paragraph does not apply in relation to the information otherwise required by paragraph 3, 7 or 21 of Schedule 4.

INFORMATION ABOUT DIRECTORS' BENEFITS: REMUNERATION (COMPANIES ACT OR IAS INDIVIDUAL OR GROUP ACCOUNTS: QUOTED AND UNQUOTED COMPANIES)

8(1) Companies Act or IAS individual or group accounts must comply with the provisions of Schedule 5 to these Regulations as to information about directors' remuneration to be given in notes to the company's accounts.

8(2) In Schedule 5–

Part 1 contains provisions applying to quoted and unquoted companies,

Part 2 contains provisions applying only to unquoted companies, and

Part 3 contains supplementary provisions.

COMPANIES ACT GROUP ACCOUNTS

9(1) Subject to paragraphs (2) and (3), where the directors of a parent company prepare Companies Act group accounts under section 403 of the 2006 Act (group accounts: applicable accounting framework), those accounts must comply with the provisions of Part 1 of Schedule 6 to these Regulations as to the form and content of the consolidated balance sheet and consolidated profit and loss account, and additional information to be provided by way of notes to the accounts.

9(2) The directors of the parent company of a banking group preparing Companies Act group accounts must do so in accordance with the provisions of Part 1 of Schedule 6 as modified by Part 2 of that Schedule.

9(3) The directors of the parent company of an insurance group preparing Companies Act group accounts must do so in accordance with the provisions of Part 1 of Schedule 6 as modified by Part 3 of that Schedule.

9(4) Accounts prepared in accordance with paragraph (2) or (3) must contain a statement that they are prepared in accordance with the provisions of these Regulations relating to banking groups or to insurance groups, as the case may be.

PART 3 – DIRECTORS' REPORT
DIRECTORS' REPORT

10(1) The report which the directors of a company are required to prepare under section 415 of the 2006 Act (duty to prepare directors' report) must disclose the matters specified in Schedule 7 to these Regulations.

10(2) In Schedule 7–

Part 1 relates to matters of a general nature including political donations and expenditure,

Part 2 relates to the acquisition by a company of its own shares or a charge on them,

Part 3 relates to the employment, training and advancement of disabled persons,

Part 4 relates to the involvement of employees in the affairs, policy and performance of the company,

Part 6 relates to certain disclosures required by publicly traded companies, and

Part 7 relates to disclosures in relation to greenhouse gas emissions.

History – Reg. 10(2) substituted by SI 2013/1970, reg. 7(1) and (2), with effect from 1 October 2013 in respect of financial years ending on or after 30 September 2013.

This version of reg. 10 applies to financial years ending on or after 30 September 2013. The version applying to financial years ending before 30 September 2013 read as follows:

"**10(1)** The report which the directors of a company are required to prepare under section 415 of the 2006 Act (duty to prepare directors' report) must disclose the matters specified in Schedule 7 to these Regulations.

10(2) In Schedule 7–
Part 1 relates to matters of a general nature, including changes in asset values and contributions for political and charitable purposes,
Part 2 relates to the acquisition by a company of its own shares or a charge on them,
Part 3 relates to the employment, training and advancement of disabled persons,
Part 4 relates to the involvement of employees in the affairs, policy and performance of the company, and
Part 5 relates to the company's policy and practice on the payment of creditors."

PART 4 – DIRECTORS' REMUNERATION REPORT
DIRECTORS' REMUNERATION REPORT (QUOTED COMPANIES)

11(1) The remuneration report which the directors of a quoted company are required to prepare under section 420 of the 2006 Act (duty to prepare directors' remuneration report) must contain the information specified in Schedule 8 to these Regulations, and must comply with any requirement of that Schedule as to how information is to be set out in the report.

11(1A) The document setting out a revised directors' remuneration policy in accordance with section 422A of the 2006 Act must contain the information specified in Schedule 8 to these Regulations, and must comply with any requirements in that Schedule as to how that information is to be set out.

11(2) [Revoked.]

11(3) For the purposes of section 497 in Part 16 of the 2006 Act (auditor's report on auditable part of directors' remuneration report), 'the auditable part' of a directors' remuneration report is the information set out in the report as identified in Part 5 of Schedule 8 to these Regulations.

History – Reg. 11(1A) inserted, 11(2) revoked and, in 11(3), 'the information set out in the report as identified in Part 5' substituted for 'the part containing the information required by Part 3' by SI 2013/1981, reg. 2, with effect from 1 October 2013 in relation to a company's financial year ending on or after 30 September 2013.

This version of reg. 11 applies to financial years ending on or after 30 September 2013. The version applying to financial years ending before 30 September 2013 read as follows:

"**11(1)** The remuneration report which the directors of a quoted company are required to prepare under section 420 of the 2006 Act (duty to prepare directors' remuneration report) must contain the information specified in Schedule 8 to these Regulations, and must comply with any requirement of that Schedule as to how information is to be set out in the report.

11(2) In Schedule 8–

Part 1 is introductory,

Part 2 relates to information about remuneration committees, performance related remuneration, consideration of conditions elsewhere in company and group and liabilities in respect of directors' contracts,

Part 3 relates to detailed information about directors' remuneration (information included under Part 3 is required to be reported on by the auditor (see subsection (3)), and

Part 4 contains interpretative and supplementary provisions.

11(3) For the purposes of section 497 in Part 16 of the 2006 Act (auditor's report on auditable part of directors' remuneration report), **'the auditable part'** of a directors' remuneration report is the part containing the information required by Part 3 of Schedule 8 to these Regulations."

PART 5 – INTERPRETATION
DEFINITION OF 'PROVISIONS'

12 Schedule 9 to these Regulations defines **'provisions'** for the purposes of these Regulations and for the purposes of–

(a) section 677(3)(a) (Companies Act accounts: relevant provisions for purposes of financial assistance) in Part 18 of the 2006 Act,

(b) section 712(2)(b)(i) (Companies Act accounts: relevant provisions to determine available profits for redemption or purchase by private company out of capital) in that Part,

(c) sections 831(3)(a) (Companies Act accounts: net asset restriction on public company distributions), 832(4)(a) (Companies Act accounts: investment companies distributions) and 836(1)(b)(i) (Companies Act accounts: relevant provisions for distribution purposes) in Part 23 of that Act, and

(d) section 841(2)(a) (Companies Act accounts: provisions to be treated as realised losses) in that Part.

Notes – Reg. 12(d) inserted by SI 2009/1581 reg 12(1) and (2): 27 June 2009 applying in relation to financial years beginning on or after 6 April 2008 which have not ended before 27 June 2009.

GENERAL INTERPRETATION

13 Schedule 10 to these Regulations contains general definitions for the purposes of these Regulations.

PART 6 – REVIEW

History – Pt. 6 inserted by SI 2016/575, reg. 67, with effect in relation to–
  (a) financial years beginning on or after 1 January 2016; and
  (b) a financial year of an LLP beginning on or after 1 January 2015, but before 1 January 2016, if–
    (i) the members of the LLP so decide; and
    (ii) copy of the LLP's accounts for that financial year has not been delivered to the registrar in accordance with CA 2006, s. 444, 445 or 446 as applied to LLPs by the 2008 Regulations before the date on which these Regulations come into force.

REVIEW

14(1) The Secretary of State must from time to time–

(a) carry out a review of the provisions of these Regulations to which amendments have been made by Part 6 of the Limited Liability Partnerships, Partnerships and Groups (Accounts and Audit) Regulations 2016 ('the 2016 Regulations'),

(b) set out the conclusions of the review in a report, and

(c) publish the report.

14(2) The report must, in particular–

(a) set out the objectives intended to be achieved by those provisions,

(b) assess the extent to which those objectives are achieved,

(c) assess whether those objectives remain appropriate, and

(d) if those objectives remain appropriate, assess the extent to which they could be achieved in another way which involves less onerous regulatory provision.

14(3) In carrying out the review, the Secretary of State must have regard to how the provisions of Directive 2013/34/EU of 26 June 2013 on the annual financial statements etc. of certain types of undertakings which are implemented by means of the provisions mentioned in paragraph (1)(a) are implemented in other Member States.

14(4) The first report under this regulation must be published before the end of the period of 5 years beginning with the date on which the 2016 Regulations come into force.

14(5) Subsequent reports under this regulation must be published at intervals not exceeding 5 years.

14(6) In this regulation, **'regulatory provision'** has the meaning given by section 32(4) of the Small Business, Enterprise and Employment Act 2015.

History – Reg. 14 inserted by SI 2016/575, reg. 67, with effect in relation to–
  (a) financial years beginning on or after 1 January 2016; and
  (b) a financial year of an LLP beginning on or after 1 January 2015, but before 1 January 2016, if–
    (i) the members of the LLP so decide; and

(ii)   copy of the LLP's accounts for that financial year has not been delivered to the registrar in accordance with CA 2006, s. 444, 445 or 446 as applied to LLPs by the 2008 Regulations before the date on which these Regulations come into force.

SCHEDULES

SCHEDULE 1 – COMPANIES ACT INDIVIDUAL ACCOUNTS: COMPANIES WHICH ARE NOT BANKING OR INSURANCE COMPANIES

Regulation 3(1)

Part 1 – General rules and formats

SECTION A – GENERAL RULES

1(1)   Subject to the following provisions of this Schedule–

(a)   every balance sheet of a company must show the items listed in either of the balance sheet formats in Section B of this Part, and

(b)   every profit and loss account must show the items listed in either of the profit and loss account formats in Section B.

1(2)   References in this Schedule to the items listed in any of the formats in Section B are to those items read together with any of the notes following the formats which apply to those items.

1(3)   Subject to paragraph 1A, the items must be shown in the order and under the headings and sub-headings given in the particular format used, but–

(a)   the notes to the formats may permit alternative positions for any particular items, and

(b)   the heading or sub-heading for any item does not have to be distinguished by any letter or number assigned to that item in the format used.

History – In para. 1(1)(b), the word 'either' substituted for the words 'any one' by SI 2015/980, reg. 27(2)(a), with effect in relation to–
(a)   financial years beginning on or after 1 January 2016, and
(b)   a financial year of a company beginning on or after 1 January 2015, but before 1 January 2016, if the directors of the company so decide.

In para. 1(3), the words 'Subject to paragraph 1A,' inserted by SI 2015/980, reg. 27(2)(b), with effect in relation to–
(a)   financial years beginning on or after 1 January 2016, and
(b)   a financial year of a company beginning on or after 1 January 2015, but before 1 January 2016, if the directors of the company so decide.

1A(1)   The company's directors may adapt one of the balance sheet formats in Section B so to distinguish between current and non-current items in a different way, provided that–

(a)   the information given is at least equivalent to that which would have been required by the use of such format had it not been thus adapted, and

(b)   the presentation of those items is in accordance with generally accepted accounting principles or practice.

1A(2)   The company's directors may adapt one of the profit and loss account formats in Section B, provided that–

(a)   the information given is at least equivalent to that which would have been required by the use of such format had it not been thus adapted, and

(b)   the presentation is in accordance with generally accepted accounting principles or practice.

1A(3)   So far as is practicable, the following provisions of Section A of this Part of this Schedule apply to the balance sheet or profit or loss account of a company notwithstanding any such adaptation pursuant to this paragraph.

History – Para. 1A inserted by SI 2015/980, reg. 27(2)(c), with effect in relation to–
   (a)   financial years beginning on or after 1 January 2016, and
   (b)   a financial year of a company beginning on or after 1 January 2015, but before 1 January 2016, if the directors of the company so decide.

2(1)   Where in accordance with paragraph 1 a company's balance sheet or profit and loss account for any financial year has been prepared by reference to one of the formats in Section B, the company's directors must use the same format in preparing Companies Act individual accounts for subsequent financial years, unless in their opinion there are special reasons for a change.

2(2)   Particulars of any such change must be given in a note to the accounts in which the new format is first used, and the reasons for the change must be explained.

3(1)   Any item required to be shown in a company's balance sheet or profit and loss account may be shown in greater detail than required by the particular format used.

3(2)   The balance sheet or profit and loss account may include an item representing or covering the amount of any asset or liability, income or expenditure not otherwise covered by any of the items listed in the format used, save that none of the following may be treated as assets in any balance sheet–

   (a)   preliminary expenses,
   (b)   expenses of, and commission on, any issue of shares or debentures, and
   (c)   costs of research.

4(1)   Where the special nature of the company's business requires it, the company's directors must adapt the arrangement, headings and sub-headings otherwise required in respect of items given an Arabic number in the balance sheet or profit and loss account format used.

4(2)   The directors may combine items to which Arabic numbers are given in any of the formats in Section B if–

   (a)   their individual amounts are not material to assessing the state of affairs or profit or loss of the company for the financial year in question, or
   (b)   the combination facilitates that assessment.

4(3)   Where sub-paragraph (2)(b) applies, the individual amounts of any items which have been combined must be disclosed in a note to the accounts.

5(1)   Subject to sub-paragraph (2), the directors must not include a heading or sub-heading corresponding to an item in the balance sheet or profit and loss account format used if there is no amount to be shown for that item for the financial year to which the balance sheet or profit and loss account relates.

5(2)   Where an amount can be shown for the item in question for the immediately preceding financial year that amount must be shown under the heading or sub-heading required by the format for that item.

6   Every profit and loss account must show the amount of a company's profit or loss before taxation.

History – In para. 6, the words 'on ordinary activities' omitted by SI 2015/980, reg. 27(2)(d), with effect in relation to–
   (a)   financial years beginning on or after 1 January 2016, and
   (b)   a financial year of a company beginning on or after 1 January 2015, but before 1 January 2016, if the directors of the company so decide.

7(1) For every item shown in the balance sheet or profit and loss account the corresponding amount for the immediately preceding financial year must also be shown.

7(2) Where that corresponding amount is not comparable with the amount to be shown for the item in question in respect of the financial year to which the balance sheet or profit and loss account relates, the former amount may be adjusted, and particulars of the non-comparability and of any adjustment must be disclosed in a note to the accounts.

8 Amounts in respect of items representing assets or income may not be set off against amounts in respect of items representing liabilities or expenditure (as the case may be), or vice versa.

9 The company's directors must, in determining how amounts are presented within items in the profit and loss account and balance sheet, have regard to the substance of the reported transaction or arrangement, in accordance with generally accepted accounting principles or practice.

9A Where an asset or liability relates to more than one item in the balance sheet, the relationship of such asset or liability to the relevant items must be disclosed either under those items or in the notes to the accounts.

History – Para. 9A inserted by SI 2015/980, reg. 27(2)(e), with effect in relation to–
  (a)   financial years beginning on or after 1 January 2016, and
  (b)   a financial year of a company beginning on or after 1 January 2015, but before 1 January 2016, if the directors of the company so decide.

SECTION B – THE REQUIRED FORMATS FOR ACCOUNTS

Balance sheet formats – Format 1

A. Called up share capital not paid [1]

B. Fixed assets

  I. Intangible assets

    1. Development costs

    2. Concessions, patents, licences, trade marks and similar rights and assets [2]

    3. Goodwill [3]

    4. Payments on account

  II. Tangible assets

    1. Land and buildings

    2. Plant and machinery

    3. Fixtures, fittings, tools and equipment

    4. Payments on account and assets in course of construction

  III. Investments

    1. Shares in group undertakings

    2. Loans to group undertakings

    3. Participating interests

    4. Loans to undertakings in which the company has a participating interest

    5. Other investments other than loans

    6. Other loans

    7. Own shares [4]

C. Current assets

  I. Stocks

    1. Raw materials and consumables

    2. Work in progress

3. Finished goods and goods for resale

4. Payments on account

II. Debtors [5]

1. Trade debtors

2. Amounts owed by group undertakings

3. Amounts owed by undertakings in which the company has a participating interest

4. Other debtors

5. Called up share capital not paid [1]

6. Prepayments and accrued income [6]

III. Investments

1. Shares in group undertakings

2. Own shares [4]

3. Other investments

IV. Cash at bank and in hand

D. Prepayments and accrued income [6]

E. Creditors: amounts falling due within one year

1. Debenture loans [7]

2. Bank loans and overdrafts

3. Payments received on account [8]

4. Trade creditors

5. Bills of exchange payable

6. Amounts owed to group undertakings

7. Amounts owed to undertakings in which the company has a participating interest

8. Other creditors including taxation and social security [9]

9. Accruals and deferred income [10]

F. Net current assets (liabilities) [11]

G. Total assets less current liabilities

H. Creditors: amounts falling due after more than one year

1. Debenture loans [7]

2. Bank loans and overdrafts

3. Payments received on account [8]

4. Trade creditors

5. Bills of exchange payable

6. Amounts owed to group undertakings

7. Amounts owed to undertakings in which the company has a participating interest

8. Other creditors including taxation and social security [9]

9. Accruals and deferred income [10]

I. Provisions for liabilities

1. Pensions and similar obligations

2. Taxation, including deferred taxation

3. Other provisions

J. Accruals and deferred income [10]

K. Capital and reserves

I. Called up share capital [12]

II. Share premium account

III. Revaluation reserve

IV. Other reserves

    1. Capital redemption reserve

    2. Reserve for own shares

    3. Reserves provided for by the articles of association

    4. Other reserves, including the fair value reserve

V. Profit and loss account

Balance sheet formats – Format 2

ASSETS

A. Called up share capital not paid [1]

B. Fixed assets

    I. Intangible assets

        1. Development costs

        2. Concessions, patents, licences, trade marks and similar rights and assets [2]

        3. Goodwill [3]

        4. Payments on account

    II. Tangible assets

        1. Land and buildings

        2. Plant and machinery

        3. Fixtures, fittings, tools and equipment

        4. Payments on account and assets in course of construction

    III. Investments

        1. Shares in group undertakings

        2. Loans to group undertakings

        3. Participating interests

        4. Loans to undertakings in which the company has a participating interest

        5. Other investments other than loans

        6. Other loans

        7. Own shares [4]

C. Current assets

    I. Stocks

        1. Raw materials and consumables

        2. Work in progress

        3. Finished goods and goods for resale

        4. Payments on account

    II. Debtors [5]

        1. Trade debtors

        2. Amounts owed by group undertakings

        3. Amounts owed by undertakings in which the company has a participating interest

        4. Other debtors

        5. Called up share capital not paid [1]

        6. Prepayments and accrued income [6]

III. Investments

    1. Shares in group undertakings

    2. Own shares [4]

    3. Other investments

IV. Cash at bank and in hand

D. Prepayments and accrued income [6]

CAPITAL, RESERVES AND LIABILITIES

A. Capital and reserves

    I. Called up share capital [12]

    II. Share premium account

    III. Revaluation reserve

    IV. Other reserves

        1. Capital redemption reserve

        2. Reserve for own shares

        3. Reserves provided for by the articles of association

        4. Other reserves, including the fair value reserve

    V. Profit and loss account

B. Provisions for liabilities

    1. Pensions and similar obligations

    2. Taxation, including deferred taxation

    3. Other provisions

C. Creditors [13]

    1. Debenture loans [7]

    2. Bank loans and overdrafts

    3. Payments received on account [8]

    4. Trade creditors

    5. Bills of exchange payable

    6. Amounts owed to group undertakings

    7. Amounts owed to undertakings in which the company has a participating interest

    8. Other creditors including taxation and social security [9]

    9. Accruals and deferred income [10]

D. Accruals and deferred income [10]

Notes on the balance sheet formats

[1] *Called up share capital not paid*

(Formats 1 and 2, items A and C.II.5.)

This item may be shown in either of the two positions given in formats 1 and 2.

[2] *Concessions, patents, licences, trade marks and similar rights and assets*

(Formats 1 and 2, item B.I.2.)

Amounts in respect of assets are only to be included in a company's balance sheet under this item if either–

(a) the assets were acquired for valuable consideration and are not required to be shown under goodwill, or

(b) the assets in question were created by the company itself.

[3] *Goodwill*

(Formats 1 and 2, item B.I.3.)

Amounts representing goodwill are only to be included to the extent that the goodwill was acquired for valuable consideration.

[4] *Own shares*

(Formats 1 and 2, items B.III.7 and C.III.2.)

The nominal value of the shares held must be shown separately.

(5) *Debtors*

(Formats 1 and 2, items C.II.1 to 6.)

The amount falling due after more than one year must be shown separately for each item included under debtors.

(6) *Prepayments and accrued income*

(Formats 1 and 2, items C.II.6 and D.)

This item may be shown in either of the two positions given in formats 1 and 2.

(7) *Debenture loans*

(Format 1, items E.1 and H.1 and format 2, item C.1.)

The amount of any convertible loans must be shown separately.

(8) *Payments received on account*

(Format 1, items E.3 and H.3 and format 2, item C.3.)

Payments received on account of orders must be shown for each of these items in so far as they are not shown as deductions from stocks.

(9) *Other creditors including taxation and social security*

(Format 1, items E.8 and H.8 and format 2, item C.8.)

The amount for creditors in respect of taxation and social security must be shown separately from the amount for other creditors.

(10) *Accruals and deferred income*

(Format 1, items E.9, H.9 and J and format 2, items C.9 and D.)

The two positions given for this item in format 1 at E.9 and H.9 are an alternative to the position at J, but if the item is not shown in a position corresponding to that at J it may be shown in either or both of the other two positions (as the case may require).

The two positions given for this item in format 2 are alternatives.

(11) *Net current assets (liabilities)*

(Format 1, item F.)

In determining the amount to be shown for this item any amounts shown under 'prepayments and accrued income' must be taken into account wherever shown.

(12) *Called up share capital*

(Format 1, item K.I and format 2, item A.I.)

The amount of allotted share capital and the amount of called up share capital which has been paid up must be shown separately.

(13) *Creditors*

(Format 2, items C.1 to 9.)

Amounts falling due within one year and after one year must be shown separately for each of these items and for the aggregate of all of these items.

Profit and loss account formats – Format 1

1. Turnover

2. Cost of sales (14)

3. Gross profit or loss

4. Distribution costs (14)

5. Administrative expenses (14)

6. Other operating income

7. Income from shares in group undertakings

8. Income from participating interests

9. Income from other fixed asset investments (15)

10. Other interest receivable and similar income (15)

11. Amounts written off investments

12. Interest payable and similar expenses (16)

13. Tax on profit or loss

14. Profit or loss after taxation

15. Omitted

16. Omitted

17. Omitted

18. Omitted

19. Other taxes not shown under the above items

20. Profit or loss for the financial year

Profit and loss account formats – Format 2

1. Turnover

2. Change in stocks of finished goods and in work in progress

3. Own work capitalised

4. Other operating income

5.

    (a) Raw materials and consumables

    (b) Other external expenses

6. Staff costs

    (a) wages and salaries

    (b) social security costs

    (c) other pension costs

7.

    (a) Depreciation and other amounts written off tangible and intangible fixed assets

    (b) Amounts written off current assets, to the extent that they exceed write-offs which are normal in the undertaking concerned

8. Other operating expenses

9. Income from shares in group undertakings

10. Income from participating interests

11. Income from other fixed asset investments [15]

12. Other interest receivable and similar income [15]

13. Amounts written off investments

14. Interest payable and similar expenses [16]

15. Tax on profit or loss

16. Profit or loss after taxation

17. Omitted

18. Omitted

19. Omitted

20. Omitted

21. Other taxes not shown under the above items

22. Profit or loss for the financial year

Notes on the profit and loss account formats

[14] *Cost of sales: distribution costs: administrative expenses*

(Format 1, items 2, 4 and 5.)

These items must be stated after taking into account any necessary provisions for depreciation or diminution in value of assets.

[15] *Income from other fixed asset investments: other interest receivable and similar income*

(Format 1, items 9 and 10; format 2, items 11 and 12.)

Income and interest derived from group undertakings must be shown separately from income and interest derived from other sources.

[16] *Interest payable and similar expenses*

(Format 1, item 12; format 2, item 14.)

The amount payable to group undertakings must be shown separately.

[17] *Format 1*

The amount of any provisions for depreciation and diminution in value of tangible and intangible fixed assets falling to be shown under item 7(a) in format 2 must be disclosed in a note to the accounts in any case where the profit and loss account is prepared using format 1.

History – In section B, the following amendments were made by SI 2015/980, reg. 27(3), with effect in relation to– (a) financial years beginning on or after 1 January 2016, and (b) a financial year of a company beginning on or after 1 January 2015, but before 1 January 2016, if the directors of the company so decide:

- in balance sheet format 1, item '4 Other reserves, including the fair value reserve' substitute for '4 Other reserves'.
- the heading 'CAPITAL, RESERVES AND LIABILITIES' substituted for the word 'LIABILITIES'.
- in balance sheet format 2, item '4 Other reserves, including the fair value reserve' substitute for '4 Other reserves'.
- in profit and loss account format 1–

  - at item 12, the word 'expenses' substitute for 'charges';
  - at item 13, the words 'on ordinary activities' omitted;
  - at item 14, the words 'on ordinary activities' omitted;
  - items 15–18 omit.
- in profit and loss account format 2–

  - at item 5(b), the word 'expenses' substitute for 'charges';
  - item 7(b) substituted;
  - at item 8, the word 'expenses' substitute for 'charges';
  - at item 14, the word 'expenses' substitute for 'charges';
  - at item 15, the words 'on ordinary activities' omitted;
  - at item 16, the words 'on ordinary activities' omitted;
  - items 17–20 omitted.
- profit and loss account format 3 omitted.
- profit and loss account format 4 omitted.
- in note (14) of 'Notes on the profit and loss account formats', the words 'and format 3, items A.1, 2 and 3' omitted.
- in note (15), the words 'format 3, items B.5 and 6 and format 4, items B.7 and 8' omitted.
- in note (16) title, the word 'expenses' substitute for 'charges'; and the words 'format 3, item A.5 and format 4, item A.7' omitted.
- note (17) title, 'Format 1' substituted; the words 'item 7(a) in format 2' substitute for 'items 7(a) and A.4(a) respectively in formats 2 and 4'; and the words 'or format 3' omitted.

Part 2 – Accounting principles and rules

SECTION A – ACCOUNTING PRINCIPLES

Preliminary

10(1) The amounts to be included in respect of all items shown in a company's accounts must be determined in accordance with the principles set out in this Section.

10(2) But if it appears to the company's directors that there are special reasons for departing from any of those principles in preparing the company's accounts in respect of any financial year they may do so, in which case particulars of the departure, the reasons for it and its effect must be given in a note to the accounts.

Accounting principles

11 The company is presumed to be carrying on business as a going concern.

12 Accounting policies and measurement bases must be applied consistently within the same accounts and from one financial year to the next.

History – In para. 12, the words 'and measurement bases' inserted by SI 2015/980, reg. 28(2)(a), with effect in relation to–
  (a) financial years beginning on or after 1 January 2016, and
  (b) a financial year of a company beginning on or after 1 January 2015, but before 1 January 2016, if the directors of the company so decide.

13 The amount of any item must be determined on a prudent basis, and in particular–

(a) only profits realised at the balance sheet date are to be included in the profit and loss account,

(b) all liabilities which have arisen in respect of the financial year to which the accounts relate or a previous financial year must be taken into account, including those which only become apparent between the balance sheet date and the date on which it is signed on behalf of the board of directors in accordance with Section 414 of the 2006 Act (approval and signing of accounts) and

(c) all provisions for diminution of value must be recognised, whether the result of the financial year is a profit or a loss.

History – Para. 13(c), (and the word 'and' preceding it) inserted; the word 'and' in para. (a) omitted by SI 2015/980, reg. 28(2)(b), with effect in relation to–
  (a) financial years beginning on or after 1 January 2016, and
  (b) a financial year of a company beginning on or after 1 January 2015, but before 1 January 2016, if the directors of the company so decide.

14 All income and charges relating to the financial year to which the accounts relate must be taken into account, without regard to the date of receipt or payment.

15 In determining the aggregate amount of any item, the amount of each individual asset or liability that falls to be taken into account must be determined separately.

15A The opening balance sheet for each financial year shall correspond to the closing balance sheet for the preceding financial year.

History – Para. 15A inserted by SI 2015/980, reg. 28(2)(c), with effect in relation to–
  (a) financial years beginning on or after 1 January 2016, and
  (b) a financial year of a company beginning on or after 1 January 2015, but before 1 January 2016, if the directors of the company so decide.

SECTION B – HISTORICAL COST ACCOUNTING RULES

Preliminary

16 Subject to Sections C and D of this Part of this Schedule, the amounts to be included in respect of all items shown in a company's accounts must be determined in accordance with the rules set out in this Section.

Fixed assets

General rules

17(1) The amount to be included in respect of any fixed asset must be its purchase price or production cost.

17(2)   This is subject to any provision for depreciation or diminution in value made in accordance with paragraphs 18 to 20.

Rules for depreciation and diminution in value

18   In the case of any fixed asset which has a limited useful economic life, the amount of–

(a)   its purchase price or production cost, or

(b)   where it is estimated that any such asset will have a residual value at the end of the period of its useful economic life, its purchase price or production cost less that estimated residual value, must be reduced by provisions for depreciation calculated to write off that amount systematically over the period of the asset's useful economic life.

19(1)   Where a fixed asset investment falling to be included under item B.III of either of the balance sheet formats set out in Part 1 of this Schedule has diminished in value, provisions for diminution in value may be made in respect of it and the amount to be included in respect of it may be reduced accordingly.

19(2)   Provisions for diminution in value must be made in respect of any fixed asset which has diminished in value if the reduction in its value is expected to be permanent (whether its useful economic life is limited or not), and the amount to be included in respect of it must be reduced accordingly.

19(3)   Provisions made under sub-paragraph (1) or (2) must be charged to the profit and loss account and disclosed separately in a note to the accounts if not shown separately in the profit and loss account.

History – Para. 19(3) substituted by SI 2015/980, reg. 28(3)(a), with effect in relation to–
(a)   financial years beginning on or after 1 January 2016, and
(b)   a financial year of a company beginning on or after 1 January 2015, but before 1 January 2016, if the directors of the company so decide.

Former para. 19(3) read as follows:
"**19(3)**   Any provisions made under sub-paragraph (1) or (2) which are not shown in the profit and loss account must be disclosed (either separately or in aggregate) in a note to the accounts."

20(1)   Where the reasons for which any provision was made in accordance with paragraph 19 have ceased to apply to any extent, that provision must be written back to the extent that it is no longer necessary.

20(1A)   But provision made in accordance with paragraph 19(2) in respect of goodwill must not be written back to any extent.

20(2)   Any amounts written back under sub-paragraph (1) must be recognised in the profit and loss account and disclosed separately in a note to the accounts if not shown separately in the profit and loss account.

History – Para. 20(1A) inserted by SI 2015/1672, reg. 4(2), with effect in relation to–
(a)   financial years beginning on or after 1 January 2016, and
(b)   a financial year of a company beginning on or after 1 January 2015 but before 1 January 2016, if the directors of the company have decided.

Para. 20(2) substituted by SI 2015/980, reg. 28(3)(b), with effect in relation to–
(a)   financial years beginning on or after 1 January 2016, and
(b)   a financial year of a company beginning on or after 1 January 2015, but before 1 January 2016, if the directors of the company so decide.

Former para. 20(2) read as follows:

"20(2) Any amounts written back in accordance with sub-paragraph (1) which are not shown in the profit and loss account must be disclosed (either separately or in aggregate) in a note to the accounts."

Intangible Assets

21(1) Where this is in accordance with generally accepted accounting principles or practice, development costs may be included in 'other intangible assets' under 'fixed assets' in the balance sheet formats set out in Section B of Part 1 of this Schedule.

21(2) If any amount is included in a company's balance sheet in respect of development costs, the note on accounting policies (see paragraph 44 of this Schedule) must include the following information–

(a) the period over which the amount of those costs originally capitalised is being or is to be written off, and

(b) the reasons for capitalising the development costs in question.

History – Para. 21 and the heading preceding it substituted by SI 2015/980, reg. 28(3)(c), with effect in relation to–

(a) financial years beginning on or after 1 January 2016, and

(b) a financial year of a company beginning on or after 1 January 2015, but before 1 January 2016, if the directors of the company so decide.

Former para. 21 read as follows:

"Development costs

21(1) Notwithstanding that an item in respect of **'development costs'** is included under **'fixed assets'** in the balance sheet formats set out in Part 1 of this Schedule, an amount may only be included in a company's balance sheet in respect of development costs in special circumstances.

21(2) If any amount is included in a company's balance sheet in respect of development costs the following information must be given in a note to the accounts–

(a) the period over which the amount of those costs originally capitalised is being or is to be written off, and

(b) the reasons for capitalising the development costs in question."

22(1) Intangible assets must be written off over the useful economic life of the intangible asset.

22(2) Where in exceptional cases the useful life of intangible assets cannot be reliably estimated, such assets must be written off over a period chosen by the directors of the company.

22(3) The period referred to in sub-paragraph (2) must not exceed ten years.

22(4) There must be disclosed in a note to the accounts the period referred to in sub-paragraph (2) and the reasons for choosing that period.

History – Para. 22 substituted by SI 2015/980, reg. 28(3)(c), with effect in relation to–

(a) financial years beginning on or after 1 January 2016, and

(b) a financial year of a company beginning on or after 1 January 2015, but before 1 January 2016, if the directors of the company so decide.

Former para. 22 read as follows:

"22(1) The application of paragraphs 17 to 20 in relation to goodwill (in any case where goodwill is treated as an asset) is subject to the following.

22(2) Subject to sub-paragraph (3), the amount of the consideration for any goodwill acquired by a company must be reduced by provisions for depreciation calculated to write off that amount systematically over a period chosen by the directors of the company.

22(3) The period chosen must not exceed the useful economic life of the goodwill in question.

22(4) In any case where any goodwill acquired by a company is shown or included as an asset in the company's balance sheet there must be disclosed in a note to the accounts–

(a) the period chosen for writing off the consideration for that goodwill, and

(b) the reasons for choosing that period."

Current assets

23 Subject to paragraph 24, the amount to be included in respect of any current asset must be its purchase price or production cost.

24(1) If the net realisable value of any current asset is lower than its purchase price or production cost, the amount to be included in respect of that asset must be the net realisable value.

24(2) Where the reasons for which any provision for diminution in value was made in accordance with sub-paragraph (1) have ceased to apply to any extent, that provision must be written back to the extent that it is no longer necessary.

Miscellaneous and supplementary provisions

Excess of money owed over value received as an asset item

25(1) Where the amount repayable on any debt owed by a company is greater than the value of the consideration received in the transaction giving rise to the debt, the amount of the difference may be treated as an asset.

25(2) Where any such amount is so treated–

(a) it must be written off by reasonable amounts each year and must be completely written off before repayment of the debt, and

(b) if the current amount is not shown as a separate item in the company's balance sheet, it must be disclosed in a note to the accounts.

Assets included at a fixed amount

26(1) Subject to sub-paragraph (2), assets which fall to be included–

(a) amongst the fixed assets of a company under the item 'tangible assets', or

(b) amongst the current assets of a company under the item 'raw materials and consumables',

may be included at a fixed quantity and value.

26(2) Sub-paragraph (1) applies to assets of a kind which are constantly being replaced where–

(a) their overall value is not material to assessing the company's state of affairs, and

(b) their quantity, value and composition are not subject to material variation.

Determination of purchase price or production cost

27(1) The purchase price of an asset is to be determined by adding to the actual price paid any expenses incidental to its acquisition and then subtracting any incidental reductions in the cost of acquisition.

27(2) The production cost of an asset is to be determined by adding to the purchase price of the raw materials and consumables used the amount of the costs incurred by the company which are directly attributable to the production of that asset.

27(3) In addition, there may be included in the production cost of an asset–

(a) a reasonable proportion of the costs incurred by the company which are only indirectly attributable to the production of that asset, but only to the extent that they relate to the period of production, and

(b)   interest on capital borrowed to finance the production of that asset, to the extent that it accrues in respect of the period of production,

provided, however, in a case within paragraph (b), that the inclusion of the interest in determining the cost of that asset and the amount of the interest so included is disclosed in a note to the accounts.

27(4)   In the case of current assets distribution costs may not be included in production costs.

History – In para. 27(1), the words 'and then subtracting any incidental reductions in the cost of acquisition' inserted by SI 2015/980, reg. 28(3)(d), with effect in relation to–
    (a)   financial years beginning on or after 1 January 2016, and
    (b)   a financial year of a company beginning on or after 1 January 2015, but before 1 January 2016, if the directors of the company so decide.

28(1)   The purchase price or production cost of–

(a)   any assets which fall to be included under any item shown in a company's balance sheet under the general item 'stocks', and

(b)   any assets which are fungible assets (including investments),

may be determined by the application of any of the methods mentioned in sub-paragraph (2) in relation to any such assets of the same class, provided that the method chosen is one which appears to the directors to be appropriate in the circumstances of the company.

28(2)   Those methods are–

(a)   the method known as 'first in, first out' (FIFO),

(b)   the method known as 'last in, first out' (LIFO),

(c)   a weighted average price, and

(d)   any other method reflecting generally accepted best practice.

28(3)   Where in the case of any company–

(a)   the purchase price or production cost of assets falling to be included under any item shown in the company's balance sheet has been determined by the application of any method permitted by this paragraph, and

(b)   the amount shown in respect of that item differs materially from the relevant alternative amount given below in this paragraph,

the amount of that difference must be disclosed in a note to the accounts.

28(4)   Subject to sub-paragraph (5), for the purposes of sub-paragraph (3)(b), the relevant alternative amount, in relation to any item shown in a company's balance sheet, is the amount which would have been shown in respect of that item if assets of any class included under that item at an amount determined by any method permitted by this paragraph had instead been included at their replacement cost as at the balance sheet date.

28(5)   The relevant alternative amount may be determined by reference to the most recent actual purchase price or production cost before the balance sheet date of assets of any class included under the item in question instead of by reference to their replacement cost as at that date, but only if the former appears to the directors of the company to constitute the more appropriate standard of comparison in the case of assets of that class.

History – In para. 28(2)(d), the words 'reflecting generally accepted best practice' substituted for the words 'similar to any of the methods mentioned above' by SI 2015/980, reg. 28(3)(e), with effect in relation to–
    (a)   financial years beginning on or after 1 January 2016, and
    (b)   a financial year of a company beginning on or after 1 January 2015, but before 1 January 2016, if the directors of the company so decide.

Substitution of original stated amount where price or cost unknown

29(1)   This paragraph applies where–

(a)   there is no record of the purchase price or production cost of any asset of a company or of any price, expenses or costs relevant for determining its purchase price or production cost in accordance with paragraph 27, or

(b)   any such record cannot be obtained without unreasonable expense or delay.

29(2)   In such a case, the purchase price or production cost of the asset must be taken, for the purposes of paragraphs 17 to 24, to be the value ascribed to it in the earliest available record of its value made on or after its acquisition or production by the company.

Equity method in respect of participating interests

29A(1)   Participating interests may be accounted for using the equity method.

29A(2)   If participating interests are accounted for using the equity method–

(a)   the proportion of profit or loss attributable to a participating interest and recognised in the profit and loss account may be that proportion which corresponds to the amount of any dividends, and

(b)   where the profit attributable to a participating interest and recognised in the profit and loss account exceeds the amount of any dividends, the difference must be placed in a reserve which cannot be distributed to shareholders.

29A(3)   The reference to **'dividends'** in sub-paragraph (2) includes dividends already paid and those whose payment can be claimed.

History – Para. 29A and the heading preceding it inserted by SI 2015/980, reg. 28(3)(f), with effect in relation to–
   (a)   financial years beginning on or after 1 January 2016, and
   (b)   a financial year of a company beginning on or after 1 January 2015, but before 1 January 2016, if the directors of the company so decide.

SECTION C – ALTERNATIVE ACCOUNTING RULES

Preliminary

30(1)   The rules set out in Section B are referred to below in this Schedule as the historical cost accounting rules.

30(2)   Those rules, with the omission of paragraphs 16, 22 and 26 to 29, are referred to below in this Part of this Schedule as the depreciation rules; and references below in this Schedule to the historical cost accounting rules do not include the depreciation rules as they apply by virtue of paragraph 33.

31   Subject to paragraphs 33 to 35, the amounts to be included in respect of assets of any description mentioned in paragraph 32 may be determined on any basis so mentioned.

Alternative accounting rules

32(1)   Intangible fixed assets, other than goodwill, may be included at their current cost.

32(2)   Tangible fixed assets may be included at a market value determined as at the date of their last valuation or at their current cost.

32(3)   Investments of any description falling to be included under item B III of either of the balance sheet formats set out in Part 1 of this Schedule may be included either–

(a)   at a market value determined as at the date of their last valuation, or

(b)   at a value determined on any basis which appears to the directors to be appropriate in the circumstances of the company.

But in the latter case particulars of the method of valuation adopted and of the reasons for adopting it must be disclosed in a note to the accounts.

32(4)   [Omitted by SI 2015/980, reg. 28(4)(a).]

32(5)   [Omitted by SI 2015/980, reg. 28(4)(a).]

History – Para. 32(4) and (5) omitted by SI 2015/980, reg. 28(4)(a), with effect in relation to–
   (a)   financial years beginning on or after 1 January 2016, and
   (b)   a financial year of a company beginning on or after 1 January 2015, but before 1 January 2016, if the directors of the company so decide.

Former reg. 32(4) and (5) read as follows:

"**32(4)**   Investments of any description falling to be included under item C III of either of the balance sheet formats set out in Part 1 of this Schedule may be included at their current cost.

32(5)   Stocks may be included at their current cost."

Application of the depreciation rules

33(1)   Where the value of any asset of a company is determined on any basis mentioned in paragraph 32, that value must be, or (as the case may require) be the starting point for determining, the amount to be included in respect of that asset in the company's accounts, instead of its purchase price or production cost or any value previously so determined for that asset.

The depreciation rules apply accordingly in relation to any such asset with the substitution for any reference to its purchase price or production cost of a reference to the value most recently determined for that asset on any basis mentioned in paragraph 32.

33(2)   The amount of any provision for depreciation required in the case of any fixed asset by paragraphs 18 to 20 as they apply by virtue of sub-paragraph (1) is referred to below in this paragraph as the adjusted amount, and the amount of any provision which would be required by any of those paragraphs in the case of that asset according to the historical cost accounting rules is referred to as the historical cost amount.

33(3)   Where sub-paragraph (1) applies in the case of any fixed asset the amount of any provision for depreciation in respect of that asset–

(a)   included in any item shown in the profit and loss account in respect of amounts written off assets of the description in question, or

(b)   taken into account in stating any item so shown which is required by note (14) of the notes on the profit and loss account formats set out in Part 1 of this Schedule to be stated after taking into account any necessary provision for depreciation or diminution in value of assets included under it,

may be the historical cost amount instead of the adjusted amount, provided that the amount of any difference between the two is shown separately in the profit and loss account or in a note to the accounts.

Additional information to be provided in case of departure from historical cost accounting rules

34(1)   This paragraph applies where the amounts to be included in respect of assets covered by any items shown in a company's accounts have been determined on any basis mentioned in paragraph 32.

34(2)   The items affected and the basis of valuation adopted in determining the amounts of the assets in question in the case of each such item must be disclosed in the note on accounting policies (see paragraph 44 of this Schedule).

34(3)   In the case of each balance sheet item affected, the comparable amounts determined according to the historical cost accounting rules must be shown in a note to the accounts.

34(4)   In sub-paragraph (3), references in relation to any item to the comparable amounts determined as there mentioned are references to–

(a)   the aggregate amount which would be required to be shown in respect of that item if the amounts to be included in respect of all the assets covered by that item were determined according to the historical cost accounting rules, and

(b)   the aggregate amount of the cumulative provisions for depreciation or diminution in value which would be permitted or required in determining those amounts according to those rules.

History – In para. 34(2), the words 'the note on accounting policies (see paragraph 44 of this Schedule)' substituted for the words 'a note to the accounts' by SI 2015/980, reg. 28(4)(b), with effect in relation to–
(a)   financial years beginning on or after 1 January 2016, and
(b)   a financial year of a company beginning on or after 1 January 2015, but before 1 January 2016, if the directors of the company so decide.

Para. 34(3) substituted by SI 2015/980, reg. 28(4)(c), with effect in relation to–
(a)   financial years beginning on or after 1 January 2016, and
(b)   a financial year of a company beginning on or after 1 January 2015, but before 1 January 2016, if the directors of the company so decide.

Former para. 34(3) read as follows:
"**34(3)**   In the case of each balance sheet item affected (except stocks) either–

(a)   the comparable amounts determined according to the historical cost accounting rules, or
(b)   the differences between those amounts and the corresponding amounts actually shown in the balance sheet in respect of that item, must be shown separately in the balance sheet or in a note to the accounts."

Revaluation reserve

35(1)   With respect to any determination of the value of an asset of a company on any basis mentioned in paragraph 32, the amount of any profit or loss arising from that determination (after allowing, where appropriate, for any provisions for depreciation or diminution in value made otherwise than by reference to the value so determined and any adjustments of any such provisions made in the light of that determination) must be credited or (as the case may be) debited to a separate reserve ('the revaluation reserve').

35(2)   The amount of the revaluation reserve must be shown in the company's balance sheet under a separate sub-heading in the position given for the item 'revaluation reserve' under 'Capital and reserves' in format 1 or 2 of the balance sheet formats set out in Part 1 of this Schedule.

35(3)   An amount may be transferred–

(a)   from the revaluation reserve–

(i)   to the profit and loss account, if the amount was previously charged to that account or represents realised profit, or
(ii)   on capitalisation,

(b)   to or from the revaluation reserve in respect of the taxation relating to any profit or loss credited or debited to the reserve.

The revaluation reserve must be reduced to the extent that the amounts transferred to it are no longer necessary for the purposes of the valuation method used.

35(4) In sub-paragraph (3)(a)(ii) **'capitalisation'**, in relation to an amount standing to the credit of the revaluation reserve, means applying it in wholly or partly paying up unissued shares in the company to be allotted to members of the company as fully or partly paid shares.

35(5) The revaluation reserve must not be reduced except as mentioned in this paragraph.

35(6) The treatment for taxation purposes of amounts credited or debited to the revaluation reserve must be disclosed in a note to the accounts.

History – In para. 35(2), the words 'under Capital and reserves' inserted; and the words 'but need not be shown under that name' omitted by SI 2015/980, reg. 28(4)(d), with effect in relation to–
(a) financial years beginning on or after 1 January 2016, and
(b) a financial year of a company beginning on or after 1 January 2015, but before 1 January 2016, if the directors of the company so decide.

SECTION D – FAIR VALUE ACCOUNTING

Inclusion of financial instruments at fair value

36(1) Subject to sub-paragraphs (2) to (5), financial instruments (including derivatives) may be included at fair value.

36(2) Sub-paragraph (1) does not apply to financial instruments that constitute liabilities unless–

(a) they are held as Part of a trading portfolio,
(b) they are derivatives, or
(c) they are financial instruments falling within sub-paragraph (4).

36(3) Unless they are financial instruments falling within sub-paragraph (4), sub-paragraph (1) does not apply to–

(a) financial instruments (other than derivatives) held to maturity,
(b) loans and receivables originated by the company and not held for trading purposes,
(c) interests in subsidiary undertakings, associated undertakings and joint ventures,
(d) equity instruments issued by the company,
(e) contracts for contingent consideration in a business combination, or
(f) other financial instruments with such special characteristics that the instruments, according to generally accepted accounting principles or practice, should be accounted for differently from other financial instruments.

36(4) Financial instruments which under international accounting standards may be included in accounts at fair value, may be so included, provided that the disclosures required by such accounting standards are made.

36(5) If the fair value of a financial instrument cannot be determined reliably in accordance with paragraph 37, sub-paragraph (1) does not apply to that financial instrument.

36(6) In this paragraph–

'associated undertaking' has the meaning given by paragraph 19 of Schedule 6 to these Regulations;

'joint venture' has the meaning given by paragraph 18 of that Schedule.

History – Para. 36(4) substituted by SI 2015/980, reg. 28(5)(a), with effect in relation to–
- (a) financial years beginning on or after 1 January 2016, and
- (b) a financial year of a company beginning on or after 1 January 2015, but before 1 January 2016, if the directors of the company so decide.

Former para. 36(4) read as follows:

"**36(4)** Financial instruments that, under international accounting standards adopted by the European Commission on or before 5th September 2006 in accordance with the IAS Regulation, may be included in accounts at fair value, may be so included, provided that the disclosures required by such accounting standards are made."

Determination of fair value

37(1) The fair value of a financial instrument is its value determined in accordance with this paragraph.

37(2) If a reliable market can readily be identified for the financial instrument, its fair value is determined by reference to its market value.

37(3) If a reliable market cannot readily be identified for the financial instrument but can be identified for its components or for a similar instrument, its fair value is determined by reference to the market value of its components or of the similar instrument.

37(4) If neither sub-paragraph (2) nor (3) applies, the fair value of the financial instrument is a value resulting from generally accepted valuation models and techniques.

37(5) Any valuation models and techniques used for the purposes of sub-paragraph (4) must ensure a reasonable approximation of the market value.

Hedged items

38 A company may include any assets and liabilities, or identified portions of such assets or liabilities, that qualify as hedged items under a fair value hedge accounting system at the amount required under that system.

Other assets that may be included at fair value

39(1) This paragraph applies to–

- (a) stocks,
- (b) investment property, and
- (c) living animals and plants.

39(2) Such stocks, investment property, and living animals and plants may be included at fair value, provided that, as the case may be, all such stocks, investment property, and living animals and plants are so included where their fair value can reliably be determined.

39(3) In this paragraph, **'fair value'** means fair value determined in accordance with generally accepted accounting principles or practice.

History – Para. 39 substituted by SI 2015/980, reg. 28(5)(b), with effect in relation to–
- (a) financial years beginning on or after 1 January 2016, and
- (b) a financial year of a company beginning on or after 1 January 2015, but before 1 January 2016, if the directors of the company so decide.

Former para. 39 read as follows:

"**39(1)** This paragraph applies to–

    (a) investment property, and

    (b) living animals and plants, that, under international accounting standards, may be included in accounts at fair value.

39(2) Such investment property and such living animals and plants may be included at fair value, provided that all such investment property or, as the case may be, all such living animals and plants are so included where their fair value can reliably be determined.

39(3) In this paragraph, **'fair value'** means fair value determined in accordance with relevant international accounting standards."

Accounting for changes in value

40(1) This paragraph applies where a financial instrument is valued in accordance with paragraph 36 or 38 or an asset is valued in accordance with paragraph 39.

40(2) Notwithstanding paragraph 13 in this Part of this Schedule, and subject to sub-paragraphs (3) and (4), a change in the value of the financial instrument or of the investment property or living animal or plant must be included in the profit and loss account.

40(3) Where–

    (a) the financial instrument accounted for is a hedging instrument under a hedge accounting system that allows some or all of the change in value not to be shown in the profit and loss account, or

    (b) the change in value relates to an exchange difference arising on a monetary item that forms part of a company's net investment in a foreign entity,

the amount of the change in value must be credited to or (as the case may be) debited from a separate reserve ('the fair value reserve').

40(4) Where the instrument accounted for–

    (a) is an available for sale financial asset, and

    (b) is not a derivative,

the change in value may be credited to or (as the case may be) debited from the fair value reserve.

The fair value reserve

41(1) The fair value reserve must be adjusted to the extent that the amounts shown in it are no longer necessary for the purposes of paragraph 40(3) or (4).

41(2) The treatment for taxation purposes of amounts credited or debited to the fair value reserve must be disclosed in a note to the accounts.

Part 3 – Notes to the accounts

PRELIMINARY

42(1) Any information required in the case of a company by the following provisions of this Part of this Schedule must be given by way of a note to the accounts.

42(2) These notes must be presented in the order in which, where relevant, the items to which they relate are presented in the balance sheet and in the profit and loss account.

History – Para. 42 substituted by SI 2015/980, reg. 29(2), with effect in relation to–

    (a) financial years beginning on or after 1 January 2016, and

(b) a financial year of a company beginning on or after 1 January 2015, but before 1 January 2016, if the directors of the company so decide.

Former para. 42 read as follows:

"42 Any information required in the case of any company by the following provisions of this Part of this Schedule must (if not given in the company's accounts) be given by way of a note to the accounts."

GENERAL

Reserves and dividends

43 There must be stated–

(a) any amount set aside or proposed to be set aside to, or withdrawn or proposed to be withdrawn from, reserves,

(b) the aggregate amount of dividends paid in the financial year (other than those for which a liability existed at the immediately preceding balance sheet date),

(c) the aggregate amount of dividends that the company is liable to pay at the balance sheet date, and

(d) the aggregate amount of dividends that are proposed before the date of approval of the accounts, and not otherwise disclosed under sub-paragraph (b) or (c).

Disclosure of accounting policies

44 The accounting policies adopted by the company in determining the amounts to be included in respect of items shown in the balance sheet and in determining the profit or loss of the company must be stated (including such policies with respect to the depreciation and diminution in value of assets).

45 It must be stated whether the accounts have been prepared in accordance with applicable accounting standards and particulars of any material departure from those standards and the reasons for it must be given (see regulation 4(2) for exemption for medium-sized companies).

INFORMATION SUPPLEMENTING THE BALANCE SHEET

46 Paragraphs 47 to 64 require information which either supplements the information given with respect to any particular items shown in the balance sheet or is otherwise relevant to assessing the company's state of affairs in the light of the information so given.

Share capital and debentures

47(1) The following information must be given with respect to the company's share capital–

(a) where shares of more than one class have been allotted, the number and aggregate nominal value of shares of each class allotted, and

(b) where shares are held as treasury shares, the number and aggregate nominal value of the treasury shares and, where shares of more than one class have been allotted, the number and aggregate nominal value of the shares of each class held as treasury shares.

47(2) In the case of any Part of the allotted share capital that consists of redeemable shares, the following information must be given–

(a) the earliest and latest dates on which the company has power to redeem those shares,

(b) whether those shares must be redeemed in any event or are liable to be redeemed at the option of the company or of the shareholder, and

(c) whether any (and, if so, what) premium is payable on redemption.

48 If the company has allotted any shares during the financial year, the following information must be given–

(a) the classes of shares allotted, and

(b) as respects each class of shares, the number allotted, their aggregate nominal value, and the consideration received by the company for the allotment.

49(1) With respect to any contingent right to the allotment of shares in the company the following particulars must be given–

(a) the number, description and amount of the shares in relation to which the right is exercisable,

(b) the period during which it is exercisable, and

(c) the price to be paid for the shares allotted.

49(2) In sub-paragraph (1) **'contingent right to the allotment of shares'** means any option to subscribe for shares and any other right to require the allotment of shares to any person whether arising on the conversion into shares of securities of any other description or otherwise.

50(1) If the company has issued any debentures during the financial year to which the accounts relate, the following information must be given–

(a) the classes of debentures issued, and

(b) as respects each class of debentures, the amount issued and the consideration received by the company for the issue.

50(2) Where any of the company's debentures are held by a nominee of or trustee for the company, the nominal amount of the debentures and the amount at which they are stated in the accounting records kept by the company in accordance with Section 386 of the 2006 Act (duty to keep accounting records) must be stated.

Fixed assets

51(1) In respect of each item which is or would but for paragraph 4(2)(b) be shown under the general item 'fixed assets' in the company's balance sheet the following information must be given–

(a) the appropriate amounts in respect of that item as at the date of the beginning of the financial year and as at the balance sheet date respectively,

(b) the effect on any amount shown in the balance sheet in respect of that item of–

(i) any revision of the amount in respect of any assets included under that item made during that year on any basis mentioned in paragraph 32,

(ii) acquisitions during that year of any assets,

(iii) disposals during that year of any assets, and

(iv) any transfers of assets of the company to and from that item during that year.

51(2) The reference in sub-paragraph (1)(a) to the appropriate amounts in respect of any item as at any date there mentioned is a reference to amounts representing the aggregate amounts determined, as at that date, in respect of assets falling to be included under that item on either of the following bases, that is to say–

(a) on the basis of purchase price or production cost (determined in accordance with paragraphs 27 and 28), or

(b) on any basis mentioned in paragraph 32,

(leaving out of account in either case any provisions for depreciation or diminution in value).

51(3) In respect of each item within sub-paragraph (1) there must also be stated–

(a) the cumulative amount of provisions for depreciation or diminution in value of assets included under that item as at each date mentioned in sub-paragraph (1)(a),

(b) the amount of any such provisions made in respect of the financial year,

(c) the amount of any adjustments made in respect of any such provisions during that year in consequence of the disposal of any assets, and

(d) the amount of any other adjustments made in respect of any such provisions during that year.

52 Where any fixed assets of the company (other than listed investments) are included under any item shown in the company's balance sheet at an amount determined on any basis mentioned in paragraph 32, the following information must be given–

(a) the years (so far as they are known to the directors) in which the assets were severally valued and the several values, and

(b) in the case of assets that have been valued during the financial year, the names of the persons who valued them or particulars of their qualifications for doing so and (whichever is stated) the bases of valuation used by them.

53 In relation to any amount which is or would but for paragraph 4(2)(b) be shown in respect of the item 'land and buildings' in the company's balance sheet there must be stated–

(a) how much of that amount is ascribable to land of freehold tenure and how much to land of leasehold tenure, and

(b) how much of the amount ascribable to land of leasehold tenure is ascribable to land held on long lease and how much to land held on short lease.

Investments

54(1) In respect of the amount of each item which is or would but for paragraph 4(2)(b) be shown in the company's balance sheet under the general item 'investments' (whether as fixed assets or as current assets) there must be stated how much of that amount is ascribable to listed investments.

54(2) Where the amount of any listed investments is stated for any item in accordance with subparagraph (1), the following amounts must also be stated–

(a) the aggregate market value of those investments where it differs from the amount so stated, and

(b) both the market value and the stock exchange value of any investments of which the former value is, for the purposes of the accounts, taken as being higher than the latter.

Information about fair value of assets and liabilities

55(1) This paragraph applies where financial instruments or other assets have been valued in accordance with, as appropriate, paragraph 36, 38 or 39.

55(2) There must be stated–

(a) the significant assumptions underlying the valuation models and techniques used to determine the fair value of the instruments or other assets,

(b) for each category of financial instrument or other asset, the fair value of the assets in that category and the changes in value–

(i) included directly in the profit and loss account, or

(ii) credited to or (as the case may be) debited from the fair value reserve, in respect of those assets, and

(c)   for each class of derivatives, the extent and nature of the instruments, including significant terms and conditions that may affect the amount, timing and certainty of future cash flows.

55(3)   Where any amount is transferred to or from the fair value reserve during the financial year, there must be stated in tabular form–

(a)   the amount of the reserve as at the date of the beginning of the financial year and as at the balance sheet date respectively,

(b)   the amount transferred to or from the reserve during the year, and

(c)   the source and application respectively of the amounts so transferred.

History – Para. 55 substituted by SI 2015/980, reg. 29(3), with effect in relation to–
(a)   financial years beginning on or after 1 January 2016, and
(b)   a financial year of a company beginning on or after 1 January 2015, but before 1 January 2016, if the directors of the company so decide.

Former para. 55 read as follows:
"**55(1)**   This paragraph applies where financial instruments have been valued in accordance with paragraph 36 or 38.
55(2)   There must be stated–

(a)   the significant assumptions underlying the valuation models and techniques used where the fair value of the instruments has been determined in accordance with paragraph 37(4),
(b)   for each category of financial instrument, the fair value of the instruments in that category and the changes in value–

(i)   included in the profit and loss account, or
(ii)   credited to or (as the case may be) debited from the fair value reserve, in respect of those instruments, and
(c)   for each class of derivatives, the extent and nature of the instruments, including significant terms and conditions that may affect the amount, timing and certainty of future cash flows.
55(3)   Where any amount is transferred to or from the fair value reserve during the financial year, there must be stated in tabular form–

(a)   the amount of the reserve as at the date of the beginning of the financial year and as at the balance sheet date respectively,
(b)   the amount transferred to or from the reserve during that year, and
(c)   the source and application respectively of the amounts so transferred."

56   Where the company has derivatives that it has not included at fair value, there must be stated for each class of such derivatives–

(a)   the fair value of the derivatives in that class, if such a value can be determined in accordance with paragraph 37, and

(b)   the extent and nature of the derivatives.

57(1)   This paragraph applies if–

(a)   the company has financial fixed assets that could be included at fair value by virtue of paragraph 36,

(b)   the amount at which those items are included under any item in the company's accounts is in excess of their fair value, and

(c)   the company has not made provision for diminution in value of those assets in accordance with paragraph 19(1) of this Schedule.

57(2)   There must be stated–

(a)   the amount at which either the individual assets or appropriate groupings of those individual assets are included in the company's accounts,

(b)   the fair value of those assets or groupings, and

(c)   the reasons for not making a provision for diminution in value of those assets, including the nature of the evidence that provides the basis for the belief that the amount at which they are stated in the accounts will be recovered.

Information where investment property and living animals and plants included at fair value

58(1) This paragraph applies where the amounts to be included in a company's accounts in respect of stocks, investment property or living animals and plants have been determined in accordance with paragraph 39.

58(2) The balance sheet items affected and the basis of valuation adopted in determining the amounts of the assets in question in the case of each such item must be disclosed in a note to the accounts.

58(3) In the case of investment property, for each balance sheet item affected there must be shown, either separately in the balance sheet or in a note to the accounts–

    (a)   the comparable amounts determined according to the historical cost accounting rules, or

    (b)   the differences between those amounts and the corresponding amounts actually shown in the balance sheet in respect of that item.

58(4) In sub-paragraph (3), references in relation to any item to the comparable amounts determined in accordance with that sub-paragraph are to–

    (a)   the aggregate amount which would be required to be shown in respect of that item if the amounts to be included in respect of all the assets covered by that item were determined according to the historical cost accounting rules, and

    (b)   the aggregate amount of the cumulative provisions for depreciation or diminution in value which would be permitted or required in determining those amounts according to those rules.

History – In para. 58(1), the word 'stocks,' inserted by SI 2015/980, reg. 29(4), with effect in relation to–
    (a)   financial years beginning on or after 1 January 2016, and
    (b)   a financial year of a company beginning on or after 1 January 2015, but before 1 January 2016, if the directors of the company so decide.

Reserves and provisions

59(1) This paragraph applies where any amount is transferred–

    (a)   to or from any reserves, or

    (b)   to any provision for liabilities, or

    (c)   from any provision for liabilities otherwise than for the purpose for which the provision was established,

and the reserves or provisions are or would but for paragraph 4(2)(b) be shown as separate items in the company's balance sheet.

59(2) The following information must be given in respect of the aggregate of reserves or provisions included in the same item in tabular form–

    (a)   the amount of the reserves or provisions as at the date of the beginning of the financial year and as at the balance sheet date respectively,

    (b)   any amounts transferred to or from the reserves or provisions during that year, and

    (c)   the source and application respectively of any amounts so transferred.

59(3) Particulars must be given of each provision included in the item 'other provisions' in the company's balance sheet in any case where the amount of that provision is material.

History – In para. 59(2), the words 'in tabular form' inserted by SI 2015/980, reg. 29(5), with effect in relation to–
    (a)   financial years beginning on or after 1 January 2016, and
    (b)   a financial year of a company beginning on or after 1 January 2015, but before 1 January 2016, if the directors of the company so decide.

Provision for taxation

60   The amount of any provision for deferred taxation must be stated separately from the amount of any provision for other taxation.

Details of indebtedness

61(1)   For the aggregate of all items shown under 'creditors' in the company's balance sheet there must be stated the aggregate of the following amounts–

  (a)   the amount of any debts included under 'creditors' which are payable or repayable otherwise than by instalments and fall due for payment or repayment after the end of the period of five years beginning with the day next following the end of the financial year, and

  (b)   in the case of any debts so included which are payable or repayable by instalments, the amount of any instalments which fall due for payment after the end of that period.

61(2)   Subject to sub-paragraph (3), in relation to each debt falling to be taken into account under sub-paragraph (1), the terms of payment or repayment and the rate of any interest payable on the debt must be stated.

61(3)   If the number of debts is such that, in the opinion of the directors, compliance with subparagraph (2) would result in a statement of excessive length, it is sufficient to give a general indication of the terms of payment or repayment and the rates of any interest payable on the debts.

61(4)   In respect of each item shown under 'creditors' in the company's balance sheet there must be stated–

  (a)   the aggregate amount of any debts included under that item in respect of which any security has been given by the company, and

  (b)   an indication of the nature and form of the securities so given.

61(5)   References above in this paragraph to an item shown under 'creditors' in the company's balance sheet include references, where amounts falling due to creditors within one year and after more than one year are distinguished in the balance sheet–

  (a)   in a case within sub-paragraph (1), to an item shown under the latter of those categories, and

  (b)   in a case within sub-paragraph (4), to an item shown under either of those categories.

References to items shown under 'creditors' include references to items which would but for paragraph 4(2)(b) be shown under that heading.

History – In para. 61(4)(b), the words 'and form' inserted by SI 2015/980, reg. 29(6), with effect in relation to–
  (a)   financial years beginning on or after 1 January 2016, and
  (b)   a financial year of a company beginning on or after 1 January 2015, but before 1 January 2016, if the directors of the company so decide.

62   If any fixed cumulative dividends on the company's shares are in arrear, there must be stated–

  (a)   the amount of the arrears, and

  (b)   the period for which the dividends or, if there is more than one class, each class of them are in arrear.

Guarantees and other financial commitments

63(1)   Particulars must be given of any charge on the assets of the company to secure the liabilities of any other person including the amount secured.

63(2)   Particulars and the total amount of any financial commitments, guarantees and contingencies that are not included in the balance sheet must be disclosed.

63(3)   An indication of the nature and form of any valuable security given by the company in respect of commitments, guarantees and contingencies within sub-paragraph (2) must be given.

63(4)   The total amount of any commitments within sub-paragraph (2) concerning pensions must be separately disclosed.

63(5)   Particulars must be given of pension commitments which are included in the balance sheet.

63(6)   Where any commitment within sub-paragraph (4) or (5) relates wholly or partly to pensions payable to past directors of the company separate particulars must be given of that commitment.

63(7)   The total amount of any commitments, guarantees and contingencies within sub-paragraph (2) which are undertaken on behalf of or for the benefit of–

(a)   any parent undertaking or fellow subsidiary undertaking of the company,

(b)   any subsidiary undertaking of the company, or

(c)   any undertaking in which the company has a participating interest

must be separately stated and those within each of paragraphs (a), (b) and (c) must also be stated separately from those within any other of those paragraphs.

History – Para. 63 substituted by SI 2015/980, reg. 29(7), with effect in relation to–
  (a)   financial years beginning on or after 1 January 2016, and
  (b)   a financial year of a company beginning on or after 1 January 2015, but before 1 January 2016, if the directors of the company so decide.

Former para. 63 read as follows:

"Guarantees and other financial commitments

63(1)   Particulars must be given of any charge on the assets of the company to secure the liabilities of any other person, including, where practicable, the amount secured.

63(2)   The following information must be given with respect to any other contingent liability not provided for–
  (a)   the amount or estimated amount of that liability,
  (b)   its legal nature, and
  (c)   whether any valuable security has been provided by the company in connection with that liability and if so, what.

63(3)   There must be stated, where practicable, the aggregate amount or estimated amount of contracts for capital expenditure, so far as not provided for.

63(4)   Particulars must be given of–
  (a)   any pension commitments included under any provision shown in the company's balance sheet, and
  (b)   any such commitments for which no provision has been made, and where any such commitment relates wholly or partly to pensions payable to past directors of the company separate particulars must be given of that commitment so far as it relates to such pensions.

63(5)   Particulars must also be given of any other financial commitments that–
  (a)   have not been provided for, and
  (b)   are relevant to assessing the company's state of affairs."

Miscellaneous matters

64(1)   Particulars must be given of any case where the purchase price or production cost of any asset is for the first time determined under paragraph 29.

64(2)   Where any outstanding loans made under the authority of Section 682(2)(b), (c) or (d) of the 2006 Act (various cases of financial assistance by a company for purchase of its own shares) are included under any item shown in the company's balance sheet, the aggregate amount of those loans must be disclosed for each item in question.

Appendix C

INFORMATION SUPPLEMENTING THE PROFIT AND LOSS ACCOUNT

65 Paragraphs 66 to 69 require information which either supplements the information given with respect to any particular items shown in the profit and loss account or otherwise provides particulars of income or expenditure of the company or of circumstances affecting the items shown in the profit and loss account (see regulation 3(2) for exemption for companies falling within Section 408 of the 2006 Act (individual profit and loss account where group accounts prepared)).

Separate statement of certain items of income and expenditure

66(1) Subject to sub-paragraph (2), there must be stated the amount of the interest on or any similar charges in respect of bank loans and overdrafts, and loans of any other kind made to the company.

66(2) Sub-paragraph (1) does not apply to interest or charges on loans to the company from group undertakings, but, with that exception, it applies to interest or charges on all loans, whether made on the security of debentures or not.

Particulars of tax

67(1) Particulars must be given of any special circumstances which affect liability in respect of taxation of profits, income or capital gains for the financial year or liability in respect of taxation of profits, income or capital gains for succeeding financial years.

67(2) The following amounts must be stated–

  (a) the amount of the charge for United Kingdom corporation tax,
  (b) if that amount would have been greater but for relief from double taxation, the amount which it would have been but for such relief,
  (c) the amount of the charge for United Kingdom income tax, and
  (d) the amount of the charge for taxation imposed outside the United Kingdom of profits, income and (so far as charged to revenue) capital gains.

These amounts must be stated separately in respect of each of the amounts which is or would but for paragraph 4(2)(b) be shown under the item 'tax on profit or loss' in the profit and loss account.

History – In para. 67(2), the words 'These amounts must be stated separately in respect of each of the amounts which is or would but for paragraph 4(2)(b) be shown under the item 'tax on profit or loss' in the profit and loss account.' substituted for the words 'These amounts must be stated separately in respect of each of the amounts which is or would but for paragraph 4(2)(b) be shown under the items 'tax on profit or loss on ordinary activities' and 'tax in extraordinary profit or loss' in the profit and loss account.' by SI 2015/980, reg. 29(8), with effect in relation to–
  (a) financial years beginning on or after 1 January 2016, and
  (b) a financial year of a company beginning on or after 1 January 2015, but before 1 January 2016, if the directors of the company so decide.

Particulars of turnover

68(1) If in the course of the financial year the company has carried on business of two or more classes that, in the opinion of the directors, differ substantially from each other, the amount of the turnover attributable to each class must be stated and the class described (see regulation 4(3)(b) for exemption for medium-sized companies in accounts delivered to registrar).

68(2) If in the course of the financial year the company has supplied markets that, in the opinion of the directors, differ substantially from each other, the amount of the turnover attributable to each such market must also be stated.

In this paragraph **'market'** means a market delimited by geographical bounds.

68(3) In analysing for the purposes of this paragraph the source (in terms of business or in terms of market) of turnover, the directors of the company must have regard to the manner in which the company's activities are organised.

68(4) For the purposes of this paragraph–

(a) classes of business which, in the opinion of the directors, do not differ substantially from each other must be treated as one class, and

(b) markets which, in the opinion of the directors, do not differ substantially from each other must be treated as one market,

and any amounts properly attributable to one class of business or (as the case may be) to one market which are not material may be included in the amount stated in respect of another.

68(5) Where in the opinion of the directors the disclosure of any information required by this paragraph would be seriously prejudicial to the interests of the company, that information need not be disclosed, but the fact that any such information has not been disclosed must be stated.

Miscellaneous matters

69(1) Where any amount relating to any preceding financial year is included in any item in the profit and loss account, the effect must be stated.

69(2) The amount, nature and effect of any individual items of income or expenditure which are of exceptional size or incidence must be stated.

History – Para. 69(2) substituted for para. 69(2) and (3) by SI 2015/980, reg. 29(9), with effect in relation to–
  (a) financial years beginning on or after 1 January 2016, and
  (b) a financial year of a company beginning on or after 1 January 2015, but before 1 January 2016, if the directors of the company so decide.

Sums denominated in foreign currencies

70 Where any sums originally denominated in foreign currencies have been brought into account under any items shown in the balance sheet format or profit and loss account formats, the basis on which those sums have been translated into sterling (or the currency in which the accounts are drawn up) must be stated.

Dormant companies acting as agents

71 Where the directors of a company take advantage of the exemption conferred by Section 480 of the 2006 Act (dormant companies: exemption from audit), and the company has during the financial year in question acted as an agent for any person, the fact that it has so acted must be stated.

Related party transactions

72(1) Particulars may be given of transactions which the company has entered into with related parties, and must be given if such transactions are material and have not been concluded under normal market conditions (see regulation 4(2B) for a modification for medium-sized companies).

72(2) The particulars of transactions required to be disclosed by sub-paragraph (1) must include–

(a) the amount of such transactions,

(b) the nature of the related party relationship, and

(c) other information about the transactions necessary for an understanding of the financial position of the company.

72(3) Information about individual transactions may be aggregated according to their nature, except where separate information is necessary for an understanding of the effects of related party transactions on the financial position of the company.

72(4) Particulars need not be given of transactions entered into between two or more members of a group, provided that any subsidiary undertaking which is a party to the transaction is whollyowned by such a member.

72(5) In this paragraph, **'related party'** has the same meaning as in international accounting standards.

History – In para. 72(1), the words 'regulation 4(2B) for a modification' substituted for the words 'regulation 4(2) for exemption' by SI 2015/980, reg. 29(10), with effect in relation to–
   (a) financial years beginning on or after 1 January 2016, and
   (b) a financial year of a company beginning on or after 1 January 2015, but before 1 January 2016, if the directors of the company so decide.

Post balance sheet events

72A The nature and financial effect of material events arising after the balance sheet date which are not reflected in the profit and loss account or balance sheet must be stated.

History – Para. 72A and the heading preceding it inserted by SI 2015/980, reg. 29(11), with effect in relation to–
   (a) financial years beginning on or after 1 January 2016, and
   (b) a financial year of a company beginning on or after 1 January 2015, but before 1 January 2016, if the directors of the company so decide.

Appropriations

72B Particulars must be given of the proposed appropriation of profit or treatment of loss or, where applicable, particulars of the actual appropriation of the profits or treatment of the losses.

History – Para. 72B and the heading preceding it inserted by SI 2015/980, reg. 29(11), with effect in relation to–
   (a) financial years beginning on or after 1 January 2016, and
   (b) a financial year of a company beginning on or after 1 January 2015, but before 1 January 2016, if the directors of the company so decide.

Part 4 – Special provision where company is a parent company or subsidiary undertaking
COMPANY'S OWN ACCOUNTS: GUARANTEES AND OTHER FINANCIAL COMMITMENTS IN FAVOUR OF GROUP UNDERTAKINGS

73 [Omitted by SI 2015/980, reg. 30.]

History – Para. 73 omitted by SI 2015/980, reg. 30, with effect in relation to–
   (a) financial years beginning on or after 1 January 2016, and
   (b) a financial year of a company beginning on or after 1 January 2015, but before 1 January 2016, if the directors of the company so decide.

Former para. 73 read as follows:

"**73** Commitments within any of sub-paragraphs (1) to (5) of paragraph 63 (guarantees and other financial commitments) which are undertaken on behalf of or for the benefit of–

   (a) any parent undertaking or fellow subsidiary undertaking, or
   (b) any subsidiary undertaking of the company, must be stated separately from the other commitments within that paragraph, and commitments within paragraph
   (a) must also be stated separately from those within paragraph (b)."

Part 5 – Special provisions where the company is an investment company

74(1) Paragraph 35 does not apply to the amount of any profit or loss arising from a determination of the value of any investments of an investment company on any basis mentioned in paragraph 32(3).

74(2) Any provisions made by virtue of paragraph 19(1) or (2) in the case of an investment company in respect of any fixed asset investments need not be charged to the company's profit and loss account provided they are either–

(a) charged against any reserve account to which any amount excluded by sub-paragraph (1) from the requirements of paragraph 35 has been credited, or

(b) shown as a separate item in the company's balance sheet under the sub-heading 'other reserves'.

74(3) For the purposes of this paragraph, as it applies in relation to any company, **'fixed asset investment'** means any asset falling to be included under any item shown in the company's balance sheet under the subdivision 'investments' under the general item 'fixed assets'.

75(1) Any distribution made by an investment company which reduces the amount of its net assets to less than the aggregate of its called-up share capital and undistributable reserves shall be disclosed in a note to the company's accounts.

75(2) For purposes of this paragraph, a company's net assets are the aggregate of its assets less the aggregate of its liabilities (including any provision for liabilities within paragraph 2 of Schedule 9 to these Regulations that is made in Companies Act accounts and any provision that is made in IAS accounts); and **'undistributable reserves'** has the meaning given by Section 831(4) of the 2006 Act.

75(3) A company shall be treated as an investment company for the purposes of this Part of this Schedule in relation to any financial year of the company if–

(a) during the whole of that year it was an investment company as defined by Section 833 of the 2006 Act, and

(b) it was not at any time during that year prohibited from making a distribution by virtue of Section 832 of the 2006 Act due to either or both of the conditions specified in Section 832(4) (a) or (b) (no distribution where capital profits have been distributed etc) not being met.

SCHEDULE 2 – BANKING COMPANIES: COMPANIES ACT INDIVIDUAL ACCOUNTS

Regulation 5(1)

Part 1 – General rules and formats

SECTION A – GENERAL RULES

1 Subject to the following provisions of this Part of this Schedule–

(a) every balance sheet of a company must show the items listed in the balance sheet format set out in Section B of this Part, and

(b) every profit and loss account must show the items listed in either of the profit and loss account formats in Section B.

2(1) References in this Part of this Schedule to the items listed in any of the formats set out in Section B, are to those items read together with any of the notes following the formats which apply to those items.

2(2) The items must be shown in the order and under the headings and sub-headings given in the particular format used, but–

(a) the notes to the formats may permit alternative positions for any particular items,

(b) the heading or sub-heading for any item does not have to be distinguished by any letter or number assigned to that item in the format used, and

(c)   where the heading of an item in the format used contains any wording in square brackets, that wording may be omitted if not applicable to the company.

3(1)   Where in accordance with paragraph 1 a company's profit and loss account for any financial year has been prepared by reference to one of the formats in Section B, the company's directors must use the same format in preparing the profit and loss account for subsequent financial years, unless in their opinion there are special reasons for a change.

3(2)   Particulars of any change must be given in a note to the accounts in which the new format is first used, and the reasons for the change must be explained.

4(1)   Any item required to be shown in a company's balance sheet or profit and loss account may be shown in greater detail than required by the particular format used.

4(2)   The balance sheet or profit and loss account may include an item representing or covering the amount of any asset or liability, income or expenditure not specifically covered by any of the items listed in the format used, save that none of the following may be treated as assets in any balance sheet–

(a)   preliminary expenses,

(b)   expenses of, and commission on, any issue of shares or debentures, and

(c)   costs of research.

5(1)   Items to which lower case letters are assigned in any of the formats in Section B may be combined in a company's accounts for any financial year if–

(a)   their individual amounts are not material for the purpose of giving a true and fair view, or

(b)   the combination facilitates the assessment of the state of affairs or profit or loss of the company for that year.

5(2)   Where sub-paragraph (1)(b) applies, the individual amounts of any items so combined must be disclosed in a note to the accounts and any notes required by this Schedule to the items so combined must, notwithstanding the combination, be given.

6(1)   Subject to sub-paragraph (2), the directors must not include a heading or sub-heading corresponding to an item in the balance sheet or profit and loss account format used if there is no amount to be shown for that item for the financial year to which the balance sheet or profit and loss account relates.

6(2)   Where an amount can be shown for the item in question for the immediately preceding financial year, that amount must be shown under the heading or sub-heading required by the format for that item.

7(1)   For every item shown in the balance sheet or profit and loss account the corresponding amount for the immediately preceding financial year must also be shown.

7(2)   Where that corresponding amount is not comparable with the amount to be shown for the item in question in respect of the financial year to which the balance sheet or profit and loss account relates, the former amount may be adjusted, and particulars of the non-comparability and of any adjustment must be disclosed in a note to the accounts.

8(1)   Subject to the following provisions of this paragraph and without prejudice to note (6) to the balance sheet format, amounts in respect of items representing assets or income may not be set off against amounts in respect of items representing liabilities or expenditure (as the case may be), or vice versa.

8(2) Charges required to be included in profit and loss account format 1, items 11(a) and 11(b) or format 2, items A7(a) and A7(b) may be set off against income required to be included in format 1, items 12(a) and 12(b) or format 2, items B5(a) and B5(b) and the resulting figure shown as a single item (in format 2 at position A7 if negative and at position B5 if positive).

8(3) Charges required to be included in profit and loss account format 1, item 13 or format 2, item A8 may also be set off against income required to be included in format 1, item 14 or format 2, item B6 and the resulting figure shown as a single item (in format 2 at position A8 if negative and at position B6 if positive).

9(1) Assets must be shown under the relevant balance sheet headings even where the company has pledged them as security for its own liabilities or for those of third parties or has otherwise assigned them as security to third parties.

9(2) A company may not include in its balance sheet assets pledged or otherwise assigned to it as security unless such assets are in the form of cash in the hands of the company.

9(3) Assets acquired in the name of and on behalf of third parties must not be shown in the balance sheet.

10 The company's directors must, in determining how amounts are presented within items in the profit and loss account and balance sheet, have regard to the substance of the reported transaction or arrangement, in accordance with generally accepted accounting principles or practice.

10A Where an asset or liability relates to more than one item in the balance sheet, the relationship of such asset or liability to the relevant items must be disclosed either under those items or in the notes to the accounts.

History – Para. 10A inserted by SI 2015/980, reg. 31(2), with effect in relation to–
  (a) financial years beginning on or after 1 January 2016, and
  (b) a financial year of a company beginning on or after 1 January 2015, but before 1 January 2016, if the directors of the company so decide.

SECTION B – THE REQUIRED FORMATS

Balance sheet format

ASSETS

1. Cash and balances at central [or post office] banks [1]
2. Treasury bills and other eligible bills [20]
    (a) Treasury bills and similar securities [2]
    (b) Other eligible bills [3]
3. Loans and advances to banks [4], [20]
    (a) Repayable on demand
    (b) Other loans and advances
4. Loans and advances to customers [5], [20]
5. Debt securities [and other fixed-income securities] [6], [20]
    (a) Issued by public bodies
    (b) Issued by other issuers
6. Equity shares [and other variable-yield securities]
7. Participating interests
8. Shares in group undertakings
9. Intangible fixed assets [7]

10. Tangible fixed assets [8]

11. Called up capital not paid [9]

12. Own shares [10]

13. Other assets

14. Called up capital not paid [9]

15. Prepayments and accrued income

Total assets

LIABILITIES

1. Deposits by banks [11], [20]

   (a) Repayable on demand

   (b) With agreed maturity dates or periods of notice

2. Customer accounts [12], [20]

   (a) Repayable on demand

   (b) With agreed maturity dates or periods of notice

3. Debt securities in issue [13], [20]

   (a) Bonds and medium term notes

   (b) Others

4. Other liabilities

5. Accruals and deferred income

6. Provisions for liabilities

   (a) Provisions for pensions and similar obligations

   (b) Provisions for tax

   (c) Other provisions

7. Subordinated liabilities [14], [20]

8. Called up share capital [15]

9. Share premium account

10. Reserves

    (a) Capital redemption reserve

    (b) Reserve for own shares

    (c) Reserves provided for by the articles of association

    (d) Other reserves

11. Revaluation reserve

12. Profit and loss account

Total liabilities

MEMORANDUM ITEMS

1. Contingent liabilities [16]

   (1) Acceptances and endorsements

   (2) Guarantees and assets pledged as collateral security [17]

   (3) Other contingent liabilities

2. Commitments [18]

   (1) Commitments arising out of sale and option to resell transactions [19]

   (2) Other commitments

Notes on the balance sheet format and memorandum items

[1] *Cash and balances at central [or post office] banks*

(Assets item 1.)

Cash is to comprise all currency including foreign notes and coins.

Only those balances which may be withdrawn without notice and which are deposited with central or post office banks of the country or countries in which the company is established may be included in this item. All other claims on central or post office banks must be shown under assets items 3 or 4.

[2] *Treasury bills and other eligible bills: Treasury bills and similar securities*

(Assets item 2.(a).)

Treasury bills and similar securities are to comprise treasury bills and similar debt instruments issued by public bodies which are eligible for refinancing with central banks of the country or countries in which the company is established. Any treasury bills or similar debt instruments not so eligible must be included under assets item 5(a).

[3] *Treasury bills and other eligible bills: Other eligible bills*

(Assets item 2.(b).)

Other eligible bills are to comprise all bills purchased to the extent that they are eligible, under national law, for refinancing with the central banks of the country or countries in which the company is established.

[4] *Loans and advances to banks*

(Assets item 3.)

Loans and advances to banks are to comprise all loans and advances to domestic or foreign credit institutions made by the company arising out of banking transactions. However loans and advances to credit institutions represented by debt securities or other fixed-income securities must be included under assets item 5 and not this item.

[5] *Loans and advances to customers*

(Assets item 4.)

Loans and advances to customers are to comprise all types of assets in the form of claims on domestic and foreign customers other than credit institutions. However loans and advances represented by debt securities or other fixed-income securities must be included under assets item 5 and not this item.

[6] *Debt securities [and other fixed-income securities]*

(Assets item 5.)

This item is to comprise transferable debt securities and any other transferable fixed-income securities issued by credit institutions, other undertakings or public bodies. Debt securities and other fixed-income securities issued by public bodies are, however, only to be included in this item if they may not be shown under assets item 2.

Where a company holds its own debt securities these must not be included under this item but must be deducted from liabilities item 3.(a) or (b), as appropriate.

Securities bearing interest rates that vary in accordance with specific factors, for example the interest rate on the inter-bank market or on the Euromarket, are also to be regarded as fixed-income securities to be included under this item.

[7] *Intangible fixed assets*

(Assets item 9.)

This item is to comprise–

(a) development costs,
(b) concessions, patents, licences, trade marks and similar rights and assets,
(c) goodwill, and
(d) payments on account.

Amounts are, however, to be included in respect of (b) only if the assets were acquired for valuable consideration or the assets in question were created by the company itself.

Amounts representing goodwill are only to be included to the extent that the goodwill was acquired for valuable consideration.

The amount of any goodwill included in this item must be disclosed in a note to the accounts.

[8] *Tangible fixed assets*

(Assets item 10.)

This item is to comprise–

(a) land and buildings,
(b) plant and machinery,
(c) fixtures and fittings, tools and equipment, and
(d) payments on account and assets in the course of construction.

The amount included in this item with respect to land and buildings occupied by the company for its own activities must be disclosed in a note to the accounts.

[9] *Called up capital not paid*

(Assets items 11 and 14.)

The two positions shown for this item are alternatives.

[10] *Own shares*

(Assets item 12.)

The nominal value of the shares held must be shown separately under this item.

(11) *Deposits by banks*

(Liabilities item 1.)

Deposits by banks are to comprise all amounts arising out of banking transactions owed to other domestic or foreign credit institutions by the company. However liabilities in the form of debt securities and any liabilities for which transferable certificates have been issued must be included under liabilities item 3 and not this item.

(12) *Customer accounts*

(Liabilities item 2.)

This item is to comprise all amounts owed to creditors that are not credit institutions. However liabilities in the form of debt securities and any liabilities for which transferable certificates have been issued must be shown under liabilities item 3 and not this item.

(13) *Debt securities in issue*

(Liabilities item 3.)

This item is to include both debt securities and debts for which transferable certificates have been issued, including liabilities arising out of own acceptances and promissory notes. (Only acceptances which a company has issued for its own refinancing and in respect of which it is the first party liable are to be treated as own acceptances.)

(14) *Subordinated liabilities*

(Liabilities item 7.)

This item is to comprise all liabilities in respect of which there is a contractual obligation that, in the event of winding up or bankruptcy, they are to be repaid only after the claims of other creditors have been met.

This item must include all subordinated liabilities, whether or not a ranking has been agreed between the subordinated creditors concerned.

(15) *Called up share capital*

(Liabilities item 8.)

The amount of allotted share capital and the amount of called up share capital which has been paid up must be shown separately.

(16) *Contingent liabilities*

(Memorandum item 1.)

This item is to include all transactions whereby the company has underwritten the obligations of a third party.

Liabilities arising out of the endorsement of rediscounted bills must be included in this item. Acceptances other than own acceptances must also be included.

(17) *Contingent liabilities: Guarantees and assets pledged as collateral security*

(Memorandum item 1(2).)

This item is to include all guarantee obligations incurred and assets pledged as collateral security on behalf of third parties, particularly in respect of sureties and irrevocable letters of credit.

(18) *Commitments*

(Memorandum item 2.)

This item is to include every irrevocable commitment which could give rise to a credit risk.

(19) *Commitments: Commitments arising out of sale and option to resell transactions*

(Memorandum item 2(1).)

This item is to comprise commitments entered into by the company in the context of sale and option to resell transactions.

(20) *Claims on, and liabilities to, undertakings in which a participating interest is held or group undertakings*

(Assets items 2 to 5, liabilities items 1 to 3 and 7.)

The following information must be given either by way of subdivision of the relevant items or by way of notes to the accounts.

The amount of the following must be shown for each of assets items 2 to 5–

(a) claims on group undertakings included therein, and
(b) claims on undertakings in which the company has a participating interest included therein.

The amount of the following must be shown for each of liabilities items 1, 2, 3 and 7–

(i) liabilities to group undertakings included therein, and
(ii) liabilities to undertakings in which the company has a participating interest included therein.

SPECIAL RULES

Subordinated assets

11(1) The amount of any assets that are subordinated must be shown either as a subdivision of any relevant asset item or in the notes to the accounts; in the latter case disclosure must be by reference to the relevant asset item or items in which the assets are included.

11(2) In the case of assets items 2 to 5 in the balance sheet format, the amounts required to be shown by note (20) to the format as sub-items of those items must be further subdivided so as to show the amount of any claims included therein that are subordinated.

11(3) For this purpose, assets are subordinated if there is a contractual obligation to the effect that, in the event of winding up or bankruptcy, they are to be repaid only after the claims of other creditors have been met, whether or not a ranking has been agreed between the subordinated creditors concerned.

Syndicated loans

12(1) Where a company is a party to a syndicated loan transaction the company must include only that part of the total loan which it itself has funded.

12(2) Where a company is a party to a syndicated loan transaction and has agreed to reimburse (in whole or in part) any other party to the syndicate any funds advanced by that party or any interest thereon upon the occurrence of any event, including the default of the borrower, any additional liability by reason of such a guarantee must be included as a contingent liability in Memorandum item 1(2).

Sale and repurchase transactions

13(1) The following rules apply where a company is a party to a sale and repurchase transaction.

13(2) Where the company is the transferor of the assets under the transaction–

(a) the assets transferred must, notwithstanding the transfer, be included in its balance sheet,

(b) the purchase price received by it must be included in its balance sheet as an amount owed to the transferee, and

(c) the value of the assets transferred must be disclosed in a note to its accounts.

13(3) Where the company is the transferee of the assets under the transaction, it must not include the assets transferred in its balance sheet but the purchase price paid by it to the transferor must be so included as an amount owed by the transferor.

14(1) The following rules apply where a company is a party to a sale and option to resell transaction.

14(2) Where the company is the transferor of the assets under the transaction, it must not include in its balance sheet the assets transferred but it must enter under Memorandum item 2 an amount equal to the price agreed in the event of repurchase.

14(3) Where the company is the transferee of the assets under the transaction it must include those assets in its balance sheet.

Managed funds

15(1) For the purposes of this paragraph, 'managed funds' are funds which the company administers in its own name but on behalf of others and to which it has legal title.

15(2) The company must, in any case where claims and obligations arising in respect of managed funds fall to be treated as claims and obligations of the company, adopt the following accounting treatment.

15(3)   Claims and obligations representing managed funds are to be included in the company's balance sheet, with the notes to the accounts disclosing the total amount included with respect to such assets and liabilities in the balance sheet and showing the amount included under each relevant balance sheet item in respect of such assets or (as the case may be) liabilities.

Profit and loss account formats – Format 1: Vertical layout

1. Interest receivable [1]

  (1) Interest receivable and similar income arising from debt securities [and other fixed-income securities]

  (2) Other interest receivable and similar income

2. Interest payable [2]

3. Dividend income

  (a) Income from equity shares [and other variable-yield securities]

  (b) Income from participating interests

  (c) Income from shares in group undertakings

4. Fees and commissions receivable [3]

5. Fees and commissions payable [4]

6. Dealing [profits] [losses] [5]

7. Other operating income

8. Administrative expenses

  (a) Staff costs

    (i) Wages and salaries

    (ii) Social security costs

    (iii) Other pension costs

  (b) Other administrative expenses

9. Depreciation and amortisation [6]

10. Other operating charges

11. Provisions

  (a) Provisions for bad and doubtful debts [7]

  (b) Provisions for contingent liabilities and commitments [8]

12. Adjustments to provisions

  (a) Adjustments to provisions for bad and doubtful debts [9]

  (b) Adjustments to provisions for contingent liabilities and commitments [10]

13. Amounts written off fixed asset investments [11]

14. Adjustments to amounts written off fixed asset investments [12]

15. [Profit] [loss] on ordinary activities before tax

16. Tax on [profit] [loss] on ordinary activities

17. [Profit] [loss] on ordinary activities after tax

18. Extraordinary income

19. Extraordinary charges

20. Extraordinary [profit] [loss]

21. Tax on extraordinary [profit] [loss]

22. Extraordinary [profit] [loss] after tax

23. Other taxes not shown under the preceding items

24. [Profit] [loss] for the financial year

Profit and loss account formats – Format 2: Horizontal layout

A. Charges

    1. Interest payable [2]

    2. Fees and commissions payable [4]

    3. Dealing losses [5]

    4. Administrative expenses

        (a) Staff costs

            (i) Wages and salaries

            (ii) Social security costs

            (iii) Other pension costs

        (b) Other administrative expenses

    5. Depreciation and amortisation [6]

    6. Other operating charges

    7. Provisions

        (a) Provisions for bad and doubtful debts [7]

        (b) Provisions for contingent liabilities and commitments [8]

    8. Amounts written off fixed asset investments [11]

    9. Profit on ordinary activities before tax

    10. Tax on [profit] [loss] on ordinary activities

    11. Profit on ordinary activities after tax

    12. Extraordinary charges

    13. Tax on extraordinary [profit] [loss]

    14. Extraordinary loss after tax

    15. Other taxes not shown under the preceding items

    16. Profit for the financial year

B. Income

    1. Interest receivable [1]

        (1) Interest receivable and similar income arising from debt securities [and other fixed-income securities]

        (2) Other interest receivable and similar income

    2. Dividend income

        (a) Income from equity shares [and other variable-yield securities]

        (b) Income from participating interests

        (c) Income from shares in group undertakings

    3. Fees and commissions receivable [3]

    4. Dealing profits [5]

    5. Adjustments to provisions

        (a) Adjustments to provisions for bad and doubtful debts [9]

        (b) Adjustments to provisions for contingent liabilities and commitments [10]

    6. Adjustments to amounts written off fixed asset investments [12]

    7. Other operating income

    8. Loss on ordinary activities before tax

    9. Loss on ordinary activities after tax

    10. Extraordinary income

    11. Extraordinary profit after tax

    12. Loss for the financial year

Notes on the profit and loss account formats

[1] *Interest receivable*

(Format 1, item 1; format 2, item B1.)

This item is to include all income arising out of banking activities, including–

(a) income from assets included in assets items 1 to 5 in the balance sheet format, however calculated,
(b) income resulting from covered forward contracts spread over the actual duration of the contract and similar in nature to interest, and
(c) fees and commissions receivable similar in nature to interest and calculated on a time basis or by reference to the amount of the claim (but not other fees and commissions receivable).

[2] *Interest payable*

(Format 1, item 2; format 2, item A1.)

This item is to include all expenditure arising out of banking activities, including–

(a) charges arising out of liabilities included in liabilities items 1, 2, 3 and 7 in the balance sheet format, however calculated,
(b) charges resulting from covered forward contracts, spread over the actual duration of the contract and similar in nature to interest, and
(c) fees and commissions payable similar in nature to interest and calculated on a time basis or by reference to the amount of the liability (but not other fees and commissions payable).

[3] *Fees and commissions receivable*

(Format 1, item 4; format 2, item B3.)

Fees and commissions receivable are to comprise income in respect of all services supplied by the company to third parties, but not fees or commissions required to be included under interest receivable (format 1, item 1; format 2, item B1).

In particular the following fees and commissions receivable must be included (unless required to be included under interest receivable)–

(a) fees and commissions for guarantees, loan administration on behalf of other lenders and securities transactions,
(b) fees, commissions and other income in respect of payment transactions, account administration charges and commissions for the safe custody and administration of securities,
(c) fees and commissions for foreign currency transactions and for the sale and purchase of coin and precious metals, and
(d) fees and commissions charged for brokerage services in connection with savings and insurance contracts and loans.

[4] *Fees and commissions payable*

(Format 1, item 5; format 2, item A2.)

Fees and commissions payable are to comprise charges for all services rendered to the company by third parties but not fees or commissions required to be included under interest payable (format 1, item 2; format 2, item A1).

In particular the following fees and commissions payable must be included (unless required to be included under interest payable)–

(a) fees and commissions for guarantees, loan administration and securities transactions;
(b) fees, commissions and other charges in respect of payment transactions, account administration charges and commissions for the safe custody and administration of securities;
(c) fees and commissions for foreign currency transactions and for the sale and purchase of coin and precious metals; and
(d) fees and commissions for brokerage services in connection with savings and insurance contracts and loans.

[5] *Dealing [profits] [losses]*

(Format 1, item 6; format 2, items B4 and A3.)

This item is to comprise–

(a) the net profit or net loss on transactions in securities which are not held as financial fixed assets together with amounts written off or written back with respect to such securities, including amounts written off or written back as a result of the application of paragraph 33(1),
(b) the net profit or loss on exchange activities, save in so far as the profit or loss is included in interest receivable or interest payable (format 1, items 1 or 2; format 2, items B1 or A1), and
(c) the net profits and losses on other dealing operations involving financial instruments, including precious metals.

[6] *Depreciation and amortisation*

(Format 1, item 9; format 2, item A5.)

This item is to comprise depreciation and other amounts written off in respect of balance sheet assets items 9 and 10.

[7] *Provisions: Provisions for bad and doubtful debts*

(Format 1, item 11(a); format 2, item A7(a).)

Provisions for bad and doubtful debts are to comprise charges for amounts written off and for provisions made in respect of loans and advances shown under balance sheet assets items 3 and 4.

[8] *Provisions: Provisions for contingent liabilities and commitments*

(Format 1, item 11(b); format 2, item A7(b).)

This item is to comprise charges for provisions for contingent liabilities and commitments of a type which would, if not provided for, be shown under Memorandum items 1 and 2.

(9) *Adjustments to provisions: Adjustments to provisions for bad and doubtful debts*

(Format 1, item 12(a); format 2, item B5(a).)

This item is to include credits from the recovery of loans that have been written off, from other advances written back following earlier write offs and from the reduction of provisions previously made with respect to loans and advances.

(10) *Adjustments to provisions: Adjustments to provisions for contingent liabilities and commitments*

(Format 1, item 12(b); format 2, item B5(b).)

This item comprises credits from the reduction of provisions previously made with respect to contingent liabilities and commitments.

(11) *Amounts written off fixed asset investments*

(Format 1, item 13; format 2, item A8.)

Amounts written off fixed asset investments are to comprise amounts written off in respect of assets which are transferable securities held as financial fixed assets, participating interests and shares in group undertakings and which are included in assets items 5 to 8 in the balance sheet format.

(12) *Adjustments to amounts written off fixed asset investments*

(Format 1, item 14; format 2, item B6.)

Adjustments to amounts written off fixed asset investments are to include amounts written back following earlier write offs and provisions in respect of assets which are transferable securities held as financial fixed assets, participating interests and group undertakings and which are included in assets items 5 to 8 in the balance sheet format.

Part 2 – Accounting principles and rules

SECTION A – ACCOUNTING PRINCIPLES

Preliminary

16(1) The amounts to be included in respect of all items shown in a company's accounts must be determined in accordance with the principles set out in this Section.

16(2) But if it appears to the company's directors that there are special reasons for departing from any of those principles in preparing the company's accounts in respect of any financial year they may do so, in which case particulars of the departure, the reasons for it and its effect must be given in a note to the accounts.

Accounting principles

17 The company is presumed to be carrying on business as a going concern.

18 Accounting policies and measurement bases must be applied consistently within the same accounts and from one financial year to the next.

History – In para. 18, the words 'and measurement bases' inserted by SI 2015/980, reg. 32(2)(a), with effect in relation to–
    (a)   financial years beginning on or after 1 January 2016, and
    (b)   a financial year of a company beginning on or after 1 January 2015, but before 1 January 2016, if the directors of the company so decide.

19 The amount of any item must be determined on a prudent basis, and in particular–

    (a)   only profits realised at the balance sheet date are to be included in the profit and loss account,

    (b)   all liabilities which have arisen in respect of the financial year to which the accounts relate or a previous financial year must be taken into account, including those which only become apparent between the balance sheet date and the date on which it is signed on behalf of the board of directors in accordance with section 414 of the 2006 Act (approval and signing of accounts) and

    (c)   all provisions for diminution of value must be recognised, whether the result of the financial year is a profit or a loss.

History – Para. 19(c), (and the word 'and' preceding it) inserted; the word 'and' in para. (a) omitted by SI 2015/980, reg. 32(2)(b), with effect in relation to–
  (a)   financial years beginning on or after 1 January 2016, and
  (b)   a financial year of a company beginning on or after 1 January 2015, but before 1 January 2016, if the directors of the company so decide.

20   All income and charges relating to the financial year to which the accounts relate must be taken into account, without regard to the date of receipt or payment.

21   In determining the aggregate amount of any item, the amount of each individual asset or liability that falls to be taken into account must be determined separately.

21A   The opening balance sheet for each financial year shall correspond to the closing balance sheet for the preceding financial year.

History – Para. 21A inserted by SI 2015/980, reg. 32(2)(c), with effect in relation to–
  (a)   financial years beginning on or after 1 January 2016, and
  (b)   a financial year of a company beginning on or after 1 January 2015, but before 1 January 2016, if the directors of the company so decide.

SECTION B – HISTORICAL COST ACCOUNTING RULES

Preliminary

22   Subject to Sections C and D of this Part of this Schedule, the amounts to be included in respect of all items shown in a company's accounts must be determined in accordance with the rules set out in this Section.

FIXED ASSETS

General rules

23(1)   The amount to be included in respect of any fixed asset is its cost.

23(2)   This is subject to any provision for depreciation or diminution in value made in accordance with paragraphs 24 to 26.

Rules for depreciation and diminution in value

24   In the case of any fixed asset which has a limited useful economic life, the amount of–

  (a)   its cost, or
  (b)   where it is estimated that any such asset will have a residual value at the end of the period of its useful economic life, its cost less that estimated residual value,

must be reduced by provisions for depreciation calculated to write off that amount systematically over the period of the asset's useful economic life.

25(1)   Where a fixed asset investment to which sub-paragraph (2) applies has diminished in value, provisions for diminution in value may be made in respect of it and the amount to be included in respect of it may be reduced accordingly.

25(2)   This sub-paragraph applies to fixed asset investments of a description falling to be included under assets item 7 (participating interests) or 8 (shares in group undertakings) in the balance sheet format, or any other holding of securities held as a financial fixed asset.

25(3)   Provisions for diminution in value must be made in respect of any fixed asset which has diminished in value if the reduction in its value is expected to be permanent (whether its useful economic life is limited or not), and the amount to be included in respect of it must be reduced accordingly.

25(4)   Provisions made under this paragraph must be charged to the profit and loss account and disclosed separately in a note to the accounts if they have not been shown separately in the profit and loss account.

History – Para. 25(4) substituted by SI 2015/980, reg. 32(3)(a), with effect in relation to–
  (a)   financial years beginning on or after 1 January 2016, and
  (b)   a financial year of a company beginning on or after 1 January 2015, but before 1 January 2016, if the directors of the company so decide.

Former para. 25(4) read as follows:
"**25(4)**   Any provisions made under this paragraph which are not shown in the profit and loss account must be disclosed (either separately or in aggregate) in a note to the accounts."

26(1)   Where the reasons for which any provision was made in accordance with paragraph 25 have ceased to apply to any extent, that provision must be written back to the extent that it is no longer necessary.

26(1A)   But provision made in accordance with paragraph 25(3) in respect of goodwill must not be written back to any extent.

26(2)   Any amounts written back under sub-paragraph (1) must be recognised in the profit and loss account and disclosed separately in a note to the accounts if not shown separately in the profit and loss account.

History – Para. 26(1A) inserted by SI 2015/1672, reg. 4(4), with effect in relation to–
  (a)   financial years beginning on or after 1 January 2016, and
  (b)   a financial year of a company beginning on or after 1 January 2015 but before 1 January 2016, if the directors of the company have decided.

Para. 26(2) substituted by SI 2015/980, reg. 32(3)(b), with effect in relation to–
  (a)   financial years beginning on or after 1 January 2016, and
  (b)   a financial year of a company beginning on or after 1 January 2015, but before 1 January 2016, if the directors of the company so decide.

Former para. 26(2) read as follows:
"**26(2)**   Any amounts written back in accordance with sub-paragraph (1) which are not shown in the profit and loss account must be disclosed (either separately or in aggregate) in a note to the accounts."

Intangible assets

27(1)   Where this is in accordance with generally accepted accounting principles or practice, development costs may be included under assets item 9 in the balance sheet format.

27(2)   If any amount is included in a company's balance sheet in respect of development costs, the note on accounting policies (see paragraph 53 of this Schedule) must include the following information–

  (a)   the period over which the amount of those costs originally capitalised is being or is to be written off, and
  (b)   the reasons for capitalising the development costs in question.

History – Para. 27 and the heading preceding it substituted by SI 2015/980, reg. 32(3)(c), with effect in relation to–
  (a)   financial years beginning on or after 1 January 2016, and
  (b)   a financial year of a company beginning on or after 1 January 2015, but before 1 January 2016, if the directors of the company so decide.

Former para. 27 read as follows:

"**Development costs**

27(1)   Notwithstanding that amounts representing 'development costs' may be included under assets item 9 in the balance sheet format, an amount may only be included in a company's balance sheet in respect of development costs in special circumstances.

27(2)   If any amount is included in a company's balance sheet in respect of development costs the following information must be given in a note to the accounts–

(a)   the period over which the amount of those costs originally capitalised is being or is to be written off, and

(b)   the reasons for capitalising the development costs in question."

Goodwill

28(1)   Intangible assets must be written off over the useful economic life of the intangible asset.

28(2)   Where in exceptional cases the useful life of intangible assets cannot be reliably estimated, such assets must be written off over a period chosen by the directors of the company.

28(3)   The period referred to in sub-paragraph (2) must not exceed ten years.

28(4)   There must be disclosed in a note to the accounts the period referred to in sub-paragraph (2) and the reasons for choosing that period.

History – Para. 28 substituted by SI 2015/980, reg. 32(3)(c), with effect in relation to–

(a)   financial years beginning on or after 1 January 2016, and

(b)   a financial year of a company beginning on or after 1 January 2015, but before 1 January 2016, if the directors of the company so decide.

Former para. 28 read as follows:

"**28(1)**   The application of paragraphs 23 to 26 in relation to goodwill (in any case where goodwill is treated as an asset) is subject to the following.

28(2)   Subject to sub-paragraph (3), the amount of the consideration for any goodwill acquired by a company must be reduced by provisions for depreciation calculated to write off that amount systematically over a period chosen by the directors of the company.

28(3)   The period chosen must not exceed the useful economic life of the goodwill in question.

28(4)   In any case where any goodwill acquired by a company is included as an asset in the company's balance sheet there must be disclosed in a note to the accounts–

(a)   the period chosen for writing off the consideration for that goodwill, and

(b)   the reasons for choosing that period."

Treatment of fixed assets

29(1)   Assets included in assets items 9 (intangible fixed assets) and 10 (tangible fixed assets) in the balance sheet format must be valued as fixed assets.

29(2)   Other assets falling to be included in the balance sheet must be valued as fixed assets where they are intended for use on a continuing basis in the company's activities.

Financial fixed assets

30(1)   Debt securities, including fixed-income securities, held as financial fixed assets must be included in the balance sheet at an amount equal to their maturity value plus any premium, or less any discount, on their purchase, subject to the following provisions of this paragraph.

30(2)   The amount included in the balance sheet with respect to such securities purchased at a premium must be reduced each financial year on a systematic basis so as to write the premium off over the period to the maturity date of the security and the amounts so written off must be charged to the profit and loss account for the relevant financial years.

30(3)   The amount included in the balance sheet with respect to such securities purchased at a discount must be increased each financial year on a systematic basis so as to extinguish the discount over the period to the maturity date of the security and the amounts by which the amount is increased must be credited to the profit and loss account for the relevant years.

30(4)   The notes to the accounts must disclose the amount of any unamortized premium or discount not extinguished which is included in the balance sheet by virtue of sub-paragraph (1).

30(5)   For the purposes of this paragraph **'premium'** means any excess of the amount paid for a security over its maturity value and **'discount'** means any deficit of the amount paid for a security over its maturity value.

Current assets

31   The amount to be included in respect of loans and advances, debt or other fixed-income securities and equity shares or other variable yield securities not held as financial fixed assets must be their cost, subject to paragraphs 32 and 33.

32(1)   If the net realisable value of any asset referred to in paragraph 31 is lower than its cost, the amount to be included in respect of that asset is the net realisable value.

32(2)   Where the reasons for which any provision for diminution in value was made in accordance with sub-paragraph (1) have ceased to apply to any extent, that provision must be written back to the extent that it is no longer necessary.

33(1)   Subject to paragraph 32, the amount to be included in the balance sheet in respect of transferable securities not held as financial fixed assets may be the higher of their cost or their market value at the balance sheet date.

33(2)   The difference between the cost of any securities included in the balance sheet at a valuation under sub-paragraph (1) and their market value must be shown (in aggregate) in the notes to the accounts.

MISCELLANEOUS AND SUPPLEMENTARY PROVISIONS

Excess of money owed over value received as an asset item

34(1)   Where the amount repayable on any debt owed by a company is greater than the value of the consideration received in the transaction giving rise to the debt, the amount of the difference may be treated as an asset.

34(2)   Where any such amount is so treated–

(a)   it must be written off by reasonable amounts each year and must be completely written off before repayment of the debt, and

(b)   if the current amount is not shown as a separate item in the company's balance sheet, it must be disclosed in a note to the accounts.

Determination of cost

35(1)   The cost of an asset that has been acquired by the company is to be determined by adding to the actual price paid any expenses incidental to its acquisition and then subtracting any incidental reductions in the cost of acquisition.

35(2)   The cost of an asset constructed by the company is to be determined by adding to the purchase price of the raw materials and consumables used the amount of the costs incurred by the company which are directly attributable to the construction of that asset.

35(3)   In addition, there may be included in the cost of an asset constructed by the company–

(a)   a reasonable proportion of the costs incurred by the company which are only indirectly attributable to the construction of that asset, but only to the extent that they relate to the period of construction, and

(b)   interest on capital borrowed to finance the construction of that asset, to the extent that it accrues in respect of the period of construction,

provided, however, in a case within paragraph (b), that the inclusion of the interest in determining the cost of that asset and the amount of the interest so included is disclosed in a note to the accounts.

History – In para. 35(1), the words 'and then subtracting any incidental reductions in the cost of acquisition' inserted by SI 2015/980, reg. 32(3)(d), with effect in relation to–
   (a)   financial years beginning on or after 1 January 2016, and
   (b)   a financial year of a company beginning on or after 1 January 2015, but before 1 January 2016, if the directors of the company so decide.

36(1)   The cost of any assets which are fungible assets (including investments), may be determined by the application of any of the methods mentioned in sub-paragraph (2) in relation to any such assets of the same class, provided that the method chosen is one which appears to the directors to be appropriate in the circumstances of the company.

36(2)   Those methods are–

(a)   the method known as 'first in, first out' (FIFO),

(b)   the method known as 'last in, first out' (LIFO),

(c)   a weighted average price, and

(d)   any other method reflecting generally accepted best practice.

36(3)   Where in the case of any company–

(a)   the cost of assets falling to be included under any item shown in the company's balance sheet has been determined by the application of any method permitted by this paragraph, and

(b)   the amount shown in respect of that item differs materially from the relevant alternative amount given below in this paragraph,

the amount of that difference must be disclosed in a note to the accounts.

36(4)   Subject to sub-paragraph (5), for the purposes of sub-paragraph (3)(b), the relevant alternative amount, in relation to any item shown in a company's balance sheet, is the amount which would have been shown in respect of that item if assets of any class included under that item at an amount determined by any method permitted by this paragraph had instead been included at their replacement cost as at the balance sheet date.

36(5)   The relevant alternative amount may be determined by reference to the most recent actual purchase price before the balance sheet date of assets of any class included under the item in question instead of by reference to their replacement cost as at that date, but only if the former appears to the directors of the company to constitute the more appropriate standard of comparison in the case of assets of that class.

History – In para. 36(2)(d), the words 'reflecting generally accepted best practice' substituted for the words 'similar to any of the methods mentioned above' by SI 2015/980, reg. 32(3)(e), with effect in relation to–
   (a)   financial years beginning on or after 1 January 2016, and
   (b)   a financial year of a company beginning on or after 1 January 2015, but before 1 January 2016, if the directors of the company so decide.

Substitution of original stated amount where price or cost unknown

37(1)   This paragraph applies where–

(a)   there is no record of the purchase price of any asset acquired by a company or of any price, expenses or costs relevant for determining its cost in accordance with paragraph 35, or

(b)   any such record cannot be obtained without unreasonable expense or delay.

37(2)   In such a case, its cost is to be taken, for the purposes of paragraphs 23 to 33, to be the value ascribed to it in the earliest available record of its value made on or after its acquisition by the company.

SECTION C – ALTERNATIVE ACCOUNTING RULES

Preliminary

38(1)   The rules set out in Section B are referred to below in this Schedule as the historical cost accounting rules.

38(2)   Paragraphs 23 to 26 and 30 to 34 are referred to below in this Section as the depreciation rules; and references below in this Schedule to the historical cost accounting rules do not include the depreciation rules as they apply by virtue of paragraph 41.

39   Subject to paragraphs 41 to 43, the amounts to be included in respect of assets of any description mentioned in paragraph 40 may be determined on any basis so mentioned.

Alternative accounting rules

40(1)   Intangible fixed assets, other than goodwill, may be included at their current cost.

40(2)   Tangible fixed assets may be included at a market value determined as at the date of their last valuation or at their current cost.

40(3)   Investments of any description falling to be included under assets items 7 (participating interests) or 8 (shares in group undertakings) of the balance sheet format and any other securities held as financial fixed assets may be included either–

(a)   at a market value determined as at the date of their last valuation, or

(b)   at a value determined on any basis which appears to the directors to be appropriate in the circumstances of the company.

But in the latter case particulars of the method of valuation adopted and of the reasons for adopting it must be disclosed in a note to the accounts.

40(4)   [Omitted by SI 2015/980, reg. 32(4)]

History – Para. 40(4) omitted by SI 2015/980, reg. 32(4)(a), with effect in relation to–
(a)   financial years beginning on or after 1 January 2016, and
(b)   a financial year of a company beginning on or after 1 January 2015, but before 1 January 2016, if the directors of the company so decide.

Former para. 40(4) read as follows:

"40(4)   Securities of any description not held as financial fixed assets (if not valued in accordance with paragraph 33) may be included at their current cost."

Application of the depreciation rules

41(1) Where the value of any asset of a company is determined in accordance with paragraph 40, that value must be, or (as the case may require) be the starting point for determining, the amount to be included in respect of that asset in the company's accounts, instead of its cost or any value previously so determined for that asset.

The depreciation rules apply accordingly in relation to any such asset with the substitution for any reference to its cost of a reference to the value most recently determined for that asset in accordance with paragraph 40.

41(2) The amount of any provision for depreciation required in the case of any fixed asset by paragraphs 24 to 26 as they apply by virtue of sub-paragraph (1) is referred to below in this paragraph as the adjusted amount, and the amount of any provision which would be required by any of those paragraphs in the case of that asset according to the historical cost accounting rules is referred to as the historical cost amount.

41(3) Where sub-paragraph (1) applies in the case of any fixed asset the amount of any provision for depreciation in respect of that asset included in any item shown in the profit and loss account in respect of amounts written off assets of the description in question may be the historical cost amount instead of the adjusted amount, provided that the amount of any difference between the two is shown separately in the profit and loss account or in a note to the accounts.

Additional information to be provided in case of departure from historical cost accounting rules

42(1) This paragraph applies where the amounts to be included in respect of assets covered by any items shown in a company's accounts have been determined in accordance with paragraph 40.

42(2) The items affected and the basis of valuation adopted in determining the amounts of the assets in question in the case of each such item must be disclosed in the note on accounting policies (see paragraph 53 of this Schedule).

42(3) In the case of each balance sheet item affected, the comparable amounts determined according to the historical cost accounting rules must be shown in a note to the accounts.

42(4) In sub-paragraph (3), references in relation to any item to the comparable amounts determined as there mentioned are references to–

    (a)   the aggregate amount which would be required to be shown in respect of that item if the amounts to be included in respect of all the assets covered by that item were determined according to the historical cost accounting rules, and

    (b)   the aggregate amount of the cumulative provisions for depreciation or diminution in value which would be permitted or required in determining those amounts according to those rules.

History – In para. 42(2), the words 'the note on accounting policies (see paragraph 53 of this Schedule)' substituted for the words 'a note to the accounts' by SI 2015/980, reg. 32(4)(b), with effect in relation to–
    (a) financial years beginning on or after 1 January 2016, and
    (b) a financial year of a company beginning on or after 1 January 2015, but before 1 January 2016, if the directors of the company so decide.

Para. 42(3) substituted by SI 2015/980, reg. 32(4)(c), with effect in relation to–
    (a) financial years beginning on or after 1 January 2016, and
    (b) a financial year of a company beginning on or after 1 January 2015, but before 1 January 2016, if the directors of the company so decide.

Former para. 42(3) read as follows:

"42(3) In the case of each balance sheet item affected either–

    (a)   the comparable amounts determined according to the historical cost accounting rules, or

    (b)   the differences between those amounts and the corresponding amounts actually shown in the balance sheet in respect of that item, must be shown separately in the balance sheet or in a note to the accounts."

Revaluation reserve

43(1)   With respect to any determination of the value of an asset of a company in accordance with paragraph 40, the amount of any profit or loss arising from that determination (after allowing, where appropriate, for any provisions for depreciation or diminution in value made otherwise than by reference to the value so determined and any adjustments of any such provisions made in the light of that determination) must be credited or (as the case may be) debited to a separate reserve ('the revaluation reserve').

43(2)   The amount of the revaluation reserve must be shown in the company's balance sheet under liabilities item 11 in the balance sheet format.

43(3)   An amount may be transferred–

    (a)   from the revaluation reserve–

        (i)   to the profit and loss account, if the amount was previously charged to that account or represents realised profit, or

        (ii) on capitalisation,

    (b)   to or from the revaluation reserve in respect of the taxation relating to any profit or loss credited or debited to the reserve.

The revaluation reserve must be reduced to the extent that the amounts transferred to it are no longer necessary for the purposes of the valuation method used.

43(4)   In sub-paragraph (3)(a)(ii) **'capitalisation'**, in relation to an amount standing to the credit of the revaluation reserve, means applying it in wholly or partly paying up unissued shares in the company to be allotted to members of the company as fully or partly paid shares.

43(5)   The revaluation reserve must not be reduced except as mentioned in this paragraph.

43(6)   The treatment for taxation purposes of amounts credited or debited to the revaluation reserve must be disclosed in a note to the accounts.

History – In para. 43(2), the words 'but need not be shown under that name' omitted by SI 2015/980, reg. 32(4)(d), with effect in relation to–

    (a)   financial years beginning on or after 1 January 2016, and

    (b)   a financial year of a company beginning on or after 1 January 2015, but before 1 January 2016, if the directors of the company so decide.

SECTION D – FAIR VALUE ACCOUNTING

Inclusion of financial instruments at fair value

44(1)   Subject to sub-paragraphs (2) to (5), financial instruments (including derivatives) may be included at fair value.

44(2)   Sub-paragraph (1) does not apply to financial instruments that constitute liabilities unless–

    (a)   they are held as part of a trading portfolio,

    (b)   they are derivatives, or

    (c)   they are financial instruments falling within sub-paragraph (4).

44(3) Unless they are financial instruments falling within sub-paragraph (4), sub-paragraph (1) does not apply to–

    (a)   financial instruments (other than derivatives) held to maturity,

    (b)   loans and receivables originated by the company and not held for trading purposes,

    (c)   interests in subsidiary undertakings, associated undertakings and joint ventures,

    (d)   equity instruments issued by the company,

    (e)   contracts for contingent consideration in a business combination, or

    (f)   other financial instruments with such special characteristics that the instruments, according to generally accepted accounting principles or practice, should be accounted for differently from other financial instruments.

44(4) Financial instruments which under international accounting standards may be included in accounts at fair value, may be so included, provided that the disclosures required by such accounting standards are made.

44(5) If the fair value of a financial instrument cannot be determined reliably in accordance with paragraph 45, sub-paragraph (1) does not apply to that financial instrument.

44(6) In this paragraph–

    'associated undertaking' has the meaning given by paragraph 19 of Schedule 6 to these Regulations;

    'joint venture' has the meaning given by paragraph 18 of that Schedule.

History – Para. 44(4) substituted by SI 2015/980, reg. 32(5)(a), with effect in relation to–
    (a)   financial years beginning on or after 1 January 2016, and
    (b)   a financial year of a company beginning on or after 1 January 2015, but before 1 January 2016, if the directors of the company so decide.

Former para. 44(4) read as follows:

"44(4) Financial instruments that, under international accounting standards adopted by the European Commission on or before 5th September 2006 in accordance with the IAS Regulation, may be included in accounts at fair value, may be so included, provided that the disclosures required by such accounting standards are made."

Determination of fair value

45(1) The fair value of a financial instrument is its value determined in accordance with this paragraph.

45(2) If a reliable market can readily be identified for the financial instrument, its fair value is determined by reference to its market value.

45(3) If a reliable market cannot readily be identified for the financial instrument but can be identified for its components or for a similar instrument, its fair value is determined by reference to the market value of its components or of the similar instrument.

45(4) If neither sub-paragraph (2) nor (3) applies, the fair value of the financial instrument is a value resulting from generally accepted valuation models and techniques.

45(5) Any valuation models and techniques used for the purposes of sub-paragraph (4) must ensure a reasonable approximation of the market value.

Hedged items

46 A company may include any assets and liabilities, or identified portions of such assets or liabilities, that qualify as hedged items under a fair value hedge accounting system at the amount required under that system.

Other assets that may be included at fair value

47(1) This paragraph applies to–

(a) investment property, and

(b) living animals and plants.

47(2) Such investment property and living animals and plants may be included at fair value, provided that, as the case may be, all such investment property or living animals and plants are so included where their fair value can be reliably determined.

47(3) In this paragraph, **'fair value'** means fair value determined in accordance with generally accepted accounting principles or practice.

History – Para. 47 substituted by SI 2015/980, reg. 32(5)(b), with effect in relation to–
(a) financial years beginning on or after 1 January 2016, and
(b) a financial year of a company beginning on or after 1 January 2015, but before 1 January 2016, if the directors of the company so decide.

Former para. 47 read as follows:
"**47(1)** This paragraph applies to–

(a) investment property, and
(b) living animals and plants, that, under international accounting standards, may be included in accounts at fair value.

47(2) Such investment property and such living animals and plants may be included at fair value, provided that all such investment property or, as the case may be, all such living animals and plants are so included where their fair value can reliably be determined.

47(3) In this paragraph, **'fair value'** means fair value determined in accordance with relevant international accounting standards."

Accounting for changes in value

48(1) This paragraph applies where a financial instrument is valued in accordance with paragraph 44 or 46 or an asset is valued in accordance with paragraph 47.

48(2) Notwithstanding paragraph 19 in this Part of this Schedule, and subject to sub-paragraphs (3) and (4), a change in the value of the financial instrument or of the investment property or living animal or plant must be included in the profit and loss account.

48(3) Where–

(a) the financial instrument accounted for is a hedging instrument under a hedge accounting system that allows some or all of the change in value not to be shown in the profit and loss account, or

(b) the change in value relates to an exchange difference arising on a monetary item that forms part of a company's net investment in a foreign entity,

the amount of the change in value must be credited to or (as the case may be) debited from a separate reserve ('the fair value reserve').

48(4) Where the instrument accounted for–

(a) is an available for sale financial asset, and

(b) is not a derivative, the change in value may be credited to or (as the case may be) debited from the fair value reserve.

The fair value reserve

49(1) The fair value reserve must be adjusted to the extent that the amounts shown in it are no longer necessary for the purposes of paragraph 48(3) or (4).

49(2) The treatment for taxation purposes of amounts credited or debited to the fair value reserve must be disclosed in a note to the accounts.

Assets and liabilities denominated in foreign currencies

50(1) Subject to the following sub-paragraphs, amounts to be included in respect of assets and liabilities denominated in foreign currencies must be in sterling (or the currency in which the accounts are drawn up) after translation at an appropriate spot rate of exchange prevailing at the balance sheet date.

50(2) An appropriate rate of exchange prevailing on the date of purchase may however be used for assets held as financial fixed assets and assets to be included under assets items 9 (intangible fixed assets) and 10 (tangible fixed assets) in the balance sheet format, if they are not covered or not specifically covered in either the spot or forward currency markets.

50(3) An appropriate spot rate of exchange prevailing at the balance sheet date must be used for translating uncompleted spot exchange transactions.

50(4) An appropriate forward rate of exchange prevailing at the balance sheet date must be used for translating uncompleted forward exchange transactions.

50(5) This paragraph does not apply to any assets or liabilities held, or any transactions entered into, for hedging purposes or to any assets or liabilities which are themselves hedged.

51(1) Subject to sub-paragraph (2), any difference between the amount to be included in respect of an asset or liability under paragraph 50 and the book value, after translation into sterling (or the currency in which the accounts are drawn up) at an appropriate rate, of that asset or liability must be credited or, as the case may be, debited to the profit and loss account.

51(2) In the case, however, of assets held as financial fixed assets, of assets to be included under assets items 9 (intangible fixed assets) and 10 (tangible fixed assets) in the balance sheet format and of transactions undertaken to cover such assets, any such difference may be deducted from or credited to any non-distributable reserve available for the purpose.

PART 3 – NOTES TO THE ACCOUNTS
PRELIMINARY

52(1) Any information required in the case of a company by the following provisions of this Part of this Schedule must be given by way of a note to the accounts.

52(2) These notes must be presented in the order in which, where relevant, the items to which they relate are presented in the balance sheet and in the profit and loss account.

History – Para. 52 substituted by SI 2015/980, reg. 33(2), with effect in relation to–
  (a) financial years beginning on or after 1 January 2016, and
  (b) a financial year of a company beginning on or after 1 January 2015, but before 1 January 2016, if the directors of the company so decide.

Former para. 52 read as follows:

"**52** Any information required in the case of any company by the following provisions of this Part of this Schedule must (if not given in the company's accounts) be given by way of a note to the accounts."

GENERAL
Disclosure of accounting policies

53 The accounting policies adopted by the company in determining the amounts to be included in respect of items shown in the balance sheet and in determining the profit or loss of the company must be stated (including such policies with respect to the depreciation and diminution in value of assets).

54   It must be stated whether the accounts have been prepared in accordance with applicable accounting standards and particulars of any material departure from those standards and the reasons for it must be given.

Sums denominated in foreign currencies

55   Where any sums originally denominated in foreign currencies have been brought into account under any items shown in the balance sheet format or profit and loss account formats, the basis on which those sums have been translated into sterling (or the currency in which the accounts are drawn up) must be stated.

Reserves and dividends

56   There must be stated—

(a)   any amount set aside or proposed to be set aside to, or withdrawn or proposed to be withdrawn from, reserves,

(b)   the aggregate amount of dividends paid in the financial year (other than those for which a liability existed at the immediately preceding balance sheet date),

(c)   the aggregate amount of dividends that the company is liable to pay at the balance sheet date, and

(d)   the aggregate amount of dividends that are proposed before the date of approval of the accounts, and not otherwise disclosed under sub-paragraph (b) or (c).

INFORMATION SUPPLEMENTING THE BALANCE SHEET

57   Paragraphs 58 to 84 require information which either supplements the information given with respect to any particular items shown in the balance sheet or is otherwise relevant to assessing the company's state of affairs in the light of the information so given.

Share capital and debentures

58(1)   Where shares of more than one class have been allotted, the number and aggregate nominal value of shares of each class allotted must be given.

58(2)   In the case of any part of the allotted share capital that consists of redeemable shares, the following information must be given—

(a)   the earliest and latest dates on which the company has power to redeem those shares,

(b)   whether those shares must be redeemed in any event or are liable to be redeemed at the option of the company or of the shareholder, and

(c)   whether any (and, if so, what) premium is payable on redemption.

59   If the company has allotted any shares during the financial year, the following information must be given—

(a)   the classes of shares allotted, and

(b)   as respects each class of shares, the number allotted, their aggregate nominal value and the consideration received by the company for the allotment.

60(1)   With respect to any contingent right to the allotment of shares in the company the following particulars must be given—

(a)   the number, description and amount of the shares in relation to which the right is exercisable,

(b)   the period during which it is exercisable, and

(c)   the price to be paid for the shares allotted.

60(2)   In sub-paragraph (1) **'contingent right to the allotment of shares'** means any option to subscribe for shares and any other right to require the allotment of shares to any person whether arising on the conversion into shares of securities of any other description or otherwise.

61(1)   If the company has issued any debentures during the financial year to which the accounts relate, the following information must be given–

(a)   the classes of debentures issued, and

(b)   as respects each class of debentures, the amount issued and the consideration received by the company for the issue.

61(2)   Where any of the company's debentures are held by a nominee of or trustee for the company, the nominal amount of the debentures and the amount at which they are stated in the accounting records kept by the company in accordance with section 386 of the 2006 Act (duty to keep accounting records) must be stated.

Fixed assets

62(1)   In respect of any fixed assets of the company included in any assets item in the company's balance sheet the following information must be given by reference to each such item–

(a)   the appropriate amounts in respect of those assets included in the item as at the date of the beginning of the financial year and as at the balance sheet date respectively,

(b)   the effect on any amount shown included in the item in respect of those assets of–

(i)   any determination during that year of the value to be ascribed to any of those assets in accordance with paragraph 40,

(ii)   acquisitions during that year of any fixed assets,

(iii) disposals during that year of any fixed assets, and

(iv)   any transfers of fixed assets of the company to and from that item during that year.

62(2)   The reference in sub-paragraph (1)(a) to the appropriate amounts in respect of any fixed assets (included in an assets item) as at any date there mentioned is a reference to amounts representing the aggregate amounts determined, as at that date, in respect of fixed assets falling to be included under the item on either of the following bases–

(a)   on the basis of cost (determined in accordance with paragraphs 35 and 36), or

(b)   on any basis permitted by paragraph 40,

(leaving out of account in either case any provisions for depreciation or diminution in value).

62(3)   In addition, in respect of any fixed assets of the company included in any assets item in the company's balance sheet, there must be stated (by reference to each such item)–

(a)   the cumulative amount of provisions for depreciation or diminution in value of those assets included under that item as at each date mentioned in sub-paragraph (1)(a),

(b)   the amount of any such provisions made in respect of the financial year,

(c)   the amount of any adjustments made in respect of any such provisions during that year in consequence of the disposal of any of those assets, and

(d)   the amount of any other adjustments made in respect of any such provisions during that year.

62(4) The requirements of this paragraph need not be complied with to the extent that a company takes advantage of the option of setting off charges and income afforded by paragraph 8(3) in Part 1 of this Schedule.

63 Where any fixed assets of the company (other than listed investments) are included under any item shown in the company's balance sheet at an amount determined in accordance with paragraph 40, the following information must be given–

(a) the years (so far as they are known to the directors) in which the assets were severally valued and the several values, and

(b) in the case of assets that have been valued during the financial year, the names of the persons who valued them or particulars of their qualifications for doing so and (whichever is stated) the bases of valuation used by them.

64 In relation to any amount which is included under assets item 10 in the balance sheet format (tangible fixed assets) with respect to land and buildings there must be stated–

(a) how much of that amount is ascribable to land of freehold tenure and how much to land of leasehold tenure, and

(b) how much of the amount ascribable to land of leasehold tenure is ascribable to land held on long lease and how much to land held on short lease.

65 There must be disclosed separately the amount of–

(a) any participating interests, and

(b) any shares in group undertakings that are held in credit institutions.

Information about fair value of assets and liabilities

66(1) This paragraph applies where financial instruments or other assets have been valued in accordance with, as appropriate, paragraph 44, 46 or 47.

66(2) There must be stated–

(a) the significant assumptions underlying the valuation models and techniques used to determine the fair value of the financial instruments or other assets,

(b) for each category of financial instrument or other asset, the fair value of the assets in that category and the changes in value–

(i) included directly in the profit and loss account, or
(ii) credited to or (as the case may be) debited from the fair value reserve,
in respect of those assets, and

(c) for each class of derivatives, the extent and nature of the instruments, including significant terms and conditions that may affect the amount, timing and certainty of future cash flows.

66(3) Where any amount is transferred to or from the fair value reserve during the financial year, there must be stated in tabular form–

(a) the amount of the reserve as at the date of the beginning of the financial year and as at the balance sheet date respectively,

(b) the amount transferred to or from the reserve during the year, and

(c) the source and application respectively of the amounts so transferred.

History – Para. 66 substituted by SI 2015/980, reg. 33(3), with effect in relation to–
(a) financial years beginning on or after 1 January 2016, and
(b) a financial year of a company beginning on or after 1 January 2015, but before 1 January 2016, if the directors of the company so decide.

Former para. 66 read as follows:

"66(1) This paragraph applies where financial instruments have been valued in accordance with paragraph 44 or 46.

66(2) There must be stated–

    (a) the significant assumptions underlying the valuation models and techniques used where the fair value of the instruments has been determined in accordance with paragraph 45(4),

    (b) for each category of financial instrument, the fair value of the instruments in that category and the changes in value–

        (i) included in the profit and loss account, or

        (ii) credited to or (as the case may be) debited from the fair value reserve, in respect of those instruments, and

    (c) for each class of derivatives, the extent and nature of the instruments, including significant terms and conditions that may affect the amount, timing and certainty of future cash flows.

66(3) Where any amount is transferred to or from the fair value reserve during the financial year, there must be stated in tabular form–

    (a) the amount of the reserve as at the date of the beginning of the financial year and as at the balance sheet date respectively,

    (b) the amount transferred to or from the reserve during that year, and

    (c) the source and application respectively of the amounts so transferred."

67 Where the company has derivatives that it has not included at fair value, there must be stated for each class of such derivatives–

    (a) the fair value of the derivatives in that class, if such a value can be determined in accordance with paragraph 45, and

    (b) the extent and nature of the derivatives.

68(1) This paragraph applies if–

    (a) the company has financial fixed assets that could be included at fair value by virtue of paragraph 44,

    (b) the amount at which those items are included under any item in the company's accounts is in excess of their fair value, and

    (c) the company has not made provision for diminution in value of those assets in accordance with paragraph 25(1) in Part 2 of this Schedule.

68(2) There must be stated–

    (a) the amount at which either the individual assets or appropriate groupings of those individual assets are included in the company's accounts,

    (b) the fair value of those assets or groupings, and

    (c) the reasons for not making a provision for diminution in value of those assets, including the nature of the evidence that provides the basis for the belief that the amount at which they are stated in the accounts will be recovered.

Information where investment property and living animals and plants included at fair value

69(1) This paragraph applies where the amounts to be included in a company's accounts in respect of investment property or living animals and plants have been determined in accordance with paragraph 47.

69(2) The balance sheet items affected and the basis of valuation adopted in determining the amounts of the assets in question in the case of each such item must be disclosed in a note to the accounts.

69(3) In the case of investment property, for each balance sheet item affected there must be shown, either separately in the balance sheet or in a note to the accounts–

(a)   the comparable amounts determined according to the historical cost accounting rules, or

(b)   the differences between those amounts and the corresponding amounts actually shown in the balance sheet in respect of that item.

69(4)   In sub-paragraph (3), references in relation to any item to the comparable amounts determined in accordance with that sub-paragraph are to–

(a)   the aggregate amount which would be required to be shown in respect of that item if the amounts to be included in respect of all the assets covered by that item were determined according to the historical cost accounting rules, and

(b)   the aggregate amount of the cumulative provisions for depreciation or diminution in value which would be permitted or required in determining those amounts according to those rules.

Reserves and provisions

70(1)   This paragraph applies where any amount is transferred–

(a)   to or from any reserves, or

(b)   to any provision for liabilities, or

(c)   from any provision for liabilities otherwise than for the purpose for which the provision was established,

and the reserves or provisions are or would but for paragraph 5(1) in Part 1 of this Schedule be shown as separate items in the company's balance sheet.

70(2)   The following information must be given in respect of the aggregate of reserves or provisions included in the same item in tabular form–

(a)   the amount of the reserves or provisions as at the date of the beginning of the financial year and as at the balance sheet date respectively,

(b)   any amounts transferred to or from the reserves or provisions during that year, and

(c)   the source and application respectively of any amounts so transferred.

70(3)   Particulars must be given of each provision included in liabilities item 6.(c) (other provisions) in the company's balance sheet in any case where the amount of that provision is material.

History – In para. 70(2), the words 'in tabular form' inserted by SI 2015/980, reg. 33(4), with effect in relation to–
(a)   financial years beginning on or after 1 January 2016, and
(b)   a financial year of a company beginning on or after 1 January 2015, but before 1 January 2016, if the directors of the company so decide.

Provision for taxation

71   The amount of any provision for deferred taxation must be stated separately from the amount of any provision for other taxation.

Maturity analysis

72(1)   A company must disclose separately for each of assets items 3.(b) and 4 and liabilities items 1.(b), 2.(b) and 3.(b) the aggregate amount of the loans and advances and liabilities included in those items broken down into the following categories–

(a)   those repayable in not more than three months,

(b)   those repayable in more than three months but not more than one year,

(c)   those repayable in more than one year but not more than five years,

(d)   those repayable in more than five years,

from the balance sheet date.

72(2)   A company must also disclose the aggregate amounts of all loans and advances falling within assets item 4 (loans and advances to customers) which are–

    (a)   repayable on demand, or

    (b)   are for an indeterminate period, being repayable upon short notice.

72(3)   For the purposes of sub-paragraph (1), where a loan or advance or liability is repayable by instalments, each such instalment is to be treated as a separate loan or advance or liability.

Debt and other fixed-income securities

73   A company must disclose the amount of debt and fixed-income securities included in assets item 5 (debt securities [and other fixed-income securities]) and the amount of such securities included in liabilities item 3.(a) (bonds and medium term notes) that (in each case) will become due within one year of the balance sheet date.

Subordinated liabilities

74(1)   The following information must be disclosed in relation to any borrowing included in liabilities item 7 (subordinated liabilities) that exceeds 10% of the total for that item–

    (a)   its amount,

    (b)   the currency in which it is denominated,

    (c)   the rate of interest and the maturity date (or the fact that it is perpetual),

    (d)   the circumstances in which early repayment may be demanded,

    (e)   the terms of the subordination, and

    (f)   the existence of any provisions whereby it may be converted into capital or some other form of liability and the terms of any such provisions.

74(2)   The general terms of any other borrowings included in liabilities item 7 must also be stated.

Fixed cumulative dividends

75   If any fixed cumulative dividends on the company's shares are in arrear, there must be stated–

    (a)   the amount of the arrears, and

    (b)   the period for which the dividends or, if there is more than one class, each class of them are in arrear.

Details of assets charged

76(1)   There must be disclosed, in relation to each liabilities and memorandum item of the balance sheet format–

    (a)   the aggregate amount of any assets of the company which have been charged to secure any liability or potential liability included under that item,

    (b)   the aggregate amount of the liabilities or potential liabilities so secured, and

    (c)   an indication of the nature of the security given.

76(2)   Particulars must also be given of any other charge on the assets of the company to secure the liabilities of any other person, including, where practicable, the amount secured.

Guarantees and other financial commitments

77(1) Particulars and the total amount of any financial commitments, guarantees and contingencies that are not included in the balance sheet must be disclosed.

77(2) An indication of the nature and form of any valuable security given by the company in respect of commitments, guarantees and contingencies within sub-paragraph (1) must be given.

77(3) The total amount of any commitments within sub-paragraph (1) concerning pensions must be separately disclosed.

77(4) Particulars must be given of pension commitments which are included in the balance sheet.

77(5) Where any commitment within sub-paragraph (3) or (4) relates wholly or partly to pensions payable to past directors of the company separate particulars must be given of that commitment.

77(6) The total amount of any commitments, guarantees and contingencies within sub-paragraph (1) which are undertaken on behalf of or for the benefit of–

(a) any parent undertaking or fellow subsidiary undertaking of the company,

(b) any subsidiary undertaking of the company, or

(c) any undertaking in which the company has a participating interest

must be separately stated and those within each of paragraphs (a), (b) and (c) must also be stated separately from those within any other of those paragraphs.

77(7) There must be disclosed the nature and amount of any contingent liabilities and commitments included in Memorandum items 1 and 2 which are material in relation to the company's activities

History – Para. 77 substituted by SI 2015/980, reg. 33(5), with effect in relation to–
- (a) financial years beginning on or after 1 January 2016, and
- (b) a financial year of a company beginning on or after 1 January 2015, but before 1 January 2016, if the directors of the company so decide.

Former para. 77 read as follows:

"77(1) There must be stated, where practicable, the aggregate amount or estimated amount of contracts for capital expenditure, so far as not provided for.

77(2) Particulars must be given of–
- (a) any pension commitments included under any provision shown in the company's balance sheet, and
- (b) any such commitments for which no provision has been made, and where any such commitment relates wholly or partly to pensions payable to past directors of the company separate particulars must be given of that commitment so far as it relates to such pensions.

77(3) Particulars must also be given of any other financial commitments, including any contingent liabilities, that–
- (a) have not been provided for,
- (b) have not been included in the memorandum items in the balance sheet format, and
- (c) are relevant to assessing the company's state of affairs.

77(4) Commitments within any of the preceding sub-paragraphs undertaken on behalf of or for the benefit of–
- (a) any parent company or fellow subsidiary undertaking of the company, or
- (b) any subsidiary undertaking of the company, must be stated separately from the other commitments within that sub-paragraph (and commitments within paragraph(a) must be stated separately from those within paragraph (b)).

77(5) There must be disclosed the nature and amount of any contingent liabilities and commitments included in Memorandum items 1 and 2 which are material in relation to the company's activities."

Memorandum items: Group undertakings

78(1) With respect to contingent liabilities required to be included under Memorandum item 1 in the balance sheet format, there must be stated in a note to the accounts the amount of such contingent liabilities incurred on behalf of or for the benefit of–

(a) any parent undertaking or fellow subsidiary undertaking, or

(b) any subsidiary undertaking,

of the company; in addition the amount incurred in respect of the undertakings referred to in paragraph (a) must be stated separately from the amount incurred in respect in respect of the undertakings referred to in paragraph (b).

78(2) With respect to commitments required to be included under Memorandum item 2 in the balance sheet format, there must be stated in a note to the accounts the amount of such commitments undertaken on behalf of or for the benefit of–

(a) any parent undertaking or fellow subsidiary undertaking, or

(b) any subsidiary undertaking,

of the company; in addition the amount incurred in respect of the undertakings referred to in paragraph (a) must be stated separately from the amount incurred in respect of the undertakings referred to in paragraph (b).

Transferable securities

79(1) There must be disclosed for each of assets items 5 to 8 in the balance sheet format the amount of transferable securities included under those items that are listed and the amount of those that are unlisted.

79(2) In the case of each amount shown in respect of listed securities under sub-paragraph (1), there must also be disclosed the aggregate market value of those securities, if different from the amount shown.

79(3) There must also be disclosed for each of assets items 5 and 6 the amount of transferable securities included under those items that are held as financial fixed assets and the amount of those that are not so held, together with the criterion used by the directors to distinguish those held as financial fixed assets.

Leasing transactions

80 The aggregate amount of all property (other than land) leased by the company to other persons must be disclosed, broken down so as to show the aggregate amount included in each relevant balance sheet item.

Assets and liabilities denominated in a currency other than sterling (or the currency in which the accounts are drawn up)

81(1) The aggregate amount, in sterling (or the currency in which the accounts are drawn up), of all assets denominated in a currency other than sterling (or the currency used) together with the aggregate amount, in sterling (or the currency used), of all liabilities so denominated, is to be disclosed.

81(2) For the purposes of this paragraph an appropriate rate of exchange prevailing at the balance sheet date must be used to determine the amounts concerned.

Sundry assets and liabilities

82 Where any amount shown under either of the following items is material, particulars must be given of each type of asset or liability included in that item, including an explanation of the nature of the asset or liability and the amount included with respect to assets or liabilities of that type–

(a)   assets item 13 (other assets),

(b)   liabilities item 4 (other liabilities).

Unmatured forward transactions

83(1)   The following must be disclosed with respect to unmatured forward transactions outstanding at the balance sheet date–

(a)   the categories of such transactions, by reference to an appropriate system of classification,

(b)   whether, in the case of each such category, they have been made, to any material extent, for the purpose of hedging the effects of fluctuations in interest rates, exchange rates and market prices or whether they have been made, to any material extent, for dealing purposes.

83(2)   Transactions falling within sub-paragraph (1) must include all those in relation to which income or expenditure is to be included in–

(a)   format 1, item 6 or format 2, items B4 or A3 (dealing [profits][losses]),

(b)   format 1, items 1 or 2, or format 2, items B1 or A1, by virtue of notes (1)(b) and (2)(b) to the profit and loss account formats (forward contracts, spread over the actual duration of the contract and similar in nature to interest).

Miscellaneous matters

84(1)   Particulars must be given of any case where the cost of any asset is for the first time determined under paragraph 37 in Part 2 of this Schedule.

84(2)   Where any outstanding loans made under the authority of section 682(2)(b), (c) or (d) of the 2006 Act (various cases of financial assistance by a company for purchase of its own shares) are included under any item shown in the company's balance sheet, the aggregate amount of those loans must be disclosed for each item in question.

INFORMATION SUPPLEMENTING THE PROFIT AND LOSS ACCOUNT

85   Paragraphs 86 to 91 require information which either supplements the information given with respect to any particular items shown in the profit and loss account or otherwise provides particulars of income or expenditure of the company or of circumstances affecting the items shown in the profit and loss account (see regulation 5(2) for exemption for companies falling within section 408 of the 2006 Act (individual profit and loss account where group accounts prepared)).

Particulars of tax

86(1)   Particulars must be given of any special circumstances which affect liability in respect of taxation of profits, income or capital gains for the financial year or liability in respect of taxation of profits, income or capital gains for succeeding financial years.

86(2)   The following amounts must be stated–

(a)   the amount of the charge for United Kingdom corporation tax,

(b)   if that amount would have been greater but for relief from double taxation, the amount which it would have been but for such relief,

(c)   the amount of the charge for United Kingdom income tax, and

(d)   the amount of the charge for taxation imposed outside the United Kingdom of profits, income and (so far as charged to revenue) capital gains.

These amounts must be stated separately in respect of each of the amounts which is shown under the following items in the profit and loss account, that is to say format 1 item 16, format 2 item A10 (tax on [profit][loss] on ordinary activities) and format 1 item 21, format 2 item A13 (tax on extraordinary [profit][loss]).

Particulars of income

87(1) A company must disclose, with respect to income included in the following items in the profit and loss account formats, the amount of that income attributable to each of the geographical markets in which the company has operated during the financial year–

(a) format 1 item 1, format 2 item B1 (interest receivable),

(b) format 1 item 3, format 2 item B2 (dividend income),

(c) format 1 item 4, format 2 item B3 (fees and commissions receivable),

(d) format 1 item 6, format 2 item B4 (dealing profits), and

(e) format 1 item 7, format 2 item B7 (other operating income).

87(2) In analysing for the purposes of this paragraph the source of any income, the directors must have regard to the manner in which the company's activities are organised.

87(3) For the purposes of this paragraph, markets which do not differ substantially from each other shall be treated as one market.

87(4) Where in the opinion of the directors the disclosure of any information required by this paragraph would be seriously prejudicial to the interests of the company, that information need not be disclosed, but the fact that any such information has not been disclosed must be stated.

Management and agency services

88 A company providing any management and agency services to customers must disclose that fact, if the scale of such services provided is material in the context of its business as a whole.

Subordinated liabilities

89 Any amounts charged to the profit and loss account representing charges incurred during the year with respect to subordinated liabilities must be disclosed.

Sundry income and charges

90 Where any amount to be included in any of the following items is material, particulars must be given of each individual component of the figure, including an explanation of their nature and amount–

(a) in format 1–

(i) items 7 and 10 (other operating income and charges),
(ii) items 18 and 19 (extraordinary income and charges);

(b) in format 2–

(i) items A6 and B7 (other operating charges and income),
(ii) items A12 and B10 (extraordinary charges and income).

Miscellaneous matters

91(1) Where any amount relating to any preceding financial year is included in any item in the profit and loss account, the effect must be stated.

91(2)   The amount, nature and effect of any individual items of income or expenditure which are of exceptional size or incidence must be stated.

History – Para. 91(2) substituted by SI 2015/980, reg. 33(6), with effect in relation to–
  (a)   financial years beginning on or after 1 January 2016, and
  (b)   a financial year of a company beginning on or after 1 January 2015, but before 1 January 2016, if the directors of the company so decide.

Former para. 91(2) read as follows:
"**91(2)**   The effect must be stated of any transactions that are exceptional by virtue of size or incidence though they fall within the ordinary activities of the company."

Related party transactions

92(1)   Particulars may be given of transactions which the company has entered into with related parties, and must be given if such transactions are material and have not been concluded under normal market conditions.

92(2)   The particulars of transactions required to be disclosed by sub-paragraph (1) must include–

  (a)   the amount of such transactions,

  (b)   the nature of the related party relationship, and

  (c)   other information about the transactions necessary for an understanding of the financial position of the company.

92(3)   Information about individual transactions may be aggregated according to their nature, except where separate information is necessary for an understanding of the effects of related party transactions on the financial position of the company.

92(4)   Particulars need not be given of transactions entered into between two or more members of a group, provided that any subsidiary undertaking which is a party to the transaction is whollyowned by such a member.

92(5)   In this paragraph, **'related party'** has the same meaning as in international accounting standards.

Post balance sheet events

92A   The nature and financial effect of material events arising after the balance sheet date which are not reflected in the profit and loss account of balance sheet must be stated.

History – Para. 92A and the heading preceding it inserted by SI 2015/980, reg. 33(7), with effect in relation to–
  (a)   financial years beginning on or after 1 January 2016, and
  (b)   a financial year of a company beginning on or after 1 January 2015, but before 1 January 2016, if the directors of the company so decide.

Appropriations

92B   Particulars must be given of the proposed appropriation of profit or treatment of loss or, where applicable, particulars of the actual appropriation of the profits or treatment of the losses.

History – Para. 92B and the heading preceding it inserted by SI 2015/980, reg. 33(7), with effect in relation to–
  (a)   financial years beginning on or after 1 January 2016, and
  (b)   a financial year of a company beginning on or after 1 January 2015, but before 1 January 2016, if the directors of the company so decide.

PART 4 – INTERPRETATION OF THIS SCHEDULE
DEFINITIONS FOR THIS SCHEDULE

93   The following definitions apply for the purposes of this Schedule.

FINANCIAL FIXED ASSETS

94 **'Financial fixed assets'** means loans and advances and securities held as fixed assets; participating interests and shareholdings in group undertakings are to be regarded as financial fixed assets.

FINANCIAL INSTRUMENTS

95 For the purposes of this Schedule, references to 'derivatives' include commodity-based contracts that give either contracting party the right to settle in cash or in some other financial instrument, except when such contracts–

(a) were entered into for the purpose of, and continue to meet, the company's expected purchase, sale or usage requirements,

(b) were designated for such purpose at their inception, and

(c) are expected to be settled by delivery of the commodity.

96(1) The expressions listed in sub-paragraph (2) have the same meaning in paragraphs 44 to 49, 66 to 68 and 95 of this Schedule as they have in Council Directives 2013/34/EU on the annual financial statements etc of certain types of undertaking and 86/635/EEC on the annual accounts and consolidated accounts of banks and other financial institutions.

96(2) Those expressions are 'available for sale financial asset', 'business combination', 'commodity-based contracts', 'derivative', 'equity instrument', 'exchange difference', 'fair value hedge accounting system', 'financial fixed asset', 'financial instrument', 'foreign entity', 'hedge accounting', 'hedge accounting system', 'hedged items', 'hedging instrument', 'held for trading purposes', 'held to maturity', 'monetary item', 'receivables', 'reliable market' and 'trading portfolio'.

History – In para. 96(1), the words '2013/34/EU on the annual financial statements etc of certain types of undertaking' substituted for the words '78/660/EEC on the annual accounts of certain types of companies' by SI 2015/980, reg. 33(8), with effect in relation to–
(a) financial years beginning on or after 1 January 2016, and
(b) a financial year of a company beginning on or after 1 January 2015, but before 1 January 2016, if the directors of the company so decide.

REPAYABLE ON DEMAND

97 **'Repayable on demand'**, in connection with deposits, loans or advances, means that they can at any time be withdrawn or demanded without notice or that a maturity or period of notice of not more than 24 hours or one working day has been agreed for them.

SALE AND REPURCHASE TRANSACTION

98(1) **'Sale and repurchase transaction'** means a transaction which involves the transfer by a credit institution or customer ('the transferor') to another credit institution or customer ('the transferee') of assets subject to an agreement that the same assets, or (in the case of fungible assets) equivalent assets, will subsequently be transferred back to the transferor at a specified price on a date specified or to be specified by the transferor.

98(2) The following are not to be regarded as sale and repurchase transactions for the purposes of sub-paragraph (1)–

(a) forward exchange transactions,

(b) options,

(c) transactions involving the issue of debt securities with a commitment to repurchase all or part of the issue before maturity, or

(d) any similar transactions.

SALE AND OPTION TO RESELL TRANSACTION

99 'Sale and option to resell transaction' means a transaction which involves the transfer by a credit institution or customer ('the transferor') to another credit institution or customer ('the transferee') of assets subject to an agreement that the transferee is entitled to require the subsequent transfer of the same assets, or (in the case of fungible assets) equivalent assets, back to the transferor at the purchase price or another price agreed in advance on a date specified or to be specified.

SCHEDULE 3 – INSURANCE COMPANIES: COMPANIES ACT INDIVIDUAL ACCOUNTS

Regulation 6(1)

Part 1 – General rules and formats

SECTION A – GENERAL RULES

1(1)   Subject to the following provisions of this Schedule–

(a)   every balance sheet of a company must show the items listed in the balance sheet format in Section B of this Part, and

(b)   every profit and loss account must show the items listed in the profit and loss account format in Section B.

1(2)   References in this Schedule to the items listed in any of the formats in Section B are to those items read together with any of the notes following the formats which apply to those items.

1(3)   The items must be shown in the order and under the headings and sub-headings given in the particular format, but–

(a)   the notes to the formats may permit alternative positions for any particular items, and

(b)   the heading or sub-heading for any item does not have to be distinguished by any letter or number assigned to that item in the format used.

2(1)   Any item required to be shown in a company's balance sheet or profit and loss account may be shown in greater detail than required by the particular format.

2(2)   The balance sheet or profit and loss account may include an item representing or covering the amount of any asset or liability, income or expenditure not specifically covered by any of the items listed in the formats set out in Section B, save that none of the following may be treated as assets in any balance sheet–

(a)   preliminary expenses,

(b)   expenses of, and commission on, any issue of shares or debentures, and

(c)   costs of research.

3(1)   The directors may combine items to which Arabic numbers are given in the balance sheet format set out in Section B (except for items concerning technical provisions and the reinsurers' share of technical provisions), and items to which lower case letters in parentheses are given in the profit and loss account format so set out (except for items within items I.1 and 4 and II.1, 5 and 6) if–

(a)   their individual amounts are not material for the purpose of giving a true and fair view, or

(b)   the combination facilitates the assessment of the state of affairs or profit or loss of the company for the financial year in question.

3(2)   Where sub-paragraph (1)(b) applies–

(a)   the individual amounts of any items which have been combined must be disclosed in a note to the accounts, and

(b)   any notes required by this Schedule to the items so combined must, notwithstanding the combination, be given.

4(1)   Subject to sub-paragraph (2), the directors must not include a heading or sub-heading corresponding to an item in the balance sheet or profit and loss account format used if there is no amount to be shown for that item for the financial year to which the balance sheet or profit and loss account relates.

4(2)   Where an amount can be shown for the item in question for the immediately preceding financial year that amount must be shown under the heading or sub-heading required by the format for that item.

5(1)   For every item shown in the balance sheet or profit and loss account the corresponding amount for the immediately preceding financial year must also be shown.

5(2)   Where that corresponding amount is not comparable with the amount to be shown for the item in question in respect of the financial year to which the balance sheet or profit and loss account relates, the former amount may be adjusted, and particulars of the non-comparability and of any adjustment must be disclosed in a note to the accounts.

6   Subject to the provisions of this Schedule, amounts in respect of items representing assets or income may not be set off against amounts in respect of items representing liabilities or expenditure (as the case may be), or vice versa.

7(1)   The provisions of this Schedule which relate to long-term business apply, with necessary modifications, to business which consists of effecting or carrying out relevant contracts of general insurance which–

(a)   is transacted exclusively or principally according to the technical principles of long-term business, and

(b)   is a significant amount of the business of the company.

7(2)   For the purposes of paragraph (1), a contract of general insurance is a relevant contract if the risk insured against relates to–

(a)   accident, or

(b)   sickness.

7(3)   Sub-paragraph (2) must be read with–

(a)   section 22 of the Financial Services and Markets Act 2000,

(b)   the Financial Services and Markets Act 2000 (Regulated Activities) Order 2001, and

(c)   Schedule 2 to that Act.

8   The company's directors must, in determining how amounts are presented within items in the profit and loss account and balance sheet, have regard to the substance of the reported transaction or arrangement, in accordance with generally accepted accounting principles or practice.

8A   Where an asset or liability relates to more than one item in the balance sheet, the relationship of such asset or liability to the relevant items must be disclosed either under those items or in the notes to the accounts.

History – Para. 8A inserted by SI 2015/980, reg. 34(2), with effect in relation to–

   (a) financial years beginning on or after 1 January 2016, and

   (b) a financial year of a company beginning on or after 1 January 2015, but before 1 January 2016, if the directors of the company so decide.

SECTION B – THE REQUIRED FORMATS

Preliminary

9(1)   Where in respect of any item to which an Arabic number is assigned in the balance sheet or profit and loss account format, the gross amount and reinsurance amount or reinsurers' share are required to be shown, a sub-total of those amounts must also be given.

9(2)   Where in respect of any item to which an Arabic number is assigned in the profit and loss account format, separate items are required to be shown, then a separate sub-total of those items must also be given in addition to any sub-total required by sub-paragraph (1).

10(1)   In the profit and loss account format set out below–

   (a) the heading 'Technical account – General business' is for business which consists of effecting or carrying out contracts of general business; and

   (b) the heading 'Technical account – Long-term business' is for business which consists of effecting or carrying out contracts of long-term insurance.

10(2)   In sub-paragraph (1), references to–

   (a) contracts of general or long-term insurance, and

   (b) the effecting or carrying out of such contracts,

must be read with section 22 of the Financial Services and Markets Act 2000, the Financial Services and Markets Act 2000 (Regulated Activities) Order 2001, and Schedule 2 to that Act.

Balance sheet format

ASSETS

A. Called up share capital not paid [1]

B. Intangible assets

   1. Development costs

   2. Concessions, patents, licences, trade marks and similar rights and assets [2]

   3. Goodwill [3]

   4. Payments on account

C. Investments

   I. Land and buildings [4]

   II. Investments in group undertakings and participating interests

      1. Shares in group undertakings

      2. Debt securities issued by, and loans to, group undertakings

      3. Participating interests

      4. Debt securities issued by, and loans to, undertakings in which the company has a participating interest

   III. Other financial investments

      1. Shares and other variable-yield securities and units in unit trusts

      2. Debt securities and other fixed-income securities [5]

      3. Participation in investment pools [6]

      4. Loans secured by mortgages [7]

      5. Other loans [7]

6. Deposits with credit institutions [8]

7. Other [9]

IV. Deposits with ceding undertakings [10]

D. Assets held to cover linked liabilities [11]

Da. Reinsurers' share of technical provisions [12]

1. Provision for unearned premiums

2. Long-term business provision

3. Claims outstanding

4. Provisions for bonuses and rebates

5. Other technical provisions

6. Technical provisions for unit-linked liabilities

E. Debtors [13]

I. Debtors arising out of direct insurance operations

1. Policyholders

2. Intermediaries

II. Debtors arising out of reinsurance operations

III. Other debtors

IV. Called up share capital not paid [1]

F. Other assets

I. Tangible assets

1. Plant and machinery

2. Fixtures, fittings, tools and equipment

3. Payments on account (other than deposits paid on land and buildings) and assets (other than buildings) in course of construction

II. Stocks

1. Raw materials and consumables

2. Work in progress

3. Finished goods and goods for resale

4. Payments on account

III. Cash at bank and in hand

IV. Own shares [14]

V. Other [15]

G. Prepayments and accrued income

I. Accrued interest and rent [16]

II. Deferred acquisition costs [17]

III. Other prepayments and accrued income

LIABILITIES

A. Capital and reserves

I. Called up share capital or equivalent funds

II. Share premium account

III. Revaluation reserve

IV. Reserves

1. Capital redemption reserve

2. Reserve for own shares

3. Reserves provided for by the articles of association

      4. Other reserves

   V. Profit and loss account

B. Subordinated liabilities [18]

Ba. Fund for future appropriations [19]

C. Technical provisions

   1. Provision for unearned premiums [20]

      (a) gross amount

      (b) reinsurance amount [12]

   2. Long-term business provision [20] [21] [26]

      (a) gross amount

      (b) reinsurance amount [12]

   3. Claims outstanding [22]

      (a) gross amount

      (b) reinsurance amount [12]

   4. Provision for bonuses and rebates [23]

      (a) gross amount

      (b) reinsurance amount [12]

   5. Equalisation provision [24]

   6. Other technical provisions [25]

      (a) gross amount

      (b) reinsurance amount [12]

D. Technical provisions for linked liabilities [26]

   (a) gross amount

   (b) reinsurance amount [12]

E. Provisions for other risks

   1. Provisions for pensions and similar obligations

   2. Provisions for taxation

   3. Other provisions

F. Deposits received from reinsurers [27]

G. Creditors [28]

   I. Creditors arising out of direct insurance operations

   II. Creditors arising out of reinsurance operations

   III. Debenture loans [29]

   IV. Amounts owed to credit institutions

   V. Other creditors including taxation and social security

H. Accruals and deferred income

Notes on the balance sheet format

[1] *Called up share capital not paid*

(Assets items A and E.IV.)

This item may be shown in either of the positions given in the format.

[2] *Concessions, patents, licences, trade marks and similar rights and assets*

(Assets item B.2.)

Amounts in respect of assets are only to be included in a company's balance sheet under this item if either–

(a) the assets were acquired for valuable consideration and are not required to be shown under goodwill, or

(b) the assets in question were created by the company itself.

(3) *Goodwill*

(Assets item B.3.)

Amounts representing goodwill are only to be included to the extent that the goodwill was acquired for valuable consideration.

(4) *Land and buildings*

(Assets item C.I.)

The amount of any land and buildings occupied by the company for its own activities must be shown separately in the notes to the accounts.

(5) *Debt securities and other fixed-income securities*

(Assets item C.III.2.)

This item is to comprise transferable debt securities and any other transferable fixed-income securities issued by credit institutions, other undertakings or public bodies, in so far as they are not covered by assets item C.II.2 or C.II.4.

Securities bearing interest rates that vary in accordance with specific factors, for example the interest rate on the inter-bank market or on the Euromarket, are also to be regarded as debt securities and other fixed-income securities and so be included under this item.

(6) *Participation in investment pools*

(Assets item C.III.3.)

This item is to comprise shares held by the company in joint investments constituted by several undertakings or pension funds, the management of which has been entrusted to one of those undertakings or to one of those pension funds.

(7) *Loans secured by mortgages and other loans*

(Assets items C.III.4 and C.III.5.)

Loans to policyholders for which the policy is the main security are to be included under 'Other loans' and their amount must be disclosed in the notes to the accounts. Loans secured by mortgage are to be shown as such even where they are also secured by insurance policies. Where the amount of 'Other loans' not secured by policies is material, an appropriate breakdown must be given in the notes to the accounts.

(8) *Deposits with credit institutions*

(Assets item C.III.6.)

This item is to comprise sums the withdrawal of which is subject to a time restriction. Sums deposited with no such restriction must be shown under assets item F.III even if they bear interest.

(9) *Other*

(Assets item C.III.7.)

This item is to comprise those investments which are not covered by assets items C.III.1 to 6. Where the amount of such investments is significant, they must be disclosed in the notes to the accounts.

(10) *Deposits with ceding undertakings*

(Assets item C.IV.)

Where the company accepts reinsurance this item is to comprise amounts, owed by the ceding undertakings and corresponding to guarantees, which are deposited with those ceding undertakings or with third parties or which are retained by those undertakings.

These amounts may not be combined with other amounts owed by the ceding insurer to the reinsurer or set off against amounts owed by the reinsurer to the ceding insurer.

Securities deposited with ceding undertakings or third parties which remain the property of the company must be entered in the company's accounts as an investment, under the appropriate item.

(11) *Assets held to cover linked liabilities*

(Assets item D.)

In respect of long-term business, this item is to comprise investments made pursuant to long-term policies under which the benefits payable to the policyholder are wholly or partly to be determined by reference to the value of, or the income from, property of any description (whether or not specified in the contract) or by reference to fluctuations in, or in an index of, the value of property of any description (whether or not so specified).

This item is also to comprise investments which are held on behalf of the members of a tontine and are intended for distribution among them.

(12) *Reinsurance amounts*

(Assets item Da: liabilities items C.1.(b), 2.(b), 3.(b), 4.(b) and 6.(b) and D.(b).)

The reinsurance amounts may be shown either under assets item Da or under liabilities items C.1.(b), 2.(b), 3.(b), 4.(b) and 6.(b) and D.(b).

The reinsurance amounts are to comprise the actual or estimated amounts which, under contractual reinsurance arrangements, are deducted from the gross amounts of technical provisions.

As regards the provision for unearned premiums, the reinsurance amounts must be calculated according to the methods referred to in paragraph 50 below or in accordance with the terms of the reinsurance policy.

(13) *Debtors*

(Assets item E.)

Amounts owed by group undertakings and undertakings in which the company has a participating interest must be shown separately as sub-items of assets items E.I, II and III.

(14) *Own shares*

(Assets item F.IV.)

The nominal value of the shares must be shown separately under this item.

(15) *Other*

(Assets item F.V.)

This item is to comprise those assets which are not covered by assets items F.I to IV. Where such assets are material they must be disclosed in the notes to the accounts.

(16) *Accrued interest and rent*

(Assets item G.I.)

This item is to comprise those items that represent interest and rent that have been earned up to the balance-sheet date but have not yet become receivable.

(17) *Deferred acquisition costs*

(Assets item G.II.)

This item is to comprise the costs of acquiring insurance policies which are incurred during a financial year but relate to a subsequent financial year ('deferred acquisition costs'), except in so far as–

(a) allowance has been made in the computation of the long-term business provision made under paragraph 52 below and shown under liabilities item C2 or D in the balance sheet, for–
  (i) the explicit recognition of such costs, or
  (ii) the implicit recognition of such costs by virtue of the anticipation of future income from which such costs may prudently be expected to be recovered, or

(b) allowance has been made for such costs in respect of general business policies by a deduction from the provision for unearned premiums made under paragraph 50 below and shown under liabilities item C.I in the balance sheet.

Deferred acquisition costs arising in general business must be distinguished from those arising in long-term business.

In the case of general business, the amount of any deferred acquisition costs must be established on a basis compatible with that used for unearned premiums.

There must be disclosed in the notes to the accounts–

(c) how the deferral of acquisition costs has been treated (unless otherwise expressly stated in the accounts), and

(d) where such costs are included as a deduction from the provisions at liabilities item C.I, the amount of such deduction, or

(e) where the actuarial method used in the calculation of the provisions at liabilities item C.2 or D has made allowance for the explicit recognition of such costs, the amount of the costs so recognised.

(18) *Subordinated liabilities*

(Liabilities item B.)

This item is to comprise all liabilities in respect of which there is a contractual obligation that, in the event of winding up or of bankruptcy, they are to be repaid only after the claims of all other creditors have been met (whether or not they are represented by certificates).

(19) *Fund for future appropriations*

(Liabilities item Ba.)

This item is to comprise all funds the allocation of which either to policyholders or to shareholders has not been determined by the end of the financial year.

Transfers to and from this item must be shown in item II.12a in the profit and loss account.

(20) *Provision for unearned premiums*

(Liabilities item C.1.)

In the case of long-term business the provision for unearned premiums may be included in liabilities item C.2 rather than in this item.

The provision for unearned premiums is to comprise the amount representing that part of gross premiums written which is estimated to be earned in the following financial year or to subsequent financial years.

(21) *Long-term business provision*

(Liabilities item C.2.)

This item is to comprise the actuarially estimated value of the company's liabilities (excluding technical provisions included in liabilities item D), including bonuses already declared and after deducting the actuarial value of future premiums.

This item is also to comprise claims incurred but not reported, plus the estimated costs of settling such claims.

⁽²²⁾ *Claims outstanding*

(Liabilities item C.3.)

This item is to comprise the total estimated ultimate cost to the company of settling all claims arising from events which have occurred up to the end of the financial year (including, in the case of general business, claims incurred but not reported) less amounts already paid in respect of such claims.

⁽²³⁾ *Provision for bonuses and rebates*

(Liabilities item C.4.)

This item is to comprise amounts intended for policyholders or contract beneficiaries by way of bonuses and rebates as defined in Note *(5)* on the profit and loss account format to the extent that such amounts have not been credited to policyholders or contract beneficiaries or included in liabilities item Ba or in liabilities item C.2.

⁽²⁴⁾ *Equalisation provision*

(Liabilities item C.5.)

This item is to comprise the amount of any equalisation reserve maintained in respect of general business by the company, in accordance with the rules made by the Financial Conduct Authority or the Prudential Regulation Authority under Part 10 of the Financial Services and Markets Act 2000.

This item is also to comprise any amounts which, in accordance with Council Directive 87/343/EEC of 22nd June 1987, are required to be set aside by a company to equalise fluctuations in loss ratios in future years or to provide for special risks.

A company which otherwise constitutes reserves to equalise fluctuations in loss ratios in future years or to provide for special risks must disclose that fact in the notes to the accounts.

⁽²⁵⁾ *Other technical provisions*

(Liabilities item C.6.)

This item is to comprise, inter alia, the provision for unexpired risks as defined in paragraph 91 below. Where the amount of the provision for unexpired risks is significant, it must be disclosed separately either in the balance sheet or in the notes to the accounts.

⁽²⁶⁾ *Technical provisions for linked liabilities*

(Liabilities item D.)

This item is to comprise technical provisions constituted to cover liabilities relating to investment in the context of long-term policies under which the benefits payable to policyholders are wholly or partly to be determined by reference to the value of, or the income from, property of any description (whether or not specified in the contract) or by reference to fluctuations in, or in an index of, the value of property of any description (whether or not so specified).

Any additional technical provisions constituted to cover death risks, operating expenses or other risks (such as benefits payable at the maturity date or guaranteed surrender values) must be included under liabilities item C.2.

This item must also comprise technical provisions representing the obligations of a tontine's organiser in relation to its members.

⁽²⁷⁾ *Deposits received from reinsurers*

(Liabilities item F.)

Where the company cedes reinsurance, this item is to comprise amounts deposited by or withheld from other insurance undertakings under reinsurance contracts. These amounts may not be merged with other amounts owed to or by those other undertakings.

Where the company cedes reinsurance and has received as a deposit securities which have been transferred to its ownership, this item is to comprise the amount owed by the company by virtue of the deposit.

⁽²⁸⁾ *Creditors*

(Liabilities item G.)

Amounts owed to group undertakings and undertakings in which the company has a participating interest must be shown separately as sub-items.

⁽²⁹⁾ *Debenture loans*

(Liabilities item G.III.)

The amount of any convertible loans must be shown separately.

History – In note (24), 'made by the Financial Conduct Authority or the Prudential Regulation Authority' substituted for 'in section 1.4 of the Prudential Sourcebook for Insurers made by the Financial Services Authority' by SI 2013/472, Sch. 2, para. 135(a), with effect from 1 April 2013.

SPECIAL RULES FOR BALANCE SHEET FORMAT

Additional items

11(1) Every balance sheet of a company which carries on long-term business must show separately as an additional item the aggregate of any amounts included in liabilities item A (capital and reserves) which are required not to be treated as realised profits under section 843 of the 2006 Act.

11(2) A company which carries on long-term business must show separately, in the balance sheet or in the notes to the accounts, the total amount of assets representing the long-term fund valued in accordance with the provisions of this Schedule.

Managed funds

12(1) For the purposes of this paragraph 'managed funds' are funds of a group pension fund–

    (a)   the management of which constitutes long-term insurance business, and

    (b)   which the company administers in its own name but on behalf of others, and

    (c)   to which it has legal title.

12(2) The company must, in any case where assets and liabilities arising in respect of managed funds fall to be treated as assets and liabilities of the company, adopt the following accounting treatment: assets and liabilities representing managed funds are to be included in the company's balance sheet, with the notes to the accounts disclosing the total amount included with respect to such assets and liabilities in the balance sheet and showing the amount included under each relevant balance sheet item in respect of such assets or (as the case may be) liabilities.

Deferred acquisition costs

13 The costs of acquiring insurance policies which are incurred during a financial year but which relate to a subsequent financial year must be deferred in a manner specified in Note *(17)* on the balance sheet format.

Profit and loss account format

I. Technical account – General business

  1. Earned premiums, net of reinsurance

    (a) gross premiums written [1]

    (b) outward reinsurance premiums [2]

    (c) change in the gross provision for unearned premiums

    (d) change in the provision for unearned premiums, reinsurers' share

  2. Allocated investment return transferred from the non-technical account (item III.6) [10]

  2a. Investment income [8] [10]

    (a) income from participating interests, with a separate indication of that derived from group undertakings

    (b) income from other investments, with a separate indication of that derived from group undertakings (aa) income from land and buildings (bb) income from other investments

    (c) value re-adjustments on investments

    (d) gains on the realisation of investments

  3. Other technical income, net of reinsurance

  4. Claims incurred, net of reinsurance [4]

    (a) claims paid

     (aa) gross amount

     (bb) reinsurers' share

    (b) change in the provision for claims

     (aa) gross amount

     (bb) reinsurers' share

  5. Changes in other technical provisions, net of reinsurance, not shown under other headings

6. Bonuses and rebates, net of reinsurance [5]

7. Net operating expenses

    (a) acquisition costs [6]

    (b) change in deferred acquisition costs

    (c) administrative expenses [7]

    (d) reinsurance commissions and profit participation

8. Other technical charges, net of reinsurance

8a. Investment expenses and charges [8]

    (a) investment management expenses, including interest

    (b) value adjustments on investments

    (c) losses on the realisation of investments

9. Change in the equalisation provision

10. Sub-total (balance on the technical account for general business) (item III.1)

II. Technical account – Long-term business

1. Earned premiums, net of reinsurance

    (a) gross premiums written [1]

    (b) outward reinsurance premiums [2]

    (c) change in the provision for unearned premiums, net of reinsurance [3]

2. Investment income [8] [10]

    (a) income from participating interests, with a separate indication of that derived from group undertakings

    (b) income from other investments, with a separate indication of that derived from group undertakings (aa) income from land and buildings (bb) income from other investments

    (c) value re-adjustments on investments

    (d) gains on the realisation of investments

3. Unrealised gains on investments [9]

4. Other technical income, net of reinsurance

5. Claims incurred, net of reinsurance [4]

    (a) claims paid

      (aa) gross amount

      (bb) reinsurers' share

    (b) change in the provision for claims

      (aa) gross amount

      (bb) reinsurers' share

6. Change in other technical provisions, net of reinsurance, not shown under other headings

    (a) Long-term business provision, net of reinsurance [3]

      (aa) gross amount

      (bb) reinsurers' share

    (b) other technical provisions, net of reinsurance

7. Bonuses and rebates, net of reinsurance [5]

8. Net operating expenses

    (a) acquisition costs [6]

    (b) change in deferred acquisition costs

    (c) administrative expenses [7]

    (d) reinsurance commissions and profit participation

9. Investment expenses and charges [8]

    (a) investment management expenses, including interest

    (b) value adjustments on investments

    (c) losses on the realisation of investments

10. Unrealised losses on investments [9]

11. Other technical charges, net of reinsurance

11a. Tax attributable to the long-term business

12. Allocated investment return transferred to the non-technical account (item III.4)

12a. Transfers to or from the fund for future appropriations

13. Sub-total (balance on the technical account – long-term business) (item III.2)

III. Non-technical account

1. Balance on the general business technical account (item I.10)

2. Balance on the long-term business technical account (item II.13)

2a. Tax credit attributable to balance on the long-term business technical account

3. Investment income [8]

    (a) income from participating interests, with a separate indication of that derived from group undertakings

    (b) income from other investments, with a separate indication of that derived from group undertakings (aa) income from land and buildings (bb) income from other investments

    (c) value re-adjustments on investments

    (d) gains on the realisation of investments

3a. Unrealised gains on investments [9]

4. Allocated investment return transferred from the long-term business technical account (item II.12) [10]

5. Investment expenses and charges [8]

    (a) investment management expenses, including interest

    (b) value adjustments on investments

    (c) losses on the realisation of investments

5a. Unrealised losses on investments [9]

6. Allocated investment return transferred to the general business technical account (item I.2) [10]

7. Other income

8. Other charges, including value adjustments

8a. Profit or loss on ordinary activities before tax

9. Tax on profit or loss on ordinary activities

10. Profit or loss on ordinary activities after tax

11. Extraordinary income

12. Extraordinary charges

13. Extraordinary profit or loss

14. Tax on extraordinary profit or loss

15. Other taxes not shown under the preceding items

16. Profit or loss for the financial year

Notes on the profit and loss account format

[1] *Gross premiums written*

(General business technical account: item I.1.(a).

Long-term business technical account: item II.1.(a).)

This item is to comprise all amounts due during the financial year in respect of insurance contracts entered into regardless of the fact that such amounts may relate in whole or in part to a later financial year, and must include inter alia–

(i)   premiums yet to be determined, where the premium calculation can be done only at the end of the year;

(ii)   single premiums, including annuity premiums, and, in long-term business, single premiums resulting from bonus and rebate provisions in so far as they must be considered as premiums under the terms of the contract;

(iii) additional premiums in the case of half-yearly, quarterly or monthly payments and additional payments from policyholders for expenses borne by the company;

(iv) in the case of co-insurance, the company's portion of total premiums;

(v)   reinsurance premiums due from ceding and retroceding insurance undertakings, including portfolio entries, after deduction of cancellations and portfolio withdrawals credited to ceding and retroceding insurance undertakings.

The above amounts must not include the amounts of taxes or duties levied with premiums.

(2) *Outward reinsurance premiums*

(General business technical account: item I.1.(b).

Long-term business technical account: item II.1.(b).)

This item is to comprise all premiums paid or payable in respect of outward reinsurance contracts entered into by the company. Portfolio entries payable on the conclusion or amendment of outward reinsurance contracts must be added; portfolio withdrawals receivable must be deducted.

(3) *Change in the provision for unearned premiums, net of reinsurance*

(Long-term business technical account: items II.1.(c) and II.6.(a).)

In the case of long-term business, the change in unearned premiums may be included either in item II.1.(c) or in item II.6.(a) of the long-term business technical account.

(4) *Claims incurred, net of reinsurance*

(General business technical account: item I.4.

Long-term business technical account: item II.5.)

This item is to comprise all payments made in respect of the financial year with the addition of the provision for claims (but after deducting the provision for claims for the preceding financial year).

These amounts must include annuities, surrenders, entries and withdrawals of loss provisions to and from ceding insurance undertakings and reinsurers and external and internal claims management costs and charges for claims incurred but not reported such as are referred to in paragraphs 53(2) and 55 below.

Sums recoverable on the basis of subrogation and salvage (within the meaning of paragraph 53 below) must be deducted.

Where the difference between–

(a)   the loss provision made at the beginning of the year for outstanding claims incurred in previous years, and

(b)   the payments made during the year on account of claims incurred in previous years and the loss provision shown at the end of the year for such outstanding claims, is material, it must be shown in the notes to the accounts, broken down by category and amount.

(5) *Bonuses and rebates, net of reinsurance*

(General business technical account: item I.6.

Long-term business technical account: item II.7.)

Bonuses are to comprise all amounts chargeable for the financial year which are paid or payable to policyholders and other insured parties or provided for their benefit, including amounts used to increase technical provisions or applied to the reduction of future premiums, to the extent that such amounts represent an allocation of surplus or profit arising on business as a whole or a section of business, after deduction of amounts provided in previous years which are no longer required.

Rebates are to comprise such amounts to the extent that they represent a partial refund of premiums resulting from the experience of individual contracts.

Where material, the amount charged for bonuses and that charged for rebates must be disclosed separately in the notes to the accounts.

(6) *Acquisition costs*

(General business technical account: item I.7.(a).

Long-term business technical account: item II.8.(a).)

This item is to comprise the costs arising from the conclusion of insurance contracts. They must cover both direct costs, such as acquisition commissions or the cost of drawing up the insurance document or including the insurance contract in the portfolio, and indirect costs, such as advertising costs or the administrative expenses connected with the processing of proposals and the issuing of policies.

In the case of long-term business, policy renewal commissions must be included under item II.8.(c) in the long-term business technical account.

(7) *Administrative expenses*

(General business technical account: item I.7.(c).

Long-term business technical account: item II.8.(c).)

This item must include the costs arising from premium collection, portfolio administration, handling of bonuses and rebates, and inward and outward reinsurance. They must in particular include staff costs and depreciation provisions in respect of office furniture and equipment in so far as these need not be shown under acquisition costs, claims incurred or investment charges.

Item II.8.(c) must also include policy renewal commissions.

[8] *Investment income, expenses and charges*

(General business technical account: items I.2a and 8a.

Long-term business technical account: items II.2 and 9.

Non-technical account: items III.3 and 5.)

Investment income, expenses and charges must, to the extent that they arise in the long-term fund, be disclosed in the long-term business technical account. Other investment income, expenses and charges must either be disclosed in the non-technical account or attributed between the appropriate technical and non-technical accounts. Where the company makes such an attribution it must disclose the basis for it in the notes to the accounts.

[9] *Unrealised gains and losses on investments*

(Long-term business technical account: items II.3 and 10.

Non-technical account: items III.3a and 5a.)

In the case of investments attributed to the long-term fund, the difference between the valuation of the investments and their purchase price or, if they have previously been valued, their valuation as at the last balance sheet date, may be disclosed (in whole or in part) in item II.3 or II.10 (as the case may be) of the long-term business technical account, and in the case of investments shown as assets under assets item D (assets held to cover linked liabilities) must be so disclosed.

In the case of other investments, the difference between the valuation of the investments and their purchase price or, if they have previously been valued, their valuation as at the last balance sheet date, may be disclosed (in whole or in part) in item III.3a or III.5a (as the case may require) of the non-technical account.

[10] *Allocated investment return*

(General business technical account: item I.2.

Long-term business technical account: item II.2.

Non-technical account: items III.4 and 6.)

The allocated return may be transferred from one part of the profit and loss account to another.

Where part of the investment return is transferred to the general business technical account, the transfer from the non-technical account must be deducted from item III.6 and added to item I.2.

Where part of the investment return disclosed in the long-term business technical account is transferred to the non-technical account, the transfer to the non-technical account shall be deducted from item II.12 and added to item III.4.

The reasons for such transfers (which may consist of a reference to any relevant statutory requirement) and the bases on which they are made must be disclosed in the notes to the accounts.

Part 2 – Accounting principles and rules

SECTION A – ACCOUNTING PRINCIPLES

Preliminary

14   The amounts to be included in respect of all items shown in a company's accounts must be determined in accordance with the principles set out in this Section.

15   But if it appears to the company's directors that there are special reasons for departing from any of those principles in preparing the company's accounts in respect of any financial year they may do so, in which case particulars of the departure, the reasons for it and its effect must be given in a note to the accounts.

Accounting principles

16   The company is presumed to be carrying on business as a going concern.

17   Accounting policies and measurement bases must be applied consistently within the same accounts and from one financial year to the next.

History – In para. 17, the words 'and measurement bases' inserted by SI 2015/980, reg. 35(2)(a), with effect in relation to–
   (a)   financial years beginning on or after 1 January 2016, and
   (b)   a financial year of a company beginning on or after 1 January 2015, but before 1 January 2016, if the directors of the company so decide.

18   The amount of any item must be determined on a prudent basis, and in particular–

(a)   subject to note (9) on the profit and loss account format, only profits realised at the balance sheet date are to be included in the profit and loss account

(b)   all liabilities which have arisen in respect of the financial year to which the accounts relate or a previous financial year must be taken into account, including those which only become apparent between the balance sheet date and the date on which it is signed on behalf of the board of directors in accordance with section 414 of the 2006 Act (approval and signing of accounts) and

(c)   all provisions for diminution of value must be recognised, whether the result of the financial year is a profit or a loss.

History – Para. 18(c), (and the word 'and' preceding it) inserted; the word 'and' in para. (a) omitted by SI 2015/980, reg. 35(2)(b), with effect in relation to–
(a)   financial years beginning on or after 1 January 2016, and
(b)   a financial year of a company beginning on or after 1 January 2015, but before 1 January 2016, if the directors of the company so decide.

19   All income and charges relating to the financial year to which the accounts relate are to be taken into account, without regard to the date of receipt or payment.

20   In determining the aggregate amount of any item, the amount of each individual asset or liability that falls to be taken into account must be determined separately.

20A   The opening balance sheet for each financial year shall correspond to the closing balance sheet for the preceding financial year.

History – Para. 20A inserted by SI 2015/980, reg. 35(2)(c), with effect in relation to–
(a)   financial years beginning on or after 1 January 2016, and
(b)   a financial year of a company beginning on or after 1 January 2015, but before 1 January 2016, if the directors of the company so decide.

Valuation

21(1)   The amounts to be included in respect of assets of any description mentioned in paragraph 22 (valuation of assets: general) must be determined either–

(a)   in accordance with that paragraph and paragraph 24 (but subject to paragraphs 27 to 29), or

(b)   so far as applicable to an asset of that description, in accordance with Section C (valuation at fair value).

21(2)   The amounts to be included in respect of assets of any description mentioned in paragraph 24 (alternative valuation of fixed-income securities) may be determined–

(a)   in accordance with that paragraph (but subject to paragraphs 27 to 29), or

(b)   so far as applicable to an asset of that description, in accordance with Section C.

21(3)   The amounts to be included in respect of assets which–

(a)   are not assets of a description mentioned in paragraph 22 or 23, but

(b)   are assets of a description to which Section C is applicable, may be determined in accordance with that Section.

21(4)   Subject to sub-paragraphs (1) to (3), the amounts to be included in respect of all items shown in a company's accounts are determined in accordance with Section C.

SECTION B – CURRENT VALUE ACCOUNTING RULES

Valuation of assets: general

22(1) Subject to paragraph 24, investments falling to be included under assets item C (investments) must be included at their current value calculated in accordance with paragraphs 25 and 26.

22(2) Investments falling to be included under assets item D (assets held to cover linked liabilities) must be shown at their current value calculated in accordance with paragraphs 25 and 26.

23(1) Intangible assets other than goodwill may be shown at their current cost.

23(2) Assets falling to be included under assets items F.I (tangible assets) and F.IV (own shares) in the balance sheet format may be shown at their current value calculated in accordance with paragraphs 25 and 26 or at their current cost.

23(3) Assets falling to be included under assets item F.II (stocks) may be shown at current cost.

Alternative valuation of fixed-income securities

24(1) This paragraph applies to debt securities and other fixed-income securities shown as assets under assets items C.II (investments in group undertakings and participating interests) and C.III (other financial investments).

24(2) Securities to which this paragraph applies may either be valued in accordance with paragraph 22 or their amortised value may be shown in the balance sheet, in which case the provisions of this paragraph apply.

24(3) Subject to sub-paragraph (4), where the purchase price of securities to which this paragraph applies exceeds the amount repayable at maturity, the amount of the difference–

(a)   must be charged to the profit and loss account, and

(b)   must be shown separately in the balance sheet or in the notes to the accounts.

24(4) The amount of the difference referred to in sub-paragraph (3) may be written off in instalments so that it is completely written off when the securities are repaid, in which case there must be shown separately in the balance sheet or in the notes to the accounts the difference between the purchase price (less the aggregate amount written off) and the amount repayable at maturity.

24(5) Where the purchase price of securities to which this paragraph applies is less than the amount repayable at maturity, the amount of the difference must be released to income in instalments over the period remaining until repayment, in which case there must be shown separately in the balance sheet or in the notes to the accounts the difference between the purchase price (plus the aggregate amount released to income) and the amount repayable at maturity.

24(6) Both the purchase price and the current value of securities valued in accordance with this paragraph must be disclosed in the notes to the accounts.

24(7) Where securities to which this paragraph applies which are not valued in accordance with paragraph 22 are sold before maturity, and the proceeds are used to purchase other securities to which this paragraph applies, the difference between the proceeds of sale and their book value may be spread uniformly over the period remaining until the maturity of the original investment.

Meaning of 'current value'

25(1)   Subject to sub-paragraph (5), in the case of investments other than land and buildings, **'current value'** means market value determined in accordance with this paragraph.

25(2)   In the case of listed investments, **'market value'** means the value on the balance sheet date or, when the balance sheet date is not a stock exchange trading day, on the last stock exchange trading day before that date.

25(3)   Where a market exists for unlisted investments, **'market value'** means the average price at which such investments were traded on the balance sheet date or, when the balance sheet date is not a trading day, on the last trading day before that date.

25(4)   Where, on the date on which the accounts are drawn up, listed or unlisted investments have been sold or are to be sold within the short term, the market value must be reduced by the actual or estimated realisation costs.

25(5)   Except where the equity method of accounting is applied, all investments other than those referred to in sub-paragraphs (2) and (3) must be valued on a basis which has prudent regard to the likely realisable value.

26(1)   In the case of land and buildings, **'current value'** means the market value on the date of valuation, where relevant reduced as provided in sub-paragraphs (4) and (5).

26(2)   **'Market value'** means the price at which land and buildings could be sold under private contract between a willing seller and an arm's length buyer on the date of valuation, it being assumed that the property is publicly exposed to the market, that market conditions permit orderly disposal and that a normal period, having regard to the nature of the property, is available for the negotiation of the sale.

26(3)   The market value must be determined through the separate valuation of each land and buildings item, carried out at least every five years in accordance with generally recognised methods of valuation.

26(4)   Where the value of any land and buildings item has diminished since the preceding valuation under sub-paragraph (3), an appropriate value adjustment must be made.

26(5)   The lower value arrived at under sub-paragraph (4) must not be increased in subsequent balance sheets unless such increase results from a new determination of market value arrived at in accordance with sub-paragraphs (2) and (3).

26(6)   Where, on the date on which the accounts are drawn up, land and buildings have been sold or are to be sold within the short term, the value arrived at in accordance with sub-paragraphs (2) and (4) must be reduced by the actual or estimated realisation costs.

26(7)   Where it is impossible to determine the market value of a land and buildings item, the value arrived at on the basis of the principle of purchase price or production cost is deemed to be its current value.

Application of the depreciation rules

27(1)   Where–

(a)   the value of any asset of a company is determined in accordance with paragraph 22 or 23, and

(b)   in the case of a determination under paragraph 22, the asset falls to be included under assets item C.I, that value must be, or (as the case may require) must be the starting point for determining, the amount to be included in respect of that asset in the company's accounts, instead of its cost or any value previously so determined for that asset.

Paragraphs 36 to 41 and 43 apply accordingly in relation to any such asset with the substitution for any reference to its cost of a reference to the value most recently determined for that asset in accordance with paragraph 22 or 23 (as the case may be).

27(2) The amount of any provision for depreciation required in the case of any asset by paragraph 37 or 38 as it applies by virtue of sub-paragraph (1) is referred to below in this paragraph as the adjusted amount, and the amount of any provision which would be required by that paragraph in the case of that asset according to the historical cost accounting rules is referred to as the historical cost amount.

27(3) Where sub-paragraph (1) applies in the case of any asset the amount of any provision for depreciation in respect of that asset included in any item shown in the profit and loss account in respect of amounts written off assets of the description in question may be the historical cost amount instead of the adjusted amount, provided that the amount of any difference between the two is shown separately in the profit and loss account or in a note to the accounts.

Additional information to be provided

28(1) This paragraph applies where the amounts to be included in respect of assets covered by any items shown in a company's accounts have been determined in accordance with paragraph 22 or 23.

28(2) The items affected and the basis of valuation adopted in determining the amounts of the assets in question in the case of each such item must be disclosed in a note to the accounts.

28(3) The purchase price of investments valued in accordance with paragraph 22 must be disclosed in the notes to the accounts.

28(4) In the case of each balance sheet item valued in accordance with paragraph 23 either–

(a)   the comparable amounts determined according to the historical cost accounting rules (without any provision for depreciation or diminution in value), or

(b)   the differences between those amounts and the corresponding amounts actually shown in the balance sheet in respect of that item,

must be shown separately in the balance sheet or in a note to the accounts.

28(5) In sub-paragraph (4), references in relation to any item to the comparable amounts determined as there mentioned are references to–

(a)   the aggregate amount which would be required to be shown in respect of that item if the amounts to be included in respect of all the assets covered by that item were determined according to the historical cost accounting rules, and

(b)   the aggregate amount of the cumulative provisions for depreciation or diminution in value which would be permitted or required in determining those amounts according to those rules.

Revaluation reserve

29(1) Subject to sub-paragraph (7), with respect to any determination of the value of an asset of a company in accordance with paragraph 22 or 23, the amount of any profit or loss arising from that determination (after allowing, where appropriate, for any provisions for depreciation or diminution in value made otherwise than by reference to the value so determined and any adjustments of any such provisions made in the light of that determination) must be credited or (as the case may be) debited to a separate reserve ('the revaluation reserve').

29(2) The amount of the revaluation reserve must be shown in the company's balance sheet under liabilities item A.III, but need not be shown under the name 'revaluation reserve'.

29(3) An amount may be transferred–

- (a) from the revaluation reserve–

  - (i) to the profit and loss account, if the amount was previously charged to that account or represents realised profit, or
  - (ii) on capitalisation,

- (b) to or from the revaluation reserve in respect of the taxation relating to any profit or loss credited or debited to the reserve.

The revaluation reserve must be reduced to the extent that the amounts transferred to it are no longer necessary for the purposes of the valuation method used.

29(4) In sub-paragraph (3)(a)(ii) **'capitalisation'**, in relation to an amount standing to the credit of the revaluation reserve, means applying it in wholly or partly paying up unissued shares in the company to be allotted to members of the company as fully or partly paid shares.

29(5) The revaluation reserve must not be reduced except as mentioned in this paragraph.

29(6) The treatment for taxation purposes of amounts credited or debited to the revaluation reserve must be disclosed in a note to the accounts.

29(7) This paragraph does not apply to the difference between the valuation of investments and their purchase price or previous valuation shown in the long-term business technical account or the non-technical account in accordance with note (9) on the profit and loss account format.

SECTION C – VALUATION AT FAIR VALUE

Inclusion of financial instruments at fair value

30(1) Subject to sub-paragraphs (2) to (5), financial instruments (including derivatives) may be included at fair value.

30(2) Sub-paragraph (1) does not apply to financial instruments that constitute liabilities unless–

- (a) they are held as part of a trading portfolio,
- (b) they are derivatives, or
- (c) they are financial instruments falling within paragraph (4).

30(3) Except where they fall within paragraph (4), or fall to be included under assets item D (assets held to cover linked liabilities), sub-paragraph (1) does not apply to–

- (a) financial instruments (other than derivatives) held to maturity,
- (b) loans and receivables originated by the company and not held for trading purposes,
- (c) interests in subsidiary undertakings, associated undertakings and joint ventures,
- (d) equity instruments issued by the company,
- (e) contracts for contingent consideration in a business combination, or
- (f) other financial instruments with such special characteristics that the instruments, according to generally accepted accounting principles or practice, should be accounted for differently from other financial instruments.

30(4) Financial instruments which under international accounting standards may be included in accounts at fair value, may be so included, provided that the disclosures required by such accounting standards are made.

30(5) If the fair value of a financial instrument cannot be determined reliably in accordance with paragraph 31, sub-paragraph (1) does not apply to that financial instrument.

30(6) In this paragraph–

'associated undertaking' has the meaning given by paragraph 19 of Schedule 6 to these Regulations; and

'joint venture' has the meaning given by paragraph 18 of that Schedule.

History – Para. 30(4) substituted by SI 2015/980, reg. 35(3)(a), with effect in relation to–
(a)   financial years beginning on or after 1 January 2016, and
(b)   a financial year of a company beginning on or after 1 January 2015, but before 1 January 2016, if the directors of the company so decide.

Former para. 30(4) read as follows:

"**30(4)**   Financial instruments that, under international accounting standards adopted by the European Commission on or before 5th September 2006 in accordance with the IAS Regulation, may be included in accounts at fair value, may be so included, provided that the disclosures required by such accounting standards are made."

Determination of fair value

31(1) The fair value of a financial instrument is its value determined in accordance with this paragraph.

31(2) If a reliable market can readily be identified for the financial instrument, its fair value is determined by reference to its market value.

31(3) If a reliable market cannot readily be identified for the financial instrument but can be identified for its components or for a similar instrument, its fair value is determined by reference to the market value of its components or of the similar instrument.

31(4) If neither sub-paragraph (2) nor (3) applies, the fair value of the financial instrument is a value resulting from generally accepted valuation models and techniques.

31(5) Any valuation models and techniques used for the purposes of sub-paragraph (4) must ensure a reasonable approximation of the market value.

Hedged items

32 A company may include any assets and liabilities, or identified portions of such assets or liabilities, that qualify as hedged items under a fair value hedge accounting system at the amount required under that system.

Other assets that may be included at fair value

33(1) This paragraph applies to–

(a)   investment property, and
(b)   living animals and plants.

33(2) Such investment property and living animals and plants may be included at fair value provided that, as the case may be, all such investment property or living animals and plants are so included where their fair value can be reliably determined.

33(3) In this paragraph, **'fair value'** means fair value determined in accordance with generally accepted accounting principles or practice.

History – Para. 33 substituted by SI 2015/980, reg. 35(3)(b), with effect in relation to–
  (a)   financial years beginning on or after 1 January 2016, and
  (b)   a financial year of a company beginning on or after 1 January 2015, but before 1 January 2016, if the directors of the company so decide.

Former para. 33 read as follows:
"33(1)   This paragraph applies to–

  (a)   investment property, and
  (b)   living animals and plants, that, under international accounting standards, may be included in accounts at fair value.

33(2)   Such investment property and such living animals and plants may be included at fair value, provided that all such investment property or, as the case may be, all such living animals and plants are so included where their fair value can reliably be determined.

33(3)   In this paragraph, **'fair value'** means fair value determined in accordance with relevant international accounting standards."

Accounting for changes in value

34(1)   This paragraph applies where a financial instrument is valued in accordance with paragraph 30 or 32 or an asset is valued in accordance with paragraph 33.

34(2)   Notwithstanding paragraph 18 in this Part of this Schedule, and subject to sub-paragraphs (3) and (4), a change in the value of the financial instrument or of the investment property or living animal or plant must be included in the profit and loss account.

34(3)   Where–

  (a)   the financial instrument accounted for is a hedging instrument under a hedge accounting system that allows some or all of the change in value not to be shown in the profit and loss account, or
  (b)   the change in value relates to an exchange difference arising on a monetary item that forms part of a company's net investment in a foreign entity,

the amount of the change in value must be credited to or (as the case may be) debited from a separate reserve ('the fair value reserve').

34(4)   Where the instrument accounted for–

  (a)   is an available for sale financial asset, and
  (b)   is not a derivative,

the change in value may be credited to or (as the case may be) debited from the fair value reserve.

The fair value reserve

35(1)   The fair value reserve must be adjusted to the extent that the amounts shown in it are no longer necessary for the purposes of paragraph 34(3) or (4).

35(2)   The treatment for taxation purposes of amounts credited or debited to the fair value reserve must be disclosed in a note to the accounts.

SECTION D – HISTORICAL COST ACCOUNTING RULES

VALUATION OF ASSETS

General rules

36(1)   The rules in this Section are 'the historical cost accounting rules'.

36(2)   Subject to any provision for depreciation or diminution in value made in accordance with paragraph 37 or 38, the amount to be included in respect of any asset in the balance sheet format is its cost.

37   In the case of any asset included under assets item B (intangible assets), C.I (land and buildings), F.I (tangible assets) or F.II (stocks) which has a limited useful economic life, the amount of–

   (a)   its cost, or
   (b)   where it is estimated that any such asset will have a residual value at the end of the period of its useful economic life, its cost less that estimated residual value,

must be reduced by provisions for depreciation calculated to write off that amount systematically over the period of the asset's useful economic life.

38(1)   This paragraph applies to any asset included under assets item B (intangible assets), C (investments), F.I (tangible assets) or F.IV (own shares).

38(2)   Where an asset to which this paragraph applies has diminished in value, provisions for diminution in value may be made in respect of it and the amount to be included in respect of it may be reduced accordingly.

38(3)   Provisions for diminution in value must be made in respect of any asset to which this paragraph applies if the reduction in its value is expected to be permanent (whether its useful economic life is limited or not), and the amount to be included in respect of it must be reduced accordingly.

38(4)   Any provisions made under sub-paragraph (2) or (3) which are not shown in the profit and loss account must be disclosed (either separately or in aggregate) in a note to the accounts.

39(1)   Where the reasons for which any provision was made in accordance with paragraph 38 have ceased to apply to any extent, that provision must be written back to the extent that it is no longer necessary.

39(1A)   But provision made in accordance with paragraph 38(2) or (3) in respect of goodwill must not be written back to any extent.

39(2)   Any amounts written back in accordance with sub-paragraph (1) which are not shown in the profit and loss account must be disclosed (either separately or in aggregate) in a note to the accounts.

History – Para. 39(1A) inserted by SI 2015/1672, reg. 4(6), with effect in relation to–
   (a)   financial years beginning on or after 1 January 2016, and
   (b)   a financial year of a company beginning on or after 1 January 2015 but before 1 January 2016, if the directors of the company have decided.

40(1)   This paragraph applies to assets included under assets items E.I, II and III (debtors) and F.III (cash at bank and in hand) in the balance sheet.

40(2)   If the net realisable value of an asset to which this paragraph applies is lower than its cost the amount to be included in respect of that asset is the net realisable value.

40(3)   Where the reasons for which any provision for diminution in value was made in accordance with sub-paragraph (2) have ceased to apply to any extent, that provision must be written back to the extent that it is no longer necessary.

Intangible assets

41(1) Where this is in accordance with generally accepted accounting principles or practice, development costs may be included under assets item B (intangible assets) in the balance sheet format.

41(2) If any amount is included in a company's balance sheet in respect of development costs, the note on accounting policies (see paragraph 61 of this Schedule) must include the following information—

  (a) the period over which the amount of those costs originally capitalised is being or is to be written off, and
  (b) the reasons for capitalising the development costs in question.

History – Para. 41 and the heading preceding it substituted by SI 2015/980, reg. 35(4)(a), with effect in relation to—
  (a) financial years beginning on or after 1 January 2016, and
  (b) a financial year of a company beginning on or after 1 January 2015, but before 1 January 2016, if the directors of the company so decide.

Former para. 41 read as follows:

"Development costs
41(1) Notwithstanding that amounts representing 'development costs' may be included under assets item B (intangible assets) in the balance sheet format, an amount may only be included in a company's balance sheet in respect of development costs in special circumstances.
41(2) If any amount is included in a company's balance sheet in respect of development costs the following information must be given in a note to the accounts—

  (a) the period over which the amount of those costs originally capitalised is being or is to be written off, and
  (b) the reasons for capitalising the development costs in question."

Goodwill

42(1) Intangible assets must be written off over the useful economic life of the intangible asset.

42(2) Where in exceptional cases the useful life of intangible assets cannot be reliably estimated, such assets must be written off over a period chosen by the directors of the company.

42(3) The period referred to in sub-paragraph (2) must not exceed ten years.

42(4) There must be disclosed in a note to the accounts the period referred to in sub-paragraph (2) and the reasons for choosing that period.

History – Para. 42 substituted by SI 2015/980, reg. 35(4)(a), with effect in relation to—
  (a) financial years beginning on or after 1 January 2016, and
  (b) a financial year of a company beginning on or after 1 January 2015, but before 1 January 2016, if the directors of the company so decide.

Former para. 42 read as follows:
"42(1) The application of paragraphs 36 to 39 in relation to goodwill (in any case where goodwill is treated as an asset) is subject to the following.
42(2) Subject to sub-paragraph (3), the amount of the consideration for any goodwill acquired by a company must be reduced by provisions for depreciation calculated to write off that amount systematically over a period chosen by the directors of the company.
42(3) The period chosen must not exceed the useful economic life of the goodwill in question.
42(4) In any case where any goodwill acquired by a company is included as an asset in the company's balance sheet, there must be disclosed in a note to the accounts—

  (a) the period chosen for writing off the consideration for that goodwill, and
  (b) the reasons for choosing that period."

MISCELLANEOUS AND SUPPLEMENTARY PROVISIONS

Excess of money owed over value received as an asset item

43(1) Where the amount repayable on any debt owed by a company is greater than the value of the consideration received in the transaction giving rise to the debt, the amount of the difference may be treated as an asset.

43(2) Where any such amount is so treated–

(a) it must be written off by reasonable amounts each year and must be completely written off before repayment of the debt, and

(b) if the current amount is not shown as a separate item in the company's balance sheet, it must be disclosed in a note to the accounts.

Assets included at a fixed amount

44(1) Subject to sub-paragraph (2), assets which fall to be included under assets item F.I (tangible assets) in the balance sheet format may be included at a fixed quantity and value.

44(2) Sub-paragraph (1) applies to assets of a kind which are constantly being replaced where–

(a) their overall value is not material to assessing the company's state of affairs, and

(b) their quantity, value and composition are not subject to material variation.

Determination of cost

45(1) The cost of an asset that has been acquired by the company is to be determined by adding to the actual price paid any expenses incidental to its acquisition and then subtracting any incidental reductions in the cost of acquisition.

45(2) The cost of an asset constructed by the company is to be determined by adding to the purchase price of the raw materials and consumables used the amount of the costs incurred by the company which are directly attributable to the construction of that asset.

45(3) In addition, there may be included in the cost of an asset constructed by the company–

(a) a reasonable proportion of the costs incurred by the company which are only indirectly attributable to the construction of that asset, but only to the extent that they relate to the period of construction, and

(b) interest on capital borrowed to finance the construction of that asset, to the extent that it accrues in respect of the period of construction,

provided, however, in a case within paragraph (b), that the inclusion of the interest in determining the cost of that asset and the amount of the interest so included is disclosed in a note to the accounts.

History – In para. 45(1), the words 'and then subtracting any incidental reductions in the cost of acquisition' inserted by SI 2015/980, reg. 35(4)(b), with effect in relation to–
(a) financial years beginning on or after 1 January 2016, and
(b) a financial year of a company beginning on or after 1 January 2015, but before 1 January 2016, if the directors of the company so decide.

46(1) The cost of any assets which are fungible assets may be determined by the application of any of the methods mentioned in sub-paragraph (2) in relation to any such assets of the same class, provided that the method chosen is one which appears to the directors to be appropriate in the circumstances of the company.

46(2)   Those methods are–

(a)   the method known as 'first in, first out' (FIFO),

(b)   the method known as 'last in, first out' (LIFO),

(c)   a weighted average price, and

(d)   any other method reflecting generally accepted best practice.

46(3)   Where in the case of any company–

(a)   the cost of assets falling to be included under any item shown in the company's balance sheet has been determined by the application of any method permitted by this paragraph, and

(b)   the amount shown in respect of that item differs materially from the relevant alternative amount given below in this paragraph,

the amount of that difference must be disclosed in a note to the accounts.

46(4)   Subject to sub-paragraph (5), for the purposes of sub-paragraph (3)(b), the relevant alternative amount, in relation to any item shown in a company's balance sheet, is the amount which would have been shown in respect of that item if assets of any class included under that item at an amount determined by any method permitted by this paragraph had instead been included at their replacement cost as at the balance sheet date.

46(5)   The relevant alternative amount may be determined by reference to the most recent actual purchase price before the balance sheet date of assets of any class included under the item in question instead of by reference to their replacement cost as at that date, but only if the former appears to the directors of the company to constitute the more appropriate standard of comparison in the case of assets of that class.

History – In para. 46(2)(d), the words 'reflecting generally accepted best practice' substituted for the words 'similar to any of the methods mentioned above' by SI 2015/980, reg. 35(4)(c), with effect in relation to–

(a)   financial years beginning on or after 1 January 2016, and

(b)   a financial year of a company beginning on or after 1 January 2015, but before 1 January 2016, if the directors of the company so decide.

Substitution of original amount where price or cost unknown

47(1)   This paragraph applies where–

(a)   there is no record of the purchase price of any asset acquired by a company or of any price, expenses or costs relevant for determining its cost in accordance with paragraph 45, or

(b)   any such record cannot be obtained without unreasonable expense or delay.

47(2)   In such a case, the cost of the asset must be taken, for the purposes of paragraphs 36 to 42, to be the value ascribed to it in the earliest available record of its value made on or after its acquisition by the company.

SECTION E – RULES FOR DETERMINING PROVISIONS

Preliminary

48   Provisions which are to be shown in a company's accounts are to be determined in accordance with this Section.

Technical provisions

49   The amount of technical provisions must at all times be sufficient to cover any liabilities arising out of insurance contracts as far as can reasonably be foreseen.

Provision for unearned premiums

50(1)   The provision for unearned premiums must in principle be computed separately for each insurance contract, save that statistical methods (and in particular proportional and flat rate methods) may be used where they may be expected to give approximately the same results as individual calculations.

50(2)   Where the pattern of risk varies over the life of a contract, this must be taken into account in the calculation methods.

Provision for unexpired risks

51   The provision for unexpired risks (as defined in paragraph 91) must be computed on the basis of claims and administrative expenses likely to arise after the end of the financial year from contracts concluded before that date, in so far as their estimated value exceeds the provision for unearned premiums and any premiums receivable under those contracts.

Long-term business provision

52(1)   The long-term business provision must in principle be computed separately for each long-term contract, save that statistical or mathematical methods may be used where they may be expected to give approximately the same results as individual calculations.

52(2)   A summary of the principal assumptions in making the provision under sub-paragraph (1) must be given in the notes to the accounts.

52(3)   The computation must be made annually by a Fellow of the Institute or Faculty of Actuaries on the basis of recognised actuarial methods, with due regard to the actuarial principles laid down in Directive 2002/83/EC of the European Parliament and of the Council of 5th November 2002 concerning life assurance.

History - In Sch. 3, para. 52(3), the words 'Directive 2009/138/EC of the European Parliament and of the Council of 25 November 2009 on the taking-up and pursuit of the business of Insurance and Reinsurance (Solvency II)' substituted for the words 'Directive 2002/83/EC of the European Parliament and of the Council of 5th November 2002 concerning life assurance' by SI 2015/575, Sch. 2, para. 26, with effect from 1 January 2016.

PROVISIONS FOR CLAIMS OUTSTANDING

General business

53(1)   A provision must in principle be computed separately for each claim on the basis of the costs still expected to arise, save that statistical methods may be used if they result in an adequate provision having regard to the nature of the risks.

53(2)   This provision must also allow for claims incurred but not reported by the balance sheet date, the amount of the allowance being determined having regard to past experience as to the number and magnitude of claims reported after previous balance sheet dates.

53(3)   All claims settlement costs (whether direct or indirect) must be included in the calculation of the provision.

53(4) Recoverable amounts arising out of subrogation or salvage must be estimated on a prudent basis and either deducted from the provision for claims outstanding (in which case if the amounts are material they must be shown in the notes to the accounts) or shown as assets.

53(5) In sub-paragraph (4), **'subrogation'** means the acquisition of the rights of policy holders with respect to third parties, and **'salvage'** means the acquisition of the legal ownership of insured property.

53(6) Where benefits resulting from a claim must be paid in the form of annuity, the amounts to be set aside for that purpose must be calculated by recognised actuarial methods, and paragraph 54 does not apply to such calculations.

53(7) Implicit discounting or deductions, whether resulting from the placing of a current value on a provision for an outstanding claim which is expected to be settled later at a higher figure or otherwise effected, is prohibited.

54(1) Explicit discounting or deductions to take account of investment income is permitted, subject to the following conditions–

(a) the expected average interval between the date for the settlement of claims being discounted and the accounting date must be at least four years;

(b) the discounting or deductions must be effected on a recognised prudential basis;

(c) when calculating the total cost of settling claims, the company must take account of all factors that could cause increases in that cost;

(d) the company must have adequate data at its disposal to construct a reliable model of the rate of claims settlements;

(e) the rate of interest used for the calculation of present values must not exceed a rate prudently estimated to be earned by assets of the company which are appropriate in magnitude and nature to cover the provisions for claims being discounted during the period necessary for the payment of such claims, and must not exceed either–

(i) a rate justified by the performance of such assets over the preceding five years, or

(ii) a rate justified by the performance of such assets during the year preceding the balance sheet date.

54(2) When discounting or effecting deductions, the company must, in the notes to the accounts, disclose–

(a) the total amount of provisions before discounting or deductions,

(b) the categories of claims which are discounted or from which deductions have been made,

(c) for each category of claims, the methods used, in particular the rates used for the estimates referred to in sub-paragraph (1)(d) and (e), and the criteria adopted for estimating the period that will elapse before the claims are settled.

Long-term business

55 The amount of the provision for claims must be equal to the sums due to beneficiaries, plus the costs of settling claims.

Equalisation reserves

56 The amount of any equalisation reserve maintained in respect of general business by the company, in accordance with the rules made by the Financial Conduct Authority or the Prudential

Regulation Authority under Part 10 of the Financial Services and Markets Act 2000, must be determined in accordance with such rules.

History – The words 'made by the Financial Conduct Authority or the Prudential Regulation Authority' substituted for 'in section 1.4 of the Prudential Sourcebook for Insurers made by the Financial Services Authority' by SI 2013/472, Sch. 2, para. 135(b), with effect from 1 April 2013.

Accounting on a non-annual basis

57(1)   Either of the methods described in paragraphs 58 and 59 may be applied where, because of the nature of the class or type of insurance in question, information about premiums receivable or claims payable (or both) for the underwriting years is insufficient when the accounts are drawn up for reliable estimates to be made.

57(2)   The use of either of the methods referred to in sub-paragraph (1) must be disclosed in the notes to the accounts together with the reasons for adopting it.

57(3)   Where one of the methods referred to in sub-paragraph (1) is adopted, it must be applied systematically in successive years unless circumstances justify a change.

57(4)   In the event of a change in the method applied, the effect on the assets, liabilities, financial position and profit or loss must be stated in the notes to the accounts.

57(5)   For the purposes of this paragraph and paragraph 58, **'underwriting year'** means the financial year in which the insurance contracts in the class or type of insurance in question commenced.

58(1)   The excess of the premiums written over the claims and expenses paid in respect of contracts commencing in the underwriting year shall form a technical provision included in the technical provision for claims outstanding shown in the balance sheet under liabilities item C.3.

58(2)   The provision may also be computed on the basis of a given percentage of the premiums written where such a method is appropriate for the type of risk insured.

58(3)   If necessary, the amount of this technical provision must be increased to make it sufficient to meet present and future obligations.

58(4)   The technical provision constituted under this paragraph must be replaced by a provision for claims outstanding estimated in accordance with paragraph 53 as soon as sufficient information has been gathered and not later than the end of the third year following the underwriting year.

58(5)   The length of time that elapses before a provision for claims outstanding is constituted in accordance with sub-paragraph (4) must be disclosed in the notes to the accounts.

59(1)   The figures shown in the technical account or in certain items within it must relate to a year which wholly or partly precedes the financial year (but by no more than 12 months).

59(2)   The amounts of the technical provisions shown in the accounts must if necessary be increased to make them sufficient to meet present and future obligations.

59(3)   The length of time by which the earlier year to which the figures relate precedes the financial year and the magnitude of the transactions concerned must be disclosed in the notes to the accounts.

Part 3 – Notes to the accounts
PRELIMINARY

60(1) Any information required in the case of a company by the following provisions of this Part of this Schedule must be given by way of a note to the accounts.

60(2) These notes must be presented in the order in which, where relevant, the items to which they relate are presented in the balance sheet and in the profit and loss account.

History – Para. 60 substituted by SI 2015/980, reg. 36(2), with effect in relation to–
   (a) financial years beginning on or after 1 January 2016, and
   (b) a financial year of a company beginning on or after 1 January 2015, but before 1 January 2016, if the directors of the company so decide.

Former para. 60 read as follows:

"**60** Any information required in the case of any company by the following provisions of this Part of this Schedule must (if not given in the company's accounts) be given by way of a note to the accounts."

GENERAL

Disclosure of accounting policies

61 The accounting policies adopted by the company in determining the amounts to be included in respect of items shown in the balance sheet and in determining the profit or loss of the company must be stated (including such policies with respect to the depreciation and diminution in value of assets).

62 It must be stated whether the accounts have been prepared in accordance with applicable accounting standards and particulars of any material departure from those standards and the reasons for it must be given.

Sums denominated in foreign currencies

63 Where any sums originally denominated in foreign currencies have been brought into account under any items shown in the balance sheet or profit and loss account format, the basis on which those sums have been translated into sterling (or the currency in which the accounts are drawn up) must be stated.

Reserves and dividends

64 There must be stated–

   (a) any amount set aside or proposed to be set aside to, or withdrawn or proposed to be withdrawn from, reserves,

   (b) the aggregate amount of dividends paid in the financial year (other than those for which a liability existed at the immediately preceding balance sheet date),

   (c) the aggregate amount of dividends that the company is liable to pay at the balance sheet date, and

   (d) the aggregate amount of dividends that are proposed before the date of approval of the accounts, and not otherwise disclosed under sub-paragraph (b) or (c).

INFORMATION SUPPLEMENTING THE BALANCE SHEET

Share capital and debentures

65(1) Where shares of more than one class have been allotted, the number and aggregate nominal value of shares of each class allotted must be given.

65(2) In the case of any part of the allotted share capital that consists of redeemable shares, the following information must be given—

(a) the earliest and latest dates on which the company has power to redeem those shares,

(b) whether those shares must be redeemed in any event or are liable to be redeemed at the option of the company or of the shareholder, and

(c) whether any (and, if so, what) premium is payable on redemption.

66 If the company has allotted any shares during the financial year, the following information must be given—

(a) the classes of shares allotted, and

(b) as respects each class of shares, the number allotted, their aggregate nominal value and the consideration received by the company for the allotment.

67(1) With respect to any contingent right to the allotment of shares in the company the following particulars must be given—

(a) the number, description and amount of the shares in relation to which the right is exercisable,

(b) the period during which it is exercisable, and

(c) the price to be paid for the shares allotted.

67(2) In sub-paragraph (1) **'contingent right to the allotment of shares'** means any option to subscribe for shares and any other right to require the allotment of shares to any person whether arising on the conversion into shares of securities of any other description or otherwise.

68(1) If the company has issued any debentures during the financial year to which the accounts relate, the following information must be given—

(a) the classes of debentures issued, and

(b) as respects each class of debentures, the amount issued and the consideration received by the company for the issue.

68(2) Where any of the company's debentures are held by a nominee of or trustee for the company, the nominal amount of the debentures and the amount at which they are stated in the accounting records kept by the company in accordance with section 386 of the 2006 Act (duty to keep accounting records) must be stated.

Assets

69(1) In respect of any assets of the company included in assets items B (intangible assets), C.I (land and buildings) and C.II (investments in group undertakings and participating interests) in the company's balance sheet the following information must be given by reference to each such item—

(a) the appropriate amounts in respect of those assets included in the item as at the date of the beginning of the financial year and as at the balance sheet date respectively,

(b) the effect on any amount included in assets item B in respect of those assets of—

(i) any determination during that year of the value to be ascribed to any of those assets in accordance with paragraph 23,

(ii) acquisitions during that year of any assets,

(iii) disposals during that year of any assets, and

(iv) any transfers of assets of the company to and from the item during that year.

69(2) The reference in sub-paragraph (1)(a) to the appropriate amounts in respect of any assets (included in an assets item) as at any date there mentioned is a reference to amounts representing the aggregate amounts determined, as at that date, in respect of assets falling to be included under the item on either of the following bases–

    (a)   on the basis of cost (determined in accordance with paragraphs 45 and 46), or

    (b)   on any basis permitted by paragraph 22 or 23,

(leaving out of account in either case any provisions for depreciation or diminution in value).

69(3)   In addition, in respect of any assets of the company included in any assets item in the company's balance sheet, there must be stated (by reference to each such item)–

    (a)   the cumulative amount of provisions for depreciation or diminution in value of those assets included under the item as at each date mentioned in sub-paragraph (1)(a),

    (b)   the amount of any such provisions made in respect of the financial year,

    (c)   the amount of any adjustments made in respect of any such provisions during that year in consequence of the disposal of any of those assets, and

    (d)   the amount of any other adjustments made in respect of any such provisions during that year.

70   Where any assets of the company (other than listed investments) are included under any item shown in the company's balance sheet at an amount determined on any basis mentioned in paragraph 22 or 23, the following information must be given–

    (a)   the years (so far as they are known to the directors) in which the assets were severally valued and the several values, and

    (b)   in the case of assets that have been valued during the financial year, the names of the persons who valued them or particulars of their qualifications for doing so and (whichever is stated) the bases of valuation used by them.

71   In relation to any amount which is included under assets item C.I (land and buildings) there must be stated–

    (a)   how much of that amount is ascribable to land of freehold tenure and how much to land of leasehold tenure, and

    (b)   how much of the amount ascribable to land of leasehold tenure is ascribable to land held on long lease and how much to land held on short lease.

Investments

72   In respect of the amount of each item which is shown in the company's balance sheet under assets item C (investments) there must be stated how much of that amount is ascribable to listed investments.

Information about fair value of assets and liabilities

73(1)   This paragraph applies where financial instruments or other assets have been valued in accordance with, as appropriate, paragraph 30, 32 or 33.

73(2)   There must be stated–

    (a)   the significant assumptions underlying the valuation models and techniques used to determine the fair value of the financial instruments or other assets,

    (b)   in the case of financial instruments, their purchase price, the items affected and the basis of valuation,

    (c)   for each category of financial instrument or other asset, the fair value of the assets in that category and the changes in value–

        (i)   included directly in the profit and loss account, or

        (ii) credited to or (as the case may be) debited from the fair value reserve,

        in respect of those assets, and

    (c)   for each class of derivatives, the extent and nature of the instruments, including significant terms and conditions that may affect the amount, timing and certainty of future cash flows.

73(3)   Where any amount is transferred to or from the fair value reserve during the financial year, there must be stated in tabular form–

    (a)   the amount of the reserve as at the date of the beginning of the financial year and as at the balance sheet date respectively,

    (b)   the amount transferred to or from the reserve during the year, and

    (c)   the source and application respectively of the amounts so transferred.

History – Para. 73 substituted by SI 2015/980, reg. 36(3), with effect in relation to–
    (a)   financial years beginning on or after 1 January 2016, and
    (b)   a financial year of a company beginning on or after 1 January 2015, but before 1 January 2016, if the directors of the company so decide.

Former para. 73 read as follows:

"**73(1)**   This paragraph applies where financial instruments have been valued in accordance with paragraph 30 or 32.

73(2)   The items affected and the basis of valuation adopted in determining the amounts of the financial instruments must be disclosed.

73(3)   The purchase price of the financial instruments must be disclosed.

73(4)   There must be stated–

    (a)   the significant assumptions underlying the valuation models and techniques used, where the fair value of the instruments has been determined in accordance with paragraph 31(4),

    (b)   for each category of financial instrument, the fair value of the instruments in that category and the changes in value–

        (i)   included in the profit and loss account, or

        (ii) credited to or (as the case may be) debited from the fair value reserve, in respect of those instruments, and

    (c)   for each class of derivatives, the extent and nature of the instruments, including significant terms and conditions that may affect the amount, timing and certainty of future cash flows.

73(5)   Where any amount is transferred to or from the fair value reserve during the financial year, there must be stated in tabular form–

    (a)   the amount of the reserve as at the date of the beginning of the financial year and as at the balance sheet date respectively,

    (b)   the amount transferred to or from the reserve during that year, and

    (c)   the source and application respectively of the amounts so transferred."

74   Where the company has derivatives that it has not included at fair value, there must be stated for each class of such derivatives–

    (a)   the fair value of the derivatives in that class, if such a value can be determined in accordance with paragraph 31, and

    (b)   the extent and nature of the derivatives.

75(1)   This paragraph applies if–

    (a)   the company has financial fixed assets that could be included at fair value by virtue of paragraph 30,

    (b)   the amount at which those assets are included under any item in the company's accounts is in excess of their fair value, and

    (c)   the company has not made provision for diminution in value of those assets in accordance with paragraph 38(2) of this Schedule.

75(2)   There must be stated–

(a)   the amount at which either the individual assets or appropriate groupings of those individual assets are included in the company's accounts,

(b)   the fair value of those assets or groupings, and

(c)   the reasons for not making a provision for diminution in value of those assets, including the nature of the evidence that provides the basis for the belief that the amount at which they are stated in the accounts will be recovered.

Information where investment property and living animals and plants included at fair value

76(1)   This paragraph applies where the amounts to be included in a company's accounts in respect of investment property or living animals and plants have been determined in accordance with paragraph 33.

76(2)   The balance sheet items affected and the basis of valuation adopted in determining the amounts of the assets in question in the case of each such item must be disclosed in a note to the accounts.

76(3)   In the case of investment property, for each balance sheet item affected there must be shown, either separately in the balance sheet or in a note to the accounts–

(a)   the comparable amounts determined according to the historical cost accounting rules, or

(b)   the differences between those amounts and the corresponding amounts actually shown in the balance sheet in respect of that item.

76(4)   In sub-paragraph (3), references in relation to any item to the comparable amounts determined in accordance with that sub-paragraph are to–

(a)   the aggregate amount which would be required to be shown in respect of that item if the amounts to be included in respect of all the assets covered by that item were determined according to the historical cost accounting rules, and

(b)   the aggregate amount of the cumulative provisions for depreciation or diminution in value which would be permitted or required in determining those amounts according to those rules.

Reserves and provisions

77(1)   This paragraph applies where any amount is transferred–

(a)   to or from any reserves,

(b)   to any provisions for other risks, or

(c)   from any provisions for other risks otherwise than for the purpose for which the provision was established,

and the reserves or provisions are or would but for paragraph 3(1) be shown as separate items in the company's balance sheet.

77(2)   The following information must be given in respect of the aggregate of reserves or provisions included in the same item–

(a)   the amount of the reserves or provisions as at the date of the beginning of the financial year and as at the balance sheet date respectively,

(b)   any amounts transferred to or from the reserves or provisions during that year, and

(c)   the source and application respectively of any amounts so transferred.

77(3)   Particulars must be given of each provision included in liabilities item E.3 (other provisions) in the company's balance sheet in any case where the amount of that provision is material.

Provision for taxation

78   The amount of any provision for deferred taxation must be stated separately from the amount of any provision for other taxation.

Details of indebtedness

79(1)   In respect of each item shown under 'creditors' in the company's balance sheet there must be stated the aggregate of the following amounts–

(a)   the amount of any debts included under that item which are payable or repayable otherwise than by instalments and fall due for payment or repayment after the end of the period of five years beginning with the day next following the end of the financial year, and

(b)   in the case of any debts so included which are payable or repayable by instalments, the amount of any instalments which fall due for payment after the end of that period.

79(2)   Subject to sub-paragraph (3), in relation to each debt falling to be taken into account under sub-paragraph (1), the terms of payment or repayment and the rate of any interest payable on the debt must be stated.

79(3)   If the number of debts is such that, in the opinion of the directors, compliance with subparagraph (2) would result in a statement of excessive length, it is sufficient to give a general indication of the terms of payment or repayment and the rates of any interest payable on the debts.

79(4)   In respect of each item shown under 'creditors' in the company's balance sheet there must be stated–

(a)   the aggregate amount of any debts included under that item in respect of which any security has been given by the company, and

(b)   an indication of the nature of the securities so given.

79(5)   References above in this paragraph to an item shown under 'creditors' in the company's balance sheet include references, where amounts falling due to creditors within one year and after more than one year are distinguished in the balance sheet–

(a)   in a case within sub-paragraph (1), to an item shown under the latter of those categories, and

(b)   in a case within sub-paragraph (4), to an item shown under either of those categories.

References to items shown under 'creditors' include references to items which would but for paragraph 3(1)(b) be shown under that heading.

80   If any fixed cumulative dividends on the company's shares are in arrear, there must be stated–

(a)   the amount of the arrears, and

(b)   the period for which the dividends or, if there is more than one class, each class of them are in arrear.

Guarantees and other financial commitments

81(1)   Particulars must be given of any charge on the assets of the company to secure the liabilities of any other person including the amount secured.

81(2) Particulars and the total amount of any financial commitments, guarantees and contingencies (excluding those which arise out of insurance contracts) that are not included in the balance sheet must be disclosed.

81(3) An indication of the nature and form of any valuable security given by the company in respect of commitments, guarantees and contingencies within sub-paragraph (2) must be given.

81(4) The total amount of any commitments within sub-paragraph (2) concerning pensions must be separately disclosed.

81(5) Particulars must be given of pension commitments which are included in the balance sheet.

81(6) Where any commitment within sub-paragraph (4) or (5) relates wholly or partly to pensions payable to past directors of the company separate particulars must be given of that commitment.

81(7) The total amount of any commitments, guarantees and contingencies within sub-paragraph (2) which are undertaken on behalf of or for the benefit of–

(a) any parent undertaking or fellow subsidiary undertaking of the company,

(b) any subsidiary undertaking of the company, or

(c) any undertaking in which the company has a participating interest

must be separately stated and those within each of paragraphs (a), (b) and (c) must also be stated separately from those within any other of those paragraphs.

History – Para. 81 substituted by SI 2015/980, reg. 36(4), with effect in relation to–
(a) financial years beginning on or after 1 January 2016, and
(b) a financial year of a company beginning on or after 1 January 2015, but before 1 January 2016, if the directors of the company so decide.

Former para. 81 read as follows:

"81(1) Particulars must be given of any charge on the assets of the company to secure the liabilities of any other person, including, where practicable, the amount secured.

81(2) The following information must be given with respect to any other contingent liability not provided for (other than a contingent liability arising out of an insurance contract)–
(a) the amount or estimated amount of that liability,
(b) its legal nature, and
(c) whether any valuable security has been provided by the company in connection with that liability and if so, what.

81(3) There must be stated, where practicable, the aggregate amount or estimated amount of contracts for capital expenditure, so far as not provided for.

81(4) Particulars must be given of–
(a) any pension commitments included under any provision shown in the company's balance sheet, and
(b) any such commitments for which no provision has been made, and where any such commitment relates wholly or partly to pensions payable to past directors of the company separate particulars must be given of that commitment so far as it relates to such pensions.

81(5) Particulars must also be given of any other financial commitments, other than commitments arising out of insurance contracts, that–
(a) have not been provided for, and
(b) are relevant to assessing the company's state of affairs.

81(6) Commitments within any of the preceding sub-paragraphs undertaken on behalf of or for the benefit of–
(a) any parent undertaking or fellow subsidiary undertaking, or
(b) any subsidiary undertaking of the company, must be stated separately from the other commitments within that sub-paragraph, and commitments within paragraph
(a) must also be stated separately from those within paragraph (b)."

Miscellaneous matters

82(1) Particulars must be given of any case where the cost of any asset is for the first time determined under paragraph 47.

82(2)   Where any outstanding loans made under the authority of section 682(2)(b)), (c) or (d) of the 2006 Act (various cases of financial assistance by a company for purchase of its own shares) are included under any item shown in the company's balance sheet, the aggregate amount of those loans must be disclosed for each item in question.

INFORMATION SUPPLEMENTING THE PROFIT AND LOSS ACCOUNT

Separate statement of certain items of income and expenditure

83(1)   Subject to sub-paragraph (2), there must be stated the amount of the interest on or any similar charges in respect of–

(a)   bank loans and overdrafts, and

(b)   loans of any other kind made to the company.

83(2)   Sub-paragraph (1) does not apply to interest or charges on loans to the company from group undertakings, but, with that exception, it applies to interest or charges on all loans, whether made on the security of debentures or not.

Particulars of tax

84(1)   Particulars must be given of any special circumstances which affect liability in respect of taxation of profits, income or capital gains for the financial year or liability in respect of taxation of profits, income or capital gains for succeeding financial years.

84(2)   The following amounts must be stated–

(a)   the amount of the charge for United Kingdom corporation tax,

(b)   if that amount would have been greater but for relief from double taxation, the amount which it would have been but for such relief,

(c)   the amount of the charge for United Kingdom income tax, and

(d)   the amount of the charge for taxation imposed outside the United Kingdom of profits, income and (so far as charged to revenue) capital gains.

Those amounts must be stated separately in respect of each of the amounts which is shown under the following items in the profit and loss account, that is to say item III.9 (tax on profit or loss on ordinary activities) and item III.14 (tax on extraordinary profit or loss).

Particulars of business

85(1)   As regards general business a company must disclose–

(a)   gross premiums written,

(b)   gross premiums earned,

(c)   gross claims incurred,

(d)   gross operating expenses, and

(e)   the reinsurance balance.

85(2)   The amounts required to be disclosed by sub-paragraph (1) must be broken down between direct insurance and reinsurance acceptances, if reinsurance acceptances amount to 10 per cent or more of gross premiums written.

85(3)   Subject to sub-paragraph (4), the amounts required to be disclosed by sub-paragraphs (1) and (2) with respect to direct insurance must be further broken down into the following groups of classes–

(a) accident and health,

(b) motor (third party liability),

(c) motor (other classes),

(d) marine, aviation and transport,

(e) fire and other damage to property,

(f) third-party liability,

(g) credit and suretyship,

(h) legal expenses,

(i) assistance, and

(j) miscellaneous,

where the amount of the gross premiums written in direct insurance for each such group exceeds 10 million Euros.

85(4) The company must in any event disclose the amounts relating to the three largest groups of classes in its business.

86(1) As regards long-term business, the company must disclose–

(a) gross premiums written, and

(b) the reinsurance balance.

86(2) Subject to sub-paragraph (3)–

(a) gross premiums written must be broken down between those written by way of direct insurance and those written by way of reinsurance, and

(b) gross premiums written by way of direct insurance must be broken down–

(i) between individual premiums and premiums under group contracts,

(ii) between periodic premiums and single premiums, and

(iii) between premiums from non-participating contracts, premiums from participating contracts and premiums from contracts where the investment risk is borne by policyholders.

86(3) Disclosure of any amount referred to in sub-paragraph (2)(a) or (2)(b)(i), (ii) or (iii) is not required if it does not exceed 10 per cent of the gross premiums written or (as the case may be) of the gross premiums written by way of direct insurance.

87(1) Subject to sub-paragraph (2), there must be disclosed as regards both general and long-term business the total gross direct insurance premiums resulting from contracts concluded by the company–

(a) in the member State of its head office,

(b) in the other member States, and

(c) in other countries.

87(2) Disclosure of any amount referred to in sub-paragraph (1) is not required if it does not exceed 5 per cent of total gross premiums.

Commissions

88 There must be disclosed the total amount of commissions for direct insurance business accounted for in the financial year, including acquisition, renewal, collection and portfolio management commissions.

Miscellaneous matters

89(1)   Where any amount relating to any preceding financial year is included in any item in the profit and loss account, the effect must be stated.

89(2)   The amount, nature and effect of any individual items of income or expenditure which are of exceptional size or incidence must be stated.

History – Para. 89(2) substituted for para. 89(2) and (3) by SI 2015/980, reg. 36(5), with effect in relation to–
- (a)   financial years beginning on or after 1 January 2016, and
- (b)   a financial year of a company beginning on or after 1 January 2015, but before 1 January 2016, if the directors of the company so decide.

Related party transactions

90(1)   Particulars may be given of transactions which the company has entered into with related parties, and must be given if such transactions are material and have not been concluded under normal market conditions.

90(2)   The particulars of transactions required to be disclosed by sub-paragraph (1) must include–

- (a)   the amount of such transactions,
- (b)   the nature of the related party relationship, and
- (c)   other information about the transactions necessary for an understanding of the financial position of the company.

90(3)   Information about individual transactions may be aggregated according to their nature, except where separate information is necessary for an understanding of the effects of related party transactions on the financial position of the company.

90(4)   Particulars need not be given of transactions entered into between two or more members of a group, provided that any subsidiary undertaking which is a party to the transaction is whollyowned by such a member.

90(5)   In this paragraph, **'related party'** has the same meaning as in international accounting standards.

Post balance sheet events

90A   The nature and financial effect of material events arising after the balance sheet date which are not reflected in the profit and loss account of balance sheet must be stated.

History – Para. 90A and the heading preceding it inserted by SI 2015/980, reg. 36(6), with effect in relation to–
- (a)   financial years beginning on or after 1 January 2016, and
- (b)   a financial year of a company beginning on or after 1 January 2015, but before 1 January 2016, if the directors of the company so decide.

Appropriations

90B   Particulars must be given of the proposed appropriation of profit or treatment of loss or, where applicable, particulars of the actual appropriation of the profits or treatment of the losses.

History – Para. 90B and the heading preceding it inserted by SI 2015/980, reg. 36(6), with effect in relation to–
- (a)   financial years beginning on or after 1 January 2016, and
- (b)   a financial year of a company beginning on or after 1 January 2015, but before 1 January 2016, if the directors of the company so decide.

Part 4 – Interpretation of this schedule

DEFINITIONS FOR THIS SCHEDULE

91   The following definitions apply for the purposes of this Schedule and its interpretation–

'general business' means business which consists of effecting or carrying out contracts of general insurance;

'long-term business' means business which consists of effecting or carrying out contracts of long-term insurance;

'long-term fund' means the fund or funds maintained by a company in respect of its long-term business in accordance with rules made by the Financial Conduct Authority or the Prudential Regulation Authority under Part 10 of the Financial Services and Markets Act 2000;

'policyholder' has the meaning given by article 3 of the Financial Services and Markets Act 2000 (Meaning of 'Policy' and 'Policyholder') Order 2001;

'provision for unexpired risks' means the amount set aside in addition to unearned premiums in respect of risks to be borne by the company after the end of the financial year, in order to provide for all claims and expenses in connection with insurance contracts in force in excess of the related unearned premiums and any premiums receivable on those contracts.

History – In the definition of 'long-term fund', 'rules made by the Financial Conduct Authority or the Prudential Regulation Authority' substituted for 'rule 1.5.22 in the Prudential Sourcebook for Insurers made by the Financial Services Authority' by SI 2013/472, Sch. 2, para. 135(c), with effect from 1 April 2013.

SCHEDULE 4 – INFORMATION ON RELATED UNDERTAKINGS REQUIRED WHETHER PREPARING COMPANIES ACT OR IAS ACCOUNTS

Regulation 7

Part 1 – Provisions applying to all companies

SUBSIDIARY UNDERTAKINGS

1(1)   The following information must be given where at the end of the financial year the company has subsidiary undertakings.

1(2)   The name of each subsidiary undertaking must be stated.

1(3)   There must be stated with respect to each subsidiary undertaking–

   (a)   the address of the undertaking's registered office (whether in or outside the United Kingdom),

   (b)   if it is unincorporated, the address of its principal place of business.

History – Para. 1(3)(a) substituted by SI 2015/980, reg. 37(2), with effect in relation to–
   (a)   financial years beginning on or after 1 January 2016, and
   (b)   a financial year of a company beginning on or after 1 January 2015, but before 1 January 2016, if the directors of the company so decide.

FINANCIAL INFORMATION ABOUT SUBSIDIARY UNDERTAKINGS

2(1)   There must be disclosed with respect to each subsidiary undertaking not included in consolidated accounts by the company–

   (a)   the aggregate amount of its capital and reserves as at the end of its relevant financial year, and

   (b)   its profit or loss for that year.

2(2) That information need not be given if the company is exempt by virtue of section 400 or 401 of the 2006 Act from the requirement to prepare group accounts (parent company included in accounts of larger group).

2(3) That information need not be given if the company's investment in the subsidiary undertaking is included in the company's accounts by way of the equity method of valuation.

2(4) That information need not be given if—

(a) the subsidiary undertaking is not required by any provision of the 2006 Act to deliver a copy of its balance sheet for its relevant financial year and does not otherwise publish that balance sheet in the United Kingdom or elsewhere, and

(b) the company's holding is less than 50% of the nominal value of the shares in the undertaking.

2(5) Information otherwise required by this paragraph need not be given if it is not material.

2(6) For the purposes of this paragraph the **'relevant financial year'** of a subsidiary undertaking is—

(a) if its financial year ends with that of the company, that year, and

(b) if not, its financial year ending last before the end of the company's financial year.

SHARES AND DEBENTURES OF COMPANY HELD BY SUBSIDIARY UNDERTAKINGS

3(1) The number, description and amount of the shares in the company held by or on behalf of its subsidiary undertakings must be disclosed.

3(2) Sub-paragraph (1) does not apply in relation to shares in the case of which the subsidiary undertaking is concerned as personal representative or, subject as follows, as trustee.

3(3) The exception for shares in relation to which the subsidiary undertaking is concerned as trustee does not apply if the company, or any of its subsidiary undertakings, is beneficially interested under the trust, otherwise than by way of security only for the purposes of a transaction entered into by it in the ordinary course of a business which includes the lending of money.

3(4) Part 5 of this Schedule has effect for the interpretation of the reference in sub-paragraph (3) to a beneficial interest under a trust.

SIGNIFICANT HOLDINGS IN UNDERTAKINGS OTHER THAN SUBSIDIARY UNDERTAKINGS

4(1) The information required by paragraphs 5 and 6 must be given where at the end of the financial year the company has a significant holding in an undertaking which is not a subsidiary undertaking of the company, and which does not fall within paragraph 18 (joint ventures) or 19 (associated undertakings).

4(2) A holding is significant for this purpose if—

(a) it amounts to 20% or more of the nominal value of any class of shares in the undertaking, or

(b) the amount of the holding (as stated or included in the company's individual accounts) exceeds one-fifth of the amount (as so stated) of the company's assets.

5(1) The name of the undertaking must be stated.

5(2) There must be stated—

(a) the address of the undertaking's registered office (whether in or outside the United Kingdom),

(b) if it is unincorporated, the address of its principal place of business.

5(3)   There must also be stated–

(a)   the identity of each class of shares in the undertaking held by the company, and

(b)   the proportion of the nominal value of the shares of that class represented by those shares.

History – Para. 5(2)(a) substituted by SI 2015/980, reg. 37(3), with effect in relation to–
(a)   financial years beginning on or after 1 January 2016, and
(b)   a financial year of a company beginning on or after 1 January 2015, but before 1 January 2016, if the directors of the company so decide.

6(1)   Subject to paragraph 14, there must also be stated–

(a)   the aggregate amount of the capital and reserves of the undertaking as at the end of its relevant financial year, and

(b)   its profit or loss for that year.

6(2)   That information need not be given in respect of an undertaking if–

(a)   the undertaking is not required by any provision of the 2006 Act to deliver a copy of its balance sheet for its relevant financial year and does not otherwise publish that balance sheet in the United Kingdom or elsewhere, and

(b)   the company's holding is less than 50% of the nominal value of the shares in the undertaking.

6(3)   Information otherwise required by this paragraph need not be given if it is not material.

6(4)   For the purposes of this paragraph the **'relevant financial year'** of an undertaking is–

(a)   if its financial year ends with that of the company, that year, and

(b)   if not, its financial year ending last before the end of the company's financial year.

MEMBERSHIP OF CERTAIN UNDERTAKINGS

7(1)   The information required by this paragraph must be given where at the end of the financial year the company is a member of an undertaking having unlimited liability.

7(2)   There must be stated–

(a)   the name and legal form of the undertaking, and

(b)   the address of the undertaking's registered office (whether in or outside the United Kingdom) or, if it does not have such an office, its head office (whether in or outside the United Kingdom).

7(3)   Where the undertaking is a qualifying partnership there must also be stated either–

(a)   that a copy of the latest accounts of the undertaking has been or is to be appended to the copy of the company's accounts sent to the registrar under section 444 of the 2006 Act, or

(b)   the name of at least one body corporate (which may be the company) in whose group accounts the undertaking has been or is to be dealt with on a consolidated basis.

7(4)   Information otherwise required by sub-paragraph (2) need not be given if it is not material.

7(5)   Information otherwise required by sub-paragraph (3)(b) need not be given if the notes to the company's accounts disclose that advantage has been taken of the exemption conferred by regulation 7 of the Partnerships (Accounts) Regulations 2008.

7(6)   [Omitted by SI 2015/980, reg. 37(4)(b).]

7(7) In this paragraph–

'dealt with on a consolidated basis' and **'qualifying partnership'** have the same meanings as in the Partnerships (Accounts) Regulations 2008;

7(8) [Omitted by SI 2015/980, reg. 37(4)(d).]

7(9) [Omitted by SI 2015/980, reg. 37(4)(e).]

7(10) [Omitted by SI 2015/980, reg. 37(4)(f).]

History – In para. (5), 'Partnerships (Accounts) Regulations 2008' substituted for 'Partnerships and Unlimited Companies (Accounts) Regulations 1993' by SI 2008/569, reg. 17(2), with effect from 6 April 2008.

Para. (6) substituted and sub-para. (7)–(10) inserted by SI 2013/2005, reg. 6, with effect from 1 September 2013 applying in relation to a financial year of a company beginning on or after 1 October 2013.

This version of para. 7 applies to financial years beginning on or after 1 October 2013. The version applying to financial years beginning before 1 October 2013 read as follows:

"7(1) The information required by this paragraph must be given where at the end of the financial year the company is a member of a qualifying undertaking.

7(2) There must be stated–

    (a) the name and legal form of the undertaking, and

    (b) the address of the undertaking's registered office (whether in or outside the United (Kingdom) or, if it does not have such an office, its head office (whether in or outside the United Kingdom).

7(3) Where the undertaking is a qualifying partnership there must also be stated either–

    (a) that a copy of the latest accounts of the undertaking has been or is to be appended to the copy of the company's accounts sent to the registrar under section 444 of the 2006 Act, or

    (b) the name of at least one body corporate (which may be the company) in whose group accounts the undertaking has been or is to be dealt with on a consolidated basis.

7(4) Information otherwise required by sub-paragraph (2) need not be given if it is not material.

7(5) Information otherwise required by sub-paragraph (3)(b) need not be given if the notes to the company's accounts disclose that advantage has been taken of the exemption conferred by regulation 7 of the Partnerships (Accounts) Regulations 2008.

7(6) In this paragraph–

'dealt with on a consolidated basis', **'member'** and **'qualifying partnership'** have the same meanings as in the Partnerships (Accounts) Regulations 2008;

'qualifying undertaking' means–
    (a) a qualifying partnership, or
    (b) an unlimited company each of whose members is–
        (i) a limited company,
        (ii) another unlimited company each of whose members is a limited company, or
        (iii) a Scottish partnership each of whose members is a limited company, and references in this paragraph to a limited company, another unlimited company or a Scottish partnership include a comparable undertaking incorporated in or formed under the law of a country or territory outside the United Kingdom.

In para. 7(1), the words 'an undertaking having unlimited liability' substituted for the words 'a qualifying undertaking' by SI 2015/980, reg. 37(4)(a), with effect in relation to–
    (a) financial years beginning on or after 1 January 2016, and
    (b) a financial year of a company beginning on or after 1 January 2015, but before 1 January 2016, if the directors of the company so decide.

Para. 7(6) omitted by SI 2015/980, reg. 37(4)(b), with effect in relation to–
    (a) financial years beginning on or after 1 January 2016, and
    (b) a financial year of a company beginning on or after 1 January 2015, but before 1 January 2016, if the directors of the company so decide.

Former para. 7(6) read as follows:

"7(6) In sub-paragraph (1) **'member'**, in relation to a qualifying undertaking which is a qualifying partnership, has the same meaning as in the Partnerships (Accounts) Regulations 2008."

In para. 7(7), the definition of 'qualifying undertaking' omitted by SI 2015/980, reg. 37(4)(c), with effect in relation to–

    (a)   financial years beginning on or after 1 January 2016, and

    (b)   a financial year of a company beginning on or after 1 January 2015, but before 1 January 2016, if the directors of the company so decide.

Para. 7(8)–(10) omitted by SI 2015/980, reg. 37(4)(d)–(f), with effect in relation to–

    (a)   financial years beginning on or after 1 January 2016, and

    (b)   a financial year of a company beginning on or after 1 January 2015, but before 1 January 2016, if the directors of the company so decide."

Former para. 7(8)–(10) read as follows:

"7(8)   In sub-paragraph (7) the references to a limited company, another unlimited company, a Scottish partnership which is not a limited partnership or a Scottish partnership which is a limited partnership include a comparable undertaking incorporated in or formed under the law of a country or territory outside the United Kingdom.

7(9)   In sub-paragraph (7) **'general partner'** means–

    (a)   in relation to a Scottish partnership which is a limited partnership, a person who is a general partner within the meaning of the Limited Partnerships Act 1907, and

    (b)   in relation to an undertaking incorporated in or formed under the law of any country or territory outside the United Kingdom and which is comparable to a Scottish partnership which is a limited partnership, a person comparable to such a general partner.

7(10)   In sub-paragraphs (7), (8) and (9) **'limited partnership'** means a partnership registered under the Limited Partnerships Act 1907."

PARENT UNDERTAKING DRAWING UP ACCOUNTS FOR LARGER GROUP

8(1)   Where the company is a subsidiary undertaking, the following information must be given with respect to the parent undertaking of–

    (a)   the largest group of undertakings for which group accounts are drawn up and of which the company is a member, and

    (b)   the smallest such group of undertakings.

8(2)   The name of the parent undertaking must be stated.

8(3)   There must be stated–

    (a)   the address of the undertaking's registered office (whether in or outside the United Kingdom),

    (b)   if it is unincorporated, the address of its principal place of business.

8(4)   If copies of the group accounts referred to in sub-paragraph (1) are available to the public, there must also be stated the addresses from which copies of the accounts can be obtained.

History – Para. 8(3)(a) substituted by SI 2015/980, reg. 37(5), with effect in relation to–

    (a)   financial years beginning on or after 1 January 2016, and

    (b)   a financial year of a company beginning on or after 1 January 2015, but before 1 January 2016, if the directors of the company so decide.

IDENTIFICATION OF ULTIMATE PARENT COMPANY

9(1)   Where the company is a subsidiary undertaking, the following information must be given with respect to the company (if any) regarded by the directors as being the company's ultimate parent company.

9(2)   The name of that company must be stated.

9(3)   If that company is incorporated outside the United Kingdom, the country in which it is incorporated must be stated (if known to the directors).

9(4)   In this paragraph **'company'** includes any body corporate.

Part 2 – Companies not required to prepare group accounts

REASON FOR NOT PREPARING GROUP ACCOUNTS

10(1)   The reason why the company is not required to prepare group accounts must be stated.

10(2)   If the reason is that all the subsidiary undertakings of the company fall within the exclusions provided for in section 405 of the 2006 Act (Companies Act group accounts: subsidiary undertakings included in the consolidation), it must be stated with respect to each subsidiary undertaking which of those exclusions applies.

HOLDINGS IN SUBSIDIARY UNDERTAKINGS

11(1)   There must be stated in relation to shares of each class held by the company in a subsidiary undertaking–

(a)   the identity of the class, and

(b)   the proportion of the nominal value of the shares of that class represented by those shares.

11(2)   The shares held by or on behalf of the company itself must be distinguished from those attributed to the company which are held by or on behalf of a subsidiary undertaking.

FINANCIAL YEARS OF SUBSIDIARY UNDERTAKINGS

12   Where–

(a)   disclosure is made under paragraph 2(1) with respect to a subsidiary undertaking, and

(b)   that undertaking's financial year does not end with that of the company,

there must be stated in relation to that undertaking the date on which its last financial year ended (last before the end of the company's financial year).

EXEMPTION FROM GIVING INFORMATION ABOUT SIGNIFICANT HOLDINGS IN NON-SUBSIDIARY UNDERTAKINGS

13(1)   The information otherwise required by paragraph 6 (significant holdings in undertakings other than subsidiary undertaking) need not be given if–

(a)   the company is exempt by virtue of section 400 or 401 of the 2006 Act from the requirement to prepare group accounts (parent company included in accounts of larger group), and

(b)   the investment of the company in all undertakings in which it has such a holding as is mentioned in sub-paragraph (1) is shown, in aggregate, in the notes to the accounts by way of the equity method of valuation.

CONSTRUCTION OF REFERENCES TO SHARES HELD BY COMPANY

14(1)   References in Parts 1 and 2 of this Schedule to shares held by a company are to be construed as follows.

14(2)   For the purposes of paragraphs 2, 11 and 12 (information about subsidiary undertakings)–

(a)   there must be attributed to the company any shares held by a subsidiary undertaking, or by a person acting on behalf of the company or a subsidiary undertaking; but

(b)   there must be treated as not held by the company any shares held on behalf of a person other than the company or a subsidiary undertaking.

14(3)   For the purposes of paragraphs 4 to 6 (information about undertakings other than subsidiary undertakings)–

(a) there must be attributed to the company shares held on its behalf by any person; but

(b) there must be treated as not held by a company shares held on behalf of a person other than the company.

14(4) For the purposes of any of those provisions, shares held by way of security must be treated as held by the person providing the security–

(a) where apart from the right to exercise them for the purpose of preserving the value of the security, or of realising it, the rights attached to the shares are exercisable only in accordance with that person's instructions, and

(b) where the shares are held in connection with the granting of loans as part of normal business activities and apart from the right to exercise them for the purpose of preserving the value of the security, or of realising it, the rights attached to the shares are exercisable only in that person's interests.

Part 3 – Companies required to prepare group accounts

INTRODUCTORY

15 In this Part of this Schedule **'the group'** means the group consisting of the parent company and its subsidiary undertakings.

SUBSIDIARY UNDERTAKINGS

16(1) In addition to the information required by paragraph 2, the following information must also be given with respect to the undertakings which are subsidiary undertakings of the parent company at the end of the financial year.

16(2) It must be stated whether the subsidiary undertaking is included in the consolidation and, if it is not, the reasons for excluding it from consolidation must be given.

16(3) It must be stated with respect to each subsidiary undertaking by virtue of which of the conditions specified in section 1162(2) or (4) of the 2006 Act it is a subsidiary undertaking of its immediate parent undertaking.

That information need not be given if the relevant condition is that specified in subsection (2)(a) of that section (holding of a majority of the voting rights) and the immediate parent undertaking holds the same proportion of the shares in the undertaking as it holds voting rights.

HOLDINGS IN SUBSIDIARY UNDERTAKINGS

17(1) The following information must be given with respect to the shares of a subsidiary undertaking held–

(a) by the parent company, and
(b) by the group,

and the information under paragraphs (a) and (b) must (if different) be shown separately.

17(2) There must be stated–

(a) the identity of each class of shares held, and
(b) the proportion of the nominal value of the shares of that class represented by those shares.

JOINT VENTURES

18(1) The following information must be given where an undertaking is dealt with in the consolidated accounts by the method of proportional consolidation in accordance with paragraph 18 of Schedule 6 to these Regulations (joint ventures)–

(a) the name of the undertaking,

(b) the address of the undertaking's registered office (whether in or outside the United Kingdom),

(c) the factors on which joint management of the undertaking is based, and

(d) the proportion of the capital of the undertaking held by undertakings included in the consolidation.

18(2) Where the financial year of the undertaking did not end with that of the company, there must be stated the date on which a financial year of the undertaking last ended before that date.

History – Para. 18(1)(a) and (b) substituted by SI 2016/575, reg. 66, with effect in relation to–

(a) financial years beginning on or after 1 January 2016; and

(b) a financial year of an LLP beginning on or after 1 January 2015, but before 1 January 2016, if–

(i) the members of the LLP so decide; and

(ii) copy of the LLP's accounts for that financial year has not been delivered to the registrar in accordance with CA 2006, s. 444, 445 or 446 as applied to LLPs by the 2008 Regulations before the date on which these Regulations come into force.

Para. 18(1)(a) substituted by SI 2015/980, reg. 38(2), with effect in relation to–

(a) financial years beginning on or after 1 January 2016, and

(b) a financial year of a company beginning on or after 1 January 2015, but before 1 January 2016, if the directors of the company so decide.

ASSOCIATED UNDERTAKINGS

19(1) The following information must be given where an undertaking included in the consolidation has an interest in an associated undertaking.

19(2) The name of the associated undertaking must be stated.

19(3) There must be stated–

(a) if the undertaking is incorporated outside the United Kingdom, the country in which it is incorporated,

(b) the address of the undertaking's registered office (whether in or outside the United Kingdom).

19(4) The following information must be given with respect to the shares of the undertaking held–

(a) by the parent company, and

(b) by the group,

and the information under paragraphs (a) and (b) must be shown separately.

19(5) There must be stated–

(a) the identity of each class of shares held, and

(b) the proportion of the nominal value of the shares of that class represented by those shares.

19(6) In this paragraph **'associated undertaking'** has the meaning given by paragraph 19 of Schedule 6 to these Regulations; and the information required by this paragraph must be given notwithstanding that paragraph 21(3) of that Schedule (materiality) applies in relation to the accounts themselves.

History – Para. 19(3)(b) substituted by SI 2015/980, reg. 38(3), with effect in relation to–
  (a) financial years beginning on or after 1 January 2016, and
  (b) a financial year of a company beginning on or after 1 January 2015, but before 1 January 2016, if the directors of the company so decide.

REQUIREMENT TO GIVE INFORMATION ABOUT OTHER SIGNIFICANT HOLDINGS OF PARENT COMPANY OR GROUP

20(1)   The information required by paragraphs 5 and 6 must also be given where at the end of the financial year the group has a significant holding in an undertaking which is not a subsidiary undertaking of the parent company and does not fall within paragraph 18 (joint ventures) or 19 (associated undertakings), as though the references to the company in those paragraphs were a reference to the group.

20(2)   A holding is significant for this purpose if–

  (a)   it amounts to 20% or more of the nominal value of any class of shares in the undertaking, or

  (b)   the amount of the holding (as stated or included in the group accounts) exceeds one-fifth of the amount of the group's assets (as so stated).

20(3)   For the purposes of those paragraphs as applied to a group the **'relevant financial year'** of an outside undertaking is–

  (a)   if its financial year ends with that of the parent company, that year, and

  (b)   if not, its financial year ending last before the end of the parent company's financial year.

GROUP'S MEMBERSHIP OF CERTAIN UNDERTAKINGS

21   The information required by paragraph 7 must also be given where at the end of the financial year the group is a member of an undertaking having unlimited liability.

History – In para. 21, the words 'an undertaking having unlimited liability' substituted for the words 'a qualifying undertaking' by SI 2015/980, reg. 38(4), with effect in relation to–
  (a) financial years beginning on or after 1 January 2016, and
  (b) a financial year of a company beginning on or after 1 January 2015, but before 1 January 2016, if the directors of the company so decide.

CONSTRUCTION OF REFERENCES TO SHARES HELD BY PARENT COMPANY OR GROUP

22(1)   References in Parts 1 and 3 of this Schedule to shares held by that parent company or group are to be construed as follows.

22(2)   For the purposes of paragraphs 4 to 6, 17, 19(4) and (5) and 12 (information about holdings in subsidiary and other undertakings)–

  (a)   there must be attributed to the parent company shares held on its behalf by any person; but

  (b)   there must be treated as not held by the parent company shares held on behalf of a person other than the company.

22(3)   References to shares held by the group are to any shares held by or on behalf of the parent company or any of its subsidiary undertakings; but any shares held on behalf of a person other than the parent company or any of its subsidiary undertakings are not to be treated as held by the group.

22(4)   Shares held by way of security must be treated as held by the person providing the security–

(a)   where apart from the right to exercise them for the purpose of preserving the value of the security, or of realising it, the rights attached to the shares are exercisable only in accordance with his instructions, and

(b)   where the shares are held in connection with the granting of loans as part of normal business activities and apart from the right to exercise them for the purpose of preserving the value of the security, or of realising it, the rights attached to the shares are exercisable only in his interests.

Part 4 – Additional disclosures for banking companies and groups

23(1)   This paragraph applies where accounts are prepared in accordance with the special provisions of Schedules 2 and 6 relating to banking companies or groups.

23(2)   The information required by paragraph 5 of this Schedule, modified where applicable by paragraph 20 (information about significant holdings of the company or group in undertakings other than subsidiary undertakings) need only be given in respect of undertakings (otherwise falling within the class of undertakings in respect of which disclosure is required) in which the company or group has a significant holding amounting to 20% or more of the nominal value of the shares in the undertaking.

In addition any information required by those paragraphs may be omitted if it is not material.

23(3)   Paragraphs 14(3) and (4) and 22(3) and (4) of this Schedule apply with necessary modifications for the purposes of this paragraph.

Part 5 – Interpretation of references to 'beneficial interest'
RESIDUAL INTERESTS UNDER PENSION AND EMPLOYEES' SHARE SCHEMES

24(1)   Where shares in an undertaking are held on trust for the purposes of a pension scheme or an employees' share scheme, there must be disregarded any residual interest which has not vested in possession, being an interest of the undertaking or any of its subsidiary undertakings.

24(2)   In this paragraph a **'residual interest'** means a right of the undertaking in question (the 'residual beneficiary') to receive any of the trust property in the event of–

(a)   all the liabilities arising under the scheme having been satisfied or provided for, or
(b)   the residual beneficiary ceasing to participate in the scheme, or
(c)   the trust property at any time exceeding what is necessary for satisfying the liabilities arising or expected to arise under the scheme.

24(3)   In sub-paragraph (2) references to a right include a right dependent on the exercise of a discretion vested by the scheme in the trustee or any other person; and references to liabilities arising under a scheme include liabilities that have resulted or may result from the exercise of any such discretion.

24(4)   For the purposes of this paragraph a residual interest vests in possession–

(a)   in a case within sub-paragraph (2)(a), on the occurrence of the event there mentioned, whether or not the amount of the property receivable pursuant to the right mentioned in that sub-paragraph is then ascertained,

(b)   in a case within sub-paragraph (2)(b) or (c), when the residual beneficiary becomes entitled to require the trustee to transfer to that beneficiary any of the property receivable pursuant to that right.

EMPLOYER'S CHARGES AND OTHER RIGHTS OF RECOVERY

25(1) Where shares in an undertaking are held on trust there must be disregarded–

(a) if the trust is for the purposes of a pension scheme, any such rights as are mentioned in sub-paragraph (2),

(b) if the trust is for the purposes of an employees' share scheme, any such rights as are mentioned in paragraph(a) of that sub-paragraph,

being rights of the undertaking or any of its subsidiary undertakings.

25(2) The rights referred to are–

(a) any charge or lien on, or set-off against, any benefit or other right or interest under the scheme for the purpose of enabling the employer or former employer of a member of the scheme to obtain the discharge of a monetary obligation due to him from the member, and

(b) any right to receive from the trustee of the scheme, or as trustee of the scheme to retain, an amount that can be recovered or retained under section 61 of the Pension Schemes Act 1993 or section 57 of the Pension Schemes (Northern Ireland) Act 1993 (deduction of contributions equivalent premium from refund of scheme contributions) or otherwise as reimbursement or partial reimbursement for any contributions equivalent premium paid in connection with the scheme under Chapter 3 of Part 3 of that Act.

TRUSTEE'S RIGHT TO EXPENSES, REMUNERATION, INDEMNITY ETC.

26 Where an undertaking is a trustee, there must be disregarded any rights which the undertaking has in its capacity as trustee including, in particular, any right to recover its expenses or be remunerated out of the trust property and any right to be indemnified out of that property for any liability incurred by reason of any act or omission of the undertaking in the performance of its duties as trustee.

SUPPLEMENTARY

27(1) This Schedule applies in relation to debentures as it applies in relation to shares.

27(2) **'Pension scheme'** means any scheme for the provision of benefits consisting of or including relevant benefits for or in respect of employees or former employees; and **'relevant benefits'** means any pension, lump sum, gratuity or other like benefit given or to be given on retirement or on death or in anticipation of retirement or, in connection with past service, after retirement or death.

27(3) In sub-paragraph (2) of this paragraph and in paragraph 25(2) **'employee'** and **'employer'** are to be read as if a director of an undertaking were employed by it.

SCHEDULE 5 – INFORMATION ABOUT BENEFITS OF DIRECTORS

Regulation 8

Part 1 – Provisions applying to quoted and unquoted companies

TOTAL AMOUNT OF DIRECTORS' REMUNERATION ETC.

1(1) There must be shown–

(a) the aggregate amount of remuneration paid to or receivable by directors in respect of qualifying services;

(b) the aggregate of the amount of gains made by directors on the exercise of share options;

(c) the aggregate of the amount of money paid to or receivable by directors, and the net value of assets (other than money and share options) received or receivable by directors, under long term incentive schemes in respect of qualifying services; and

(d)   the aggregate value of any company contributions–

   (i)   paid, or treated as paid, to a pension scheme in respect of directors' qualifying services, and

   (ii)   by reference to which the rate or amount of any money purchase benefits that may become payable will be calculated.

1(2)   There must be shown the number of directors (if any) to whom retirement benefits are accruing in respect of qualifying services–

(a)   under money purchase schemes, and

(b)   under defined benefit schemes.

1(3)   In the case of a company which is not a quoted company and whose equity share capital is not listed on the market known as AIM–

(a)   sub-paragraph (1) has effect as if paragraph (b) were omitted and, in paragraph (c), 'assets' did not include shares; and

(b)   the number of each of the following (if any) must be shown, namely–

   (i)   the directors who exercised share options, and

   (ii)   the directors in respect of whose qualifying services shares were received or receivable under long term incentive schemes.

Part 2 – Provisions applying only to unquoted companies

DETAILS OF HIGHEST PAID DIRECTOR'S EMOLUMENTS ETC.

2(1)   Where the aggregates shown under paragraph 1(1)(a), (b) and (c) total £200,000 or more, there must be shown–

(a)   so much of the total of those aggregates as is attributable to the highest paid director, and

(b)   so much of the aggregate mentioned in paragraph 1(1)(d) as is so attributable.

2(2)   Where sub-paragraph (1) applies and the highest paid director has performed qualifying services during the financial year by reference to which the rate or amount of any defined benefits that may become payable will be calculated, there must also be shown–

(a)   the amount at the end of the year of his accrued pension, and

(b)   where applicable, the amount at the end of the year of his accrued lump sum.

2(3)   Subject to sub-paragraph (4), where sub-paragraph (1) applies in the case of a company which is not a listed company, there must also be shown–

(a)   whether the highest paid director exercised any share options, and

(b)   whether any shares were received or receivable by that director in respect of qualifying services under a long term incentive scheme.

2(4)   Where the highest paid director has not been involved in any of the transactions specified in sub-paragraph (3), that fact need not be stated.

EXCESS RETIREMENT BENEFITS OF DIRECTORS AND PAST DIRECTORS

3(1)   Subject to sub-paragraph (2), there must be shown the aggregate amount of–

(a)   so much of retirement benefits paid to or receivable by directors under pension schemes, and

(b)   so much of retirement benefits paid to or receivable by past directors under such schemes, as (in each case) is in excess of the retirement benefits to which they were respectively entitled on the date on which the benefits first became payable or 31st March 1997, whichever is the later.

3(2)   Amounts paid or receivable under a pension scheme need not be included in the aggregate amount if–

(a)   the funding of the scheme was such that the amounts were or, as the case may be, could have been paid without recourse to additional contributions, and

(b)   amounts were paid to or receivable by all pensioner members of the scheme on the same basis.

3(3)   In sub-paragraph (2), **'pensioner member'**, in relation to a pension scheme, means any person who is entitled to the present payment of retirement benefits under the scheme.

3(4)   In this paragraph–

(a)   references to retirement benefits include benefits otherwise than in cash, and

(b)   in relation to so much of retirement benefits as consists of a benefit otherwise than in cash, references to their amount are to the estimated money value of the benefit,

and the nature of any such benefit must also be disclosed.

COMPENSATION TO DIRECTORS FOR LOSS OF OFFICE

4(1)   There must be shown the aggregate amount of any compensation to directors or past directors in respect of loss of office.

4(2)   This includes compensation received or receivable by a director or past director–

(a)   for loss of office as director of the company, or

(b)   for loss, while director of the company or on or in connection with his ceasing to be a director of it, of–

(i)   any other office in connection with the management of the company's affairs, or

(ii)   any office as director or otherwise in connection with the management of the affairs of any subsidiary undertaking of the company.

4(3)   In this paragraph references to compensation for loss of office include–

(a)   compensation in consideration for, or in connection with, a person's retirement from office, and

(b)   where such a retirement is occasioned by a breach of the person's contract with the company or with a subsidiary undertaking of the company–

(i)   payments made by way of damages for the breach, or

(ii)   payments made by way of settlement or compromise of any claim in respect of the breach.

4(4)   In this paragraph–

(a)   references to compensation include benefits otherwise than in cash, and

(b)   in relation to such compensation references to its amount are to the estimated money value of the benefit.

The nature of any such compensation must be disclosed.

SUMS PAID TO THIRD PARTIES IN RESPECT OF DIRECTORS' SERVICES

5(1)   There must be shown the aggregate amount of any consideration paid to or receivable by third parties for making available the services of any person–

    (a)   as a director of the company, or

    (b)   while director of the company–

        (i)   as director of any of its subsidiary undertakings, or

        (ii)   otherwise in connection with the management of the affairs of the company or any of its subsidiary undertakings.

5(2)   In sub-paragraph (1)–

    (a)   the reference to consideration includes benefits otherwise than in cash, and

    (b)   in relation to such consideration the reference to its amount is to the estimated money value of the benefit.

The nature of any such consideration must be disclosed.

5(3)   For the purposes of this paragraph a **'third party'** means a person other than–

    (a)   the director himself or a person connected with him or a body corporate controlled by him, or

    (b)   the company or any of its subsidiary undertakings.

Part 3 – Supplementary provisions

GENERAL NATURE OF OBLIGATIONS

6(1)   This Schedule requires information to be given only so far as it is contained in the company's books and papers or the company has the right to obtain it from the persons concerned.

6(2)   For the purposes of this Schedule any information is treated as shown if it is capable of being readily ascertained from other information which is shown.

PROVISIONS AS TO AMOUNTS TO BE SHOWN

7(1)   The following provisions apply with respect to the amounts to be shown under this Schedule.

7(2)   The amount in each case includes all relevant sums, whether paid by or receivable from the company, any of the company's subsidiary undertakings or any other person.

7(3)   References to amounts paid to or receivable by a person include amounts paid to or receivable by a person connected with him or a body corporate controlled by him (but not so as to require an amount to be counted twice).

7(4)   Except as otherwise provided, the amounts to be shown for any financial year are–

    (a)   the sums receivable in respect of that year (whenever paid), or

    (b)   in the case of sums not receivable in respect of a period, the sums paid during that year.

7(5)   Sums paid by way of expenses allowance that are charged to United Kingdom income tax after the end of the relevant financial year must be shown in a note to the first accounts in which it is practicable to show them and must be distinguished from the amounts to be shown apart from this provision.

7(6)   Where it is necessary to do so for the purpose of making any distinction required in complying with this Schedule, the directors may apportion payments between the matters in respect of which they have been paid or are receivable in such manner as they think appropriate.

EXCLUSION OF SUMS LIABLE TO BE ACCOUNTED FOR TO COMPANY ETC.

8(1) The amounts to be shown under this Schedule do not include any sums that are to be accounted for–

(a) to the company or any of its subsidiary undertakings, or

(b) by virtue of sections 219 and 222(3) of the 2006 Act (payments in connection with share transfers: duty to account) to persons who sold their shares as a result of the offer made.

8(2) Where–

(a) any such sums are not shown in a note to the accounts for the relevant financial year on the ground that the person receiving them is liable to account for them, and

(b) the liability is afterwards wholly or partly released or is not enforced within a period of two years,

those sums, to the extent to which the liability is released or not enforced, must be shown in a note to the first accounts in which it is practicable to show them and must be distinguished from the amounts to be shown apart from this provision.

MEANING OF 'REMUNERATION'

9(1) In this Schedule **'remuneration'** of a director includes–

(a) salary, fees and bonuses, sums paid by way of expenses allowance (so far as they are chargeable to United Kingdom income tax), and

(b) subject to sub-paragraph (2), the estimated money value of any other benefits received by the director otherwise than in cash.

9(2) The expression does not include–

(a) the value of any share options granted to the director or the amount of any gains made on the exercise of any such options,

(b) any company contributions paid, or treated as paid, under any pension scheme or any benefits to which the director is entitled under any such scheme, or

(c) any money or other assets paid to or received or receivable by the director under any long term incentive scheme.

MEANING OF 'HIGHEST PAID DIRECTOR'

10 In this Schedule, **'the highest paid director'** means the director to whom is attributable the greatest part of the total of the aggregates shown under paragraph 1(1)(a),(b) and (c).

MEANING OF 'LONG TERM INCENTIVE SCHEME'

11(1) In this Schedule **'long term incentive scheme'** means an agreement or arrangement–

(a) under which money or other assets may become receivable by a director, and

(b) which includes one or more qualifying conditions with respect to service or performance which cannot be fulfilled within a single financial year.

11(2) For this purpose the following must be disregarded–

(a) bonuses the amount of which falls to be determined by reference to service or performance within a single financial year;

(b) compensation for loss of office, payments for breach of contract and other termination payments; and

(c) retirement benefits.

MEANING OF 'SHARES' AND 'SHARE OPTION' AND RELATED EXPRESSIONS

12   In this Schedule–

(a)   **'shares'** means shares (whether allotted or not) in the company, or any undertaking which is a group undertaking in relation to the company, and includes a share warrant as defined by section 779(1) of the 2006 Act; and

(b)   **'share option'** means a right to acquire shares.

MEANING OF 'PENSION SCHEME' AND RELATED EXPRESSIONS

13(1)   In this Schedule–

'pension scheme' means a retirement benefits scheme as defined by section 611 of the Income and Corporation Taxes Act 1988; and

'retirement benefits' has the meaning given by section 612(1) of that Act.

13(2)   In this Schedule **'accrued pension'** and **'accrued lump sum'**, in relation to any pension scheme and any director, mean respectively the amount of the annual pension, and the amount of the lump sum, which would be payable under the scheme on his attaining normal pension age if–

(a)   he had left the company's service at the end of the financial year,

(b)   there was no increase in the general level of prices in the United Kingdom during the period beginning with the end of that year and ending with his attaining that age,

(c)   no question arose of any commutation of the pension or inverse commutation of the lump sum, and

(d)   any amounts attributable to voluntary contributions paid by the director to the scheme, and any money purchase benefits which would be payable under the scheme, were disregarded.

13(3)   In this Schedule, **'company contributions'**, in relation to a pension scheme and a director, means any payments (including insurance premiums) made, or treated as made, to the scheme in respect of the director by a person other than the director.

13(4)   In this Schedule, in relation to a director–

'defined benefits' means retirement benefits payable under a pension scheme that are not money purchase benefits;

'defined benefit scheme' means a pension scheme that is not a money purchase scheme;

'money purchase benefits' means retirement benefits payable under a pension scheme the rate or amount of which is calculated by reference to payments made, or treated as made, by the director or by any other person in respect of the director and which are not average salary benefits; and

'money purchase scheme' means a pension scheme under which all of the benefits that may become payable to or in respect of the director are money purchase benefits.

13(5)   In this Schedule, **'normal pension age'**, in relation to any pension scheme and any director, means the age at which the director will first become entitled to receive a full pension on retirement of an amount determined without reduction to take account of its payment before a later age (but disregarding any entitlement to pension upon retirement in the event of illness, incapacity or redundancy).

13(6)   Where a pension scheme provides for any benefits that may become payable to or in respect of any director to be whichever are the greater of–

(a) money purchase benefits as determined by or under the scheme; and

(b) defined benefits as so determined,

the company may assume for the purposes of this paragraph that those benefits will be money purchase benefits, or defined benefits, according to whichever appears more likely at the end of the financial year.

13(7) For the purpose of determining whether a pension scheme is a money purchase or defined benefit scheme, any death in service benefits provided for by the scheme are to be disregarded.

REFERENCES TO SUBSIDIARY UNDERTAKINGS

14(1) Any reference in this Schedule to a subsidiary undertaking of the company, in relation to a person who is or was, while a director of the company, a director also, by virtue of the company's nomination (direct or indirect) of any other undertaking, includes that undertaking, whether or not it is or was in fact a subsidiary undertaking of the company.

14(2) Any reference to a subsidiary undertaking of the company–

(a) for the purposes of paragraph 1 (remuneration etc.) is to an undertaking which is a subsidiary undertaking at the time the services were rendered, and

(b) for the purposes of paragraph 4 (compensation for loss of office) is to a subsidiary undertaking immediately before the loss of office as director.

OTHER MINOR DEFINITIONS

15(1) In this Schedule–

'net value', in relation to any assets received or receivable by a director, means value after deducting any money paid or other value given by the director in respect of those assets;

'qualifying services', in relation to any person, means his services as a director of the company, and his services while director of the company–

(a) as director of any of its subsidiary undertakings; or

(b) otherwise in connection with the management of the affairs of the company or any of its subsidiary undertakings.

15(2) References in this Schedule to a person being 'connected' with a director, and to a director 'controlling' a body corporate, are to be construed in accordance with sections 252 to 255 of the 2006 Act.

15(3) For the purposes of this Schedule, remuneration paid or receivable or share options granted in respect of a person's accepting office as a director are treated as emoluments paid or receivable or share options granted in respect of his services as a director.

SCHEDULE 6 – COMPANIES ACT GROUP ACCOUNTS
Regulation 9

Part 1 – General rules
GENERAL RULES

1(1) Group accounts must comply so far as practicable with the provisions of Schedule 1 to these Regulations as if the undertakings included in the consolidation ('the group') were a single company (see Parts 2 and 3 of this Schedule for modifications for banking and insurance groups).

1(2) Where the parent company is treated as an investment company for the purposes of Part 5 of Schedule 1 (special provisions for investment companies) the group must be similarly treated.

2(1) The consolidated balance sheet and profit and loss account must incorporate in full the information contained in the individual accounts of the undertakings included in the consolidation, subject to the adjustments authorised or required by the following provisions of this Schedule and to such other adjustments (if any) as may be appropriate in accordance with generally accepted accounting principles or practice.

2(1A) Group accounts must be drawn up as at the same date as the accounts of the parent company.

2(2) If the financial year of a subsidiary undertaking included in the consolidation does not end with that of the parent company, the group accounts must be made up–

(a) from the accounts of the subsidiary undertaking for its financial year last ending before the end of the parent company's financial year, provided that year ended no more than three months before that of the parent company, or

(b) from interim accounts prepared by the subsidiary undertaking as at the end of the parent company's financial year.

History – Para. 2(1A) inserted by SI 2015/980, reg. 39(2), with effect in relation to–
(a) financial years beginning on or after 1 January 2016, and
(b) a financial year of a company beginning on or after 1 January 2015, but before 1 January 2016, if the directors of the company so decide.

3(1) Where assets and liabilities to be included in the group accounts have been valued or otherwise determined by undertakings according to accounting rules differing from those used for the group accounts, the values or amounts must be adjusted so as to accord with the rules used for the group accounts.

3(2) If it appears to the directors of the parent company that there are special reasons for departing from sub-paragraph (1) they may do so, but particulars of any such departure, the reasons for it and its effect must be given in a note to the accounts.

3(3) The adjustments referred to in this paragraph need not be made if they are not material for the purpose of giving a true and fair view.

4 Any differences of accounting rules as between a parent company's individual accounts for a financial year and its group accounts must be disclosed in a note to the latter accounts and the reasons for the difference given.

5 Amounts that in the particular context of any provision of this Schedule are not material may be disregarded for the purposes of that provision.

ELIMINATION OF GROUP TRANSACTIONS

6(1) Debts and claims between undertakings included in the consolidation, and income and expenditure relating to transactions between such undertakings, must be eliminated in preparing the group accounts.

6(2) Where profits and losses resulting from transactions between undertakings included in the consolidation are included in the book value of assets, they must be eliminated in preparing group accounts.

6(3) The elimination required by sub-paragraph (2) may be effected in proportion to the group's interest in the shares of the undertakings.

6(4) Sub-paragraphs (1) and (2) need not be complied with if the amounts concerned are not material for the purpose of giving a true and fair view.

ACQUISITION AND MERGER ACCOUNTING

7(1)   The following provisions apply where an undertaking becomes a subsidiary undertaking of the parent company.

7(2)   That event is referred to in those provisions as an 'acquisition', and references to the 'undertaking acquired' are to be construed accordingly.

8   An acquisition must be accounted for by the acquisition method of accounting unless the conditions for accounting for it as a merger are met and the merger method of accounting is adopted.

9(1)   The acquisition method of accounting is as follows.

9(2)   The identifiable assets and liabilities of the undertaking acquired must be included in the consolidated balance sheet at their fair values as at the date of acquisition.

9(3)   The income and expenditure of the undertaking acquired must be brought into the group accounts only as from the date of the acquisition.

9(4)   There must be set off against the acquisition cost of the interest in the shares of the undertaking held by the parent company and its subsidiary undertakings the interest of the parent company and its subsidiary undertakings in the adjusted capital and reserves of the undertaking acquired.

9(5)   The resulting amount if positive must be treated as goodwill, and if negative as a negative consolidation difference.

9(6)   Negative goodwill may be transferred to the consolidated profit and loss account where such a treatment is in accordance with the principles and rules of Part 2 of Schedule 1 to these Regulations.

History – Para. 9(6) inserted by SI 2015/980, reg. 39(3), with effect in relation to–
   (a)   financial years beginning on or after 1 January 2016, and
   (b)   a financial year of a company beginning on or after 1 January 2015, but before 1 January 2016, if the directors of the company so decide.

10   The conditions for accounting for an acquisition as a merger are–

   (a)   that the undertaking whose shares are acquired is ultimately controlled by the same party both before and after the acquisition,

   (b)   that the control referred to in paragraph (a) is not transitory, and

   (c)   that adoption of the merger method accords with generally accepted accounting principles or practice.

History – Para. 10 substituted by SI 2015/980, reg. 39(4), with effect in relation to–
   (a)   financial years beginning on or after 1 January 2016, and
   (b)   a financial year of a company beginning on or after 1 January 2015, but before 1 January 2016, if the directors of the company so decide.

Former para. 10 read as follows:
"10(1)   The conditions for accounting for an acquisition as a merger are–

   (a)   that at least 90% of the nominal value of the relevant shares in the undertaking acquired (excluding any shares in the undertaking held as treasury shares) is held by or on behalf of the parent company and its subsidiary undertakings,

   (b)   that the proportion referred to in paragraph (a) was attained pursuant to an arrangement providing for the issue of equity shares by the parent company or one or more of its subsidiary undertakings,

    (c)   that the fair value of any consideration other than the issue of equity shares given pursuant to the arrangement by the parent company and its subsidiary undertakings did not exceed 10% of the nominal value of the equity shares issued, and

    (d)   that adoption of the merger method of accounting accords with generally accepted accounting principles or practice.

10(2)   The reference in sub-paragraph (1)(a) to the **'relevant shares'** in an undertaking acquired is to those carrying unrestricted rights to participate both in distributions and in the assets of the undertaking upon liquidation."

11(1)   The merger method of accounting is as follows.

11(2)   The assets and liabilities of the undertaking acquired must be brought into the group accounts at the figures at which they stand in the undertaking's accounts, subject to any adjustment authorised or required by this Schedule.

11(3)   The income and expenditure of the undertaking acquired must be included in the group accounts for the entire financial year, including the period before the acquisition.

11(4)   The group accounts must show corresponding amounts relating to the previous financial year as if the undertaking acquired had been included in the consolidation throughout that year.

11(5)   There must be set off against the aggregate of–

    (a)   the appropriate amount in respect of qualifying shares issued by the parent company or its subsidiary undertakings in consideration for the acquisition of shares in the undertaking acquired, and

    (b)   the fair value of any other consideration for the acquisition of shares in the undertaking acquired, determined as at the date when those shares were acquired,

the nominal value of the issued share capital of the undertaking acquired held by the parent company and its subsidiary undertakings.

11(6)   The resulting amount must be shown as an adjustment to the consolidated reserves.

11(7)   In sub-paragraph (5)(a) **'qualifying shares'** means–

(a)   in relation to which any of the following provisions applies (merger relief), and in respect of which the appropriate amount is the nominal value–

    (i)   section 131 of the Companies Act 1985,

    (ii)   Article 141 of the Companies (Northern Ireland) Order 1986, or

    (iii)   section 612 of the 2006 Act, or

(b)   shares in relation to which any of the following provisions applies (group reconstruction relief), and in respect of which the appropriate amount is the nominal value together with any minimum premium value within the meaning of that section–

    (i)   section 132 of the Companies Act 1985,

    (ii)   Article 142 of the Companies (Northern Ireland) Order 1986, or

    (iii)   section 611 of the 2006 Act.

12(1)   Where a group is acquired, paragraphs 9 to 11 apply with the following adaptations.

12(2)   References to shares of the undertaking acquired are to be construed as references to shares of the parent undertaking of the group.

12(3)   Other references to the undertaking acquired are to be construed as references to the group; and references to the assets and liabilities, income and expenditure and capital and reserves of the undertaking acquired must be construed as references to the assets and liabilities, income and expenditure and capital and reserves of the group after making the set-offs and other adjustments required by this Schedule in the case of group accounts.

13(1) The following information with respect to acquisitions taking place in the financial year must be given in a note to the accounts.

13(2) There must be stated–

(a) the name of the undertaking acquired or, where a group was acquired, the name of the parent undertaking of that group, and

(b) whether the acquisition has been accounted for by the acquisition or the merger method of accounting;

and in relation to an acquisition which significantly affects the figures shown in the group accounts, the following further information must be given.

13(3) The composition and fair value of the consideration for the acquisition given by the parent company and its subsidiary undertakings must be stated.

13(4) Where the acquisition method of accounting has been adopted, the book values immediately prior to the acquisition, and the fair values at the date of acquisition, of each class of assets and liabilities of the undertaking or group acquired must be stated in tabular form, including a statement of the amount of any goodwill or negative consolidation difference arising on the acquisition, together with an explanation of any significant adjustments made.

13(5) In ascertaining for the purposes of sub-paragraph (4) the profit or loss of a group, the book values and fair values of assets and liabilities of a group or the amount of the assets and liabilities of a group, the set-offs and other adjustments required by this Schedule in the case of group accounts must be made.

14(1) There must also be stated in a note to the accounts the cumulative amount of goodwill resulting from acquisitions in that and earlier financial years which has been written off otherwise than in the consolidated profit and loss account for that or any earlier financial year.

14(2) That figure must be shown net of any goodwill attributable to subsidiary undertakings or businesses disposed of prior to the balance sheet date.

15 Where during the financial year there has been a disposal of an undertaking or group which significantly affects the figure shown in the group accounts, there must be stated in a note to the accounts–

(a) the name of that undertaking or, as the case may be, of the parent undertaking of that group, and

(b) the extent to which the profit or loss shown in the group accounts is attributable to profit or loss of that undertaking or group.

16 The information required by paragraph 13, 14 or 15 need not be disclosed with respect to an undertaking which–

(a) is established under the law of a country outside the United Kingdom, or

(b) carries on business outside the United Kingdom,

if in the opinion of the directors of the parent company the disclosure would be seriously prejudicial to the business of that undertaking or to the business of the parent company or any of its subsidiary undertakings and the Secretary of State agrees that the information should not be disclosed.

16A Where an acquisition has taken place in the financial year and the merger method of accounting has been adopted, the notes to the accounts must also disclose–

(a) the address of the registered office of the undertaking acquired (whether in or outside the United Kingdom),

(b) the name of the party referred to in paragraph 10(a),

(c)   the address of the registered office of that party (whether in or outside the United Kingdom), and

(d)   the information referred to in paragraph 11(6).

History – Para. 16A inserted by SI 2015/980, reg. 39(5), with effect in relation to–
(a)   financial years beginning on or after 1 January 2016, and
(b)   a financial year of a company beginning on or after 1 January 2015, but before 1 January 2016, if the directors of the company so decide.

NON-CONTROLLING INTERESTS

17(1)   The formats set out in Schedule 1 to these Regulations have effect in relation to group accounts with the following additions.

17(2)   In the balance sheet formats there must be shown, as a separate item and under the heading 'non-controlling interests', the amount of capital and reserves attributable to shares in subsidiary undertakings included in the consolidation held by or on behalf of persons other than the parent company and its subsidiary undertakings.

17(3)   In the profit and loss account formats there must be shown, as a separate item and under the heading 'non-controlling interests', the amount of any profit or loss attributable to shares in subsidiary undertakings included in the consolidation held by or on behalf of persons other than the parent company and its subsidiary undertakings.

17(4)   For the purposes of paragraph 4(1) and (2) of Schedule 1 (power to adapt or combine items)–

(a)   the additional item required by sub-paragraph (2) above is treated as one to which a letter is assigned, and

(b)   the additional item required by sub-paragraph (3) above is treated as one to which an Arabic number is assigned.

History – Para. 17 and the heading preceding it substituted by SI 2015/980, reg. 39(6), with effect in relation to–
(a)   financial years beginning on or after 1 January 2016, and
(b)   a financial year of a company beginning on or after 1 January 2015, but before 1 January 2016, if the directors of the company so decide.

Former para. 17 read as follows:

"MINORITY INTERESTS

17(1)   The formats set out in Schedule 1 to these Regulations have effect in relation to group accounts with the following additions.

17(2)   In the balance sheet formats there must be shown, as a separate item and under an appropriate heading, the amount of capital and reserves attributable to shares in subsidiary undertakings included in the consolidation held by or on behalf of persons other than the parent company and its subsidiary undertakings.

17(3)   In the profit and loss account formats there must be shown, as a separate item and under an appropriate heading–

(a)   the amount of any profit or loss on ordinary activities, and
(b)   the amount of any profit or loss on extraordinary activities, attributable to shares in subsidiary undertakings included in the consolidation held by or on behalf of persons other than the parent company and its subsidiary undertakings.

17(4)   For the purposes of paragraph 4(1) and (2) of Schedule 1 (power to adapt or combine items)–

(a)   the additional item required by sub-paragraph (2) above is treated as one to which a letter is assigned, and
(b)   the additional items required by sub-paragraph (3)(a) and (b) above are treated as ones to which an Arabic number is assigned."

JOINT VENTURES

18(1)   Where an undertaking included in the consolidation manages another undertaking jointly with one or more undertakings not included in the consolidation, that other undertaking ('the joint venture') may, if it is not–

(a)   a body corporate, or

(b)   a subsidiary undertaking of the parent company,

be dealt with in the group accounts by the method of proportional consolidation.

18(2)   The provisions of this Schedule relating to the preparation of consolidated accounts and sections 402 and 405 of the 2006 Act apply, with any necessary modifications, to proportional consolidation under this paragraph.

18(3)   In addition to the disclosure of the average number of employees employed during the financial year (see section 411(7) of the 2006 Act), there must be a separate disclosure in the notes to the accounts of the average number of employees employed by undertakings that are proportionately consolidated.

History – In para. 18(2), the words 'and sections 402 and 405 of the 2006 Act' inserted by SI 2015/980, reg. 39(7), with effect in relation to–
(a)   financial years beginning on or after 1 January 2016, and
(b)   a financial year of a company beginning on or after 1 January 2015, but before 1 January 2016, if the directors of the company so decide.

Para. 18(3) inserted by SI 2015/980, reg. 39(8), with effect in relation to–
(a)   financial years beginning on or after 1 January 2016, and
(b)   a financial year of a company beginning on or after 1 January 2015, but before 1 January 2016, if the directors of the company so decide.

ASSOCIATED UNDERTAKINGS

19(1)   An **'associated undertaking'** means an undertaking in which an undertaking included in the consolidation has a participating interest and over whose operating and financial policy it exercises a significant influence, and which is not–

(a)   a subsidiary undertaking of the parent company, or

(b)   a joint venture dealt with in accordance with paragraph 18.

19(2)   Where an undertaking holds 20% or more of the voting rights in another undertaking, it is presumed to exercise such an influence over it unless the contrary is shown.

19(3)   The voting rights in an undertaking means the rights conferred on shareholders in respect of their shares or, in the case of an undertaking not having a share capital, on members, to vote at general meetings of the undertaking on all, or substantially all, matters.

19(4)   The provisions of paragraphs 5 to 11 of Schedule 7 to the 2006 Act (parent and subsidiary undertakings: rights to be taken into account and attribution of rights) apply in determining for the purposes of this paragraph whether an undertaking holds 20% or more of the voting rights in another undertaking.

20(1)   The formats set out in Schedule 1 to these Regulations have effect in relation to group accounts with the following modifications.

20(2)   In the balance sheet formats replace the items headed 'Participating interests', that is–

(a)   in format 1, item B.III.3, and

(b)   in format 2, item B.III.3 under the heading 'ASSETS',

by two items: 'Interests in associated undertakings' and 'Other participating interests'.

20(3)   In the profit and loss account formats replace the items headed 'Income from participating interests', that is–

(a)   in format 1, item 8, and

(b)   in format 2, item 10.

History – Para. 20(3)(c) and (d) omitted; and the word 'and' in para. (a) inserted by SI 2015/980, reg. 39(9), with effect in relation to–
(a) financial years beginning on or after 1 January 2016, and
(b) a financial year of a company beginning on or after 1 January 2015, but before 1 January 2016, if the directors of the company so decide.

21(1) The interest of an undertaking in an associated undertaking, and the amount of profit or loss attributable to such an interest, must be shown by the equity method of accounting (including dealing with any goodwill arising in accordance with paragraphs 17 to 20 and 22 of Schedule 1 to these Regulations).

21(2) Where the associated undertaking is itself a parent undertaking, the net assets and profits or losses to be taken into account are those of the parent and its subsidiary undertakings (after making any consolidation adjustments).

21(3) The equity method of accounting need not be applied if the amounts in question are not material for the purpose of giving a true and fair view.

RELATED PARTY TRANSACTIONS

22 Paragraph 72 of Schedule 1 to these Regulations applies to transactions which the parent company, or other undertakings included in the consolidation, have entered into with related parties, unless they are intra group transactions.

TOTAL AMOUNT OF DIRECTORS' REMUNERATION ETC

22A Paragraph 1 of Schedule 5 to these Regulations applies to group accounts with the modification that only the amounts and values referred to in that paragraph received or receivable by the directors of the parent company from the parent company and any of its subsidiary undertakings must be disclosed in the notes to the accounts.

History – Para. 22A inserted by SI 2015/980, reg. 39(10), with effect in relation to–
(a) financial years beginning on or after 1 January 2016, and
(b) a financial year of a company beginning on or after 1 January 2015, but before 1 January 2016, if the directors of the company so decide.

DEFERRED TAX BALANCES

22B Deferred tax balances must be recognised on consolidation where it is probable that a charge to tax will arise within the foreseeable future for one of the undertakings included in the consolidation.

History – Para. 22B inserted by SI 2015/980, reg. 39(10), with effect in relation to–
(a) financial years beginning on or after 1 January 2016, and
(b) a financial year of a company beginning on or after 1 January 2015, but before 1 January 2016, if the directors of the company so decide.

Part 2 – Modifications for banking groups
GENERAL APPLICATION OF PROVISIONS APPLICABLE TO INDIVIDUAL ACCOUNTS

23 In its application to banking groups, Part 1 of this Schedule has effect with the following modifications.

24 In paragraph 1 of this Schedule–

(a) the reference in sub-paragraph (1) to the provisions of Schedule 1 to these Regulations is to be construed as a reference to the provisions of Schedule 2 to these Regulations, and
(b) sub-paragraph (2) is to be omitted.

24A In paragraph 9 of this Schedule, the reference in sub-paragraph (6) to Schedule 1 is to these Regulations is to be construed as a reference to Schedule 2.

History – Para. 24A inserted by SI 2015/980, reg. 39(11), with effect in relation to–
(a) financial years beginning on or after 1 January 2016, and
(b) a financial year of a company beginning on or after 1 January 2015, but before 1 January 2016, if the directors of the company so decide.

NON-CONTROLLING INTERESTS AND ASSOCIATED UNDERTAKINGS

History – In heading, the words 'NON-CONTROLLING INTERESTS AND ASSOCIATED UNDERTAKINGS' substituted for the words 'MINORITY INTERESTS AND ASSOCIATED UNDERTAKINGS' by SI 2015/980, reg. 39(12), with effect in relation to–
(a) financial years beginning on or after 1 January 2016, and
(b) a financial year of a company beginning on or after 1 January 2015, but before 1 January 2016, if the directors of the company so decide.

25(1) This paragraph adapts paragraphs 17 and 20 (which require items in respect of 'non-controlling interests' and associated undertakings to be added to the formats set out in Schedule 1 to these Regulations) to the formats prescribed by Schedule 2 to these Regulations.

25(2) In paragraph 17–

(a) in sub-paragraph (1), for the reference to Schedule 1 to these Regulations, substitute a reference to Schedule 2,

(b) sub-paragraph (3) is to apply as if the reference to **'a separate item'** were a reference to **'separate items'** and the reference to **'the amount of any profit or loss'** were a reference to the following–

(i) the amount of any profit or loss on ordinary activities, and
(ii) the amount of any profit or loss on extraordinary activities, and

(c) sub-paragraph (4) is not to apply, but for the purposes of paragraph 5(1) of Part 1 of Schedule 2 to these Regulations (power to combine items) the additional items required by the foregoing provisions of this paragraph are to be treated as items to which a letter is assigned.

25(3) Paragraph 20(2) is to apply with respect to a balance sheet prepared under Schedule 2 to these Regulations as if it required assets item 7 (participating interests) in the balance sheet format to be replaced by the two replacement items referred to in that paragraph.

25(4) Paragraph 20(3) is not to apply, but the following items in the profit and loss account formats–

(a) format 1 item 3(b) (income from participating interests),
(b) format 2 item B2(b) (income from participating interests),

are replaced by the following–

(i) 'Income from participating interests other than associated undertakings', to be shown at position 3(b) in format 1 and position B2(b) in format 2, and
(ii) 'Income from associated undertakings', to be shown at an appropriate position.

History – Para. 25 substituted by SI 2015/980, reg. 39(12), with effect in relation to–
(a) financial years beginning on or after 1 January 2016, and
(b) a financial year of a company beginning on or after 1 January 2015, but before 1 January 2016, if the directors of the company so decide.

Former para. 25 read as follows:

"**25(1)** This paragraph adapts paragraphs 17 and 20 (which require items in respect of 'Minority interests' and associated undertakings to be added to the formats set out in Schedule 1 to these Regulations) to the formats prescribed by Schedule 2 to these Regulations.

25(2) In paragraph 17–

(a) in sub-paragraph (1), for the reference to Schedule 1 to these Regulations, substitute a reference to Schedule 2, and

(b) paragraph 17(4) is not to apply, but for the purposes of paragraph 5(1) of Part I of

Schedule 2 to these Regulations (power to combine items) the additional items required by the foregoing provisions of this paragraph are to be treated as items to which a letter is assigned.

25(3) Paragraph 20(2) is to apply with respect to a balance sheet prepared under Schedule 2 to these Regulations as if it required assets item 7 (participating interests) in the balance sheet format to be replaced by the two replacement items referred to in that paragraph.

25(4) Paragraph 20(3) is not to apply, but the following items in the profit and loss account formats–

(a) format 1 item 3(b) (income from participating interests),

(b) format 2 item B2(b) (income from participating interests), are replaced by the following–

(i) 'Income from participating interests other than associated undertakings', to be shown at position 3(b) in format 1 and position B2(b) in format 2, and

(ii) 'Income from associated undertakings', to be shown at an appropriate position."

26 In paragraph 21(1) of this Schedule, for the references to paragraphs 17 to 20 and 22 of Schedule 1 to these Regulations substitute references to paragraphs 23 to 26 and 28 of Schedule 2 to these Regulations.

RELATED PARTY TRANSACTIONS

27 In paragraph 22 of this Schedule, for the reference to paragraph 72 of Schedule 1 to these Regulations substitute a reference to paragraph 92 of Schedule 2 to these Regulations.

FOREIGN CURRENCY TRANSLATION

28 Any difference between–

(a) the amount included in the consolidated accounts for the previous financial year with respect to any undertaking included in the consolidation or the group's interest in any associated undertaking, together with the amount of any transactions undertaken to cover any such interest, and

(b) the opening amount for the financial year in respect of those undertakings and in respect of any such transactions, arising as a result of the application of paragraph 50 of Schedule 2 to these Regulations may be credited to (where (a) is less than (b)), or deducted from (where (a) is greater than (b)), (as the case may be) consolidated reserves.

29 Any income and expenditure of undertakings included in the consolidation and associated undertakings in a foreign currency may be translated for the purposes of the consolidated accounts at the average rates of exchange prevailing during the financial year.

INFORMATION AS TO UNDERTAKING IN WHICH SHARES HELD AS A RESULT OF FINANCIAL ASSISTANCE OPERATION

30(1) The following provisions apply where the parent company of a banking group has a subsidiary undertaking which–

(a) is a credit institution of which shares are held as a result of a financial assistance operation with a view to its reorganisation or rescue, and

(b) is excluded from consolidation under section 405(3)(c) of the 2006 Act (interest held with a view to resale).

30(2) Information as to the nature and terms of the operations must be given in a note to the group accounts, and there must be appended to the copy of the group accounts delivered to the registrar in accordance with section 441 of the 2006 Act a copy of the undertaking's latest individual accounts and, if it is a parent undertaking, its latest group accounts.

If the accounts appended are required by law to be audited, a copy of the auditor's report must also be appended.

30(3) Any requirement of Part 35 of the 2006 Act as to the delivery to the registrar of a certified translation into English must be met in relation to any document required to be appended by subparagraph (2).

30(4) The above requirements are subject to the following qualifications–

    (a)   an undertaking is not required to prepare for the purposes of this paragraph accounts which would not otherwise be prepared, and if no accounts satisfying the above requirements are prepared none need be appended;

    (b)   the accounts of an undertaking need not be appended if they would not otherwise be required to be published, or made available for public inspection, anywhere in the world, but in that case the reason for not appending the accounts must be stated in a note to the consolidated accounts.

30(5) Where a copy of an undertaking's accounts is required to be appended to the copy of the group accounts delivered to the registrar, that fact must be stated in a note to the group accounts.

Part 3 – Modifications for insurance groups

GENERAL APPLICATION OF PROVISIONS APPLICABLE TO INDIVIDUAL ACCOUNTS

31 In its application to insurance groups, Part 1 of this Schedule has effect with the following modifications.

32 In paragraph 1 of this Schedule–

    (a)   the reference in sub-paragraph (1) to the provisions of Schedule 1 to these Regulations is to be construed as a reference to the provisions of Schedule 3 to these Regulations, and

    (b)   sub-paragraph (2) is to be omitted.

FINANCIAL YEARS OF SUBSIDIARY UNDERTAKINGS

33 In paragraph 2(2)(a), for 'three months' substitute 'six months'.

ASSETS AND LIABILITIES TO BE INCLUDED IN GROUP ACCOUNTS

34 In paragraph 3, after sub-paragraph (1) insert–

"3(1A) Sub-paragraph (1) is not to apply to those liabilities items the valuation of which by the undertakings included in a consolidation is based on the application of provisions applying only to insurance undertakings, nor to those assets items changes in the values of which also affect or establish policyholders' rights.

3(1B) Where sub-paragraph (1A) applies, that fact must be disclosed in the notes to the consolidated accounts."

ELIMINATION OF GROUP TRANSACTIONS

35 For sub-paragraph (4) of paragraph 6 substitute–

"6(4) Sub-paragraphs (1) and (2) need not be complied with–

   (a)   where a transaction has been concluded according to normal market conditions and a policyholder has rights in respect of the transaction, or

   (b)   if the amounts concerned are not material for the purpose of giving a true and fair view.

6(5)   Where advantage is taken of sub-paragraph (4)(a) that fact must be disclosed in the notes to the accounts, and where the transaction in question has a material effect on the assets, liabilities, financial position and profit or loss of all the undertakings included in the consolidation that fact must also be so disclosed."

35A   In paragraph 9 of this Schedule, the reference in sub-paragraph (6) to Schedule 1 to these Regulations is to be construed as a reference to Schedule 3 to these Regulations.

History – Para. 35A inserted by SI 2015/980, reg. 39(13), with effect in relation to–
   (a)   financial years beginning on or after 1 January 2016, and
   (b)   a financial year of a company beginning on or after 1 January 2015, but before 1 January 2016, if the directors of the company so decide.

NON-CONTROLLING INTERESTS

36   In paragraph 17–

   (a)   in sub-paragraph (1), for the reference to Schedule 1 to these Regulations, substitute a reference to Schedule 3,

   (b)   sub-paragraph (3) is to apply as if the reference to **'a separate item'** were a reference to **'separate items'** and as if the reference to **'the amount of any profit or loss'** were a reference to the following–

      (i)   the amount of any profit or loss on ordinary activities, and
      (ii)   the amount of any profit or loss on extraordinary activities, and

   (c)   for sub-paragraph (4), substitute–

"17(4)   Paragraph 3(1) of Schedule 3 to these Regulations (power to combine items) does not apply in relation to the additional items required by the above provisions of this paragraph."

History – Para. 36 and the heading preceding it substituted by SI 2015/980, reg. 39(14), with effect in relation to–
   (a)   financial years beginning on or after 1 January 2016, and
   (b)   a financial year of a company beginning on or after 1 January 2015, but before 1 January 2016, if the directors of the company so decide.

Former para. 36 read as follows:

MINORITY INTERESTS

36   In paragraph 17–

   (a)   in sub-paragraph (1), for the reference to Schedule 1 to these Regulations, substitute a reference to Schedule 3, and
   (b)   for sub-paragraph (4) substitute–

"17(4)   Paragraph 3(1) of Schedule 3 to these Regulations (power to combine items) does not apply in relation to the additional items required by the above provisions of this paragraph."

ASSOCIATED UNDERTAKINGS

37   In paragraph 20–

   (a)   in sub-paragraph (1), for the reference to Schedule 1 to these Regulations substitute a reference to Schedule 3 to these Regulations, and

   (b)   for sub-paragraphs (2) and (3) substitute–

"20(2)   In the balance sheet format, replace asset item C.II.3 (participating interests) with two items, 'Interests in associated undertakings' and 'Other participating interests'.

20(3)   In the profit and loss account format, replace items II.2.(a) and III.3.(a) (income from participating interests, with a separate indication of that derived from group undertakings) with–

(a)   'Income from participating interests other than associated undertakings, with a separate indication of that derived from group undertakings', to be shown as items II.2.(a) and III.3.(a), and

(b)   'Income from associated undertakings', to be shown as items II.2.(aa) and III.3.(aa)."

38   In paragraph 21(1) of this Schedule, for the references to paragraphs 17 to 20 and 22 of Schedule 1 to these Regulations, substitute references to paragraphs 36 to 39 and 42 of Schedule 3 to these Regulations.

RELATED PARTY TRANSACTIONS

39   In paragraph 22 of this Schedule, for the reference to paragraph 72 of Schedule 1 to these Regulations substitute a reference to paragraph 90 of Schedule 3 to these Regulations.

MODIFICATIONS OF SCHEDULE 3 TO THESE REGULATIONS FOR PURPOSES OF PARAGRAPH 31

40(1)   For the purposes of paragraph 31 of this Schedule, Schedule 3 to these Regulations is to be modified as follows.

40(2)   The information required by paragraph 11 (additional items) need not be given.

40(3)   In the case of general business, investment income, expenses and charges may be disclosed in the non-technical account rather than in the technical account.

40(4)   In the case of subsidiary undertakings which are not authorised to carry on long-term business in the United Kingdom, notes (8) and (9) to the profit and loss account format have effect as if references to investment income, expenses and charges arising in the long-term fund or to investments attributed to the long-term fund were references to investment income, expenses and charges or (as the case may be) investments relating to long-term business.

40(5)   In the case of subsidiary undertakings which do not have a head office in the United Kingdom, the computation required by paragraph 52 must be made annually by an actuary or other specialist in the field on the basis of recognised actuarial methods.

40(6)   The information required by paragraphs 85 to 88 need not be shown.

SCHEDULE 7 – MATTERS TO BE DEALT WITH IN DIRECTORS' REPORT

Regulation 10

Part 1 – Matters of a general nature

INTRODUCTION

1   In addition to the information required by section 416 of the 2006 Act, the directors' report must contain the following information.

1A   Where a company has chosen in accordance with section 414C(11) to set out in the company's strategic report information required by this Schedule to be contained in the directors' report it shall state in the directors' report that it has done so and in respect of which information it has done so.

History – Para. 1A inserted by SI 2013/1970, reg. 7(1) and (3)(a), with effect from 1 October 2013 in respect of financial years ending on or after 30 September 2013.

ASSET VALUES

2 [Repealed.]

History – Para. 2 repealed by SI 2013/1970, reg. 7(1) and (3)(b), with effect from 1 October 2013 in respect of financial years ending on or after 30 September 2013. Prior to repeal, para. 2 read as follows:

"2(1) If, in the case of such of the fixed assets of the company as consist in interests in land, their market value (as at the end of the financial year) differs substantially from the amount at which they are included in the balance sheet, and the difference is, in the directors' opinion, of such significance as to require that the attention of members of the company or of holders of its debentures should be drawn to it, the report must indicate the difference with such degree of precision as is practicable.

2(2) In relation to a group directors' report sub-paragraph (1) has effect as if the reference to the fixed assets of the company was a reference to the fixed assets of the company and of its subsidiary undertakings included in the consolidation."

POLITICAL DONATIONS AND EXPENDITURE

3(1) If–

(a) the company (not being the wholly-owned subsidiary of a company incorporated in the United Kingdom) has in the financial year–

(i) made any political donation to any political party or other political organisation,
(ii) made any political donation to any independent election candidate, or
(iii) incurred any political expenditure, and

(b) the amount of the donation or expenditure, or (as the case may be) the aggregate amount of all donations and expenditure falling within paragraph (a), exceeded £2000,

the directors' report for the year must contain the following particulars.

3(2) Those particulars are–

(a) as respects donations falling within sub-paragraph (1)(a)(i) or (ii)–

(i) the name of each political party, other political organisation or independent election candidate to whom any such donation has been made, and
(ii) the total amount given to that party, organisation or candidate by way of such donations in the financial year; and

(b) as respects expenditure falling within sub-paragraph (1)(a)(iii), the total amount incurred by way of such expenditure in the financial year.

3(3) If–

(a) at the end of the financial year the company has subsidiaries which have, in that year, made any donations or incurred any such expenditure as is mentioned in sub-paragraph (1)(a), and

(b) it is not itself the wholly-owned subsidiary of a company incorporated in the United Kingdom,

the directors' report for the year is not, by virtue of sub-paragraph (1), required to contain the particulars specified in sub-paragraph (2).

But, if the total amount of any such donations or expenditure (or both) made or incurred in that year by the company and the subsidiaries between them exceeds £2000, the directors' report for the year must contain those particulars in relation to each body by whom any such donation or expenditure has been made or incurred.

3(4) Any expression used in this paragraph which is also used in Part 14 of the 2006 Act (control of political donations and expenditure) has the same meaning as in that Part.

4(1)   If the company (not being the wholly-owned subsidiary of a company incorporated in the United Kingdom) has in the financial year made any contribution to a non-EU political party, the directors' report for the year must contain–

(a)   a statement of the amount of the contribution, or

(b)   (if it has made two or more such contributions in the year) a statement of the total amount of the contributions.

4(2)   If–

(a)   at the end of the financial year the company has subsidiaries which have, in that year, made any such contributions as are mentioned in sub-paragraph (1), and

(b)   it is not itself the wholly-owned subsidiary of a company incorporated in the United Kingdom,

the directors' report for the year is not, by virtue of sub-paragraph (1), required to contain any such statement as is there mentioned, but it must instead contain a statement of the total amount of the contributions made in the year by the company and the subsidiaries between them.

4(3)   In this paragraph, **'contribution'**, in relation to an organisation, means–

(a)   any gift of money to the organisation (whether made directly or indirectly);

(b)   any subscription or other fee paid for affiliation to, or membership of, the organisation; or

(c)   any money spent (otherwise than by the organisation or a person acting on its behalf) in paying any expenses incurred directly or indirectly by the organisation.

4(4)   In this paragraph, **'non-EU political party'** means any political party which carries on, or proposes to carry on, its activities wholly outside the member States.

CHARITABLE DONATIONS

5   [Repealed.]

History – Para. 5 repealed by SI 2013/1970, reg. 7(1) and (3)(b), with effect from 1 October 2013 in respect of financial years ending on or after 30 September 2013. Prior to repeal, para. 5 read as follows:

"5(1)   If–

(a)   the company (not being the wholly-owned subsidiary of a company incorporated in the United Kingdom) has in the financial year given money for charitable purposes, and

(b)   the money given exceeded £2000 in amount, the directors' report for the year must contain, in the case of each of the purposes for which money has been given, a statement of the amount of money given for that purpose.

5(2)   If–

(a)   at the end of the financial year the company has subsidiaries which have, in that year, given money for charitable purposes, and

(b)   it is not itself the wholly owned subsidiary of a company incorporated in the United Kingdom, sub-paragraph (1) does not apply to the company. But, if the amount given in that year for charitable purposes by the company and the subsidiaries between them exceeds £2000, the directors' report for the year must contain, in the case of each of the purposes for which money has been given by the company and the subsidiaries between them, a statement of the amount of money given for that purpose.

5(3)   Money given for charitable purposes to a person who, when it was given, was ordinarily resident outside the United Kingdom is to be left out of account for the purposes of this paragraph.

5(4)   For the purposes of this paragraph, **'charitable purposes'** means purposes which are exclusively charitable, and as respects Scotland a purpose is charitable if it is listed in section 7(2) of the Charities and Trustee Investment (Scotland) Act 2005."

FINANCIAL INSTRUMENTS

6(1)   In relation to the use of financial instruments by a company, the directors' report must contain an indication of–

(a) the financial risk management objectives and policies of the company, including the policy for hedging each major type of forecasted transaction for which hedge accounting is used, and

(b) the exposure of the company to price risk, credit risk, liquidity risk and cash flow risk,

unless such information is not material for the assessment of the assets, liabilities, financial position and profit or loss of the company.

6(2) In relation to a group directors' report sub-paragraph (1) has effect as if the references to the company were references to the company and its subsidiary undertakings included in the consolidation.

6(3) In sub-paragraph (1) the expressions **'hedge accounting'**, **'price risk'**, **'credit risk'**, **'liquidity risk'** and **'cash flow risk'** have the same meaning as they have in Council Directive 78/660/EEC on the annual accounts of certain types of companies, and in Council Directive 83/349/EEC on consolidated accounts.

MISCELLANEOUS

7(1) The directors' report must contain–

(a) particulars of any important events affecting the company which have occurred since the end of the financial year,

(b) an indication of likely future developments in the business of the company,

(c) an indication of the activities (if any) of the company in the field of research and development, and

(d) (unless the company is an unlimited company) an indication of the existence of branches (as defined in section 1046(3) of the 2006 Act) of the company outside the United Kingdom.

7(2) In relation to a group directors' report paragraphs (a), (b) and (c) of sub-paragraph (1) have effect as if the references to the company were references to the company and its subsidiary undertakings included in the consolidation.

Part 2 – Disclosure required by company acquiring its own shares etc.

8 This Part of this Schedule applies where shares in a public company–

(a) are purchased by the company or are acquired by it by forfeiture or surrender in lieu of forfeiture, or in pursuance of any of the following provisions (acquisition of own shares by company limited by shares)–

   (i) section 143(3) of the Companies Act 1985,
   (ii) Article 153(3) of the Companies (Northern Ireland) Order 1986, or
   (iii) section 659 of the 2006 Act, or

(b) are acquired by another person in circumstances where paragraph (c) or (d) of any of the following provisions applies (acquisition by company's nominee, or by another with company financial assistance, the company having a beneficial interest)–

   (i) section 146(1) of the Companies Act 1985,
   (ii) Article 156(1) of the Companies (Northern Ireland) Order 1986, or
   (iii) section 662(1) of the 2006 Act applies, or

(c) are made subject to a lien or other charge taken (whether expressly or otherwise) by the company and permitted by any of the following provisions (exceptions from general rule against a company having a lien or charge on its own shares)–

   (i) section 150(2) or (4) of the Companies Act 1985,
   (ii) Article 160(2) or (4) of the Companies (Northern Ireland) Order 1986, or
   (iii) section 670(2) or (4) of the 2006 Act.

History – In the opening words, 'public' inserted by SI 2013/1970, reg. 7(1) and (3)(c), with effect from 1 October 2013 in respect of financial years ending on or after 30 September 2013.

9 The directors' report for a financial year must state–

(a) the number and nominal value of the shares so purchased, the aggregate amount of the consideration paid by the company for such shares and the reasons for their purchase;

(b) the number and nominal value of the shares so acquired by the company, acquired by another person in such circumstances and so charged respectively during the financial year;

(c) the maximum number and nominal value of shares which, having been so acquired by the company, acquired by another person in such circumstances or so charged (whether or not during that year) are held at any time by the company or that other person during that year;

(d) the number and nominal value of the shares so acquired by the company, acquired by another person in such circumstances or so charged (whether or not during that year) which are disposed of by the company or that other person or cancelled by the company during that year;

(e) where the number and nominal value of the shares of any particular description are stated in pursuance of any of the preceding sub-paragraphs, the percentage of the called-up share capital which shares of that description represent;

(f) where any of the shares have been so charged the amount of the charge in each case; and

(g) where any of the shares have been disposed of by the company or the person who acquired them in such circumstances for money or money's worth the amount or value of the consideration in each case.

Part 3 – Disclosure concerning employment etc. Of disabled persons

10(1) This Part of this Schedule applies to the directors' report where the average number of persons employed by the company in each week during the financial year exceeded 250.

10(2) That average number is the quotient derived by dividing, by the number of weeks in the financial year, the number derived by ascertaining, in relation to each of those weeks, the number of persons who, under contracts of service, were employed in the week (whether throughout it or not) by the company, and adding up the numbers ascertained.

10(3) The directors' report must in that case contain a statement describing such policy as the company has applied during the financial year–

(a) for giving full and fair consideration to applications for employment by the company made by disabled persons, having regard to their particular aptitudes and abilities,

(b) for continuing the employment of, and for arranging appropriate training for, employees of the company who have become disabled persons during the period when they were employed by the company, and

(c) otherwise for the training, career development and promotion of disabled persons employed by the company.

10(4) In this Part–

(a) **'employment'** means employment other than employment to work wholly or mainly outside the United Kingdom, and 'employed' and 'employee' are to be construed accordingly; and

(b) **'disabled person'** means the same as in the Disability Discrimination Act 1995.

Part 4 – Employee involvement

11(1) This Part of this Schedule applies to the directors' report where the average number of persons employed by the company in each week during the financial year exceeded 250.

11(2) That average number is the quotient derived by dividing, by the number of weeks in the financial year, the number derived by ascertaining, in relation to each of those weeks, the number of persons who, under contracts of service, were employed in the week (whether throughout it or not) by the company, and adding up the numbers ascertained.

11(3) The directors' report must in that case contain a statement describing the action that has been taken during the financial year to introduce, maintain or develop arrangements aimed at–

 (a) providing employees systematically with information on matters of concern to them as employees,

 (b) consulting employees or their representatives on a regular basis so that the views of employees can be taken into account in making decisions which are likely to affect their interests,

 (c) encouraging the involvement of employees in the company's performance through an employees' share scheme or by some other means,

 (d) achieving a common awareness on the part of all employees of the financial and economic factors affecting the performance of the company.

11(4) In sub-paragraph (3) **'employee'** does not include a person employed to work wholly or mainly outside the United Kingdom; and for the purposes of sub-paragraph (2) no regard is to be had to such a person.

Part 5 – Policy and practice on payment of creditors

12 [Repealed.]

History – Para. 12 repealed by SI 2013/1970, reg. 7(1) and (3)(d), with effect from 1 October 2013 in respect of financial years ending on or after 30 September 2013. Prior to repeal, para. 12 read as follows:

"12(1) This Part of this Schedule applies to the directors' report for a financial year if–

 (a) the company was at any time within the year a public company, or

 (b) the company did not qualify as small or medium-sized in relation to the year by virtue of section 382 or 465 of the 2006 Act and was at any time within the year a member of a group of which the parent company was a public company.

12(2) The report must state, with respect to the next following financial year–

 (a) whether in respect of some or all of its suppliers it is the company's policy to follow any code or standard on payment practice and, if so, the name of the code or standard and the place where information about, and copies of, the code or standard can be obtained,

 (b) whether in respect of some or all of its suppliers it is the company's policy–

  (i) to settle the terms of payment with those suppliers when agreeing the terms of each transaction,

  (ii) to ensure that those suppliers are made aware of the terms of payment, and

  (iii) to abide by the terms of payment,

 (c) where the company's policy is not as mentioned in paragraph (a) or (b) in respect of some or all of its suppliers, what its policy is with respect to the payment of those suppliers; and if the company's policy is different for different suppliers or classes of suppliers, the report must identify the suppliers to which the different policies apply.

In this sub-paragraph references to the company's suppliers are references to persons who are or may become its suppliers.

12(3) The report must also state the number of days which bears to the number of days in the financial year the same proportion as X bears to Y where–

X = the aggregate of the amounts which were owed to trade creditors at the end of the year; and

Y = the aggregate of the amounts in which the company was invoiced by suppliers during the year.

12(4) For the purposes of sub-paragraphs (2) and (3) a person is a supplier of the company at any time if–

 (a) at that time, he is owed an amount in respect of goods or services supplied, and

 (b) that amount would be included under the heading corresponding to item E.4 (trade creditors) in format 1 if–

    (i)   the company's accounts fell to be prepared as at that time,

    (ii)   those accounts were prepared in accordance with Schedule 1 to these Regulations, and

    (iii) that format were adopted.

12(5) For the purpose of sub-paragraph (3), the aggregate of the amounts which at the end of the financial year were owed to trade creditors is taken to be–

    (a)   where in the company's accounts format 1 of the balance sheet formats set out in Part 1 of Schedule 1 to these Regulations is adopted, the amount shown under the heading corresponding to item E.4 (trade creditors) in that format,

    (b)   where format 2 is adopted, the amount which, under the heading corresponding to item C.4 (trade creditors) in that format, is shown as falling due within one year, and

    (c)   where the company's accounts are prepared in accordance with Schedule 2 or 3 to these Regulations or the company's accounts are IAS accounts, the amount which would be shown under the heading corresponding to item E.4 (trade creditors) in format 1 if the company's accounts were prepared in accordance with Schedule 1 and that format were adopted."

Part 6 – Disclosure required by certain publicly-traded companies

13(1) This Part of this Schedule applies to the directors' report for a financial year if the company had securities carrying voting rights admitted to trading on a regulated market at the end of that year.

13(2) The report must contain detailed information, by reference to the end of that year, on the following matters–

    (a)   the structure of the company's capital, including in particular–

        (i)   the rights and obligations attaching to the shares or, as the case may be, to each class of shares in the company, and

        (ii) where there are two or more such classes, the percentage of the total share capital represented by each class;

    (b)   any restrictions on the transfer of securities in the company, including in particular–

        (i)   limitations on the holding of securities, and

        (ii) requirements to obtain the approval of the company, or of other holders of securities in the company, for a transfer of securities;

    (c)   in the case of each person with a significant direct or indirect holding of securities in the company, such details as are known to the company of–

        (i)   the identity of the person,

        (ii) the size of the holding, and

        (iii) the nature of the holding;

    (d)   in the case of each person who holds securities carrying special rights with regard to control of the company–

        (i)   the identity of the person, and

        (ii) the nature of the rights;

    (e)   where–

        (i)   the company has an employees' share scheme, and

        (ii) shares to which the scheme relates have rights with regard to control of the company that are not exercisable directly by the employees, how those rights are exercisable;

    (f)   any restrictions on voting rights, including in particular–

        (i)   limitations on voting rights of holders of a given percentage or number of votes,

        (ii) deadlines for exercising voting rights, and

        (iii) arrangements by which, with the company's co-operation, financial rights carried by securities are held by a person other than the holder of the securities;

(g)　any agreements between holders of securities that are known to the company and may result in restrictions on the transfer of securities or on voting rights;

(h)　any rules that the company has about–

(i)　appointment and replacement of directors, or
(ii)　amendment of the company's articles of association;

(i)　the powers of the company's directors, including in particular any powers in relation to the issuing or buying back by the company of its shares;

(j)　any significant agreements to which the company is a party that take effect, alter or terminate upon a change of control of the company following a takeover bid, and the effects of any such agreements;

(k)　any agreements between the company and its directors or employees providing for compensation for loss of office or employment (whether through resignation, purported redundancy or otherwise) that occurs because of a takeover bid.

13(3)　For the purposes of sub-paragraph (2)(a) a company's capital includes any securities in the company that are not admitted to trading on a regulated market.

13(4)　For the purposes of sub-paragraph (2)(c) a person has an indirect holding of securities if–

(a)　they are held on his behalf, or

(b)　he is able to secure that rights carried by the securities are exercised in accordance with his wishes.

13(5)　Sub-paragraph (2)(j) does not apply to an agreement if–

(a)　disclosure of the agreement would be seriously prejudicial to the company, and

(b)　the company is not under any other obligation to disclose it.

13(6)　In this paragraph–

'securities' means shares or debentures;

'takeover bid' has the same meaning as in the Takeovers Directive;

'the Takeovers Directive' means Directive 2004/25/EC of the European Parliament and of the Council;

'voting rights' means rights to vote at general meetings of the company in question, including rights that arise only in certain circumstances.

14　The directors' report must also contain any necessary explanatory material with regard to information that is required to be included in the report by this Part.

Part 7 – Disclosures Concerning Greenhouse Gas Emissions

15(1)　This Part of this Schedule applies to the directors' report for a financial year if the company is a quoted company.

15(2)　The report must state the annual quantity of emissions in tonnes of carbon dioxide equivalent from activities for which that company is responsible including–

(a)　the combustion of fuel; and

(b)　the operation of any facility.

15(3)　The report must state the annual quantity of emissions in tonnes of carbon dioxide equivalent resulting from the purchase of electricity, heat, steam or cooling by the company for its own use.

15(4) Sub-paragraphs (2) and (3) apply only to the extent that it is practical for the company to obtain the information in question; but where it is not practical for the company to obtain some or all of that information, the report must state what information is not included and why.

16 The directors' report must state the methodologies used to calculate the information disclosed under paragraph 15(2) and (3).

17 The directors' report must state at least one ratio which expresses the quoted company's annual emissions in relation to a quantifiable factor associated with the company's activities.

18 With the exception of the first year for which the directors' report contains the information required by paragraphs 15(2) and (3) and 17, the report must state not only the information required by paragraphs 15(2) and (3) and 17, but also that information as disclosed in the report for the preceding financial year.

19 The directors' report must state if the period for which it is reporting the information required by paragraph 15(2) and (3) is different to the period in respect of which the directors' report is prepared.

20 The following definitions apply for the purposes of this Part of this Schedule–

'emissions' means emissions into the atmosphere of a greenhouse gas as defined in section 92 of the Climate Change Act 2008 which are attributable to human activity;

'tonne of carbon dioxide equivalent' has the meaning given in section 93(2) of the Climate Change Act 2008.

History – Pt. 7 inserted by SI 2013/1970, reg. 7(1) and (3)(e), with effect from 1 October 2013 in respect of financial years ending on or after 30 September 2013.

SCHEDULE 8 – QUOTED COMPANIES: DIRECTORS' REMUNERATION REPORT

Regulation 11

Part 1 – Introductory

1(1) In the directors' remuneration report for a financial year ('the relevant financial year') there must be shown, subject to sub-paragraph (2), the information specified in Parts 2, 3, and 4.

1(2) The directors' remuneration policy as specified in Part 4, may, subject to subparagraph (3), be omitted from the directors' remuneration report for a financial year, if the company does not intend, at the accounts meeting at which the report is to be laid, to move a resolution to approve the directors' remuneration policy in accordance with section 439A of the 2006 Act.

1(3) Where the directors' remuneration policy is omitted from the report in accordance with sub-paragraph (2), there must be set out in the report the following information–

    (a)   the date of the last general meeting of the company at which a resolution was moved by the company in respect of that directors' remuneration policy and at which that policy was approved; and

    (b)   where, on the company's website or at some other place, a copy of that directors' remuneration policy may be inspected by the members of the company.

2(1) Information required to be shown in the report for or in respect of a particular person must be shown in the report in a manner that links the information to that person identified by name.

2(2)   Nothing in this Schedule prevents the directors setting out in the report any such additional information as they think fit, and any item required to be shown in the report may be shown in greater detail than required by the provisions of this Schedule.

2(3)   Where the requirements of this Schedule make reference to a "director" those requirements may be complied with in such manner as to distinguish between directors who perform executive functions and those who do not.

2(4)   Any requirement of this Schedule to provide information in respect of a director may, in respect of those directors who do not perform executive functions, be omitted or otherwise modified where that requirement is not applicable to such a director and in such a case, particulars of, and the reasons for, the omission or modification must be given in the report.

2(5)   Any requirement of this Schedule to provide information in respect of performance measures or targets does not require the disclosure of information which, in the opinion of the directors, is commercially sensitive in respect of the company.

2(6)   Where information that would otherwise be required to be in the report is not included in reliance on sub-paragraph (5), particulars of, and the reasons for, the omission must be given in the report and an indication given of when (if at all) the information is to be reported to the members of the company.

2(7)   Where any provision of this Schedule requires a sum or figure to be given in respect of any financial year preceding the relevant financial year, in the first directors' remuneration report prepared in accordance with this Schedule, that sum or figure may, where the sum or figure is not readily available from the reports and accounts of the company prepared for those years, be given as an estimate and a note of explanation provided in the report.

Part 2 – Annual Statement

3   The directors' remuneration report must contain a statement by the director who fulfils the role of chair of the remuneration committee (or, where there is no such person, by a director nominated by the directors to make the statement) summarising for the relevant financial year–

(a)   the major decisions on directors' remuneration;

(b)   any substantial changes relating to directors' remuneration made during the year; and

(c)   the context in which those changes occurred and decisions have been taken.

Part 3 – Annual Report on Remuneration

SINGLE TOTAL FIGURE OF REMUNERATION FOR EACH DIRECTOR

4(1)   The directors' remuneration report must, for the relevant financial year, for each person who has served as a director of the company at any time during that year, set out in a table in the form set out in paragraph 5 ('the single total figure table') the information prescribed by paragraphs 6 and 7 below.

4(2)   The report may set out in separate tables the information to be supplied in respect of directors who perform executive functions and those who do not.

4(3)   Unless otherwise indicated the sums set out in the table are those in respect of the relevant financial year and relate to the director's performance of, or agreement to perform, qualifying services.

5(1) The form of the table required by paragraph 4 is–

Single total figure table

	a	b	c	d	e	Total
Director 1	xxx	xxx	xxx	xxx	xxx	xxx
Director 2	xxx	xxx	xxx	xxx	xxx	xxx

5(2) The directors may choose to display the table using an alternative orientation, in which case references in this Schedule to columns are to be read as references to rows.

6(1) In addition to the columns described in paragraph 7, columns–

(a) must be included to set out any other items in the nature of remuneration (other than items required to be disclosed under paragraph 15) which are not set out in the columns headed '(a)' to '(e)'; and

(b) may be included if there are any sub-totals or other items which the directors consider necessary in order to assist the understanding of the table.

6(2) Any additional columns must be inserted before the column marked 'Total'.

7(1) Subject to paragraph 9, in the single total figure table, the sums that are required to be set out in the columns are–

(a) in the column headed 'a', the total amount of salary and fees;

(b) in the column headed 'b', all taxable benefits;

(c) in the column headed 'c', money or other assets received or receivable for the relevant financial year as a result of the achievement of performance measures and targets relating to a period ending in that financial year other than–

  (i) those which result from awards made in a previous financial year and where final vesting is determined as a result of the achievement of performance measures or targets relating to a period ending in the relevant financial year; or

  (ii) those receivable subject to the achievement of performance measures or targets in a future financial year;

(d) in the column headed 'd', money or other assets received or receivable for periods of more than one financial year where final vesting–

  (i) is determined as a result of the achievement of performance measures or targets relating to a period ending in the relevant financial year; and

  (ii) is not subject to the achievement of performance measures or targets in a future financial year;

(e) in the column headed 'e', all pension related benefits including–

  (i) payments (whether in cash or otherwise) in lieu of retirement benefits;

  (ii) all benefits in year from participating in pension schemes;

(f) in the column headed 'Total', the total amount of the sums set out in the previous columns.

7(2) Where it is necessary to assist the understanding of the table by the creation of subtotals the columns headed 'a' to 'e' may be set out in an order other than the one set out in paragraph 5.

8(1) In respect of any items in paragraph 7(1)(c) or (d) where the performance measures or targets are substantially (but not fully) completed by the end of the relevant financial year–

(a) the sum given in the table may include sums which relate to the following financial year; but

(b) where such sums are included, those sums must not be included in the corresponding column of the single total figure table prepared for that following financial year; and

(c) a note to the table must explain the basis of the calculation.

8(2)   Where any money or other assets reported in the single total figure table in the directors' remuneration report prepared in respect of any previous financial year are the subject of a recovery of sums paid or the withholding of any sum for any reason in the relevant financial year–

(a)   the recovery or withholding so attributable must be shown in a separate column in the table as a negative value and deducted from the column headed 'Total'; and

(b)   an explanation for the recovery or withholding and the basis of the calculation must be given in a note to the table.

8(3)   Where the calculations in accordance with paragraph 10 (other than in respect of a recovery or withholding) result in a negative value, the result must be expressed as zero in the relevant column in the table.

9(1)   Each column in the single total figure table must contain, in such manner as to permit comparison, two sums as follows–

(a)   the sum set out in the corresponding column in the report prepared in respect of the financial year preceding the relevant financial year; and

(b)   the sum for the relevant financial year.

9(2)   When, in the single total figure table, a sum is given in the column which relates to the preceding financial year and that sum, when set out in the report for that preceding year was given as an estimated sum, then in the relevant financial year–

(a)   it must be given as an actual sum;

(b)   the amount representing the difference between the estimate and the actual must not be included in the column relating to the relevant financial year; and

(c)   details of the calculation of the revised sum must be given in a note to the table.

10(1)   The methods to be used to calculate the sums required to be set out in the single total figure table are–

(a)   for the column headed 'a', cash paid to or receivable by the person in respect of the relevant financial year;

(b)   for the column headed 'b', the gross value before payment of tax;

(c)   for column 'c', the total cash equivalent including any amount deferred, other than where the deferral is subject to the achievement of further performance measures or targets in a future financial year;

(d)   for column 'd'–

(i)   the cash value of any monetary award;

(ii)   the value of any shares or share options awarded, calculated by–

(aa)   multiplying the original number of shares granted by the proportion that vest (or an estimate);

(bb)   multiplying the total arrived at in (aa) by the market price of shares at the date on which the shares vest; and

(iii)   the value of any additional cash or shares receivable in respect of dividends accrued (actually or notionally);

(e)   for the column headed 'e',–

(i)   for the item in paragraph 7(1)(e)(i), the cash value;

(ii)   for the item in paragraph 7(1)(e)(ii), what the aggregate pension input amount would be across all the pension schemes of the company or group in which the director accrues benefits, calculated using the method set out in section 229 of the Finance Act 2004 where–

(aa) references to **'pension input period'** are to be read as references to the company's financial year, or where a person becomes a director during the financial year, the period starting on the date the person became a director and ending at the end of the financial year;

(bb) all pension schemes of the company or group which provide relevant benefits to the director are deemed to be registered schemes;

(cc) all pension contributions paid by the director during the pension input period are deducted from the pension input amount;

(dd) in the application of section 234 of that Act, the figure 20 is substituted for the figure 16 each time it appears;

(ee) subsections 229(3) and (4) do not apply; and

(ff) section 277 of that Act is read as follows–

Valuation assumptions

For the purposes of this Part the valuation assumptions in relation to a person, benefits and a date are–

(a) if the person has not left the employment to which the arrangement relates on or before the date, that the person left that employment on the date with a prospective right to benefits under the arrangement,

(b) if the person has not reached such age (if any) as must have been reached to avoid any reduction in the benefits on account of age, that on the date the person is entitled to receive the benefits without any reduction on account of age, and

(c) that the person's right to receive the benefits had not been occasioned by physical or mental impairment.

10(2) For the item in paragraph 7(1)(e)(ii) where there has not been a company contribution to the pension scheme in respect of the director, but if such a contribution had been made it would have been measured for pension input purposes under section 233(1)(b) of the Finance Act 2004, when calculating the pension input amount for the purposes of subparagraph (1)(e)(ii) it should be calculated as if the cash value of any contribution notionally allocated to the scheme in respect of the person by or on behalf of the company including any adjustment made for any notional investment return achieved during the relevant financial year were a contribution paid by the employer in respect of the individual for the purposes of section 233(1)(b) of the Finance Act 2004.

For the purposes of the calculation in sub-paragraph (1)(d)(ii)–

(a) where the market price of shares at the date on which the shares vest is not ascertainable by the date on which the remuneration report is approved by the directors, an estimate of the market price of the shares shall be calculated on the basis of an average market value over the last quarter of the relevant financial year; and

(b) where the award was an award of shares or share options, the cash amount the individual was or will be required to pay to acquire the share must be deducted from the total.

DEFINITIONS APPLICABLE TO THE SINGLE TOTAL FIGURE TABLE

11(1) In paragraph 7(1)(b) **'taxable benefits'** includes–

(a) sums paid by way of expenses allowance that are–

(i) chargeable to United Kingdom income tax (or would be if the person were an individual, or would be if the person were resident in the United Kingdom for tax purposes), and

(ii) paid to or receivable by the person in respect of qualifying services; and

(b)   any benefits received by the person, other than salary, (whether or not in cash) that–

   (i)   are emoluments of the person, and
   (ii)   are received by the person in respect of qualifying services.

11(2)   A payment or other benefit received in advance of a director commencing qualifying services, but in anticipation of performing qualifying services, is to be treated as if received on the first day of performance of the qualifying services.

ADDITIONAL REQUIREMENTS IN RESPECT OF THE SINGLE TOTAL FIGURE TABLE

12(1)   In respect of the sum required to be set out by paragraph 7(1)(b), there must be set out after the table a summary identifying–

(a)   the types of benefits the value of which is included in the sum set out in the column headed 'b'; and
(b)   the value (where significant).

12(2)   For every component the value of which is included in the sums required to be set out in the columns headed 'c' and 'd' of the table by paragraphs 7(1)(c) and (d), there must be set out after the table the relevant details.

12(3)   In sub-paragraph (2) **'the relevant details'** means–

(a)   details of any performance measures and the relative weighting of each;
(b)   within each performance measure, the performance targets set at the beginning of the performance period and corresponding value of the award achievable;
(c)   for each performance measure, details of actual performance relative to the targets set and measured over the relevant reporting period, and the resulting level of award; and
(d)   where any discretion has been exercised in respect of the award, particulars must be given of how the discretion was exercised and how the resulting level of award was determined.

12(4)   For each component the value of which is included in the sum set out in the column headed 'c' of the table, the report must state if any amount was deferred, the percentage deferred, whether it was deferred in cash or shares, if relevant, and whether the deferral was subject to any conditions other than performance measures.

12(5)   Where additional columns are included in accordance with paragraph 6(1)(a), there must be set out in a note to the table the basis on which the sums in the column were calculated, and other such details as are necessary for an understanding of the sums set out in the column, including any performance measures relating to that component of remuneration or if there are none, an explanation of why not.

TOTAL PENSION ENTITLEMENTS

13(1)   The directors' remuneration report must, for each person who has served as a director of the company at any time during the relevant financial year, and who has a prospective entitlement to defined benefits or cash balance benefits (or to benefits under a hybrid arrangement which includes such benefits) in respect of qualifying services, contain the following information in respect of pensions–

(a)   details of those rights as at the end of that year, including the person's normal retirement date;
(b)   a description of any additional benefit that will become receivable by a director in the event that that director retires early; and
(c)   where a person has rights under more than one type of pension benefit identified in column headed 'e' of the single total figure table, separate details relating to each type of pension benefit.

13(2) For the purposes of this paragraph, 'defined benefits', 'cash balance benefits' and 'hybrid arrangement' have the same meaning as in section 152 of the Finance Act 2004.

13(3) **'Normal retirement date'** means an age specified in the pension scheme rules (or otherwise determined) as the earliest age at which, while the individual continues to accrue benefits under the pension scheme, entitlement to a benefit arises–

(a) without consent (whether of an employer, the trustees or managers of the scheme or otherwise), and

(b) without an actuarial reduction,

but disregarding any special provision as to early repayment on grounds of ill health, redundancy or dismissal.

SCHEME INTERESTS AWARDED DURING THE FINANCIAL YEAR

14(1) The directors' remuneration report must for each person who has served as a director of the company at any time during the relevant financial year contain a table setting out–

(a) details of the scheme interests awarded to the person during the relevant financial year; and

(b) for each scheme interest–

(i) a description of the type of interest awarded;

(ii) a description of the basis on which the award is made;

(iii) the face value of the award;

(iv) the percentage of scheme interests that would be receivable if the minimum performance was achieved;

(v) for a scheme interest that is a share option, an explanation of any difference between the exercise price per share and the price specified under paragraph 14(3);

(vi) the end of the period over which the performance measures and targets for that interest have to be achieved (or if there are different periods for different measures and targets, the end of whichever of those periods ends last); and

(vii) a summary of the performance measures and targets if not set out elsewhere in the report.

14(2) In respect of a scheme interest relating to shares or share options, **'face value'** means the maximum number of shares that would vest if all performance measures and targets are met multiplied by either–

(a) the share price at date of grant or

(b) the average share price used to determine the number of shares awarded.

14(3) Where the report sets out the face value of an award in respect of a scheme interest relating to shares or share options, the report must specify–

(a) whether the face value has been calculated using the share price at date of grant or the average share price;

(b) where the share price at date of grant is used, the amount of that share price and the date of grant;

(c) where the average share price is used, what that price was and the period used for calculating the average.

PAYMENTS TO PAST DIRECTORS

15   The directors' remuneration report must, for the relevant financial year, contain details of any payments of money or other assets to any person who was not a director of the company at the time the payment was made, but who had been a director of the company before that time, excluding–

(a)   any payments falling within paragraph 16;

(b)   any payments which are shown in the single total figure table;

(c)   any payments which have been disclosed in a previous directors' remuneration report of the company;

(d)   any payments which are below a *de minimis* threshold set by the company and stated in the report;

(e)   payments by way of regular pension benefits commenced in a previous year or dividend payments in respect of scheme interests retained after leaving office; and

(f)   payments in respect of employment with or any other contractual service performed for the company other than as a director.

PAYMENTS FOR LOSS OF OFFICE

16   The directors' remuneration report must for the relevant financial year set out, for each person who has served as a director of the company at any time during that year, or any previous year, excluding payments which are below a *de minimis* threshold set by the company and stated in the report–

(a)   the total amount of any payment for loss of office paid to or receivable by the person in respect of that financial year, broken down into each component comprised in that payment and the value of each component;

(b)   an explanation of how each component was calculated;

(c)   any other payments paid to or receivable by the person in connection with the termination of qualifying services, whether by way of compensation for loss of office or otherwise, including the treatment of outstanding incentive awards that vest on or following termination; and

(d)   where any discretion was exercised in respect of the payment, an explanation of how it was exercised.

STATEMENT OF DIRECTORS' SHAREHOLDING AND SHARE INTERESTS

17   The directors' remuneration report for the relevant financial year must contain, for each person who has served as a director of the company at any time during that year–

(a)   a statement of any requirements or guidelines for the director to own shares in the company and state whether or not those requirements or guidelines have been met;

(b)   in tabular form or forms–

(i)   the total number of interests in shares in the company of the director including interests of connected persons (as defined for the purposes of section 96B(2) of the Financial Services and Markets Act 2000);

(ii)   total number of scheme interests differentiating between–

(aa)   shares and share options; and

(bb)   those with or without performance measures;

(iii)   details of those scheme interests (which may exclude any details included elsewhere in the report); and

(iv)   details of share options which are–

(aa)   vested but unexercised; and

(bb)   exercised in the relevant financial year.

PERFORMANCE GRAPH AND TABLE

18(1) The directors' remuneration report must–

    (a) contain a line graph that shows for each of–

        (i) a holding of shares of that class of the company's equity share capital whose listing, or admission to dealing, has resulted in the company falling within the definition of 'quoted company', and

        (ii) a hypothetical holding of shares made up of shares of the same kinds and number as those by reference to which a broad equity market index is calculated,

    a line drawn by joining up points plotted to represent, for each of the financial years in the relevant period, the total shareholder return on that holding; and

    (b) state the name of the index selected for the purposes of the graph and set out the reasons for selecting that index.

18(2) The report must also set out in tabular form the following information for each of the financial years in the relevant period in respect of the director undertaking the role of chief executive officer–

    (a) total remuneration as set out in the single total figure table;

    (b) the sum set out in the table in column headed 'c' in the single total figure table expressed as a percentage of the maximum that could have been paid in respect of that component in the financial year; and

    (c) the sum set out in column headed 'd' in the single total figure table restated as a percentage of the number of shares vesting against the maximum number of shares that could have been received, or, where paid in money and other assets, as a percentage of the maximum that could have been paid in respect of that component in the financial year.

18(3) For the purposes of sub-paragraphs (1), (2) and (6), **'relevant period'** means the specified period of financial years of which the last is the relevant financial year.

18(4) Where the relevant financial year–

    (a) is the company's first financial year for which the performance graph is prepared in accordance with this paragraph, **'specified'** in sub-paragraph (3) means 'five';

    (b) is the company's 'second', 'third', 'fourth', 'fifth' financial year in which the report is prepared in accordance with this Schedule, **'specified'** in sub-paragraph (3) means 'six', 'seven', 'eight', 'nine' as the case may be; and

    (c) is any financial year after the fifth financial year in which the report is prepared in accordance with this Schedule, **'specified'** means 'ten'.

18(5) Sub-paragraph (2) may be complied with by use of either–

    (a) a sum based on the information supplied in the directors' remuneration reports for those previous years, or,

    (b) where no such report has been compiled, a suitable corresponding sum.

18(6) For the purposes of sub-paragraph (1), the 'total shareholder return' for a relevant period on a holding of shares must be calculated using a fair method that–

    (a) takes as its starting point the percentage change over the period in the market price of the holding;

    (b) involves making–
        (i) the assumptions specified in sub-paragraph (7) as to reinvestment of income, and
        (ii) the assumption specified in sub-paragraph (9) as to the funding of liabilities; and

    (c) makes provision for any replacement of shares in the holding by shares of a different description;

and the same method must be used for each of the holdings mentioned in sub-paragraph (1).

18(7)   The assumptions as to reinvestment of income are–

(a)   that any benefit in the form of shares of the same kind as those in the holding is added to the holding at the time the benefit becomes receivable; and

(b)   that any benefit in cash, and an amount equal to the value of any benefit not in cash and not falling within paragraph (a), is applied at the time the benefit becomes receivable in the purchase at their market price of shares of the same kind as those in the holding and that the shares purchased are added to the holding at that time.

18(8)   In sub-paragraph (7) **'benefit'** means any benefit (including, in particular, any dividend) receivable in respect of any shares in the holding by the holder from the company of whose share capital the shares form part.

18(9)   The assumption as to the funding of liabilities is that, where the holder has a liability to the company of whose capital the shares in the holding form part, shares are sold from the holding–

(a)   immediately before the time by which the liability is due to be satisfied, and

(b)   in such numbers that, at the time of the sale, the market price of the shares sold equals the amount of the liability in respect of the shares in the holding that are not being sold.

18(10)   In sub-paragraph (9) **'liability'** means a liability arising in respect of any shares in the holding or from the exercise of a right attached to any of those shares.

PERCENTAGE CHANGE IN REMUNERATION OF DIRECTOR UNDERTAKING THE ROLE OF CHIEF EXECUTIVE OFFICER

19(1)   The directors' remuneration report must set out (in a manner which permits comparison) in relation to each of the kinds of remuneration required to be set out in each of the columns headed 'a', 'b' and 'c' of the single total figure table the following information–

(a)   the percentage change from the financial year preceding the relevant financial year in respect of the director undertaking the role of the chief executive officer; and

(b)   the average percentage change from the financial year preceding the relevant financial year in respect of the employees of the company taken as a whole.

19(2)   Where for the purposes of sub-paragraph (1)(b), a comparator group comprising the employees taken as a whole is considered by the company as an inappropriate comparator group of employees, the company may use such other comparator group of employees as the company identifies, provided the report contains a statement setting out why that group was chosen.

19(3)   Where the company is a parent company, the statement must relate to the group and not the company, and the director reported on is the director undertaking the role of chief executive officer of the parent company, and the employees are the employees of the group.

RELATIVE IMPORTANCE OF SPEND ON PAY

20(1)   The directors' remuneration report must set out in a graphical or tabular form that shows in respect of the relevant financial year and the immediately preceding financial year the actual expenditure of the company, and the difference in spend between those years, on–

(a)   remuneration paid to or receivable by all employees of the group;

(b)   distributions to shareholders by way of dividend and share buyback; and

(c)   any other significant distributions and payments or other uses of profit or cashflow deemed by the directors to assist in understanding the relative importance of spend on pay.

20(2)   There must be set out in a note to the report an explanation in respect of subparagraph (1)(c) why the particular matters were chosen by the directors and how the amounts were calculated.

20(3) Where the matters chosen for the report in respect of sub-paragraph (1)(c) in the relevant financial year are not the same as the other items set out in the report for previous years, an explanation for that change must be given.

STATEMENT OF IMPLEMENTATION OF REMUNERATION POLICY IN THE FOLLOWING FINANCIAL YEAR

21(1) The directors' remuneration report must contain a statement describing how the company intends to implement the approved directors' remuneration policy in the financial year following the relevant financial year.

21(2) The statement must include, where applicable, the–

(a) performance measures and relative weightings for each; and

(b) performance targets determined for the performance measures and how awards will be calculated.

21(3) Where this is not the first year of the approved remuneration policy, the statement should detail any significant changes in the way that the remuneration policy will be implemented in the next financial year compared to how it was implemented in the relevant financial year.

21(4) This statement need not include information that is elsewhere in the report, including any disclosed in the directors' remuneration policy.

CONSIDERATION BY THE DIRECTORS OF MATTERS RELATING TO DIRECTORS' REMUNERATION

22(1) If a committee of the company's directors has considered matters relating to the directors' remuneration for the relevant financial year, the directors' remuneration report must–

(a) name each director who was a member of the committee at any time when the committee was considering any such matter;

(b) state whether any person provided to the committee advice, or services, that materially assisted the committee in their consideration of any such matter and name any person that has done so;

(c) in the case of any person named under paragraph (b), who is not a director of the company (other than a person who provided legal advice on compliance with any relevant legislation), state–

(i) the nature of any other services that that person has provided to the company during the relevant financial year;

(ii) by whom that person was appointed, whether or not by the committee and how they were selected;

(iii) whether and how the remuneration committee has satisfied itself that the advice received was objective and independent; and

(iv) the amount of fee or other charge paid by the company to that person for the provision of the advice or services referred to in paragraph (b) and the basis on which it was charged.

22(2) In sub-paragraph (1)(b) **'person'** includes (in particular) any director of the company who does not fall within sub-paragraph (1)(a).

22(3) Sub-paragraph (1)(c) does not apply where the person was, at the time of the provision of the advice or service, an employee of the company.

22(4) This paragraph also applies to a committee which considers remuneration issues during the consideration of an individual's nomination as a director.

STATEMENT OF VOTING AT GENERAL MEETING

23   The directors' remuneration report must contain a statement setting out in respect of the last general meeting at which a resolution of the following kind was moved by the company–

(a)   in respect of a resolution to approve the directors' remuneration report, the percentage of votes cast for and against and the number of votes withheld;

(b)   in respect of a resolution to approve the directors' remuneration policy, the percentage of votes cast for and against and the number of votes withheld; and,

(c)   where there was a significant percentage of votes against either such resolution, a summary of the reasons for those votes, as far as known to the directors, and any actions taken by the directors in response to those concerns.

Part 4 – Directors' Remuneration Policy
INTRODUCTORY

24(1)   The information required to be included in the directors' remuneration report by the provisions of this Part must be set out in a separate part of the report and constitutes the directors' remuneration policy of the company.

24(2)   (2) Where a company intends to move a resolution at a meeting of the company to approve a directors' remuneration policy and it is intended that some or all of the provisions of the last approved directors' remuneration policy are to continue to apply after the resolution is approved, this fact must be stated in the policy which is the subject of the resolution and it must be made clear which provisions of the last approved policy are to continue to apply and for what period of time it is intended that they shall apply.

24(3)   Notwithstanding the requirements of this Part, the directors' remuneration policy part of the report must set out all those matters for which the company requires approval for the purposes of Chapter 4A of Part 10 of the 2006 Act.

24(4)   Where any provision of the directors' remuneration policy provides for the exercise by the directors of a discretion on any aspect of the policy, the policy must clearly set out the extent of that discretion in respect of any such variation, change or amendment.

24(5)   The directors' remuneration policy (or revised directors' remuneration policy) of a company in respect of which a company moves a resolution for approval in accordance with section 439A of the 2006 Act must, on the first occasion that such a resolution is moved after 1st October 2013 set out the date from which it is intended by the company that that policy is to take effect.

FUTURE POLICY TABLE

25(1)   The directors' remuneration report must contain in tabular form a description of each of the components of the remuneration package for the directors of the company which are comprised in the directors' remuneration policy of the company.

25(2)   Where the report complies with sub-paragraph (1) by reference to provisions which apply generally to all directors, the table must also include any particular arrangements which are specific to any director individually.

25(3)   References in this Part to **'component parts of the remuneration package'** include, but are not limited to, all those items which are relevant for the purposes of the single total figure table.

26   In respect of each of the components described in the table there must be set out the following information–

(a)   how that component supports the short and long-term strategic objectives of the company (or, where the company is a parent company, the group);

(b)   an explanation of how that component of the remuneration package operates;

(c)   the maximum that may be paid in respect of that component (which may be expressed in monetary terms, or otherwise);

(d)   where applicable, a description of the framework used to assess performance including–

  (i)   a description of any performance measures which apply and, where more than one performance measure applies, an indication of the weighting of the performance measure or group of performance measures;

  (ii)   details of any performance period; and

  (iii)   the amount (which may be expressed in monetary terms or otherwise) that may be paid in respect of–

    (aa)   the minimum level of performance that results in any payment under the policy, and

    (bb)   any further levels of performance set in accordance with the policy;

(e)   an explanation as to whether there are any provisions for the recovery of sums paid or the withholding of the payment of any sum.

27   There must accompany the table notes which set out–

(a)   in respect of any component falling within paragraph 26(d)(i)–(iii), an explanation of why any performance measures were chosen and how any performance targets are set;

(b)   in respect of any component (other than salary, fees, benefits or pension) which is not subject to performance measures, an explanation of why there are no such measures;

(c)   if any component did not form part of the remuneration package in the last approved directors' remuneration policy, why that component is now contained in the remuneration package;

(d)   in respect of any component which did form a part of such a package, what changes have been made to it and why; and

(e)   an explanation of the differences (if any) in the company's policy on the remuneration of directors from the policy on the remuneration of employees generally (within the company, or where the company is a parent company, the group).

28   The information required by paragraph 25 may, in respect of directors not performing an executive function, be set out in a separate table and there must be set out in that table the approach of the company to the determination of–

(a)   the fee payable to such directors;

(b)   any additional fees payable for any other duties to the company;

(c)   such other items as are to be considered in the nature of remuneration.

APPROACH TO RECRUITMENT REMUNERATION

29(1)   The directors' remuneration policy must contain a statement of the principles which would be applied by the company when agreeing the components of a remuneration package for the appointment of directors.

29(2)   The statement must set out the various components which would be considered for inclusion in that package and the approach to be adopted by the company in respect of each component.

29(3)   The statement must, subject to sub-paragraph (4), set out the maximum level of variable remuneration which may be granted (which can be expressed in monetary terms or otherwise).

29(4) Remuneration which constitutes compensation for the forfeit of any award under variable remuneration arrangements entered into with a previous employer is not included within sub-paragraph (3) of this paragraph, but is subject to the requirements of subparagraphs (1) and (2).

SERVICE CONTRACTS

30 The directors' remuneration policy must contain a description of any obligation on the company which–

(a) is contained in all directors' service contracts;

(b) is contained in the service contracts of any one or more existing directors (not being covered by paragraph (a)); or

(c) it is proposed would be contained in directors' service contracts to be entered into by the company

and which could give rise to, or impact on, remuneration payments or payments for loss of office but which is not disclosed elsewhere in this report.

31 Where the directors' service contracts are not kept available for inspection at the company's registered office, the report must give details of where the contracts are kept, and if the contracts are available on a website, a link to that website.

32 The provisions of paragraphs 30 and 31 relating to directors' service contracts apply in like manner to the terms of letters of appointment of directors.

ILLUSTRATIONS OF APPLICATION OF REMUNERATION POLICY

33 The directors' remuneration report must, in respect of each person who is a director (other than a director who is not performing an executive function), set out in the form of a bar chart an indication of the level of remuneration that would be received by the director in accordance with the directors' remuneration policy in the first year to which the policy applies.

34(1) The bar chart must contain separate bars representing–

(a) minimum remuneration receivable, that is to say, including, but not limited to, salary, fees, benefits and pension;

(b) the remuneration receivable if the director was, in respect of any performance measures or targets, performing in line with the company's expectation;

(c) maximum remuneration receivable (not allowing for any share price appreciation).

34(2) Each bar of the chart must contain separate parts which represent–

(a) salary, fees, benefits, pension and any other item falling within sub-paragraph 34(1)(a);

(b) remuneration where performance measures or targets relate to one financial year;

(c) remuneration where performance measures or targets relate to more than one financial year.

34(3) Each bar must show–

(a) percentage of the total comprised by each of the parts; and

(b) total value of remuneration expected for each bar.

35(1) A narrative description of the basis of calculation and assumptions used to compile the bar chart must be set out to enable an understanding of the charts presented.

35(2) In complying with sub-paragraph (1) it is not necessary for any matter to be included in the narrative description which has been set out in the future policy table required by paragraph 25.

POLICY ON PAYMENT FOR LOSS OF OFFICE

36 The directors' remuneration policy must set out the company's policy on the setting of notice periods under directors' service contracts.

37 The directors' remuneration policy must also set out the principles on which the determination of payments for loss of office will be approached including–

(a) an indication of how each component of the payment will be calculated;

(b) whether, and if so how, the circumstances of the director's loss of office and performance during the period of qualifying service are relevant to any exercise of discretion; and

(c) any contractual provision agreed prior to 27th June 2012 that could impact on the quantum of the payment.

STATEMENT OF CONSIDERATION OF EMPLOYMENT CONDITIONS ELSEWHERE IN COMPANY

38 The directors' remuneration policy must contain a statement of how pay and employment conditions of employees (other than directors) of the company and, where the company is a parent company, of the group of other undertakings within the same group as the company, were taken into account when setting the policy for directors' remuneration.

39 The statement must also set out–

(a) whether, and if so, how, the company consulted with employees when drawing up the directors' remuneration policy set out in this part of the report;

(b) whether any remuneration comparison measurements were used and if so, what they were, and how that information was taken into account.

STATEMENT OF CONSIDERATION OF SHAREHOLDER VIEWS

40 The directors' remuneration policy must contain a statement of whether, and if so how, any views in respect of directors' remuneration expressed to the company by shareholders (whether at a general meeting or otherwise) have been taken into account in the formulation of the directors' remuneration policy.

Part 5 – Provisions of the Directors' Remuneration Report Which are Subject to Audit

41 The information contained in the directors' remuneration report which is subject to audit is the information required by paragraphs 4 to 17 (inclusive) of Part 3 of this Schedule.

Part 6 – Revised Directors' Remuneration Policy

42 A revised directors' remuneration policy prepared in accordance with section 422A of the 2006 Act must contain all those matters required by Part 4 of this Schedule to be in the directors' remuneration policy.

43 A revised directors' remuneration policy must be set out in the same manner as required by Part 4 of this Schedule in respect of that part of the directors' remuneration report.

Part 7 – Interpretation and Supplementary

44(1) In this Schedule–

'amount', in relation to a gain made on the exercise of a share option, means the difference between–

(a) the market price of the shares on the day on which the option was exercised; and

(b) the price actually paid for the shares;

'company contributions', in relation to a pension scheme and a person, means any payments (including insurance premiums) made, or treated as made, to the scheme in respect of the person by anyone other than the person;

'emoluments' of a person–

(a) include salary, fees and bonuses, sums paid by way of expenses allowance (so far as they are chargeable to United Kingdom income tax or would be if the person were an individual or would be if the person were resident in the United Kingdom for tax purposes), but

(b) do not include any of the following, namely–

    (i) the value of any share options granted to him or the amount of any gains made on the exercise of any such options;

    (ii) any company contributions paid, or treated as paid, in respect of him under any pension scheme or any benefits to which he is entitled under any such scheme; or

    (iii) any money or other assets paid to or received or receivable by him under any scheme;

'pension scheme' means a retirement benefits scheme within the meaning given by section 150(1) of the Finance Act 2004 which is–

(a) one in which the company participates or

(b) one to which the company paid a contribution during the financial year;

'performance measure' is the measure by which performance is to be assessed, but does not include any condition relating to service:

'performance target' is the specific level of performance to be attained in respect of that performance measure;

"qualifying services", in relation to any person, means his services as a director of the company, and his services at any time while he is a director of the company–

(a) as a director of an undertaking that is a subsidiary undertaking of the company at that time;

(b) as a director of any other undertaking of which he is a director by virtue of the company's nomination (direct or indirect); or

(c) otherwise in connection with the management of the affairs of the company or any such subsidiary undertaking or any such other undertaking;

'remuneration committee' means a committee of directors of the company having responsibility for considering matters related to the remuneration of directors;

'retirement benefits' means relevant benefits within the meaning given by section 393B of the Income Tax (Earnings and Pensions) Act 2003 read as if subsection (2) were omitted;

'scheme' (other than a pension scheme) means any agreement or arrangement under which money or other assets may become receivable by a person and which includes one or more qualifying conditions with respect to service or performance that cannot be fulfilled within a single financial year, and for this purpose the following must be disregarded, namely–

(a) any payment the amount of which falls to be determined by reference to service or performance within a single financial year;

(b) compensation in respect of loss of office, payments for breach of contract and other termination payments; and

(c) retirement benefits;

'scheme interest' means an interest under a scheme;

'shares' means shares (whether allotted or not) in the company, or any undertaking which is a group undertaking in relation to the company, and includes a share warrant as defined by section 779(1) of the 2006 Act;

'share option' means a right to acquire shares;

'value' in relation to shares received or receivable on any day by a person who is or has been a director of a company, means the market price of the shares on that day.

44(2) In this Schedule **'compensation in respect of loss of office'** includes compensation received or receivable by a person for—

(a) loss of office as director of the company, or

(b) loss, while director of the company or on or in connection with his ceasing to be a director of it, of—

  (i) any other office in connection with the management of the company' affairs; or
  (ii) any office as director or otherwise in connection with the management of the affairs of any undertaking that, immediately before the loss, is a subsidiary undertaking of the company or an undertaking of which he is a director by virtue of the company's nomination (direct or indirect);

(c) compensation in consideration for, or in connection with, a person's retirement from office; and

(d) where such a retirement is occasioned by a breach of the person's contract with the company or with an undertaking that, immediately before the breach, is a subsidiary undertaking of the company or an undertaking of which he is a director by virtue of the company's nomination (direct or indirect)—

  (i) payments made by way of damages for the breach; or
  (ii) payments made by way of settlement or compromise of any claim in respect of the breach.

44(3) References in this Schedule to compensation include benefits otherwise than in cash; and in relation to such compensation references in this Schedule to its amounts are to the estimated money value of the benefit.

44(4) References in this Schedule to a person being **'connected'** with a director, and to a director **'controlling'** a body corporate, are to be construed in accordance with sections 252 to 255 of the 2006 Act.

45 For the purposes of this Schedule emoluments paid or receivable or share options granted in respect of a person's accepting office as a director are to be treated as emoluments paid or receivable or share options granted in respect of his services as a director.

46(1) The following applies with respect to the amounts to be shown under this Schedule.

46(2) The amount in each case includes all relevant sums paid by or receivable from—

(a) the company; and

(b) the company's subsidiary undertakings; and

(c) any other person,

except sums to be accounted for to the company or any of its subsidiary undertakings or any other undertaking of which any person has been a director while director of the company, by virtue of section 219 of the 2006 Act (payment in connection with share transfer: requirement of members' approval), to past or present members of the company or any of its subsidiaries or any class of those members.

46(3)   Reference to amounts paid to or receivable by a person include amounts paid to or receivable by a person connected with the person or a body corporate controlled by the person (but not so as to require an amount to be counted twice).

47(1)   The amounts to be shown for any financial year under Part 3 of this Schedule are the sums receivable in respect of that year (whenever paid) or, in the case of sums not receivable in respect of a period, the sums paid during that year.

47(2)   But where—

(a)   any sums are not shown in the directors' remuneration report for the relevant financial year on the ground that the person receiving them is liable to account for them as mentioned in paragraph 46(2), but the liability is thereafter wholly or partly released or is not enforced within a period of 2 years; or

(b)   any sums paid by way of expenses allowance are charged to United Kingdom income tax after the end of the relevant financial year or, in the case of any such sums paid otherwise than to an individual, it does not become clear until the end of the relevant financial year that those sums would be charged to such tax were the person an individual,

those sums must, to the extent to which the liability is released or not enforced or they are charged as mentioned above (as the case may be), be shown in the first directors' remuneration report in which it is practicable to show them and must be distinguished from the amounts to be shown apart from this provision.

48   Where it is necessary to do so for the purpose of making any distinction required by the preceding paragraphs in an amount to be shown in compliance with this Schedule, the directors may apportion any payments between the matters in respect of which these have been paid or are receivable in such manner as they think appropriate.

49   The Schedule requires information to be given only so far as it is contained in the company's books and papers, available to members of the public or the company has the right to obtain it.

History – Sch. 8 substituted by SI 2013/1981, reg. 3 and Sch., with with effect from 1 October 2013. The following transitional provision is made by SI 2013/1981, reg. 4:

"**4(1)**   The amendments made by these Regulations to the 2008 Regulations do not apply to a company in respect of a financial year ending before 30th September 2013.

4(2)   The provisions of the 2008 Regulations as they stood immediately before 1st October 2013 continue to apply in respect of a financial year ending before 30th September 2013.

4(3)   The provisions of Part 6 of Schedule 8 apply to a revised directors' remuneration policy set out in a document in accordance with section 422A (3) of the Companies Act 2006 on or after 1st October 2013."

Prior to substitution, Sch. 8 read as follows:

"SCHEDULE 8 – QUOTED COMPANIES: DIRECTORS' REMUNERATION REPORT

Regulation 11

Part 1 – Introductory

1(1)   In the directors' remuneration report for a financial year ('the relevant financial year') there must be shown the information specified in Parts 2 and 3.

1(2)   Information required to be shown in the report for or in respect of a particular person must be shown in the report in a manner that links the information to that person identified by name.

Part 2 – Information not subject to audit

CONSIDERATION BY THE DIRECTORS OF MATTERS RELATING TO DIRECTORS' REMUNERATION

2(1) If a committee of the company's directors has considered matters relating to the directors' remuneration for the relevant financial year, the directors' remuneration report must–

    (a) name each director who was a member of the committee at any time when the committee was considering any such matter;

    (b) name any person who provided to the committee advice, or services, that materially assisted the committee in their consideration of any such matter;

    (c) in the case of any person named under paragraph (b), who is not a director of the company, state–

        (i) the nature of any other services that that person has provided to the company during the relevant financial year; and

        (ii) whether that person was appointed by the committee.

2(2) In sub-paragraph (1)(b) **'person'** includes (in particular) any director of the company who does not fall within sub-paragraph (1)(a).

STATEMENT OF COMPANY'S POLICY ON DIRECTORS' REMUNERATION

3(1) The directors' remuneration report must contain a statement of the company's policy on directors' remuneration for the following financial year and for financial years subsequent to that.

3(2) The policy statement must include–

    (a) for each director, a detailed summary of any performance conditions to which any entitlement of the director–

        (i) to share options, or

        (ii) under a long term incentive scheme, is subject;

    (b) an explanation as to why any such performance conditions were chosen;

    (c) a summary of the methods to be used in assessing whether any such performance conditions are met and an explanation as to why those methods were chosen;

    (d) if any such performance condition involves any comparison with factors external to the company–

        (i) a summary of the factors to be used in making each such comparison, and

        (ii) if any of the factors relates to the performance of another company, of two or more other companies or of an index on which the securities of a company or companies are listed, the identity of that company, of each of those companies or of the index;

    (e) a description of, and an explanation for, any significant amendment proposed to be made to the terms and conditions of any entitlement of a director to share options or under a long term incentive scheme; and

    (f) if any entitlement of a director to share options, or under a long term incentive scheme, is not subject to performance conditions, an explanation as to why that is the case.

3(3) The policy statement must, in respect of each director's terms and conditions relating to remuneration, explain the relative importance of those elements which are, and those which are not, related to performance.

3(4) The policy statement must summarise, and explain, the company's policy on–

    (a) the duration of contracts with directors, and

    (b) notice periods, and termination payments, under such contracts.

3(5) In sub-paragraphs (2) and (3), references to a director are to any person who serves as a director of the company at any time in the period beginning with the end of the relevant financial year and ending with the date on which the directors' remuneration report is laid before the company in general meeting.

STATEMENT OF CONSIDERATION OF CONDITIONS ELSEWHERE IN COMPANY AND GROUP

4 The directors' remuneration report must contain a statement of how pay and employment conditions of employees of the company and of other undertakings within the same group as the company were taken into account when determining directors' remuneration for the relevant financial year.

PERFORMANCE GRAPH

5(1) The directors' remuneration report must–

    (a) contain a line graph that shows for each of–

        (i) a holding of shares of that class of the company's equity share capital whose listing, or admission to dealing, has resulted in the company falling within the definition of **'quoted company'**, and

        (ii) a hypothetical holding of shares made up of shares of the same kinds and number as those by reference to which a broad equity market index is calculated, a line drawn by joining up points plotted to represent, for each of the financial years in the relevant period, the total shareholder return on that holding; and

    (b) state the name of the index selected for the purposes of the graph and set out the reasons for selecting that index.

5(2) For the purposes of sub-paragraphs (1) and (4), **'relevant period'** means the five financial years of which the last is the relevant financial year.

5(3) Where the relevant financial year—

(a) is the company's second, third or fourth financial year, sub-paragraph (2) has effect with the substitution of 'two', 'three' or 'four' (as the case may be) for 'five'; and

(b) is the company's first financial year, **'relevant period'**, for the purposes of subparagraphs (1) and (4), means the relevant financial year.

5(4) For the purposes of sub-paragraph (1), the **'total shareholder return'** for a relevant period on a holding of shares must be calculated using a fair method that—

(a) takes as its starting point the percentage change over the period in the market price of the holding;

(b) involves making—

(i) the assumptions specified in sub-paragraph (5) as to reinvestment of income, and

(ii) the assumption specified in sub-paragraph (7) as to the funding of liabilities, and

(c) makes provision for any replacement of shares in the holding by shares of a different description; and the same method must be used for each of the holdings mentioned in sub-paragraph (1).

5(5) The assumptions as to reinvestment of income are—

(a) that any benefit in the form of shares of the same kind as those in the holding is added to the holding at the time the benefit becomes receivable; and

(b) that any benefit in cash, and an amount equal to the value of any benefit not in cash and not falling within paragraph (a), is applied at the time the benefit becomes receivable in the purchase at their market price of shares of the same kind as those in the holding and that the shares purchased are added to the holding at that time.

5(6) In sub-paragraph (5) **'benefit'** means any benefit (including, in particular, any dividend) receivable in respect of any shares in the holding by the holder from the company of whose share capital the shares form part.

5(7) The assumption as to the funding of liabilities is that, where the holder has a liability to the company of whose capital the shares in the holding form part, shares are sold from the holding—

(a) immediately before the time by which the liability is due to be satisfied, and

(b) in such numbers that, at the time of the sale, the market price of the shares sold equals the amount of the liability in respect of the shares in the holding that are not being sold.

5(8) In sub-paragraph (7) **'liability'** means a liability arising in respect of any shares in the holding or from the exercise of a right attached to any of those shares.

SERVICE CONTRACTS

6(1) The directors' remuneration report must contain, in respect of the contract of service or contract for services of each person who has served as a director of the company at any time during the relevant financial year, the following information—

(a) the date of the contract, the unexpired term and the details of any notice periods;

(b) any provision for compensation payable upon early termination of the contract; and

(c) such details of other provisions in the contract as are necessary to enable members of the company to estimate the liability of the company in the event of early termination of the contract.

6(2) The directors' remuneration report must contain an explanation for any significant award made to a person in the circumstances described in paragraph 15.

Part 3 – Information subject to audit

AMOUNT OF EACH DIRECTOR'S EMOLUMENTS AND COMPENSATION IN THE RELEVANT FINANCIAL YEAR

7(1) The directors' remuneration report must for the relevant financial year show, for each person who has served as a director of the company at any time during that year, each of the following—

(a) the total amount of salary and fees paid to or receivable by the person in respect of qualifying services;

(b) the total amount of bonuses so paid or receivable;

(c) the total amount of sums paid by way of expenses allowance that are—

(i) chargeable to United Kingdom income tax (or would be if the person were an individual), and

(ii) paid to or receivable by the person in respect of qualifying services;

(d) the total amount of—

(i) any compensation for loss of office paid to or receivable by the person, and

(ii) any other payments paid to or receivable by the person in connection with the termination of qualifying services;

(e) the total estimated value of any benefits received by the person otherwise than in cash that—

(i) do not fall within any of paragraphs (a) to (d) or paragraphs 8 to 12,

(ii) are emoluments of the person, and

(iii) are received by the person in respect of qualifying services; and

(f) the amount that is the total of the sums mentioned in paragraphs (a) to (e).

7(2)   The directors' remuneration report must show, for each person who has served as a director of the company at any time during the relevant financial year, the amount that for the financial year preceding the relevant financial year is the total of the sums mentioned in paragraphs (a) to (e) of sub-paragraph (1).

7(3)   The directors' remuneration report must also state the nature of any element of a remuneration package which is not cash.

7(4)   The information required by sub-paragraphs (1) and (2) must be presented in tabular form.

SHARE OPTIONS

8(1)   The directors' remuneration report must contain, in respect of each person who has served as a director of the company at any time in the relevant financial year, the information specified in paragraph 9.

8(2)   Sub-paragraph (1) is subject to paragraph 10 (aggregation of information to avoid excessively lengthy reports).

8(3)   The information specified in sub-paragraphs (a) to (c) of paragraph 9 must be presented in tabular form in the report.

8(4)   In paragraph 9 **'share option'**, in relation to a person, means a share option granted in respect of qualifying services of the person.

9   The information required by sub-paragraph (1) of paragraph 8 in respect of such a person as is mentioned in that sub-paragraph is–

  (a)   the number of shares that are subject to a share option–

    (i)   at the beginning of the relevant financial year or, if later, on the date of the appointment of the person as a director of the company, and
    (ii)   at the end of the relevant financial year or, if earlier, on the cessation of the person's appointment as a director of the company, in each case differentiating between share options having different terms and conditions;

  (b)   information identifying those share options that have been awarded in the relevant financial year, those that have been exercised in that year, those that in that year have expired unexercised and those whose terms and conditions have been varied in that year;

  (c)   for each share option that is unexpired at any time in the relevant financial year–

    (i)   the price paid, if any, for its award,
    (ii)   the exercise price,
    (iii)   the date from which the option may be exercised, and
    (iv)   the date on which the option expires;

  (d)   a description of any variation made in the relevant financial year in the terms and conditions of a share option;

  (e)   a summary of any performance criteria upon which the award or exercise of a share option is conditional, including a description of any variation made in such performance criteria during the relevant financial year;

  (f)   for each share option that has been exercised during the relevant financial year, the market price of the shares, in relation to which it is exercised, at the time of exercise; and

  (g)   for each share option that is unexpired at the end of the relevant financial year–

    (i)   the market price at the end of that year, and
    (ii)   the highest and lowest market prices during that year, of each share that is subject to the option.

10(1)   If, in the opinion of the directors of the company, disclosure in accordance with paragraphs 8 and 9 would result in a disclosure of excessive length then, (subject to subparagraphs (2) and (3))–

  (a)   information disclosed for a person under paragraph 9(a) need not differentiate between share options having different terms and conditions;

  (b)   for the purposes of disclosure in respect of a person under paragraph 9(c)(i) and (ii) and (g), share options may be aggregated and (instead of disclosing prices for each share option) disclosure may be made of weighted average prices of aggregations of share options;

  (c)   for the purposes of disclosure in respect of a person under paragraph 9(c)(iii) and (iv), share options may be aggregated and (instead of disclosing dates for each share option) disclosure may be made of ranges of dates for aggregation of share options.

10(2)   Sub-paragraph (1)(b) and (c) does not permit the aggregation of–

  (a)   share options in respect of shares whose market price at the end of the relevant financial year is below the option exercise price, with

  (b)   share options in respect of shares whose market price at the end of the relevant financial year is equal to, or exceeds, the option exercise price.

10(3)   Sub-paragraph (1) does not apply (and accordingly, full disclosure must be made in accordance with paragraphs 8 and 9) in respect of share options that during the relevant financial year have been awarded or exercised or had their terms and conditions varied.

LONG TERM INCENTIVE SCHEMES

11(1)   The directors' remuneration report must contain, in respect of each person who has served as a director of the company at any time in the relevant financial year, the information specified in paragraph 12.

11(2)   Sub-paragraph (1) does not require the report to contain share option details that are contained in the report in compliance with paragraphs 8 to 10.

11(3)   The information specified in paragraph 12 must be presented in tabular form in the report.

11(4)   For the purposes of paragraph 12–

(a)   **'scheme interest'**, in relation to a person, means an interest under a long term incentive scheme that is an interest in respect of which assets may become receivable under the scheme in respect of qualifying services of the person; and

(b)   such an interest **'vests'** at the earliest time when–

    (i)   it has been ascertained that the qualifying conditions have been fulfilled, and

    (ii)   the nature and quantity of the assets receivable under the scheme in respect of the interest have been ascertained.

11(5)   In this Schedule **'long term incentive scheme'** means any agreement or arrangement under which money or other assets may become receivable by a person and which includes one or more qualifying conditions with respect to service or performance that cannot be fulfilled within a single financial year, and for this purpose the following must be disregarded, namely–

(a)   any bonus the amount of which falls to be determined by reference to service or performance within a single financial year;

(b)   compensation in respect of loss of office, payments for breach of contract and other termination payments; and

(c)   retirement benefits.

12(1)   The information required by sub-paragraph (1) of paragraph 11 in respect of such a person as is mentioned in that sub-paragraph is–

(a)   details of the scheme interests that the person has at the beginning of the relevant financial year or if later on the date of the appointment of the person as a director of the company;

(b)   details of the scheme interests awarded to the person during the relevant financial year;

(c)   details of the scheme interests that the person has at the end of the relevant financial year or if earlier on the cessation of the person's appointment as a director of the company;

(d)   for each scheme interest within paragraphs (a) to (c)–

    (i)   the end of the period over which the qualifying conditions for that interest have to be fulfilled (or if there are different periods for different conditions, the end of whichever of those periods ends last); and

    (ii)   a description of any variation made in the terms and conditions of the scheme interests during the relevant financial year; and

(e)   for each scheme interest that has vested in the relevant financial year–

    (i)   the relevant details (see sub-paragraph (3)) of any shares,

    (ii)   the amount of any money, and

    (iii)   the value of any other assets, that have become receivable in respect of the interest.

12(2)   The details that sub-paragraph (1)(b) requires of a scheme interest awarded during the relevant financial year include, if shares may become receivable in respect of the interest, the following–

(a)   the number of those shares;

(b)   the market price of each of those shares when the scheme interest was awarded; and

(c)   details of qualifying conditions that are conditions with respect to performance.

12(3)   In sub-paragraph (1)(e)(i) **'the relevant details'**, in relation to any shares that have become receivable in respect of a scheme interest, means–

(a)   the number of those shares;

(b)   the date on which the scheme interest was awarded;

(c)   the market price of each of those shares when the scheme interest was awarded;

(d)   the market price of each of those shares when the scheme interest vested; and

(e)   details of qualifying conditions that were conditions with respect to performance.

PENSIONS

13(1)   The directors' remuneration report must, for each person who has served as a director of the company at any time during the relevant financial year, contain the information in respect of pensions that is specified in sub-paragraphs (2) and (3).

13(2)   Where the person has rights under a pension scheme that is a defined benefit scheme in relation to the person and any of those rights are rights to which he has become entitled in respect of qualifying services of his–

(a)   details–

    (i)   of any changes during the relevant financial year in the person's accrued benefits under the scheme, and

    (ii)   of the person's accrued benefits under the scheme as at the end of that year;

[version of sub-paragraph (b) applying in relation to financial years beginning on or after 6 April 2008 and ending before 26 June 2009]

(b)   the transfer value, calculated in a manner consistent with 'Retirement Benefit Schemes – Transfer Values (GN 11)' published by the Institute of Actuaries and the Faculty of Actuaries and dated 6th April 2001, of the person's accrued benefits under the scheme at the end of the relevant financial year;

[version of sub-paragraph (b) applying in relation to financial years beginning on or after 6 April 2008 and not ending before 26 June 2009]

(b)   the transfer value, calculated in accordance with regulations 7 to 7E of the Occupational Pension Schemes (Transfer Values) Regulations 1996, of the person's accrued benefits under the scheme at the end of the relevant financial year;

(c)   the transfer value of the person's accrued benefits under the scheme that in compliance with paragraph (b) was contained in the directors' remuneration report for the previous financial year or, if there was no such report or no such value was contained in that report, the transfer value, calculated in such a manner as is mentioned in paragraph (b), of the person's accrued benefits under the scheme at the beginning of the relevant financial year;

(d)   the amount obtained by subtracting–

(i)   the transfer value of the person's accrued benefits under the scheme that is required to be contained in the report by paragraph (c), from

(ii)   the transfer value of those benefits that is required to be contained in the report by paragraph (b), and then subtracting from the result of that calculation the amount of any contributions made to the scheme by the person in the relevant financial year.

13(3) Where–

(a)   the person has rights under a pension scheme that is a money purchase scheme in relation to the person, and

(b)   any of those rights are rights to which he has become entitled in respect of qualifying services of his, details of any contribution to the scheme in respect of the person that is paid or payable by the company for the relevant financial year or paid by the company in that year for another financial year.

Notes – Para. (2)(b) substituted by SI 2009/1581 reg 12(1) and (3): 27 June 2009 applying in relation to financial years beginning on or after 6 April 2008 which have not ended before 27 June 2009

EXCESS RETIREMENT BENEFITS OF DIRECTORS AND PAST DIRECTORS

14(1) Subject to sub-paragraph (3), the directors' remuneration report must show in respect of each person who has served as a director of the company–

(a)   at any time during the relevant financial year, or

(b)   at any time before the beginning of that year, the amount of so much of retirement benefits paid to or receivable by the person under pension schemes as is in excess of the retirement benefits to which he was entitled on the date on which the benefits first became payable or 31st March 1997, whichever is the later.

14(2) In subsection (1) **'retirement benefits'** means retirement benefits to which the person became entitled in respect of qualifying services of his.

14(3) Amounts paid or receivable under a pension scheme need not be included in an amount required to be shown under sub-paragraph (1) if–

(a)   the funding of the scheme was such that the amounts were or, as the case may be, could have been paid without recourse to additional contributions; and

(b)   amounts were paid to or receivable by all pensioner members of the scheme on the same basis; and in this sub-paragraph **'pensioner member'**, in relation to a pension scheme, means any person who is entitled to the present payment of retirement benefits under the scheme.

14(4) In this paragraph–

(a)   references to retirement benefits include benefits otherwise than in cash; and

(b)   in relation to so much of retirement benefits as consists of a benefit otherwise than in cash, references to their amount are to the estimated money value of the benefit, and the nature of any such benefit must also be shown in the report.

COMPENSATION FOR PAST DIRECTORS

15   The directors' remuneration report must contain details of any significant award made in the relevant financial year to any person who was not a director of the company at the time the award was made but had previously been a director of the company, including (in particular) compensation in respect of loss of office and pensions but excluding any sums which have already been shown in the report under paragraph 7(1)(d).

SUMS PAID TO THIRD PARTIES IN RESPECT OF A DIRECTOR'S SERVICES

16(1) The directors' remuneration report must show, in respect of each person who served as a director of the company at any time during the relevant financial year, the aggregate amount of any consideration paid to or receivable by third parties for making available the services of the person–

(a)   as a director of the company, or

(b)   while director of the company–

    (i)   as director of any of its subsidiary undertakings, or

    (ii)   as director of any other undertaking of which he was (while director of the company) a director by virtue of the company's nomination (direct or indirect), or

    (iii) otherwise in connection with the management of the affairs of the company or any such other undertaking.

16(2)   The reference to consideration includes benefits otherwise than in cash; and in relation to such consideration the reference to its amount is to the estimated money value of the benefit.

The nature of any such consideration must be shown in the report.

16(3)   The reference to third parties is to persons other than–

   (a)   the person himself or a person connected with him or a body corporate controlled by him, and

   (b)   the company or any such other undertaking as is mentioned in sub-paragraph (1)(b)(ii).

Part 4 – Interpretation and supplementary

17(1)   In this Schedule–

'amount', in relation to a gain made on the exercise of a share option, means the difference between–

   (a)   the market price of the shares on the day on which the option was exercised; and

   (b)   the price actually paid for the shares;

'company contributions', in relation to a pension scheme and a person, means any payments (including insurance premiums) made, or treated as made, to the scheme in respect of the person by anyone other than the person;

'defined benefit scheme', in relation to a person, means a pension scheme which is not a money purchase scheme in relation to the person;

'emoluments' of a person–

   (a)   includes salary, fees and bonuses, sums paid by way of expenses allowance (so far as they are chargeable to United Kingdom income tax or would be if the person were an individual), but

   (b)   does not include any of the following, namely–

      (i)   the value of any share options granted to him or the amount of any gains made on the exercise of any such options;

      (ii) any company contributions paid, or treated as paid, in respect of him under any pension scheme or any benefits to which he is entitled under any such scheme; or

      (iii) any money or other assets paid to or received or receivable by him under any long term incentive scheme;

'long term incentive scheme' has the meaning given by paragraph 11(5); **'money purchase benefits'**, in relation to a person, means retirement benefits the rate or amount of which is calculated by reference to payments made, or treated as made, by the person or by any other person in respect of that person and which are not average salary benefits;

'money purchase scheme', in relation to a person, means a pension scheme under which all of the benefits that may become payable to or in respect of the person are money purchase benefits in relation to the person;

'pension scheme' means a retirement benefits scheme within the meaning given by section 611 of the Income and Corporation Taxes Act 1988;

'qualifying services', in relation to any person, means his services as a director of the company, and his services at any time while he is a director of the company–

   (a)   as a director of an undertaking that is a subsidiary undertaking of the company at that time;

   (b)   as a director of any other undertaking of which he is a director by virtue of the company's nomination (direct or indirect); or

   (c)   otherwise in connection with the management of the affairs of the company or any such subsidiary undertaking or any such other undertaking;

'retirement benefits' means relevant benefits within the meaning given by section 612(1) of the Income and Corporation Taxes Act 1988;

'shares' means shares (whether allotted or not) in the company, or any undertaking which is a group undertaking in relation to the company, and includes a share warrant as defined by section 779(1) of the 2006 Act;

'share option' means a right to acquire shares;

'value', in relation to shares received or receivable on any day by a person who is or has been a director of the company, means the market price of the shares on that day.

17(2)   In this Schedule **'compensation in respect of loss of office'** includes compensation received or receivable by a person for–

(a) loss of office as director of the company, or

(b) loss, while director of the company or on or in connection with his ceasing to be a director of it, of–

(i) any other office in connection with the management of the company's affairs, or

(ii) any office as director or otherwise in connection with the management of the affairs of any undertaking that, immediately before the loss, is a subsidiary undertaking of the company or an undertaking of which he is a director by virtue of the company's nomination (direct or indirect);

(c) compensation in consideration for, or in connection with, a person's retirement from office; and

(d) where such a retirement is occasioned by a breach of the person's contract with the company or with an undertaking that, immediately before the breach, is a subsidiary undertaking of the company or an undertaking of which he is a director by virtue of the company's nomination (direct or indirect)–

(i) payments made by way of damages for the breach; or

(ii) payments made by way of settlement or compromise of any claim in respect of the breach.

17(3) References in this Schedule to compensation include benefits otherwise than in cash; and in relation to such compensation references in this Schedule to its amounts are to the estimated money value of the benefit.

17(4) References in this Schedule to a person being 'connected' with a director, and to a director 'controlling' a body corporate, are to be construed in accordance with sections 252 to 255 of the 2006 Act.

18(1) For the purposes of this Schedule emoluments paid or receivable or share options granted in respect of a person's accepting office as a director are to be treated as emoluments paid or receivable or share options granted in respect of his services as a director.

18(2) Where a pension scheme provides for any benefits that may become payable to or in respect of a person to be whichever are the greater of–

(a) such benefits determined by or under the scheme as are money purchase benefits in relation to the person; and

(b) such retirement benefits determined by or under the scheme to be payable to or in respect of the person as are not money purchase benefits in relation to the person, the company may assume for the purposes of this Schedule that those benefits will be money purchase benefits in relation to the person, or not, according to whichever appears more likely at the end of the relevant financial year.

18(3) In determining for the purposes of this Schedule whether a pension scheme is a money purchase scheme in relation to a person or a defined benefit scheme in relation to a person, any death in service benefits provided for by the scheme are to be disregarded.

19(1) The following applies with respect to the amounts to be shown under this Schedule.

19(2) The amount in each case includes all relevant sums paid by or receivable from–

(a) the company; and

(b) the company's subsidiary undertakings; and

(c) any other person, except sums to be accounted for to the company or any of its subsidiary undertakings or any other undertaking of which any person has been a director while director of the company, by virtue of section 219 of the 2006 Act (payment in connection with share transfer: requirement of members' approval), to past or present members of the company or any of its subsidiaries or any class of those members.

19(3) Reference to amounts paid to or receivable by a person include amounts paid to or receivable by a person connected with him or a body corporate controlled by him (but not so as to require an amount to be counted twice).

20(1) The amounts to be shown for any financial year under Part 3 of this Schedule are the sums receivable in respect of that year (whenever paid) or, in the case of sums not receivable in respect of a period, the sums paid during that year.

20(2) But where–

(a) any sums are not shown in the directors' remuneration report for the relevant financial year on the ground that the person receiving them is liable to account for them as mentioned in paragraph 19(2), but the liability is thereafter wholly or partly released or is not enforced within a period of 2 years; or

(b) any sums paid by way of expenses allowance are charged to United Kingdom income tax after the end of the relevant financial year or, in the case of any such sums paid otherwise than to an individual, it does not become clear until the end of the relevant financial year that those sums would be charged to such tax were the person an individual, those sums must, to the extent to which the liability is released or not enforced or they are charged as mentioned above (as the case may be), be shown in the first directors' remuneration report in which it is practicable to show them and must be distinguished from the amounts to be shown apart from this provision.

21 Where it is necessary to do so for the purpose of making any distinction required by the preceding paragraphs in an amount to be shown in compliance with this Part of this Schedule, the directors may apportion any payments between the matters in respect of which these have been paid or are receivable in such manner as they think appropriate.

22 The Schedule requires information to be given only so far as it is contained in the company's books and papers, available to members of the public or the company has the right to obtain it."

SCHEDULE 9 – INTERPRETATION OF TERM 'PROVISIONS'

Regulation 12

Part 1 – Meaning for purposes of these regulations

DEFINITION OF 'PROVISIONS'

1(1) In these Regulations, references to provisions for depreciation or diminution in value of assets are to any amount written off by way of providing for depreciation or diminution in value of assets.

1(2) Any reference in the profit and loss account formats or the notes to them set out in Schedule 1, 2 or 3 to these Regulations to the depreciation of, or amounts written off, assets of any description is to any provision for depreciation or diminution in value of assets of that description.

2 References in these Regulations to provisions for liabilities or, in the case of insurance companies, to provisions for other risks are to any amount retained as reasonably necessary for the purpose of providing for any liability the nature of which is clearly defined and which is either likely to be incurred, or certain to be incurred but uncertain as to amount or as to the date on which it will arise.

2A At the balance sheet date, a provision must represent the best estimate of the expenses likely to be incurred or, in the case of a liability, of the amount required to meet that liability.

History – Para. 2A inserted by SI 2015/980, reg. 40, with effect in relation to–
  (a) financial years beginning on or after 1 January 2016, and
  (b) a financial year of a company beginning on or after 1 January 2015, but before 1 January 2016, if the directors of the company so decide.

2B Provisions must not be used to adjust the value of assets.

History – Para. 2B inserted by SI 2015/980, reg. 40, with effect in relation to–
  (a) financial years beginning on or after 1 January 2016, and
  (b) a financial year of a company beginning on or after 1 January 2015, but before 1 January 2016, if the directors of the company so decide.

Part 2 – Meaning for purposes of Parts 18 and 23 of the 2006 Act

FINANCIAL ASSISTANCE FOR PURCHASE OF OWN SHARES

3 The specified provisions for the purposes of section 677(3)(a) of the 2006 Act (Companies Act accounts: relevant provisions for purposes of financial assistance) are provisions within paragraph 2 of this Schedule.

REDEMPTION OR PURCHASE BY PRIVATE COMPANY OUT OF CAPITAL

4 The specified provisions for the purposes of section 712(2)(b)(i)1162(2) of the 2006 Act (Companies Act accounts: relevant provisions to determine available profits for redemption or purchase out of capital) are provisions of any of the kinds mentioned in paragraphs 1 and 2 of this Schedule.

NET ASSET RESTRICTION ON PUBLIC COMPANIES DISTRIBUTIONS

5 The specified provisions for the purposes of section 831(3)(a) of the 2006 Act (Companies Act accounts: net asset restriction on public company distributions) are–

(a) provisions within paragraph 2 of this Schedule, and

(b) in the case of an insurance company, any amount included under liabilities items Ba (fund for future appropriations), C (technical provisions) and D (technical provisions for linked liabilities) in a balance sheet drawn up in accordance with Schedule 3 to these Regulations.

DISTRIBUTIONS BY INVESTMENT COMPANIES

6   The specified provisions for the purposes of section 832(4)(a) of the 2006 Act (Companies Act accounts: investment companies distributions) are provisions within paragraph 2 of this Schedule.

JUSTIFICATION OF DISTRIBUTION BY REFERENCES TO ACCOUNTS

7   The specified provisions for the purposes of section 836(1)(b)(i) of the 2006 Act (Companies Act accounts: relevant provisions for distribution purposes)–

(a)   are provisions of any of the kinds mentioned in paragraphs 1 and 2 of this Schedule, and

(b)   in the case of an insurance company, any amount included under liabilities items Ba (fund for future appropriations), C (technical provisions) and D (technical provisions for linked liabilities) in a balance sheet drawn up in accordance with Schedule 3 to these Regulations.

REALISED LOSSES

8   The specified provisions for the purposes of section 841(2)(a) of the 2006 Act (Companies Act accounts: treatment of provisions as realised losses) are provisions of any of the kinds mentioned in paragraphs 1 and 2 of this Schedule.

Notes – Para. 8 inserted by SI 2009/1581 reg 12(1) and (4): 27 June 2009 applying in relation to financial years beginning on or after 6 April 2008 which have not ended before 27 June 2009.

SCHEDULE 10 – GENERAL INTERPRETATION
Regulation 13

CAPITALISATION

1   **'Capitalisation'**, in relation to work or costs, means treating that work or those costs as a fixed asset.

FINANCIAL INSTRUMENTS

2   Save in Schedule 2 to these Regulations, references to **'derivatives'** include commodity-based contracts that give either contracting party the right to settle in cash or in some other financial instrument, except where such contracts–

(a)   were entered into for the purpose of, and continue to meet, the company's expected purchase, sale or usage requirements,

(b)   were designated for such purpose at their inception, and

(c)   are expected to be settled by delivery of the commodity (for banking companies, see the definition in paragraph 94 of Schedule 2 to these Regulations).

3(1)   Save in Schedule 2 to these Regulations, the expressions listed in sub-paragraph (2) have the same meaning as they have in Directive 2013/34/EC of the European Parliament and of the Council of 26 June 2013 on the annual financial statements etc of certain types of undertakings and Council Directive 91/674/EEC of 19 December 1991 on the annual accounts and consolidated accounts of insurance undertakings (for banking companies, see the definition in paragraph 96 of Schedule 2 to these Regulations).

3(2)   Those expressions are 'available for sale financial asset', 'business combination', 'commodity-based contracts', 'derivative', 'equity instrument', 'exchange difference', 'fair value hedge accounting system', 'financial fixed asset', 'financial instrument', 'foreign entity', 'hedge accounting', 'hedge accounting system', 'hedged items', 'hedging instrument', 'held for trading purposes', 'held to maturity', 'monetary item', 'receivables', 'reliable market' and 'trading portfolio'.

History – Para. 3(1) substituted by SI 2015/980, reg. 41, with effect in relation to–

   (a) financial years beginning on or after 1 January 2016, and

   (b) a financial year of a company beginning on or after 1 January 2015, but before 1 January 2016, if the directors of the company so decide.

Former para. 3(1) read as follows:

"**3(1)** Save in Schedule 2 to these Regulations, the expressions listed in sub-paragraph (2) have the same meaning as they have in Council Directive 78/660/EEC on the annual accounts of certain types of companies(a) and 91/674/EEC on the annual accounts and consolidated accounts of insurance undertakings(b) (for banking companies, see the definition in paragraph 96 of Schedule 2 to these Regulations)."

FIXED AND CURRENT ASSETS

4 **'Fixed assets'** means assets of a company which are intended for use on a continuing basis in the company's activities, and **'current assets'** means assets not intended for such use.

FUNGIBLE ASSETS

5 **'Fungible assets'** means assets of any description which are substantially indistinguishable one from another.

HISTORICAL COST ACCOUNTING RULES

6 References to the historical cost accounting rules are to be read in accordance with paragraph 30 of Schedule 1, paragraph 38 of Schedule 2 and paragraph 36(1) of Schedule 3 to these Regulations.

LEASES

7(1) **'Long lease'** means a lease in the case of which the portion of the term for which it was granted remaining unexpired at the end of the financial year is not less than 50 years.

7(2) **'Short lease'** means a lease which is not a long lease.

7(3) **'Lease'** includes an agreement for a lease.

LISTED INVESTMENTS

8(1) **'Listed investment'** means an investment as respects which there has been granted a listing on–

(a) a recognised investment exchange other than an overseas investment exchange, or

(b) a stock exchange of repute outside the United Kingdom.

8(2) **'Recognised investment exchange'** and **'overseas investment exchange'** have the meaning given in Part 18 of the Financial Services and Markets Act 2000(a).

LOANS

9 A loan or advance (including a liability comprising a loan or advance) is treated as falling due for repayment, and an instalment of a loan or advance is treated as falling due for payment, on the earliest date on which the lender could require repayment or (as the case may be) payment, if he exercised all options and rights available to him.

MATERIALITY

10 Amounts which in the particular context of any provision of Schedules 1, 2 or 3 to these Regulations are not material may be disregarded for the purposes of that provision.

PARTICIPATING INTERESTS

11(1) A **'participating interest'** means an interest held by an undertaking in the shares of another undertaking which it holds on a long-term basis for the purpose of securing a contribution to its activities by the exercise of control or influence arising from or related to that interest.

11(2) A holding of 20% or more of the shares of the undertaking is to be presumed to be a participating interest unless the contrary is shown.

11(3) The reference in sub-paragraph (1) to an interest in shares includes–

(a) an interest which is convertible into an interest in shares, and

(b) an option to acquire shares or any such interest, and an interest or option falls within paragraph (a) or (b) notwithstanding that the shares to which it relates are, until the conversion or the exercise of the option, unissued.

11(4) For the purposes of this regulation an interest held on behalf of an undertaking is to be treated as held by it.

11(5) In the balance sheet and profit and loss formats set out in Schedules 1, 2 and 3 to these Regulations, 'participating interest' does not include an interest in a group undertaking.

11(6) For the purpose of this regulation as it applies in relation to the expression 'participating interest'–

(a) in those formats as they apply in relation to group accounts, and
(b) in paragraph 19 of Schedule 6 (group accounts: undertakings to be accounted for as associated undertakings),

the references in sub-paragraphs (1) to (4) to the interest held by, and the purposes and activities of, the undertaking concerned are to be construed as references to the interest held by, and the purposes and activities of, the group (within the meaning of paragraph 1 of that Schedule).

PURCHASE PRICE

12 **'Purchase price'**, in relation to an asset of a company or any raw materials or consumables used in the production of such an asset, includes any consideration (whether in cash or otherwise) given by the company in respect of that asset or those materials or consumables, as the case may be.

REALISED PROFITS AND REALISED LOSSES

13 **'Realised profits'** and **'realised losses'** have the same meaning as in section 853(4) and (5) of the 2006 Act.

STAFF COSTS

14(1) **'Social security costs'** means any contributions by the company to any state social security or pension scheme, fund or arrangement.

14(2) **'Pension costs'** includes–

(a) any costs incurred by the company in respect of any pension scheme established for the purpose of providing pensions for persons currently or formerly employed by the company,

(b) any sums set aside for the future payment of pensions directly by the company to current or former employees, and

(c) any pensions paid directly to such persons without having first been set aside.

14(3)   Any amount stated in respect of the item **'social security costs'** or in respect of the item **'wages and salaries'** in the company's profit and loss account must be determined by reference to payments made or costs incurred in respect of all persons employed by the company during the financial year under contracts of service.

SCOTS LAND TENURE

15   In the application of these Regulations to Scotland, **'land of freehold tenure'** means land in respect of which the company is the owner; **'land of leasehold tenure'** means land of which the company is the tenant under a lease.

Appendix D   Glossary of terms used in FRS 102

The following terms are used in FRS 102.

accounting policies	The specific principles, bases, conventions, rules and practices applied by an entity in preparing and presenting **financial statements**.
accrual basis (of accounting)	The effects of transactions and other events are recognised when they occur (and not as **cash** or its equivalent is received or paid) and they are recorded in the accounting records and reported in the **financial statements** of the periods to which they relate.
accumulating compensated absences	Compensated absences that are carried forward and can be used in future periods if the current period's entitlement is not used in full.
acquisition date	The date on which the acquirer obtains **control** of the acquiree.
Act	The *Companies Act* 2006
active market	A market in which all the following conditions exist: (a) the items traded in the market are homogeneous; (b) willing buyers and sellers can normally be found at any time; and (c) prices are available to the public.
actuarial assumptions	An entity's unbiased and mutually compatible best estimates of the demographic and financial variables that will determine the ultimate cost of providing post-employment benefits.
actuarial gains and losses	Changes in the **present value** of the **defined benefit obligation** resulting from: (a) experience adjustments (the effects of differences between the previous **actuarial assumptions** and what has actually occurred); and (b) the effects of changes in actuarial assumptions.
agent	An entity is acting as an agent when it does not have exposure to the significant risks and rewards associated with the sale of goods or the rendering of services. One feature indicating that an entity is acting as an agent is that the amount the entity earns is predetermined, being either a fixed fee per transaction or a stated percentage of the amount billed to the customer.
agricultural activity	The management by an entity of the biological transformation of **biological assets** for sale, into agricultural produce or into additional biological assets.
agricultural produce	The harvested product of the entity's **biological assets.**
amortisation	The systematic allocation of the **depreciable amount** of an **asset** over its **useful life**.
amortised cost (of a financial asset or financial liability)	The amount at which the **financial asset** or **financial liability** is measured at initial **recognition** minus principal repayments, plus or minus the cumulative **amortisation** using the **effective interest method** of any difference between that initial amount and the maturity amount, and minus any reduction (directly or through the use of an allowance account) for impairment or uncollectability.
asset	A resource controlled by the entity as a result of past events and from which future economic benefits are expected to flow to the entity.

asset held by a long-term employee benefit fund	An **asset** (other than non-transferable financial instruments issued by the reporting entity) that:
	(a) is held by an entity (a fund) that is legally separate from the reporting entity and exists solely to pay or fund **employee benefits**; and
	(b) is available to be used only to pay or fund employee benefits, is not available to the reporting entity's own creditors (even in bankruptcy), and cannot be returned to the reporting entity, unless either:
	  (i) the remaining assets of the fund are sufficient to meet all the related employee benefit obligations of the plan or the reporting entity; or
	  (ii) the assets are returned to the reporting entity to reimburse it for employee benefits already paid.

associate	An entity, including an unincorporated entity such as a partnership, over which the investor has **significant influence** and that is neither a **subsidiary** nor an interest in a **joint venture**.
biological asset	A living animal or plant.
borrowing costs	Interest and other costs incurred by an entity in connection with the borrowing of funds.
business	An integrated set of activities and **assets** conducted and managed for the purpose of providing: (a) a return to investors; or (b) lower costs or other economic benefits directly and proportionately to policyholders or participants. A business generally consists of inputs, processes applied to those inputs, and resulting outputs that are, or will be, used to generate **revenues**. **If goodwill** is present in a transferred set of activities and assets, the transferred set shall be presumed to be a business.
business combination	The bringing together of separate entities or **businesses** into one reporting entity.
carrying amount	The amount at which an **asset** or **liability** is recognised in the **statement of financial position**.
cash	Cash on hand and demand and deposits.
cash equivalents	Short-term, highly liquid investments that are readily convertible to known amounts of **cash** and that are subject to an insignificant risk of changes in value.
cash flows	Inflows and outflows of **cash** and **cash equivalents**.
cash-generating unit	The smallest identifiable group of **assets** that generates cash inflows that are largely independent of the cash inflows from other assets or groups of assets.
cash-settled share-based payment transaction	A **share-based payment transaction** in which the entity acquires goods or services by incurring **liability** to transfer **cash** or other **assets** to the supplier of those goods or services for amounts that are based on the price (or value) of the entity's shares or other equity instruments of the entity or another group entity.
change in accounting estimate	An adjustment of the **carrying amount** of an **asset** or a **liability,** or the amount of the periodic consumption of an asset, that results from the assessment of the present status of, and expected future benefits and obligations associated with, assets and liabilities. Changes in accounting estimates result from new information or new developments and, accordingly, are not corrections of **errors**.
class of assets	A grouping of **assets** of a similar nature and use in an entity's operations.

close members of the family of a person	Those family members who may be expected to influence, or be influenced by, that person in their dealings with the entity including: (a) that person's children and spouse or domestic partner; (b) children of that person's spouse or domestic partner; and (c) dependants of that person or that person's spouse or domestic partner.
closing rate	The spot exchange rate at the end of the **reporting period**.
combination that is in substance is a gift	A combination carried out at nil or nominal consideration that is not a fair value exchange but in substance the gift of one entity to another.
commencement of lease term	The date from which the lessee is entitled to exercise its right to use the leased asset. It is the date of initial **recognition** of the **lease** (i.e. the **recognition** of the **assets**, **liabilities**, **income** or **expenses** resulting from the lease, as appropriate).
component of an entity	Operations and **cash flows** that can be clearly distinguished, operationally and for financial reporting purposes, from the rest of the entity.
compound financial instrument	A financial instrument that, from the issuer's perspective, contains both a **liability** and an **equity** element.
consolidated financial statements	The financial statements of a **parent** and its **subsidiaries** presented as those of a single economic entity.
construction contract	A contract specifically negotiated for the construction of an **asset** or a combination of assets that are closely interrelated or interdependent in terms of their design, technology and function or their ultimate purpose or use.
constructive obligation	An obligation that derives from an entity's actions where: (a) by an established pattern of past practice, published policies or a sufficiently specific current statement, the entity has indicated to other parties that it will accept certain responsibilities; and (b) as a result, the entity has created a valid expectation on the part of those other parties that it will discharge those responsibilities.
contingent asset	A possible **asset** that arises from past events and whose existence will be confirmed only by the occurrence or non-occurrence of one or more uncertain future events not wholly within the control of the entity.
contingent liability	(a) a possible obligation that arises from past events and whose existence will be confirmed only by the occurrence or non-occurrence of one or more uncertain future events not wholly within the control of the entity; or (b) a present obligation that arises from past events but is not recognised because: 　(i) it is not probable that an outflow of resources embodying economic benefits will be required to settle the obligation; or 　(ii) the amount of the obligation cannot be measured with sufficient **reliability**.
contingent rent	That portion of the lease payments that is not fixed in amount but is based on the future amount of a factor that changes other than with the passage of time (e.g. percentage of future sales, amount of future use, future price indices, and future market rates of interest).
control (of an entity)	The power to govern the financial and operating policies of an entity so as to obtain benefits from its activities.
credit risk	The risk that one party to a financial instrument will cause a financial loss for the other party by failing to discharge an obligation.
current assets	**Assets** of an entity which are not intended for use on a continuing basis in the entity's activities.
current tax	The amount of income tax payable (refundable) in respect of the taxable profit (tax loss) for the current period or past **reporting periods**.

date of transition	The beginning of the earliest period for which an entity presents full comparative information in a given standard in its first **financial statements** that comply with that standard.
deemed cost	An amount used as a surrogate for cost or depreciated cost at a given date. Subsequent **depreciation** or **amortisation** assumes that the entity had initially recognised the **asset** or **liability** at the given date and that its cost was equal to the deemed cost.
deferred acquisition costs	Costs arising from the conclusion of **insurance contracts** that are incurred during a **reporting period** but which relate to a subsequent reporting period.
deferred tax	Income tax payable (recoverable) in respect of the **taxable profit (tax loss)** for future **reporting periods** as a result of past transactions or events.
deferred tax assets	Income tax recoverable in future **reporting periods** in respect of: (a) future tax consequences of transactions and events recognised in the **financial statements** of the current and previous periods; (b) the carry forward of unused tax losses; and (c) the carry forward of unused tax credits.
deferred tax liabilities	Income tax payable in future **reporting periods** in respect of future tax consequences of transactions and events recognised in the **financial statements** of the current and previous periods.
defined benefit obligation (present value of)	The **present value,** without deducting any **plan assets,** of expected future payments required to settle the obligation resulting from employee service in the current and prior periods.
defined benefit plans	**Post-employment benefit plans** other than **defined contribution plans**.
defined contribution plans	**Post-employment benefit plans** under which an entity pays fixed contributions into a separate entity (a fund) and has no legal or **constructive obligation** to pay further contributions or to make direct benefit payments to employees if the fund does not hold sufficient **assets** to pay all **employee benefits** relating to employee service in the current and prior periods.
depreciable amount	The cost of an **asset,** or other amount substituted for cost (in the **financial statements**), less its residual value.
depreciated replacement cost	The most economic cost required for the entity to replace the **service potential** of an **asset** (including the amount that the entity will receive from its disposal at the end of its **useful life**) at the **reporting date**.
depreciation	The systematic allocation of the **depreciable amount** of an **asset** over its **useful life**.
derecognition	The removal of a previously recognised **asset** or **liability** from an entity's **statement of financial position**.
derivative	A financial instrument or other contract with all three of the following characteristics: (a) its value changes in response to the change in a specified interest rate, financial instrument price, commodity price, foreign exchange rate, index of prices or rates, credit rating or credit index, or other variable (sometimes called the 'underlying'), provided in the case of a non-financial variable that the variable is not specific to a party to the contract; (b) it requires no initial net investment or an initial net investment that is smaller than would be required for other types of contracts that would be expected to have a similar response to changes in market factors; and (c) it is settled at a future date.
development	The application of **research** findings or other knowledge to a plan or design for the production of new or substantially improved materials, devices, products, processes, systems or services before the start of commercial production or use.

discontinued operation	A **component of an entity** that has been disposed of and: (a) represented a separate major line of **business** or geographical area of operations; (b) was part of a single co-ordinated plan to dispose of a separate major line of business or geographical area of operations; or (c) was a **subsidiary** acquired exclusively with a view to resale.

discretionary participation feature	A contractual right to receive, as a supplement to guaranteed benefits, additional benefits:
	(a) that are likely to be a significant portion of the total contractual benefits;
	(b) whose amount or timing is contractually at the discretion of the issuer; and
	(c) that are contractually based on:
	
	    (i) the performance of a specified pool of contracts or a specified type of contract;
	
	    (ii) realised and/or unrealised investment returns on a specified pool of **assets** held by the issuer; or
	
	    (iii) the **profit or loss** of the company, fund or other entity that issues the contract.

disposal group	A group of **assets** to be disposed of, by sale or otherwise, together as a group in a single transaction, and **liabilities** directly associated with those assets that will be transferred in the transaction. The group includes **goodwill** acquired in a **business combination** if the group is a **cash-generating unit** to which goodwill has been allocated in accordance with the requirements of paragraphs 27.24 to 27.27 of this FRS.
effective interest method	A method of calculating the **amortised cost** of **financial asset** or a **financial liability** (or a group of financial assets or financial liabilities) and of allocating the interest income or interest expense over the relevant period.
effective interest rate	The rate that exactly discounts estimated future cash payments or receipts through the expected life of the financial instrument or, when appropriate, a shorter period to the **carrying amount** of the **financial asset** or **financial liability**.
effectiveness of a hedge	The degree to which changes in the **fair value** or **cash flows** of the **hedged item** that are attributable to a hedged risk are offset by changes in the fair value or cash flows of the **hedging instrument**.
employee benefits	All forms of consideration given by an entity in exchange for service rendered by employees.
entity combination	See **business combination**.
equity	The residual interest in the **assets** of the entity after deducting all its **liabilities**.
equity-settled share-based payment transaction	A **share-based payment transaction** in which the entity: (a) receives goods or services as consideration for its own equity instruments (including shares or **share options**); or (b) receives goods or services but has no obligation to settle the transaction with the supplier.
errors	Omissions from, and misstatements in, the entity's **financial statements** for one or more prior periods arising from a failure to use, or misuse of, reliable information that: (a) was available when financial statements for those periods were authorised for issue; and (b) could reasonably be expected to have been obtained and taken into account in the preparation and presentation of those financial statements.
expenses	Decreases in economic benefits during the **reporting period** in the form of outflows or depletions of **assessor** incurrences of **liabilities** that result in decreases **inequity**, other than those relating to distributions to equity investors.

EU-adopted IFRS	IFRS that have been adopted in the European Union in accordance with EU Regulation 1606/2002.
fair presentation	Faithful representation of the effects of transactions, other events and conditions in accordance with the definitions and **recognition** criteria for **assets, liabilities, income** and **expenses** unless the override stated in paragraph 3.4 applies.
fair value	The amount for which an **asset** could be exchanged, a **liability** settled, or an equity instrument granted could be exchanged, between knowledgeable, willing parties in an arm's length transaction. In the absence of any specific guidance provided in the relevant section of this FRS, the guidance in paragraphs 11.27 to 11.32 shall be used in determining fair value.
fair value less costs to sell	The amount obtainable from the sale of an **asset** or **cash-generating unit** in an arm's length transaction between knowledgeable, willing parties, less the costs of disposal.
finance lease	A **lease** that transfers substantially all the risks and rewards incidental to ownership of an **asset**. Title may or may not eventually be transferred. A lease that is not a finance lease is an operating lease.

financial asset	Any **asset** that is:
	(a) **cash**;
	(b) an equity instrument of another entity;
	(c) a contractual right:
	   (i) to receive cash or another financial asset from another entity, or
	   (ii) to exchange financial assets or **financial liabilities** with another entity under conditions that are potentially favourable to the entity; or
	(d) a contract that will or may be settled in the entity's own equity instruments and:
	   (i) under which the entity is or may be obliged to receive a variable number of the entity's own equity instruments; or
	   (ii) that will or may be settled other than by the exchange of a fixed amount of cash or another financial asset for a fixed number of the entity's own equity instruments. For this purpose the entity's own equity instruments do not include instruments that are themselves contracts for the future receipt or delivery of the entity's own equity instruments.

financial guarantee contract	A contract that requires the issuer to make specified payments to reimburse the holder for a loss it incurs because a specified debtor fails to make payments when due in accordance with the original or modified terms of a debt instrument.

financial institution	Any of the following:
	(a) a bank which is:
	   (i) a firm with a Part IV permission which includes accepting deposits and:
	      (a) which is a credit institution; or
	      (b) whose Part IV permission includes a requirement that it complies with the rules in the General Prudential sourcebook and the Prudential sourcebook for Banks, Building Societies and Investment Firms relating to banks, but which is not a building society, a friendly society or a credit union;
	   (ii) an EEA bank which is a full credit institution;
	(b) a building society which is defined in the *Building Societies Act* 1986, s. 119(1) as a building society incorporated (or deemed to be incorporated) under that Act;

	(c) a credit union, being a body corporate registered under the *Industrial and Provident Societies Act* 1965 as a credit union in accordance with the *Credit Unions Act* 1979, which is an authorised person;
	(d) custodian bank, broker-dealer or stockbroker;
	(e) an entity that undertakes the business of effecting or carrying out **insurance contracts**, including general and life assurance entities;
	(f) an incorporated friendly society incorporated under the *Friendly Societies Act* 1992 or a registered friendly society registered under the *Friendly Societies Act* 1974, s. 7(1)(a) or any enactment which it replaced, including any registered branches;
	(g) an investment trust, Irish Investment Company, venture capital trust, mutual fund, exchange traded fund, unit trust, open-ended investment company (OEIC);
	(h) a **retirement benefit plan**; or
	(i) any other entity whose principal activity is to generate wealth or manage risk through financial instruments. This is intended to cover entities that have business activities similar to those listed above but are not specifically included in the list above.
	A **parent** entity whose sole activity is to hold investments in other group entities is not a financial institution.
financial instrument	A contract that gives rise to a **financial asset** of one entity and a **financial liability** or equity instrument of another entity.
financial liability	Any **liability** that is:
	(a) a contractual obligation:
	(i) to deliver **cash** or another **financial asset** to another entity; or
	(ii) to exchange financial assets or financial liabilities with another entity under conditions that are potentially unfavourable to the entity; or
	(b) a contract that will or may be settled in the entity's own equity instruments and:
	(i) under which the entity is or may be obliged to deliver a variable number of the entity's own equity instruments; or
	(ii) will or may be settled other than by the exchange of a fixed amount of cash or another financial asset for a fixed number of the entity's own equity instruments. For this purpose, the entity's own equity instruments do not include instruments that are themselves contracts for the future receipt or delivery of the entity's own equity instruments.
financial position	The relationship of the **assets, liabilities** and **equity** of an entity as reported in the **statement of financial position**.
financial statements	Structured representation of the **financial position,** financial **performance** and **cash flows** of an entity.
financial risk	The risk of a possible future change in one or more of a specified interest rate, financial instrument price, commodity price, foreign exchange rate, index of prices or rates, credit rating or credit index or other variable, provided in the case of a non-financial variable that the variable is not specific to a party to the contract.
financial activities	Activities that result in changes in the size and composition of the contributed **equity** and borrowings of the entity.
firm commitment	A binding agreement for the exchange of a specified quantity of resources at a specified price on a specified future date or dates.
first-time adopter of this FRS	An entity that presents its first annual **financial statements** that conform to this FRS, regardless of whether its previous accounting framework was **EU-adopted IFRS** or another set of accounting standards.

fixed assets	**Assets** of an entity which are intended for use on a continuing basis in the entity's activities.
forecast transaction	An uncommitted but anticipated future transaction.
foreign operation	An entity that is a **subsidiary, associate, joint venture** or branch of a reporting entity, the activities of which are based or conducted in a country or currency other than those of the reporting entity.
FRS 100	FRS 100 *Application of Financial Reporting Requirements.*
FRS 101	FRS 101 *Reduced Disclosure Framework.*
FRS 102	FRS 102 *The Financial Reporting Standard applicable in the UK and Republic of Ireland.*
FRS 103	FRS 103 *Insurance Contracts.*
FRSSE	The extant version of the *Financial Reporting Standard for Smaller Entities.*
functional currency	The currency of the primary economic environment in which the entity operates.
funding (of post-employment benefits)	Contributions by an entity, and sometimes its employees, into an entity, or fund, that is legally separate from the reporting entity and from which the **employee benefits** are paid.
gains	Increases in economic benefits that meet the definition of **income** but are not **revenue.**
general purpose financial statements (generally referred to simply as financial statements)	**Financial statements** directed to the general financial information needs of a wide range of users who are not in a position to demand reports tailored to meet their particular information needs.
going concern	An entity is a going concern unless management either intends to liquidate the entity or to cease trading, or has no realistic alternative but to do so.
goodwill	Future economic benefits arising from **assets** that are not capable of being individually identified and separately recognised.
government grant	Assistance by government in the form of a transfer of resources to an entity in return for past or future compliance with specified conditions relating to the **operating activities** of the entity. Government refers to government, government agencies and similar bodies whether local, national or international.
grant date	The date at which the entity and another party (including an employee) agree to a share-based payment arrangement, being when the entity and the counterparty have a shared understanding of the terms and conditions of the arrangement. At grant date the entity confers on the counterparty the right to cash, other **assets,** or equity instruments of the entity, provided the specified vesting conditions, if any, are met. If that agreement is subject to an approval process (for example, by shareholders), grant date is the date when that approval is obtained.
gross investment in a lease	The aggregate of: (a) the **minimum lease payments** receivable by the lessor under a **finance lease**; and (b) any unguaranteed **residual value** accruing to the lessor.
group	A **parent** and all its **subsidiaries**.

group reconstruction	Any one of the following arrangements: (a) the transfer of an equity holing in a **subsidiary** from one group entity to another; (b) the addition of a new **parent** entity to a **group**; (c) the transfer of equity holdings in one or more subsidiaries of a group to a new entity that is not a group entity but whose equity holders are the same as those of the group's parent; or (d) the combination into a group of two or more entities that before the combination had the same equity holders.
hedged item	For the purpose of special hedge accounting under s. 12 of this FRS, a hedged item is: (a) interest rate risk of a debt instrument measured at **amortised cost**; (b) foreign exchange or interest rate risk in a **firm commitment** or a **highly probable forecast transaction**; (c) price risk of a commodity that the entity holds or price risk in a firm commitment or highly probable forecast transaction to purchase or sell a commodity; or (d) foreign exchange risk in a **net investment in a foreign operation**.

hedging instrument	For the purpose of special hedge accounting under section 12 of this FRS, a hedging instrument is a financial instrument that meets all of the following terms and conditions:
	(a) it is an interest rate swap, a foreign currency swap, a cross currency interest rate swap, a forward or future foreign currency exchange contract, a forward or future commodity exchange contract, or any financial instrument used to hedge foreign exchange risk in **ante investment in a foreign operation**; provided it is expected to be highly effective in offsetting the designated hedged risk(s) identified in paragraph 12.17;
	(b) it involves a party external to the reporting entity (i.e. external to the **group**, segment or individual entity being reported on);
	(c) its **notional amount** is equal to the designated amount of the principal or notional amount of the **hedged item**;
	(d) it has a specified maturity date not later than:
	   (i) the maturity of the financial instrument being hedged;
	   (ii) the expected settlement of the commodity purchase or sale commitment; or
	   (iii) the later of the occurrence and settlement of the **highly probable** forecast foreign currency or commodity transaction being hedged;
	(e) it has no prepayment, early termination or extension features other than at **fair value**.
	
	An entity that chooses to apply IAS 39 *Financial Instruments: Recognition and Measurement* (as adopted in the EU) in accounting for financial instruments shall apply the definition of a hedging instrument in that standard rather than this definition.

held exclusively with a view to subsequent resale	An interest: (a) for which a purchaser has been identified or is being sought, and which is reasonably expected to be disposed of within approximately one year of its date of acquisition; or (b) that was acquired as a result of the enforcement of a security, unless the interest has become part of the continuing activities of the **group** or the holder acts as if it intends the interest to become so; or (c) which is **held as part of an investment portfolio**.

held as part of an investment portfolio	An interest is held as part of an investment portfolio if its value to the investor is through **fair value** as part of a directly or indirectly held basket of investments rather than as media through which the investor carries out **business**. A basket of investments is indirectly held if an investment fund holds a single investment in a second investment fund which, in turn, holds a basket of investments.
heritage assets	Tangible and **intangible assets** with historic, artistic, scientific, technological, geophysical, or environmental qualities that are held and maintained principally for their contribution to knowledge and culture.
highly probable	Significantly more likely than **probable**.
IAS Regulation	EU Regulation 1606/2002.
IFRS (International Financial Reporting Standards)	Standards and interpretations issued (or adopted) by the International Accounting Standards Board (IASB). They comprise: (a) International Financial Reporting Standards; (b) International Accounting Standards; and (c) Interpretations developed by the IFRS Interpretations Committee (IFRIC) or the former Standing Interpretations Committee (SIC).
impairment loss	The amount by which the **carrying amount** of an **asset** exceeds: (a) in the case of **inventories**, its selling price less costs to complete and sell; or (b) in the case of other assets, its **recoverable amount**.
impracticable	Applying a requirement is impracticable when the entity cannot apply it after making every reasonable effort to do so.
imputed rate of interest	The more clearly determinable of either: (a) the prevailing rate for a similar instrument of an issuer with a similar credit rating; or (b) a rate of interest that discounts the nominal amount of the instrument to the current cash sales price of the goods or services.
inception of the lease	The earlier of the date of the lease agreement and the date of commitment by the parties to the principal provisions of the **lease**.
income	Increases in economic benefits during the **reporting period** in the form of inflows or enhancements of **assets** or decreases of **liabilities** that result in increases in **equity**, other than those relating to contributions from equity investors.
income and expenditure	The total of **income** less **expenses**, excluding the components of **other comprehensive income**. In the for-profit sector this is known as **profit or loss**.
income statement	**Financial statement** that presents all items of **income** and **expense** recognised in a **reporting period,** excluding the items of **other comprehensive income** (referred to as the profit and loss account in the **Act**).
income tax	All domestic and foreign taxes that are based on **taxable profits**. Income tax also includes taxes, such as withholding taxes, that are payable by **subsidiary, associate** or **joint venture** on distributions to the reporting entity.
individual financial statements	The accounts that are required to be prepared by an entity in accordance with the Act or relevant legislation, for example: (a) 'individual accounts', as set out in s. 394 of the Act; (b) 'statement of accounts', as set out in the *Charities Act* 2011, s. 132; or (c) 'individual accounts', as set out in the *Building Societies Act* 1986, s. 72A. **Separate financial statements** are included in the meaning of this term.
infrastructure assets	Infrastructure for public services, such as roads, bridges, tunnels, prisons, hospitals, airports, water distribution facilities, energy supply and telecommunications networks.

insurance contract	A contract under which one party (the insurer) accepts significant insurance risk from another party (the policyholder) by agreeing to compensate the policyholder if a specified uncertain future event (the insured event) adversely affects the policyholder.
intangible asset	An identifiable non-monetary asset without physical substance. Such an **asset** is identifiable when: (a) it is separable, i.e. capable of being separated or divided from the entity and sold, transferred, licensed, rented or exchanged, either individually or together with a related contract, asset or **liability**; or (b) it arises from contractual or other legal rights, regardless of whether those rights are transferable or separable from the entity or from other rights and obligations.

interest rate implicit in the lease	The discount rate that, at the **inception of the lease,** causes the aggregate **present value** of:
	(a) the **minimum lease payments**; and
	(b) the unguaranteed **residual value** to be equal to the sum of:
	   (i) the **fair value** of the leased asset; and
	   (ii) any initial direct costs of the lessor.

interim financial report	A financial report containing either a complete set of **financial statements** or a set of condensed financial statements for an **interim period.**
interim period	A financial **reporting period** shorter than a full financial year.
intrinsic value	The difference between the fair value of the shares to which the counterparty has the (conditional or unconditional) right to subscribe or which it has the right to receive, and the price (if any) the counterparty is (or will be) required to pay for those shares. For example, a share option with an exercise price of CU15, on a share with a fair value of CU20, has an intrinsic value of CU5.
inventories	**Assets**: (a) held for sale in the ordinary course of business; (b) in the process of production for such sale; or (c) in the form of materials or supplies to be consumed in the production process or in the rendering of services.
inventories held for distribution at no or nominal consideration	**Assets** that are: (a) held for distribution at no or nominal consideration in the ordinary course of operations; (b) in the process of production for distribution at no or nominal consideration in the ordinary course of operations; or (c) in the form of material or supplies to be consumed in the production process or in the rendering of services at no or nominal consideration.
investing activities	The acquisition and disposal of long-term assets and other investments not included in **cash equivalents**.
investment property	Property (land or a building, or part of a building, or both) held by the owner or by the lessee under **finance lease** to earn rentals or for capital appreciation or both, rather than for: (a) use in the production or supply of goods or services or for administrative purposes; or (b) sale in the ordinary course of **business**.
joint control	The contractually agreed sharing of **control** over an economic activity. It exists only when the strategic financial and operating decisions relating to the activity require the unanimous consent of the parties sharing control (the **venturers**).
joint venture	A contractual arrangement whereby two or more parties undertake an economic activity that is subject to **joint control**. Joint ventures can take the form of jointly controlled operations, jointly controlled assets, or **jointly controlled entities**.

jointly controlled entity	**A joint venture** that involves the establishment of a corporation, partnership or other entity in which each **venturer** has an interest. The entity operates in the same way as other entities, except that a contractual arrangement between the venturers establishes **joint control** over the economic activity of the entity.
key management personnel	Those persons having authority and responsibility for planning, directing and controlling the activities of the entity, directly or indirectly, including any director (whether executive or otherwise) of that entity.
lease	An agreement whereby the lessor conveys to the lessee in return for a payment or series of payments the right to use an **asset** for an agreed period of time.
lease incentives	Incentives provided by the lessor to the lessee to enter into a new or renew an operating lease. Examples of such incentives include up-front cash payments to the lessee, the reimbursement or assumption by the lessor of costs of the lessee (such as relocation costs, leasehold improvements and costs associated with pre-existing lease commitments of the lessee), or initial periods of the **lease** provided by the lessor rent-free or at a reduced rent.
lease term	The non-cancellable period for which the lessee has contracted to **lease** the **asset** together with any further terms for which the lessee has the option to continue to lease the asset, with or without further payment, when at the **inception of the lease** it is reasonably certain that the lessee will exercise the option.
lessee's incremental borrowing rate (of interest)	The rate of interest the lessee would have to pay on a similar **lease** or, if that is not determinable, the rate that, at the **inception of the lease**, the lessee would incur to borrow over a similar term, and with a similar security, the funds necessary to purchase the **asset**.
liability	A present obligation of the entity arising from past events, the settlement of which is expected to result in an outflow from the entity of resources embodying economic benefits.
liquidity risk	The risk that an entity will encounter difficulty in meeting obligations associated with **financial liabilities** that are settled by delivering **cash** or another **financial asset**.
LLP Regulations	The *Large and Medium-sized Limited Liability Partnerships (Accounts) Regulations* 2008 (SI 2008/1913).
loans payable	**Financial liabilities** other than short-term trade payables on normal credit terms.
market condition	A condition upon which the exercise price, vesting or exercisability of an equity instrument depends that is related to the market price of the entity's equity instruments, such as attaining a specified share price or a specified amount of **intrinsic value of a share option**, or achieving a specified target that is based on the market price of the entity's equity instruments relative to an index of market prices of equity instruments of other entities.
market risk	The risk that the **fair value** or future **cash flows** of a financial instrument will fluctuate because of changes in market prices. Market risk comprises three types of risk: currency risk, interest rate risk and other price risk.
	Interest rate risk – the risk that the fair value or future cash flows of a financial instrument will fluctuate because of changes in market interest rates.
	Currency risk – the risk that the fair value or future cash flows of a financial instrument will fluctuate because of changes in foreign exchange rates.
	Other price risk – the risk that the fair value or future cash flows of a financial instrument will fluctuate because of changes in market prices (other than those arising from interest rate risk or currency risk), whether those changes are caused by factors specific to the financial instrument or its issuer, or factors affecting all similar financial instruments traded in the market.

material	Omissions or misstatements of items are material if they could, individually or collectively, influence the economic decisions of users taken on the basis of the **financial statements**. Materiality depends on the size and nature of the omission or misstatement judged in the surrounding circumstances. The size or nature of the item, or a combination of both, could be the determining factor.
measurement	The process of determining the monetary amounts at which the elements of the **financial statements** are to be recognised and carried in the **statement of financial position** and **statement of comprehensive income**.
merger	An **entity combination** that results in the creation of a new reporting entity formed from the combining parties, in which the controlling parties of the combining entities come together in a partnership for the mutual sharing of risks and benefits of the newly formed entity and in which no party to the combination in substance obtains **control** over any other, or is otherwise seen to be dominant. All of the following criteria must be met for an entity combination to meet the definition of a merger: (a) no party to the combination is portrayed as either acquirer or acquiree, either by its own board or management or by that of another party to the combination; (b) there is no significant change to the classes of beneficiaries of the combining entities or the purpose of the benefits provided as a result of the combination; and (c) all parties to the combination, as represented by the members of the board, participate in establishing the management structure of the combined entity and in selecting the management personnel, and such decisions are made on the basis of a consensus between the parties to the combination rather than purely by exercise of voting rights.
minimum lease payments	The payments over the **lease term** that the lessee is or can be required to make, excluding **contingent rent**, costs for services and taxes to be paid by and reimbursed to the lessor, together with: (a) for a lessee, any amounts guaranteed by the lessee or by a party related to the lessee; or (b) for a lessor, any **residual value** guaranteed to the lessor by: 　(i) the lessee; 　(ii) a party related to the lessee; or 　(iii) a third party unrelated to the lessor that is financially capable of discharging the obligations under the guarantee. However, if the lessee has an option to purchase the **asset** at a price that is expected to be sufficiently lower than **fair value** at the date the option becomes exercisable for it to be reasonably certain, at the **inception of the lease**, that the option will be exercised, the minimum lease payments comprise the minimum payments payable over the lease term to the expected date of exercise of this purchase option and the payment required to exercise it.
monetary items	Units of currency held and **assets** and **liabilities** to be received or paid in a fixed or determinable number of units of currency.
multi-employer (benefit) plans	**Defined contribution plans** (other than **state plans**) or **defined benefit plans** (other than state plans) that: (a) pool the **assets** contributed by various entities that are not under common control; and (b) use those assets to provide benefits to employees of more than one entity, on the basis that contribution and benefit levels are determined without regard to the identity of the entity that employs the employees concerned.
net assets available for benefits	The **assets** of a plan less **liabilities** other than the actuarial **present value** of promised retirement benefits.

net defined benefit liability	The **present value** of the **defined benefit obligation** at the **reporting date** minus the **fair value** at the reporting date of **plan assets** (if any) out of which the obligations are to be settled.
net investment in a foreign operation	The amount of the reporting entity's interest in the net assets of that operation.
net investment in a lease	The **gross investment in a lease** discounted at the **interest rate implicit in the lease**.
non-controlling interest	The **equity** in a **subsidiary** not attributable, directly or indirectly, to a **parent**.
non-exchange transaction	A transaction whereby an entity receives value from another entity without directly giving approximately equal value in exchange, or gives value to another entity without directly receiving approximately equal value in exchange.
notes (to financial statements)	Notes contain information in addition to that presented in the **statement of financial position, statement of comprehensive income, income statement** (if presented), combined **statement of income and retained earnings** (if presented), **statement of changes in equity** and **statement of cash flows.** Notes provide narrative descriptions or disaggregation of items presented in those statements and information about items that do not qualify for **recognition** in those statements.
notional amount	The quantity of currency units, shares, bushels, pounds or other units specified in a financial instrument contract.
objective of financial statements	To provide information about the **financial position, performance** and **cash flows** of an entity that is useful for economic decision-making by a broad range of users who are not in a position to demand reports tailored to meet their particular information needs.
onerous contract	A contract in which the unavoidable costs of meeting the obligations under the contract exceed the economic benefits expected to be received under it.
operating activities	The principal revenue-producing activities of the entity and other activities that are not investing or **financing activities**.
operating lease	A **lease** that does not transfer substantially all the risks and rewards incidental to ownership. A lease that is not an operating lease is a **finance lease**.
operating segment	An operating segment is a **component of an entity:** (a) that engages in business activities from which it may earn **revenues** and incur **expenses** (including revenues and expenses relating to transactions with other components of the same entity); (b) whose operating results are regularly reviewed by the entity's chief operating decision maker to make decisions about resources to be allocated to the segment and assess its **performance**; and (c) for which discrete financial information is available.
ordinary share	An equity instrument that is subordinate to all other classes of equity instrument.
other comprehensive income	Items of **income** and **expense** (including reclassification adjustments) that are not recognised in **profit or loss** as required or permitted by this FRS.
owners	Holders of instruments classified as **equity.**
parent	An entity that has one or more **subsidiaries.**
performance	The relationship of the **income** and **expenses** of an entity, as reported in the **statement of comprehensive income.**
performance-related condition	A condition that requires the performance of a particular level of service or units of output to be delivered, with payment of, or entitlement to, the resources conditional on that performance.
permanent differences	Differences between an entity's **taxable profits** and its **total comprehensive income** as stated in the **financial statements,** other than **timing differences.**

plan assets (of an employee benefit plan)	(a) **assets held by a long-term employee benefit fund;** and (b) **qualifying insurance policies.**
post-employment benefits	**Employee benefits** (other than **termination benefits** and short-term employee benefits) that are payable after the completion of employment.
post-employment benefit plans	Formal or informal arrangements under which an entity provides **post-employment benefits** for one or more employees.
potential ordinary share	A financial instrument or other contract that may entitle its holder to **ordinary shares.**
present value	A current estimate of the present discounted value of the future net **cash flows** in the normal course of **business.**
presentation currency	The currency in which the **financial statements** are presented.
prevailing market rate	The rate of interest that would apply to the entity in an open market for a similar financial instrument.
principal	An entity is acting as a principal when it has exposure to the significant risks and rewards associated with the sale of goods or the rendering of services. Features that indicate that an entity is acting as a principal include: (a) the entity has the primary responsibility for providing the goods or services to the customer or for fulfilling the order, for example by being responsible for the acceptability of the products or services ordered or purchased by the customer; (b) the entity has inventory risk before or after the customer order, during shipping or on return; (c) the entity has latitude in establishing prices, either directly or indirectly, for example by providing additional goods or services; and (d) the entity bears the customer's credit risk for the amount receivable from the customer.
probable	More likely than not.
profit or loss	The total of **income** less **expenses,** excluding the components of **other comprehensive income.**
projected unit credit method	An actuarial valuation method that sees each period of service as giving rise to an additional unit of benefit entitlement and measures each unit separately to build up the final obligation (sometimes known as the accrued benefit method pro-rated on service or as the benefit/years of service method).
property, plant and equipment	Tangible assets that: (a) are held for use in the production or supply of goods or services, for rental to others, or for administrative purposes; and (b) are expected to be used during more than one period.
prospectively (applying a change in accounting policy)	Applying the new **accounting policy** to transactions, other events and conditions occurring after the date as at which the policy is changed.
provision	A **liability** of uncertain timing or amount.
prudence	The inclusion of a degree of caution in the exercise of the judgments needed in making the estimates required under conditions of uncertainty, such that **assets** or **income** are not overstated and **liabilities** or **expenses** are not understated.
public benefit entity	An entity whose primary objective is to provide goods or services for the general public, community or social benefit and where any **equity** is provided with a view to supporting the entity's primary objectives rather than with a view to providing a financial return to equity providers, shareholders or members.

public benefit entity concessionary loan	A loan made or received between a **public benefit entity** or an entity within a **public benefit entity group** and another party: (a) at below the **prevailing market rate** of interest; (b) that is not repayable on demand; and (c) is for the purposes of furthering the objectives of the public benefit entity or public benefit entity **parent.**
public benefit entity group	**A public benefit entity parent** and all of its wholly-owned **subsidiaries.**
publicly traded (debt or equity instruments)	Traded, or in process of being issued for trading, in a public market (a domestic or foreign stock exchange or an over-the-counter market, including local and regional markets).
qualifying asset	An **asset** that necessarily takes a substantial period of time to get ready for its intended use or sale. Depending on the circumstances any of the following may be qualifying assets: (a) **inventories;** (b) manufacturing plants; (c) power generation facilities; (d) **intangible assets;** and (e) **investment properties.** **Financial assets,** and inventories that are produced over a short period of time, are not qualifying assets. Assets that are ready for their intended use or sale when acquired are not qualifying assets.
qualifying entity (for the purposes of this FRS)	A member of a **group** where the **parent** of that group prepares publicly available **consolidated financial statements** which are intended to give a true and fair view (of the **assets, liabilities, financial position** and **profit or loss**) and that member is included in the consolidation.
qualifying insurance policies	An insurance policy issued by an insurer that is not a **related party** of the reporting entity, if the proceeds of the policy: (a) can be used only to pay or fund **employee benefits** under a **defined benefit plan;** and (b) are not available to the reporting entity's own creditors (even in bankruptcy) and cannot be paid to the reporting entity, unless either: (i) the proceeds represent surplus **assets** that are not needed for the policy to meet all the related employee benefit obligations; or (ii) the proceeds are returned to the reporting entity to reimburse it for employee benefits already paid.
recognition	The process of incorporating in the **statement of financial position** or **statement of comprehensive income** an item that meets the definition of an asset, liability, equity, income or expense and satisfies the following criteria: (a) it is **probable** that any future economic benefit associated with the item will flow to or from the entity; and (b) the item has a cost or value that can be measured with **reliability.**
recoverable amount	The higher of an **asset's** (or **cash-generating unit's) fair value less costs to sell** and its value in use.
Regulations	The *Large and Medium-sized Companies and Groups (Accounts and Reports) Regulations* 2008 (SI 2008/410).
reinsurance contract	An **insurance contract** issued by one insurer (the reinsurer) to compensate another insurer (the cedant) for losses on one or more contracts issued by the cedant.

related party	A related party is a person or entity that is related to the entity that is preparing its **financial statements** (the reporting entity).
	(a) A person or a close member of that person's family is related to a reporting entity if that person:
	(i) has **control** or **joint control** over the reporting entity;
	(ii) has **significant influence** over the reporting entity; or
	(iii) is a member of the **key management personnel** of the reporting entity or of a **parent** of the reporting entity.
	(b) An entity is related to a reporting entity if any of the following conditions apply:
	(i) the entity and the reporting entity are members of the same **group** (which means that each parent, **subsidiary** and fellow subsidiary is related to the others);
	(ii) one entity is an **associate** or **joint venture** of the other entity (or of a member of a group of which the other entity is a member);
	(iii) both entities are joint ventures of the same third entity;
	(iv) one entity is a joint venture of a third entity and the other entity is an associate of the third entity;
	(v) the entity is a **post-employment benefit plan** for the benefit of employees of either the reporting entity or an entity related to the reporting entity. If the reporting entity is itself such a plan, the sponsoring employers are also related to the reporting entity;
	(vi) the entity is controlled or jointly controlled by a person identified in (a);
	(vii) a person identified in (a)(i) has significant influence over the entity or is a member of the key management personnel of the entity (or of a parent of the entity).
related party transaction	A transfer of resources, services or obligations between a reporting entity and a **related party,** regardless of whether a price is charged.
relevance	The quality of information that allows it to influence the economic decisions of users by helping them evaluate past, present or future events or confirming, or correcting, their past evaluations.
reliability	The quality of information that makes it free from **material error** and bias and represents faithfully that which it either purports to represent or could reasonably be expected to represent.
reporting date	The end of the latest period covered by **financial statements** or by an interim financial report.
reporting period	The period covered by **financial statements** or by an **interim financial report.**
research	Original and planned investigation undertaken with the prospect of gaining new scientific or technical knowledge and understanding.
residual value (of an asset)	The estimated amount that an entity would currently obtain from disposal of an **asset,** after deducting the estimated costs of disposal, if the asset were already of the age and in the condition expected at the end of its **useful life.**
restriction	A requirement that limits or directs the purposes for which a resource may be used that does not meet the definition of a **performance-related condition.**
restructuring	A restructuring is a programme that is planned and controlled by management and materially changes either:
	(a) the scope of a business undertaken by an entity; or
	(b) the manner in which that business is conducted.

retirement benefit plan	Arrangements whereby an entity provides benefits for employees on or after termination of service (either in the form of an annual **income** or as a lump sum) when such benefits, or the contributions towards them, can be determined or estimated in advance of retirement from the provisions of a document or from the entity's practice.
retrospective application (of an accounting policy)	Applying a new **accounting policy** to transactions, other events and conditions as if that policy had always been applied.
revenue	The gross inflow of economic benefits during the period arising in the course of the ordinary activities of an entity when those inflows result in increases in **equity**, other than increases relating to contributions from equity participants.
separate financial statements	Those presented by a **parent** in which the investments in **subsidiaries, associates** or **jointly controlled entities** are accounted for either at cost or **fair value** rather than on the basis of the reported results and net assets of the investees. Separate financial statements are included within the meaning of individual **financial statements.**
service concession arrangement	An arrangement whereby a public sector body or a **public benefit entity** (the grantor) contracts with a private sector entity (the operator) to construct (or upgrade), operate and maintain **infrastructure assets** for a specified period of time (the concession period).
service potential	The economic utility of an **asset,** based on the total benefit expected to be derived by the entity from use (and/or through sale) of the asset.
share-based payment transaction	A transaction in which the entity: (a) receives goods or services (including employee services) as consideration for its own equity instruments (including shares or **share options**); or (b) receives goods or services but has no obligation to settle the transaction with supplier; or (c) acquires goods or services by incurring **liabilities** to the supplier of those goods or services for amounts that are based on the price (or value) of the entity's shares or other equity instruments of the entity or another group entity.
share option	A contract that gives the holder the right, but not the obligation, to subscribe to the entity's shares at a fixed or determinable price for a specific period of time.
significant influence	Significant influence is the power to participate in the financial and operating policy decisions of the **associate** but is not **control** or **joint control** over those policies.
Statement of Recommended Practice (SORP)	An extant Statement of Recommended Practice developed in accordance with *SORPs: Policy and Code of Practice*. SORPs recommend accounting practices for specialised industries or sectors. They supplement accounting standards and other legal and regulatory requirements in the light of the special factors prevailing or transactions undertaken in a particular industry or sector.
state	A national, regional, or local government.
state (employee benefit) plan	Employee benefit plans established by legislation to cover all entities (or all entities in a particular category, for example a specific industry) and operated by national or local government or by another body (for example an autonomous agency created specifically for this purpose) which is not subject to control or influence by the reporting entity.
statement of cash flows	**Financial statement** that provides information about the changes in **cash** and **cash equivalents** of an entity for a period, showing separately changes during the period from operating, investing and **financing activities.**

statement of comprehensive income	**Financial statement** that presents all items of **income** and **expense** recognised in a period, including those items recognised in determining **profit or loss** (which is a subtotal in the statement of comprehensive income) and items of **other comprehensive income.** If an entity chooses to present both an **income statement** and a statement of comprehensive income, the statement of comprehensive income begins with profit or loss and then displays the items of other comprehensive income.
statement of financial position	**Financial statement** that presents the relationship of an entity's **assets, liabilities** and **equity** as of a specific date (referred to as the balance sheet in the **Act**).
statement of income and retained earnings	**Financial statement** that presents the **profit or loss** and changes in retained earnings for a **reporting period**.
subsidiary	An entity, including an unincorporated entity such as a partnership, that is **controlled** by another entity (known as the **parent**).
substantively enacted	Tax rates shall be regarded as substantively enacted when the remaining stages of the enactment process historically have not affected the outcome and are unlikely to do so. A UK tax rate shall be regarded as having been substantively enacted if it is included in either:
	(a) a Bill that has been passed by the House of Commons and is awaiting only passage through the House of Lords and Royal Assent; or
	(b) a resolution having statutory effect that has been passed under the *Provisional Collection of Taxes Act* 1968. (Such a resolution could be used to collect taxes at a new rate before that rate has been enacted. In practice, corporation tax rates are now set a year ahead to avoid having to invoke the Provisional Collection of Taxes Act for the quarterly payment system.)
	A Republic of Ireland tax rate can be regarded as having been substantively enacted if it is included in a Bill that has been passed by the Dáil.
tax expense	The aggregate amount included in **total comprehensive income** or **equity** for the **reporting period** in respect of **current tax** and **deferred tax.**
taxable profit (tax loss)	The profit (loss) for a **reporting period** upon which income taxes are payable or recoverable, determined in accordance with the rules established by the taxation authorities. Taxable profit equals taxable income less amounts deductible from taxable income.
termination benefits	**Employee benefits** provided in exchange for the termination of an employee's employment as a result of either:
	(a) an entity's decision to terminate an employee's employment before the normal retirement date; or
	(b) an employee's decision to accept voluntary redundancy in exchange for those benefits.
timing differences	Differences between **taxable profits** and **total comprehensive income** as stated in the **financial statements** that arise from the inclusion of **income** and **expenses** in tax assessments in periods different from those in which they are recognised in financial statements.
timelines	Providing the information in **financial statements** within the decision time frame.
total comprehensive income	The change in **equity** during a period resulting from transactions and other events, other than those changes resulting from transactions from equity participants (equal to the sum of **profit or loss** and **other comprehensive income**).

transaction costs (financial instruments)	Incremental costs that are directly attributable to the acquisition, issue or disposal of a **financial asset** or **financial liability,** or the issue or reacquisition of an entity's **own equity instrument**. An incremental cost is one that would not have been incurred if the entity had not acquired, issued or disposed of the financial asset or financial liability, or had not issued or reacquired its own equity instrument.
treasury shares	An entity's own equity instruments, held by that entity or other members of the consolidated group.
turnover	The amounts derived from the provision of goods and services falling within the entity's ordinary activities, after deduction of: (a) trade discounts; (b) value added tax; and (c) any other taxes based on the amounts so derived.
understandability	The presentation of information in a way that makes it comprehensible by users who have a reasonable knowledge of **business** and economic activities and accounting and a willingness to study the information with reasonable diligence.
useful life	The period over which an **asset** is expected to be available for use by an entity or the number of production or similar units expected to be obtained from the asset by an entity.
value in use	The **present value** of the future **cash flows** expected to be derived from an **asset** or **cash-generating unit.**
value in use (in respect of assets held for their service potential)	When the future economic benefits of an **asset** are not primarily dependent on the asset's ability to generate net cash inflows, **value in use** (in respect of assets held for their **service potential**) is the **present value** to the entity of the asset's remaining service potential if it continues to be used, plus the net amount that the entity will receive from its disposal at the end of its **useful life.**
venturer	A party to a **joint venture** that has **joint control** over that joint venture.
vest	Become an entitlement. Under a share-based payment arrangement, a counterparty's right to receive **cash,** other **assets** or equity instruments of the entity vests when the counterparty's entitlement is no longer conditional on the satisfaction of any vesting conditions.
vested benefits	Benefits, the rights to which, under the conditions of **retirement benefit plan,** are not conditional on continued employment.

Appendix E Selected reading and reference material

This appendix provides a selection of the websites and literature to which this book might form a companion.

Wolters Kluwer online resources and Accounting and Auditing Standards

CCH daily including Accountancy Live	www.cchdaily.co.uk
Navigate GAAP	Your comprehensive easy-to-search New UK GAAP online resource
CCH Online	The professional online library for tax, audit, accounting and finance
Accounting Standards 2016–17	Wolters Kluwer (UK) Ltd
Auditing Standards 2016–17	Wolters Kluwer (UK) Ltd

Checklists and other useful publications

Company Accounts Disclosure Checklist and the Interactive Companies Accounts Disclosure Checklist	SWAT UK Ltd	Wolters Kluwer (UK) Ltd
New UK GAAP: An at a glance comparison	Helen Lloyd	Wolters Kluwer (UK) Ltd
Applying New UK GAAP (focus on FRS 102)	Various technical writers	Wolters Kluwer (UK) Ltd
CCH Preparing Company Accounts – Small and Micros	SWAT UK Ltd	Wolters Kluwer (UK) Ltd
Preparing FRS 101 Accounts	Helen Lloyd	Wolters Kluwer (UK) Ltd
Deloitte UK GAAP Commentary	Deloitte LLP	Wolters Kluwer (UK) Ltd
Implementing GAAS 2016–17	BDO LLP	Wolters Kluwer (UK) Ltd
Preparing Audit Reports	David Duvall	Wolters Kluwer (UK) Ltd

Useful websites

Financial Reporting Council	www.frc.org.uk
International Accounting Standard Board	www.ifrs.org
International Auditing and Assurance Standards Board	www.iaasb.org
The International Federation of Accountants	www.ifac.org
Federation of European Accountants (Fédération des Experts-comptables Européens)	www.fee.be
Department for Business, Innovation and Skills (BIS)	www.bis.gov.uk
Companies House	www.companieshouse.gov.uk
Legislation and statutory instruments	www.legislation.gov.uk
European legislation	www.eur-lex.europa.eu
Institute of Chartered Accountants in England and Wales	www.icaew.com
Institute of Chartered Accountants of Scotland	www.icas.org.uk

FRC guidance

Compendium of Illustrative Auditor's Reports on United Kingdom Public Sector Financial Statements for periods ended on or after 15 December 2010 (Revised)	APB Bulletin 2010/2 (Revised March 2012 and updated by Bulletin 4 below)
Recent Developments in Company Law, The Listing Rules and Auditing Standards that affect United Kingdom Auditor's Reports	Financial Reporting Council Bulletin 4 (June 2015)

Index

Abbreviated accounts
individual accounts 14.1
medium-sized companies 14.1
statutory accounts 14.1

Accounting principles
accruals 3.5, Appendix D
consistency 3.5
going concern 3.5, Appendix D
individual determination 3.5
netting 3.5
prudence 3.5, 7.2, Appendix D
substance of transaction 3.5

Accounts information
qualitative characteristics 7.2

Accounts presentation
aggregation 8.7
comparative information 8.5
compliance with FRS 102 8.3
composition of set of accounts 8.2
   FRS 102.1A 8.2.2
   FRS 102 8.2.1
consistency principle 8.6
fair presentation ('true and fair view') 8.1, Appendix D
   FRS 102.1A, small companies 8.1.1
frequency of reporting 8.5
going concern – see Going concern
materiality 8.7, Appendix D

Amended accounts
on CA 2006 (s. 454-459) 15.7
Companies House 15.7
contents, details 15.7
statements, required of 15.7

Asset
accounting principles 3.5
meaning 7.3, Appendix D
measurement of 7.6
offsetting 7.7
recognition of 7.5, Appendix D

Auditor's report
on CA 2006, Pt. 16 13.1.1
CA 2006, s. 495 and 496 13.1.3, Table 13.1
directors and auditors, responsibilities of Appendix A
elements of 13.1.2
generally 13.1
identifying annual accounts subject to audit 13.1.4
independent auditor's report Appendix A
ISAs (UK and Ireland) 700 13.2.1
matters on Appendix A
medium-sized (or large) company, example of 13.3
opinion on Appendix A
signature of 13.1.5
small company, example of 13.4

Business combinations – see also **Financial Reporting Standards (FRS 102), disclosure requirements**

Companies Act accounts
FRS 102 disclosure checklist Appendix B
structure of SI 2008/409 2.2.2, Table 2.2
structure of SI 2008/410 2.1, Table 2.1, Appendix C

Companies Act 2006
accounts and reports, Part 15 (Sections 380–474) 2.1.3
annual accounts 2.1
audit, Part 16 (Sections 475–539) 2.1.3
'commencement orders', statutory instrument 2.1.2
CA 2006 s. 380 2.1.1
companies legislation 2.1.1

Companies Act 2006 – contd
contents and reports 2.3, Appendix C
elements of audit report 2.4
group accounts 3.8, Appendix C
implementation, commencing on or after 6 April 2008 2.1.2
provisions of 2.1.1
reforms and company laws 2.1.1
small companies 2.1.1
'think small first' approach 2.1.1

Companies House
amended accounts 15.7
common reasons for accounts rejection, listing 15.5
electronic tagging of accounts (iXBRL) 15.9
filing accounts 15.4, Table 15.2
Registrar's Rules 2009 Table 15.2

Concepts and pervasive principles
financial position – see Financial position
measurement of assets, liabilities, income and expenses 7.6
objective of accounts 7.1
offsetting 7.7
performance – see Performance
qualitative characteristics of accounts information 7.2
recognition of assets, liabilities, income and expenses 7.5

Consolidated and separate accounts (FRS 102 section 9)
individual and separate accounts, difference of 10.4
intermediate payment arrangements 10.5
parent and subsidiary, defined 10.1, Appendix D
requirement to present 10.2
   intermediate parent entities 10.2.1
   small groups 10.2.2
   subsidiaries excluded from consolidation 10.2.3
specific disclosures 10.3

Definitions and meanings
asset 7.3, 11.2.1, Appendix D
associate 11.4, Appendix D
balance between benefit and cost 7.2
business combinations 11.9, Appendix D
comparability 7.2
completeness 7.2
employee benefits 11.16, Appendix D
equity 7.3, 11.2.1, Appendix D
events after end of reporting period 11.20
expenses 7.4, Appendix D
financial instruments 11.2.1, Appendix D
goodwill 11.9, Appendix D
government grants 11.13, Appendix D
impairment of assets 11.15
income 7.4, Appendix D
intangible asset 11.8, Appendix D
leases (section 20) 11.10, Appendix D
liability 7.3, 11.2.1, Appendix D
materiality 7.2, Appendix D
parent and subsidiary 10.1, Appendix D
provisions and contingencies 11.11
prudence 7.2, Appendix D
relevance 7.2, Appendix D
reliability 7.2, Appendix D
share-based payment 11.14, Appendix D
substance over form 7.2
timeliness 7.2, Appendix D
understandability 7.2, Appendix D

Director's report – see also **Strategic report**
content of 12.2.1
generally 12.2
remuneration report 3.7, 3.9, Appendix B
statement of directors' responsibilities 12.2.3, Appendix A
statement of disclosure of information to auditors 12.2.2,
    Appendix A, Appendix B

Index

Electronic tagging of accounts (iXBRL) – *see also* **Filing of accounts**

Employee benefits – *see also* **Financial Reporting Standards (FRS 102), disclosure requirements**
  other long-term 11.16.3
  post-employment 11.16.2, Appendix D
  short-term 11.16.1
  termination 11.16.4

Equity
  meaning 7.3, 11.2.1, Appendix D

Expenses
  meaning 7.4
  measurement of 7.6
  offsetting 7.7
  recognition of 7.5
  relationship with income 7.4

Filing of accounts – *see also* **Companies House**
  amended accounts 15.7
  deadlines 15.2
    private companies – see Private companies
    public companies – see Public companies
  electronic filing 15.1
  electronic form 15.6
  electronic tagging of accounts (iXBRL) 15.9
  in paper form 15.4
  Registrar of Companies 15.3

Financial instruments
  at fair value through profit or loss 11.2.2
  disclosure requirements
    accounting policies 11.2.2
    collateral 11.2.2
    derecognition 11.2.2, Appendix D
    hedge accounting 11.2.2
    items of income, expense, gain or losses 11.2.2
    statement of financial position 11.2.2, Appendix D
  FRS 102, sections 11, 12 and 22 11.2, Appendix A, Appendix D
  meaning 11.2.1

Financial position
  relationship of assets, liabilities and equity 7.3, Appendix D

Financial reporting framework in UK and Ireland
  consistency with company law 4.5
  effective date and transitional arrangements 4.6
  FRS 100 requirements, application of 4.2
  new standards 4.1
  statement of compliance 4.4
  summary of 4.3, Table 4.1

Financial Reporting Standards (FRS 102), disclosure requirements
  accounting policies, estimates and errors (section 10) 11.1, Appendix D
    accounting policies 11.1.1
    changes in accounting estimates 11.1.2
    corrections of prior period errors 11.1.3
    small companies 11.1.4
  business combinations and goodwill (section 19) Appendix D
    small companies 11.9
  employee benefits (section 28) 11.16, Appendix A
    other long-term benefits 11.16.3
    post-employment benefits 11.16.2, Appendix D
    short-term employee benefits 11.16.1, Appendix B
    small companies 11.16.5
    termination benefits 11.16.4, Appendix D
  events after end of reporting period (section 32) 11.20
  financial instruments (sections 11, 12 and 22) 11.2, Appendix A, Appendix D
    definitions and meanings – see Definitions and meanings
    disclosure requirements – see also Financial instruments
    small companies 11.2.3
  foreign currency translation (section 30) 11.18
  government grants (section 24) 11.13, Appendix D
  hyperinflation (section 31) 11.19
  impairment of assets (section 27)
    small companies 11.15
  income tax (section 29) 11.17, Appendix D

Financial Reporting Standards (FRS 102), disclosure requirements – contd
  intangible assets other than goodwill (section 18) Appendix A
    small companies 11.8
  inventories (section 13) Appendix D
    small companies 11.3
  investment property (section 16) Appendix D
    small companies 11.6
    true and fair override 11.6
  investments in associates (section 14) Appendix D
    small companies 11.4, 11.5
  investments in joint ventures (section 15) 11.5
  leases (section 20) Appendix D
    lessees 11.10.1
    lessors 11.10.2
    small companies 11.10.3
  property, plant and equipment (section 17)
    small companies 11.7
  provisions and contingencies (section 21) 11.11
    commitments 11.11.5
    contingent assets 11.11.3, Appendix D
    contingent liabilities 11.11.2, Appendix D
    prejudicial disclosures 11.11.4
    provisions 11.11.1
    small companies 11.11.6
  related party disclosures (section 33) 11.21
    disclosure of key management personnel compensation 11.21.2
    information about directors' benefits: advances, credit and guarantees 11.21.4
    parent-subsidiary relationships 11.21.1
    small companies 11.21.5
    transactions 11.21.3
  revenue (section 23) 11.12, Appendix D
    particulars of turnover 11.12.1
  share-based payment (section 26) 11.14
  specialised activities (section 34) 11.22
  transition to FRS 102 (section 35) 11.23

Financial Reporting Standards (FRS) 102 in UK and Ireland
  basis of preparation of accounts 6.2
  reduced disclosures for subsidiaries and ultimate parents
    specific disclosure exemptions 6.3, Table 6.1
  scope 6.1

Foreign currency translation and hyperinflation – *see also* **Financial Reporting Standards (FRS 102), disclosure requirements**

Format of accounts
  accounts, example 9.6, Appendix A
  notes to accounts – see Notes to accounts
  small companies: abridged accounts 9.7, Table 9.1, Table 9.2, Table 9.3, Table 9.4
  statement of cash flows – see Statement of cash flows
  statement of changes in equity – see Statement of changes in equity
  statement of comprehensive income – see Statement of comprehensive income
  statement of financial position – see Statement of financial position
  statement of income and retained earnings – see Statement of income and retained earnings

General accounting provisions
  accounting principles – see Accounting principles
  adequate accounting records 3.10, Table 3.2
  annual accounts 3.2
  approval and signature of accounts 3.11
  audit reports 2.4
  audit requirements 3.9
  format of accounts 3.4
  generally 3.1, Table 3.1
  group accounts 3.8
  notes to accounts – disclosures 3.6
  publication of statutory and non-statutory accounts 3.12
  strategic and directors' report – content and requirements 3.7
  true and fair view 3.3

Going concern
accounting principle 3.5
accounts preparation 8.4

Government grants – *see also* **Financial Reporting Standards (FRS 102), disclosure requirements**

Group accounts
Companies Act 3.1, 3.8, Table 2.1

HMRC
electronic tagging of account (iXBRL) format 15.9
filing of accounts 15.8

Impairment of assets – *see also* **Financial Reporting Standards (FRS 102), disclosure requirements**

Income
meaning 7.4, Appendix D
measurement of 7.6, Appendix D
offsetting 7.7
recognition of 7.5
relationship with expense 7.4

Income tax – *see also* **Financial Reporting Standards (FRS 102), disclosure requirements**

Individual accounts
Companies Act 3.1, Table 2.1, Table 3.1
true and fair view 3.3

Intangible assets
FRS 102 (section 18) 11.8
meaning 11.8

International accounting standards
CA 2006 s. 395 2.1.4

ISAs (UK and Ireland) 700
generally 13.2.1

Inventories
FRS 102 (section 13) 11.3, Appendix D

Investments
associates, FRS 102 (section 14) 11.4, Appendix D
joint ventures, FRS 102 (section 15) 11.5, Appendix D
property, FRS 102 (section 16) 11.6

Large and medium-sized companies and groups (accounts and reports)
content and structure 2.2, 3.4, Table 2.1, Appendix C

Leases – *see also* **Financial Reporting Standards (FRS 102), disclosure requirements**
lessees 11.10.1
lessors 11.10.2

Liabilities
cash or cash equivalents 7.6, Appendix D
meaning 7.3, Appendix D
offsetting 7.7

Notes to accounts 9.5
accounting policies 9.5.2, Appendix A, Appendix C
key sources of estimation uncertainty 9.5.3
structure 9.5.1

Performance
relationship of income and expenses 7.4, Appendix D

Private companies
filing of accounts, deadline 15.2.1

Property, plant and equipment
FRS 102 (section 17) 11.7
tangible assets 11.7

Provisions and contingencies – *see also* **Financial Reporting Standards (FRS 102), disclosure requirements**
assets 11.11.3, Appendix D
commitments 11.11.5
liabilities 11.11.2
prejudicial disclosures 11.11.4
provisions 11.11.1

Public companies
'think small first' approach 2.1.1
filing of accounts, deadline 15.2.2

Quoted public companies
'think small first' approach 2.1.1

Reduced disclosure framework
consolidated accounts 5.4
criteria 5.2
equivalent disclosures 5.5
financial institutions 5.3, Appendix D
qualifying entities 5.1, Appendix D
specific disclosure exemptions 5.6, Table 5.1

Registrar of Companies
filing of accounts 15.3
Registrar's Rules Table 15.1

Related party disclosures – *see also* **Financial Reporting Standards (FRS 102), disclosure requirements**
disclosure of key management personnel compensation 11.21.2
information about directors' benefits: advances, credit and guarantees 11.21.4
parent-subsidiary relationships 11.21.1
small companies 11.21.5
transactions 11.21.3

Revenue – *see also* **Financial Reporting Standards (FRS 102), disclosure requirements**
particulars of turnover 11.12.1

Share-based payment – *see also* **Financial Reporting Standards (FRS 102), disclosure requirements**

Small companies
abbreviated accounts 14.1
filing exemptions 14.2
abridged accounts 14.2.1
audit report 14.2.3
CA 2006, s. 444 14.2.2
directors' report 14.2.2
income statement 14.2.2, Appendix D
'think small first' approach 2.1.1

Small companies and groups (accounts and director's report) 2.2.2, Table 2.2

Statement of cash flows 9.4, Table 9.7, Appendix A, Appendix D
cash and cash equivalents, components 9.4.10, Appendix D
cash equivalents 9.4.1, Appendix A, Appendix D
categories 9.4.2
financing activities 9.4.2.3
investing activities 9.4.2.2, Appendix D
operating activities 9.4.2.1, Appendix D
foreign currency 9.4.6, Appendix A
income tax 9.4.8, Appendix D
interest and dividends 9.4.7
non-cash transactions 9.4.9
operating activities: direct vs indirect 9.4.3
other disclosures 9.4.11
reporting from investing and financing activities 9.4.4
reporting on net basis 9.4.5

Statement of changes in equity 9.3, Table 9.5, Appendix A
information to be presented 9.3.1

Statement of comprehensive income
discontinued operations 9.2.2, Appendix A, Appendix D
exceptional items 9.2.4
formats 9.2.1, Table 9.4
generally 9.2.1, Appendix A, Appendix D
operating profit 9.2.5
prior period adjustments 9.2.3

Index

Statement of financial position
    creditors: amounts falling due within one year 9.1.3,
        Appendix A
    debtors due after more than one year 9.1.2
    formats 9.1.1, Table 9.1, Table 9.2
    major disposal of assets or a disposal group 9.1.5,
        Appendix D
    share capital and reserves 9.1.4, Appendix A
    small companies 9.1.6, Table 9.3

**Statement of income and retained earnings 9.3,
Appendix A, Appendix D**
    information to be presented 9.3.2, Table 9.6

Strategic report
    generally 12.1, Appendix A
        content of 12.1.1

'True and fair' view
    audit report 2.4
    individual accounts 3.3